Psychological, Social, and Cultural Aspects of Internet Addiction

Bahadir Bozoglan
IF Weinheim Institute, Germany

A volume in the Advances in Human and Social
Aspects of Technology (AHSAT) Book Series

IGI Global
DISSEMINATOR OF KNOWLEDGE

Published in the United States of America by
   IGI Global
   Information Science Reference (an imprint of IGI Global)
   701 E. Chocolate Avenue
   Hershey PA, USA 17033
   Tel: 717-533-8845
   Fax: 717-533-8661
   E-mail: cust@igi-global.com
   Web site: http://www.igi-global.com

Library of Congress Cataloging-in-Publication Data

Names: Bozoglan, Bahadir, 1979- editor.
Title: Psychological, social, and cultural aspects of Internet addiction /
  Bahadir Bozoglan, editor.
Description: Hershey, PA : Information Science Reference, [2018]
Identifiers: LCCN 2017017435| ISBN 9781522534778 (hardcover) | ISBN
  9781522534785 (ebook)
Subjects: LCSH: Internet addiction.
Classification: LCC RC569.5.I54 P764 2018 | DDC 362.19685/84--dc23 LC record available at https://lccn.loc.gov/2017017435

This book is published in the IGI Global book series Advances in Human and Social Aspects of Technology (AHSAT) (ISSN: 2328-1316; eISSN: 2328-1324)

British Cataloguing in Publication Data
A Cataloguing in Publication record for this book is available from the British Library.

All work contributed to this book is new, previously-unpublished material. The views expressed in this book are those of the authors, but not necessarily of the publisher.

For electronic access to this publication, please contact: eresources@igi-global.com.

Advances in Human and Social Aspects of Technology (AHSAT) Book Series

Ashish Dwivedi
The University of Hull, UK

ISSN:2328-1316
EISSN:2328-1324

MISSION

In recent years, the societal impact of technology has been noted as we become increasingly more connected and are presented with more digital tools and devices. With the popularity of digital devices such as cell phones and tablets, it is crucial to consider the implications of our digital dependence and the presence of technology in our everyday lives.

The **Advances in Human and Social Aspects of Technology (AHSAT) Book Series** seeks to explore the ways in which society and human beings have been affected by technology and how the technological revolution has changed the way we conduct our lives as well as our behavior. The AHSAT book series aims to publish the most cutting-edge research on human behavior and interaction with technology and the ways in which the digital age is changing society.

COVERAGE

- Technology adoption
- Technology and Social Change
- Technology and Freedom of Speech
- Cyber Bullying
- Cyber Behavior
- Technoself
- Activism and ICTs
- Cultural Influence of ICTs
- Human-Computer Interaction
- Philosophy of technology

IGI Global is currently accepting manuscripts for publication within this series. To submit a proposal for a volume in this series, please contact our Acquisition Editors at Acquisitions@igi-global.com or visit: http://www.igi-global.com/publish/.

Titles in this Series

For a list of additional titles in this series, please visit: www.igi-global.com/book-series

701 East Chocolate Avenue, Hershey, PA 17033, USA
Tel: 717-533-8845 x100 • Fax: 717-533-8661
E-Mail: cust@igi-global.com • www.igi-global.com

I dedicate this book to my little daughter,
who is the sun of our family at our tough times.

Table of Contents

Section 5
Putting It Together

Detailed Table of Contents

Section 1
Internet Addiction as a Global Phenomenon

This section provides an introduction to internet addiction as a global phenomenon.

Chapter 1

> *Shilpa Suresh Bisen, Visvesvaraya National Institute of Technology Nagpur, India*
> *Yogesh Deshpande, Visvesvaraya National Institute of Technology Nagpur, India*

In the era of digital technology, the internet has its significant role in sprouting vulnerability toward the different form of addictions and psychiatric disorders as well as providing the platform to manage them effectively. The internet provides ready access to illicit drugs, nonprescription medications which facilitate a sale of controlled substances over the Internet without a valid prescription which contributed to the rise of several forms of addictions. Studies have linked the severity of Problematic Internet Use to increase chances of substance Use disorder. Utilization of internet for longer durations serves as a booster for behavioral addictions like online gambling. Web based interventions on the positive side provides a cost effective, readily accessible and user-friendly platform to reach out majority of patients to help them in seeking treatment of Addictions and various psychiatric disorders. The aim of this chapter is to discuss the contribution of the internet in a positive and negative way to develop as well as resolve Psychiatric disorder.

Chapter 2

> *Shaun Joseph Smyth, Ulster University, UK*
> *Kevin Curran, Ulster University, UK*
> *Nigel Mc Kelvey, Letterkenny Institute of Technology, Ireland*

Internet addiction is a recent phenomenon which describes a state where people become so involved in online behaviour to the detriment of other aspects of their lives. Treatment camps for young people have sprung up around in a bid to address this contemporary issue. This chapter examines the factors in Internet addiction, its definition, the complications which exist in the various diagnostic methods of successfully diagnosing Internet addiction and the criticism directed towards some of these diagnostic methods. We also examine which individuals are at risk of developing this condition. We look at positive diagnosis of the addiction and the resultant effects it has on an individual's family life, employment, social life and personal wellbeing before finally looking at possible methods and treatments that can be used in treating Internet addiction.

Section 2
Psychological Aspects of Internet Addiction

This section covers psychological aspects of internet addiction.

Research into technological addictions, such as Internet addiction, smartphone addiction and social networking addiction has greatly increased. It is important to understand how technological addictions may be related to different personality types and key individual differences associated to personality. This chapter provides empirical and conceptual insights into how technological addictions may be related to different personality types and key individual differences associated to personality. This chapter focuses on a number of technological addictions and illustrates how research and theory in this area has developed in relation to commonly researched personality traits (e.g., extraversion, introversion, neuroticism, conscientiousness, openness to experience, and narcissism) and key individual differences related to personality (e.g., personality disorders). The complex nature of personality and technological addictions is discussed together with areas for future research.

Internet use has become an integral part of our lives. It provides a lot of benefits; however, excessive use can have serious consequences for one's well-being. Therefore, the aim of this chapter is to explore well-being of heavy Internet users. Empirical research was conducted on 500 students of engineering, who were divided into groups based on the total time per day reported spending in various online activities. The comparison of subjective well-being and sources of life satisfaction and dissatisfaction showed that heavy Internet users were less happy compared to light users. Heavy Internet users found more satisfaction in various entertainment activities, while light users found more satisfaction in love life and family. Findings of this research provide some important theoretical findings, but also point out that the continuing research is needed to further explore the relation between Internet addiction, time spent online, and well-being.

Internet use enhances one's quality of life; yet, excessive use may lead to various problems for their healthy development and wellbeing. Understanding the risk and protective factors in internet addiction has importance to promote individuals' positive development and wellbeing. Therefore, the purpose of the present chapter is to explore the role of psychological maltreatment in the development of the internet addiction. Psychological maltreatment is a significant public health problems associated with a range of short and long–term undesirable mental health and wellbeing outcomes in childhood to adulthood. Considering the outcomes supporting the significant role of child maltreatment on the development of internet addiction, it is clear that maltreated individuals are at–risk to develop internet addiction, and psychological maltreatment, as a risk factor, has a crucial role in the development of internet addiction. However, evidences here are relatively limited, and there is need further research investigated long–term impacts of psychological maltreatment on internet addiction.

The present study was designed to determine the relationship between loneliness and Internet addiction, based on a sample of young generation from Turkey. Participants in this study were students of the Hacettepe University in Ankara, Turkey (n = 440). Findings show that there is a statistically significant relationship (p <0.05) between students' Internet addiction and only the grade they are studying. According to the correlation analysis, it was found that there is a negative relationship between the loneliness of students and the time they spend on the internet, and a positive relationship between internet addiction and age of students. Moreover, it was found that the age, time spent on the Internet and loneliness of university students were important determinants of Internet addiction.

Section 3
Social Aspects of Internet Addiction

This section covers social aspects of internet addiction.

Chapter 7

From a social epidemiological perspective, this chapter presents a new approach to conceptualizing the socioeconomic determinants of Internet Addiction (IA) in adolescents, followed by a rapid scoping review of the empirical research literature on the same topic which aims to provide an overview of the current body of knowledge. With a strict adherence to the established procedures, fifteen original research articles were retrieved for review and analysis. A wide range of socioeconomic risk factors was identified. The theoretical pathways of socioeconomic determinants suggested in the included studies were also tabulated and discussed. Finally, the chapter closes with several recommendations for future research on the potential socioeconomic determinants of IA based on the retrieved findings.

Chapter 8

Bahadir Bozoglan, IF Weinheim Institute, Germany

As the Internet becomes increasingly integrated into everyday life, there is a growing concern on the antecedents that contribute to some of the adverse effects such as Internet addiction. Parents are important and influential agents, and their parenting practices may promote or prevent the development of Internet-related problems. This chapter provides a review of family factors surrounding child and adolescent Internet addiction such as parental monitoring and parental guidance, parental mediation, Internet parenting styles, parental norms and behaviors, parent and child characteristics, family functioning and parent marital conflict, quality of the parent-child and peer relationship and culture as highlighted in previous research. Common limitations on past research on family factors and child and adolescent Internet addiction are noted and future research directions are suggested. Finally, family-based solutions and recommendations to prevent children and adolescents from developing Internet addiction are provided in the light of previous findings.

Chapter 9

Jonathan Bishop, Crocels Community Media Group, UK

Digital addiction is a phenomenon where people who might take up addictive substances or other self-medicating activities do so instead with information and communications technology. The environment in which someone finds themselves is known to influence their behaviour. This might be as a result of the environment placing more demands on people with one cognitive set-up compared to those with a different one. One might not normally think of education environments as addictive, but the introduction of technology into them can affect different learners in different ways. Through computing a measure of brain activity called knol (k), this paper seeks to explore how learners with different learning styles react in environments that are differentiated according to the intensity of ICTs used and the physical architecture of the learning environment in which those ICTs are used.

Chapter 10

Manisha J. Nene, Defence Institute of Advanced Technology (DIAT), India
Prashant Gupta, Defence Institute of Advanced Technology (DIAT), India

The Internet has become a platform for different campaigns like political, social, cultural and marketing. Researchers are working on the effect of these services on human behavior and how the use of Internet and social network persuade the environment. This chapter focuses on the causes and effects of persuasive messages based on current trending news and events which can influence an individual's behavior. Cyberspace plus Psychological effect equals to CyberPsycho Effect leading to CyberPsycho attacks. In CyberPsycho attacks, an attacker uses cyberspace and social network to affect attitude or behavior of an individual or a targeted society, and achieve certain goals to attain political, religious, economical, and social gains. It motivates social media users towards a certain objective by spreading the persuasive messages in the form of texts, images or videos. The study is unique, valuable and compels the experts to understand the impact of Internet addiction.

Section 4
Cultural Aspects of Internet Addiction

This section covers cultural aspects of internet addiction.

This chapter presents a review of Internet addiction on the basis of different countries between the years of 2007 and 2017. For this purpose, the term "addiction" is explained, some addiction types are examined, the differences between Internet addiction and the other ones are given and the Internet addiction status of different countries are presented. In today's world, Internet addiction is a privileged problem in almost all of the countries but especially a few countries have important number of studies about the subject. The most studies are completed in China, Turkey, Taiwan, Hong Kong and Korea. In this chapter, studies about these countries and some other ones are investigated. These studies show that the "Far East" is suffering from the problem a bit more than the others.

Internet addiction (IA) has emerged as a universal issue, but its international estimates vary due to different screening instruments and different samples. The present study aims to estimate the risk of IA in a school-based nationally representative sample of Slovenian adolescents and ascertain the interplay between IA, sociodemographic factors, free-time activities, self-control, and perceived satisfaction with life. Overall, the present study found that adolescents at greater risk for developing IA tend to be more passive in their free time, since they watch TV and play video games more than their peers, as well as chat on social media. Adolescents presenting high risk of IA displayed poorer levels of self-control in most cases and reported to be generally less satisfied with their lives in comparison to adolescents presenting low risk of IA.

The advent of the social media in Nigeria has given rise to a plurality of information technology syndromes as well as multiple forms of social leprosies. One of these social leprosies has been selfie-objectification manifested by naked and highly sexualized selfies. As a form of social pathology, selfie-objectification has particularly engulfed the youths, corrupting the latter's innocence and affecting the positive relationship culture among them. Using observations and secondary sources, this chapter explores two opposing perspectives on selfie-objectification in Nigeria namely conservative and liberal.

It criticizes the conservative reading of the self-objectification paradigm, arguing that any interpretation of selfie-objectification by Nigerian youths solely as a culturally insensitive act and a western cultural import is myopic and objectionable. The phenomenon should rather be read along the line of Nigerian youths' visible embrace of a liberal and postmodern philosophy of life.

Chapter 14

Valentina Boursier, University of Naples Federico II, Italy
Valentina Manna, Association for Social Promotion Roots in Action, Italy

Internet usage represents a risky opportunity for the youngest. Due to its social, communicative and emotional function in adolescents' lives, it may provide benefits and facilitations to their relationships. On the other hand, the excessive use of the Internet can harmfully affect their daily routines, with negative effects on their psychological state. Considering the widespread use of the Internet in everyday life during this developmental stage, the authors question the applicability of the concept of "addiction" and provide empirical data about the adaption of a useful instrument to measure problematic relationships with the Internet. The establishment of a cut-off procedure is proposed for screening purpose to identify at risk and problematic users. Moreover, differences by gender and age are explored and discussed. A comprehensive model of the Problematic Relationships with the Internet is presented and analyzed in comparison with the main perspectives and measures in literature.

Section 5
Putting It Together

This section provides a conclusion to internet addiction with treatment strategies and future research directions.

Chapter 15

Libi Shen, University of Phoenix, USA

The birth of the Internet in 1969 has changed people's lives immensely in the past 48 years. Over the years, this invention has brought people connection, information, communication, business, entertainment, and so forth; however, researchers have found the impact of the Internet's byproduct, namely Internet addiction, in the past two decades as well. It was argued that Internet addiction might be detrimental to people's mental and physical health. The problem is that Internet addiction is not clearly defined, nor has it been included in Diagnostic and Statistical Manual for Mental Disorders (DSM-5) by American Psychiatric Association. If the definition is not clear and the symptoms are varied, the treatment for Internet addiction would become an issue. In this chapter, the researcher will focus on different approaches to the treatment of Internet addiction based on research after reviewing the definitions, theories, causes, consequences, and symptoms of Internet addiction.

Foreword

Internet addiction began as a pet project in a young researcher's one-bedroom apartment in Rochester, New York. I was that young researcher. It was 1995 and a friend of mine's husband was seemingly addicted to AOL Chat Rooms spending 40, 50, 60 hours online at a time when it was still $2.95 per hour to dial into the Internet. Not only did they suffer financial burdens but their marriage ended in divorce when he met women in online chat rooms.

The first study on Internet addiction shortly followed as I collected over 600 similar case studies of people who suffered from relationship problems, academic problems, financial problems, and job loss because they were unable to control their Internet use (Young, 1998). The research grew very quickly into a rapidly evolving new field. Psychologists such as Drs. David Greenfield and Marissa Hecht Orzack were early pioneers in the field. They wrote the most prolifically in the late 1990s, which led to new areas of research to be developed. Studies in China, Korea, and Taiwan emerged in the early 2000s. Historically, this was a pivotal moment as the research lead to the development of the first inpatient treatment.

In 2006, the first inpatient center to treat Internet Addiction opened in Beijing, China (Jiang, 2009). The Asian cultures seemingly had significant problems dealing with problem Internet use compared to the rest of the world, although that same year the US found through its first national study that 1 in 8 Americans suffered from one criteria of problem Internet use.

In this time, new online applications such as Facebook and Twitter evolved making technology part of everyday life and blurring the distinction between addictive and functional Internet use.

By the late 2000s, studies predominantly came from Asian cultures regarding this problem, which led to comprehensive prevention programs in some countries. For instance, Korea has developed an entire master plan to prevent and treat Internet addiction including national screening days to identify children at risk, early prevention programs offered in schools, and hundreds of inpatient units to treat Internet addiction. Comparatively, America had seemingly fallen behind with no government-based or national intervention plans to deal with Internet addiction such as screenings, prevention programs, or inpatient care.

Studies began to identity what were considered 'digitally potent' online applications such as online role-playing games, online gambling, or online pornography that were more addictive than email, database searches, or texting. In 2013, Internet Addiction Gaming disorder was singled out as the most potent problem categorized in the revised Diagnostic and Statistical Manual of Mental Disorders as a condition for further study (American Psychiatric Association, 2013). Later that year, the first inpatient hospital program in the United States for Internet addiction opened in Pennsylvania at the Bradford Regional Medical Center in Bradford, Pa treating all forms of Internet addiction applying concepts of digital diet and digital nutrition.

New statistical models also emerged that identified moderating factors such as coping styles and Internet expectancies that determined functional and dysfunctional Internet use among adult populations (Brand, Laier, and Young, 2014). Research on Internet addiction had turned from clinical observation to more statistically and empirically grounded studies. Furthermore, a growing body of neurological and neuroimaging studies showed that the prefrontal cortex played a significant role in the development of Internet addition (Brand, Young, and Laier, 2014) suggesting a biological causation for the disorder similar to other addictive syndromes.

New outcome studies have been done showing Cognitive-Behavioral Therapy for Internet Addiction or CBT-IA is effective at long-term treatment efficacy. This has turned into a standard of care by developing RESTORE RECOVERY, the first empirically-based training program for therapists interested in learning how to assess and treat Internet addiction disorders. Based on CBT-IA, treatment includes areas such as pornography addiction, Internet gambling addiction, online shopping addiction, addictions to social media, and Internet Gaming Disorder (RestoreRecovery.net). The training program is based on 20 years of research in the field and uses the acronym RESTORE to provide step-by-step approach in treatment and relapse prevention for patients.

Today, the question has shifted from how much time online is too much to how young is too young for children to go online. According to the Pew Internet Project in the U.S., more than 30% of children under the age of 2 have used a tablet or smartphone and 75% of kids age 8 and younger live with one or more mobile devices in the home. Because technology is used so frequently in child play, the creativity and imaginations of our youth are left idle, and studies suggest their opportunities to achieve optimal motor and sensory development are diminished. Compounding the problem, children react with defiance, disobedience, and in some cases, violence when parents try to limit or stop screen time.

These risks raise new concerns about technology addiction among children and adolescents. Already, the American Academy of Pediatrics warns against children under two years old having any access to technology or any media and only limited amounts thereafter.

Given the attention to Internet addiction among most cultures, Bahadır Bozoğlan book on Internet Addiction as a Global Phenomenon provides a comprehensive overview of Internet Addiction as a modern societal and clinical problem. This book is written by experts in their respective countries to review how Internet Addiction on the global basis. The book gathers important research that examines the psychological aspects of Internet Addiction and risk factors such as loneliness and personality traits that impact the well-being and main sources of life dis/satisfaction of heavy Internet users. It also examines the addictive properties of e-dating narratives. As much of the research shows, there are social aspects of Internet Addiction such as online multi-user role-playing games that also play an important role in the development of problem online behavior. This book examines those social and cultural impact of this condition and addresses the role of parents, parenting and other Mediating variables on child Internet use.

This book examines the psychological, social, and cultural Aspects of Internet Addiction and the individual differences in developing Internet Addiction based on national studies conducted in several countries. The book also provides treatment strategies based on the research to examine how to approach prevention and recovery of Internet addiction. The book is intended to provide an opportunity for academics, health care professionals, teachers, social workers, community leaders, members from parent school associations, government officials, politicians, and the public to better understand the signs of Internet addiction and the preventive responses.

As a society, we struggle with finding a balance with technology prowess and the battle against addiction. We can learn from leading countries that provide national screening days to identify children at young ages with problems related to Internet use and they are the leader in providing school-based prevention programs and more Internet addiction programs to give parents more options for treatment. What this book does is provide greater awareness of the problems associated with Internet addiction and strategies for how therapists can intervene early with adolescents and families on ways to balance technology use without being consumed by it.

Kimberly S. Young
Netaddiction.com, USA & Center for Internet Addiction, USA

REFERENCES

Brand, M., Laier, C., & Young, K. S. (2014). Internet addiction: coping styles, expectancies, and treatment implications. *Frontiers in Psychology: Psychpathology*. doi: 10.3389/fpsyg.2014.01256

Brand, M., Young, K. S., & Laier, C. (2014). Prefrontal control and Internet addiction: A theoretical model and review of neuropsychological and neuroimaging findings. *Frontiers in Human Neuroscience*, 8, 375–390. doi:10.3389/fnhum.2014.00375 PMID:24904393

Young, K. S. (1998). Internet Addiction: The emergence of a new disorder. *Cyberpsychology & Behavior*, 1(3), 237–244. doi:10.1089/cpb.1998.1.237

Preface

INTRODUCTION

The Internet has made our lives easier in the twenty-first century (Shek & Yu, 2012). It has become an integral part of our modern day living and a crucial means of communication and socialization. Along with the several conveniences the Internet has brought to our lives, several negative effects have also appeared on academic, work, and family lives, social relationships, physical health, and psychological well-being (Shek & Yu, 2012; Yen, Ko, Yen, Wu, & Yang, 2007). Although there are no agreed-upon definition of "Internet addiction" or "pathological use of the Internet" (Shek & Yu, 2012), it is broadly defined as the case when a person cannot control his/her use of the Internet, resulting in noticeable sorrow and functional impairment (Young, 1999). Since the end of the 1990s (Young, 1999), Internet addiction has been noted as one of the most serious behavioral problems among all age groups (Yang et al., 2014).

All over the world, Internet use has been the focus of a myriad of studies investigating the associations between Internet addiction and psychological, social and cultural factors (Douglas et al., 2008; Kuss, Griffiths, Karila, & Billieux, 2014). Some of these factors can be listed as depression (Bozoglan, Demirer, & Sahin, 2014; Dalbudak et al., 2013; Ko et al., 2014; Kraut et al., 1998; Pontes, Patrão, & Griffiths, 2014; Scimeca et al., 2014; Young & Rogers, 1998), attention deficit and hyperactive disorder (Yen et al., 2007), loneliness (Bozoglan et al., 2013; Kraut et al., 1998; Morahan-Martin & Schumacher, 2000; Yao & Zhong, 2014), poor mental health (Yang, 2001), low self-esteem (Bozoglan et al., 2013; Ko et al., 2005), life satisfaction (Bozoglan et al., 2013), alexithymia (Dalbudak et al., 2013; Scimeca et al., 2014), low family function (Armstrong et al., 2000), sensation seeking and pleasure experiencing (Chou & Hsiao, 2000; Lavin, Marvin, McLarney, Nola, & Scott, 1999) and shyness (Caplan, 2002).

The studies so far have revealed that Internet use might predict various changes in psychological well-being and that social resources and cultural variables might moderate the changes (Bessière et al., 2008; Bozoglan Demirer, 2015). In this respect, this book sheds light on the relationship between psychosocial variables and Internet addiction and examines each variable in detail. Each chapter introduces the relationship between the elicited psychological, social or cultural variable and Internet addiction, describes the causal relationship in the light of the related literature and suggests possible solutions. I believe an understanding of psychological, social and cultural aspects of Internet addiction will help to answer, "How do people get addicted?" and "How can we help the Internet addicts?". This book will be of interest to the researchers, clinicians and students who work and study in the field of psychology, psychiatry, psychotherapy, psychological counseling, sociology, anthropology, computer sciences, education, Internet and family issues.

ORGANIZATION OF THE BOOK

Internet Addiction as a Global Phenomenon

The first section of the book makes an introduction to Internet addiction as a global phenomenon and shows how Internet has become such a fundamental part of our daily lives to the extent where it has become an addiction and a disorder to our once orderly lives. The first chapter in this section is "Impact of the Internet in Twenty-First Century Addictions: An Overview". This chapter, by Shilpa Suresh Bisen and Yogesh Deshpande, describes how the Internet has the impact on fulfilling the craving for various types of addiction. In this context, the author focuses on Internet influence on addictions and discusses Internet as a platform for illegal drug trafficking. Next, the relationship between Internet addiction, substance use and behavioral addictions is explored. Finally, mode of treating addictions, Internet influence on psychiatric disorders and mode of treating psychiatric disorders are covered.

The next chapter in this section is "Internet Addiction: A Modern Societal Problem" by Shaun Joseph Smyth, Kevin Curran, and Nigel Mc Kelvey. This chapter while defining the term known as Internet addiction also looks at how it has grown playing a necessary role in both business and education and many other areas of our lives also. This chapter provides a synopsis of how the Internet can affect our lives for the better and at the same time has the ability to affect different areas of our lives from employees at work to students in educational settings. The authors explain both the signs and symptoms of Internet addiction while discussing possible treatments and looking to the future and the growing roles the Internet will play, from online shopping, communication networks and the ever-increasing online activities which rule our lives.

Psychological Aspects of Internet Addiction

Section 2 covers psychological aspects of Internet addiction. This section opens with Chapter 3, titled "Personality, Internet Addiction, and Other Technological Addictions: A Psychological Examination of Personality Traits and Technological Addictions". This chapter, by Zaheer Hussain and Halley M Pontes, focuses on a number of technological addictions (e.g. Internet addiction, videogame addiction, SNS addiction, and smart phone addiction) and illustrates how research and theory in this area has developed in relation to commonly researched personality traits (e.g., extraversion, introversion, neuroticism, conscientiousness, openness to experience, and narcissism) and key individual differences related to personality (e.g., personality disorders). The complex nature of personality and technological addictions is discussed together with areas for future research.

The next chapter in this section is "I'm Always Online: Well-Being and Main Sources of Life Dis/Satisfaction of Heavy Internet Users". This chapter, by Tihana Brkljačić, Filip Majetić, and Anja Wertag, focuses on excessive Internet use and its relation to well-being of a particularly vulnerable group - students of electrical engineering and computing, who are, due to the nature of their study, forced to be online much more in comparison with an average population of emerging adults. Through an empirical research design, the authors compare subjective well-being and sources of life satisfaction and dissatisfaction among heavy users and light users. This study provides important theoretical findings and underlines the need for continuing research to further explore the relation between Internet addiction, time spent online, and well-being.

This chapter is followed by "Psychological Maltreatment and Internet Addiction: Is Psychological Maltreatment a Risk Factor?" This chapter, by Gökmen Arslan, seeks to understand the role of psychological maltreatment in the development of the Internet addiction. The chapter highlights the role of psychological maltreatment as a significant public health problem associated with a range of short and long–term undesirable mental health and wellbeing outcomes during the period from childhood to adulthood. The author notes that maltreated individuals are at risk to develop Internet addiction disorder, and psychological maltreatment, as a risk factor, is important to better understand the development of Internet addiction. Among the limited literature on short and long–term impacts of psychological maltreatment on Internet addiction, this chapter paves the way for future studies.

The final chapter in this section is titled "Loneliness and Internet Addiction Among University Students". This chapter, by Ayfer Aydiner Boylu and Gülay Günay, seeks to determine the relationship between loneliness and Internet addiction among university students in Turkey. The findings indicate that age, time spent on the Internet and loneliness of university students are important determinants of Internet addiction. The authors aim at contributing to preserving or improving university students' quality of life and to formulating services and policies for them.

Social Aspects of Internet Addiction

This section focuses on social aspects of Internet addiction. It starts with Chapter 7, titled "Socioeconomic Determinants of Internet Addiction: A Scoping Review". This chapter, by Francisco T.T. Lai and Joyce L.Y. Kwan, presents a new social epidemiological approach to conceptualizing the potential socioeconomic determinants of Internet addiction and describes the findings of a scoping review of the relevant literature. The authors review and analyze fifteen original research articles. The chapter also provides a tabulation and discussion on the theoretical pathways of socioeconomic determinants suggested in the covered studies. It serves as an overview of the existing knowledge on the socioeconomic factors in the shaping of Internet addiction and makes recommendations on further research to be conducted on the topic.

The next chapter in this section, by me, is "The Role of Family Factors in Internet Addiction Among Children and Adolescents: An Overview". This chapter seeks to provide an overview of the risk and protection factors for the occurrence of Internet addiction during childhood and adolescence in relation to family context and parenting behaviors. In this context, past research concerning family factors and child Internet addiction have been reviewed and frequently occurring points are explained. Family factors put forward in previous research on child Internet addiction such as parental monitoring and parental guidance, parental mediation, Internet parenting styles, parental norms and behaviors, parent and child characteristics, parent marital conflict, quality of the parent-child and peer relationship and culture are revisited in this chapter.

Following this chapter is Chapter 9, "Evaluating the Risk of Digital Addiction in Blended Learning Environments: Considering ICT Intensity, Learning Style, and Architecture". This chapter, by Jonathan Bishop, investigates the effect of the environment in which a person is situated has on their propensity to be compulsive in their use of digital technologies. More specifically, the chapter aims to explore how learners with different learning styles react in environments that are differentiated according to the intensity of ICTs used and the physical architecture of the learning environment in which those ICTs are used by computing a measure of brain activity called knol (k). Within an ethnographic design, Jonathan Bishop has looked heavily at questionnaire-derived data from a total of 10 teaching sessions that occurred over 4 iterations, namely a fieldtrip and church hall, a cybercafé, an ICT laboratory and augmented technology approach. The chapter contributes to the understanding of digital addiction, and shows that different environments offer different levels of engagement, which by using the measure of knol can assess the risk of each learning style compulsively using a particular intensity of ICT.

The final chapter in this section is "CyberPsycho Effect: A Critical Study on the Impact of Internet Addiction". This chapter, by Manisha Nene and Prashant Gupta, looks at the causes and effects of persuasive messages based on current trending news and events which effectively can influence an individual's behavior. The authors call this "Cyberpsycho Effect" leading to "CyberPsycho attacks". As different from previous descriptions of cyber attacks, in cyberpsycho attacks an attacker makes use of cyber space and social network to influence the victims' mental attitude or psychological behavior to achieve political, religious, economical and social gains. The study presented in this chapter is unique and compels the experts in academia, researchers, technologists and end-users to understand and acknowledge the serious impact of psychological, social and cultural aspects of Internet addiction.

Cultural Aspects of Internet Addiction

This section covers cultural aspects of Internet addiction. The first chapter in this section is Chapter 11, titled "A Review of Internet Addiction on the Basis of Different Countries: 2007–2017". This chapter, by Ruya Samli, provides a review of Internet addiction on the basis of different countries between the years of 2007 and 2017. The author explains the term "addiction" and examines some different types of addiction. Later, the status of Internet addiction in different countries including China, Turkey, Taiwan, Hong Kong, Korea, Italy, Greece, India, Germany, Japan, Jordan, Singapore, Norway, Australia, Vietnam, Portugal and Poland is investigated.

The next chapter in this section is "Individual Differences in Developing Internet Addiction: A Nationally Representative Study" by Mirna Macur and Halley M. Pontes. The authors investigate the risk of Internet addiction among Slovenian adolescents and the interplay between Internet addiction, sociodemographic factors, free-time activities, self-control, and perceived satisfaction with life. They find that adolescents presenting high risk of Internet addiction tend to be more passive in their free time and display poorer levels of self-control, and they also report to be generally less satisfied with their lives in comparison to adolescents presenting low risk of Internet addiction. Macur and Pontes highlight the problem of Internet addiction in adolescence and provides important insights into how Internet addiction may affect several aspects of life during this developmental stage.

The next chapter is "Selfie-Objectification as a Facet of the Social Media Craze Among Youths in Nigeria: A Socio-Cultural Discourse". This chapter, by Floribert Patrick Calvain Endong, reviews social interpretations of selfie-objectification in Nigeria. It illustrates the fact that, in spite of its apparent incompatibility with the conservative and doctrinaire religious paradigms (which continues to govern the Nigerian society), the selfie-objectification is an index of the Nigerian youths' increasing fascination by foreign – mostly western – cultures and models of self-imaging. In its first section, the chapter provides illuminations on some key conceptual and theoretical issues (namely self-objectification, social media craze, liberalism and African conservatism). In its second part, the chapter shows how the selfie culture is progressively becoming a social "syndrome" in the Nigerian socio-cultural ecology. In its third section, the chapter provides a conservative perspective on self-objectification in Nigeria while the last section of the chapter critically discusses selfie-objectification as the manifestation of Nigerian youths' adherence to liberalism.

The final chapter in this section is "Problematic Linkages in Adolescents: Italian Adaptation of a Measure for Internet-Related Problems". This chapter, by Valentina Boursier and Valentina Manna, contributes to the ongoing debate about the usefulness of generally defining the Internet misuse as an "addiction". The issue is particularly explored with reference to adolescents, who largely use technologies in a stage of life commonly predisposed to risks. Moreover, taking in account the need for clarification of measures and related perspectives on the phenomenon, a contribution to this organization is proposed and here expanded. Moving from this debate, this study proposes a review of perspectives and measures to assess problematic relationships with the Internet and then presents the validation of a psychometric tool to assess problematic relationships with the Internet among Italian preadolescents/adolescents. The tool overcomes the shortcomings of extant instruments and the findings reveal that a clear profile of the "addicted" adolescent is not identified. To the best of the authors' knowledge, this is the first study to provide empirical information about the measurement of a cut-off threshold for identifying maladaptive relationships with the Internet among preadolescents/adolescents.

Putting It Together

The final chapter in this book aims to put the pieces of the puzzle together. This section provides a conclusion to Internet addiction with treatment strategies and future research directions. "Treatment of Internet Addiction", by Libi Shen, provides a broad review of definitions, theories, causes, consequences, and symptoms of Internet addiction. Next, the chapter examines different approaches for treating the Internet addicts. The author notes that there is a need to identify the definitions of Internet addiction, the symptoms and their treatment, the appropriate strategies or approaches to tackle with Internet addiction, and the right types of medicine for different types of Internet addiction. Thus, this chapter is important for parents, Internet addicts, policy makers, educators, and healthcare providers as it highlights the importance and effectiveness of the treatment for Internet addiction.

REFERENCES

Armstrong, L., Phillips, J. G., & Saling, L. L. (2000). Potential determinants of heavier Internet usage. *International Journal of Human-Computer Studies*, *53*(4), 537–550. doi:10.1006/ijhc.2000.0400

Bessière, K., Kiesler, S., Kraut, R., & Boneva, B. S. (2008). Effects of Internet use and social resources on changes in depression. *Information Communication and Society*, *11*(1), 47–70. doi:10.1080/13691180701858851

Bozoglan, B., & Demirer, V. (2015). The Association between Internet Addiction and Psychosocial Variables. In *Psychological and Social Implications Surrounding Internet and Gaming Addiction* (pp. 171–185). IGI Global. doi:10.4018/978-1-4666-8595-6.ch010

Bozoglan, B., Demirer, V., & Sahin, I. (2013). Loneliness, self-esteem, and life satisfaction as predictors of Internet addiction: A cross-sectional study among Turkish university students. *Scandinavian Journal of Psychology*, *54*(4), 313–319. doi:10.1111/sjop.12049 PMID:23577670

Bozoglan, B., Demirer, V., & Sahin, I. (2014). Problematic Internet use: Functions of use, cognitive absorption, and depression. *Computers in Human Behavior, 37*, 117–123. doi:10.1016/j.chb.2014.04.042

Caplan, S. E. (2002). Problematic Internet use and psychosocial well-being: Development of a theory based cognitive behavioral measurement instrument. *Computers in Human Behavior, 18*(5), 553–575. doi:10.1016/S0747-5632(02)00004-3

Chou, C., & Hsiao, M. C. (2000). Internet addiction, usage, gratifications, and pleasure experience: The Taiwan college students' case. *Computers & Education, 35*(1), 65–80. doi:10.1016/S0360-1315(00)00019-1

Dalbudak, E., Evren, C., Aldemir, S., Coskun, K. S., Ugurlu, H., & Yildirim, F. G. (2013). Relationship of Internet addiction severity with depression, anxiety, and alexithymia, temperament and character in university students. *Cyberpsychology, Behavior, and Social Networking, 16*(4), 272–278. doi:10.1089/cyber.2012.0390 PMID:23363230

Douglas, A. C., Mills, J. E., Niang, M., Stepchenkova, S., Byun, S., Ruffini, C., & Blanton, M. et al. (2008). Internet addiction: Meta-synthesis of qualitative research for the decade 1996–2006. *Computers in Human Behavior, 24*(6), 3027–3044. doi:10.1016/j.chb.2008.05.009

Ko, C. H., Liu, T. L., Wang, P. W., Chen, C. S., Yen, C. F., & Yen, J. Y. (2014). The exacerbation of depression, hostility, and social anxiety in the course of Internet addiction among adolescents: A prospective study. *Comprehensive Psychiatry, 55*(6), 1377–1384. doi:10.1016/j.comppsych.2014.05.003 PMID:24939704

Ko, C. H., Yen, J. Y., Chen, C. C., Chen, S. H., & Yen, C. F. (2005). Gender differences and related factors affecting online gaming addiction among Taiwanese adolescents. *The Journal of Nervous and Mental Disease, 193*(4), 273–277. doi:10.1097/01.nmd.0000158373.85150.57 PMID:15805824

Kraut, R., Patterson, M., Lundmark, V., Kiesler, S., Mukophadhyay, T., & Scherlis, W. (1998). Internet paradox: A social technology that reduces social involvement and psychological well-being? *The American Psychologist, 53*(9), 1017–1031. doi:10.1037/0003-066X.53.9.1017 PMID:9841579

Kuss, J., Griffiths, M., Karila, L., & Billieux, J. (2014). Internet addiction: A systematic review of epidemiological research for the last decade. *Current Pharmaceutical Design, 20*(25), 4026–4052. doi:10.2174/13816128113199990617 PMID:24001297

Morahan-Martin, J., & Schumacher, P. (2000). Incidence and correlates of pathological Internet use among college students. *Computers in Human Behavior, 16*(1), 13–29. doi:10.1016/S0747-5632(99)00049-7

Pontes, H. M., Griffiths, M. D., & Patrão, I. M. (2014). Internet addiction and loneliness among children and adolescents in the education setting: an empirical pilot study. *Aloma: Revista de Psicologia, Ciències de l'Educació i de l'Esport, 32*(1).

Scimeca, G., Bruno, A., Cava, L., Pandolfo, G., Muscatello, M. R. A., & Zoccali, R. (2014). The Relationship between Alexithymia, Anxiety, Depression, and Internet Addiction Severity in a Sample of Italian High School Students. *The Scientific World Journal*. PMID:25401143

Shek, D. T., & Yu, L. (2012). Internet addiction phenomenon in early adolescents in Hong Kong. *The Scientific World Journal.* PMID:22778694

Yang, C. K. (2001). Sociopsychiatric characteristics of adolescents who use computers to excess. *Acta Psychiatrica Scandinavica, 104*(3), 217–222. doi:10.1034/j.1600-0447.2001.00197.x PMID:11531659

Yao, M. Z., & Zhong, Z.-J. (2014). Loneliness, social contacts and Internet addiction: A cross-lagged panel study. *Computers in Human Behavior, 30,* 164–170. doi:10.1016/j.chb.2013.08.007

Yen, J. Y., Ko, C. H., Yen, C. F., Wu, H. Y., & Yang, M. J. (2007). The comorbid psychiatric symptoms of Internet addiction: Attention deficit and hyperactivity disorder (ADHD), depression, social phobia, and hostility. *The Journal of Adolescent Health, 41*(1), 93–98. doi:10.1016/j.jadohealth.2007.02.002 PMID:17577539

Young, K. S. (1999). The research and controversy surrounding Internet addiction. *Cyberpsychology & Behavior, 2*(5), 381–383. doi:10.1089/cpb.1999.2.381 PMID:19178209

Young, K. S., & Rogers, R. C. (1998). The relationship between depression and Internet addiction. *Cyberpsychology & Behavior, 1*(1), 25–28. doi:10.1089/cpb.1998.1.25

Acknowledgment

First and foremost, I would like to thank IGI Global for inviting me to edit a book on internet addiction. I am grateful for their valuable support and assistance throughout this project. A prominent acknowledgement goes to Marianne Caesar, Assistant Development Editor at IGI Global. Marianne provided me with responsive and expert guidance whenever I had an inquiry.

Second, I acknowledge my indebtedness to the chapter authors who welcomed and contributed to this project. My sincere gratitude goes to the chapter authors who contributed their time and expertise to this book. They tried their best to comply with the content and organization of the outline. Most of the authors also served as referees and I highly appreciate their double task. Without their support, this book would not have become a reality. This was a real team work. I would also like to acknowledge the help of the external reviewers, who carefully reviewed the assigned chapters and made valuable improvement suggestions. Specifically, I would like to thank Kimberly Young for graciously writing the Forward for this book.

Special thanks to my beloved daughter and wife, who provided the inspiration and support I needed to complete this project. Without them, this endeavour would have never been possible.

Bahadır Bozoglan
IF Weinheim Institute, Germany

Section 1
Internet Addiction as a Global Phenomenon

This section provides an introduction to internet addiction as a global phenomenon.

Chapter 1
The Impact of the Internet in Twenty-First Century Addictions:
An Overview

Shilpa Suresh Bisen
Visvesvaraya National Institute of Technology Nagpur, India

Yogesh Deshpande
Visvesvaraya National Institute of Technology Nagpur, India

ABSTRACT

In the era of digital technology, the internet has its significant role in sprouting vulnerability toward the different form of addictions and psychiatric disorders as well as providing the platform to manage them effectively. The internet provides ready access to illicit drugs, nonprescription medications which facilitate a sale of controlled substances over the Internet without a valid prescription which contributed to the rise of several forms of addictions. Studies have linked the severity of Problematic Internet Use to increase chances of substance Use disorder. Utilization of internet for longer durations serves as a booster for behavioral addictions like online gambling. Web based interventions on the positive side provides a cost effective, readily accessible and user-friendly platform to reach out majority of patients to help them in seeking treatment of Addictions and various psychiatric disorders. The aim of this chapter is to discuss the contribution of the internet in a positive and negative way to develop as well as resolve Psychiatric disorder.

INTRODUCTION

The word Internet originates from the words "Internet Connection Network" (Greenfield, 1999), which connects computers around the world with a standard protocol. Internet created a completely different and consumer friendly way to communicate and gradually evolved into the most important prop to the

DOI: 10.4018/978-1-5225-3477-8.ch001

personal, professional and social life of a significant proportion of the world population. Its use ranges from very basic search engines, socializing, shopping to sophisticated research aids, banking, business to name a few. At the same time, it has also come with its share of misuse like accessing inappropriate sites, hacking, stalking, spamming, etc. The Internet has become a basic tool for trading, entertainment, communication, as well as education in the contemporary world. Nevertheless, despite the high speed of information flow and potential educational value of the Internet, there are several attributes of the Internet which may foster addictive behavior. Of all the revolutions that have influenced mankind in the course of its evolution mass communication has been the most remarkable one and internet has catalyses the process to an extent that even Charles Darwin would have been left wonder-struck, for those who make their living forecasting change in social institutions are frequently humbled by the actual flow of events. Developments that seem inevitable (such as "artificial intelligence") seem to take forever to happen, while seemingly unstoppable institutions or innovations (such as physician practice, management firms) suddenly collapse. Sometimes, however, innovations spring, full blown and unheralded, seemingly from out of nowhere.

The objective of this chapter is to discuss how the internet has the impact on fulfilling the craving for various types of addiction among the larger section of the population. As well as the role of the internet is serving the mode of treatment for various addictions and psychiatric disorders.

As per the outline of whole chapter, researcher will be discussing in the following sections, the neutral role of internet in increasing the risk of addictions and various psychiatric disorders as well as contribution to the management of psychiatric illness by helping in increasing awareness, web based interventions, web based counseling, etc., on the whole, the influence of internet on 21st century has been immense in all aspects of humanity and obviously mental health hasn't remained untouched by it

BACKGROUND

Addiction of any kind is traditionally associated with an uncontrollable urge, often accompanied by a loss of control, a preoccupation and continued use despite negative consequences.

In the era of digital technology, the internet has its very significant role in sprouting vulnerability toward the different form of addiction, whether it's chemical or behavioral addiction, at the same time providing the platform to manage it well.

INTERNET: A PLATFORM FOR ILLEGAL DRUG TRAFFICKING

It has been revealed in researches that the internet provides ready access to drugs, including prescription medications. A study in the United states, Jena AB & Goldman DP (2011) estimated that for every 10% increase in high-speed Internet use from 2000 to 2007 (a proxy for access to Internet-based pharmacies), associated with admissions to treatment centers for opioid, sedative, hypnotic, and stimulant abuse increased by 1% each, whereas admissions for abuse of substances that are not purchasable online (alcohol, heroin, and cocaine) were unaffected. Due to increase in internet connectivity, an emergence of the new psychoactive substance called "legal highs" has increased. These drugs are specially designed to be legal alternatives to the established illegal drugs (Gibbons, 2012). Most of these are amphetamine- or ecstatic-like stimulants, hallucinogens or synthetic cannabinoids. They are widely sold on the internet without any information regarding safety content, interactions, and side-effects (Schmidt et al, 2011).

The Internet has been used to facilitate the illicit sale of controlled substances. No-prescription websites (NPWs) offer and then actually sell controlled substances over the Internet without a valid prescription which has facilitated the illicit sale of controlled substances. A basic Google or Yahoo search, simply using the term "Vicodin" return 40% to 50% NPWs in the top 100 sites. Thus, NPWs represent an important development in the sale of illicit drugs because of the ease with which controlled substances can be sold with relative anonymity (Forman et al., 2006). In the report published by the international narcotics control board in 2005, it was proposed that internet pharmacy has promoted the use of illicit substances like 3,4-methylenedioxy-methamphetamine(MDMA), Methoxetamine (MXE), amphetamines, fenethylline, Rohypnol, etc. Drug enforcement agency and general accounting office (GAO) identified 8 illegitimate online pharmacies that shipped Hydrocodone from US based pharmacies to GAO investigator purporting to be a patient, without any communication between the investigator and the physician who ultimately prescribed the medication. The continued presence of illegitimate Internet-based pharmacies prompted federal and private efforts to tackle the problem. The US Congress passed the Ryan Haight Online Pharmacy Consumer Protection Act in 2008 prohibiting the distribution of controlled prescription medications over the Internet without a prescription from a physician who directly examined the patient. Still, many of such NPWs continue their operations in several countries where similar acts are yet to be instated.

INTERNET: RELATION WITH SUBSTANCE USE DISORDER

Over the recent years, it has been postulated that there is a positive association between problematic internet use and substance use disorders with a severity of Problematic Internet Use adversely affecting the substance use disorder as concluded from numerous researches done in the recent past, till date.

In one of the earliest studies, alcohol consumption behavior in students was extensively studied and results showed that students with Problematic Internet Use consumed more alcohol (32.1%) compared to the non-Problematic Internet Use group (20.4%) (Young et al., 1999). There is ample proof that Problematic Internet Use is a predictor for future risk of cigarette smoking and alcohol intake (Chi Chiao et al., 2014). People who sit online and in front of their computers for long periods have shown a definite pattern of addictive behavior like cigarette smoking.

Recently, it has been concluded that common clinical characteristics such as craving and over engagement despite negative consequences between internet gaming disorder (IGD) and alcohol dependence might be present in certain groups of individuals in close proximity to high-level internet use and this group may also share common deficit in executive functioning. Unrestricted media exposures are known to be strongly associated with marijuana and alcohol intake among adolescent groups. Among the various categories of media exposure, music was independently associated with marijuana use, however, exposure to movies showed an independent association with alcohol use. (Primack et al., 2009)

Several studies have linked the severity of Problematic Internet Use to increase chances of having used an illicit substance. The biological basis of addictive behavior in Problematic Internet Use groups has shown the subjects showing similar vulnerable brain regions like substance addiction patients, which may include dorsolateral and orbitofrontal cortices. On the psychological interface, it has been seen that adolescents indulging in the use of illicit substances share common personality characteristics with those involved in Problematic Internet Use and together this can be classified under "psychoticism" in the Eysenck's personality model. (Fisoun v., 2012)

With the proliferation of social networking sites like Twitter and Facebook, there is a provision of a larger and virtual platform to discuss drug use and provide information on better sources to procure illicit substances across seas and beyond geographical borders. It also provides a safe haven from the law and can be done in a stealthy manner. It is also increasing promiscuous behavior among adolescents that backgrounds substance use like dating strangers, unhealthy sexual behavior, increasing incidence of sexual assaults and sexually transmitted disease. It has been seen that teens who spend more time indulging in social networking online are five times more likely to use tobacco, three times more likely to use alcohol, and two times more likely to use marijuana. (Califano J.A., 2008)

INTERNET: RELATION WITH BEHAVIORAL ADDICTION

Participating in a virtual environment like the internet for longer durations serves as a "booster" for several behavioral addictions like online gambling, online gaming, compulsive shopping, and cyber sex etc. as can be seen from data collected in recent times.

Problematic Internet Use

Many terms have been used to describe problematic Internet use, including "Internet addiction," "Internet addiction disorder," "Internet dependency," "compulsive Internet use," "pathological Internet use," and "compulsive computer use"(Liu & Potenza, 2007) Regardless of the term used, these behaviors have been defined as non-chemical or behavioral addictions which involve human-machine interactions (Griffiths, 1995).Studies have been conducted in many countries but due to the lack of a standardized definition is a significant limitation in estimating the prevalence of problematic Internet use. The range of prevalence rates has been estimated to be 3% to 11% of Internet users (DeAngelis, 2000). Research describes a typical problematic Internet users as technologically sophisticated male loners (Shotton, 1991). These people typically spend substantial time on non-work-related Internet activities and consequently neglect other social or vocational obligations. It not only consumes time, but also disrupts major areas of life functioning (Morahan& Schumacher, 2000). The most widely used criteria for diagnosis is:

The Young's Diagnostic Questionnaire (1996)

1.   Do you feel preoccupied with the internet (think about the previous online activity or anticipate next online session)?
2.   Do you feel the need to use the internet with increasing amounts of time in order to achieve satisfaction?
3.   Have you repeatedly made unsuccessful efforts to control, cut back or stop internet use?
4.   Do you feel restless, moody, depressed or irritable when attempting to cut down or stop internet use?
5.   Do you stay online longer than originally intended?

6. Have you jeopardized or risked the loss of significant relationship, job, educational or career opportunity because of the internet?
7. Have you lied to family members, therapists or others to conceal the extent of involvement with the internet?
8. Do you use the internet as a way of escaping from problems or of relieving a dysphoric mood (e.g., feelings of helplessness, guilt, anxiety, and depression)?

Psychiatric Co-Morbidities With Problematic Internet Use

Psychiatric disorders have not been carefully assessed in conjunction with problematic Internet use among large community samples. However, published case series and surveys have shown associations between psychiatric symptoms/disorders and problematic use of the Internet (Ha et al, 2006). Psychological impairments associated with excessive Internet use include depression, loneliness, and social isolation (Young & Rogers, 1998). Obsessive-compulsive symptoms were associated with excessive internet use (Yang et al, 2005) & so was ADHD to explain the deficiency in self-regulation, stimulation-seeking cognitive style, and poor social skills as a reason for associating with problematic Internet use. Other psychiatric disorders included substance use disorders, personality disorders, anxiety disorders, and psychotic disorders (Shapira et al, 2000). Thirty-eight percent of patients in the Black and colleagues' series carried a lifetime diagnosis of a substance use disorder and substance use disorders were the most common lifetime disorders identified. They (Black et al, 1999) also found personality disorders to be common, with cluster B disorders (narcissistic, borderline, and antisocial personality disorders) most frequently observed. In general, psychotic disorders were relatively less common (<10%), consistent with other reports (Mitchell, 2000). Thus, co-occurrence is the norm rather than the exception for problematic internet use (Timothy & Marc, 2007)

Online Gaming

Amongst the various subtypes of internet addiction disorders, online gaming is the most commonly found in Asian countries (Yen et al, 2010). Factors which could be responsible for online gaming are aural and visual stimulus rewards, peer group attention and/or approval, the requirement of total concentration, the keeping of a digital score, and incremental rewards for winning which reinforces "correct" behavior. A major factor of online gaming is that it adds social context and social interaction to this mix, that is, you can show off in-game rewards in a virtual environment. Additionally, online games often demand more time from the game than offline games. Among them, online role-playing games (in which the gamer develops a character over time) are very time to consume (Antonius et al, 2010). In fact, Western researchers specifically report Massive Multiplayer Online Role Playing Games as the main culprit in cases of online video game addiction (Chappell et al, 2006).

Internet gaming addiction is seen in close association with mental health disorders and pre morbid symptoms, including depression and insomnia (Cheung and Wong, 2011), suicidal ideation (Fu et al.,2010), attention-deficit hyperactivity disorder, social phobia, and hostility (Ko et al., 2009a), schizophrenia, obsessive–compulsive disorder (Ha et al., 2006), aggression (Ko et al., 2009b), drug use (Gong et al., 2009), and problematic alcohol use (Ko et al., 2008; Kuss et al., 2013).

Compulsive Cybersex

To the most common, restrictive use of the term, cybersex refers to a sequence of visual or textual exchanges with a partner for the purposes of sexual pleasure, which frequently culminates in masturbation (Cooper et al, 2004). Such cyber behavior typically occurs between consenting partners in private spaces accessed through e-mail, instant messaging, real-time exchanges via Web sites, or other consensual means. Compulsive cybersex is distinguished from problematic behavior based on perceptions of lack of control or choice and experiences of negative consequences by patients for whom the cybersex behavior is dystonic or unacceptable. Negative consequences of compulsive cyber sex affect familial, social, and vocational functioning, as well as physical and spiritual domains. Typically, persons who engage in cybersex find each other on the Internet and have never met before in real life (IRL). The conversations vary and range from flirting and "talking dirty" to giving very detailed descriptions of having intercourse. This way of having "virtual" sex enables people to explore their own sexuality, to try new things they have not yet tried offline, or in other cases have no intention of trying offline. It could be sharing secret sexual fantasies or creating an interactive sex novel. Children and adolescents are more prone to become "sexually reactive" in response to cyber sex exposure with engaging in compulsive masturbation, developing sexual variance, or perpetrating sexual aggression (Zilman, 2000). Treatment of compulsive cyber sex is based on the function of the problem behavior. Some couples seek therapy for sexual dysfunction or dissatisfaction in which cybersex interferes with normal sexual function (Southern, 2008).

Online pornography, cybersex, and cyber relationships are an important part of the internet landscape (Cooper, 1998). It indicates that a significant number of people are at a risk of cybersex addiction due to accessibility, affordability, and anonymity. Many people having a Problematic Internet Use are also misled by promises made by anonymous characters online and fall into traps from which it can be difficult to come out. This includes drug cartels, terrorist groups, flesh trade and all these groups have addictions in various forms within. Online bullying, sexual self-disclosure messages through Whatsapp, Facebook associated depression, digital footprints are potential risks that are posed by cyber addiction.

Internet Gambling

Gambling disorder is recognized under non-substance related disorders in DSM-5. Internet gambling can be described as continued online gambling despite the knowledge of the negative consequences of losing and putting oneself in a financially difficult position and added the loss of productive time. It is as serious as pathological "real world" gambling which is defined as a continuous or periodic loss of control over gambling and is highlighted by irrational thinking and erroneous cognition with the idea of giving up whatever one has for the euphoria surrounding a win or reward. It is a preoccupation with gambling and with obtaining money to gamble, continuation with gambling despite adverse consequences, and inability to stop gambling despite having the desire to do so (American Psychiatry Association,1994). Internet based gambling appears to be an incredibly profitable market with several governmental agencies becoming actively involved and legalizing their operation, for example, Australia, New Zealand and Holland. The researcher has highlighted the ease with which the gambling websites may be accessed by young people as well as the visually inviting aspect may contribute to increase in internet gambling (Griffith et al., 2000).

It is an impulse-control disorder characterized by preoccupation with gambling, a need to bet more, 'chasing' lost money and continued gambling in spite of escalating negative consequences (APA, 1994).

One type of gambling that is now widely available throughout the world, even without legalization, is Internet gambling. Ladd &Petry (2002) in their study of medical patients estimate only a small minority (7%) of gambling on the internet. Younger age and male gender were related to increased rates of Internet gambling similar to individuals with pathological gambling in the general community (Petry, 2005). Adolescents appear particularly vulnerable to the appeal of Internet gambling as they find gambling enjoyment (Dickson et al, in press), are particularly attracted to the colorful, fast-paced video game-like qualities, view themselves as highly intelligent, and perceive themselves as invulnerable to a gambling problem. It is seen that Internet gambling is associated with emotional distress, even among non-regular Internet gamblers & more substantial involvement has an additive and independent effect on poor physical and emotional health (Petry, 2006) as the youth from engaging in gambling are for entertainment, excitement and the possibility of winning money (Derevensky& Gupta, 1998).

Derevensky& Gupta (1998) has proposed few public health goals to address problem gambling. Denormalization, within the context of youth gambling, which implies social denormalization, where society begins to question and assess underage gambling. Governments, industry and the public have to take a responsibility to protect children and adolescents through effective institutional policy, legislation and through a reduction in the accessibility and availability of all forms of regulated gambling to underage youth. Prevention can consist of increasing knowledge and awareness of the risk of gambling (including online gambling on practice sites) among youth, parents, and professionals. Developing harm-reduction programs targeting those youth who are already gambling excessively, but who have not reached the level of pathological gambling, in order to prevent the progression as the presence of pathological gambling has been suggested to be a risk factor for suicide (Bourget & Gagne, 2003).

The person with IGD shows impaired risk evaluation and decision making which is similar to those having a substance use disorder and pathological gambling. In this scenario the player also has a compulsive urge to win and spends hours online to fuel such an obsession. There is a growing ease in the commercial participation with which the games are played and this includes rewards for points, free products, coupons to make online purchases and money in all forms and currencies to create an addiction. For the player, the convenience lies in making easy online payments, gaming on credit, speed, anonymity, and interactivity. (Griffiths 2000)

Internet Sex Addiction

Internet sex addiction typically involves viewing, downloading, and trading online pornography or engagement in adult fantasy role-play rooms as a compulsive behavior that persists despite serious negative consequences for personal, social, or occupational function. As users become comfortable with virtual forms of sex, they experience changes in their behavior or warning signs that they have become hooked (Young, 2008). Some of them are:

1. They routinely spend significant amounts of time in chat rooms and private messaging with the sole purpose of finding online pornography or cybersex.
2. They feel preoccupied with using the Internet to find online sex activities.
3. They frequently use anonymous communication to engage in sexual fantasies not typically carried out in real life.
4. They anticipate the next online session with the expectation that they will find sexual arousal or gratification.

5.   They frequently move from cybersex to phone sex (or even real-life meetings).
6.   They hide their online interactions from their significant others.
7.   They feel guilt or shame about their online use.
8.   They masturbate while online while engaged looking at porn or having erotic chat.
9.   They are less invested with their real-life sexual partners only to prefer online pornography or cybersex as a primary form of sexual gratification.

Cooper (1998) suggested three primary factors: Accessibility, affordability, and anonymity that facilitates increased online sexuality & termed it the "Triple A Engine". Accessibility makes millions of adult sites available 24 hours a day, 7 days a week; Affordability is the competition on the Web that keeps prices low along with many ways to access "free" sex, and Anonymity is what people perceive their communications. According to Young, Anonymity is one of the most seductive lures of Internet sex. Another risk factor could be the emotional & interpersonal problems such as stress, depression, loneliness, anxiety, or burnout which can lead to an addict's need to go online.

Compulsive Online Shopping

Earlier people had a free will to walk into physical shops and make choices before making a purchase. Being online for long hours has started limiting the time a person can make for his or her personal shopping needs. With a human tendency in "getting more for less irrespective of quality" and "easy availability", a dangerous pattern of compulsive buying has taken birth. With increasing logistics and ease of delivery, there are also businesses which allow schemes like "cash on delivery" and "buy now pay later" which makes the person online bite more than they can chew. The person making the purchases will rarely leave his desk and is not interested in the quality of goods either, it's just the momentary impulsiveness of purchasing online that gives them satisfaction, even if they regret their purchase a few hours later, only to place new orders within hours and this forms a vicious circle from which the person finds difficult to exit. Compulsive buying corresponds to a repetitive uncontrolled urge to buy items that are not needed. High prevalence of substance use disorders in the compulsive buying group was found to be 21%-53% and there is also the positive relationship between compulsive buying and Problematic Internet Use. (Mueller et al., 2011)

Recently there have been websites offering high-end phones and internet devices to people who earn maximum points online by listening and downloading songs. This can create a preoccupation in the Problematic Internet Use population and make them addicted to listening songs, even at times when they require maintaining a high degree of alertness at work or study. They also end up spending pounds for a penny.

INTERNET: MODE OF TREATING ADDICTIONS

Web based interventions are primarily self-guided intervention program that is executed by means of a perspective online program operated through a website and used by consumers seeking health and mental health related assistance. These are categorized into web based psycho-education intervention; self-guided web based therapeutic intervention; Human supported web based therapeutic interventions. The advantages of internet based interventions are high-cost effectiveness, increased access to evidence based treatment and greater opportunity to reach patients in the remote location. (Carlbring & Andersson, 2006). Symptomatic deterioration, an emergence of new psychological symptoms, high dropout rate, lack of predicted a positive effect on target symptoms and frustration caused by technical issues are some of the negative effects of web based interventions. (Boettcher et al., 2014) there are some interventions to manage substance use disorders mentioned below

Alcohol electronic screening and brief intervention aimed to reduce the unhealthy/excessive alcohol consumption in alcohol dependence patients. The patient completes a web based AUDIT questionnaire and a personalized feedback along with brief intervention is provided to the patient via email. Alcohol anonymous is a form of self-help therapy, which is now available online also. Numerous studies have found AA online participation to be related to improved alcohol use outcomes. (Humphreys et al., 1997) Large scale use of web based interventions for smoking cessation, very famous one (Quitnet) showed that sustained use of Quitnet was associated with better abstinence. Intervention is provided through interactive websites and tailored emails for which benefits have been found. Internet based intervention for smoking can be provided in conjunction with individual or group counseling or pharmacotherapy. (Graham et al, 2005) Cognitive behavioral therapy and motivational enhancement therapy is the main intervention used in treating cannabis dependence and are available online. Web based intervention for cannabis and other illegal drugs are still at a premature stage, nevertheless, its effectiveness in reducing the short term cannabis use has been supported by a few studies (Tait et al, 2013).

INTERNET: INFLUENCE ON PSYCHIATRIC DISORDERS

The Internet is beneficial in its moderate usage for the well-being of individuals. Rather than usage exceeding a certain daily threshold, concerns have been raised for Problematic Internet Use. Internet use is considered as problematic when it becomes compulsive, interferes with the normal activity of daily living and the individual finds difficulty in controlling his usage. In an opinion of some researchers, it is not a true addiction, but may be the product of other existing disorders like depression or phase of life problem. While excessive use of the internet can become associated with a various psychiatric disorder, on the other side internet is also being developed as an effective tool to treat such mental health issues.

Depression

Excessive Internet use has been proven in research to be associated with depression, but determining temporality of which came first is difficult. It is well known that increasing number of people are spending more time online at the cost of their real world relationships leading to social deprivation syndrome and early signs of depression. Also diverting time otherwise meant for social and family meetings to the internet may isolate an individual and predispose him to depression (Young and Rogers, 1998). Persons suffering social deprivation develop irritability, mood swings, poor concentration, increased restlessness, aggressive behavior, impulsivity and relationship problems. Lee et al., (2014) found a level of depression and suicide ideation highest on the Internet-addicts group. Teague E S (2004) in a study found that females with high neuroticism used Facebook more frequently and had depressive symptoms, while Facebook use was not related to depression in males. Several studies have demonstrated the association between depression and Internet Addiction (Ko et al, 2012, Fisher et al., 2010).On one hand, Loneliness, low self-esteem, and lack of motivation may drive a depressed individual to net addiction while at the other end Problematic Internet Use may serve as an easy means of getting social approval and thus improving an otherwise low self-esteem in such subjects (Wartberg et al., 2011).

Anxiety

Addiction to the internet, many people don't realize, causes anxiety. It could either be apprehensions about being hooked to the cyber world or the fear of being judged online. Musarrat Azher et al (2014) in the latest study using Internet addiction scale and Beck anxiety scale showed a positive correlation between anxiety and Problematic Internet Use among students. Loneliness, social anxiety, and shyness tend to drive an individual to internet owing to the comfort of anonymity, easy approachability and no need of nonverbal communication. (Casale & Fioravanti., 2011)

Social Phobia

Social phobia is a strong fear of being judged by others and being embarrassed. This fear can be so strong that it gets in the way of going to work or school or doing other everyday things. Lee & Stapinski (2012) suggest that problematic internet use may serve to worsen or reinforce social fears and avoidance of face-to-face social interactions Persons with social anxiety feel a greater sense of control in online rather than offline interactions. Also, a perception of having a high likelihood of threat in face-to-face interactions leads to problematic internet use among persons with high social anxiety. (Campbell et al., 2006) He argued that "chat" users who are socially fearful may be using the internet to rehearse social behavior and communication skills, in order to improve their social interaction.

Obsessive Compulsive Disorder

A person with OCD has tremendous anxiety and discomfort throughout their daily life. A person with OCD is susceptible to the different addictions and internet addiction are more devastating in it. OCD patients constantly search for websites providing the types of thrill seeking material, such as Gambling, Auction, and Pornography. OCD patients with inappropriate sexual thoughts have been noticed visiting pornographic sites with alarming frequency. Persons with OCD have unique reactions when exposed to sites such as ebay.com, and in an effort to suppress emotion and problem, they have a competitive urge to outbid others and excessively purchase items from a huge selection option. (Cooper A., 2013)

Attention Deficit Hyperactivity Disorder

Attention deficit hyperactivity disorder is most common psychiatric disorder in adolescents with internet addiction. Rapid response and immediate reward are characteristic of internet usage, which may provide immediate stimulation and reward for people with core ADHD symptoms of being easily bored and having an aversion for the delayed reward. Internet games are designed with the incentive of "get to the next level" which makes ADHD patients more vulnerable to them. Yen et al., (2014) in a study on Taiwanese adolescent diagnosed with ADHD found that severe physical anxiety symptom, low harm avoidance, depressive symptom and lower self-esteem were significantly associated with severity of internet addiction symptoms.

Personality Factors

An abundance of literature proving internet use and its link to various personality disorders have explored. Around 52% of Internet addicts met criteria for at least one personality disorder, the most frequent being borderline, schizotypal and narcissistic personality disorders. Mittal et al (2007) suggests that people with the schizotypal personality disorder would spend a greater amount of time in online chat rooms and online games as to compensate his anxiety in the social situation and forming a relationship. Bernardi & Pallanti., (2009) linked borderline and avoidant personality to internet addiction. A person with borderline personality disorder has impulsivity and feeling of boredom and emptiness frequently so while involving oneself in online activities increases chances of getting addicted to the internet. A person with Narcissistic personality disorder is more prone to involve in cybersex and pornography due to his excessive fantasies and exploit interpersonal relationship as found in several studies more Facebook friends was associated with more clinical symptoms of bipolar-mania, narcissism, and histrionic personality disorder but fewer symptoms of dysthymia and schizoid personality disorders(Rosen et al.,2013) Aggression, poor self-control and narcissistic personality traits were also found to predispose individuals to internet gaming addiction (Kim et al., 2008). In a meta-analysis of all studies done by Floros et al (2014) found positive correlations of Internet addiction scores with the traits of psychoticism, sensation seeking & neuroticism and negative correlations with the traits of extraversion, conscientiousness, reward dependence, agreeableness, and self-directedness.

INTERNET: MODE OF TREATING PSYCHIATRIC DISORDERS

Treatment for Depression

1. **Problem-Solving Technique:** Problem-solving techniques are used to improve a problem-solving ability of a person while addressing depressive symptoms too. The five-week program with one session per week is generally carried out via email. The core elements of such technique targets to solve the problem by describing the problem, brainstorming, choosing the best solution, making the plan for carrying out the solution, actually carrying out the solution, evaluation. (Warmerdam et al., 2010)
2. **Internet Based Cognitive Behavior Therapy:** It is a clinician assisted treatment which consists of Eight illustrated online lessons and a corresponding lesson summary which include practical homework exercise and is completed over eight weeks period, one lesson a week using text exercises, audio, and video conferencing techniques. The therapist communicates to the client via email. The specific components are psycho-education, self-monitoring, cognitive restructuring, behavioral activation, structural problem solving, relaxation techniques and social skill training. (Warmerdam et al., 2010)
3. **Acceptance and Commitment Therapy:** Its therapeutic target is psychological flexibility which is defined as 'the ability to contact the present moment more fully as a conscious human being and to change the persisting behavior when doing so serves valued ends. (Hayes et al., 2006) It is based on six processes cognitive defusion, acceptance, contact with the present moment, self-as-context, value and committed action. The modules consist of text, video, narrated animations and the patient is also provided with a workbook and CD. (Segal et al, 2002).

4. **Mindfulness Based Therapy:** It is an empirically supported intervention to teach participants emotion-regulation skills to reduce residual depressive symptoms and avoid relapse triggers which contribute to a chronic illness course. It is an 8-week program with ten interactive sessions were under instructions, participants learn to use formal meditation skills (body scan, mindful movement, seated meditation, three-minute breathing space) and informal mindfulness technique (incorporating mindfulness into daily activities like mindful eating) through downloadable video, audio clips, assignments, and emails. (Segal et al, 2012)

Participants are requested to complete one module each week and to conduct mindfulness exercises twice a day for 6 days a week. Participants get access to the next module once they had completed the previous one. Mindful mood balance most uses mindfulness technique over the internet. It has 8 sessions of 60-90 minute programs with each session integrating mindfulness meditation and principles of cognitive behavioral therapy. (Segal et al., 2014). Currently, three depression Interventional application is accessible on the web without charge to consumers- ODIN, moodGYM, Blue pages.

Treatment for Anxiety Disorder

Web based cognitive behavioral therapy have increasingly become a popular empirical evidence based therapy for various anxiety spectrum disorders. Evidence suggests that internet delivered CBT works for Panic disorder (Carlbring et al, 2001) Social anxiety disorder (Anderson et al, 2006), Generalized anxiety disorder (Titov et al, 2009), Post-traumatic stress disorder (Lange et al, 2003) and Specific phobia (Anderson et al., 2009).

Internet Based Cognitive Behavioral Therapy

It is a form of text based guided self-help treatment consisting of ten treatment modules with the eleven-week treatment given over the internet under therapist guidance. The session is targeted cognitive restructuring, exposure exercises, self-focused attention, social skills and relapse prevention. Clients are given short quizzes and homework. Feedback is provided within 24 hours. (Hedman et al., 2012).

LIMITATIONS AND RECOMMENDATIONS

On the Basis of review of the included studies, there seemed several limitations in the existing literature of how the internet is affecting different sphere of psychiatry. Even though the availability of the huge literature on how the internet is providing platform for psychological intervention in form of Psychological testing and psychotherapy, Researcher unable to compile and systematically organized within the restricted formatting of the chapter. The diagnostic criterion for problematic internet use is still not consistent across studies. This is because there is currently no official diagnosis of IA as a mental or psychiatric disorder. Due to the uncertainty of including Problematic Internet Use as a psychiatric disorder is still the matter of debate, hence the definition and operationalization of the concept may vary within a cultural framework. Multiple limitations of the current literature on Problematic Internet Use aroused from the absence of an operational definition of Problematic Internet Use. The most notable limitation is the inconsistency in the adoption of various instruments for the measurement of Problematic Internet

Use in research studies. Due to this inconsistency, Treatment for Problematic Internet Use is also difficult to modulate. Therefore, the Researcher recommend strongly to work toward establishment of the official diagnostic criteria of Problematic Internet Use.

CONCLUSION

In researcher's opinion, the greatest concern facing this field of research is a general complacency toward the internet. In some cases, this complacency is born of ignorance. Too many parents are simply unaware of what their children are doing online and what risks it might pose. At the same time, many physicians are unaware of the power of the internet. In an era of an empowered public and patients, the internet may be a more powerful determinant of health-seeking behavior than medical opinion. It may provide more information for various kinds of drugs than was ever available to the public domain in the past. The internet is effected across cultural and geographical boundaries. In addition, it has a significant impact in assisting and promoting substance abuse. It provides services and information ranging from general information to online orders of prescription drugs or other poisons that bypass government regulations and custom controls. This bridges the gaps of locality and accessibility, which previously formed a natural divide in accessing and grabbing drugs which were not so feasible earlier. In addition to these negative effects, there is a vast potential to harness these properties to a beneficial effect. The wide acceptance of the internet makes it a powerful tool for recognition of the at-risk individual, for preventing and supporting survivors, with the different mode of treating options.

ACKNOWLEDGMENT

This research received no specific grant from any funding agency in the public, commercial, or not-for-profit sectors.

REFERENCES

American Psychiatric Association. (1994). *APA Diagnostic and Statistical Manual of Mental Disorders*. Author.

Andersson, E., Enander, J., Andrén, P., Hedman, E., Ljótsson, B., Hursti, T., & Rück, C. et al. (2012). Internet-based cognitive behavior therapy for obsessive–compulsive disorder: A randomized controlled trial. *Psychological Medicine*, 42(10), 2193–2203. doi:10.1017/S0033291712000244 PMID:22348650

Antonius, J., Schoenmakers, T. M., & Regina, J. J. M. et al.. (2010). Compulsive Internet Use: The Role of Online Gaming and Other Internet Applications. *The Journal of Adolescent Health*, 47(1), 51–57. doi:10.1016/j.jadohealth.2009.12.021 PMID:20547292

Azher, M., Khan, R. B., Salim, M., Bilal, M., Hussain, A., & Haseeb, M. (2014). The relationship between internet addiction and anxiety among students of the University of Sargodha. *International Journal of Humanities and Social Science*, 4(1), 288–293.

Bernardi, S., & Pallanti, S. (2009). Internet addiction: A descriptive clinical study focusing on comorbidities and dissociative symptoms. *Comprehensive Psychiatry, 50*(6), 510–516. doi:10.1016/j.comppsych.2008.11.011 PMID:19840588

Black, D. W., Belsare, G., & Schlosser, S. (1999). Clinical features, psychiatric comorbidity, and health-related quality of life in persons reporting compulsive computer use behavior. *The Journal of Clinical Psychiatry, 60*(12), 839–844. doi:10.4088/JCP.v60n1206 PMID:10665630

Boettcher, J., Åström, V., Påhlsson, D., Schenström, O., Andersson, G., & Carlbring, P. (2014). Internet-based mindfulness treatment for anxiety disorders: A randomized controlled trial. *Behavior Therapy, 45*(2), 241–253. doi:10.1016/j.beth.2013.11.003 PMID:24491199

Bourget, D., Ward, H., & Gagne, P. (2003). Characteristics of 75 gambling-related suicides in Quebec. *Canadian Psychiatric Association Bulletin, 35*, 17–21.

Califano, J. A. Jr. (2008). *High society: How substance abuse ravages America and what to do about it*. Public Affairs.

Campbell, A. J., Cumming, S. R., & Hughes, I. (2006). Internet use of the socially fearful: Addiction or therapy? *Cyberpsychology & Behavior, 9*(1), 69–81. doi:10.1089/cpb.2006.9.69 PMID:16497120

Carlbring, P., & Andersson, G. (2006). The Internet and psychological treatment. How well can they be combined? *Computers in Human Behavior, 22*(3), 545–553. doi:10.1016/j.chb.2004.10.009

Carlbring, P., Westling, B.E., Ljungstrand, P., Ekselius, L., & Andersson, G. (2001) Treatment of panic disorder via the Internet: A randomized trial of a self-help program. *Behavior Therapy, 32*(4), 751-64.

Chappell, D., Eatough, V., Davies, M. N., & Griffiths, M. (2006). Everquest—It's just a computer game right? An interpretative phenomenological analysis of online gaming addiction. *International Journal of Mental Health and Addiction, 4*(3), 205–216. doi:10.1007/s11469-006-9028-6

Chiao, C., Yi, C. C., & Ksobiech, K. (2014). Adolescent Internet use and its relationship to cigarette smoking and alcohol use: A prospective cohort study. *Addictive Behaviors, 39*(1), 7–12. doi:10.1016/j.addbeh.2013.09.006 PMID:24140305

Choi, Y. H. (2007). Advancement of IT and seriousness of youth Internet addiction. In *2007 International Symposium on the Counseling and Treatment of Youth Internet Addiction* (Vol. 20, pp. 279-298). Seoul, South Korea: National Youth Commission .

Cooper, A. (1998). Sexuality and the Internet: Surfing into the new millennium. *Cyberpsychology & Behavior, 1*(2), 187–193. doi:10.1089/cpb.1998.1.187

Cooper, A. (Ed.). (2013). *Cybersex: The dark side of the force: A special issue of the Journal Sexual Addiction and Compulsion*. Routledge.

Cooper, A., Delmonico, D. L., & Griffin, S. E. (2004). Online sexual activity: An examination of potentially problematic behaviors. *Sexual Addiction & Compulsivity, 11*(3), 129–143. doi:10.1080/10720160490882642

DeAngelis, T. (2000). Is Internet addiction real? Monitor on Psychology. *American Psychological Association Publication, 31*, 4.

Derevensky, J., & Gupta, R. (1998). Child, and adolescent gambling problems: *A program of research. Canadian Journal of School Psychology, 14*, 55–58. doi:10.1177/082957359801400106

Dickson, L., Derevensky, J., & Gupta, R. (2004). Harm reduction in the prevention of youth gambling problems: Lessons Learned from Adolescent High-Risk Behavior Prevention Programs. *Journal of Adolescent Research, 19*(2), 233–263. doi:10.1177/0743558403258272

Fioravanti, G., Dèttore, D., & Casale, S. (2012). Adolescent Internet addiction: Testing the association between self-esteem, the perception of Internet attributes, and preference for online social interactions. *Cyberpsychology, Behavior, and Social Networking, 15*(6), 318–323. doi:10.1089/cyber.2011.0358 PMID:22703038

Fisher, D. R., & Boekkooi, M. (2010). Mobilizing Friends and Strangers: Understanding the role of the Internet in the Step It Up day of action. *Information Communication and Society, 13*(2), 193–208. doi:10.1080/13691180902878385

Fisoun, V., Floros, G., Siomos, K., Geroukalis, D., & Navridis, K. (2012). Internet addiction as an important predictor in early detection of adolescent drug use experience—implications for research and practice. *Journal of Addiction Medicine, 6*(1), 77–84. doi:10.1097/ADM.0b013e318233d637 PMID:22227578

Floros, G., & Siomos, K. (2014). Excessive Internet use and personality traits. *Current Behavioral Neuroscience Reports, 1*(1), 19–26. doi:10.1007/s40473-014-0006-1

Forman, R. F., Marlowe, D. B., & McLellan, A. T. (2006). The Internet as a source of drugs of abuse. *Current Psychiatry Reports, 8*(5), 377–382. doi:10.1007/s11920-006-0039-6 PMID:16968618

Fu, K. W., Chan, W. S., Wong, P. W., & Yip, P. S. (2010). Internet addiction: Prevalence, discriminant validity and correlates among adolescents in Hong Kong. *The British Journal of Psychiatry, 196*(6), 486–492. doi:10.1192/bjp.bp.109.075002 PMID:20513862

Gibbons, R. D., Brown, C. H., Hur, K., Davis, J. M., & Mann, J. J. (2012). Suicidal thoughts and behavior with antidepressant treatment: Reanalysis of the randomized placebo-controlled studies of fluoxetine and venlafaxine. *Archives of General Psychiatry, 69*(6), 580–587. doi:10.1001/archgenpsychiatry.2011.2048 PMID:22309973

Gong, J., Chen, X., Zeng, J., Li, F., Zhou, D., & Wang, Z. (2009). Adolescent addictive Internet use and drug abuse in Wuhan, China. *Addiction Research and Theory, 17*(3), 291–305. doi:10.1080/16066350802435152

Graham, A. L., Cobb, N. K., Raymond, L., Sill, S., & Young, J. (2007). The effectiveness of an Internet-based worksite smoking cessation intervention at 12 months. *Journal of Occupational and Environmental Medicine, 49*(8), 821–828. doi:10.1097/JOM.0b013e3180d09e6f PMID:17693778

Greenfield, D. N. (1999). Psychological characteristics of compulsive Internet use: A preliminary analysis. *Cyberpsychology & Behavior, 2*(5), 403–412. doi:10.1089/cpb.1999.2.403 PMID:19178212

Griffiths, M. (1995) Technological addictions. *Clinical Psychology Forum, 76,* 14-19.

Griffiths, M. (2000). Does Internet and computer" addiction" exist? Some case study evidence. *Cyberpsychology & Behavior, 3*(2), 211–218. doi:10.1089/109493100316067

Griffiths, M. (2003). Internet gambling: Issues, concerns, and recommendations. *Cyberpsychology & Behavior, 6*(6), 557–568. doi:10.1089/109493103322725333 PMID:14756922

Ha, J. H., Yoo, H. J., Cho, I. H., Chin, B., Shin, D., & Kim, J. H. (2006). Psychiatry comorbidity assessed in Korean children and adolescents who screen positive for Internet addiction. *The Journal of Clinical Psychiatry, 67*(05), 821–826. doi:10.4088/JCP.v67n0517 PMID:16841632

Hayes, S. C., Luoma, J. B., Bond, F. W., Masuda, A., & Lillis, J. (2006). Acceptance and commitment therapy: Model, processes, and outcomes. *Behaviour Research and Therapy, 44*(1), 1–25. doi:10.1016/j.brat.2005.06.006 PMID:16300724

Hedman, E., Ljótsson, B., & Lindefors, N. (2012). Cognitive behavior therapy via the Internet: A systematic review of applications, clinical efficacy, and cost–effectiveness. *Expert Review of Pharmacoeconomics & Outcomes Research, 12*(6), 745–764. doi:10.1586/erp.12.67 PMID:23252357

Humphreys, K., & Tucker, J. A. (2002). Toward a more responsive and effective intervention systems for alcohol-related problems. *Addiction (Abingdon, England), 97*(2), 126–132. doi:10.1046/j.1360-0443.2002.00004.x PMID:11860378

Jena, A. B., & Goldman, D. P. (2011). Growing Internet use may help explain the rise in prescription drug abuse in the United States. *Health Affairs*, 10–1377. PMID:21565838

Kim, E. J., Namkoong, K., Ku, T., & Kim, S. J. (2008). The relationship between online game addiction and aggression, self-control and narcissistic personality traits. *European Psychiatry, 23*(3), 212–218. doi:10.1016/j.eurpsy.2007.10.010 PMID:18166402

Ko, C. H., Yen, J. Y., Chen, C. C., Chen, S. H., & Yen, C. F. (2005). Proposed diagnostic criteria for Internet addiction for adolescents. *The Journal of Nervous and Mental Disease, 193*(11), 728–733. doi:10.1097/01.nmd.0000185891.13719.54 PMID:16260926

Ko, C. H., Yen, J. Y., Yen, C. F., Chen, C. S., Weng, C. C., & Chen, C. C. (2008). The association between Internet addiction and problematic alcohol use in adolescents: The problem behavior model. *Cyberpsychology & Behavior, 11*(5), 571–576. doi:10.1089/cpb.2007.0199 PMID:18785835

Krusche, A., Cyhlarova, E., & Williams, J. M. G. (2013). Mindfulness online: An evaluation of the feasibility of a web-based mindfulness course for stress, anxiety, and depression. *BMJ Open, 3*(11), e003498. doi:10.1136/bmjopen-2013-003498 PMID:24293203

Kuss, D. J. (2013). Internet gaming addiction: Current perspectives. *Psychology Research and Behavior Management, 6*, 125. doi:10.2147/PRBM.S39476 PMID:24255603

Ladd, G. T., & Petry, N. M. (2002). Disordered gambling among university-based medical and dental patients: A focus on Internet gambling. *Psychology of Addictive Behaviors, 16*(1), 76–79. doi:10.1037/0893-164X.16.1.76 PMID:11934091

Lam, L. T., Peng, Z. W., Mai, J. C., & Jing, J. (2009). Factors associated with Internet addiction among adolescents. *Cyberpsychology & Behavior*, *12*(5), 551–555. doi:10.1089/cpb.2009.0036 PMID:19619039

Lange, A., Rietdijk, D., Hudcovicova, M., Van De Ven, J. P., Schrieken, B., & Emmelkamp, P. M. (2003). Interapy: A controlled randomized trial of the standardized treatment of posttraumatic stress through the internet. *Journal of Consulting and Clinical Psychology*, *71*(5), 901–909. doi:10.1037/0022-006X.71.5.901 PMID:14516238

Lee, Y. S., Han, D. H., Kim, S. M., & Renshaw, P. F. (2013). Substance abuse precedes internet addiction. *Addictive Behaviors*, *38*(4), 2022–2025. doi:10.1016/j.addbeh.2012.12.024 PMID:23384457

Leiner, B. M., Cerf, V. G., Clark, D. D., Kahn, R. E., Kleinrock, L., Lynch, D. C., & Wolff, S. S. (1997). The past and future history of the Internet. *Communications of the ACM*, *40*(2), 102–108. doi:10.1145/253671.253741

Liu, T., & Potenza, M. N. (2007). Problematic Internet use: Clinical implications. *CNS Spectrums*, *12*(6), 453–466. doi:10.1017/S1092852900015339 PMID:17545956

Mitchell, P. (2000). Internet addiction: Genuine diagnosis or not? *Lancet*, *355*(9204), 632. doi:10.1016/S0140-6736(05)72500-9 PMID:10696991

Morahan, M. J., & Schumacher, P. (2000). Incidence and correlates of pathological Internet use among college students. *Computers in Human Behavior*, *16*(1), 13–29. doi:10.1016/S0747-5632(99)00049-7

Mueller, A., Mitchell, J. E., Peterson, L. A., Faber, R. J., Steffen, K. J., Crosby, R. D., & Claes, L. (2011). Depression, materialism, and excessive Internet use in relation to compulsive buying. *Comprehensive Psychiatry*, *52*(4), 420–424. doi:10.1016/j.comppsych.2010.09.001 PMID:21683178

Petry, N. M. (2005). *Pathological Gambling: Etiology, Comorbidity, and Treatments*. Washington, DC: American Psychological Association Press. doi:10.1037/10894-000

Petry, N. M. (2006). Internet gambling: An emerging concern in family practice medicine? *Family Practice*, *23*(4), 421–426. doi:10.1093/fampra/cml005 PMID:16621919

Primack, B. A., Swanier, B., Georgiopoulos, A. M., Land, S. R., & Fine, M. J. (2009). Association between media use in adolescence and depression in young adulthood: A longitudinal study. *Archives of General Psychiatry*, *66*(2), 181–188. doi:10.1001/archgenpsychiatry.2008.532 PMID:19188540

Rosen, L. D., Whaling, K., Rab, S., Carrier, L. M., & Cheever, N. A. (2013). Is Facebook creating "iDisorders"? The link between clinical symptoms of psychiatric disorders and technology use, attitudes, and anxiety. *Computers in Human Behavior*, *29*(3), 1243–1254. doi:10.1016/j.chb.2012.11.012

Schmidt, M. M., Sharma, A., Schifano, F., & Feinmann, C. (2011). "Legal highs" on the net—Evaluation of UK-based Web sites, products, and product information. *Forensic Science International*, *206*(1), 92–97. doi:10.1016/j.forsciint.2010.06.030 PMID:20650576

Segal, Z. V., Teasdale, J. D., Williams, J. M., & Gemar, M. C. (2002). The mindfulness-based cognitive therapy adherence scale: Inter-rater reliability, adherence to protocol and treatment distinctiveness. *Clinical Psychology & Psychotherapy*, *9*(2), 131–138. doi:10.1002/cpp.320

Segal, Z. V., Teasdale, J. D., & Williams, J. M. G. (2004). Mindfulness-based cognitive therapy: Theoretical rationale and empirical status. In S. Hayes, V. Follette, & M. Linehan (Eds.), *Mindfulness and acceptance: Expanding the cognitivebehavioral tradition.* New York: Guilford Press.

Shapira, N. A., Goldsmith, T. D., Keck, P. E. Jr, Khosla, U. M., & McElroy, S. L. (2000). Psychiatric features of individuals with problematic internet use. *Journal of Affective Disorders, 57*(1-3), 267–272. doi:10.1016/S0165-0327(99)00107-X PMID:10708842

Shotton, M. A. (1991). The costs and benefits of "computer addiction". *Behaviour & Information Technology, 10*(3), 219–230. doi:10.1080/01449299108924284

Southern, S. (2008). Treatment of compulsive cybersex behavior. *The Psychiatric Clinics of North America, 31*(4), 697–712. doi:10.1016/j.psc.2008.06.003 PMID:18996308

Tait, R. J., Spijkerman, R., & Riper, H. (2013). Internet and computer based interventions for cannabis use: A meta-analysis. *Drug and Alcohol Dependence, 133*(2), 295–304. doi:10.1016/j.drugalcdep.2013.05.012 PMID:23747236

Teague, E., Simoncic, K., & Vargas, J. (2014). On the internet no one knows I am Introvert''.Extraversion, Neuroticism and Internet Interaction. *Cyberpsychology & Behavior, 5*(2), 125–128.

Timothy, L., & Marc, N. (2007). Problematic Internet Use: Clinical Implications. *CNS Spectrums, 12*(6), 453–466. doi:10.1017/S1092852900015339 PMID:17545956

Titov, N., Andrews, G., Davies, M., McIntyre, K., Robinson, E., & Solley, K. (2010). Internet treatment for depression: A randomized controlled trial comparing clinician vs. technician assistance. *PLoS One, 5*(6), e10939. doi:10.1371/journal.pone.0010939 PMID:20544030

Warmerdam, L., Riper, H., Klein, M. C., van de Ven, P., Rocha, A., Henriques, M. R., & Cuijpers, P. et al. (2012). Innovative ICT solutions to improve treatment outcomes for depression: The ICT4Depression project. *Annual Review of Cybertherapy and Telemedicine, 181*(1), 339–343. PMID:22954884

Wartberg, L., Kammerl, R., Bröning, S., Hauenschild, M., Petersen, K. U., & Thomasius, R. (2015). Gender-related consequences of Internet use perceived by parents in a representative quota sample of adolescents. *Behaviour & Information Technology, 34*(4), 341–348. doi:10.1080/0144929X.2014.928746

Williams, J. M., Teasdale, J. D., Segal, Z. V., & Soulsby, J. (2000). Mindfulness-based cognitive therapy reduces over general autobiographical memory in formerly depressed patients. *Journal of Abnormal Psychology, 109*(1), 150–155. doi:10.1037/0021-843X.109.1.150 PMID:10740947

Yang, C. K., Choe, B. M., Baity, M., Lee, J.-H., & Cho, J.-S. (2005). SCL-90-R and 16PF profiles of senior high school students with excessive internet use. *Canadian Journal of Psychiatry, 50*(7), 407–414. doi:10.1177/070674370505000704 PMID:16086538

Yen, J. Y., Yen, C. F., Chen, C. S., Tang, T. C., & Ko, C. H. (2009). The association between adult ADHD symptoms and internet addiction among college students: The gender difference. *Cyberpsychology & Behavior, 12*(2), 187–191. doi:10.1089/cpb.2008.0113 PMID:19072077

Young, K. S. (1998). Internet addiction: The emergence of a new clinical disorder. *Cyberpsychology & Behavior, 1*(3), 237–244. doi:10.1089/cpb.1998.1.237

Young, K. S. (1999). Internet addiction: Symptoms, evaluation, and treatment. *Innovations in Clinical Practice: A Source Book, 17,* 19-31.

Young, K. S. (2008). Internet Sex Addiction: Risk Factors, Stages of Development, and treatment. *The American Behavioral Scientist, 52*(1), 21–37. doi:10.1177/0002764208321339

Young, K. S., & Rogers, R. C. (1998). The relationship between depression and Internet addiction. *Cyberpsychology & Behavior, 1*(1), 25–28. doi:10.1089/cpb.1998.1.25

Zilman, D. (2000). Influence of unrestrained access to erotica on adolescents' and young adults' dispositions toward sexuality. *The Journal of Adolescent Health, 27*(2), 41–44. doi:10.1016/S1054-139X(00)00137-3 PMID:10904205

KEY TERMS AND DEFINITIONS

Behavioral Addiction: Behavioral addiction is a form of addiction that involves a compulsion to engage in a rewarding non-drug-related behavior despite knowledge of negative consequences to the person's physical, mental and social well-being.

Gambling Disorder: Internet gambling can be described as continued online gambling despite the knowledge of the negative consequences of losing and putting oneself in a financially difficult position and added the loss of productive time.

Internet Sex Addiction: It involves viewing, downloading, and trading online pornography or engagement in adult fantasy role-play rooms as a compulsive behavior that persists despite serious negative consequences for personal, social, or occupational function.

Problematic Internet Use: Problematic Internet use is a behavior defined as non-chemical or behavioral addictions which involve human-machine interactions, can be is also called as compulsive Internet use (CIU), Internet overuse, problematic computer use, or pathological computer use (PCU) or Internet addiction disorder (IAD).

Psychiatric Co Morbidity: Psychiatric Co morbidity is the presence of one or more additional psychiatric diseases or disorders co-occurring with primary Psychiatric disease or disorder.

Psychiatric Disorder: A Psychiatric disorder is a syndrome characterized by clinically significant disturbance in an individual's cognition, emotion or behavior that reflects a dysfunction in the person's psychological, biological, or developmental well being.

Substance Use Disorder: Substance use disorder is a condition in which the excessive use of one or more substances leads to a clinically significant impairment or distress.

Web Based Management: Web based interventions are primarily self-guided intervention program that is executed by means of a perspective online program operated through a website and used by consumers seeking health and mental health related assistance.

Chapter 2
Internet Addiction:
A Modern Societal Problem

Shaun Joseph Smyth
Ulster University, UK

Kevin Curran
Ulster University, UK

Nigel Mc Kelvey
Letterkenny Institute of Technology, Ireland

ABSTRACT

Internet addiction is a recent phenomenon which describes a state where people become so involved in online behaviour to the detriment of other aspects of their lives. Treatment camps for young people have sprung up around in a bid to address this contemporary issue. This chapter examines the factors in Internet addiction, its definition, the complications which exist in the various diagnostic methods of successfully diagnosing Internet addiction and the criticism directed towards some of these diagnostic methods. We also examine which individuals are at risk of developing this condition. We look at positive diagnosis of the addiction and the resultant effects it has on an individual's family life, employment, social life and personal wellbeing before finally looking at possible methods and treatments that can be used in treating Internet addiction.

INTRODUCTION

While the 20th century proved to be the century which provided us with a time of great advances in both information and communication technologies the 21st century however is proving to be the age of the Internet as we enjoy access to vast amounts of information from all over the World and many different forums for communication. The Internet plays an integral part of our modern lives and as advances are continually being made in the world of information Technology (IT), it becomes substantially easier to access. As it's uses continually increase, especially among the younger generation (Akin and Iskender, 2011), the Internet means that we no longer need to go searching for information but rather information

DOI: 10.4018/978-1-5225-3477-8.ch002

arrives at our homes on a computer screen via the simple click of a computer key. The Internet provides a wealth of services at our fingertips, including online gaming, shopping, gambling communication with friends, social media sites as well as an abundance of information for research purposes and it enables businesses to carry out operations in the form of Electronic Commerce (e-commerce) (Hersh,1999; Poon, 2000). These and many other services are all readily available through the very accessible Internet which can be accessed without leaving the comfort of our chair at home.

Most people make use of the Internet as a functional tool performing their day-to-day personal objectives which may include booking hotels or making airline reservations. However certain individuals experience an inability to control their Internet use resulting in distressful symptoms of psychological dependence (Brand et al. 2014). The limits however, to which many individuals are engaging with the Internet and its many functions such as a means for communication is a subject of much discussion, as the topic of Internet addiction (IA) continues to be the subject of much debate among researchers in mental health (Young, 2004). Despite the vast numbers of Internet users which exist the benefits of the Internet are reported to far outweigh the opposing consequences which result from extreme use such as Internet addiction which reportedly is not yet recognised by the ICD-10 (International classification of Diseases) or the DSM-IV which is the 4th edition of the Diagnostic and Statistical Manual of Mental Disorders (Murali and George, 2007). Internet addiction is referred to in several different ways and the terms "Internet addiction disorder (IAD)," "Problematic Internet Use (PIU)," "Excessive Internet Use," "Compulsive Internet Use," "Pathological Internet Use," and "Computer Addiction" have all been used to refer to the same notion which is that an individual gets so involved in their online use to such an extent that it leaves other areas of their lives neglected (Griffiths, 1998; Cash et al. 2012; Yan et al. 2014; Li et al. 2014).

The remainder of this chapter looks at what constitutes an addiction, the definition of Internet addiction, the complications which exist in the various diagnostic methods of successfully diagnosing Internet addiction, the criticism some of these diagnostic methods have taken and the effects of excessive Internet use by both students and employees. This chapter also highlights those individuals which are of increased risk of developing this condition including positive diagnosis of the addiction and the resultant effects it has on the individual's family life, employment, social life and personal wellbeing before finally looking at possible methods and treatments that can be employed for treating Internet addiction.

BACKGROUND

Even though the last 15 years has witnessed the number of Internet users increase by 1000% research into Internet addiction is however, still in it's infancy (Kuss and Lopez-Fernandez, 2016). With the growth of the Internet over the last two decades the number of Internet users and individuals experiencing problems as they have lost control over their Internet use and experienced negative issues in their daily lives such as problems at work or school, has risen extensively (Brand et al. 2014). There are currently over three billion Internet users worldwide which accounts for 40% of the world's population. The first billion was reached in 2005 as 2010 witnessed the second billion and the level reach three billion in 2014 as the growth in smartphones and other devices enables online and Internet connectivity (Zafar, 2016). A recent nationwide study in 11 European countries reported the occurrence of obsessive Internet users to range from 11.8% in Israel to 1.2% in Italy (Lai et al. 2013).

Internet addiction (IA) is typically defined as a condition where an individual has lost control of their Internet use and proceeds to use the Internet excessively to the point where he/she experiences problematic consequences which ultimately have a negative effect on his/her life (Kardefelt-Winther, 2014; Scimeca et al 2013). Young (1998) has been credited with devising the term Internet addiction disorder (IAD) which was used to describe excessive and problematic Internet use displaying features such as preoccupation and an inability to cut back on their usage of the Internet (Murali and George, 2007). Internet addiction refers to using the Internet for more than 38 hours per week and even though the real extent of Internet addiction is not known, the estimated figure is reported to be between 5 and 10% of all online users (Murali and George, 2007). Researchers have endeavoured to classify Internet addiction (IA) into several different categories and as Murali and George (2007) explain, this feat was achieved by Young (1999) who categorised (IA) into the following five categories: cybersexual addiction, cyberrelationship addiction, computer addiction (which includes activities such as game-playing), information overload (including uncontrollable database searching) and finally Net compulsion (which includes tasks such as gambling or shopping on the Net).

However, Griffiths (2000) argues that many of these are not Internet addicts but merely using the Internet as a medium to fuel a different addiction completely and highlights how there is a need to distinguish and differentiate between addiction to the Internet as opposed to addictions on the Internet.

Young (1996) highlights those Internet applications most utilised by both dependent and non-dependent users. The results show that applications accessed by non-dependent and dependent users differs from that of non-dependent users using aspects of the Internet such as Information protocols and the World Wide Web (W.W.W.) to enable them to gather information compared to dependent users who mainly used the two-way communication functions of the Internet such as chat rooms, e-mail, news groups and MUDs which differs from chat rooms was originally Multi-User Dungeon with later variants such as Multi-User Domain a spin-off of the old Dungeon and Dragons game which seen players take on character roles (Young, 1996).

Table 1 displays values recorded from Young's research in 1996 for different Internet applications used by both dependent and non-dependent computer users, although with the huge changes in aspects of Internet use these figures will have changed greatly also with the introduction of newer computers, smartphones and hand-held devices etc.

Due to the relative newness of the disorder referred to as Internet addiction, there is still however very little information which clearly highlights the habit-forming nature of the Internet and the conse-

Table 1. Internet applications most utilized by dependents and non-dependents

Application	Type of Computer User	
	Dependents	Non-Dependents
Chat Rooms	35%	7%
B vMUDs	28%	5%
News Groups	15%	10%
E-mail	13%	30%
WWW	7%	25%
Information Protocols	2%	24%

(Young, 1996)

quences that are associated with it (Young, 2004). Despite this claim by Young (2004) the past decade as highlighted by Romano et al. (2013) has witnessed much debate in medical literature with the term being regarded by many as a novel psychopathology which may indeed effect many individuals. There are many varied uses of the Internet by Internet addicts but using it for gambling and pornography are common among this group of individuals resulting in a negative impact across areas of the individual's personal life and family functioning (Romano et al, 2013). There has been minimal research to explore the immediate psychological impact of exposure to the Internet on 'Internet addicts' which can act as a driver in cases of such problematic behaviour (Romano et al., 2013).

Due to a lack of research, testing and validity of the term 'Internet addiction' many critics have suggested that maladaptive, excessive or problematic Internet use (PIU) should replace the term 'Internet addiction' (Murali and George, 2007). Once the principle that people can become addicted to the Internet is accepted a further problem exists as the Internet consists of many different activities such as e-mailing, browsing information, file transferring, etc. and some Internet activities are more addictive than others (Griffiths, 1997).

DEFINING ADDICTION AND INTERNET ADDICTION

In the same manner as an alcoholic who needs to consume large amounts of alcohol to achieve satisfaction, an Internet addict routinely spends a significant amount of time online and may go to great lengths to disguise their online activity and the extent of their Internet behaviour (Young, 2004).

The Internet which was originally designed for the facilitation of research among both academic and military agencies however, prolonged use by some people has created an awareness among the mental health community which has caused much debate about Internet addiction (Young, 2004). The term Internet addiction has been described by Fu et al. (2010) as a growing psychiatric disorder although much debate exists as to this description. Regarding Internet addiction and its definition there are many health care professionals and researchers who are uncertain as to the validity in terming it a legitimate mental health disorder (Fu et al, 2010).

A well-defined definition is required for both Internet addiction in children and adolescents (Christakis, 2010). The addictive use of the Internet is a new experience which is developing in a rapid manner (Young, 1999a). The term addiction must firstly be defined before it can be decided as to whether Internet addiction is in fact a problem and truly does exist in some of today's Internet users.

Young (2004) defines an addiction as the following:

Addiction of any kind is traditionally associated with an uncontrollable urge, often accompanied by a loss of control, a preoccupation with use, and continued use despite problems the behavior causes.

The Internet is capable of and does create obvious changes in mood with almost 30% of Internet users having admitted to Internet use in a bid to reduce negative feelings or mood, hence they are using the Internet like a drug (Greenfield, 1999).

Many believe that addiction is a term which should only be applied to the ingestion of a drug (Young, 1999a; Griffiths and Pontes, 2014). Although some individuals' views have moved on to include several different behaviours which do not involve the use of an intoxicant and include compulsive behaviour such as gambling, playing video games, overeating, exercise, love relationships as linking the term addiction solely to drugs does not prohibit its use for similar conditions which do not involve drugs. Despite the restrictive definition of addiction there is however no grounds for linking the word addiction solely to drug habits and there is no basis to assume that the most severe addictions automatically involve the use of drugs and therefore the term should not be limited solely to drug use (Alexander and Schweighofer, 1988; Griffiths and Pontes, 2014).

The American Society of Addiction Medicine (ASAM) defines addiction as a chronic brain disorder which officially proposes that for the first time ever that addiction is not limited to substance abuse only. Addictions, whether they are chemical or behavioural do share certain characteristics which include salience, compulsive use (loss of control) modifications in the individual's mood, alleviation of distress, tolerance, withdrawal and the continuation despite the negative consequences (Cash et al, 2012).

Abuse is different in that it is a milder form of an addiction which can worry and create problems for the user but the user is better equipped and has better control over their behaviour allowing them to set limits and regulate their use (Young, 2004). Addiction and abuse of the Internet will both result in consequences such as the student who is obsessively using social media sites to chat with friends loses valuable study time resulting in poor academic performance and the employee who spends too much time surfing the Internet during his/her working hours will result in poor job productivity and may lead to further actions such as job loss.

The major elements which make up an addiction include the fixation on a specific substance or activity which the individual partakes in despite continual, failed attempts to decrease it and the development of mood disturbances as a direct result of these failed attempts (Christakis, 2010). Christakis (2010) also highlights that signs of an addiction are both a greater usage than expected or wanted which can lead to possible loss of employment, jeopardizing both relationships and education or lying about actual usage. While instances such as these are present and can be seen within Internet usage there is a strong foundation that there is an issue with pathological Internet usage and the argument is no longer about the existence of Internet addiction as a condition but rather how widespread it is (Christakis, 2010).

WHAT ARE INTERNET ADDICTS ADDICTED TO?

There remains no clear and concise reason as to what Internet addicts become addicted to however many suggestions have been proposed including: the physical process of typing, the communication properties the Internet offers, information attained from a wide range of different Internet sites and the allure of applications such as e-mail, gambling, pornographic material, video games are just a few of the many possibilities to attract addicts to the Internet along with the anonymity that it also offers (Murali and George, 2007). Past studies have revealed an association with Internet addiction and psychological variables including shyness, loneliness, self-consciousness, anxiety, depression and interpersonal relations (Ahmadi et al. 2014; Weinstein et al. 2014; Zhu et al. 2015).

Individuals who experience social anxiety may compensate for these feelings of loneliness which they experience by socializing in a game or via social networking sites as they feel safer in online environments due to the sense of anonymity. Such cases where using the Internet relieves an unfulfilled, real-life problem may lead to problematic outcomes and debate as to whether this can be called Internet addiction are ongoing (Kardefelt-Winther, 2014).

The Internet is used by many shy individuals to avoid face to face interaction. They often choose to engage with others in Internet relay chat and virtual multiuser domains (Murali and George, 2007). The addictive potential offered by these massive multiplayer online roles playing games (MMORPGs) has led some people to refer to them as heroin ware (Murali and George, 2007). Christakis (2010) highlights how reality games which allow people to assume different identities or join forces with team members from all over the globe may pose the greatest risk of addiction. In these worlds, a continuous online presence is vital and going offline may often incur penalties. Such games have a large profit margin and the makers of such games have an incentive to create games which are addictive in nature.

Whether it may be playing games online or the use of the Internet as a medium for communication, there is a differentiation in those which are addicted to the Internet itself as against those using the Internet as a means of fuelling a different addiction (Griffiths, 1998).

DIFFICULTIES IN DIAGNOSING INTERNET ADDICTION

Universally the Internet is looked upon as a technical instrument which is very much encouraged thus rendering both the detection and diagnosis of addiction as difficult tasks (Young, 2004). The understanding of the criteria which differentiate a normal Internet user from a pathological Internet user (PIU) is essential before a correct diagnosis of this addiction can be achieved (Young, 2004; Young and Rodgers, 1998).

However, the concept and the definition of Internet addiction are still under debate from an academic and clinical point of view (Fu et al., 2010). There is both a sheer lack of evidence-based standardisation and clinical clear-cut clinical assessment criteria for Internet addiction and there is no aetiological explanation for the condition known as Internet addiction and it would be premature to determine the validity of Internet addiction as a condition (Fu et al., 2010).

The achievement of a successful diagnosis of individuals with Internet addiction is complex and further complicated due to the absence of an accepted set of standards for this condition in the Diagnostic and Statistical Manual of Mental Disorders- Fourth Edition (DSM-IV) (Young, 1999a; Cash et al. 2012; Young, 1996; Young, 2004; Murali and George, 2007; Young and Rodgers,1998). Despite the lack of the inclusion of Internet addiction in the DSM-IV many other different conditions are however listed and within this list Pathological Gambling was regarded as the condition whose pathological nature closely resembles that of Internet use (Young, 1996; Young, 1999a; Christakis, 2010; Cash et al. 2012; Griffiths, 1998; Young, 2004; Young and Rodgers, 1998; Tao et al. 2010; Ko et al. 2005; Greenfield, 1999). Employing the use of the condition known as Pathological Gambling as a template for Internet addiction it has been consequently possible to define Internet addiction as an impulse- control disorder which does not feature an intoxicant (Young, 1996; Young, 1999a; Young, 2004; Young and Rodgers, 1998).

Numerous different approaches have been employed in both the assessment and evaluation of the disorder commonly known as Internet addiction and they include: Young's Internet Addiction Test, the Problematic Internet Use Questionnaire (PIUQ) and the Compulsive Internet Use Scale (CIUS) (Cash et al. 2012). Through modifications to the criteria for pathological gambling Young (1996a) managed to create a short 8 item questionnaire which could be used as a screening instrument for addictive Internet use referred to as a Diagnostic Questionnaire (DQ) (Young, 1999a; Young, 1996; Young, 2004; Liu and Luo, 2015; Zhu et al. 2015; Lai et al. 2013). The 8 item questionnaire involved questioning the individual to determine if they felt preoccupied with the Internet; used it to feel satisfied; thought about their previous session online; anticipated their next session on-line; made unsuccessful attempts to cease or reduce Internet usage; use the Internet longer than planned; felt changes in their mood if they attempted to reduce or stop Internet usage; affected employment, education or relationship; lied as to extent of Internet usage and finally do they use the Internet as an escape from problems such as mood or feelings of depression, anxiety, guilt or helplessness (Young, 1996; Young, 1999a; Tao et al. 2010; Murali and George, 2007).

Individuals who took part in the 8-question questionnaire and replied 'yes' to five or more of the questions were termed as addicted Internet users or dependents while the remainder were non-dependents (Widyanto and Griffiths, 2007; Young, 1996; Young, 1999).

The score of five was the same measure used in pathological gambling and was viewed as a sufficient number to make the difference between either normal or compulsive addictive use of the Internet (Young, 1996; Young, 1996a, Young and Rodgers, 1998).

Young (2004) however, recommended that only nonessential computer or Internet use such as that which is neither business nor academic related should be assessed and an individual should only be classified as dependent or an addicted Internet user when they reply 'yes' to five or more of the eight questions over a time frame of 6 months.

In a bid to achieve a definition for addiction which would encompass Internet addiction Griffiths (1998) suggested that six conditions need to be fulfilled and they include salience, alteration in mood, symptoms upon withdrawal, tolerance, conflict and finally relapse. Although this method appears in theory to be both sensible and simple to use it has however lacks sufficient testing and has not been proven (Murali and George, 2007).

Internet addiction is difficult to diagnose as arguments exist regarding many of the diagnostic measures which are available as there is limited agreement on the crucial component, dimensions of Internet addiction and most instruments are self-report and are reliant on the person answering the questions on questionnaires to be honest and as people who suffer from Internet addiction are prone to lying about Internet usage a 'lie scale' which none operate is required to correct this aspect. Also, none of the methods proposed for the diagnosis of Internet addiction specify which actual Internet application (e.g. e-mail, chat rooms, pornography etc.) the Internet user is addicted to (Murali and George, 2007).

There is much controversy surrounding Internet addiction and it also remains unclear to the present time as to whether the underlying mechanisms which are responsible for the addictive behaviour are the same in the various types of Internet Addiction Disorders (IAD) (e.g. online sexual addiction, online gaming and excessive surfing) (Cash et al. 2012).

Successful diagnosis of Internet addiction is further complicated as Internet addiction does not seem to exist independently but rather it is comorbid with other psychopathological conditions (Fu et al. 2010). Internet addiction has been found to be associated with attention-deficit hyperactivity disorder (ADHD), depression symptoms, low self-esteem, impulsivity, social anxiety, shyness, suicidality and stress, (Akin and Iskender, 2011; Fu et al. 2010; Romano et al. 2013). Such findings suggest that a new label of Internet addiction may lead to an underdiagnosis of primary psychiatric disorders (Fu et al. 2010). Many health care professionals view excessive Internet use as a symptom of another disorder such as depression or anxiety and think that Internet addiction could be viewed as an impulse control disorder and used to alleviate the anxiety, stress or depression from which they suffer (Cash et al. 2012).

MEDICAL CONDITIONS AND INTERNET ADDICTION

The current research which exists about Internet addiction not only validates the presence of a condition/ disorder commonly known as 'Internet addiction', how it can be related with other social conditions such as substance abuse but it also highlights certain areas of the population which prove to be of an increased risk of being diagnosed with Internet addiction (Christakis, 2010). Such individuals include those with other psychological illnesses, including attention-deficit/hyperactivity disorder (ADHD), depression and social isolation (Christakis, 2010; Thorens et al. 2013) and these views are backed up by (Fu et al., 2010) who believe that Internet addiction should not be looked upon as a standalone psychiatric disorder but rather it does not seem to exist independently in individuals and it is more often in existence simultaneously with other psychopathological conditions.

Other conditions which Internet addiction has been known to be present with include depressive symptoms, depressive disorder, social anxiety, shyness, impulsivity, low self-esteem, anxiety disorder and even suicidality (Fu et al,2010; Wu et al. 2015). These findings highlight how labelling an individual with Internet addiction may lead to the under diagnosis of primary psychiatric disorders for which there is both proven and effective interventions available (Fu et al,2010). Since many researchers and clinicians have noticed a large variety of mental disorders co- occurring with Internet addiction disorder (IAD) it raises the debate as to whether the IAD or the co- occurring disorder came first (Cash et al,2012).

However, there is a relationship between Internet addiction and depression, anxiety and stress as the more addictive to the Internet an individual is the more stress or anxiety he or she would experience (Akin and Iskender, 2011).

BIOLOGICAL PREDISPOSITION TO INTERNET ADDICTION

Addictions are responsible for activating a combination of areas within the brain known as the 'reward centre' or the 'pleasure pathway' of the brain and when they are activated the release of dopamine is increased along with opiates and a group of other neurochemicals. Over a period, the associated receptors may become affected producing a tolerance or a need for increasing the stimulation of the reward centre to produce a 'high' leading to subsequent behavioural patterns which are required to prevent withdrawal. The use of Internet may also be responsible for the release of dopamine into the nucleus accumbens which is one of the reward structures of the brain which is specifically involved in other addictions (Cash et al. 2012).

There are underlying neurochemical changes, most likely dopamine plays a major role in Internet addiction disorder (IAD) as a neuro transmitter in the brain and occurs during any pleasurable act and have proven themselves to be habit forming on a brain behavioural level (Greenfield, 1999; Liu and Luo, 2015). Each time there is a highly pleasurable human behaviour which can be acquired without human interface (as can be achieved on the Net) there seems to be a greater risk of abuse. The ease at which purchasing of stock, gambling and online shopping via the Internet allows for both a limitless and disinhibited experience. As there is no human interaction in these areas there is a heightened risk of abusive and/or compulsive behaviour in these areas (Greenfield, 1999).

Cash et al (2012) highlights the rewarding nature of technology by quoting the following statement made by a 21-year-old male undergoing treatment for Internet addiction disorder (IAD):

I feel technology has brought so much joy into my life. No other activity relaxes me or stimulates me like technology. However, when depression hits, I tend to use technology as a way of retreating and isolating.

PATHOLOGICAL USE OF THE INTERNET

The key components of addiction include factors such as the preoccupation with a substance or behaviour with the failure of repeated attempts to reduce it, mood disturbances because of failed attempts to reduce it, a greater usage than anticipated or desired, jeopardizing employment, education or lying about actual usage (Christakis, 2010). With most of these criteria evident in Internet usage and given the strong basis to believe that there could possibly be a strong problem with Internet usage the debate is not about whether it exists but rather just how prevalent it is (Christakis, 2010). There has been considerable debate regarding both the terms and definitions of pathological Internet behaviour and many terms used include Internet abuse, Internet addiction and compulsive Internet use (Greenfield, 1999).

Despite the definition of pathological Internet use (PIU) as an impulse- control disorder which does not employ the use of an intoxicant (Young, 1996) professionals in the field of pathology provide a more restrictive definition for the classification of Internet usage, highlighting that according to the pathological concept an individual who reportedly uses the Internet for 2 to 3 hours per week is considered as a normal user whereas any individual registering 8.5 hours or above per week is classified as a pathological user (Chebbi et al. 2001). Even though 8.5 hours a week online does not seem like an excessive figure Griffiths (1998) explains that authors argued that it was indicative of problems surfacing in relatively short periods of being online.

Research has shown that specific applications seemed to play a substantial role in the development of pathological Internet use (PIU) and dependents were less likely to control their usage of highly interactive features compared to other online applications (Young and Rodgers, 1998). On-line users presenting with a more extreme danger of pathological Internet use include those individuals which tend to lead more unsociable or lonely lifestyles (Young and Rodgers, 1998). Pathological users of the Internet used it to meet new people for emotional reasons and to play interactive games and these types of people are more inclined to be more socially disinhibited (Griffiths, 1998). However, as the Internet becomes ever-present in society today it is obvious that some of the assumed ''symptoms'' of Internet addiction (IA) can be construed as the normal movement in how the younger generations entertain or communicate and as an indication of Internet use in everyday life rather than pathological behaviour (Kardefelt-Winther, 2014).

There is a possibility that a unique reinforcement exists which displays that such anonymous on-line relationships gathered using the Internet's interactive applications have the powerful ability to provide the fulfilment of unmet real-life social needs which would otherwise not be met and would remain unfulfilled (Young and Rodgers, 1998).

The prevalence of pathological Internet usage (PIU) is high with Young and Rodgers (1998) highlighting that research on PIU among self-proclaimed 'addicted' users displayed many similar traits such as: they were always anticipating their next session on-line; they felt nervous when they were off-line;

they lied regarding their activity on-line; lost track of time when on-line; they believed that the Internet caused difficulties with their careers, finances and in a social capacity

Surveys to test for the effects of pathological Internet use were carried out in both the University of Texas and Bryant College in the USA and the results from both campuses documented that pathological Internet use is both problematic for both academic performance and relationship functioning (Young and Rodgers, 1998).

Family Issues of Internet Addiction

Family plays an important role in an individuals' ability to deal with stress as the family provides the main spiritual and material support system for college students especially in Eastern cultures such as China's (Yan et al. 2014). Possibly one of the most damaging effects of Internet addiction is that as unwarranted time is spent on-line the consequences are that neglect frequently occurs within the family circle. Time spent on-line takes the place of social activities, family social life and interests and ultimately disrupting family relationships (Murali and George, 2007; Griffiths, 1998; Akin and Iskender, 2011; Young, 1999a). The occurrence of Internet addiction in adolescents in Asia was reported to be 13.8% in Taiwan, South Korea reported to be 10.7%, Hong Kong a reported 6.7% with China reporting 2.4% (Lai et al. 2013)

Online affairs are highlighted as one of the most common consequences associated with the Internet and Internet addiction (Young, 2004). The problem experienced because of online affairs is that the addicted member of the relationship will isolate himself or herself and refuse to engage in activities such as going out for dinner or attending sports events which they previously enjoyed together as a couple (Young,1999a). Cyber sexual infidelity is reported to be a common reason for couples looking for advice or marriage counselling and it is the most upsetting aspect of Internet-based sexual infidelity as it violates both the marital and family space (Greenfield,1999). Individuals develop online relationships which over time overshadow the time spent with real people to the point where matrimonial lawyers have witnessed a significant increase in divorce cases solely from information of such cyberaffairs (Young, 1999a). Such cyberaffairs are defined as romantic or sexual relationships which originate through contact online and continue mainly by electronic discussions via e-mails, chat rooms or interactive games (Young, 2004).

Using these virtual groups strangers from all over the world can meet up instantly 24 hours a day and 7 days a week and it is a breeding ground for the development of online affairs causing problems in marriages that were once solid and cyberaffairs have caused the destruction of many marriages. Serious relationship problems in 53% of Internet addicts surveyed resulted in marital discord, separation and in some cases even led to divorce proceedings. explains how online affairs differ dynamically from real-life affairs with the potential to be more seductive and due to the global nature of the Internet online affairs can be more glamorous than the partner they already have in their day to day life enabling users to interact with other individuals without the fear of rejection (Watson, 2015; Young, 2004).

Electronic communication can accelerate the intimacy and people are more open and honest online allowing intimacy which may take months or years to create offline to be created in a matter of weeks or days in an online relationship. Seemingly harmless online relationships can easily progress to secret phone calls, letters and meeting offline and can see what was once an online affair ultimately turn what was a happy marriage or relationship into a possible divorce (Young, 2004). Unlike affairs which happen outside the home the online affair has the possibility to start in the marital home while the unsuspecting spouse has been sitting in the next room (Young, 2004). The question is there a limit to how much time spent at a computer is too much and how can a wife or husband know if their partner is having an online affair while at the computer.

The following indications are possible signals of an online affair:

- **Altered Sleeping Patterns:** The change in an individual's sleeping habits is one of the first warning signs of an online affair as chat rooms and other such meeting places which are used for cybersex do not heat up until late at night so the unfaithful person in the relationship may start staying up later to be part of the action (Young, 2004). The unfaithful partner starts to go to bed in the early hours of the morning or the unfaithful person in the relationship suspected of having an online affair may start getting up 1 or 2 hours earlier each morning to use the computer and have an e-mail exchange with their new online romantic partner before they go to work. Thomas (2014) describes how the Internet makes cybersex a particularly exciting type of sex addiction due to its accessibility, affordability and the anonymity that it offers and is often referred to as the Triple- A Engine as a result.

- **Demanding Privacy:** When a person starts, an affair be it online or offline the usually go to extreme lengths to hide this from their partner and the same is true for cyberaffairs as they lead to the greater need for privacy and secrecy for their use of their computer. The person having a cyberaffair will generally move the computer from the view of others in the household, especially their partner and may even change the password of the computer or laptop they are using or hide their online activities in a bid to keep their affair from their partner. The person having the affair will react with anger or be defensive in a bid to hide his or her online activity (Young 2004).

- **Ignoring Their Daily Responsibilities:** As the Internet user increases their time spent online this results in responsibilities within their day to day lives suffering. This is not automatically a sign of a cyberaffair. The person spending more time at the office than usual or neglecting housework that is normally done or tasks such as mowing the lawn may indicate that somebody else is competing for the suspected person's attention and time as the novelty and excitement that are created by an online affair and the husband or wife does not feel the same sense of responsibility to household tasks as they felt before the computer came into his or her life.

- **Evidence of Lying:** The partner having the affair on the Internet tends to lie about the length of time length of time their Internet sessions last (Young, 2004; Fu et al. 2010; Young 1999a; Young 1996). The person involved in the cyberaffair will lie about Internet charges and hide bills such as credit card bills to conceal their Internet usage (Young, 2004; Young, 1999a; Young 1996). Such behaviours create distrust between the couple in a relationship and over time this will damage the quality of what was once a happy relationship (Young, 2004) Those involved in online affairs find themselves telling bigger lies in a bid to conceal the existence of their online relationship (Young, 2004). Such behaviours create distrust in what was once a stable relationship (Young, 1996) which finds both partners arguing about computer usage and trust in the relationship is broken (Young, 2004).

- **Change in Personality:** The mood in the person engaging in the Internet affair changes and they may become withdrawn and cold in what was once a warm and happy relationship. If a person is questioned about their Internet usage they often respond in denial and sometimes consciously or not they shift the blame to the person not engaging in the cyberaffair (Young,2004).

- **Lose Interest in Sex:** In some cases, online affairs can lead to either phone sex or meetings in real-life. The process of sharing secrets of sexual fantasies online can change an individual's pattern of sexual interest with their real-life partner (Young, 2004). Those who engage in online affairs are less enthusiastic to their real-life partner.
- **Reduced Investment in the Relationship:** Individuals who pursue online affairs have less energy to put into their real-life relationship with their partner. The excitement of going on vacation together is not what it once was and they avoid making any long-range plans with their real-life partner.

The discovery that you have an unfaithful partner is difficult especially as it is with someone that your unfaithful partner has not actually met in real-life. In many case the faithful partner will try to take charge of the situation by not disclosing it to close friends and family. Through sheer frustration and jealousy many faithful partners try to control the situation by controlling the partner's time spent online, taking measures such as changing passwords on online devices within the house and in severe cases cancelling the Internet provider to the home or dismantling the computer itself to rebuild the relationship they once had with their partner (Young, 2004) with the ignored or unloved partners of Internet addicts often referred to as a 'cyberwidow' (Murali and George, 2007).

Student Internet Abuse

The Internet is an essential tool providing a wealth of information and enabling lectures to be viewed online to view at our leisure. It enables research to be carried out on many different devices by students and teaching staff alike and has been advertised as an important educational tool which has led to the integration by many schools of Internet services within the classroom environment. Even though the Internet is an ideal tool for carrying out research both psychologists and educators alike have been aware of the negative impacts which accompany this tool, especially the over use or misuse of the Internet (Murali & George, 2007; Young, 1996). One survey carried out revealed that a total of 86% of teachers, librarians and computer coordinators that responded believed that the usage of the Internet by children does not improve the child's performance arguing that information on the Internet is too disorganised and it is unrelated to the school curriculum to assist students and the Internet can serve as a distraction (Barber, 1997).

In a study by Young (1998), 58% of students suffered from a result of poor study habits and poor grades or even failed school because of excessive Internet use. Many students are unable to control their Internet usage and as a result there has been a reported decline in their study habits due to extreme Internet use resulting in a substantial decline in student grades, class attendance and in severe cases students being placed on probation due to their excessive Internet use (Young, 1996a).

Colleges are now beginning to recognise the possible influence of Internet use as counsellors at the University of Texas-Austin began to realise that the leading issue for many students was their inability to regulate their Internet use, a view that was confirmed when a study of student Internet abuse at the campus revealed that 14% displayed the conditions of Internet addiction (Young, 2004).

Despite the merits of the Internet which is an ideal research tool for students if used correctly many students experienced significant academic problems as they found themselves surfing inappropriate web sites, taking part in chat room gossip, communicating with pen-pals and playing interactive games online all of which affected the result of their own studies. Due to these activities, many students encountered difficulty completing homework assignments, studying for upcoming exams, getting sufficient sleep to be alert for the next day's classes and those not able to control their Internet use found themselves achieving poor grades, receiving academic expulsion and sometimes resulting in expulsion for university entirely (Young, 1996; Young, 2007).

The high dependence of the younger generation on the Internet for learning, leisure and social activities is recognised as a social problem and this generation are also more vulnerable to the influences of the media (Fu et al. 2010).

When compared to other sections of society college students are regarded as being more susceptible to Internet addiction due to psychological and developmental characteristics of adolescence and early adulthood and easy access to and expected use of the Internet. Stress, family support or the lack of it and the harmful use of alcohol use among college students are all factors in the development of Internet addiction (IA) (Yan et al. 2014; Weinstein et al. 2014).

College administrators are however now starting to see the possible impact of which Internet usage can have on their students/younger generation with many realising that they have invested money into what they believed to be a great educational tool only to find out that it can be misused and very easily abused (Young, 2004).

When the head of Alfred University in USA looked further into the reasons why normally successful students had been dismissed to his amazement he found that 43% of these students had failed school due to lengthy night-time logins to the university's computer system (Young 2004; Young 1999a)

The University of Texas Austin was one of the first campuses to carry out a study on student Internet abuse as counsellors at the University began seeing students whose primary problem was an inability to control their Internet use (Young, 1999a; Young, 2004). Findings revealed that from 531 valid responses from students there was a total of 14% which met the criteria which qualified them for Internet addiction (Young, 2004).

Internet addiction (IA) is both a newly evolving social and mental health issue among youths today attracting much attention worldwide, particularly in certain Asian countries such as South Korea and China have already recognised Internet addiction as a public health problem with reports that China which is ranked as the largest Internet broadband market worldwide claiming that one in every six Chinese Internet users may have already developed some degree of Internet addiction (Fu et al. 2010; Yan et al. 2014; Block, 2008). The average South Korean high school student spends about 23 hours every week online gaming, a further 1.2 million are believed to be at risk of addiction and require basic counselling (Block, 2008).

A 2009 National report on Internet Addiction of the Chinese youth community carried out by the China Youth Association for Network Development revealed that 14.1% of young people in China aged 13-29 years old (i.e. at least 24 million youths) were possibly addicted to the Internet with more than half of these college or high school students (Yan et al. 2014).

Factors Contributing to Student Internet Abuse

With such a widespread existence of Internet abuse the question which needs answering is what are the factors contributing to student Internet abuse. Young (2004) attributes the following factors for abuse of the Internet by students.

- **Unlimited Internet Access:** When students enrol in universities today they receive their student ID card. However, despite receiving their ID card they more importantly they also more importantly receive a free personal e-mail account with no online service fees to pay, no limits as to the amount of time they can remain logged on and the luxury of computer labs which are available for 24 hours a day which equates to any Internet user's dream scenario.
- **Large Volume of Unstructured Time:** With the large amount of unstructured time students have time to explore the campus and activities at the campus they are attending but many choose to forget this and concentrate on one activity: The Internet.
- **Freedom From Parental Control:** Many students are experiencing life away from home for the first time without the watchful eyes of their parents. The use of chat rooms at all hours of the night is not checked by their parents.
- **Lack of Monitoring and Censorship of Online Activities:** While in college or university the monitors of the computer labs are usually senior volunteer students whose responsibility is to help students, who require assistance using the Internet and not telling students what they cannot do while on the Internet.
- **Encouragement From Faculty and Administrators:** Students are under the presumption that the faculty wants them to make full use of the resources supplied. There is usually no option when it comes to not using online facilities as with large classes most course material such as lectures is placed online, many assignments are submitted via e-mail and if a student required to contact a lecturer out of class time to ask a question this is also carried out online. Administrators must be seen to justify the financial outlay they invest in computers and Internet access on campus.
- **Social Intimidation and Alienation:** Many campuses can have up to 30,000 students on campus and it is very easy for some students to feel lost in the crowd. When these students reach out they invariably run into tighter clicks than those they experienced in high school. To hide from the difficult feelings of anxiety, depression, pressure of making top grades, fulfilling parental expectations, graduation and the competition of finding a good job they join the faceless community of the Internet which allows them to find friends worldwide.

Employee Internet Abuse

The benefits of employees having access to the Internet is a benefit for the employee and the company alike enabling the employee to carry out tasks such as market research and business communication (Young, 1999a). However, despite these benefits (Murali and George, 2007) report that employees with access to the Internet at their desk spend a lot of their time during a business working day engaged in Internet use which is completely non-work related.

Employers are inclined to underestimate the amount of time employees spend on their mobile phones and underestimate the amount of time spent on social media. Such flexible anytime, anyplace attitude to working on mobile devices can very quickly become 'all the time and everywhere' (Jeske et al. 2016).

Since approximately 70% of companies provide Internet access to more than half of their employees and due to the widespread reliance, that we as individuals have on the Internet in the world today there has been a drive to carry out surveys within the industry sector to investigate the prevalence of employee Internet abuse while at work (Young, 2004).

The wrongful use of the Internet in the workplace by employees is of grave concern for managers at work, with a survey of the nation's leading 1,000 companies highlighting that 55% of company executives were of the belief that time spent on the Internet for non-business reasons was detrimental to the efficiency by which their employees could carry out the tasks involved in their job (Young, 1999). The use of new monitoring devices enables employers to track Internet usage and one company which carried this out practice had its worst fears confirmed, revealing that only 23% of the Internet usage within the company was for business purposes (Young, 1999).

The rise in employee Internet usage has resulted in the development of new electronic monitoring companies such as Cyber Surveillance, Websense and Spector Pro which include features such as logging Internet conversations, web activity and the tracking the history of employee Internet usage either weekly or daily (Young, 1999).

Employee abuse of the Internet during working hours has the potential to create Internet addiction among the workforce and have further consequences for the business which include the following:

- **Business Epidemic:** A survey by an online analyst firm of 1439 workers revealed that 37% of workers admitted to surfing the Net continually at work, while 32% admitted to surfing a few times a day and 21% admitting to surfing the Net a few times a week (Young and Case, 2004; Young, 2004)
- **Disciplining & Termination of Employees:** A further survey of 224 companies by the electronic monitoring firm Websense Inc, revealed that a total of 64% of these companies have disciplined employees while a further 30% have had their contracts terminated for improper Internet usage. The main reasons requiring termination or disciplinary action to be taken included (42%) accessing pornography, (13%) chatting online, (12%) involved in gaming, (8%) sports-related, (7%) investing and finally (7%) shopping from work (Young and Case, 2004, Young, 2004). A report on online usage carried out in the year 2000 reports how in the USA 73% of active adult Internet users confess to having accessed the Web at least once from work, while 41% do most of their online activity from work and 15% go online solely from work (Young and Case, 2004).
- **Lost Productivity:** Internet usage by employees at work equates to billions in lost revenue for employers with Vault.com estimating that the figure for employee Internet abuse costs the U.S. $54 billion in lost productivity each year (Young and Case, 2004).
- **Negative Publicity:** A survey covering a diverse range of industries and employees within these different industries found that a total of 83% of companies were concerned over the inappropriate Internet usage by employees and the resultant negative publicity from employee termination because of abuse of the Internet makes potential customers less trustful of the integrity of such companies (Young and Case, 2004).
- **Legal Liability:** Even though Internet is invaluable resource in companies today the wrongful termination of employee contracts for using a tool which the company has supplied and the diagnosis of Internet addiction leaves companies open to being sued in a court of law.

Treatment Strategies for Pathological Internet Use

In today's world, the use of the Internet is both essential and increasing in use both in business and in households. Given that the Internet has numerous positive uses and advantages in day-to-day life such as electronic correspondences to venders regarding orders in the world of business and the practice of Internet banking in the home environment (Young, 1999a; Murali and George, 2007). Due to the many positive uses of the Internet in our daily lives, customary examples of the standard treatment which include abstinence as used for individuals presenting with substance addictions is not the focus of treatment for Internet use as treatment for individuals who display excessive Internet use should be moderation and controlled use (Murali and George, 2007; Young, 1999). There is a consensus that total abstinence from the Internet should not be the goal of any interventions in the treatment of Internet addiction but rather the goal should be to achieve an abstinence from problematic applications and both a controlled and balanced Internet usage should be the desired outcome (Cash et al. 2012). A significant finding shows that individuals which present with Internet addiction (IA) are associated with poor impulse control so understanding the neural basis which underlies poor impulse control in IA subjects may be of great importance in firstly the diagnosis and secondly the treatment of this disorder (Li et al. 2014).

Internet addiction disorder displays a resistance to treatment, involves significant risks, demonstrates high relapse rates while making other disorders less reactive to therapy (Block, 2008). However, evidence based intervention for the intervention in a stand-alone diagnosis of Internet addiction is not currently available as further treatment studies are required to examine Internet addiction as a secondary outcome measure (Fu et al., 2010).

Approaches for treating pathological Internet use are very much in their infancy as there is little research in this area with no recognised or effective treatments available. However, initial indications despite being early point to the effective nature of behavioural strategies in the treatment of Internet addiction (Murali and George, 2007).

Based upon individual practitioners who have worked with individuals with Internet addiction and research findings from other addictions there are several different techniques employed to treat Internet addiction and they include the following eight strategies which as Cash et al (2012) explains are already known from the cognitive-behavioural approach.

1.   Practising the opposite. Once the patient's usual pattern of logging on to the Internet is realised, interrupt this pattern by proposing they use the Internet at alternative times by proposing a different schedule.
2.   Employing external stoppers. Employ the use of actual events or real goings-on in a bid to encourage the patient to log off from their current use.
3.   Set goals.
4.   Abstain from an application.
5.   Use reminder cards.
6.   Develop a personal inventory.
7.   Enter a support group.
8.   Family therapy.

The first three methods for dealing with Internet addiction are however only methods for the management of the Internet addict's time and upon failure of these fail there is a requirement to adopt a more approach. Those patients which discover positive methods of managing in their day-to-day lives should no longer rely on the Internet to control frustrations, however within the early stages of recovery these patients will have a void in their lives with the loss of the lengthy periods which they previously spent online. For most patients that derive a great source of pleasure from the Internet the adjustment to no longer having it as the central part of their lives anymore can be very difficult (Young, 1999a).

- **Practising the Opposite:** A major factor in the treatment of an Internet addict is the restructuring of the way in which the Internet addict manages their time. When treating, the Internet addict the clinician should take time to ask questions to understand the addict's current habits of using the Internet. In a bid to ascertain the extent of the Internet addict's current problem the clinician should find out: which days of the week the Internet addict usually goes online; what time of the day do they normally start their online usage; the length of time they spend in a typical on-line session and finally where they carry out their computer use (Young, 1999a).

Once evaluation of the patient's Internet use has been achieved it is essential to create a new timetable with the client which practices the opposite to what they are currently practicing. The ultimate objective of this is to disrupt the client's current routine in a bid to adjust to new time patterns of use and disrupt their old on-line habit. If an addict checked their e-mails first thing every morning, then change this and have their shower followed by breakfast before logging on and if the addict has an established pattern of coming home and logging on and sitting in front of the computer then they should change this and have dinner and watch the news before logging on. For those patients who never take breaks then he or she should be reminded to take a break from the Internet every half hour. Addicts that use the Internet all weekend should change this pattern to just weekdays. This simple tool helps Internet addicts in the step to changing an online practice use which is opposite to what they are used to (Young. 1999a).

- **Employing External Stoppers:** This technique uses real things such as places the Internet user needs to go to as ways of assisting him or her log off such as leaving for work although this is fraught with danger as there is the possibility that the patient may disregard such natural alarms. If this happens then the placement of an alarm clock which is pre-set to determine when the Internet session should finish nearby so when the alarm rings it is time to log off (Young. 1999a; Cash et al. 2012).
- **Setting Goals:** Attempts to limit online usage in many cases fail as users rely on an unclear plan to trim hours without defining firstly when their remaining online slots will come. In a bid to prevent relapse occurring the Internet addict should have a program of sensible goals such as 20 hours in place of the current 40 and those 20 hours should be written on a weekly planner so Internet sessions have time slots which are brief but frequent thus helping to evade longings for the Internet and withdrawal. For example, a 20-hour schedule could be split into the following slots, 8p.m. to 10p.m. every weekday and 1p.m. to 6p.m. on Saturday and Sunday. Using a schedule such as this will give the patient/addict the feeling that they are in control rather than allowing the Internet to take control of them (Young, 1999a; Cash et al. 2012).
- **Abstinence:** A clinician's assessment will diagnose an application such as chat rooms, interactive games, World Wide Web (W.W.W.) or news groups as the most problematic for the patient. Upon identification of the application which is most problematic to the user the next course of action is restrained use of this application and if this course of action fails then abstaining from it completely is the next stage in the Internet addict's treatment. While abstaining from the application completely the Internet user is still allowed to use other applications which the user finds less interesting or those which the user has a genuine reason for using. This means that a patient who finds chat rooms addictive should abstain from them but that they can still use the W.W.W. to make holiday reservations or shop for a new car (Young, 1999a). Abstinence is most appropriate for those patients who

present with a previous history of a prior addiction such as alcoholism or drug use. Many patients with such a previous history find the Internet a safe substitute to their addiction and many become obsessed with the Internet thus preventing a relapse into drug use or drinking. Although such patients justify the Internet as a safe addiction they still avoid dealing with the unpleasant situation which has triggered this new addictive behaviour. The introduction of previous approaches which have been effective for each individual Internet addict it will allow him or her to manage their Internet usage efficiently enabling them to focus on their underlying issues (Young, 1999a; Cash et al. 2012).

- **Reminder Cards:** In a bid to support patients so that their concentration remains focused on the end goal of either reduced abstinence or complete abstinence from an Internet application the Internet addict is encouraged to make a list, firstly of five major problems which Internet addiction causes and secondly five major reasons for reducing Internet use or abstaining completely from a specific Internet application (Young, 1999a; Cash et al. 2012).

Problems may include things such as marital problems, problems at work, poor academic grades whereas benefits will include a better home life, more time with family, better grades at school and more productivity in the workplace (Young, 1999a). By putting these points on a card and carrying the card in their wallet, trouser pocket, coat or purse the patient when tempted to use the Internet should look at the card and make a point of taking this card out several times a week to reflect on the problems that Internet overuse causes. Young (1999a) highlights how making decisions about what is included on the cards should be both as broad and as honest as possible. This tool is useful later as the patient has cut down on Internet usage or quit it completely as it prevents relapse into a state of Internet addiction again and (Young, 1999a).

- **Personal Inventory:** Young (1999a) highlights that whether a patient is trying to reduce their usage of an application or achieve abstinence from it the clinician treating them should tell the patient to take time to make a personal inventory of activities such as fishing, hiking or golf that he or she has had to cut down on due to their increased time spent on the Internet. The clinician should make the patient list all activities and practices which have been neglected or curtailed due to their Internet use and rank them as follows: very important, important and finally not very important as this exercise shows the patient exactly what they are missing out on due to their increased time spent online. Such practices are beneficial to patients that feel euphoric when engaged in online activity as it cultivates pleasant feelings achieved from real-life activities thus reducing their need for emotional fulfilment on-line.

- **Support Groups:** The absence of real life social support in the lives of individuals has been responsible for propelling these individuals towards the addictive Internet use from which they now suffer. Individuals who spend long periods of time alone and adopt lonely lifestyles such as single, retired or disabled individuals turn to online applications such as chat rooms to replace the absence of real life social support in their own lives (Young, 1999a). Akin and Iskender (2011) highlights how loneliness, depression and a reduction in the size of the individual's social circle all give rise to the use of the Internet. Young (1999) highlights how patients who have experienced the loss of loved ones, job loss, divorce may respond by turning to the Internet as a mental distraction from their real- life problems as their on-line world makes their real-life problems fade into the background.

Clinicians who carry out a life assessment on their patients and uncover this problem should assist the client in finding a support group that best addresses his or her situation. Clinicians should search out private practices that offer support groups which include those addicted to the Internet as these will be especially useful to those with feelings of inadequacy, low self-esteem. As Young (1999a) highlights addiction recovery groups deal with the Internet user's poor thoughts providing an opportunity to form real life relationships allowing them relief of their social shyness and ultimately their requirement for companionship on the Internet. Such groups enable the Internet addict to find support to help them in challenging changes in their lives like AA sponsors.

- **Family Therapy:** Family therapy may be required for addicts whose marriages and family relationships have been negatively affected because of Internet addiction. Family intervention should focus on the following areas:
  - Educating the family on the addictive nature of the Internet.
  - Reducing blame on addicts for their behaviour.
  - Improve communication within the family including problems which caused the on-line addiction initially.
  - Encouragement within the family to assist with the addict's recovery such as finding new hobbies or taking an overdue vacation.

A strong sense of support and encouragement from within the family network can be an important tool in the process of recovering from Internet addiction (Young, 1999a).

According to Chebbi et al. (2001) there exists two major kinds of treatment that individuals with Internet addiction can benefit from and they include motivational enhancement therapy (MET) and cognitive behavioural therapy (CBT) with the latter being the more favourable of the two. CBT is a treatment based upon the premise that thoughts determine feelings and patients are taught to monitor their thoughts and identify those thoughts which trigger addictive feelings and actions as they learn new coping mechanisms to prevent a relapse. CBT usually requires three months of treatment or 12 weekly sessions (Young, 2007; Brand et al. 2014). CBT has been shown to be an effective treatment for compulsive disorders such as intermittent explosive disorder, pathological gambling and it has also been effective in the treatment of substance abuse, emotional disorders and eating disorders (Young, 2007). CBT is just one treatment approach and further research is required to investigate the long-term effects of this treatment with larger populations along with matching which types of Internet addiction respond best to which treatment types best as this will ultimately lead to long-term recovery. Reality therapy (RT) is a further method used for the treatment of Internet addiction. The goal of Reality Therapy is to encourage the individual to choose to improve their own lives by committing to change their behaviour (Cash et al, 2012). This form of therapy includes sessions which show clients that the addiction they have is a choice and it trains them in management of their time and introduces them to alternative activities to their problematic behaviour (Cash et al, 2012).

The use of psychopharmacotherapy was also used in treatment which involved administering selective serotonin reuptake inhibitors (SSRIs) typically used in treating anxiety disorders including OCD, stimulants for treating ADHD and antipsychotics used for schizophrenia has also reported a decrease of Internet addiction symptomatology and Internet/gaming use times (Kuss, 2016).

FUTURE RESEARCH DIRECTIONS

Asian countries such as China and Korea have already recognised Internet addiction as a public health problem and China which is ranked as the largest broadband market in the World reports that a possible one in every six Internet users may have developed some level of Internet addiction (Fu et al., 2010). Internet addiction is viewed upon as a social problem in the younger generation as they depend upon it for learning, leisure and social activities and are more susceptible to media influences and appear to be less self-regulative.

With no one diagnosis many therapists are unsure that they are looking for Internet addiction and thus it is unlikely to be detected but in Asia where cases are more prevalent therapists are taught to screen for it automatically (Block, 2008).

The year 2006 saw the first opening of the first inpatient treatment centre in Beijing, China with Korea having over an estimated 140 Internet addiction treatment recovery centres. The United States saw the opening of the first inpatient residential care centre in Redmond Washington. A basic understanding of this disorder is required by psychiatrists so early recognition and intervention can take place especially in individuals with other underlying problems (Murali and George, 2007). Due to the ever-increasing use of the Internet in our day-to-day lives, criteria for the successful diagnosis of this disorder are necessary and the recognition of it as disorder by the Diagnostic and Statistical Manual of Mental Disorders is needed so those affected can receive treatment and those diagnosing individuals know the signs of Internet addiction.

CONCLUSION

People have an increasing reliance on the Internet and it plays an essential part of their everyday lives (Chebbi et al., 2001). Even though this disorder is still in its infancy the problems associated with it are set to rise. With the rapid rise in Internet use, millions more are coming online which has the potential to create a real clinical threat due to the rise in a disorder about which very little is known. Since Internet addiction disorder (IAD) is such a new and innovative condition which causes laughter among many people when mentioned many individuals suffering from this addiction are therefore hesitant about seeking treatment from their clinician as they are afraid that their complaints will not be treated seriously and their current condition will worsen as a result (Young, 1999a). Many find it difficult to comprehend how a tool which is so beneficial in our day-to-day lives as a means of both information and communication could be classified as addictive (Young, 2010).

There is a major requirement to establish an agreement on diagnostic criteria for Internet addiction as this is needed for both the purpose of diagnosis and correct intervention to enable effective and efficient treatment approaches. The American Psychiatric Association (APA) is proposing the inclusion of "pathological Internet use" in the DSM-IV revision concluding that this is the broadest term to use (Young, 2010; Kuss and Lopez-Fernandez, 2016). In 2013, the American Psychiatric Association included Internet Gaming Disorder (IGD) in the appendix of the updated (DSM-V) as a condition which requires additional research prior to its official inclusion in the main manual (Kuss, 2016; Kuss and Lopez-Fernandez, 2016; Zhu et al. 2015). The term Internet addiction is currently being considered for inclusion in the DSM-V as a psychiatric diagnosis which indicates that professionals are beginning to take the matter of Internet addiction seriously (Fu et al., 2010).

REFERENCES

Ahmadi, J., Amiri, A., Ghanizadeh, A., Khademalhosseini, M., Khademalhosseini, Z., Gholami, Z., & Sharifian, M. (2014). Prevalence of addiction to the Internet, computer games, DVD, and video and its relationship to anxiety and depression in a sample of Iranian high school students. *Iranian Journal of Psychiatry and Behavioral Sciences*, *8*(2), 75. PMID:25053960

Akin, A., & Iskender, M. (2011). Internet addiction and depression, anxiety and stress. *International Online Journal of Educational Sciences*, *3*(1), 138-148.

Alexander, B. K., & Schweighofer, A. R. (1988). Defining addiction. *Canadian Psychology*, *29*(2), 151–162. doi:10.1037/h0084530

Barber, A. (1997). Net's educational value questioned. *USA Today*, 4.

Block, J. J. (2008). *Issues for DSM-V: Internet addiction*. Academic Press.

Brand, M., Young, K. S., & Laier, C. (2014). Prefrontal control and Internet addiction: A theoretical model and review of neuropsychological and neuroimaging findings. *Frontiers in Human Neuroscience*, 8. PMID:24904393

Cash, H. D., Rae, C. H., Steel, A., & Winkler, A. (2012). Internet addiction: A brief summary of research and practice. *Current Psychiatry Reviews*, *8*(4), 292–298. doi:10.2174/157340012803520513 PMID:23125561

Chebbi, P., Koong, K. S., Liu, L., & Rottman, R. (2001). Some observations on Internet addiction disorder research. *Journal of Information Systems Education*, *1*(1), 3–4.

Christakis, D. A., & Moreno, M. A. (2009). Trapped in the net: Will Internet addiction become a 21st-century epidemic? *Archives of Pediatrics & Adolescent Medicine*, *163*(10), 959–960. doi:10.1001/archpediatrics.2009.162 PMID:19805719

Fu, K. W., Chan, W. S., Wong, P. W., & Yip, P. S. (2010). Internet addiction: Prevalence, discriminant validity and correlates among adolescents in Hong Kong. *The British Journal of Psychiatry*, *196*(6), 486–492. doi:10.1192/bjp.bp.109.075002 PMID:20513862

Greenfield, D. N. (1999). *Virtual addiction: Sometimes new technology can create new problems*. Academic Press.

Griffiths, M. (1997). Psychology of computer use: XLIII. Some comments on 'addictive use of the Internet' by Young. *Psychological Reports*, *80*(1), 81–82. doi:10.2466/pr0.1997.80.1.81 PMID:9122355

Griffiths, M. (1998). Internet addiction: does it really exist? *Psychology and the Internet*, 61-75.

Griffiths, M. (2000). Internet addiction-time to be taken seriously? *Addiction Research*, *8*(5), 413–418. doi:10.3109/16066350009005587

Hersh, W. (1999). A world of knowledge at your fingertips": The promise, reality, and future directions of on-line information retrieval. *Academic Medicine*, *74*(3), 240–243. doi:10.1097/00001888-199903000-00012 PMID:10099643

Jeske, D., Briggs, P., & Coventry, L. (2016). Exploring the relationship between impulsivity and decision-making on mobile devices. *Personal and Ubiquitous Computing, 20*(4), 545–557. doi:10.1007/s00779-016-0938-4

Kardefelt-Winther, D. (2014). A conceptual and methodological critique of Internet addiction research: Towards a model of compensatory Internet use. *Computers in Human Behavior, 31*, 351–354. doi:10.1016/j.chb.2013.10.059

Ko, C. H., Yen, J. Y., Chen, C. C., Chen, S. H., & Yen, C. F. (2005). Proposed diagnostic criteria of Internet addiction for adolescents. *The Journal of Nervous and Mental Disease, 193*(11), 728–733. doi:10.1097/01.nmd.0000185891.13719.54 PMID:16260926

Kuss, D. J. (2016). Internet Addiction: The Problem and Treatment. *Addicta-The Turkish Journal on Addictions, 3*(2), 185–192. doi:10.15805/addicta.2016.3.0106

Kuss, D. J., & Lopez-Fernandez, O. (2016). Internet addiction and problematic Internet use: A systematic review of clinical research. *World Journal of Psychiatry, 6*(1), 143. doi:10.5498/wjp.v6.i1.143 PMID:27014605

Lai, C. M., Mak, K. K., Watanabe, H., Ang, R. P., Pang, J. S., & Ho, R. C. (2013). Psychometric properties of the Internet addiction test in Chinese adolescents. *Journal of Pediatric Psychology, 38*(7), 794–807. doi:10.1093/jpepsy/jst022 PMID:23671059

Li, B., Friston, K. J., Liu, J., Liu, Y., Zhang, G., Cao, F., & Hu, D. et al. (2014). Impaired frontal-basal ganglia connectivity in adolescents with Internet addiction. *Scientific Reports, 4*. PMID:24848380

Liu, M., & Luo, J. (2015). Relationship between peripheral blood dopamine level and Internet addiction disorder in adolescents: A pilot study. *International Journal of Clinical and Experimental Medicine, 8*(6), 9943. PMID:26309680

Murali, V., & George, S. (2007). Lost online: An overview of Internet addiction. *Advances in Psychiatric Treatment, 13*(1), 24–30. doi:10.1192/apt.bp.106.002907

Pontes, H. M., & Griffiths, M. D. (2014). Internet addiction disorder and Internet gaming disorder are not the same. *Journal of Addiction Research & Therapy, 5*(4).

Poon, S. (2000). Business environment and Internet commerce benefit—a small business perspective. *European Journal of Information Systems, 9*(2), 72–81. doi:10.1057/palgrave.ejis.3000361

Romano, M., Osborne, L. A., Truzoli, R., & Reed, P. (2013). Differential psychological impact of Internet exposure on Internet addicts. *PLoS One, 8*(2), e55162. doi:10.1371/journal.pone.0055162 PMID:23408958

Scimeca, G., Bruno, A., Cava, L., Pandolfo, G., Muscatello, M. R. A., & Zoccali, R. (2014). The relationship between alexithymia, anxiety, depression, and Internet addiction severity in a sample of Italian high school students. *The Scientific World Journal.* PMID:25401143

Thomas, J. C. (2016). A humanistic approach to problematic online sexual behavior. *Journal of Humanistic Psychology, 56*(1), 3–33. doi:10.1177/0022167814542286

Thorens, G., Achab, S., Billieux, J., Khazaal, Y., Khan, R., Pivin, E., & Zullino, D. et al. (2014). Characteristics and treatment response of self-identified problematic Internet users in a behavioral addiction outpatient clinic. *Journal of Behavioral Addictions, 3*(1), 78–81. doi:10.1556/JBA.3.2014.008 PMID:25215217

Watson, J. C. (2015). Internet addiction. *Treatment Strategies for Substance Abuse and Process Addictions, 293.*

Weinstein, A., & Lejoyeux, M. (2010). Internet addiction or excessive Internet use. *The American Journal of Drug and Alcohol Abuse, 36*(5), 277–283. doi:10.3109/00952990.2010.491880 PMID:20545603

Wu, C. Y., Lee, M. B., Liao, S. C., & Chang, L. R. (2015). Risk factors of Internet addiction among Internet users: An online questionnaire survey. *PLoS One, 10*(10), e0137506. doi:10.1371/journal.pone.0137506 PMID:26462196

Yan, W., Li, Y., & Sui, N. (2014). The relationship between recent stressful life events, personality traits, perceived family functioning and Internet addiction among college students. *Stress and Health, 30*(1), 3–11. doi:10.1002/smi.2490 PMID:23616371

Young, K. (2010). Internet addiction over the decade: A personal look back. *World Psychiatry; Official Journal of the World Psychiatric Association (WPA), 9*(2), 91–91. doi:10.1002/j.2051-5545.2010.tb00279.x PMID:20671891

Young, K. S. (1998). Internet addiction: The emergence of a new clinical disorder. *Cyberpsychology & Behavior, 1*(3), 237–244. doi:10.1089/cpb.1998.1.237

Young, K. S. (1999). Internet addiction: symptoms, evaluation and treatment. *Innovations in Clinical Practice: A Source Book, 17,* 19-31.

Young, K. S. (2004). Internet addiction: A new clinical phenomenon and its consequences. *The American Behavioral Scientist, 48*(4), 402–415. doi:10.1177/0002764204270278

Young, K. S. (2007). Cognitive behavior therapy with Internet addicts: Treatment outcomes and implications. *Cyberpsychology & Behavior, 10*(5), 671–679. doi:10.1089/cpb.2007.9971 PMID:17927535

Young, K. S., & Case, C. J. (2004). Internet abuse in the workplace: New trends in risk management. *Cyberpsychology & Behavior, 7*(1), 105–111. doi:10.1089/109493104322820174 PMID:15006175

Young, K. S., & Rodgers, R. C. (1998, April). Internet addiction: Personality traits associated with its development. *69th annual meeting of the Eastern Psychological Association,* 40-50.

Zafar, S. N. (2016). Internet Addiction or Problematic Internet Use: Current Issues and Challenges in Conceptualization, Measurement and Treatment. *Journal of Islamic International Medical College, 11*(2), 46–47.

Zhu, Y., Zhang, H., & Tian, M. (2015). Molecular and functional imaging of Internet addiction. *BioMed Research International.* PMID:25879023

KEY TERMS AND DEFINITIONS

Addiction: An addiction is a medical condition which is portrayed by compulsive use in a pleasing stimulus which it may offer despite the long-term negative consequences which it may result in.

Diagnosis: This refers to the identification of a disease or illness through an evaluation of the signs and symptoms individual presents with.

Disorder: A disturbance in body function, structure or both which is inherited or results from development failure from such factors as disease, trauma or poison.

Dysphoric: A feeling of unease, unhappiness or anxiety about oneself as opposed to euphoria which describes a state of extreme happiness.

Internet: A global system of interconnected computer networks which use Internet protocols to link devices worldwide. The Internet carries a vast array of information enabling the passage of information through services and applications of the World Wide Web W.W.W.

Pathological: The behaviour of a person can be described as pathological when he or she behaves in a way that is extreme and unacceptable and displays powerful feelings that they are unable to control.

Predisposition: The state of being likely to behave in a certain way or suffer from a disease or condition.

Psychopathological Conditions: This refers to the development of conditions which manifest themselves because of a mental or behavioural disorder.

Reliance: This refers to the placement of one's dependence or trust in a person or a thing which leads to that individual becoming reliant on that person or thing.

Section 2
Psychological Aspects of Internet Addiction

This section covers psychological aspects of internet addiction.

Chapter 3
Personality, Internet Addiction, and Other Technological Addictions:
A Psychological Examination of Personality Traits and Technological Addictions

Zaheer Hussain
University of Derby, UK

Halley M. Pontes
Nottingham Trent University, UK

ABSTRACT

Research into technological addictions, such as Internet addiction, smartphone addiction and social networking addiction has greatly increased. It is important to understand how technological addictions may be related to different personality types and key individual differences associated to personality. This chapter provides empirical and conceptual insights into how technological addictions may be related to different personality types and key individual differences associated to personality. This chapter focuses on a number of technological addictions and illustrates how research and theory in this area has developed in relation to commonly researched personality traits (e.g., extraversion, introversion, neuroticism, conscientiousness, openness to experience, and narcissism) and key individual differences related to personality (e.g., personality disorders). The complex nature of personality and technological addictions is discussed together with areas for future research.

INTRODUCTION

Recent figures suggest that 40% of the world's population have access to the Internet, worldwide Internet usage has increased with 499 million Internet users in Europe, 647 million users in the Americas, 240 million users in Africa and 1.7 billion users in Asia and the Pacific region (International Telecom-

DOI: 10.4018/978-1-5225-3477-8.ch003

munication Union [ITU], 2016). When considering country specific data, 74% of individuals use the Internet in the United States of America (USA), 91% in the United Arab Emirates (UAE), 93% in Japan and 89% in South Korea (ITU, 2016). Although Internet use is usually beneficial and advantageous for most people (Howard, Wilding & Guest, 2016; Heo et al. 2015; Roy & Ferguson, 2016; Wiederhold, 2017), increased availability and high penetration rates across the globe can facilitate the emergence of excessive and addictive behaviors related to Internet use. Furthermore, many people appear to display impulsive, narcissistic and aggressive personalities online which can be nurtured by various Internet technologies (Aboujaoude, 2017).

Internet addiction has been defined as "excessive or poorly controlled preoccupations, urges or behaviours regarding computer use and Internet access that lead to impairment or distress" (Weinstein & Lejoyeux, 2010, p277). Studies have systematically shown that excessive use of the Internet can lead to Internet addiction (Durkee et al. 2012; Pontes & Griffiths, 2016a; Pontes & Griffiths, 2017; Lortie & Guitton, 2013), which comprises a heterogeneous spectrum of Internet-related activities with a potential to cause problems for the individual, such as gaming, shopping, gambling, or social networking. In fact, the phenomenon of Internet addiction has been recognized since the mid-1990s as a new type of addiction and a mental health problem that exhibits signs and symptoms like those of other established addictions. Young (1996) and Griffiths (1996) were among the first researchers to investigate Internet addiction from a scientific perspective by publishing case study accounts of individuals who suffered from this condition based on an adapted criterion for pathological gambling as defined in the *Diagnostic and Statistical Manual for Mental Disorders* (DSM-IV; American Psychiatric Association, 1994). In one of the earliest studies published in the field, Young (1998) investigated a sample of 396 dependent Internet users who endorsed a minimum of five out of eight criteria adapted from the diagnostic criteria for pathological gambling in the DSM-IV, and 100 non-dependent Internet users. The results of this study indicated that on average, the dependent users spent eight times more hours online than the controls, and used chat rooms and Multi User Dungeons (MUDs). With regards to online gaming addiction diagnostic approaches, researchers and clinicians are now utilizing the nine diagnostic criteria for Internet Gaming Disorder that was developed by the American Psychiatric Association in the last revision of the *Diagnostic and Statistical Manual of Mental Disorders* (5th ed.; DSM–5; American Psychiatric Association, 2013). According to the APA (2013), the clinical diagnosis of Internet Gaming Disorder comprises a behavioral pattern encompassing persistent and recurrent use of the Internet to engage in online games, leading to significant impairment or distress over a period of 12 months as specified by the endorsement of at least five out of the following nine criteria: (i) preoccupation with Internet games; (ii) withdrawal symptoms when Internet gaming is taken away; (iii) tolerance, resulting in the need to spend increasing amounts of time engaged in Internet games; (iv) unsuccessful attempts to control participation in Internet games; (v) loss of interest in previous hobbies and entertainment as a result of, and with the exception of, Internet games; (vi) continued excessive use of Internet games despite knowledge of psychosocial problems; (vii) deceiving family members, therapists, or others regarding the amount of Internet gaming; (viii) use of Internet games to escape or relieve negative moods; and (ix) jeopardizing or losing a significant relationship, job, or education or career opportunity because of participation in Internet games (APA, 2013). Given these recent advances, researchers have now developed several standardized psychometric assessment tools to assess both Internet Gaming Disorder (Pontes et al., 2014; Pontes & Griffiths, 2015; Pontes, 2016) and generalized Internet addiction (Pontes & Griffiths, 2016a, 2016b, 2017) based on the nine Internet Gaming Disorder criteria.

Various terms have been used to name the condition of Internet addiction, including compulsive computer use (Black, Belsare, & Schlosser, 1999), Internet dependency (te Wildt, 2011), pathological Internet use (Morahan-Martin & Schumacher, 2000), problematic Internet use (Davis, Flett, & Besser, 2002), virtual addiction (Greenfield, 1999), and Internet addiction disorder (Ko, Yen, Chen, Chen, & Yen, 2005). Internet use has substantially increased with adolescents becoming progressively addicted to social networking sites (SNS) such as Facebook, this assertion is supported by research (Jafarkarimi et al. 2016) showing that 47% of a student sample in Malaysia were classified as addicted to Facebook. There is increasing research evidence to suggest that mental health is impacted by technology (Rosen, Whaling, Rab, Carrier, & Cheever, 2013) and various Internet activities appear to be linked to problematic Internet use (Bruno et al. 2014). Given the relevance of technological addictions (e.g., Internet addiction) as a potential public health issue and the existing conflicting findings concerning the role of personality in technological addictions, this chapter will provide empirical and conceptual insights into how technological addictions may be related to different personality types and key individual differences associated to personality. The present chapter will focus on several technological addictions (e.g. Internet addiction, videogame addiction, SNS addiction, and smartphone addiction) and illustrate how research and theory in this area has developed in relation to commonly researched personality traits (e.g., extraversion, introversion, neuroticism, conscientiousness, openness to experience, and narcissism) and key individual differences related to personality (e.g., personality disorders). It is envisaged that this chapter will help inform future research and will shed light on the intricacies between personality and technological addictions.

BACKGROUND

Internet addiction has been traditionally defined as an uncontrollable and damaging use of the Internet, and conceptually framed as a compulsive-impulsive phenomenon, one of those in the spectrum of impulse-control disorders as discussed in the literature (Beutel et al. 2011). More recently, Pontes and Griffiths (2017) have conducted a large-scale study in a sample of 1,105 Internet users, and were able to empirically conceptualize Internet addiction via four distinct domains: (i) escapism and dysfunctional emotional coping, (ii) withdrawal symptoms, (iii) impairments and dysfunctional self-regulation, and (iv) dysfunctional Internet-related self-control.

Research evidence suggests that Internet addicts experience a number of biopsychosocial symptoms and consequences (Beutel et al. 2011) that can include symptoms traditionally associated with substance-related addictions (Kuss & Billieux, 2016; Rücker, Akre, Berchtold, & Suris, 2015;) and a similar set of common defining criteria, namely salience, mood modification, tolerance, withdrawal symptoms, conflict, and relapse (Griffiths, 2005). More specifically, Internet addiction has been linked to social anxiety in young adults (Weinstein, Dorani, Elhadif, Bukovza, & Yarmulnik, 2015), lower levels of family functioning, life satisfaction, and problems in family interactions (Wartberg, Kriston, Kammerl, Petersen, & Thomasius, 2015), attention deficit/hyperactivity disorder and depression (Sariyska, Reuter, Lachmann, & Montag, 2015), higher incidence of substance use, poor emotional well-being, and decreased academic performance in adolescents (Rücker, Akre, Berchtold, & Suris, 2015), increased academic stress (Jun & Choi, 2015), impulsive behaviours (Reed, Osborne, Romano, & Truzoli, 2015), introversion (McIntyre, Wiener, & Saliba, 2015), and higher levels of loneliness, alexithymia, and suicide (Alpaslan, Avci, Soylu, & Guzel, 2015).

Although Internet addiction is not currently recognized as a *bona fide* addiction and numerous scholarly debates have questioned its legitimacy (Block, 2008; Pies, 2009; Starcevic & Aboujaoude, 2016; Starcevic, 2013; Starcevic, 2016), recent review studies have shown that Internet addiction may pose a serious health hazard to a minority of people (Pontes, Kuss & Griffiths, 2015). Moreover, Pontes et al. (2015) recently reviewed a total of 12 robust empirical studies that estimated prevalence rates of Internet addiction in a wide range of cultural backgrounds using nationally representative samples, and found that prevalence rates ranged from a minimum of 1% in Germany (Rumpf et al. 2014) to a maximum of 18.7% in Taiwan (Lin et al. 2014). Pontes et al. (2015) also noted that such disparity in the prevalence rates reported may have been a result of heterogeneity in the assessment of Internet addiction, adoption of arbitrary cut-off points to ascertain prevalence rates (even when researchers adopt the same instrument), and utilization of assessment criteria that are not psychometrically or clinically validated. While studies have indicated that people suffering from Internet addiction are mostly young males with introverted personality (e.g., Mottram & Fleming, 2009; Van der Aa et al. 2009), findings concerning gender differences are mixed, with some studies reporting higher prevalence rates among males (Király et al. 2014), and females (Rücker et al. 2015) and other studies reporting no significant differences across both genders (Blinka et al. 2017; Rumpf et al. 2014).

Internet addiction amongst adolescents has become a serious public health problem in some countries (especially in Asian countries) (Oberst et al. 2017). Since adolescents usually have fixed class schedules, more freedom of time, and less excessive parental intervention, they are more vulnerable to Internet addiction in general (Lai & Kwan, 2014; Yu & Chao, 2016), including addiction to Social Networking Sites (SNSs), which can negatively impact upon their mental health (Bányai et al. 2017) and academic performance (Kirschner & Karpinski, 2010). In fact, a recent report found that 71% of teenage social media users access more than one social media site, and 24% of adolescents are 'almost constantly' online due to the widespread use of smartphones (Lenhart et al. 2015). The general prevalence for SNS users remains relatively balanced across both genders, with an ever-growing 93% of American young adults aged 18-29 using social media for communication, and 72% of individuals in this age group also use the Internet to search for online health information, including that of depression (Lenhart, Purcell, Smith, & Zickuhr, 2010).

PERSONALITY FACTORS AND ADDICTIVE PROCESSES

Issues, Controversies, Problems

The role of personality in the study of substance-based addictions has been significantly better understood in comparison to behavioral addictions. One of the potential reasons for this might be because the field of substance use disorder is more established at medical and societal levels. Since the field of behavioral addictions, especially technological addictions are relatively recent in comparison to other more established fields, it is paramount to understand how addictive processes related to these new forms addictions might be facilitated or mitigated in the context of personality research as personality in general can contribute to both chemical and behavioral addictions (Andreassen et al. 2013; Grant et al. 2010).

Several personality traits appear to be associated with various Internet-related activities such as SNS, online gaming, and online gambling. The findings of some studies (e.g., Ross et al. 2009; Zywica et al. 2008) indicate that people with large offline social networks, who are more extroverted, and who have higher self-esteem, use Facebook for social enhancement. People higher in narcissistic personality traits tend to be more active on Facebook and other SNSs in order to present themselves favourably online because the virtual environment empowers them to construct their ideal selves (Buffardi & Campbell, 2008; Mehdizadeh, 2010). Research suggested that people with different personality traits differ in their usage of SNSs (Correa et al. 2010) and prefer to use distinct functions of SNSs such as Facebook.

Personality traits influence individual's cognitions, motivation, and behaviours in a variety of situations, with SNS use closely related to specific personality traits (Ryan & Xenos, 2011). According to research conducted by Ryan and Xenos (2011), Facebook users tend to be more extraverted and narcissistic, but less conscientious and socially lonely, than non-users. Furthermore, frequency of Facebook use and preferences for specific SNS features appear to vary as a result of certain characteristics, such as neuroticism, loneliness, shyness and narcissism (Ryan & Xenos, 2011). Ross et al. (2009) have supported these findings by suggesting in their work that people with different personality traits use specific functions of Facebook. More recently, studies found that SNS use and certain personality traits may have important implications for work performance. For instance, the study conducted by Kim and Chung (2014) in a sample of 1,452 employees in Korea found that SNS use moderated the association between extraversion and neuroticism with employees' job satisfaction. Additionally, Kim and Chung (2014) found that SNS use increases job satisfaction of employees that are extraverted, while it also affects job satisfaction of those exhibiting low agreeableness.

Extraversion

Extraversion relates to how individuals socialize with each other. Moreover, individuals high on this trait are very sociable, energetic, optimistic, friendly and assertive (Maltby et al. 2010). Extraversion plays an important role in the context of Internet use as the Internet is a highly interactive and social tool, especially in the context of SNS use where users tend to be more open in the way they portray themselves. Since extraversion predicts a variety of positive social behaviors (Eaton & Funder, 2003) and extroverts report increased levels of social support and larger social networks (Swickert, Rosentreter, Hittner & Mushrush, 2002), it is possible that this extends to many online social behaviors as well. People high in extraversion and openness to experience use SNSs more frequently, with the former being true for mature and the latter for young people (Correa et al. 2010). Given that SNS use facilitates social interactions and provides social support for individuals, extraverts have a chance to increase their social connections further through SNS activities (Kim & Chung. 2014). Furthermore, extraverts and individuals open to experiences are members of significantly more groups on Facebook, use socializing functions more (Ross et al. 2009), and have more Facebook friends than introverts (Amichai-Hamburger & Vinitzky, 2010) which defines the former's higher sociability in general.

In terms of addictive SNS use, extraversion (together with depression) has been found to be linked to Facebook addiction (Hwang, 2014). Research by Wang et al. (2015) revealed that extraversion was associated with SNS addiction. Additionally, research by Servidio (2014) examining Internet addiction amongst Italian students found that extraversion was negatively related to Internet addiction. Hsiao et al. (2016) explored the links between personality traits and compulsive mobile application usage. The results showed that extraversion had significant effects on compulsive usage of mobile applications. In terms of smartphone use and Internet addiction, Bianchi and Phillips (2005) reported that extraversion was linked to problematic smartphone use.

Several studies support the notion that gamers exhibit higher extraversion than those who do not play videogames (Teng, 2008; Yee, 2006). This may be because these extraverts have high higher chances than less extraverted players to achieve success in games, and improve their self-efficacy (Klimmt & Hartmann, 2006). Moreover, highly extraverted players can enjoy social activities within online games that can match their social motivations (Jansz & Tanis, 2007; Teng, 2008). However, the relationship between extraversion and videogame play may not be straightforward. Collins and Freeman (2013) investigated the role of extraversion, trait empathy, social capital and prosocial tendencies in a sample of 416 gamers and reported that extraversion did not differ significantly between problematic gamers, non-problematic gamers, and non-gamers despite previous reports suggesting that problematic gamers are low in extraversion (e.g., Peters & Malesky, 2008). In terms of smartphone addiction, previous studies have found important correlates with smoking habits and low health practices in males, suggesting that the intensity of smartphone use may be related to unhealthy lifestyles (Toda, Monden, Kubo & Morimoto, 2006). Notwithstanding this, when considering all these studies together, it appears that extraversion plays a role in how people interact with newer forms of technological applications (i.e., SNS and smartphones) even though this personality trait appears to affect videogame play in a distinct way.

Introversion

The psychological trait of introversion is one that is inward focused where one is directed towards his/her own thoughts (Jung, 1964; Maltby et al. 2010). Individuals with high levels of introversion are described as reserved, independent rather than followers socially, even-paced rather than sluggish in terms of their pace of work (Maltby et al. 2010). Previous research found consistent links between Internet addiction and loneliness, and that Internet addicts were less satisfied with life, and experienced greater levels of depression and had lower self-esteem (Meerkerk et al. 2010; Pontes, Griffiths, & Patrão, 2014; Pontes, Patrão, & Griffiths, 2014; Pontes, Kuss, & Griffiths, 2015). This finding is of concern for those who are introverted as it has been shown that they use the Internet more frequently for social interaction and have higher rates of compulsive Internet use (McIntyre et al. 2015; van der Aa et al. 2009).

With regards to SNS use, there is evidence suggesting that introverts disclose more personal information on their SNSs profiles (Amichai-Hamburger & Vinitzky, 2010) and may thus be using it for social compensation in order to meet specific psychosocial needs. Additionally, it appears that particularly shy people spend large amounts of time on Facebook and have large amounts of friends on this SNS (Orr et al. 2009). Therefore, SNSs may appear beneficial for those whose real-life networks are limited because of the possibility of easy access to peers without the demands of real-life proximity and intimacy. This ease of access entails a higher time commitment for this group, which may possibly result in addictive use. Research by Van der Aa et al. (2009) amongst a sample of 7,888 Dutch adolescents revealed that compulsive Internet use was associated with loneliness in introverted, low agreeable, less emotionally stable participants. Another recent study found that introversion partially mediated the relationship between compulsive Internet use and social connectedness (McIntyre et al. 2015), further emphasizing the role of introversion in the context of Internet use.

Introversion in the context of videogame play has been found to be associated with massively multiplayer online role-playing games (MMORPGs) and social compensation as these games can help players increase their social capital acquisition (Reer & Krämer, 2017). Furthermore, MMORPGs in general present the potential to help introverts build up new social relationships and gather further social capital. For this reason, introverts who realize these potentials, who take the chance to participate in in-game social activities such as team play, using videogames as a starting point for social interactions with other gamers, could benefit socially from playing videogames (Reer & Krämer, 2017). Studies examining the effects of introversion on Internet addiction has produced mixed findings in terms of how this personality trait impacts on users' online experiences. On the one hand, introversion appears to be consistently associated with problematic Internet use. However, studies have also shown that introverted individuals can benefit socially from using the Internet and playing videogames for social purposes.

Neuroticism

Neuroticism is one of the key personality traits implicated in excessive and addictive Internet use. Neuroticism measures emotional stability and personal psychological adjustment in individuals (Maltby et al. 2010). Individuals showing high levels of neuroticism usually experience wide swings in their mood and are more volatile in their emotions (Maltby et al. 2010). In a study of Internet addiction amongst a Taiwanese sample, Tsai et al. (2009) surveyed 1,360 University students and found that 17.9% of the sample were classified as Internet addicts, scoring high on neuroticism increased the odds for Internet addiction. Interestingly, men and women with higher levels of neurotic personality traits use SNSs differently, with men using SNSs more frequently than women with neurotic traits (Correa et al. 2010). A study by Ross et al. (2009) revealed that neurotics favoured the wall function of Facebook, whereas those low on neuroticism preferred posting photos. Opposite findings were reported by Amichai-Hamburger and Vinitzky (2010) where highly neurotic individuals were found to be more inclined to post their photos on their Facebook profile than less neurotic individuals.

In regard to addictive use of Internet applications, research by Ehrenberg et al. (2008) showed that more neurotic individuals reported stronger mobile phone addictive tendencies. Hardie and Tee's (2007) online survey study of 96 adults showed that 40% of the sample could be classified as average internet users, 52% of the sample could be classified as problem over-users and 8% as pathologically addicted to the Internet. The problem over-users and addicts spent increasingly more time in online activities, were more neurotic and less extraverted, more socially anxious and emotionally lonely, and gained more support from SNSs than average Internet users. The results also revealed that only neuroticism and perceived support from online SNS were significant predictors of excessive Internet use. Research on a Chinese adolescent sample (n = 2,620) by Cao and Su (2006) exploring psychological features associated with Internet addiction revealed that 2.4% of the sample were classified as Internet addicts who had significantly higher scores on the neuroticism, psychoticism and lie subscales of personality.

More recent studies have also revealed findings linking Internet addiction to neuroticism and related traits. Yan, Li and Sui (2014) investigated the relationship between Internet addiction, personality, stressful life events and family functioning in 892 college students. The researchers reported that compared with non-addicted participants, participants with severe Internet addiction (9%) had lower family functioning, lower extraversion, higher neuroticism and psychoticism, and more stressful life events. Additionally, participants with mild Internet addiction (11%) had higher neuroticism and more health and adaptation problems. Yan et al. (2014) concluded that neuroticism, health and adaptation problems were potential predictors of Internet addiction. Similar findings were reported by Dong et al. (2013) as neuroticism and psychoticism were both linked to Internet addiction.

Mehroof and Griffiths' (2010) study revealed that neuroticism was associated with online gaming addiction. Other research studies (e.g., Dalbudak & Evren, 2014; Tsai et al. 2009) have reported similar findings showing that neuroticism and Internet addiction are associated. In their cross-cultural study,

Blachnio et al. (2017) reported that in a sample of Ukrainian Internet users, lower emotional stability was associated with Facebook addiction. With the prevalence of mobile devices, people can now connect to SNSs anytime regardless of their physical location. Tang et al. (2016) investigated Facebook addiction by surveying 894 college students in Taiwan and found that only 1% was classified as addicted while approximately 80% of students used Facebook every day and 10% spent more than 8 hours a day using this SNS. Online interpersonal relationships and neuroticism were found to be prominent predictors of Facebook addiction, and other researchers (Osturk & Ozmen, 2016; Yao et al. 2014) have reported that psychoticism and neuroticism were both positively related to Internet addiction. When examining personality and compulsive mobile application use, Hsiao et al. (2016) reported that neuroticism was linked to compulsive use.

Recent research by Li et al. (2016) revealed that 4.8% of participants in their Chinese sample of 651 participants were identified as online game addicts, these addicts had higher neuroticism scores than non-addicts and were apt to use avoidant coping styles. Higher neuroticism has been associated with Internet addiction and SNS addiction (Wang et al. 2015). Muller et al. (2013) took a different stance on investigating Internet addiction, they compared the profiles of 70 patients who met the criteria for Internet addiction against 48 patients suffering from alcohol dependence. It was shown that patients with Internet addiction can be discriminated from others by high neuroticism scores. All together these studies suggest that neuroticism is an important personality trait in the acquisition, development and maintenance of Internet related addictions.

Conscientiousness

Conscientiousness is a strong predictor of health behaviors and better health outcomes and is a trait describing (at higher levels) an individual's degree of self-discipline and control, with people showing high levels of this personality trait being characterized as being highly determined and organized (Maltby et al. 2010). Several studies have emphasized the effect of conscientiousness as a risk factor across different types of addictions, including substance abuse (Montag & Reuter, 2015; Kotov, Gamez, Schmidt, & Watson, 2010), alcoholism (Alminhana & Farias, 2014; Kuntsche, von Fischer, & Gmel, 2008) and smoking (Terracciano & Costa, 2004). Kuss et al. (2013) reported that 3.7% of their study sample (N = 3,105) were potentially addicted to the Internet, one of the risk factors for addiction was low conscientiousness. A recent 2-year longitudinal study (i.e., Stavropoulos, Kuss, Griffiths & Motti-Stefanidi, 2017) that has investigated the role of conscientiousness and class hostility in the development of Internet addiction in a sample of adolescents, found that lower levels of conscientiousness were associated with Internet addiction and this did not change over time, suggesting that the contribution of individual and context Internet addiction factors may differ across both genders.

In a research study by Amichai-Hamburger and Vinitzky (2010) it was revealed that high conscientiousness individuals have a greater number of friends than individuals who scored lower on the trait of conscientiousness. Blachnio et al. (2017) reported that in their Turkish and Ukrainian samples, lower conscientiousness was associated with Facebook addiction. In support of these findings, Wang et al. (2015) reported that lower conscientiousness was associated with Internet and gaming addiction. Research by Muller et al. (2013) showed that lower conscientiousness was a risk factor for Internet addiction. Buckner, Castille and Sheets (2012) explored personality and problem and pathological technology (Internet and text-messaging) use in the workplace. The findings showed that conscientiousness was negatively related to problem Internet use and that conscientiousness may also predict other excessive use tendencies.

Overall, the findings of the aforementioned studies suggest that conscientiousness is an important personality that can act as a protective or risk factor for addictive behaviors related to technology use. More specifically, conscientiousness can facilitate the emergence and maintenance of addictive processes (i.e., at lower levels) or help protect individuals from engaging in addictive behaviors (i.e., at higher levels).

Openness to Experience

Openness to experience at a higher level, is a personality trait describing individuals that are sophisticated, knowledgeable, cultured, artistic, curious, analytical and more liberal in general (Maltby et al. 2010). Openness as a personality trait has been extensively investigated in substance-based addictions (e.g., Kornør, & Nordvik, 2007; Brooner, Schmidt & Herbst, 1994) and it has also been implicated in other behavioral addictions such as pathological gambling (e.g., Hwang et al. 2012; Kaare, Mõttus, & Konstabel, 2009) and workaholism (e.g., Aziz & Tronzo, 2011).

Although little is known with regards to the role of openness in technological addictions, studies often present mixed findings. For instance, Andreassen et al. (2013) conducted a comprehensive empirical study in a sample of psychology undergraduate students (N = 218) to investigate the role of the five-factor model of personality in several behavioral addictions including Facebook addiction, videogame addiction, Internet addiction, and smartphone addiction. With regards to openness, the authors found that this trait was inversely associated with Facebook addiction and smartphone addiction. In other words, lower levels of openness was associated with higher levels of addictive Facebook and smartphone use. Additionally, openness did not seem to have an influence on videogame addiction and Internet addiction. This finding does not support the results found in previous studies showing that higher levels of openness is related to increased frequency of SNS use (Correa et al. 2010).

Kuss et al. (2013) reported that a combination of online gaming and openness to experience increased Internet addiction risk. Amichai-Hamburger and Vinitzky (2010) reported that individuals who scored higher on the trait of openness to experience used more features from the personal information section of Facebook than individuals who scored lower on the trait of openness to experience. This finding suggested that people exhibiting higher levels of openness are more expressive when using Facebook. More recently, Blachnio et al. (2017) reported that in their Polish sample, lower openness was associated with Facebook addiction and Wang et al. (2015) also found that low openness was significantly associated with gaming addiction. Servidio (2014) reported that there was a positive association between openness and Internet addiction. Ko et al. (2010) reported that novelty seeking, which is part of openness, was related to Internet addiction, the authors concluded that college students with a high rate of novelty-seeking might appreciate Internet activities with higher motivation and excitement; this behavioural involvement may make students prone to problematic Internet use. Taken together, these research studies suggest that further research should be carried out to ascertain the role of openness in technological addictions as findings appear mixed. Furthermore, these studies also show that specific structural characteristics of SNS, such as the Facebook personal information section, may encourage openness (Vaknin, 2003).

Narcissism

Narcissism as a personality trait can be defined as a pattern of traits and behaviors suggesting an obsession with the self to the exclusion of all others, and the egotistic pursuit of gratification, dominance, and ambition (Vaknin, 2003). Furthermore, narcissism can also be defined as an individual difference reflecting an excessive love or admiration of oneself or grandiose and inflated sense of self (Campbell, Rudich & Sedikides, 2002). Narcissism as a personality has been associated with addictions in general (La Barbera et al. 2009) and has been widely investigated in behavioral addictions such as exercise dependence (e.g., Miller & Mesagno, 2014) and technological addictions such as Internet addiction (e.g., Odacı & Çelik, 2013) and online gaming addiction (e.g., Kim, Namkoong, Ku & Kim, 2008).

Similarly, to previous studies on individual differences related to different personality traits in technological addictions, findings from studies investigating the specific link between narcissism and technological addictions remain inconclusive. For instance, studies investigating SNS use found that people presenting higher levels of narcissistic personality traits tend to be more active on SNSs in order to present themselves favorably online (Buffardi & Campbell, 2008; Mehdizadeh, 2010). Furthermore, the relationship between narcissism and Facebook activity may be related to the fact that narcissists have an imbalanced sense of self, fluctuating between grandiosity with regards to explicit agency and low self-esteem concerning implicit communion and vulnerability (Cain et al. 2008).

A more recent study conducted by Eşkisu, Hoşoğlu and Rasmussen (2017) examining the relationship between narcissism and Facebook usage in a sample of 492 Turkish students found that students spending more time on Facebook and who had a greater number of friends and used Facebook to meet new people displayed high levels of narcissism, leading the authors to suggest that SNS use might provide an outlet for users high in narcissism to present and reinforce their inflated self-image. Andreassen, Pallesen and Griffiths (2017) examined the association between addictive use of social media, narcissism and self-esteem amongst a sample of 23,532 Norwegian participants. The results showed that addictive social media use was related to lower age, being a woman, not being in a relationship, lower education, being a student, lower income, having narcissistic traits, and negative self-esteem. When online games are brought into the discussion, research (Kim et al. 2008) suggests that narcissistic personality traits may predispose some individuals to become addicted to online games. Wu et al. (2016) examined personality disorders and gender differences amongst college students (n = 556) with Internet addiction, their study revealed that males with Internet addiction showed a higher frequency of narcissistic personality disorder, whereas females showed higher frequency of borderline narcissistic, avoidant, or dependent personality disorder when compared with those without Internet addiction.

Overall, the existing findings suggest that high frequency technology use and technology addiction appear to be linked with increased levels of narcissism. However, this finding is not straightforward as recent studies have failed to replicate this finding in the context of generalized Internet addiction (e.g., Odaci & Çelik, 2013), suggesting that the interplay between narcissism and technological addiction is rather complex and may be mediated by additional variables.

OTHER KEY PERSONALITY TRAITS, INDIVIDUAL DIFFERENCES AND PERSONALITY DISORDERS

There are other personality traits other than the Big-Five traits that merit further consideration as they may help to understand how technological addictions can be explained by additional personality traits often neglected by research. For instance, Floros et al. (2014) assessed the underlying links between personality, defense styles, Internet addiction and psychopathology. The results of this study showed that impulsivity, sensation seeking, neuroticism/anxiety, and aggression-hostility contributed to the prediction of variability in Internet addiction. In contrast to these findings, Lavin et al. (1999) reported that dependent Internet users scored significantly lower on sensation seeking than non-dependent Internet users.

Research by Servidio (2014) reported that agreeableness was negatively related to Internet addiction. Interestingly, Yang and Tung's (2007) research highlighted that people can have personalities that are characterized by dependence, shyness, depression, and low self-esteem. Such personalities have a higher tendency to become addicted to the Internet. In support of these findings Chak and Leung (2004) reported shyness was linked to Internet addiction. In a Turkish study of Internet addiction, Odaci and Celik (2013) found positive associations between shyness and Internet addiction. To add to this finding, research by Huan, Ang and Chye (2014) demonstrated that social anxiety mediated the relationship between shyness and loneliness and problematic Internet use.

A personality trait that has not been researched extensively is that of self-directedness. Low self-directed humans can be described by low self-esteem, low satisfaction with their own personalities and problems in handling everyday life (Hahn, Reuter, Spinath, & Montag, 2017). Sariyska et al. (2014) conducted a cross-cultural comparison study of seven countries and reported that self-directedness was negatively correlated with Internet addiction in all samples. A more recent study conducted by Hahn et al. (2017) in samples of adult monozygotic and dizygotic twins and non-twin siblings found that self-directedness accounted for 20% to 65% of the genetic variance in specific Internet addiction facets through overlapping genetic pathways. Although the relationship between personality and Internet addiction is complex, it has been established that it is influenced by both genetic and environmental factors (Hahn & Spinath, 2017). However, only a few studies have investigated Internet addiction using genetic-based designs. With regards to Internet addiction, if the environmental factors do not vary in a relevant way, all phenotypic variation related to environmental variation will be cancelled out, and the only variation left will be associated with genetic differences (Hahn & Spinath, 2017).

Another critical personality trait that has received little scientific attention in the technological addictions literature is agreeableness. This personality trait relates to characteristics of the individual that are relevant for social interaction, with higher levels on this trait being often described as trusting, helpful, softhearted, and sympathetic (Maltby et al. 2010). The study of agreeableness in the context of technological addictions is of utmost importance given that addiction to technology often represents poor communication and interpersonal skills with increased levels of preference for online social interaction (Caplan, 2003; Kim, 2017; Yu et al. 2017). It has also been suggested by communication researchers (e.g., Tokunaga, 2015) that maladaptive Internet use is unmistakably a communication research problem. In light of this, many studies have linked technological addiction with agreeableness. Collins, Freeman and Chamarro-Premuzic (2012) investigated the associations between personality traits and MMORPGs and found that problematic players were found to score lower in agreeableness, leading the authors to suggest that agreeableness may be implicated in the development and maintenance of problematic MMORPG use. A recent study on Internet use in Slovakia found that agreeableness was negatively associated with Internet addiction and that this personality trait explained 5% of the unique variance in Internet addiction (Holdoš, 2016).

Deficient self-regulation is a key individual difference that has been implicated in the development of problematic Internet use as it reflects the interplay between compulsive behavioral symptoms and obsessive cognitive symptoms of generalized problematic Internet use (Caplan, 2010). LaRose, Lin and Eastin (2003) defined deficient self-regulation "as a state in which conscious self-control is relatively diminished" (p. 232). LaRose et al. (2003) have also suggested that the process of technology addiction may be interpreted as the struggle to maintain effective self-regulation over problematic media behavior.

Caplan (2010) conducted a study in a sample of 424 undergraduate students and found that deficient self-regulation predicted negative outcomes arising from one's Internet use, a finding that has been corroborated by several studies (Assunção & Matos, 2017; Haagsma, Caplan, Peters, & Pieterse, 2013; Pontes, Caplan, & Griffiths, 2016; Gámez-Guadix, Calvete, Orue, & Las Hayas, 2015).

Research on technological addictions has also investigated the role of abnormal personality in addition to healthy personality. Personality disorders are an example of abnormal personality and can be conceptualized as extreme variants of normal personality domains (Saulsman & Page, 2004). A recent study conducted by Zadra et al. (2016) found that in individuals meeting the diagnostic criteria for Internet addiction showed higher frequencies of personality disorders compared to regular Internet users. Moreover, it was also found that cluster C personality disorders (i.e., avoidant, dependent, and obsessive-compulsive personality disorders) were more prevalent in males than females, and that rates of remission of Internet addiction were found to be lower in participants presenting with cluster B personality disorders (i.e., antisocial, borderline, histrionic, and narcissistic personality disorders). Research by Laconi, Andreoletti, Chauchard, Rodgers and Chabrol (2016) revealed that cluster A personality traits (schizoid and schizotypal) and cluster B personality traits (borderline and antisocial) played important roles in problematic Internet use among men. Borderline personality disorder (BPD) (i.e., emotionally unstable personality disorder characterized by unstable relationships with other people, unstable sense of self and emotions) was linked to Internet addiction in recent research by Wu, Ko, Tung, and Li (2016). The researchers set out to examine whether BPD features would increase the risk for Internet addiction severity in a sample of 1,826 Taiwanese college students. The results showed that BPD was significantly correlated with Internet addiction severity a year later.

SOLUTIONS AND RECOMMENDATIONS

There is evidence showing that different personality traits are associated with different online activities (Wang et al. 2015). Thus, psychosocial interventions for the prevention of addiction needs to consider the sensitivity of individual differences. At the clinical level, many studies have revealed that Internet addiction is related to unique patterns of behavior, especially amongst clinical patients (Muller et al. 2013), so treatment approaches that meet the specific requirements of people suffering with Internet addiction is required. One suggested approach to treatment is to assess an individual's coping style and cognitions and improve biased thinking (e.g., cognitive distortions) to reduce symptoms of Internet addiction (Brand, Laier & Young, 2014; Gervasi et al. 2017). Similarly, Noh and Kim (2016) also propose a focus on cognition when administering treatment. Skills based treatments which incorporate rational problem-solving skills and practical life skills are among the best treatments for alcohol dependency (Kwee, Komoru-Venovic & Kwee, 2010) and could be adapted to help prevent addiction to technology by educators, parents, and social media developers. These treatments could involve face-face sessions or even short online tutorials. Such treatments would equip individuals with important long-term competencies that can be adapted to tackle various addictive behaviours.

FUTURE RESEARCH DIRECTIONS

The present chapter has revealed that there are some dissimilar findings amongst research studies. Billieux, Schimmenti, Khazaal, Maurage and Heeren (2015) have argued that there is a tendency to easily overpathologise some everyday behaviours and consider them behavioural addictions. They argue that most research fails to consider the factors of functional impairment and stability of the dysfunctional behavior. Future addiction research should consider these factors. Further analysis of technology users who are classed as introverts and their network of friends is an area which will delve light on their risks of developing technological addictions such as Internet addiction. The trait of neuroticism warrants further investigation, particularly in the context of SNS use as it has been found that neuroticism affects how individuals use SNSs (Skues, Williams, & Wise, 2012; Ryan & Xenos, 2011; Eşkisu, Hoşoğlu & Rasmussen, 2017). For instance, Ross et al. (2009) found that SNSs users with higher levels of neuroticism were less willing to share personal information on Facebook but preferred posting on their timeline more frequently compared to uploading pictures onto their profiles.

Higher usage associated with narcissists, neurotics, extraverts and introverts may implicate that each of these groups of users are particularly at risk for developing an addiction to Internet applications. The use of different Internet applications tends to have an influence on whether one will experience problematic use. A large number of studies that has been reviewed tends to support initial research (e.g., Leung, 2004) showing that specific online activities can lead to addictive use. This finding appears to support more recent empirical studies that have found that the Internet may be just a means used by individuals to fuel addiction to specific Internet applications and services (Griffiths & Szabo, 2014; Pontes, Szabo, & Griffiths, 2015).

It is important to note that technological addictions present with distinct cultural features and addiction to specific Internet applications can be experienced differently across different cultures. Blachnio et al. (2017) showed that different personality traits were associated with Facebook addiction across three different cultures (i.e., Turkish, Polish and Ukrainian cultures). Future research must consider these findings. There are other influential variables that also need to be considered as research (Yao et al. 2014) has shown that parental behavior can affect the risk of being addicted to the Internet. Furthermore, future studies should investigate the role of specific personality traits in terms of prevention of relapse in technological addictions as research on substance abuse has shown that the risk of relapsing is increased for patients both low in conscientiousness and high in neuroticism, suggesting that these two broad personality dimensions are relevant to the development and maintenance of addiction processes (Fisher, Elias, & Ritz, 1998).

CONCLUSION

The present chapter focused on several technological addictions (e.g. Internet addiction, videogame addiction, SNS addiction, and smartphone addiction) and personality traits (e.g., extraversion, introversion, neuroticism, conscientiousness, openness to experience, and narcissism) alongside specific individual differences related to personality (e.g., personality disorders). After reviewing the scientific literature on personality and technological addictions, it can be argued that greater use of technology and addiction to technology is associated with specific personality traits, disorders, and characteristics. Although the relationship between technological addictions and personality traits has been consistently identified by a large number of empirical studies, it is likely that the causal pathway between these two constructs may be bi-directional (i.e., one can potentiate the other) and not exclusively unidirectional (i.e., one causing the other). The bi-directional approach to understanding the relationship between technological addictions and personality traits is supported by the lack of robust evidence as well as the fact that the vast majority of studies employed cross-sectional designs and non-probability sampling techniques. This finding may implicate that individuals presenting specific personality features may be particularly at risk for developing technological addictions. For instance, personality traits such as neuroticism, extraversion, openness to experience, agreeableness, and conscientiousness were found to explain between 6% and 17% of the variance in different types of technological addictions such as Facebook addiction, videogame addiction, Internet addiction, and smartphone addiction (Andreassen et al. 2013). Research and theory in personality and technological addictions has developed considerably but further research is needed into investigating the intricate relationship personality and technological addiction.

REFERENCES

Aboujaoude, E. (2017). The Internet's effect on personality traits: An important casualty of the "Internet addiction" paradigm. *Journal of Behavioral Addictions*, *6*(1), 1–4. doi:10.1556/2006.6.2017.009 PMID:28301969

Adalier, A. (2012). The relationship between Internet addiction and psychological symptoms. *International Journal of Global Education*, *1*, 42–49.

Alminhana, L. O., & Farias, M. (2014). The missing link: What mediates the relationship between religiosity and alcohol use? *Revista Brasileira de Psiquiatria (Sao Paulo, Brazil)*, *36*(1), 3–3. doi:10.1590/1516-4446-2014-3602 PMID:24604457

Alpaslan, A. H., Avci, K., Soylu, N., & Guzel, H. I. (2015). The association between problematic Internet use, suicide probability, alexithymia and loneliness among Turkish medical students. *Journal of Psychiatry*, *18*(208).

American Psychiatric Association. (1994). *Diagnostic and Statistical Manual for Mental Disorders* (4th ed.). Washington, DC: American Psychiatric Association.

Amichai-Hamburger, Y., & Vinitzky, G. (2010). Social network use and personality. *Computers in Human Behavior*, *26*(6), 1289–1295. doi:10.1016/j.chb.2010.03.018

Andreassen, C. S., Griffiths, M. D., Gjertsen, S. R., Krossbakken, E., Kvam, S., & Pallesen, S. (2013). The relationships between behavioral addictions and the five-factor model of personality. *Journal of Behavioral Addictions*, *2*(2), 90–99. doi:10.1556/JBA.2.2013.003 PMID:26165928

Andreassen, C. S., Pallesen, S., & Griffiths, M. D. (2017). The relationship between addictive use of social media, narcissism, and self-esteem: Findings from a large national survey. *Addictive Behaviors*, *64*, 287–293. doi:10.1016/j.addbeh.2016.03.006 PMID:27072491

Assunção, R. S., & Matos, P. M. (2017). The Generalized Problematic Internet Use Scale 2: Validation and test of the model to Facebook use. *Journal of Adolescence*, *54*, 51–59. doi:10.1016/j.adolescence.2016.11.007 PMID:27871015

Aziz, S., & Tronzo, C. L. (2011). Exploring the relationship between workaholism facets and personality traits: A replication in American workers. *The Psychological Record*, *61*(2), 269–286. doi:10.1007/BF03395760

Bakken, I. J., Wenzel, H. G., Götestam, K. G., Johansson, A., & Øren, A. (2009). Internet addiction among Norwegian adults: A stratified probability sample study. *Scandinavian Journal of Psychology*, *50*(2), 121–127. doi:10.1111/j.1467-9450.2008.00685.x PMID:18826420

Bányai, F., Zsila, Á., Király, O., Maraz, A., Elekes, Z., Griffiths, M. D., & Demetrovics, Z. et al. (2017). Problematic social media use: Results from a large-scale nationally representative adolescent sample. *PLoS One*, *12*(1), e0169839. doi:10.1371/journal.pone.0169839 PMID:28068404

Bernardi, S., & Pallanti, S. (2009). Internet addiction: A descriptive clinical study focusing on comorbidities and dissociative symptoms. *Comprehensive Psychiatry*, *50*(6), 510–516. doi:10.1016/j.comppsych.2008.11.011 PMID:19840588

Beutel, M. E., Hoch, C., Woelfing, K., & Mueller, K. W. (2011). Clinical characteristics of computer game and Internet addiction in persons seeking treatment in an outpatient clinic for computer game addiction. *Psychosomatic Medecine & Psychotherapy*, *57*, 77–90. PMID:21432840

Bianchi, A., & Phillips, J. G. (2005). Psychological predictors of problem mobile phone use. *Cyberpsychology & Behavior*, *8*(1), 39–51. doi:10.1089/cpb.2005.8.39 PMID:15738692

Billieux, J., Schimmenti, A., Khazaal, Y., Maurage, P., & Heeren, A. (2015). Are we overpathologizing everyday life? A tenable blueprint for behavioral addiction research. *Journal of Behavioral Addictions*, *4*(3), 119–123. doi:10.1556/2006.4.2015.009 PMID:26014667

Blachnio, A., Przepiorka, A., Senol-Durak, E., Durak, M., & Sherstyuk, L. (2017). The role of personality traits in Facebook and Internet addictions: A study on Polish, Turkish, and Ukrainian samples. *Computers in Human Behavior*, *68*, 269–275. doi:10.1016/j.chb.2016.11.037

Blinka, L., Škařupová, K., Ševčíková, A., Wölfling, K., Müller, K. W., & Dreier, M. (2015). Excessive Internet use in European adolescents: What determines differences in severity? *International Journal of Public Health*, *60*(2), 249–256. doi:10.1007/s00038-014-0635-x PMID:25532555

Block, J. J. (2008). Issues for DSM-V: Internet addiction. *The American Journal of Psychiatry*, *165*(3), 306–307. doi:10.1176/appi.ajp.2007.07101556 PMID:18316427

Brand, M., Laier, C., & Young, K. S. (2014). Internet addiction: Coping styles, expectancies, and treatment implications. *Frontiers in Psychology*, *5*, 1256. doi:10.3389/fpsyg.2014.01256 PMID:25426088

Brooner, R. K., Schmidt, C. W., Jr., & Herbst, J. H. (1994). Personality trait characteristics of opioid abusers with and without comorbid personality disorders. In Personality disorders and the five-factor model of personality (pp. 131-148). Washington, DC: American Psychological Association. doi:10.1037/10140-025

Bruno, A., Scimeca, G., Cava, L., Pandolfo, G., Zoccali, R. A., & Muscatello, M. R. (2014). Prevalence of internet addiction in a sample of southern Italian high school students. *International Journal of Mental Health and Addiction*, *12*(6), 708–715. doi:10.1007/s11469-014-9497-y

Buckner, J. E., Castille, C. M., & Sheets, T. L. (2012). The Five Factor Model of personality and employees' excessive use of technology. *Computers in Human Behavior*, *28*(5), 1947–1953. doi:10.1016/j. chb.2012.05.014

Buffardi, E. L., & Campbell, W. K. (2008). Narcissism and social networking web sites. *Perspectives in Social Psychology*, *34*, 1303–1314. PMID:18599659

Cain, N. M., Pincus, A. L., & Ansell, E. B. (2008). Narcissism at the crossroads: Phenotypic description of pathological narcissism across clinical theory, social/personality psychology, and psychiatric diagnosis. *Clinical Psychology Review*, *28*(4), 638–656. doi:10.1016/j.cpr.2007.09.006 PMID:18029072

Campbell, W. K., Rudich, E. A., & Sedikides, C. (2002). Narcissism, self-esteem, and the positivity of self-views: Two portraits of self-love. *Personality and Social Psychology Bulletin*, *28*(3), 358–368. doi:10.1177/0146167202286007

Cao, F. L., & Su, L. Y. (2007). Internet addiction among Chinese adolescents: Prevalence and psychological features. *Child: Care, Health and Development*, *33*(3), 275–281. doi:10.1111/j.1365-2214.2006.00715.x PMID:17439441

Caplan, S. E. (2003). Preference for online social interaction A theory of problematic Internet use and psychosocial well-being. *Communication Research*, *30*(6), 625–648. doi:10.1177/0093650203257842

Caplan, S. E. (2010). Theory and measurement of generalized problematic Internet use: A two-step approach. *Computers in Human Behavior*, *26*(5), 1089–1097. doi:10.1016/j.chb.2010.03.012

Chak, K., & Leung, L. (2004). Shyness and locus of control as predictors of internet addiction and internet use. *Cyberpsychology & Behavior*, *7*(5), 559–570. doi:10.1089/cpb.2004.7.559 PMID:15667051

Chou, C., & Hsiao, M. C. (2000). Internet addiction, usage, gratification, and pleasure experience: The Taiwan college students' case. *Computers & Education*, *35*(1), 65–80. doi:10.1016/S0360-1315(00)00019-1

Collins, E., Freeman, J., & Chamarro-Premuzic, T. (2012). Personality traits associated with problematic and non-problematic massively multiplayer online role playing game use. *Personality and Individual Differences*, *52*(2), 133–138. doi:10.1016/j.paid.2011.09.015

Correa, T., Hinsley, A. W., & de Zuniga, H. G. (2010). Who interacts on the Web?: The intersection of users' personality and social media use. *Computers in Human Behavior*, *26*(2), 247–253. doi:10.1016/j. chb.2009.09.003

Dalbudak, E., & Evren, C. (2014). The relationship of Internet addiction severity with Attention Deficit Hyperactivity Disorder symptoms in Turkish University students; impact of personality traits, depression and anxiety. *Comprehensive Psychiatry*, *55*(3), 497–503. doi:10.1016/j.comppsych.2013.11.018 PMID:24374171

Dong, G., Wang, J., Yang, X., & Zhou, H. (2013). Risk personality traits of Internet addiction: A longitudinal study of Internet-addicted Chinese university students. *Asia-Pacific Psychiatry*, *5*(4), 316–321. doi:10.1111/j.1758-5872.2012.00185.x PMID:23857796

Durkee, T., Kaess, M., Carli, V., Parzer, P., Wasserman, C., Floderus, B., & Bobes, J. et al. (2012). Prevalence of pathological internet use among adolescents in Europe: Demographic and social factors. *Addiction (Abingdon, England)*, *107*(12), 2210–2222. doi:10.1111/j.1360-0443.2012.03946.x PMID:22621402

Eaton, L. G., & Funder, D. C. (2003). The creation and consequences of the social world: An interactional analysis of extraversion. *European Journal of Personality*, *17*(5), 375–395. doi:10.1002/per.477

Ehrenberg, A., Juckes, S., White, K. M., & Walsh, S. P. (2008). Personality and self-esteem as predictors of young people's technology use. *Cyberpsychology & Behavior*, *11*(6), 739–741. doi:10.1089/cpb.2008.0030 PMID:18991531

Ellison, N. B. (2007). Social network sites: Definition, history, and scholarship. *Journal of Computer-Mediated Communication*, *13*(1), 210–230. doi:10.1111/j.1083-6101.2007.00393.x

Eşkisu, M., Hoşoğlu, R., & Rasmussen, K. (2017). An investigation of the relationship between Facebook usage, Big Five, self-esteem and narcissism. *Computers in Human Behavior*, *69*, 294–301. doi:10.1016/j.chb.2016.12.036

Farmer, A. D., Holt, C. B., Cook, M. J., & Hearing, S. D. (2009). Social networking sites: A novel portal for communication. *Postgraduate Medical Journal*, *85*(1007), 455–459. doi:10.1136/pgmj.2008.074674 PMID:19734511

Fisher, L. A., Elias, J. W., & Ritz, K. (1998). Predicting relapse to substance abuse as a function of personality dimensions. *Alcoholism, Clinical and Experimental Research*, *22*(5), 1041–1047. doi:10.1111/j.1530-0277.1998.tb03696.x PMID:9726270

Floros, G., Siomos, K., Stogiannidou, A., Giouzepas, I., & Garyfallos, G. (2014). The relationship between personality, defense styles, internet addiction disorder, and psychopathology in college students. *Cyberpsychology, Behavior, and Social Networking*, *17*(10), 672–676. doi:10.1089/cyber.2014.0182 PMID:25225916

Gámez-Guadix, M., Calvete, E., Orue, I., & Las Hayas, C. (2015). Problematic Internet use and problematic alcohol use from the cognitive–behavioral model: A longitudinal study among adolescents. *Addictive Behaviors*, *40*, 109–114. doi:10.1016/j.addbeh.2014.09.009 PMID:25244690

Gervasi, A. M., La Marca, L., Lombardo, E., Mannino, G., Iacolino, C., & Schimmenti, A. (2017). Maladaptive Personality Traits and Internet Addiction Symptoms among Young Adults: A Study based on the alternative DSM-5 Model for Personality Disorders. *Clinical Neuropsychiatry*, *14*(1), 20–28.

Grant, J. E., Potenza, M. N., Weinstein, A., & Gorelick, D. A. (2010). Introduction to behavioral addictions. *The American Journal of Drug and Alcohol Abuse*, *36*(5), 233–241. doi:10.3109/00952990.2010.491884 PMID:20560821

Griffiths, M. D. (1996). Internet addiction: An issue for clinical psychology? *Clinical Psychology Forum, 97*, 32-6.

Griffiths, M. D. (2005). A components model of addiction within a biopsychosocial framework. *Journal of Substance Use, 10*(4), 191–197. doi:10.1080/14659890500114359

Griffiths, M. D., & Szabo, A. (2014). Is excessive online usage a function of medium or activity? An empirical pilot study. *Journal of Behavioral Addictions, 3*(1), 74–77. doi:10.1556/JBA.2.2013.016 PMID:25215216

Haagsma, M. C., Caplan, S. E., Peters, O., & Pieterse, M. E. (2013). A cognitive-behavioral model of problematic online gaming in adolescents aged 12–22 years. *Computers in Human Behavior, 29*(1), 202–209. doi:10.1016/j.chb.2012.08.006

Hahn, E., Reuter, M., Spinath, F. M., & Montag, C. (2017). Internet addiction and its facets: The role of genetics and the relation to self-directedness. *Addictive Behaviors, 65*, 137–146. doi:10.1016/j.addbeh.2016.10.018 PMID:27816039

Hahn, E., & Spinath, F. M. (2017). Quantitative behavior genetics of Internet addiction. In C. Montag & M. Reuter (Eds.), *Internet addiction: Neuroscientific approaches and therapeutical implications including smartphone addiction* (2nd ed.; pp. 125–140). Cham, Switzerland: Springer International Publishing. doi:10.1007/978-3-319-46276-9_8

Hardie, E., & Tee, M. Y. (2007). Excessive Internet use: The role of personality, loneliness and social support networks in Internet Addiction. *Australian Journal of Emerging Technologies and Society, 5*(1).

Heo, J., Chun, S., Lee, S., Lee, K. H., & Kim, J. (2015). Internet use and well-being in older adults. *Cyberpsychology, Behavior, and Social Networking, 18*(5), 268–272. doi:10.1089/cyber.2014.0549 PMID:25919967

Holdoš, J. (2016). Type D personality in the prediction of Internet addiction in the young adult population of Slovak Internet users. *Current Psychology (New Brunswick, N.J.)*, 1–8.

Howard, C. J., Wilding, R., & Guest, D. (2016). Light video game play is associated with enhanced visual processing of rapid serial visual presentation targets. *Perception, 46*, 2. PMID:27697909

Hsiao, K. L., Lee, C. H., Chiang, H. S., & Wang, J. Y. (2016). Exploring the Antecedents of Technostress and Compulsive Mobile Application Usage: Personality Perspectives. In *International Conference on Human Aspects of IT for the Aged Population* (pp. 320-328). Springer International Publishing. doi:10.1007/978-3-319-39943-0_31

Huan, V. S., Ang, R. P., & Chye, S. (2014). Loneliness and shyness in adolescent problematic internet users: The role of social anxiety. *Child and Youth Care Forum, 43*(5), 539–551. doi:10.1007/s10566-014-9252-3

Hwang, J. Y., Shin, Y. C., Lim, S. W., Park, H. Y., Shin, N. Y., Jang, J. H., & Kwon, J. S. et al. (2012). Multidimensional comparison of personality characteristics of the Big Five Model, impulsiveness, and affect in pathological gambling and obsessive–compulsive disorder. *Journal of Gambling Studies, 28*(3), 351–362. doi:10.1007/s10899-011-9269-6 PMID:21938524

Hwang, Y. (2014). Personal Characters and Addictive Use of Facebook. *Journal of the Korea Society of IT Services, 13*(4), 45-63.

International Telecommunication Union. (2012). *Internet users*. International Telecommunication Union. Retrieved 14 December 2016 from http://www.itu.int/ITU-D/ict/statistics/index.html

Jafarkarimi, H., Sim, A. T. H., Saadatdoost, R., & Hee, J. M. (2016). Facebook addiction among Malaysian students. *International Journal of Information and Education Technology (IJIET), 6*(6), 465–469. doi:10.7763/IJIET.2016.V6.733

Jansz, J., & Tanis, M. (2007). Appeal of playing online first person shooter games. *Cyberpsychology & Behavior, 10*(1), 133–136. doi:10.1089/cpb.2006.9981 PMID:17305460

Jun, S., & Choi, E. (2015). Academic stress and Internet addiction from general strain theory framework. *Computers in Human Behavior, 49*, 282–287. doi:10.1016/j.chb.2015.03.001

Jung, C. G. (1964). *Man and his symbols*. New York: Dell.

Kaare, P. R., Mõttus, R., & Konstabel, K. (2009). Pathological gambling in Estonia: Relationships with personality, self-esteem, emotional states and cognitive ability. *Journal of Gambling Studies, 25*(3), 377–390. doi:10.1007/s10899-009-9119-y PMID:19234772

Kim, E. J., Namkoong, K., Ku, T., & Kim, S. J. (2008). The relationship between online game addiction and aggression, self-control and narcissistic personality traits. *European Psychiatry, 23*(3), 212–218. doi:10.1016/j.eurpsy.2007.10.010 PMID:18166402

Kim, H., & Chung, Y. W. (2014). The use of social networking services and their relationship with the Big Five personality model and job satisfaction in Korea. *Cyberpsychology, Behavior, and Social Networking, 17*(10), 658–663. doi:10.1089/cyber.2014.0109 PMID:25127246

Kim, J. H. (2017). Smartphone-mediated communication vs. face-to-face interaction: Two routes to social support and problematic use of smartphone. *Computers in Human Behavior, 67*, 282–291. doi:10.1016/j.chb.2016.11.004

Király, O., Griffiths, M. D., Urbán, R., Farkas, J., Kökönyei, G., Elekes, Z., & Demetrovics, Z. et al. (2014). Problematic Internet use and problematic online gaming are not the same: Findings from a large nationally representative adolescent sample. *Cyberpsychology, Behavior, and Social Networking, 17*(12), 749–754. doi:10.1089/cyber.2014.0475 PMID:25415659

Kirschner, P. A., & Karpinski, A. C. (2010). Facebook and academic performance. *Computers in Human Behavior, 26*(6), 1237–1245. doi:10.1016/j.chb.2010.03.024

Klimmt, C., & Hartmann, T. (2006). Effectance, self-efficacy, and the motivation to play video games. *Playing Video Games: Motives, Responses, and Consequences*, 133-145.

Ko, C. H., Hsiao, S., Liu, G. C., Yen, J. Y., Yang, M. J., & Yen, C. F. (2010). The characteristics of decision making, potential to take risks, and personality of college students with Internet addiction. *Psychiatry Research, 175*(1), 121–125. doi:10.1016/j.psychres.2008.10.004 PMID:19962767

Kornør, H., & Nordvik, H. (2007). Five-factor model personality traits in opioid dependence. *BMC Psychiatry*, *7*(1), 37. doi:10.1186/1471-244X-7-37 PMID:17683593

Kotov, R., Gamez, W., Schmidt, F., & Watson, D. (2010). Linking "big" personality traits to anxiety, depressive, and substance use disorders: A meta-analysis. *Psychological Bulletin*, *136*(5), 768–821. doi:10.1037/a0020327 PMID:20804236

Kuntsche, E., von Fischer, M., & Gmel, G. (2008). Personality factors and alcohol use: A mediator analysis of drinking motives. *Personality and Individual Differences*, *45*(8), 796–800. doi:10.1016/j.paid.2008.08.009

Kuss, D. J., & Billieux, J. (2016). Technological addictions: Conceptualisation, measurement, etiology and treatment. *Addictive Behaviors*, *30*(16), 147–152. PMID:27136694

Kuss, D. J., Griffiths, M. D., & Binder, J. F. (2013). Internet addiction in students: Prevalence and risk factors. *Computers in Human Behavior*, *29*(3), 959–966. doi:10.1016/j.chb.2012.12.024

Kuss, D. J., Van Rooij, A. J., Shorter, G. W., Griffiths, M. D., & van de Mheen, D. (2013). Internet addiction in adolescents: Prevalence and risk factors. *Computers in Human Behavior*, *29*(5), 1987–1996. doi:10.1016/j.chb.2013.04.002

Kwee, A. W., Komoru-Venovic, E., & Kwee, J. L. (2010). Treatment Implications from Etiological and Diagnostic Considerations of Internet Addiction: Cautions with the Boot Camp Approach. *Proceedings of the International Conference of e-CASE*.

La Barbera, D., La Paglia, F., & Valsavoia, R. (2009). Social network and addiction. *Cyberpsychology & Behavior*, *12*, 628–629. PMID:19592725

Laconi, S., Andréoletti, A., Chauchard, E., Rodgers, R. F., & Chabrol, H. (2016). Problematic Internet use, time spent online and personality traits. *L'Encéphale*, *42*(3), 214–218. doi:10.1016/j.encep.2015.12.017 PMID:26827120

Lai, F. T. T., & Kwan, J. L. Y. (2017). Socioeconomic influence on adolescent problematic Internet use through school-related psychosocial factors and pattern of Internet use. *Computers in Human Behavior*, *68*, 121–136. doi:10.1016/j.chb.2016.11.021

Lavin, M., Marvin, K., McLarney, A., Nola, V., & Scott, L. (1999). Sensation seeking and collegiate vulnerability to Internet dependence. *Cyberpsychology & Behavior*, *2*(5), 425–430. doi:10.1089/cpb.1999.2.425 PMID:19178215

Lenhart, A., Duggan, M., Perrin, A., Stepler, R., Rainie, H., & Parker, K. (2015). *Teens, social media and technology overview 2015. Smartphones facilitate shifts in communication landscape for teens*. Washington, DC: Pew Internet & American Life Project.

Lenhart, A., Purcell, K., Smith, A., & Zickuhr, K. (2010). *Social Media and Young Adults*. Retrieved 14 November 2016 from http://www.pewinternet.org/2010/02/03/social-media-and-young-adults/

Leung, L. (2004). Net-generation attributes and seductive properties of the Internet as predictors of online activities and Internet addiction. *Cyberpsychology & Behavior*, *7*(3), 333–348. doi:10.1089/1094931041291303 PMID:15257834

Li, H., Zou, Y., Wang, J., & Yang, X. (2016). Role of Stressful Life Events, Avoidant Coping Styles, and Neuroticism in Online Game Addiction among College Students: A Moderated Mediation Model. *Frontiers in Psychology*, 7. PMID:27920734

Lin, I. H., Ko, C. H., Chang, Y. P., Liu, T. L., Wang, P. W., Lin, H. C., & Yen, C. F. et al. (2014). The association between suicidality and internet addiction and activities in Taiwanese adolescents. *Comprehensive Psychiatry*, 55(3), 504–510. doi:10.1016/j.comppsych.2013.11.012 PMID:24457034

Liu, T., & Potenza, M. N. (2007). Problematic Internet use: Clinical implications. *CNS Spectrums*, 12(06), 453–466. doi:10.1017/S1092852900015339 PMID:17545956

Lortie, C. L., & Guitton, M. J. (2013). Internet addiction assessment tools: Dimensional structure and methodological status. *Addiction (Abingdon, England)*, 108(7), 1207–1216. doi:10.1111/add.12202 PMID:23651255

Maltby, J., Day, L., & Macaskill, A. (2010). *Personality, individual differences and intelligence* (2nd ed.). Essex, UK: Pearson Education Limited.

McIntyre, E., Wiener, K. K. K., & Saliba, A. J. (2015). Compulsive Internet use and relations between social connectedness, and introversion. *Computers in Human Behavior*, 48, 569–574. doi:10.1016/j.chb.2015.02.021

Meerkerk, G. J., Van den Eijnden, R. J. J. M., Franken, I. H. A., & Garretsen, H. F. L. (2010). Is compulsive Internet use related to sensitivity to reward and punishment, and impulsivity? *Computers in Human Behavior*, 26(4), 729–735. doi:10.1016/j.chb.2010.01.009

Mehdizadeh, S. (2010). Self-presentation 2.0: Narcissism and self-esteem on Facebook. *Cyberpsychology, Behavior, and Social Networking*, 13(4), 357–364. doi:10.1089/cyber.2009.0257 PMID:20712493

Mehroof, M., & Griffiths, M. D. (2010). Online gaming addiction: The role of sensation seeking, self-control, neuroticism, aggression, state anxiety, and trait anxiety. *Cyberpsychology, Behavior, and Social Networking*, 13(3), 313–316. doi:10.1089/cyber.2009.0229 PMID:20557251

Miller, K. J., & Mesagno, C. (2014). Personality traits and exercise dependence: Exploring the role of narcissism and perfectionism. *International Journal of Sport and Exercise Psychology*, 12(4), 368–381. doi:10.1080/1612197X.2014.932821

Montag, C., & Reuter, M. (2015). Molecular Genetics, Personality and Internet Addiction. In C. Montag & M. Reuter (Ed.), Internet Addiction (pp. 93–109). Springer International Publishing.

Mottram, A. J., & Fleming, M. J. (2009). Extraversion, impulsivity, and online group membership as predictors of problematic Internet use. *Cyberpsychology & Behavior*, 12(3), 319–321. doi:10.1089/cpb.2007.0170 PMID:19445635

Müller, K. W., Koch, A., Dickenhorst, U., Beutel, M. E., Duven, E., & Wölfling, K. (2013). Addressing the question of disorder-specific risk factors of internet addiction: A comparison of personality traits in patients with addictive behaviors and comorbid internet addiction. *BioMed Research International*, 2013, 1–7. doi:10.1155/2013/546342 PMID:23865056

Noh, D., & Kim, S. (2016). Dysfunctional attitude mediates the relationship between psychopathology and Internet addiction among Korean college students: A cross-sectional observational study. *International Journal of Mental Health Nursing*, 25(6), 588–597. doi:10.1111/inm.12220

Oberst, U., Wegmann, E., Stodt, B., Brand, M., & Chamarro, A. (2017). Negative consequences from heavy social networking in adolescents: The mediating role of fear of missing out. *Journal of Adolescence*, 55, 51–60. doi:10.1016/j.adolescence.2016.12.008 PMID:28033503

Odacı, H., & Çelik, Ç. B. (2013). Who are problematic internet users? An investigation of the correlations between problematic internet use and shyness, loneliness, narcissism, aggression and self-perception. *Computers in Human Behavior*, 29(6), 2382–2387. doi:10.1016/j.chb.2013.05.026

Orr, E. S., Ross, C., Simmering, M. G., Arseneault, J. M., & Orr, R. R. (2009). The influence of shyness on the use of Facebook in an undergraduate sample. *Cyberpsychology & Behavior*, 12(3), 337–340. doi:10.1089/cpb.2008.0214 PMID:19250019

Öztürk, E., & Özmen, S. K. (2016). The relationship of self-perception, personality and high school type with the level of problematic internet use in adolescents. *Computers in Human Behavior*, 65, 501–507. doi:10.1016/j.chb.2016.09.016

Peters, C. S., & Malesky, L. A. Jr. (2008). Problematic usage among highly-engaged players of massively multiplayer online role playing games. *Cyberpsychology & Behavior*, 11(4), 481–484. doi:10.1089/cpb.2007.0140 PMID:18721098

Pies, R. (2009). Should DSM-V designate "Internet addiction" a mental disorder? *Psychiatry (Edgmont)*, 6(2), 31–37. PMID:19724746

Pontes, H. M. (2016). Current practices in the clinical and psychometric assessment of internet gaming disorder in the era of the DSM-5: A mini review of existing assessment tools. *Mental Health and Addiction Research*, 1(1), 18–19. doi:10.15761/MHAR.1000105

Pontes, H. M., Caplan, S. E., & Griffiths, M. D. (2016). Psychometric validation of the Generalized Problematic Internet Use Scale 2 in a Portuguese sample. *Computers in Human Behavior*, 63, 823–833. doi:10.1016/j.chb.2016.06.015

Pontes, H. M., & Griffiths, M. D. (2015). Measuring DSM-5 Internet Gaming Disorder: Development and validation of a short psychometric scale. *Computers in Human Behavior*, 45, 137–143. doi:10.1016/j.chb.2014.12.006

Pontes, H. M., & Griffiths, M. D. (2016a). The development and psychometric properties of the Internet Disorder Scale-Short Form (IDS9-SF). *Addicta: The Turkish Journal on Addictions*, 3(2), 1–16.

Pontes, H. M., & Griffiths, M. D. (2016b). Portuguese validation of the Internet Gaming Disorder Scale–Short-Form. *Cyberpsychology, Behavior, and Social Networking*, 19(4), 288–293. doi:10.1089/cyber.2015.0605 PMID:26974853

Pontes, H. M., & Griffiths, M. D. (2017). The development and psychometric evaluation of the Internet Disorder Scale (IDS-15). *Addictive Behaviors*, 64, 261–268. doi:10.1016/j.addbeh.2015.09.003 PMID:26410796

Pontes, H. M., Griffiths, M. D., & Patrão, I. M. (2014). Internet addiction and loneliness among children and adolescents in the education setting: An empirical pilot study. *Aloma: Revista de Psicologia, Ciències de l'Educació I de l'Esport, 32*(1), 91-98.

Pontes, H. M., Király, O., Demetrovics, Z., & Griffiths, M. D. (2014). The conceptualisation and measurement of DSM-5 Internet Gaming Disorder: The development of the IGD-20 Test. *PLoS One, 9*(10), e110137. doi:10.1371/journal.pone.0110137 PMID:25313515

Pontes, H. M., Kuss, D. J., & Griffiths, M. D. (2015). Clinical psychology of Internet addiction: A review of its conceptualization, prevalence, neuronal processes, and implications for treatment. *Neuroscience and Neuroeconomics, 4*, 11–23.

Pontes, H. M., Kuss, D. J., & Griffiths, M. D. (2015). Clinical psychology of Internet addiction: A review of its conceptualization, prevalence, neuronal processes, and implications for treatment. *Neuroscience and Neuroeconomics, 4*, 11–23.

Pontes, H. M., Patrão, I. M., & Griffiths, M. D. (2014). Portuguese validation of the Internet Addiction Test: An empirical study. *Journal of Behavioral Addictions, 3*(2), 107–114. doi:10.1556/JBA.3.2014.2.4 PMID:25215221

Pontes, H. M., Szabo, A., & Griffiths, M. D. (2015). The impact of Internet-based specific activities on the perceptions of Internet addiction, quality of life, and excessive usage: A cross-sectional study. *Addictive Behaviors Reports, 1*, 19–25. doi:10.1016/j.abrep.2015.03.002

Reed, P., Osborne, L. A., Romano, M., & Truzoli, R. (2015). Higher impulsivity after exposure to the Internet for individuals with high but not low levels of self-reported problematic Internet behaviours. *Computers in Human Behavior, 49*, 512–516. doi:10.1016/j.chb.2015.03.064

Reer, F., & Krämer, N. C. (2017). The connection between introversion/extraversion and social capital outcomes of playing World of Warcraft. *Cyberpsychology, Behavior, and Social Networking, 20*(2), 97–103. doi:10.1089/cyber.2016.0439 PMID:28170308

Rosen, L. D., Whaling, K., Rab, S., Carrier, L. M., & Cheever, N. A. (2013). Is Facebook creating "iDisorders"? The link between clinical symptoms of psychiatric disorders and technology use, attitudes and anxiety. *Computers in Human Behavior, 29*(3), 1243–1254. doi:10.1016/j.chb.2012.11.012

Ross, C., Orr, E. S., Sisic, M., Arseneault, J. M., Simmering, M. G., & Orr, R. R. (2009). Personality and Motivations associated with Facebook Use. *Computers in Human Behavior, 25*(2), 578–586. doi:10.1016/j.chb.2008.12.024

Roy, A., & Ferguson, C. J. (2016). Competitively versus cooperatively? An analysis of the effect of game play on levels of stress. *Computers in Human Behavior, 56*, 14–20. doi:10.1016/j.chb.2015.11.020

Rücker, J., Akre, C., Berchtold, A., & Suris, J. C. (2015). Problematic Internet use is Associated with substance use in young adolescents. *Acta Paediatrica (Oslo, Norway), 104*(5), 504–507. doi:10.1111/apa.12971 PMID:25662370

Ruggiero, T. E. (2000). Uses and gratifications theory in the 21st century. *Mass Communication & Society, 3*(1), 3–37. doi:10.1207/S15327825MCS0301_02

Rumpf, H. J., Vermulst, A. A., Bischof, A., Kastirke, N., Gürtler, D., Bischof, G., & Meyer, C. et al. (2014). Occurence of Internet addiction in a general population sample: A latent class analysis. *European Addiction Research*, *20*(4), 159–166. doi:10.1159/000354321 PMID:24401314

Ryan, T., & Xenos, S. (2011). Who uses Facebook? An investigation into the relationship between the Big Five, shyness, narcissism, loneliness, and Facebook usage. *Computers in Human Behavior*, *27*(5), 1658–1664. doi:10.1016/j.chb.2011.02.004

Sariyska, R., Reuter, M., Bey, K., Sha, P., Li, M., Chen, Y. F., & Feldmann, M. et al. (2014). Self-esteem, personality and Internet addiction: A cross-cultural comparison study. *Personality and Individual Differences*, *61*, 28–33. doi:10.1016/j.paid.2014.01.001

Sariyska, R., Reuter, M., Lachmann, B., & Montag, C. (2015). Attention deficit/hyperactivity disorder is a better predictor for problematic Internet use than depression: Evidence from Germany. *Journal of Addiction Research & Therapy*, *6*(209), 1–6. PMID:26925299

Saulsman, L. M., & Page, A. C. (2004). The five-factor model and personality disorder empirical literature: A meta-analytic review. *Clinical Psychology Review*, *23*(8), 1055–1085. doi:10.1016/j.cpr.2002.09.001 PMID:14729423

Servidio, R. (2014). Exploring the effects of demographic factors, Internet usage and personality traits on Internet addiction in a sample of Italian university students. *Computers in Human Behavior*, *35*, 85–92. doi:10.1016/j.chb.2014.02.024

Shaw, W., & Black, D. W. (2008). Internet addiction: Definition, assessment, epidemiology and clinical management. *CNS Drugs*, *22*(5), 353–365. doi:10.2165/00023210-200822050-00001 PMID:18399706

Siomos, K. E., Dafouli, E. D., Braimiotis, D. A., Mouzas, O. D., & Angelopoulos, N. V. (2008). Internet addiction among Greek adolescent students. *Cyberpsychology & Behavior*, *11*(6), 653–657. doi:10.1089/cpb.2008.0088 PMID:18991535

Skues, J. L., Williams, B., & Wise, L. (2012). The effects of personality traits, self-esteem, loneliness, and narcissism on Facebook use among university students. *Computers in Human Behavior*, *28*(6), 2414–2419. doi:10.1016/j.chb.2012.07.012

Starcevic, V. (2013). Is Internet addiction a useful concept? *The Australian and New Zealand Journal of Psychiatry*, *47*(1), 16–19. doi:10.1177/0004867412461693 PMID:23293309

Starcevic, V. (2016). *Internet addiction: Rarely an addiction and not the Internet that one is addicted to*. Paper presented at the 3rd International Conference on Behavioral Addictions, Geneva, Switzerland.

Starcevic, V., & Aboujaoude, E. (2016). Internet addiction: Reappraisal of an increasingly inadequate concept. *CNS Spectrums*, 1–7. PMID:26831456

Stavropoulos, V., Kuss, D. J., Griffiths, M. D., & Motti-Stefanidi, F. (2016). A longitudinal study of adolescent Internet addiction: The role of conscientiousness and classroom hostility. *Journal of Adolescent Research*, *31*(4), 442–473. doi:10.1177/0743558415580163

Swickert, R. J., Rosentreter, C. J., Hittner, J. B., & Mushrush, J. E. (2002). Extraversion, social support processes, and stress. *Personality and Individual Differences, 32*(5), 877–891. doi:10.1016/S0191-8869(01)00093-9

Tang, J. H., Chen, M. C., Yang, C. Y., Chung, T. Y., & Lee, Y. A. (2016). Personality traits, interpersonal relationships, online social support, and Facebook addiction. *Telematics and Informatics, 33*(1), 102–108. doi:10.1016/j.tele.2015.06.003

Teng, C. I. (2008). Personality Differences between Online Game Players and Nonplayers in a Student Sample. *Cyberpsychology & Behavior, 11*(2), 232–234. doi:10.1089/cpb.2007.0064 PMID:18422420

Terracciano, A., & Costa, P. T. Jr. (2004). Smoking and the Five-Factor Model of personality. *Addiction (Abingdon, England), 99*(4), 472–481. doi:10.1111/j.1360-0443.2004.00687.x PMID:15049747

Toda, M., Monden, K., Kubo, K., & Morimoto, K. (2006). Mobile phone dependence and health-related lifestyle of university students. *Social Behavior and Personality, 34*(10), 1277–1284. doi:10.2224/sbp.2006.34.10.1277

Tokunaga, R. S. (2015). Perspectives on Internet addiction, problematic Internet use, and deficient self-regulation: Contributions of communication research. In E. L. Cohen (Ed.), *Communication Yearbook 30* (pp. 131–161). New York, NY: Routledge. doi:10.1080/23808985.2015.11679174

Tsai, H. F., Cheng, S. H., Yeh, T. L., Shih, C. C., Chen, K. C., Yang, Y. C., & Yang, Y. K. (2009). The risk factors of Internet addiction—a survey of university freshmen. *Psychiatry Research, 167*(3), 294–299. doi:10.1016/j.psychres.2008.01.015 PMID:19395052

Vaknin, S. (2003). *Malignant self-love: Narcissism revisited.* Prague: Narcissus Publications.

Van der Aa, N., Overbeek, G., Engels, R. C., Scholte, R. H., Meerkerk, G. J., & Van den Eijnden, R. J. (2009). Daily and compulsive internet use and well-being in adolescence: A diathesis-stress model based on big five personality traits. *Journal of Youth and Adolescence, 38*(6), 765–776. doi:10.1007/s10964-008-9298-3 PMID:19636779

Wang, C. W., Ho, R. T., Chan, C. L., & Tse, S. (2015). Exploring personality characteristics of Chinese adolescents with internet-related addictive behaviors: Trait differences for gaming addiction and social networking addiction. *Addictive Behaviors, 42,* 32–35. doi:10.1016/j.addbeh.2014.10.039 PMID:25462651

Wartberg, L., Kriston, L., Kammerl, R., Petersen, K. U., & Thomasius, R. (2015). Prevalence of pathological Internet use in a representative German sample of adolescents: Results of a latent profile analysis. *Psychopathology, 48*(1), 25–30. doi:10.1159/000365095 PMID:25342152

Weinstein, A., Dorani, D., Elhadif, R., Bukovza, Y., & Yarmulnik, A. (2015). Internet addiction is associated with social anxiety in young adults. *Annals of Clinical Psychiatry, 27*(1), 4–9. PMID:25696775

Weinstein, A., & Lejoyeux, M. (2010). Internet addiction or excessive internet use. *The American Journal of Drug and Alcohol Abuse, 36*(5), 277–283. doi:10.3109/00952990.2010.491880 PMID:20545603

Wiederhold, B. K. (2017). Beyond direct benefits: Indirect health benefits of social media use. *Cyberpsychology, Behavior, and Social Networking, 20*(1), 1–2. doi:10.1089/cyber.2016.29059.bkw PMID:28080148

Wu, J. Y. W., Ko, H. C., & Lane, H. Y. (2016). Personality disorders in female and male college students with internet addiction. *The Journal of Nervous and Mental Disease, 204*(3), 221–225. doi:10.1097/NMD.0000000000000452 PMID:26731123

Wu, J. Y. W., Ko, H. C., Tung, Y. Y., & Li, C. C. (2016). Internet use expectancy for tension reduction and disinhibition mediates the relationship between borderline personality disorder features and Internet addiction among college students–One-year follow-up. *Computers in Human Behavior, 55*, 851–855. doi:10.1016/j.chb.2015.09.047

Xiuqin, H., Huimin, Z., Mengchen, L., Jinan, W., Ying, Z., & Ran, T. (2010). Mental health, personality, and parental rearing styles of adolescents with Internet addiction disorder. *Cyberpsychology, Behavior, and Social Networking, 13*(4), 401–406. doi:10.1089/cyber.2009.0222 PMID:20712498

Yan, W., Li, Y., & Sui, N. (2014). The relationship between recent stressful life events, personality traits, perceived family functioning and internet addiction among college students. *Stress and Health, 30*(1), 3–11. doi:10.1002/smi.2490 PMID:23616371

Yang, S. C., & Tung, C. J. (2007). Comparison of Internet addicts and non-addicts in Taiwanese high school. *Computers in Human Behavior, 23*(1), 79–96. doi:10.1016/j.chb.2004.03.037

Yao, M. Z., He, J., Ko, D. M., & Pang, K. (2014). The influence of personality, parental behaviors, and self-esteem on Internet addiction: A study of Chinese college students. *Cyberpsychology, Behavior, and Social Networking, 17*(2), 104–110. doi:10.1089/cyber.2012.0710 PMID:24003966

Yee, N. (2006). Motivations for play in online games. *Cyberpsychology & Behavior, 9*(6), 772–775. doi:10.1089/cpb.2006.9.772 PMID:17201605

Young, K. (1996). Psychology of computer use. Addictive use of the Internet: A case that breaks the stereotype. *Psychological Reports, 79*(3), 899–902. doi:10.2466/pr0.1996.79.3.899 PMID:8969098

Young, K. (1998). Internet addiction: The emergence of a new clinical disorder. *Cyberpsychology & Behavior, 3*(3), 237–244. doi:10.1089/cpb.1998.1.237

Yu, Q., Zhang, L., Wu, S., Guo, Y., Jin, S., & Sun, Y. (2017). The influence of juvenile preference for online social interaction on problematic Internet use: The moderating effect of sibling condition and the moderated moderating effect of age cohort. *Computers in Human Behavior, 68*, 345–351. doi:10.1016/j.chb.2016.11.026

Yu, T. K., & Chao, C. M. (2016). Internet misconduct impact adolescent mental health in Taiwan: The moderating roles of Internet addiction. *International Journal of Mental Health and Addiction, 14*(6), 921–936. doi:10.1007/s11469-016-9641-y

Zywica, J., & Danowski, J. (2008). The faces of Facebookers: Investigating social enhancement and social compensation hypotheses: Predicting Facebook and offline popularity from sociability and self-esteem, and mapping the meanings of popularity with semantic networks. *Journal of Computer-Mediated Communication, 14*(1), 1–34. doi:10.1111/j.1083-6101.2008.01429.x

KEY TERMS AND DEFINITIONS

Conscientiousness: A personality trait that is characterized with being highly determined and organized.

Extraversion: A personality trait which refers to how individuals socialize with each other. Extraverts tend to be sociable, energetic, optimistic, friendly and assertive.

Introversion: A personality trait which when displayed in individuals would make one inward focused, focusing more on internal thoughts, feelings and moods.

Massively Multi-Player Online Role-Playing Games: Internet connected video games in which very large numbers of people interact with one another within a virtual world.

Multi-User Dungeons: A multi-player real time virtual world, usually text-based.

Narcissism: A personality trait can be defined as a pattern of traits and behaviors suggesting an obsession with the self to the exclusion of all others, and the egotistic pursuit of gratification, dominance, and ambition.

Neuroticism: A personality trait that measures emotional stability and personal psychological adjustment in individuals. Individuals scoring high in neuroticism are more likely to experience negative mood states such as anxiety, anger, and frustration.

Openness to Experience: A personality trait, people with high levels of openness to experience tend to be sophisticated, knowledgeable, cultured, artistic, curious, analytical and more liberal in general.

Wall Function of Facebook: An area on a profile or page where friends and 'fans' can post their thoughts and opinions for everyone to see.

Chapter 4
I'm Always Online:
Well–Being and Main Sources of Life Dis/Satisfaction of Heavy Internet Users

Tihana Brkljačić
Institute of Social Sciences Ivo Pilar, Croatia

Filip Majetić
Institute of Social Sciences Ivo Pilar, Croatia

Anja Wertag
Institute of Social Sciences Ivo Pilar, Croatia

ABSTRACT

Internet use has become an integral part of our lives. It provides a lot of benefits; however, excessive use can have serious consequences for one's well-being. Therefore, the aim of this chapter is to explore well-being of heavy Internet users. Empirical research was conducted on 500 students of engineering, who were divided into groups based on the total time per day reported spending in various online activities. The comparison of subjective well-being and sources of life satisfaction and dissatisfaction showed that heavy Internet users were less happy compared to light users. Heavy Internet users found more satisfaction in various entertainment activities, while light users found more satisfaction in love life and family. Findings of this research provide some important theoretical findings, but also point out that the continuing research is needed to further explore the relation between Internet addiction, time spent online, and well-being.

INTRODUCTION

The role of the Internet has risen exponentially in our lives. While at the end of the 20th and in the beginning of the 21st century online activities were mostly used as an additional social and business tool, nowadays they have become an integral part of all life aspects among various groups of people – especially among younger generations. Not only an increasing number of people (regularly) uses the Internet, but

DOI: 10.4018/978-1-5225-3477-8.ch004

for an increasing number of them being available online 24/7 (through smart-phones and tablets) has become a common, acceptable, even desirable behavior.

However, certain forms of Internet use are related to non-beneficial health outcomes. The term Internet Addiction Disorder was first introduced by Goldberg (1996) to describe pathological and compulsive use of the Internet. This kind of addiction is defined as an impulse-control disorder that does not involve an intoxicant (Young, 1996) or as a form of obsessive-compulsive disorder (Bastani, 2008). Morahan-Martin (2007) and Widyanto and Griffiths (2007) define *problematic Internet use (PIU)* as a syndrome that consists of cognitive, emotional, and behavioral symptoms related to difficulties with managing one's offline life. Although Internet addiction is not included in the official manual of American Psychiatric Association (2013), Internet gaming disorder is listed in it as a disorder requiring further study (Section III - Conditions for Further Study). Chou and Hsiao (2000) claim that Internet addiction represents a global mental health problem, and epidemiological studies showed that the international prevalence rate of Internet addiction among adolescents varied significantly from 0.9% to 38% (Xu et al., 2012).

This chapter will not focus on the Internet addiction per se, but on one of its symptoms: excessive Internet use and its relation to well-being of a particularly vulnerable group - students of electrical engineering and computing. Namely, due to the nature of their study, they are forced to be online much more in comparison with an average population of emerging adults.

BACKGROUND

Time Spent Online and Internet Addiction

Various research confirmed positive relationship between higher consumption and a higher level of addiction (e.g. Chen & Fu, 2009, Beutel et al., 2011; Frangos, Frangos & Sotiropoulos, 2011). Likewise, an increased amount of time spent on the Internet, i.e. excessive Internet use represents a fundamental indicator of Internet addiction (Chou, Condron, & Belland, 2005). As an illustration, amount of time spent on the Internet was an item in the Young's (1996) Internet Addiction Diagnostic Questionnaire. To investigate Internet addiction of adolescents, Müller et al. (2016) explored, among other things, the frequency of their online activities (e.g. gambling, pornography). Furthermore, Soule, Shell, and Kleen (2003, p. 66) emphasized "long hours" of Internet use as one of the Internet addiction symptoms, while Weinstein and Lejoyeux (2010) highlighted "higher frequency of Internet use" as a factor "predictive of problematic Internet use" (p. 280). Finally, Young's (1998) research results show that Internet dependents spent an average of 39.5 hours per week on Internet activities, while Internet non-dependents spent an average of 4.9 hours. According to Chou, Condron, and Belland (2005), Chen and Chou (1999) reported that the Internet addiction "high-risk" group spent about 20 hours per week online, while the "non–high-risk" group spent about 9 hours online.

Well-Being

The concept of well-being refers to optimal psychological functioning and experience (Ryan & Deci, 2001). Well-being is a multi-faceted and subjective concept; it is related to various domains of individuals' life such as health, social relations, achievement, leisure, material status, and mental health (Diener, Scollon, & Lucas, 2009). Subjective well-being refers to one's own satisfaction with those aspects, but importance of single aspect varies across individuals. Since the Internet has become integrated into virtually all activities of a modern human life, it seems reasonable to presume that it has significant effects on various domains of life and, eventually, on the well-being in general. While it is easy to name numerous domains of life where Internet helped us to perform more efficiently, possible negative effects of excessive Internet use are still far from being thoroughly investigated.

Furthermore, the hedonistic approach argues that well-being consists of three elements: life satisfaction, the presence of positive mood, and the absence of negative mood (e.g. Lyubomirsky & Lepper, 1999). On the other hand, the eudaimonic well-being is defined via actions essential for psychological growth such as recognition or achievement (see Ryan & Deci, 2001). Various online activities can satiate hedonistic or eudaimonic needs. For example, if a user is getting satisfaction from some amusing content, his/her hedonistic needs are fulfilled. On the other hand, if someone uses the Internet to promote him/herself, he/she enjoys the feeling of recognition which is an eudaimonic need. Playing online games (or computer games in general) often gives an instant reward (a hedonistic need), but can also fulfill a need for achievement (though sometimes misplaced) and act as (a compensation for) eudemonic reward. Finally, online social contacts that someone creates/maintains can satiate both hedonistic and eudemonic needs.

Time Spent Online and Well-Being

One of the first, but also the most worrying finding was presented by Kraut et al. (1998) who reported that using the Internet for as little as three hours per week led to increased levels of depression and reductions in offline social contacts among teenagers. They proposed a concept of "Internet paradox" suggesting that, although the Internet is often used for social interaction, it reduces social involvement and leads to social isolation and depression. Stepanikova, Nie, and He (2010) also found that time spent online was related to increased loneliness and decreased life satisfaction; while Nie, Hillygus, and Erbring (2002) found that those who spent more time online spent less time with their family and friends, felt lonelier, and more depressed. However, a lot has changed in almost 20 years from Kraut et al.'s (1998) research, and nowadays it is virtually impossible to find adolescents who are online less than three hours per week. Since the use of Internet was strongly facilitated by a widespread availability of smart-phones, it became an unavoidable part of life for both youth and adults. Lenhart (2015) states that more than 50% of 13 to 17 year-olds go online several times per day and almost 25% claim to be online "almost constantly". Similarly, Waldo (2014) reported that 16% of adolescents spend 5-6 hours per day on the Internet, while additional 11% spend more than 7 hours.

During the last twenty years, the differences between ways people use the Internet have changed not only in quantitative, but also in qualitative manner. Kraut et al. (1998) explained their results speculating that teenagers switched from real-life (i.e. offline) social contacts to online communication with strangers. Nowadays, the expansion of social networks resulted in shifting online communication towards friends. As an illustration, compared to a popular phenomenon of anonymous chat-groups at the end of the 20th century, today's social networks represent a space where identities are usually preserved and where social contacts get maintained for a longer period. Boyd (2014) suggests three affordances that motivate youth to use social networks: social connections (family, friends, peers, and adults), visibility and recognition (to see and be seen), and freedom to explore (privacy and autonomy).

Several studies reported positive effects of Internet use on people's expansion of social networks and increasement of well-being (e.g. Campbell, Cumming, & Hughes, 2006, Shaw & Gant, 2002). For example, Bryant, Sanders-Jackson, and Smallwood (2006), and Valkenburg and Peter (2007) revealed positive relationship between use of the Internet, social relations, and well-being. Other studies reported that effects of Internet use on well-being depend on what people use it for; usage for communication purposes was associated with beneficial effects, and usage for non-social purposes led to detrimental outcomes (e.g. Morgan & Cotten, 2003). Moreover, there are evidences that the engagement in specific online behaviors, such as gaming and social networking, might lead to symptoms associated with addiction (see Kuss & Griffiths, 2012; Schou Andreassen & Pallesen, 2014).

MAIN FOCUS OF THE CHAPTER

Despite the fact that many research has already explored well-being indicators of heavy Internet users, most of it defined well-being in terms of absence of mental illness and distress, such as loneliness, depression, and social isolation (Whang, Lee, & Chang, 2003). Therefore, this empirical study defined psychological well-being as a concept of positive mental health (life satisfaction and happiness), in order to gain more detailed insights into the relationship between Internet use and subjective well-being. Moreover, it seems important to analyze main sources of life satisfaction, as well sources of dissatisfaction of specific groups of Internet users.

It should be noted that the focus will not be on the Internet addiction per se, but on one of its symptoms: heavy Internet use. Therefore, the aims of this study were as follows:

1. To explore differences in well-being between light and heavy Internet users
2. To explore differences in sources of life dis/satisfaction between light and heavy Internet users

Method

This study was a part of a larger survey focused on exploring habits of students. The survey was conducted during the regularly-scheduled classes, and the students were provided with detailed information about the purpose and the procedure of the study. Students were asked to complete the self-report pen and paper questionnaires, by giving honest self-ratings about their thoughts and behaviors. Participation in the study was voluntary and anonymous, the whole procedure took about 20 minutes, and the approval of the institutional review board was obtained for all the aspects of the study.

Participants

The research was conducted on the sample of $N=500$ students of Faculty of Electrical Engineering and Computing, University of Zagreb. There were 112 (22.4%) women. Age range was 18-32 years, with $M = 20.2$ years ($SD = 2.18$), while dominant age was 19 years (Table 1). For the purpose of this research, participants were divided into three groups on the basis of the average time they reported to spend on the Internet: (1) light Internet users spent up to three hours per day on the Internet ($N=100$, 20%), (2) moderate users spend between 3 and 9 hours per day on the Internet ($N=286$, 57.2%), and (3) heavy users spend at least 9 hours per day on the Internet ($N=114$, 22.8%). The differences in average Internet use between the three groups were statistically significant ($F(2,497)= 633.2\ p<.01$). However, no significant differences regarding gender ($X^2(2)=0.2$, $p>.05$) or age ($F(2,497)= 0.767\ p>.05$) of the participants were found between the groups.

Table 1. Groups of participants regarding reported average daily Internet use (minutes per day), gender and mean age

Group	Average Internet Use	N	Woman (%)	Mean Age
Light (≤3 hrs)	91.3±60.52	100	21.0	20.3±2.36
Moderate	331.9±90.04	286	23.1	20.3±2.20
Heavy (≥9 hrs)	786.6±270.07	114	21.9	20.0±1.94
TOTAL	387.5±278.61	500	22.4	20.2±2.18

Measures

1. Time Spent on the Internet: Participants were asked to approximate average time per day they spend in the following activities: online chatting; using social networks or similar platforms for content sharing (Instagram etc.); playing computer games; surfing the Web for entertainment (e.g. hobbies); Internet activities for studies/work or other work-related obligations; e-mailing.

    According to the focus groups conducted prior to this research these were by far the most popular online activities among students and all Internet related activities can fit into these categories. Activities such as online listening to music, reading e-books, or watching movies/videos, although popular, are not typical Internet activities. Namely, people usually do not label time spent on them as "time spent online" because Internet represents just a tool to reach a desired content.

2. Total Amount of Time on the Internet: Total amount of time spent on the Internet per day was computed by summing time in all the above-mentioned categories. It is very likely that some of these activities sometimes overlap with each other, resulting in overestimation of online time (for 4 participants total time on the Internet per day exceeds 24 hours). However, as displayed in Table 2, correlations between times in various activities, though almost all significant, are low to moderate in magnitude, implying that all the activities were, at least to some extent, autonomous. Expectedly, social networking and online chatting showed highest correlation (sharing almost 20% of common variance), suggesting that social networks are often used for conversation. However, this way of measuring time spent on the Internet gives better approximation than estimation of the total amount of time because respondents are reminded on different activities they use the Internet for. In addition, during focus groups, almost all the participants claimed to be online all the time (not even turning off their mobile phones when going to sleep), so a global measure of online time probably would not be useful for making a distinction between participants. Finally, the aim of this research was not to assess the amount of time students spend online on average, but to differentiate between heavy, moderate, and light users.

3. Forming Groups According to Amount of Time on the Internet: In line with aims of this research, it was necessary to form groups of heavy and light Internet users. As it is important to make clear distinction between heavy and light users, it was opted for a variant of extreme group analysis (Alf & Abrahams, 1975). Since the total number of participants was 500, about 20% of them (100 students) was needed in each group to ensure valid statistical conclusions. Therefore, it was decided to create two extreme groups of about 20% students each; regarding time they spent on the Internet. This resulted in formation of three groups: heavy users (*n*=114) who were online at least 9 hours

Table 2. Correlations and descriptive statistics of reported time (minutes per day) spent in various online activities

Type of Activity	1.	2.	3.	4.	5.	6.
1. Chatting						
2. Social networking	.44**					
3. Playing on computer	.16**	.21**				
4. Surfing for entertainment	.26**	.29**	.24**			
5. Internet for studies	.13**	.19**	.02	.24**		
6. E-mail	.22**	.16**	.03	.15**	.16**	
M	69.1	71.8	51.4	98.1	84.8	12.3
SD	83.75	92.39	81.01	101.98	80.19	26.57

*Note. N = 500. * p<.05, ** p<.01*

per day, light users (n=100) who were online up to 3 hours per day, and moderate users (n=286) who used the Internet between 3 and 9 hours per day. Although the results for all three groups will be presented in the following tables, the comparisons will be oriented only towards two extreme groups. As the "moderate" users captured a wide range of online time, which might distort the results, we opted for this analytic approach.

4. Well-Being Measures: Well-being was defined as happiness and positive evaluation of one's life in general (Diener, Suh, Lucas, & Lucas 1999).
   a. **Happiness:** Overall happiness was measured by the question: "In general, how happy do you feel?" which participants rated on the 10-point scale ranging from 1 as "extremely unhappy" to 10 as "extremely happy". The measure was adapted from the Fordyce Happiness Scale (Fordyce, 1988).
   b. **Life Satisfaction:** Life satisfaction was measured by the question adapted from Diener, Emmons, Larsen, and Griffin (1985) scale: "All things considered, how satisfied are you with your life as a whole nowadays?" which participants rated on the 10-point scale ranging from 1 as "extremely dissatisfied" to 10 as "extremely satisfied".
5. Sources of Satisfaction and Dissatisfaction With Life: To measure sources of satisfaction and dissatisfaction with life, participants were asked (open ended question) to declare three main sources of satisfaction and three main sources of dissatisfaction in their lives. Answers were analyzed, open-coded and grouped into 16 categories: Family, Love, Friends, University, Money, Politics, Religion, Art, Sport, Fun, Health, Hobbies, Stress, Working/Studying, Free time, and Personal characteristics. While categories Family, Love, Friends, University, Money, Politics, Fun, Health, Hobbies, Stress, Working, Free time, and Personal characteristics were pre-determined, Religion, Art, and Sport emerged as independent categories during the coding process.

Data Analysis

The data was analyzed by using Statistical package for social sciences (SPSS v-20). Statistical techniques used for analyzing data were: t-tests for independent samples and chi-square tests. The statistical significance value was set at $p<.05$.

To answer the first research question, the groups of heavy and light Internet users were compared with the regard to well-being indicators using *t*-test for independent samples.

To answer second research question, chi-square test was used to compare heavy and light Internet users regarding:1. Total number of listed sources of satisfaction and dissatisfaction

2.   Frequencies of listings of specific topic as a source of satisfaction and dissatisfaction.

Results

Before analyzing the differences between specific types of Internet users, it should be mentioned that, in general, students showed high levels of both happiness and life satisfaction, about 2 points (20%) from theoretical average of 5.5 (Table 3). Additional *t*-tests were performed to test for possible differences between male and female students regarding well-being indices, but those didn't prove to be significant neither for life satisfaction ($t=2.0$; $p>.05$), nor for happiness ($t=2.8$, $p>.05$), although females outscored males for about 0.5 point (5%) on both scales.

Differences in Well-Being Among Heavy and Light Users

Regarding the first research problem, Table 3 shows ratings of happiness and life satisfaction among three groups of students.

A brief look at the table shows the tendency of decrease in well-being indices with an increase of time spent on the Internet. Group of heavy Internet users showed about half point difference compared to light users, and this difference was significant for both happiness ($t(212)= 2.4$; $p<.05$), and life satisfaction ($t(212)=2$, $p<.05$), indicating that light users, on average, reported higher levels of well-being compared to heavy users.

Sources of Life Satisfaction and Dissatisfaction

Since every student was asked to report up to three sources of both satisfaction and dissatisfaction, there were 1500 possible statements in each category (Table 4). Students in general listed almost two times more sources of life satisfaction (1259) than sources of life dissatisfaction (783). Most satisfaction students found in family (16.7% of statements), friends (16.1%), university (9.3%), love (7.9%), and fun (6.4%) while the main sources of dissatisfaction were politics (9.7%), university (8.5%), and various personal characteristics (6.3%). Although all categories appeared as both sources of satisfaction and sources of dissatisfaction it is obvious that for the most of them one is prevalent. For example, family was much

Table 3. Average ratings of life satisfaction and happiness among light, moderate and heavy Internet users

Group	Life Satisfaction	Happiness
Light (≤3 hrs)	8.1±1.82	7.9±1.56
Moderate	7.7±1.86	7.4±1.99
Heavy (≥9 hrs)	7.6±2.09	7.3±2.08
TOTAL	7.7±1.92	7.5±1.96

Table 4. Percentages of specific sources of life satisfaction/dissatisfaction that were mentioned

| Sources | Satisfaction | | | | Dissatisfaction | | | |
| | Type of Users | | | | Type of Users | | | |
	Light	Moderate	Heavy	Total	Light	Moderate	Heavy	Total
Family	19.7	16.4	14.6	16.7	1.0	1.8	0.3	1.3
Love	9.0	8.9	4.7	7.9	1.3	2.3	1.2	1.9
Friends	13.0	16.1	19.0	16.1	1.3	1.9	1.5	1.7
University	9.0	9.9	7.9	9.3	8.0	8.0	10.2	8.5
Money	2.0	2.8	3.2	2.7	4.7	6.1	5.0	5.6
Politics	1.0	1.1	0.6	1.0	9.3	9.5	10.3	9.7
Religion	1.7	1.3	0	1.1	0.7	0.2	0	0.3
Art	1.7	2.0	3.5	2.3	0.3	0.2	0	0.2
Sport	3.0	3.6	4.4	3.7	0.7	0.4	0.6	0.5
Fun	5.7	5.8	8.5	6.4	0.7	1.2	2.1	1.3
Health	5.3	4.3	6.4	5.0	1.7	2.2	2.4	2.1
Hobby	1.3	2.4	3.2	2.4	0	0.9	0.3	0.6
Fatigue, Stress	0.3	0	0	0.1	4.7	4.9	4.1	4.7
Work	4.0	2.5	2.9	2.9	2.7	3.7	3.5	3.5
Free time	2.0	1.9	2.0	1.9	3.7	4.3	4.1	4.1
Personal characteristics	4.3	4.3	5.0	4.7	5.3	5.9	7.9	6.3
Art, Sport, Fun, Hobby	11.7	13.8	19.6	14.8	1.7	2.7	3.0	2.0
No answer	17.0	16.5	14.0	16.1	54.0	46.0	46.8	47.8

more often listed as a source of satisfaction while stress was much more often listed as a source of dissatisfaction (meaning that students did not mention absence of stress as a source of life satisfaction).

University was the only category frequently mentioned for both satisfaction (9.3%) and dissatisfaction (8.5%), while politics was the only category related much more to the dissatisfaction than to satisfaction (9.7% versus 1%). The other categories that were predominantly reported as sources of dissatisfaction were Money (5.6% versus 2.7%), Stress (4.7% versus 0.1%), Free time (4.1% versus 1.9%), and Personal Characteristics (6.3% versus 4.7%).

No significant differences were found regarding total number of reported sources of satisfaction or dissatisfaction among three groups of students, although there was a tendency of heavy Internet users to provide more sources of both satisfaction and dissatisfaction. Furthermore, regarding most categories there were no significant differences between the groups. However, heavy Internet users found less satisfaction in love compared to the group of light Internet users ($X^2(3)=4.8$, $p<.05$), but more satisfaction in friendships ($X^2(3)=4.2$, $p<.05$). Moreover, there was a tendency of heavy Internet users to find less satisfaction in family relations, but this difference didn't reach the level of significance ($X^2(3)=2.89$, $p=.09$). For the rest of the categories differences between groups were not significant.

However, since a lot of categories were represented only with a small number of responses, it was opted to merge categories related to various entertainment activities (Sport, Art, Hobby, and Fun). Category "Free time" was left out of this newly-formed category because it was the most often mentioned source in the context of getting satisfaction from an absence of activities (idleness). The newly-formed category was significantly more often mentioned as a source of satisfaction among heavy than light Internet users ($X^2(3)=9.2$, $p<.05$). Regarding sources of dissatisfaction, no significant differences were found between light and heavy Internet users. Since only about half of 1500 responses was retrieved, small number of frequencies for a specific source might have biased the results. However, a closer inspection of the Table 4 indicates that there were not even stable tendencies that would indicate a direction of any specific source of life dissatisfaction related to the amount of Internet use.

In summary, these results suggest that heavy Internet users found more satisfaction in various entertainment activities, while light Internet users found more satisfaction in close relations with family and partner.

General Discussion

The aims of this study were to explore differences in well-being between light and heavy Internet users, as well as to explore differences in sources of life dis/satisfaction between light and heavy Internet users. On average, participants had both indices of well-being well above theoretical average (5.5). These differences, about 2 points from the theoretical average on the 10-point scale (20%), are in accordance with previous research results on well-being of adolescents. Moreover, the results suggest that, on average, participants are happy and satisfied with their lives, which is consistent with finding that people are on average moderately happy (for details see Myers & Diener; 1996). In our research, this was further confirmed by reported sources of life satisfaction and dissatisfaction where, in general, our respondents reported more sources of life satisfaction (84%) than dissatisfaction (52%).

Furthermore, in line with previous findings on no gender differences in Internet addiction among adolescents (Waldo, 2014; Kawa & Shafi, 2015), no significant differences between male and female students regarding time spent on the Internet were found in the present study. However, some studies found higher levels of Internet addiction among male adolescents (e.g. Sato, 2009; Beutel et al., 2011). A possible explanation of the research findings presented in this chapter may lie in the fact that females in this study were preselected by the university that was oriented towards computers. Therefore, the study was investigating females whose interest in various computer related activities, including online behaviors, was above the average.

Moreover, no significant gender differences regarding well-being measures were found, which is consistent with the results of many previous research (e.g. Myers & Diener, 1996; Sharma, 2014).

Some studies from the beginning of the 21st century were mostly oriented towards identifying negative correlates (such as loneliness or depression) of time spent online. For example, Stepanikova et al. (2010) and Nie et al. (2002) reported that those who spent more time online reported increased loneliness, decreased life satisfaction, and felt more depressed. Although it was shown that the life satisfaction is inversely related to depression, the lack of depression shouldn't be used as a sole predictor of one's well-being. In other words, the fact that someone is not suffering from depression is not enough to conclude that his/her well-being is high. However, many studies focused on depression, as one of the most widespread illnesses in the developed world, when assessing correlates of heavy Internet use and Internet addiction. Therefore, the empirical research presented in this chapter was oriented towards more general and positive evaluations of well-being: life satisfaction, and happiness.

The results suggest that there are both quantitative and qualitative differences between light and heavy Internet users. Namely, they differed on both well-being measures, but also reported different sources of life satisfaction. First, a tendency of lower happiness and life satisfaction of heavy Internet users was found. The difference between light and heavy users was about 0.5 points on the 10-point scale (5%). These findings are in accordance with previous research. For example, Cardaks (2013) found that students with higher levels of Internet addiction are more likely to be low in psychological well-being, while Gross et al. (2002) and Wastlund, Norlander and Archer (2001) reported negative correlations between adolescents' time online and psychological well-being (e.g., dispositional or daily well-being, loneliness, depression).

Regarding sources of life satisfaction, regardless of online behavior, participants in this study claimed that social contacts (family and friends) are the most important sources of satisfaction. It is well known that close social relations with family and friends (Argyle, 2001) are among the most important factors of subjective well-being. However, for heavy Internet users, friends were more often mentioned as a source of life satisfaction (19%) than for light users (13%), while light users more often mentioned family contacts as a source of life satisfaction (20% compared to 15% in heavy users). For both heavy and light Internet users, the university was an important source of life satisfaction. This finding is consistent with Diener et al. (1999), who claim that education, job satisfaction, productivity, the feeling of success, and the ability to apply skills are positively related to happiness. However, the university was equally often mentioned as a source of life dissatisfaction. It seems that, unlike friends, love, and family that are all related almost exclusively to satisfaction, university related issues affect life in both positive and negative manner. Regarding sources of life dissatisfaction, there were no differences between light and heavy Internet users, while the main sources of dissatisfaction were related to political issues (10%), university features, demands and teachers' attitudes (9%), and personal characteristics (6%).

The open coding system that was used to group obtained qualitative data, proved to be too specific for entertainment related issues. During the coding, it was opted to keep specific codes that emerged from reports; to distinguish various types of entertainment such as art, sport, fun, and hobby. It was presumed that a specific type of entertainment might be associated with a specific online behavior. However, during the data analysis, it became obvious that those codes are too specific, since they were all capturing small percentages of responses. Therefore, it was decided to merge those four categories related to free time activities. However, the category "free time" was not added to the newly formed category because it captured responses oriented towards passive leisure (idling) and reports regarding amount of free time without mentioning any activity. Once the responses in categories art, sport, fun, and hobby were summed, another significant difference between light and heavy Internet users emerged. While light Internet users reported these activities in 12% of cases, heavy Internet users reported them in 20% of cases. A substantial body of research found strong connections between participation in structured leisure activities and well-being (e.g., Fredericks & Eccles, 2006; Palen & Coatsworth, 2007). Therefore, it is not surprising that the group of all these free time activities represents the third (after family and friends) most important contributor to life satisfaction.

To summarize, it seems that light and heavy Internet users have similar, but not the same sources of life satisfaction. Namely, while light users find more satisfaction in more intimate and closer relations (love life and family), heavy users find more satisfaction in various leisure activities. As being online can represent a leisure activity itself, and Internet addiction is related to use of Internet as a coping mechanism against some psychological issues (see Ko et al., 2006), heavy Internet users represent a risk group for developing Internet addiction. Putting more emphasis on forming and maintaining intimate and closer relationships, especially offline, is important for this group of Internet users, in order to prevent them to become Internet addicts.

Important theoretical finding of the research presented in this chapter is related to dichotomy of sources of satisfaction and dissatisfaction. This research confirmed that some aspects of life (e.g. money, (absence of) stress) are much more contributing to dissatisfaction than to satisfaction, while some others are almost exclusively cited as sources of satisfaction (e.g. family, friends). Moreover, important finding for practical implications are the differences in the sources of life satisfaction among light and heavy Internet users discussed above.

Limitations

Sample

The sample in this empirical study was very specific: students of the Faculty of Electrical Engineering and Computing, who were predominantly male (79% in this research). However, it was purposely opted for this sample, since the intention of this study was to capture a group of emerging adults who are heavy Internet users in order to get a sample large enough to be able to produce valid conclusions. Since there was over 100 students who used Internet at least 9 hours per day, the intention related to sample choice seems justified. Moreover, additional group of 100 students who used Internet less than 3 hours per day was optimal comparison group (especially because they came from the same university and there were no significant gender nor age differences).

Time Measures

Instead of asking participants about total amount of time they spent on the Internet, they were asked to report the time spent in different activities such as online chatting or surfing the Web. Although there is no particular reason participants would give incorrect data (other than all controversies related to self-reports), some of Internet activities happen simultaneously (such as social networking and online chatting or social networking and playing games) which leads to artificial overestimation of total Internet time. Therefore, this research doesn't provide reliable information on total time spent on the Internet, but rather on differences between heavy and light Internet users in well-being and sources of life dis/satisfaction.

Analysis of Extreme Groups

The decision was to analyze differences between light and heavy Internet users. Alternative methods would be performing correlational analyses on the whole sample or ANOVA tests between all three user groups (light, moderate, and heavy users). However, the approach used in this research is similar to the one implemented by Cummins, Walter, and Woerner (2007), who compared groups with highest and lowest well-being predictors. This type of analysis was preferred because (1) as mentioned previously, time measures were not fully reliable due to possible time overlaps, and therefore more robust approach was needed; (2) since this study was dealing with students of engineering, who are above average Internet users, it was important to clearly discriminate light users who were not frequent among the studied sample.

Assessed Online Activities

This research measured time spent in various Internet activities: online chatting (including video-chat and forum discussions); usage of social networks including various platforms for content exchange (such as Instagram); playing computer games; surfing the Web for entertainment; Internet activities for studies/ work or other work-related obligations; and e-mailing. However, some popular Internet activities such as watching movies, reading online books or listening to online music were not included. Although these activities are taking serious amount of time (as mentioned in the focus group discussions that were conducted prior to this research), they are not exclusively Internet activities. For that reason, the research opted to capture only those activities that are Internet specific.

Internet Addiction vs. Time on the INTERNET

The main purpose of this book is to present relevant theoretical approaches and empirical findings regarding psychological, social, and cultural aspects of Internet addiction. However, the research presented in this chapter focused on heavy Internet users who are not necessarily addicts. Although time spent online is certainly one of the manifestations of Internet addiction, it is not possible to diagnose Internet addiction by simply measuring time spent on the Internet. However, studying heavy Internet users is as important as studying addiction per se, since excessive use itself can be result of or lead to certain well-being or social circumstances, no matter if it is a part of addiction or not.

Well-Being Measures

Although there are many specific measures, the overall assessment of well-being was used in the research. Donovan, Halpern, and Sargeant (2002) and Layard (2011) argued that the reliability of items rating overall life satisfaction is satisfactory, providing evidence such as comparison of interview ratings and self-completion questionnaire or comparison of physiological indicators of happiness and self-ratings.

SOLUTIONS AND RECOMMENDATIONS

It is quite difficult to correctly assess amount of time people spend per day in various (not exclusively Internet) activities. Namely, certain activities often happen simultaneously, and it is well-known that perception of time in humans depends on many factors, such as involvement and interest in a certain task. In other words, time flies when we are occupied with something we enjoy doing, while it crawls when we are bored. Observational method would solve this problem, but observational studies are extremely time consuming so it wouldn't be possible to conduct a research on a large sample for a long period. Moreover, it would be very difficult and ethically questionable to monitor respondents in the privacy of their homes. Therefore, for the future research aiming to assess correct amount of time in various (online) activities it can be suggested to employ diaries as a combination of self-reports and observations. Participants' task in that case would be to observe their own online behavior, including passive time when they are available but not occupied with online activities, and simultaneous activities (such as online chatting while networking). Although this method would provide more accurate time measures, it would still be biased by self-reports and individual judgments. For example, people may sit with friends in a restaurant, or read a book, but still be online and check social networks or e-mail every few minutes. In cases like these, which are quite frequent, it is very hard to distinguish between activities and to specify amount of time spent in each of them. Therefore, the best measure should include main activity (e.g. dining and chatting with friends), but also background activities that happen at the same time (e.g. checking for new posts on Facebook every few minutes). Researchers should further distinguish between "being online passively", defined as being ready to response to an online stimuli such as a message, while preoccupied with other activity and not seeking for online stimuli; "occasionally checking", defined as being occupied with something else, but actively checking for new content from time to time; and "being online actively" when the main activity happens online, such as surfing the Web or online chatting.

FUTURE RESEARCH DIRECTIONS

The research presented in this chapter provides some useful information on general well-being and sources of satisfaction of heavy Internet users. It seems that heavy users are less happy and that they seek life satisfaction in less intimate sources such as various entertainment activities, while light users find more satisfaction in romantic relations and family. However, the difference in happiness between heavy and light Internet users, found in this research, although significant, is not big in magnitude (5%).

The design of this research doesn't allow casual interpretation, but future research should try to identify weather less happy individuals are more likely to be heavy Internet users, or excessive Internet use decreases happiness, or is there a mediation factor that is associated with both happiness and amount of time on the Internet (e.g. less satisfaction in love life). Further research should aim to distinguish between causes, consequences and moderating factors. Longitudinal research that would follow participants from their teenage years up to early adulthood would give better insight into cause-effect relations.

Finally, there are more and more adolescents and emerging adults whose study or work demand continuous Internet use. For that reason, it is of great importance to orient a significant part of research towards this population, since, unlike "voluntary" or free time Internet users, those individuals are obliged to spend their time online. Some interesting research questions regarding this phenomenon would include analysis of their daily routines i.e. engagement in online and offline social and societal activities; as well as process of Internet addiction development and possible methods of its prevention. From practical point of view, it is extremely important for policy makers to develop programs that would prevent educational institutions, as well as work organizations, to push their members into the addiction. To build or maintain healthy society, finding the right balance between Internet strengths, weaknesses, opportunities, and threats is of great importance.

CONCLUSION

The role of the Internet and its use has risen exponentially in our lives. As the excessive use can have serious consequences for one's well-being, the main aim of this chapter was to distinguish heavy Internet users from light Internet users in the terms of well-being. Empirical research that was carried out on 500 students in the Faculty of Electrical Engineering and Computing at the University of Zagreb, showed that, in general, students express high levels of happiness and life satisfaction. Students also reported more sources of life satisfaction (84%) than dissatisfaction (52%), which was consistent with overall ratings of well-being indices.

Heavy Internet users were defined as those who spent on average at least 9 hours per day on the Internet, while light Internet users were those who spent less than 3 hours. Heavy Internet users were found to be less happy and satisfied compared to light Internet users. Group of heavy Internet users showed about half point difference compared to light users, and this difference was significant for both happiness ($t(212)= 2.4$; $p<.05$), and life satisfaction ($t(212)=2$, $p<.05$), indicating that light users, on average, reported higher levels of well-being. Regarding sources of life satisfaction, heavy Internet users found more satisfaction in various entertainment activities, while light Internet users found more satisfaction in family and love life. No difference was found in the number of reported sources of satisfaction, or dissatisfaction between light and heavy users.

Continuing research is needed to further explore relation between Internet addiction, time spent online, and well-being. Aside from studying Internet addiction and its causes and consequences, it is important to study the growing population of emerging adults who are, by the nature of their work or study, obliged to spend most of their time online.

REFERENCES

Alf, E. F. Jr, & Abrahams, N. M. (1975). The use of extreme groups in assessing relationships. *Psychometrika*, *40*(4), 563–572. doi:10.1007/BF02291557

American Psychiatric Association. (2013). *Diagnostic and statistical manual of mental disorders* (5th ed.). Arlington, VA: American Psychiatric Publishing.

Argyle, M. (2001). *The Psychology of Happiness* (2nd ed.). London: Routledge.

Bastani, S. (2008). Gender Division in Computer and Internet Application: Investigation of the Students of Tehran Universities. *Women's Studies*, *5*, 45–64.

Beutel, M. E., Brähler, E., Glaesmer, H., Kuss, D. J., Wölfling, K., & Müller, K. W. (2011). Regular and problematic leisure-time Internet use in the community: Results from a German population-based survey. *Cyberpsychology, Behavior, and Social Networking*, *14*(5), 291–296. doi:10.1089/cyber.2010.0199 PMID:21067277

Boyd, D. (2014). *It's complicated: The social lives of networked teens*. Yale University Press.

Bryant, J. A., Sanders-Jackson, A., & Smallwood, A. K. (2006). IMing, Text Messaging, and Adolescent Social Networks. *Journal of Computer-Mediated Communication*, *11*(2), 577–592. doi:10.1111/j.1083-6101.2006.00028.x

Campbell, A. J., Cumming, S. R., & Hughes, I. (2006). Internet use by the socially fearful: Addiction or therapy? *Cyberpsychology & Behavior*, *9*(1), 69–81. doi:10.1089/cpb.2006.9.69 PMID:16497120

Cardak, M. (2013). Psychological well-being and Internet addiction among university students. *TOJET: The Turkish Online Journal of Educational Technology*, *12*(3), 134–141.

Chen, S. Y., & Fu, Y. C. (2009). Internet use and academic achievement: Gender differences in early adolescence. *Adolescence*, *44*(176), 797–812. PMID:20432601

Chou, C., Condron, L., & Belland, J. C. (2005). A Review of the Research on Internet Addiction. *Educational Psychology Review*, *17*(4), 363–388. doi:10.1007/s10648-005-8138-1

Chou, C., & Hsiao, M. C. (2000). Internet Addiction, Usage, Gratification, and Pleasure Experience: The Taiwan College Students' Case. *Computers & Education*, *35*(1), 65–80. doi:10.1016/S0360-1315(00)00019-1

Cummins, R. A., Walter, J., & Woerner, J. (2007). *Australian Unity Wellbeing Index: Report 16.1—The wellbeing of Australians—Groups with the highest and lowest wellbeing in Australia.* Melbourne: Australian Centre on Quality of Life, School of Psychology, Deakin University.

Diener, E., Emmons, R. A., Larsen, R. J., & Griffin, S. (1985). The satisfaction with life scale: A measure of life satisfaction. *Journal of Personality Assessment*, *49*(1), 71–75. doi:10.1207/s15327752jpa4901_13 PMID:16367493

Diener, E., Scollon, C. N., & Lucas, R. E. (2009). The evolving concept of subjective well-being: The multifaceted nature of happiness. In E. Diener (Ed.), *Assessing well-being* (pp. 67–100). Springer Netherlands; . doi:10.1007/978-90-481-2354-4_4

Diener, E., Suh, E. M., Lucas, R. E., & Lucas, H. E. (1999). Subjective well-being: Three decades of progress. *Psychological Bulletin*, *125*(2), 276–302. doi:10.1037/0033-2909.125.2.276

Donovan, N., Halpern, D., & Sargeant, R. (2002). *Life satisfaction: The state of knowledge and implications for government.* Cabinet Office, Strategy Unit.

Fordyce, M. W. (1988). A review of research on the happiness measures: A sixty second index of happiness and mental health. *Social Indicators Research*, *20*(4), 355–381. doi:10.1007/BF00302333

Frangos, C. C., Frangos, C. C., & Sotiropoulos, I. (2011). Problematic Internet use among Greek university students: An ordinal logistic regression with risk factors of negative psychological beliefs, pornographic sites, and online games. *Cyberpsychology, Behavior, and Social Networking*, *14*(1-2), 51–58. doi:10.1089/cyber.2009.0306 PMID:21329443

Fredricks, J. A., & Eccles, J. S. (2006). Is extracurricular participation associated with beneficial outcomes? Concurrent and longitudinal relationships. *Developmental Psychology*, *42*(4), 698–713. doi:10.1037/0012-1649.42.4.698 PMID:16802902

Goldberg, I. (1996). *Internet addictive disorder (IAD) diagnostic criteria.* Retrieved March 17, 2017 from http://www.webcitation.org/query?url=http%3A%2F%2Fwww.psycom.net%2Fiadcriteria.html&date=2013-02-06

Gross, E. F. (2004). Adolescent Internet use: What we expect, what teens report. *Journal of Applied Developmental Psychology*, *25*(6), 633–649. doi:10.1016/j.appdev.2004.09.005

Gross, E. F., Juvonen, J., & Gable, S. L. (2002). Internet use and well-being in adolescence. *The Journal of Social Issues*, *58*(1), 75–90. doi:10.1111/1540-4560.00249

Kawa, M. H., & Shafi, H. (2015). Evaluation of Internet addiction and psychological distress among university students. *International Journal of Modern Social Sciences*, *4*(1), 29–41.

Ko, C. H., Yen, J. Y., Chen, C. C., Chen, S. H., Wu, K., & Yen, C. F. (2006). Tridimensional personality of adolescents with Internet addiction and substance use experience. *Canadian Journal of Psychiatry*, *51*(14), 887–894. doi:10.1177/070674370605101404 PMID:17249631

Kraut, R., Patterson, M., Lundmark, V., Kiesler, S., Mukophadhyay, T., & Scherlis, W. (1998). Internet paradox: A social technology that reduces social involvement and psychological well-being? *The American Psychologist*, *53*(9), 1017–1031. doi:10.1037/0003-066X.53.9.1017 PMID:9841579

Kuss, D. J., & Griffiths, M. D. (2012). Internet gaming addiction: A systematic review of empirical research. *International Journal of Mental Health and Addiction*, *10*(2), 278–296. doi:10.1007/s11469-011-9318-5

Layard, R. (2011). *Happiness: Lessons from a new science*. Penguin UK.

Lenhart, A. (2015). *Teens, Social Media & Technology: Overview 2015*. Retrieved March 17 2017 from http://www.pewInternet.org/2015/04/09/teens-social-media-technology-2015/

Lyubomirsky, S., & Lepper, H. S. (1999). A measure of subjective happiness: Preliminary reliability and construct validation. *Social Indicators Research*, *46*(2), 137–155. doi:10.1023/A:1006824100041

Morahan-Martin, J. (2007). Internet use and abuse and psychological problems. In J. Joinson, K. McKenna, T. Postmes, & U. Reips (Eds.), *Oxford Handbook of Internet Psychology* (pp. 331–345). Oxford, UK: Oxford University Press.

Morgan, C., & Cotten, S. R. (2003). The relationship between Internet activities and depressive symptoms in a sample of college freshmen. *Cyberpsychology & Behavior*, *6*(2), 133–142. doi:10.1089/109493103321640329 PMID:12804025

Müller, K. W., Dreier, M., Beutel, M. E., Duven, E., Giralt, S., & Wölfling, K. (2016). A hidden type of Internet addiction? Intense and addictive use of social networking sites in adolescents. *Computers in Human Behavior*, *55*, 172–177. doi:10.1016/j.chb.2015.09.007

Myers, D. G., & Diener, E. (1996). The pursuit of happiness. *Scientific American*, *274*(5), 70–72. doi:10.1038/scientificamerican0596-70 PMID:8934647

Nie, N., Hillygus, D. S., & Erbring, L. (2002). Internet use, interpersonal relations, and sociability: A time diary study. In B. Wellman & C. Haythornthwaite (Eds.), *The Internet in Everyday Life* (pp. 215–243). Oxford, UK: Blackwell. doi:10.1002/9780470774298.ch7

Palen, L. A., & Coatsworth, J. D. (2007). Activity-based identity experiences and their relations to problem behaviour and psychological well-being in adolescence. *Journal of Adolescence*, *30*(5), 721–737. doi:10.1016/j.adolescence.2006.11.003 PMID:17222899

Rehman, A., Shafi, H., & Rizvi, T. (2016). Internet Addiction and Psychological Well-being among Youth of Kashmir. *The International Journal of Indian Psychology, 3*(3), 6–11.

Ryan, R. M., & Deci, E. L. (2001). On happiness and human potentials: A review of research on hedonic and eudaimonic well-being. *Annual Review of Psychology, 52*(1), 141–166. doi:10.1146/annurev. psych.52.1.141 PMID:11148302

Sato, T. (2009). *Internet Addiction among Students: Prevalence and Psychological Problems in Japan.* Retrieved March 17, 2017 from www.med.or.jp/english/pdf/2006_07+/279_283.pdf

Schou Andreassen, C., & Pallesen, S. (2014). Social network site addiction-an overview. *Current Pharmaceutical Design, 20*(25), 4053–4061. doi:10.2174/13816128113199990616 PMID:24001298

Sharma, G. (2014). Effect of demographic variables on psychological well-being and quality of life. *International Journal of Social Science and Humanities Research, 2*(3), 290–298.

Shaw, L. H., & Gant, L. M. (2002). In defense of the Internet: The relationship between Internet communication and depression, loneliness, self-esteem, and perceived social support. *Cyberpsychology & Behavior, 5*(2), 157–171. doi:10.1089/109493102753770552 PMID:12025883

Soule, L. C., Shell, L. W., & Kleen, B. A. (2003). Exploring Internet addiction: Demographic characteristics and stereotypes of heavy Internet users. *Journal of Computer Information Systems, 44*(1), 64–73.

Stepanikova, I., Nie, N. H., & He, X. (2010). Time on the Internet at home, loneliness, and life satisfaction: Evidence from panel time-diary data. *Computers in Human Behavior, 26*(3), 329–338. doi:10.1016/j. chb.2009.11.002

Valkenburg, P. M., & Peter, J. (2007). Online communication and adolescent well-being: Testing the stimulation versus the displacement hypothesis. *Journal of Computer-Mediated Communication, 12*(4), 1169–1182. doi:10.1111/j.1083-6101.2007.00368.x

van den Eijnden, R. J., Meerkerk, G. J., Vermulst, A. A., Spijkerman, R., & Engels, R. C. (2008). Online communication, compulsive Internet use, and psychosocial well-being among adolescents: A longitudinal study. *Developmental Psychology, 44*(3), 655–665. doi:10.1037/0012-1649.44.3.655 PMID:18473634

Waldo, A. (2014). Correlates of Internet addiction among adolescents. *Psychology (Irvine, Calif.), 5*(18), 1999–2008. doi:10.4236/psych.2014.518203

Wästlund, E., Norlander, T., & Archer, T. (2001). Internet blues revisited: Replication and extension of an Internet paradox study. *Cyberpsychology & Behavior, 4*(3), 385–391. doi:10.1089/109493101300210295 PMID:11710264

Weinstein, A., & Lejoyeux, M. (2010). Internet Addiction or Excessive Internet Use. *The American Journal of Drug and Alcohol Abuse, 36*(5), 277–283. doi:10.3109/00952990.2010.491880 PMID:20545603

Whang, L. S. M., Lee, S., & Chang, G. (2003). Internet over-users' psychological profiles: A behavior sampling analysis on Internet addiction. *Cyberpsychology & Behavior*, *6*(2), 143–150. doi:10.1089/109493103321640338 PMID:12804026

Widyanto, L., & Griffiths, M. (2007). Internet addiction: Does it really exist? (revisited). In J. Gackenbach (Ed.), *Psychology and the Internet: Intrapersonal, interpersonal, and transpersonal implications* (2nd ed.; pp. 141–163). San Diego, CA: Academic Press. doi:10.1016/B978-012369425-6/50025-4

Xu, J., Shen, L. X., Yan, C. H., Hu, H., Yang, F., Wang, L., & Ouyang, F. X. et al. (2012). Personal characteristics related to the risk of adolescent Internet addiction: A survey in Shanghai, China. *BMC Public Health*, *12*(1), 1106–1116. doi:10.1186/1471-2458-12-1106 PMID:23259906

Young, K. S. (1996). *Internet addiction: The emergence of a new clinical disorder*. Poster presented at the 104th American Psychological Association Annual Convention, Toronto, Canada.

Young, K. S. (1996). Psychology of computer use: XL. Addictive use of the Internet: a case that breaks the stereotype. *Psychological Reports*, *79*(3), 899–902. doi:10.2466/pr0.1996.79.3.899 PMID:8969098

Young, K. S. (1998). Internet addiction: The emergence of a new clinical disorder. *Cyberpsychology & Behavior*, *1*(3), 237–244. doi:10.1089/cpb.1998.1.237

KEY TERMS AND DEFINITIONS

Emerging Adults: Individuals in a time period after adolescence, but prior to the independent adult stage of life, when they still don't take on full adult responsibilities but explore possible life-styles.

Happiness: The experience of joy, contentment, or positive well-being, combined with a sense that one's life is good, meaningful, and worthwhile.

Heavy Internet Users: Internet users who spend a large amount of time online engaging in online activities such as chatting, social networking, playing, surfing for entertainment, activities related to studies/work or other obligations, and e-mailing.

Life Satisfaction: The way individuals evaluate their lives.

Sources of Life Dissatisfaction: Various aspects of life, reported by an individual, that decrease his/her life satisfaction.

Sources of Life Satisfaction: Various aspects of life, reported by an individual, that increase his/her life satisfaction.

Subjective Well-Being: A way how people experience the quality of their lives, which includes both emotional reactions and cognitive judgments.

Chapter 5
Psychological Maltreatment and Internet Addiction:
Is Psychological Maltreatment a Risk Factor?

Gökmen Arslan
Independent Researcher, Turkey

ABSTRACT

Internet use enhances one's quality of life; yet, excessive use may lead to various problems for their healthy development and wellbeing. Understanding the risk and protective factors in internet addiction has importance to promote individuals' positive development and wellbeing. Therefore, the purpose of the present chapter is to explore the role of psychological maltreatment in the development of the internet addiction. Psychological maltreatment is a significant public health problems associated with a range of short and long–term undesirable mental health and wellbeing outcomes in childhood to adulthood. Considering the outcomes supporting the significant role of child maltreatment on the development of internet addiction, it is clear that maltreated individuals are at–risk to develop internet addiction, and psychological maltreatment, as a risk factor, has a crucial role in the development of internet addiction. However, evidences here are relatively limited, and there is need further research investigated long–term impacts of psychological maltreatment on internet addiction.

INTRODUCTION

Internet use has become a prominent part of individuals' daily life, and people can solve many day-to-day problems and obtain knowledge using the internet (e.g. taking online courses, finding specific information, and talking with others; Tsai & Lin, 2001; 2003). Given these benefits of internet use, internet use enhances individuals' quality–of–life; however, excessive use may lead to various problems for their healthy development and wellbeing (Arslan, 2017a). In recent years, a growing number research have demonstrated that internet addiction is associated with psychopathology, such as depression, anxiety, social adaptation problems, physiological dysfunction (e.g., Akın & Iskender, 2011; Arslan, 2017a; Cao,

DOI: 10.4018/978-1-5225-3477-8.ch005

Sun, Wan, Hao, & Tao, 2011; Şahin, 2014; Özdemir, Kuzucu, & Ak, 2014; Young & Rodgers, 1998), personality traits (Celik, Atak, & Basal, 2012; Kim, Namkoong, Ku, & Kim, 2008; Dong, Wang, Yang, & Zhou, 2013), psychosocial variables, including shyness, compassion, loneliness (Ayas, 2012; Iskender & Akin, 2011; Özdemir et al., 2014), and wellbeing indicators, such as psychological wellbeing, life satisfaction (Bozoglan, Demirer, & Sahin, 2013; Cardak, 2013; Cao et al., 2011; Çelik & Odacı, 2013; Odacı, & Çıkrıkçı, 2014; Telef, 2016). In addition, many other research aimed to explore the diagnostic criteria and treatment of internet addiction disorder (e.g., Beard, 2011; Beard & Wolf, 2001; Caldwell & Cunningham, 2010; Chrismore, Betzelberger, Bier, & Camacho, 2011; Griffiths, 2005; Shaw & Black, 2008; Şenormanci, Konkan, & Sungur, 2012; Toa et al., 2010; Young, 1998; 2007; 2011; 2015).

Despite this increasing literature of the internet addiction, there is no consensus on the definition and diagnostic criteria of internet addiction. Moreover, given the literature, many terms have been used to describe the internet addiction, such as excessive internet use, pathological internet use, problematic internet use, and compulsive internet use (Widyanto & Griffiths, 2006). Young (1998) has defined the internet addiction using the set of diagnostic criteria of pathological gambling, modeled them on the Diagnostic and Statistical Manual of Mental Disorders (DSM IV), and she defined the internet addiction as "an impulse-control disorder which does not involve an intoxicant" (p. 238). In this regard, internet addiction is considered as an impulse-control disorder with no involvement of an intoxicant; thus, it is akin to pathological gambling (Young, 2004; Whang, Lee, & Chang, 2003). Another study by Griffiths (2005) has described a components model of the internet addiction within a biopsychosocial framework, and proposed that internet addiction consists of several distinct common components (i.e., salience, tolerance, mood modification, conflict, withdrawal, and relapse). Chrismore, Betzelberger, Bier, and Camacho (2011) have defined the internet addiction as, like chemical addictions, a primary, progressive disease. Therefore, individuals with internet addiction use the internet excessively that creates psychological, social, school, and/or work difficulties in their life (Beard & Wolf, 2001). Young (2011) has stated three subtypes (excessive gaming, sexual preoccupations, and e-mail/text messaging), four components (excessive use, withdrawal, tolerance, negative repercussions), and eight criteria (see Table 1) for defining internet addiction.

More recently, Toa et al. (2010) have identified several internet addiction disorder symptoms, and they proposed a diagnostic criterion for internet addiction as follows;

Table 1. Young's criteria for Internet Addiction Disorder

1. Do you feel preoccupied with the Internet (think about previous online activity or anticipate next online session)?
2. Do you feel the need to use the Internet with increasing amounts of time in order to achieve satisfaction?
3. Have you repeatedly made unsuccessful efforts to control, cut back, or stop Internet use?
4. Do you feel restless, moody, depressed, or irritable when attempting to cut down or stop Internet use?
5. Do you stay online longer than originally intended?
6. Have you jeopardized or risked the loss of a significant relationship, job, or educational or career opportunity because of the Internet?
7. Have you lied to family members, therapists, or others to conceal the extent of involvement with the Internet?
8. Do you use the Internet as a way of escaping from problems or of relieving a dysphoric mood (e.g., feelings of helplessness, guilt, anxiety, depression)?

1. Symptom criterion (all the following must be present): preoccupation and withdrawal symptoms and at least one (or more) of these criteria: tolerance, persistent desire and/or unsuccessful attempts to control, cut back or discontinue internet use, continued excessive use of internet despite problems, loss of interests, uses the internet to escape or relieve a dysphoric mood,

2. Clinically significant impairment criterion: functional impairments (reduced social, academic, working ability), including loss of a significant relationship, job, educational or career opportunities,

3. Course criterion: duration of internet addiction must have lasted for an excess of 3 months, with at least 6 hours of internet usage (non-business/non-academic) per day.

In Diagnostic and Statistical Manual of Mental Disorders (DSM-V; 2013), internet addiction is not defined as a psychological disorder; and, it is stated that internet gaming disorder is also referred to as internet use disorder or internet addiction. However, internet gaming disorder or problematic gaming is not the same as internet addiction (see, Griffiths & Pontes, 2014). For example, Király and colleagues (2014) investigated the interrelationship and the overlap between internet addiction disorder and internet gaming disorder in terms of gender, psychological well-being (e.g., depression, self–esteem), time spent using the Internet and/or online gaming, school achievement, and preferred online activities. Their outcomes indicated that internet gaming disorder was much more strongly related to being male, and that Internet addiction was positively related to online gaming, online chatting, and social networking while Internet gaming disorder was only associated with online gaming. Based on these outcomes, they argued that internet gaming disorder appears to be a conceptually different behavior from internet addiction and thus their data supports the notion that internet addiction and internet gaming disorder are separate nosological entities. Griffiths and Pontes (2014) have argued that internet gaming disorder and internet addiction are not the same, and they reported differences between internet gaming disorder and internet addiction based on the empirical and conceptual evidences. Considering the literature, there is need for further research to define the internet addiction and identify its diagnostic criteria for research and practice.

CONSEQUENCES OF INTERNET ADDICTION

Although internet use provides many advantages in daily life and enhances one's quality–of–life, excessive use of the internet may cause significant undesirable outcomes. In this regard, individuals with internet addiction face with various challenges, and this excessive and uncontrollable internet use negatively influences their healthy development and wellbeing. Previous research indicated that individuals with internet addiction had more emotional, social, behavioral problems (e.g. Bozoglan, Demirer, & Sahin, 2014; Kamal & Mosallem, 2013; Lin et al., 2014; Milani, Osualdella, & Di Blasio, 2009; Müller et al., 2015; Odacı, 2013; Tahiroğlu et al., 2010; Yoo et al., 2004) and academic or occupational difficulties (e.g. Akhter, 2013; Eldeleklioğlu & Vural, 2013; Odacı, 2013) as well as less psychological and subjective wellbeing (e.g. Bozoglan, Demirer, & Sahin, 2013; Çardak, 2013; Morsünbül, 2014) compared to those with non–addiction. For instance, Bozoglan and Demirer (2015) documented the association between internet addiction and psychosocial variables, demonstrating that internet addiction is related to depression, loneliness, poor mental health, low self–esteem, shyness, life satisfaction, social anxiety, social support. Yen, Ko, Yen, Wu, and Yang (2007) demonstrated that youths with internet addiction reported more psychopathological problems including attention deficit and hyperactivity disorder symptoms, social phobia, depression, and hostility. A study by Tahiroğlu et el. (2010) investigated the relationship between excessive internet use and psychopathology in adolescents, and they compared the community and psychiatric sample. Their outcomes indicated that adolescents with a psychiatric disorder (e.g. attention deficit hyperactivity disorder, anxiety disorders) reported more problematic internet use than those with no disorder. In this regard, internet addiction is a significant risk factor for individual mental health and wellbeing (Ceyhan, 2008), and individuals with internet addiction are more likely to develop psychopathology compared to normal internet users. A related study by Cao et al. (2011) documented that adolescents with internet addiction reported more lack of physical energy, physiological dysfunction, weakened immunity, emotional symptoms, behavioral symptoms, and social adaptation problems as well as less life satisfaction than those who were non–addicts. Gámez-Guadix, Calvete, Orue, and Las Hayas (2015) investigated the longitudinal effect of problematic internet use on the problematic alcohol use among adolescents, and they found a significant association between problematic internet use and problematic alcohol use. Lin et al. (2014) examined the association between internet addiction activities and suicidality among Taiwanese adolescents, and they reported a significant association between internet addiction and suicidal ideation and suicidal attempt after controlling demographic variables, family support, depression, and self-esteem. Internet addiction activities (e.g. online gaming, online searching for information, or MSN) were found significant factors associated with an increased risk of suicidal ideation. In addition, many studies focused on the wellbeing indicators, and they demonstrated that happiness and emotions were significant factors associated with internet addiction or problematic internet use (Çelik & Odacı, 2013; Odacı, & Çıkrıkçı, 2014; Telef, 2016). For example, Çelik & Odacı (2013) noted the significant and negative predictive effect of life satisfaction on internet addiction. Taken together, these outcomes support that individuals with internet addiction face with various psychological, social, school, and/or work difficulties in their life, and; thereby, internet addiction influences their positive development and wellbeing.

PSYCHOLOGICAL MALTREATMENT AND INTERNET ADDICTION

Understanding the risk and protective factors in internet addiction has importance to promote individuals' positive development and wellbeing from childhood to adulthood (Arslan, 2017a; Young, Yue, & Ying, 2011). Research investigating the risk and protective factors of internet addiction demonstrated many personal, internet-related, and family or parental risk factors for internet addiction disorder (e.g. Arslan, 2017a; Kabasakal, 2015; Şaşmaz et al., 2013; Yen, Yen, Chen, Chen, & Ko, 2007). For example, male individuals were commonly documented more likely suffer from internet addiction compared to females (Balcı & Gülnar, 2009; Krishnamurthy & Chetlapalli, 2015; Şaşmaz et al., 2013). A related study by Tsai et al. (2009) found a significant role of gender, deficient social support, mental health morbidity, and neurotic personality characteristics as risk factors in internet addiction among young adults. Specifically, internet–related factors were found to be important in development of internet addiction disorder (Kuss, van Rooij, Shorter, Griffiths, & van de Mheen, 2013; Mazhari, 2012). Duration of daily computer use and internet use time were reported as significant predictors and risk factors of internet addiction (Şaşmaz et al., 2013; Wu, Lee, Liao, & Chang, 2015). Kabasakal (2015) indicated the predictive effect of gender, age, gambling behavior, the quality of relationship between parents, internet use time, length of daily internet use, purpose of the internet use (e.g. academic), and family functioning (e.g. problem solving, roles, behavioral controls). Another study by Park, Kim, and Cho (2008) demonstrated a link between family risk factors and internet addiction indicating the importance of family communication, parenting attitudes, family cohesion, and family violence exposure with regard to internet addiction.

Despite the literature supporting the importance of investigating and understanding risk factors of internet addiction, few have focused on the role of stressful life events as risk factors in the etiology of pathological internet use. However, stressful life events (e.g., psychological maltreatment) play a significant role in development of internet–related problems, and individuals with internet addiction and internet–related addictions reported a greater number of life stressors (e.g. Bergevin, Gupta, Derevensky, & Kaufman, 2006; Li, Zhang, Li, Zhen, & Wang, 2010). Psychological maltreatment is a common form of child maltreatment and a stressful experience associated with a range of short and long–term undesirable mental health and wellbeing outcomes (e.g., Arslan, 2016; Gross & Keller, 1992; Miller-Perrin & Perrin, 2007; Mullen, Martin, Anderson, Romans, & Herbison, 1996; Norman, Byambaa, Butchart, Scott, & Vos, 2012). Psychological maltreatment thwarts the fulfillment of fundamental human needs (e.g. belonging, safety, and esteem; Hart, Binggeli, & Brassard, 1998), and consists of both omission and commission behaviors that is defined as "a repeated pattern of caregiver behavior or a serious incident that transmits to the child that s/he is worthless, flawed, unloved, unwanted, endangered, or only of value in meeting another's needs" (The American Professional Society on the Abuse of Children [APSAC]; Scannapieco & Connell-Carrick, 2005; p. 17). It is actually potentially harmful by causing impairment to the child's mental health and wellbeing (Glaser, 2002; Infurna, Reichl, Parzer, Schimmenti, Bifulco, & Kaess, 2016). It comprises of negative interactions between child and parent, such as spurning (e.g. belittling, shaming, degrading, or ridiculing a child), terrorizing (e.g. committing life-threatening acts; setting unrealistic expectations with threat of loss, harm, or danger if they are not met), denying emotional responsiveness (e.g. failing to express affection, caring, and love for a child) corrupting (e.g. modeling, permitting, or encouraging developmentally inappropriate behavior), or rejecting experiences (Kairys et al., 2002).

Psychological maltreatment is a harmful event that negatively influences child healthy development and wellbeing. Individuals with these experiences face with various challenges in development process, and report more social, emotional and behavioral problems from childhood to adulthood (see Iwaniec, Larkin, & Higgins, 2006; Miller-Perrin & Perrin, 2007). Individuals with higher levels of psychological maltreatment, for example, have reported higher levels of emotional and behavioral problems, such as depression, somatization, substance use, antisocial behavior (Arslan, 2016; Arslan & Balkıs, 2016; Kim & Cicchetti, 2014; Özge, & Gölge, 2015; Wingo et al., 2011) as well as lower levels of wellbeing, including psychological wellbeing, life satisfaction (Arslan, 2017b; Bellis, Hughes, Jones, Perkins, & McHale 2003; Brodski & Hutz 2012; Oshio, Umeda, & Kawakami 2011). In particular, many research support significant effects of psychological maltreatment on mental health and wellbeing compared to other child maltreatment forms, such as psychical maltreatment (Brown, Fite, Stone, & Bortolato, 2016; Gross & Keller, 1992; Kabasakal & Erdem, 2015). Research has also demonstrated that psychological maltreated individuals develop more addictive behaviors (e.g. alcohol or nicotine; Arslan, 2016; Elliott et al., 2014; Hyman, Garcia, & Sinha, 2006). A study by Rosenkranz, Muller, and Henderson (2012), for example, has documented the significant role of psychological maltreatment on predicting the level of substance use problem among youths, comparing the other forms of child maltreatment. Considering the conceptualization by Griffiths (2005), all addictions have particular and idiosyncratic characteristics. However, they reflect a common etiology of addictive behavior (e.g., mood modification, salience, withdrawal symptoms; Griffiths, 2005; Griffiths & Pontes, 2014). In this regard, psychological maltreatment may play a critical role in the development of internet addiction disorder. In brief, the outcomes demonstrate that individuals who have maltreatment experiences are more likely to suffer from various social, emotional, and behavioral difficulties. Thus, psychologically maltreated individuals may have more internet-related problems–e.g. internet addiction– than non–maltreated ones.

THEORETICAL FRAMEWORK AND EMPIRICAL EVIDENCE

Childhood experiences are considered to have important influences on later social, behavioral, and emotional functioning of individuals (Shaffer & Kipp, 2010), and quality of child interaction with parents plays a crucial role in child healthy development and wellbeing (Thompson, 2008). For example, individuals learn to cope with stressors at early ages (Compas, Banez, Malcarne, & Worsham, 1991), and these early experiences influence their development of coping strategies and problem solving skills (Lerner, Rothbaum, Boulos, & Castellino, 2002). Individuals who use more adaptive coping strategies have been reported to develop more positive relationships with their parents (Zimmer-Gembeck & Locke, 2007) and less mental health and internet–related problems (e.g. Arslan, 2017c; Brand, Laier, & Young, 2014; Dowling, Merkouris, Greenwood, Oldenhof, Toumbourou, & Youssef, 2017). In this regard, the quality–of–interaction between child and parent may influence the development of internet addiction. However, psychological maltreatment is negative in nature (Iwaniec, 2006), and refers to a harmful interaction between child and parent or caregiver (Glasser, 2002). This negative interaction between child and parent leads to a range of short and long–term problems in the development of individuals (see Miller-Perrin & Perrin, 2007) and leads to an increased risk for internet addiction disorder (Arslan, 2017a). For example, individuals with low family functioning and inappropriate parental rearing styles (e.g. being over-intrusive or lacking in responsiveness) were found to have higher levels of internet addiction disorder (Kabasakal, 2015; Xiuqin, Huimin, Mengchen, Jinan, Ying, & Ran, 2010). A study by Şenormancı, Şenormancı, Güçlü, and Konkan (2014) investigated the attachment styles and family functioning in patients with internet addiction, and they documented that individuals with internet addiction had more depression symptoms, anxious attachment styles, and problems of family functioning compared to those with non–addiction. These outcomes support that the quality–of–interaction between child–parent is a significant factor for development of the internet addiction and individuals with positive relations and interaction have lower levels of internet addiction.

A theoretical framework by Davis (2001) identified the risk factors of internet addiction based on the cognitive-behavioral model. Within this framework, the distal contributory causes of internet addiction are explained in a diathesis-stress model, and abnormal behaviors such as internet addiction are explained as resulting from vulnerability (e.g., diathesis, and a stressful life event, such as child maltreatment). Given the model, child maltreatment experiences play a critical role in development of pathological internet use, and psychologically maltreated individuals have higher levels of internet addiction than those who are non–maltreated (Arslan, 2017a). Another theoretical framework for pathological gambling proposed by Blaszczynski and Nower (2002) describes pathological gambling using pathway model in three pathways:

1.   Behaviourally conditioned problem gamblers,
2.   Emotionally vulnerable problem gamblers
3.   Antisocial, impulsivist problem gamblers.

According to this model, for example, emotionally vulnerable pathway comprises of individuals who had psychopathological problems (e.g. depression, anxiety) or stressful life experiences prior to developing a gambling disorder, and individual on this path generally use gambling as a coping strategy in face of the emotional problems (Turner, Jain, Spence, & Zangeneh, 2008). On the other hand, in line with the components theoretical background of internet addiction, internet addiction consists of seven distinct–yet–related common components (i.e., salience, tolerance, mood modification, conflict, withdrawal, and relapse; modified from Brown, 1993) and descripted the internet addiction as a part of the biopsychosocial process (Griffiths, 2005). The model suggests that the internet addiction has a complex nature; therefore, it may be more pragmatic to use an eclectic approach when studying internet addiction for research and practice. Despite these theoretical frameworks of internet addiction or internet–related addictions, there is no consensus on a single model identifying the internet addiction. However, Griffiths and Larkin (2004) have suggested the components of a successful model of internet addiction, and they have proposed that a successful model of addiction must comprise of the following core components:

1. Synthesizing pharmacological, cultural, situational and personality factors,
2. Accounting for the varying nature of addiction across cultures, individuals and time,
3. Accounting for commonalities between all addictions,
4. Being faithful to lived human experience (Griffiths, 2005).

Given this suggestion and theoretical framework sketched above, it appears that there is need for further evidence to demonstrate the usefulness of these theoretical frameworks.

Additionally, ecological perspective particularly presents a more comprehensive theoretical framework to understand and explain the risk and protective factors of psychological maltreatment (Cicchetti & Lynch, 1993). The ecological framework defines individual development in terms of different ecologic levels (e.g. microsystem, macrosystem) and interactions between these ecologic systems (Bronfenbrenner & Morris 2006; Cicchetti & Lynch, 1993). Moreover, each ecologic system includes risk and protective factors for mental health and wellbeing (Arslan, 2017b). Therefore, this model helps us to better understand the range of factors that put individuals at risk for psychological maltreatment or protect them from experiencing or perpetrating psychological maltreatment, and its impacts on individuals' mental health and wellbeing. For example, the ontogenic system has important impacts on one's positive development and positive adaptation, and includes various factors that influence mental health and wellbeing (Cicchetti & Lynch, 1993). Some of these factors promote the positive adaptation and protect the mental health, while others may make things worse and lead to undesirable outcomes (Arslan, 2017b), such as internet addiction. Therefore, many individual, familial, and social risk factors are associated with the development of internet addiction–such as psychological maltreatment. In this regard, psychologically maltreated individuals may be more vulnerable and at risk to develop internet addiction and other online addictions. General Theory of Addictions (Jacobs, 1986) is consistent with this notion, identifying the physiological and psychological risk factors of addictions, and the model has proposed that childhood negative life experiences are risk factors in the development of internet addiction and internet–related problems (Felsher, Derevensky, & Gupta, 2010). For example, Jacobs (1986) identified the sense of rejection as a psychological risk factor that is consistent with the role of psychological maltreatment in the development of internet addiction. Overall, given these theoretical frameworks, psychological maltreatment is considered as a risk factors for internet addiction, and it may increase vulnerability to internet addiction and internet–related problems.

Despite growing number of research focusing on child maltreatment experiences and their associated factors and consequences, only a few have focused on the association between maltreatment experiences and internet addiction or internet–related addictions. Moreover, to our knowledge, only one study investigated the association between psychological maltreatment and internet addiction (Arslan, 2017a). The outcomes indicated significant and positive predictive effect of psychological maltreatment on internet addiction in young adults, and individuals who were at-risk group for internet addiction reported higher levels of psychological maltreatment than those who were the typical group. Many of these studies investigated the association between other forms of child maltreatment and internet addiction disorder. For instance, Hsieh, Shen, Wei, Feng, Huang, and Hwa (2016) found the predictive effect of psychological and physical neglect, paternal physical violence, maternal physical violence, and sexual violence on internet addiction and post-traumatic stress disorder. A related study by Yates, Gregor, and Haviland (2012) investigated the association between child maltreatment, including physical maltreatment, sexual maltreatment, and neglectful/negative household environment and problematic internet use with a large collage sample, and their outcomes demonstrated that child maltreatment was a significant and negative predictor of problematic internet use. Further, several other research examined the impact of child maltreatment on internet gambling addiction, and they demonstrated that child maltreatment experiences increased the risk of pathological gambling (Hodgins et al., 2010; Petry & Steinberg, 2005). Felsher and colleagues (2010) in their study investigated the role of child maltreatment, including psychological, physical and sexual maltreatment and neglect in gambling problems among young adults, and they reported that adults with gambling problems had higher levels of these maltreatment experiences compared to those who were non gamblers and social gamblers. They also underlined that psychological maltreatment has a significant role in the development of psychological gambling, yet it is commonly ignored compared to other maltreatment forms. Further, a systematic review study by Lane, Sacco, Downton, Ludeman, Levy, & Tracy (2016) explored the role of child maltreatment experiences in increased risk for gambling problems. Their outcomes showed that child maltreatment is related to increased risk of gambling problems; moreover, problem gamblers may be more likely to maltreat their children. Zhang, Yang, Hao, Huang, Zhang, and Sun (2012) reported the significant predictive effect of physical maltreatment on the internet addiction disorder in adolescents. Taken together, considering the theoretical frameworks and the literature sketched above, psychological maltreatment is a factor associated with increased risk for internet addiction, and maltreated individuals are at risk to develop internet addiction disorder. However, evidences here are relatively limited; therefore, there is need for further research to investigate short and long–term impacts of psychological maltreatment on internet addiction or other internet–related addictions.

CONCLUSION

In recent years, a growing number of the research has focused on the internet use or internet–related problems, such as internet addiction and internet gaming disorder. Internet use provides various advantages to enhance the life quality of the individuals, yet excessive use is associated with significant social, emotional, and behavioral problems. In particular, although a growing number of research has focused on excessive internet use as a psychological problem (e.g. internet addiction), and supports that individuals with internet addiction disorder face with various difficulties, there is no agreed definition and diagnostic criteria of the internet addiction disorder in the literature. Therefore, it seems that further research should be conducted to define the internet addiction and identify its diagnostic criteria for research and practice. In addition, despite the evidences demonstrating the association between internet addiction and various psychological, social, and behavioral variables, such as depression, social support, attention deficit and hyperactivity disorder, and social phobia, most of this research is based on the cross-sectional approach. There is need further research, particularly longitudinal, to establish causal association between internet addiction disorder and these variables.

Additionally, understanding the risk and protective factors of internet addiction has importance to promote individuals' healthy development and wellbeing and provide mental health services for individuals with internet addiction disorder. The literature has discussed many personal, internet-related, and family or parental risk factors for internet addiction. Despite the large volume of the literature of internet addiction, the risk factors that lead to internet addiction disorder are relatively unexplored, and only a few studies have focused on the role of child maltreatment experiences as risk factors in in the etiology of internet addiction or other internet-related addictions. In particular, many recent research has focused on the relationship between stressful life events and the internet addiction and concluded that individuals with internet addiction disorder have more negative life experiences or stressors than those who are typical internet users. A few research has also investigated the effects of child maltreatment on the internet addiction or pathological internet use, and their results support the significant role of child maltreatment experiences on the internet addiction and other internet–related addictions. Generally, these studies have focused on the association between child maltreatment, particularly sexual and psychical maltreatment, and gambling disorder, and they have not directly investigated the effect of these experiences on the internet addiction disorder. Therefore, the effects of psychological maltreatment on the development of pathological internet use have been relatively ignored. However, considering the outcomes and theoretical frameworks supporting the significant role of child maltreatment on the development of internet addiction, it is clear that psychologically maltreated individuals are at–risk to develop pathological internet use, and psychological maltreatment, as a risk factor, has a crucial role in the development of internet addiction disorder. However, evidences here are relatively limited, and there is need for further research to investigate short and long–term impacts of psychological maltreatment on internet addiction or other internet–related addictions. Finally, given the research on the internet addiction has commonly been conducted in Asian countries, the effects of psychological maltreatment on internet addiction should be investigated in different countries or cultures with diverse and large samples. Taken all together, the literature demonstrates that further research should be conducted to define the internet addiction and identify its diagnostic criteria for research and practice. Moreover, the literature and theoretical frameworks support the significant role of psychological maltreatment in the development of internet addiction disorder; however, there is need for further research to investigate the influences of psychological maltreatment on internet addiction and other internet–related addictions, such as smartphone addiction or internet gaming disorder. Particularly, it is clear that there is need for longitudinal research investigating the effects of psychological maltreatment experiences in the development of internet addiction disorder.

REFERENCES

Akhter, N. (2013). Relationship between internet addiction and academic performance among university undergraduates. *Educational Research Review, 8*(19), 1793–1796.

Akin, A., & Iskender, M. (2011). Internet addiction and depression, anxiety and stress. *International Online Journal of Educational Sciences, 3*(1), 138–148.

American Psychiatric Association. (2013). *Diagnostic and statistical manual of mental disorders (DSM-5®)*. Arlington, VA: American Psychiatric Pub.

Arslan, G. (2016). Psychological maltreatment, emotional and behavioral problems in adolescents: The mediating role of resilience and self-esteem. *Child Abuse & Neglect, 52*, 200–209. doi:10.1016/j.chiabu.2015.09.010 PMID:26518981

Arslan, G. (2017a). Psychological maltreatment, forgiveness, mindfulness, and internet addiction among young adults: A study of mediation effect. *Computers in Human Behavior, 72*, 57–66. doi:10.1016/j.chb.2017.02.037

Arslan, G. (2017b). Psychological maltreatment, social acceptance, social connectedness, and subjective well-being in adolescents. *Journal of Happiness Studies*. doi:10.1007/s10902-017-9856-z

Arslan, G. (2017c). Psychological maltreatment, coping strategies, and mental health problems: A brief and effective measure of psychological maltreatment in adolescents. *Child Abuse & Neglect, 68*, 96–106. doi:10.1016/j.chiabu.2017.03.023 PMID:28427000

Arslan, G., & Balkis, M. (2016). Ergenlerde Duygusal İstismar, Problem Davranışlar, Öz-Yeterlik ve Psikolojik Sağlamlık Arasındaki İlişki. *Sakarya University Journal of Education, 6*(1), 8–22. doi:10.19126/suje.35977

Ayas, T. (2012). The relationship between Internet and computer game addiction level and shyness among high school students. *Educational Sciences: Theory and Practice, 12*(2), 632–636.

Balci, Ş., & Gülnar, B. (2009). Üniversite öğrencileri arasında internet bağımlılığı ve internet bağımlılarının profili. *Selçuk Üniversitesi İletişim Fakültesi Akademik Dergisi, 6*(1), 5–22.

Beard, K. W. (2011). Working with adolescents addicted to the Internet. In K. S. Young (Ed.), *Internet addiction: A handbook and guide to evaluation and treatment* (pp. 173–189). Hoboken, NJ: John Wiley & Sons, Inc.

Beard, K. W., & Wolf, E. M. (2001). Modification in the proposed diagnostic criteria for Internet addiction. *Cyberpsychology & Behavior, 4*(3), 377–383. doi:10.1089/109493101300210286 PMID:11710263

Bellis, M. A., Hughes, K., Jones, A., Perkins, C., & McHale, P. (2013). Childhood happiness and violence: A retrospective study of their impacts on adult well-being. *BMJ Open, 3*(9), 1–10. doi:10.1136/bmjopen-2013-003427 PMID:24056485

Bergevin, T., Gupta, R., Derevensky, J., & Kaufman, F. (2006). Adolescent gambling: Understanding the role of stress and coping. *Journal of Gambling Studies, 22*(2), 195–208. doi:10.1007/s10899-006-9010-z PMID:16838102

Blaszczynski, A., & Nower, L. (2002). A pathways model of problem and pathological gambling. *Addiction (Abingdon, England)*, *97*(5), 487–499. doi:10.1046/j.1360-0443.2002.00015.x PMID:12033650

Bozoglan, B., & Demirer, V. (2015). The Association between internet addiction and psycho-social variables. In J. Bishop (Ed.), *Psychological and social issues surrounding internet and gaming addiction* (pp. 171–185). Hershey, PA: IGI Global. doi:10.4018/978-1-4666-8595-6.ch010

Bozoglan, B., Demirer, V., & Sahin, I. (2013). Loneliness, self-esteem, and life satisfaction as predictors of Internet addiction: A cross-sectional study among Turkish university students. *Scandinavian Journal of Psychology*, *54*(4), 313319. doi:10.1111/sjop.12049 PMID:23577670

Bozoglan, B., Demirer, V., & Sahin, I. (2014). Problematic Internet use: Functions of use, cognitive absorption, and depression. *Computers in Human Behavior*, *37*, 117–123. doi:10.1016/j.chb.2014.04.042

Brand, M., Laier, C., & Young, K. S. (2014). Internet addiction: Coping styles, expectancies, and treatment implications. *Frontiers in Psychology*, *5*, 1–14. doi:10.3389/fpsyg.2014.01256 PMID:25426088

Brodski, S. K., & Hutz, C. S. (2012). The repercussions of emotional abuse and parenting styles on self-esteem, subjective well-being: A retrospective study with university students in Brazil. *Journal of Aggression, Maltreatment & Trauma*, *21*(3), 256–276. doi:10.1080/10926771.2012.666335

Bronfenbrenner, U., & Morris, P. A. (2006). The bioecological model of human development. In R. M. Lerner (Ed.), Handbook of child development: Vol. 1. Theoretical models of human development (6th ed.; pp. 793 – 828). Hoboken, NJ: Wiley.

Brown, R. I. F. (1993). Some contributions of the study of gambling to the study of other addictions. In W. R. Eadington & J. Cornelius (Eds.), *Gambling behavior and problem gambling*. Reno, NV: University of Nevada Press.

Brown, S., Fite, P. J., Stone, K., & Bortolato, M. (2016). Accounting for the associations between child maltreatment and internalizing problems: The role of alexithymia. *Child Abuse & Neglect*, *52*, 20–28. doi:10.1016/j.chiabu.2015.12.008 PMID:26774529

Caldwell, C. D., & Cunningham, T. J. (2010). *Internet addiction and students: Implications for school counselors*. American Counseling Association. Retrieved from http://www.counseling.org/resources/library/vistas/2010-v-online/Article_61.pdf

Cao, H., Sun, Y., Wan, Y., Hao, J., & Tao, F. (2011). Problematic Internet use in Chinese adolescents and its relation to psychosomatic symptoms and life satisfaction. *BMC Public Health*, *11*(1), 2–8. doi:10.1186/1471-2458-11-802 PMID:21995654

Cardak, M. (2013). Psychological well-being and Internet addiction among university students. *TOJET: The Turkish Online Journal of Educational Technology*, *12*(3), 134–141.

Çelik, Ç. B., & Odacı, H. (2013). The relationship between problematic internet use and interpersonal cognitive distortions and life satisfaction in university students. *Children and Youth Services Review*, *35*(3), 505–508. doi:10.1016/j.childyouth.2013.01.001

Çelik, S., Atak, H., & Başal, A. (2012). Predictive role of personality traits on Internet addiction. *Turkish Online Journal of Distance Education*, *13*(4), 10-24.

Ceyhan, E. (2008). Ergen ruh sağlığı açısından bir risk faktörü: İnternet bağımlılığı. *Çocuk ve Gençlik Ruh Sağliği Dergisi, 15*(2), 109–116.

Chrismore, S., Betzelberger, E., Bier, L., & Camacho, T. (2011). Twelve-step recovery in inpatient treatment for Internet addiction. In K. S. Young (Ed.), *Internet addiction: A handbook and guide to evaluation and treatment* (pp. 205–222). Hoboken, NJ: John Wiley & Sons, Inc.

Cicchetti, D., & Lynch, M. (1993). Toward an ecological/transactional model of community violence and child maltreatment: Consequences for children's development. *Psychiatry, 56*(1), 96–118. doi:10.1 080/00332747.1993.11024624 PMID:8488217

Compas, B. E., Banez, G. A., Malcarne, V., & Worsham, N. (1991). Perceived control and coping with stress: A developmental perspective. *The Journal of Social Issues, 47*(4), 23–34. doi:10.1111/j.1540-4560.1991. tb01832.x

Davis, R. A. (2001). A cognitive-behavioral model of pathological Internet use. *Computers in Human Behavior, 17*(2), 187–195. doi:10.1016/S0747-5632(00)00041-8

Dong, G., Wang, J., Yang, X., & Zhou, H. (2013). Risk personality traits of Internet addiction: A longitudinal study of Internet-addicted Chinese university students. *Asia-Pacific Psychiatry, 5*(4), 316–321. doi:10.1111/j.1758-5872.2012.00185.x PMID:23857796

Dowling, N. A., Merkouris, S. S., Greenwood, C. J., Oldenhof, E., Toumbourou, J. W., & Youssef, G. J. (2017). Early risk and protective factors for problem gambling: A systematic review and meta-analysis of longitudinal studies. *Clinical Psychology Review, 51*, 109–124. doi:10.1016/j.cpr.2016.10.008 PMID:27855334

Eldeleklioğlu, J., & Vural, M. (2013). Predictive effects of academic achievement, internet use duration, loneliness and shyness on internet addiction. *Hacettepe Üniversitesi Eğitim Fakültesi Dergisi, 28*(1), 141–152.

Elliott, J. C., Stohl, M., Wall, M. M., Keyes, K. M., Goodwin, R. D., Skodol, A. E., & Hasin, D. S. et al. (2014). The risk for persistent adult alcohol and nicotine dependence: The role of childhood maltreatment. *Addiction (Abingdon, England), 109*(5), 842–850. doi:10.1111/add.12477 PMID:24401044

Felsher, J. R., Derevensky, J. L., & Gupta, R. (2010). Young adults with gambling problems: The impact of childhood maltreatment. *International Journal of Mental Health and Addiction, 8*(4), 545–556. doi:10.1007/s11469-009-9230-4

Gámez-Guadix, M., Calvete, E., Orue, I., & Las Hayas, C. (2015). Problematic Internet use and problematic alcohol use from the cognitive–behavioral model: A longitudinal study among adolescents. *Addictive Behaviors, 40*, 109–114. doi:10.1016/j.addbeh.2014.09.009 PMID:25244690

Glaser, D. (2002). Emotional abuse and neglect (psychological maltreatment): A conceptual framework. *Child Abuse & Neglect, 26*(6), 697–714. doi:10.1016/S0145-2134(02)00342-3 PMID:12201163

Griffiths, M. (2005). A 'components' model of addiction within a biopsychosocial framework. *Journal of Substance Use, 10*(4), 191–197. doi:10.1080/14659890500114359

Griffiths, M. D., & Larkin, M. (2004). Conceptualizing addiction: The case for a 'complex systems' account. *Addiction Research and Theory*, *12*(2), 99–102. doi:10.1080/1606635042000193211

Griffiths, M. D., & Pontes, H. M. (2014). Internet addiction disorder and internet gaming disorder are not the same. *Addiction Research & Therapy*, *5*(4), 1-3. DOI: 10.4172/2155-6105.1000e124

Gross, A. B., & Keller, H. R. (1992). Long-term consequences of childhood physical and psychological maltreatment. *Aggressive Behavior*, *18*(3), 171–185. doi:10.1002/1098-2337(1992)18:3<171::AID-AB2480180302>3.0.CO;2-I

Hart, S. N., Binggeli, N. J., & Brassard, M. R. (1998). Evidence for the effects of psychological maltreatment. *Journal of Emotional Abuse*, *1*(1), 27–58. doi:10.1300/J135v01n01_03

Hodgins, D. C., Schopflocher, D. P., el-Guebaly, N., Casey, D. M., Smith, G. J., Williams, R. J., & Wood, R. T. (2010). The association between childhood maltreatment and gambling problems in a community sample of adult men and women. *Psychology of Addictive Behaviors*, *24*(3), 548–554. doi:10.1037/a0019946 PMID:20853942

Hsieh, Y. P., Shen, A. C. T., Wei, H. S., Feng, J. Y., Huang, S. C. Y., & Hwa, H. L. (2016). Associations between child maltreatment, PTSD, and internet addiction among Taiwanese students. *Computers in Human Behavior*, *56*, 209–214. doi:10.1016/j.chb.2015.11.048

Hyman, S. M., Garcia, M., & Sinha, R. (2006). Gender specific associations between types of childhood maltreatment and the onset, escalation and severity of substance use in cocaine dependent adults. *The American Journal of Drug and Alcohol Abuse*, *32*(4), 655–664. doi:10.1080/10623320600919193 PMID:17127554

Infurna, M. R., Reichl, C., Parzer, P., Schimmenti, A., Bifulco, A., & Kaess, M. (2016). Associations between depression and specific childhood experiences of abuse and neglect: A meta-analysis. *Journal of Affective Disorders*, *190*, 47–55. doi:10.1016/j.jad.2015.09.006 PMID:26480211

Iwaniec, D. (2006). *The emotionally abused and neglected child: Identification, assessment and intervention: A practice handbook*. Chichester, UK: John Wiley & Son,Ltd.

Iwaniec, D., Larkin, E., & Higgins, S. (2006). Research review: Risk and resilience in cases of emotional abuse. *Child & Family Social Work*, *11*(1), 73–82. doi:10.1111/j.1365-2206.2006.00398.x

Jacobs, D. F. (1986). A general theory of addictions: A new theoretical model. *Journal of Gambling Behavior*, *2*(1), 15-31.

Kabasakal, Z. (2015). Life satisfaction and family functions as-predictors of problematic Internet use in university students. *Computers in Human Behavior*, *53*, 294–304. doi:10.1016/j.chb.2015.07.019

Kabasakal, Z., & Erdem, Ş. (2015). Üniversite öğrencilerinde çocukluk dönemi istismar yaşantilari ve psikolojik iyi olma. *Eğitim ve Öğretim Araştırmaları Dergisi*, *4*(1), 14–23.

Kairys, S. W., & Johnson, C. F. (2002). The psychological maltreatment of children—Technical report. *Pediatrics*, *109*(4), 1–3. doi:10.1542/peds.109.4.e68 PMID:11927741

Kairys, S. W., & Johnson, C. F. (2002). The psychological maltreatment of children: Technical report. *Pediatrics, 109*(4), e68–e72. doi:10.1542/peds.109.4.e68 PMID:11927741

Kamal, N. N., & Mosallem, F. A. E. H. (2013). Determinants of problematic internet use among el-minia high school students, Egypt. *International Journal of Preventive Medicine, 4*(12), 1429–1437. PMID:24498499

Kim, E. J., Namkoong, K., Ku, T., & Kim, S. J. (2008). The relationship between online game addiction and aggression, self-control and narcissistic personality traits. *European Psychiatry, 23*(3), 212–218. doi:10.1016/j.eurpsy.2007.10.010 PMID:18166402

Kim, J., & Cicchetti, D. (2004). A longitudinal study of child maltreatment, mother–child relationship quality and maladjustment: The role of self-esteem and social competence. *Journal of Abnormal Child Psychology, 32*(4), 341–354. doi:10.1023/B:JACP.0000030289.17006.5a PMID:15305541

Király, O., Griffiths, M. D., Urbán, R., Farkas, J., Kökönyei, G., Elekes, Z., & Demetrovics, Z. et al. (2014). Problematic internet use and problematic online gaming are not the same: Findings from a large nationally representative adolescent sample. *Cyberpsychology, Behavior, and Social Networking, 17*(12), 749–754. doi:10.1089/cyber.2014.0475 PMID:25415659

Krishnamurthy, S., & Chetlapalli, S. K. (2015). Internet addiction: Prevalence and risk factors: A cross-sectional study among college students in Bengaluru, the Silicon Valley of India. *Indian Journal of Public Health, 59*(2), 115–121. doi:10.4103/0019-557X.157531 PMID:26021648

Kuss, D. J., van Rooij, A., Shorter, G. W., Griffiths, M. D., & van de Mheen, D. (2013). Internet addiction in adolescents: Prevalence and risk factors. *Computers in Human Behavior, 29*(5), 1987–1996. doi:10.1016/j.chb.2013.04.002

Lam, L. T. (2014). Risk factors of Internet addiction and the health effect of Internet addiction on adolescents: A systematic review of longitudinal and prospective studies. *Current Psychiatry Reports, 16*(11), 1–9. doi:10.1007/s11920-014-0508-2 PMID:25212714

Lane, W., Sacco, P., Downton, K., Ludeman, E., Levy, L., & Tracy, J. K. (2016). Child maltreatment and problem gambling: A systematic review. *Child Abuse & Neglect, 58*, 24–38. doi:10.1016/j.chiabu.2016.06.003 PMID:27337693

Lerner, R. M., Rothbaum, F., Boulos, S., & Castellino, D. R. (2002). Developmental systems perspective on parenting. In M. H. Bornstein (Ed.), Handbook of parenting (2nd ed.; pp. 315–344). Mahwah, NJ: Erlbaum.

Li, D., Zhang, W., Li, X., Zhen, S., & Wang, Y. (2010). Stressful life events and problematic Internet use by adolescent females and males: A mediated moderation model. *Computers in Human Behavior, 26*(5), 1199–1207. doi:10.1016/j.chb.2010.03.031

Lin, I. H., Ko, C. H., Chang, Y. P., Liu, T. L., Wang, P. W., Lin, H. C., & Yen, C. F. et al. (2014). The association between suicidality and Internet addiction and activities in Taiwanese adolescents. *Comprehensive Psychiatry, 55*(3), 504–510. doi:10.1016/j.comppsych.2013.11.012 PMID:24457034

Mazhari, S. (2012). The prevalence of problematic internet use and the related factors in medical students, Kerman, Iran. *Addiction & Health, 4*(3-4), 87. PMID:24494141

Milani, L., Osualdella, D., & Di Blasio, P. (2009). Quality of interpersonal relationships and problematic Internet use in adolescence. *Cyberpsychology & Behavior, 12*(6), 681–684. doi:10.1089/cpb.2009.0071 PMID:19788382

Miller-Perrin, C. L., & Perrin, R. D. (2007). *Child maltreatment: An introduction*. London: Sage Publications.

Morsünbül, Ü. (2014). The association of internet addiction with attachment styles, personality traits, loneliness and life satisfaction. *Journal of Human Sciences, 11*(1), 357–372.

Mullen, P. E., Martin, J. L., Anderson, J. C., Romans, S. E., & Herbison, G. P. (1996). The long-term impact of the physical, emotional, and sexual abuse of children: A community study. *Child Abuse & Neglect, 20*(1), 7–21. doi:10.1016/0145-2134(95)00112-3 PMID:8640429

Müller, K. W., Janikian, M., Dreier, M., Wölfling, K., Beutel, M. E., Tzavara, C., & Tsitsika, A. et al. (2015). Regular gaming behavior and internet gaming disorder in European adolescents: Results from a cross-national representative survey of prevalence, predictors, and psychopathological correlates. *European Child & Adolescent Psychiatry, 24*(5), 565–574. doi:10.1007/s00787-014-0611-2 PMID:25189795

Norman, R. E., Byambaa, M., De, R., Butchart, A., Scott, J., & Vos, T. (2012). The long-term health consequences of child physical abuse, emotional abuse, and neglect: A systematic review and meta-analysis. *PLoS Medicine, 9*(11), e1001349. doi:10.1371/journal.pmed.1001349 PMID:23209385

Odacı, H. (2013). Risktaking behavior and academic selfefficacy as variables accounting for problematic internet use in adolescent university students. *Children and Youth Services Review, 35*(1), 183–187. doi:10.1016/j.childyouth.2012.09.011

Odacı, H., & Çıkrıkçı, Ö. (2014). Problematic internet use in terms of gender, attachment styles and subjective well-being in university students. *Computers in Human Behavior, 32*, 61–66. doi:10.1016/j.chb.2013.11.019

Oshio, T., Umeda, M., & Kawakami, N. (2011). *Childhood adversity and adulthood happiness: Evidence from Japan (No. 529)*. Center for Intergenerational Studies, Institute of Economic Research, Hitotsubashi University.

Özdemir, Y., Kuzucu, Y., & Ak, Ş. (2014). Depression, loneliness and Internet addiction: How important is low self-control? *Computers in Human Behavior, 34*, 284–290. doi:10.1016/j.chb.2014.02.009

Özge, E., & Gölge, Z. B. (2015). Üniversite öğrencilerinde riskli davranışlar ile çocukluk çağı istismar, dürtüsellik ve riskli davranışlar arasındaki ilişki. *Journal of Psychiatry, 16*(3), 189–197.

Park, S. K., Kim, J. Y., & Cho, C. B. (2008). Prevalence of Internet addiction and correlations with family factors among South Korean adolescents. *Adolescence, 43*(172), 895–909. PMID:19149152

Petry, N. M., & Steinberg, K. L. (2005). Childhood maltreatment in male and female treatment-seeking pathological gamblers. *Psychology of Addictive Behaviors*, *19*(2), 226–229. doi:10.1037/0893-164X.19.2.226 PMID:16011396

Rosenkranz, S. E., Muller, R. T., & Henderson, J. L. (2012). Psychological maltreatment in relation to substance use problem severity among youth. *Child Abuse & Neglect*, *36*(5), 438–448. doi:10.1016/j.chiabu.2012.01.005 PMID:22622223

Şahin, C. (2014). An analysis of the relationship between Internet addiction and depression levels of high school students. *Participatory Educational Research*, *1*(2), 53–67. doi:10.17275/per.14.10.1.2

Şaşmaz, T., Öner, S., Kurt, A. Ö., Yapıcı, G., Buğdaycı, R., & Şiş, M. (2013). Prevalence and risk factors of Internet addiction in high school students. *European Journal of Public Health*, *24*(1), 15–20. doi:10.1093/eurpub/ckt051 PMID:23722862

Scannapieco, M., & Connell-Carrick, K. (2005). *Understanding child maltreatment: An ecological and developmental perspective*. New York, NY: Oxford University Press. doi:10.1093/acprof:oso/9780195156782.001.0001

Şenormancı, Ö., Konkan, R., & Sungur, M. Z. (2012) Internet addiction and its cognitive behavioral therapy. In Standard and Innovative Strategies in Cognitive Behavior Therapy. Intech.

Şenormancı, Ö., Şenormancı, G., Güçlü, O., & Konkan, R. (2014). Attachment and family functioning in patients with internet addiction. *General Hospital Psychiatry*, *36*(2), 203–207. doi:10.1016/j.genhosppsych.2013.10.012 PMID:24262601

Shaffer, D. R., & Kipp, K. (2013). *Developmental psychology: Childhood and adolescence*. Wadsworth, Cengage Learning.

Shaw, M., & Black, D. W. (2008). Internet addiction: Definition, assessment, epidemiology and clinical management. *CNS Drugs*, *22*(5), 353–365. doi:10.2165/00023210-200822050-00001 PMID:18399706

Tahiroğlu, A. Y., Çelik, G. G., Fettahoğlu, Ç., Yildirim, V., Toros, F., Avci, A., ... Uzel, M. (2010). Psikiyatrik Bozukluğu Olan ve Olmayan Ergenlerde Problemli İnternet Kullanımı. *Archives of Neuropsychiatry/Noropsikiatri Arsivi*, *47*(3), 241-246.

Tao, R., Huang, X., Wang, J., Zhang, H., Zhang, Y., & Li, M. (2010). Proposed diagnostic criteria for internet addiction. *Addiction (Abingdon, England)*, *105*(3), 556–564. doi:10.1111/j.1360-0443.2009.02828.x PMID:20403001

Telef, B. B. (2016). Investigating the relationship among internet addiction, positive and negative effects, and life satisfaction in Turkish adolescents. *International Journal of Progressive Education*, *12*(1), 128–135.

Thompson, R. A. (2008). Early attachment and later development. In J. Cassidy & P. R. Shaver (Eds.), *Handbook of attachment: Theory, research, and clinical applications* (pp. 265–286). New York: Guilford.

Tsai, C. C., & Lin, S. S. (2001). Analysis of attitudes toward computer networks and Internet addiction of Taiwanese adolescents. *Cyberpsychology & Behavior*, *4*(3), 373–376. doi:10.1089/109493101300210277 PMID:11710262

Tsai, C. C., & Lin, S. S. (2003). Internet addiction of adolescents in Taiwan: An interview study. *Cyberpsychology & Behavior*, *6*(6), 649–652. doi:10.1089/109493103322725432 PMID:14756931

Tsai, H. F., Cheng, S. H., Yeh, T. L., Shih, C. C., Chen, K. C., Yang, Y. C., & Yang, Y. K. (2009). The risk factors of Internet addiction—a survey of university freshmen. *Psychiatry Research*, *167*(3), 294–299. doi:10.1016/j.psychres.2008.01.015 PMID:19395052

Turner, N. E., Jain, U., Spence, W., & Zangeneh, M. (2008). Pathways to pathological gambling: Component analysis of variables related to pathological gambling. *International Gambling Studies*, *8*(3), 281–298. doi:10.1080/14459790802405905

Whang, L. S. M., Lee, S., & Chang, G. (2003). Internet over-users' psychological profiles: A behavior sampling analysis on internet addiction. *Cyberpsychology & Behavior*, *6*(2), 143–150. doi:10.1089/109493103321640338 PMID:12804026

Widyanto, L., & Griffiths, M. (2006). 'Internet addiction': A critical review. *International Journal of Mental Health and Addiction*, *4*(1), 31–51. doi:10.1007/s11469-006-9009-9

Wingo, A. P., Wrenn, G., Pelletier, T., Gutman, A. R., Bradley, B., & Ressler, K. J. (2010). Moderating effects of resilience on depression in individuals with a history of childhood abuse or trauma exposure. *Journal of Affective Disorders*, *126*(3), 411–414. doi:10.1016/j.jad.2010.04.009 PMID:20488545

Wu, C. Y., Lee, M. B., Liao, S. C., & Chang, L. R. (2015). Risk factors of internet addiction among internet users: An online questionnaire survey. *PLoS One*, *10*(10), 1–10. doi:10.1371/journal.pone.0137506 PMID:26462196

Xiuqin, H., Huimin, Z., Mengchen, L., Jinan, W., Ying, Z., & Ran, T. (2010). Mental health, personality, and parental rearing styles of adolescents with internet addiction disorder. *Cyberpsychology, Behavior, and Social Networking*, *13*(4), 401–406. doi:10.1089/cyber.2009.0222 PMID:20712498

Yates, T. M., Gregor, M. A., & Haviland, M. G. (2012). Child maltreatment, alexithymia, and problematic internet use in young adulthood. *Cyberpsychology, Behavior, and Social Networking*, *15*(4), 219–225. doi:10.1089/cyber.2011.0427 PMID:22313343

Yen, J. Y., Ko, C. H., Yen, C. F., Wu, H. Y., & Yang, M. J. (2007). The comorbid psychiatric symptoms of Internet addiction: Attention deficit and hyperactivity disorder (ADHD), depression, social phobia, and hostility. *The Journal of Adolescent Health*, *41*(1), 93–98. doi:10.1016/j.jadohealth.2007.02.002 PMID:17577539

Yen, J. Y., Yen, C. F., Chen, C. C., Chen, S. H., & Ko, C. H. (2007). Family factors of internet addiction and substance use experience in Taiwanese adolescents. *Cyberpsychology & Behavior*, *10*(3), 323–329. doi:10.1089/cpb.2006.9948 PMID:17594255

Yoo, H. J., Cho, S. C., Ha, J., Yune, S. K., Kim, S. J., Hwang, J., & Lyoo, I. K. et al. (2004). Attention deficit hyperactivity symptoms and internet addiction. *Psychiatry and Clinical Neurosciences*, *58*(5), 487–494. doi:10.1111/j.1440-1819.2004.01290.x PMID:15482579

Young, K. (2015). The evolution of Internet addiction disorder. In C. Montag & M. Reuter (Eds.), *Internet addiction: Neuroscientific approaches and therapeutical interventions* (pp. 3–17). New York, NY: Springer International Publishing.

Young, K. S. (1998). Internet addiction: The emergence of a new clinical disorder. *Cyberpsychology & Behavior, 1*(3), 237–244. doi:10.1089/cpb.1998.1.237

Young, K. S. (2004). Internet addiction a new clinical phenomenon and its consequences. *The American Behavioral Scientist, 48*(4), 402–415. doi:10.1177/0002764204270278

Young, K. S. (2007). Cognitive behavior therapy with Internet addicts: Treatment outcomes and implications. *Cyberpsychology & Behavior, 10*(5), 671–679. doi:10.1089/cpb.2007.9971 PMID:17927535

Young, K. S. (2011). Clinical assessment of Internet-addicted clients. In K. S. Young (Ed.), *Internet addiction: A handbook and guide to evaluation and treatment* (pp. 19–34). Hoboken, NJ: John Wiley & Sons, Inc.

Young, K. S., & Rogers, R. C. (1998). The relationship between depression and Internet addiction. *Cyberpsychology & Behavior, 1*(1), 25–28. doi:10.1089/cpb.1998.1.25

Young, K. S., Yue, X. D., & Ying, L. (2011). Prevalence estimates and etiologic models of Internet addiction. In K. S. Young & C. N. de Abreu (Eds.), *Internet addiction: A handbook and guide to evaluation and treatment* (pp. 3–18). Hoboken, NJ: John Wiley & Sons.

Zhang, Z. H., Yang, L. S., Hao, J. H., Huang, F., Zhang, X. J., & Sun, Y. H. (2012). Relationship of childhood physical abuse and Internet addiction disorder in adolescence: The mediating role of self-esteem. *Zhonghua liu xing bing xue za zhi= Zhonghua liuxingbingxue zazhi, 33*(1), 50-53.

Zimmer-Gembeck, M. J., & Locke, E. M. (2007). The socialization of adolescent coping behaviours: Relationships with families and teachers. *Journal of Adolescence, 30*(1), 1–16. doi:10.1016/j.adolescence.2005.03.001 PMID:16837040

KEY TERMS AND DEFINITIONS

Component Model: A theoretical background of internet addiction proposed internet addiction consists of seven distinct–yet–related common components (i.e., salience, tolerance, mood modification, conflict, withdrawal, and relapse) and descripts the internet addiction as a part of the biopsychosocial process.

General Theory of Addictions: A theoretical framework that identifies the physiological and psychological risk factors of addictions, and the model has proposed that childhood negative life experiences are risk factors in the development of pathological internet use.

Gambling Addiction Disorder: A psychological disorder that is described as the "persistent and recurrent problematic gambling behavior leading to clinically significant impairment or distress".

Internet Addiction: A psychological disorder that is described as an impulse-control disorder which does not involve an intoxicant.

Pathways Model: A theoretical framework that defines the internet addiction and pathological gambling in three pathways.

Protective Factors: Variables that decrease or eliminate the likelihood of developing the internet addiction or pathological internet use, and help individuals cope more effectively with stressful life events.

Psychological Maltreatment: Psychological maltreatment is one of the most common form of child maltreatment. It is a stressful life event associated with a range of short and long–term undesirable mental health and wellbeing outcomes.

Risk Factors: Variables that are associated with an increased risk for the internet addiction or pathological internet use.

Chapter 6
Loneliness and Internet Addiction Among University Students

Ayfer Aydiner Boylu
Hacettepe University, Turkey

Gülay Günay
Karabük University, Turkey

ABSTRACT

The present study was designed to determine the relationship between loneliness and Internet addiction, based on a sample of young generation from Turkey. Participants in this study were students of the Hacettepe University in Ankara, Turkey (n = 440). Findings show that there is a statistically significant relationship (p <0.05) between students' Internet addiction and only the grade they are studying. According to the correlation analysis, it was found that there is a negative relationship between the loneliness of students and the time they spend on the internet, and a positive relationship between internet addiction and age of students. Moreover, it was found that the age, time spent on the Internet and loneliness of university students were important determinants of Internet addiction.

INTRODUCTION

Advances in technology have made the Internet an indispensible part of our lives. The Internet brings the world so close together today, by its positive aspects such as conducting research, performing business transactions & communications, accessing library journals, and communicating with social relations, etc. (Sukunesan, 1999). However, it has also turned out to be an important source of risk. In spite of the widely perceived merits of this tool, psychologists and educators have been aware of the negative impacts of its use, especially the over or misuse (Bricolo, Gentile, Smelser and Serpelloni, 2007; Greenfield, 2000; Hur, 2006).

DOI: 10.4018/978-1-5225-3477-8.ch006

BACKGROUND

Internet Addiction

Excessive Internet use is discussed by many researchers with different concepts. "Internet Addiction" (Young and Rodgers, 1998), "Internet Dependency" (Wang, 2001), "Pathological Internet Use" (Davis, 2001), "Problematic Internet Use" (Kaltiala-Heino, Lintonen and Rimpela, 2004), "Internet Abuse" (Young and Case, 2004), "Excessive Internet Use" (Yang et al., 2005), "Internet Addiction Disorder" (Gonzalez, 2002), are many of these. Griffiths (2000) has described Internet addiction as a kind of technology addiction and a behavioral addiction similar to a gambling habit. Internet addiction can be defined in general as excessive use of the Internet; it is the inability to resist the desire to use it, loss of the importance of time spent without being connected to it, extreme nervousness and aggression when deprived of it, and increased deterioration of one's business, social, and family life (Young, 2004).

The literature suggests that there are several components of Internet addiction. Young (1999), while collecting the component for Internet addiction under 8 headings, argued that of these eight component, a person could be regarded as addicted who matched five of them. These component are: (a) excessive thoughts related to the Internet, thinking about the Internet; (b) an increasing proportion of Internet use is expected for pleasure; (c) unsuccessful attempts at quitting or decreasing Internet use; (d) restlessness, depression, or anger occur in the absence of Internet usage; (e) being online longer than planned; (f) experiencing problems with family, school, work, and friends due to excessive Internet usage; (g) lying to others (family, friends, therapist, etc.) about time spent on the Internet; (h) using the Internet to get away from negative feelings or to escape from problems. According Block (2008) Internet addiction has four components: (1) excessive Internet use, often associated with a loss of the sense of time or a neglect of basic drives; (2) withdrawal, including feelings of anger, tension, and/or depression when the computer is inaccessible; (3) tolerance, including the need for better computer equipment, more software, or more hours of use; and (4) negative repercussions, including arguments, lying, poor achievement, social isolation, and fatigue.

In literature, there are a number of studies demonstrating the relationship between Internet addiction and the Internet use purposes. When the findings of these studies (Ceyhan, 2008; Ceyhan & Ceyhan, 2008; Leung, 2004; Keser Özcan & Buzlu, 2007; Kesici & Şahin, 2009; Morahan-Martin & Schumacher, 2003; Yang & Tung, 2007) are taken into consideration, it is seen that the Internet use purpose acts as a significant determiner in distinguishing unhealthy/problematic Internet users from healthy users in terms of their Internet use, and the Internet users who do not have problematic Internet use behavior prefer to use the Internet primarily to obtain information, while problematic Internet users tend to use the Internet more for entertainment, social activities, and interactive virtual games.

Researchers have described a wide range impacts of Internet addiction such as excessive amounts of time spent online, feeling that the world outside of the Internet is boring, becoming irritated if disturbed while online, and decreased social interaction with "real" people (Kraut et al., 1998). They have also characterized Internet addiction by psychomotor agitation, anxiety, craving (Ferraro, Caci, D'Amico, and Di Blasi, 2007), loss of control, intolerance, withdrawal, impairment of function, reduced decision-making ability (Ko, Yen, Chen, Chen, and Yen, 2005), and migraine or headache, sleep pattern disrupt etc (Jeon, 2005; You, 2007; Yang and Tung, 2007). Moreover, Shapira et al. (2000) stated that Internet addiction might result in financial problems.

Internet Addiction and University Students

Internet addiction is a type of addiction that can be seen at any age. Psychological and environmental factors related to the lives of university students may cause them to be affected by Internet addiction (Hall and Parsons, 2001). Because university students may face a variety of life challenges or problems such as meeting their needs such as accommodation, nutrition, health, participating in a social group, self-confidence, adapting and developing close relationships with their surroundings (Ceyhan, 2011). Perhaps for the first time, the individual is separated from his or her parents as nearby emotional support becomes scarce; family contact becomes limited; and the individual faces the difficulty of having to develop a whole new set of relationships (Shaver et al., 1985). At the same time, the vast majority of students who come to the university from different social, cultural and physical environments enter a transitional period in their lives and experience a temporary sense of loneliness due to the different sentiments of being in a different environment (Aral and Gürsoy, 2000). In addition in terms of their daily lives, university student schedules provide them with a lot of flexibility and free time resulting in the flexibility to spend long epochs on various Internet applications. Moreover, university students have easy access through direct Internet connections in dorms, libraries, and computer labs (Kandell, 1998).

Loneliness, University Students and Internet Addiction

Events that can affect a college student, such as leaving family and friends for college, the breakup of a romantic relationship, problems with friends and roommates, and difficulties with schoolwork, may create a discrepancy between actual and desired interpersonal relationships, which could lead to loneliness (Cutrona, 1982). In parallel with this view, Weiss (1973) stated that loneliness does not come from being alone but from the lack of a certain set of relationships that are clearly needed. In other words, there may be a lack of intimate connections, friendships, or other social bonds. Loneliness generally is viewed not as a feeling in individuals; it is seen as a phenomenon different from being alone and as an unexplained fear, problem, or hopelessness that can be seen sometimes for a short while and sometimes for longer (Duy, 2003; Öz, 2010). Similarly, the feeling of loneliness is expressed as an unwanted and unpleasant experience accompanied by feeling different than other people and by feeling anxiety, anger, and sadness (Russell et al., 1980); it appears to be more intense in adolescence and young adulthood, although it exists as a feeling that can be seen in almost every period of human life.

As time passes, some students overcome the feeling of loneliness, but some continue to live this sentiment even in the last class (Aral and Gürsoy, 2000). According to the study by McWhirter (1990), loneliness seems to be especially prevalent among university students. In McWhirters' study with an estimated 30% of university students reporting loneliness as a problem. In a study of university freshmen, 75% of the students report some degree of loneliness in the first 2 weeks of school, with 47% of these students classified as having moderate to severe loneliness. After 7 months, 25% still reported feelings of loneliness (Cutrona, 1982).

Spending time on the Internet is one of the defensive mechanisms developed to constantly face loneliness, such as continuously and exceedingly eating, purchasing things senselessly and constantly, continuously watching TV without making a choice, watching storefronts without purpose (Geçtan, 1997: 109). Some of the factors that make the Internet attractive can be listed as being able to establish relationships through the Internet that could not happen in real life, being able to communicate risk-free with other people, expressing one's thoughts and feelings freely, and while masking, showing one's identity how one wants to be seen, being able to hide one's true identity, and being able to get in contact whenever one wants (King, 1996). Lone individuals are more inclined to using the Internet (Caplan 2007; Yellowlees and Marks 2007; Young and Rodgers 1998), and it is also likely that they get an opportunity to decrease their loneliness by setting up social relationships (Ando and Sakamoto 2008; Sum, Mathews, Hughes and Campbell 2008). In the findings of many of the studies have also demonstrated that (Erdoğan, 2008; Hamburger & Artzi, 2003; Gu, 2012; Kelleci & İnal, 2010), loneliness as an important determinant in Internet addiction.

Considering the young population in Turkey, it is imperative to explore the effects of loneliness on Internet addiction among university students. This will contribute to not only preserving or improving university students' quality of life but also formulating services and policies for them. Although there have been previous studies on Internet addiction, in contrast to studies that have been done, this is the first study focused on the influence of loneliness on Internet addiction of university students studying in Ankara. Further the data were collected with the "Turkish Internet Addiction Scale" which is more suitable for Turkish culture and structure. The present study was designed to help fill this gap. In this regard, the aim of this study is to investigate the effects of loneliness on Internet addiction among university students studying in Ankara using the "Turkish Internet Addiction Scale".

METHOD

Participants

The data of the study were collected in Hacettepe University (HU) using a cross-sectional questionnaire. Hacettepe University is a major state university in Ankara, Turkey. HU offers over 150 different undergraduate programs. According to the list taken from Registrar's office in 2016, 49582 students' registered at the HU. The numbers of samples that can represent the universe, calculate with sample size formula. The sample size was determined as 381, however to decrease sampling error and to take missing value situation under control, the researcher reached to 500 students (Çıngı, 1994). Data were collected via face-to-face interviews. All participants were informed of the purpose of the study and assured that their answers would be anonymously used for research purposes only. The research forms were filled in 30 to 40 minutes. Five hundred interviews were conducted. However, 60 research forms filled imperfectly or inadequately were excluded from the analysis; thus, 440 forms were included for the evaluation.

Measurement Variables

The questionnaire form consist three sections. The first part of the questionnaire included demographic variables such as age, gender, grade, people living together, the average time spent on the Internet in a day, for what purpose the Internet is used, and the recreational activity level. The second part comprise The University of California Los Angeles Loneliness Scale (UCLA-LS) (Russell, Peplau, and Ferguson, 1980). The third part of the questionnaire form included the dependent variable Turkish Internet Addiction Scale (Günüç, 2009).

Independent Variables

- **Demographic Variables:** The study included demographic variables such as age, gender, grade, people living together, the average time spent on the Internet in a day, for what purpose the Internet is used, and the recreational activity level.

- **University of California Los Angeles Loneliness Scale (UCLA-LS):** UCLA-LS, which aims to determine an individual's general state and level of loneliness, is an instrument consisting of 20 items (10 straight and 10 reverse items). This scale is self-evaluating, using 4-point Likert-type responses. The total score a person receives from the scale is obtained while totaling the points from the forward-and reverse-scored items. A high total score received on the scale indicates a high level of loneliness. The UCLA-LS, which aims to measure loneliness (being an important problem that is experienced in social relations in everyday life) through social and emotional dimensions, was first developed by Russell, Peplau, and Ferguson (1980). Later it was revised to its current form after Russell et al. (1980) reviewed it. The scale was first used while translated to Turkish by Yaparel in 1984. Demir (1989) later conducted a reliability and validity study of the scale's translation; internal consistency was found as 0.96, and the test-retest correlation coefficient was found as 0.94. The Cronbach's alpha (α) reliability coefficient of the UCLA-LS scale was .78 for this study performed to determine the relationship between Internet addiction and loneliness levels of university students.

Dependent Variables

- **Turkish Internet Addiction Scale:** The Turkish Internet Addiction Scale was developed by Günüç (2009) and includes 35 items which cover four dimensions; Withdrawal, Controlling Difficulty, Disorder in Functionality and Social Isolation. Each item is rated on a five-point Likert-type response format (1 = very strongly disagree; 5 = very strongly agree). All items in the scale are for addiction, and transposing is not required. Cronbach alpha internal consistency coefficient of the scale was found as .94. The lowest score that can be obtained from the scale is 35, the highest score is 175, and as the score increases, the Internet addiction also increases. The Cronbach's alpha (α) reliability coefficients for the four sub-factors were found to be .88, .86, .83 and .79, respectively. In this study, the lowest score obtained from the scale was determined as 56, the highest score as 175, and the scale average as 130.8 (S: 21.4). The internal consistency coefficient of the scale was calculated as .94 for this study. For each subscale, Cronbach's alpha (α) reliability coefficients were calculated as .86 (Withdrawal), .84 (Controlling Difficulty), .86 (Disorder in Functionality) and .84 (Social Isolation).

Data Analysis

The information collected with the questionnaire form was evaluated with "SPSS for Windows 18.0" statistical package program. For the analysis of the data obtained in the study, firstly descriptive analyzes, number and percentage distributions, averages, standard deviations are calculated. Validity and reliability analyzes of independent and dependent variables were performed.

"One Way Variance Analysis (ANOVA)" was applied to test whether the difference between Internet addiction levels of students in study and independent variables (grade, individuals they are living with, Internet use purposes, recreational activity levels) was statistically significant. The "Multiple Comparison Test (LSD test)" was used to check which groups cause difference when the difference is found significant as a result of ANOVA analysis and its results are given in tables (Büyüköztürk, 2007:67).

A correlation analysis was conducted to determine the level or amount and direction of the relationship between dependent and independent variables. Spearman correlation analysis was used to determine whether there was a significant relationship between Internet addiction levels of university students and demographic variables and loneliness. Multiple Regression Analysis was applied in order to determine the relationship between independent variables such as age, time spent on the Internet, loneliness and Internet addiction scores of the students. Regression analysis is a widely used statistical method in the social sciences and research. Regression analysis provides an estimate of how independent variable or variables predict the variance of the dependent variable (Büyüköztürk, 2007:98). In this statistical analysis, two or more independent variables predicting the dependent variable is called multiple linear regression analysis. Before the analysis, it was observed whether extreme values existed and regression analysis was found to meet the assumptions of "linearity" and "multivariate normality".

RESULTS

Table 1 contains demographic information about the students participating in the study. 287 (65.2%) of the participants were female and 153 (34.8%) were male students. It is observed that 35.9% of the students are Sophomore, 30.5% Senior, 23.4% Junior and only 10.2% are Freshmen. 36.1% of the students stated that they live together with their friends; these are followed by those stated that they live with their parents (31.1%), staying at a dorm (25.7%) and living alone (7.1%), respectively. The time spent daily by the participants in the Internet varies between 60 - 960 minutes and they spend an average of 236 minutes on the Internet per day (S = 135.9). The use of social media (59.1%) is at the forefront among purposes of using Internet, followed by entertainment with 23.4%. There is a high percentage of students who say that they participate in recreational activities at medium (46.4%) level.

In the study, when the relationship between Internet addiction levels of students and various demographic variables (grade, the individuals they live with, the purpose of Internet use and the level of participation in recreational activities) are evaluated statistically; it is observed that the relationship between only the grade and Internet addiction was significant (F=3.191; df=3-436; p<0.05). According to the LSD test, the relation between freshman (M=121.6; S=20.5) and Sophomore (M=131.3; S=19.3); freshman (M=121.6; S=20.5) and junior (M=132.0; S=22.3), freshman (M=121.6; S=20.5) and senior (M=132.3; S=22.8) were determined as significant. The relationships between gender (t=1.509; df=438; p>.05), individuals living with (F=0.006; df=3-436; p>0.05), purpose of Internet use (F=0.717; df=3-436; p>0.05) and participation level to recreational activities (F=0.994; df=4-435; p>0.05) and Internet addiction are statistically insignificant.

"Pearson Correlation" analysis was applied to examine the relation between dependent variable (Internet addiction) and independent variables (age, time spent on the Internet, level of loneliness). The results of the correlation analysis are shown in Table 3. There is a significant positive relationship between Internet addiction and age (r = .169; p <0.01). The relationship between Internet addiction and time spent on the Internet (r = -. 333; p <0.01) and loneliness (r = -. 238; p <0.01) was found to be negative and significant. In other words, as the age increases, the Internet addiction also increases, and Internet addiction decreases as the time spent on the Internet and loneliness increases (Table 3).

Table 1. Demographic variables

Demographic Variables	F	%
Age (M=21,1; S=1.6)		
Gender		
Female	287	65,2
Male	153	34,8
Grade		
Freshmen	45	10,2
Sophomore	158	35,9
Junior	103	23,4
Senior	134	30,5
Individuals Living With		
With their families	137	31,1
With their friends	159	36,1
Live alone	31	7,1
Dormitory	113	25,7
Students' Internet Usage Purposes		
To do research	40	9,1
To read news	37	8,4
To join social media	260	59,1
To have fun	103	23,4
Recreational Activity Level		
Very low	29	6,6
Low	59	13,4
Middle	204	46,4
High	116	26,3
Too high	32	7,3

The results of multiple regression analysis of independent variables (age, time spent on the Internet, level of loneliness) that may be effective on the Internet addiction of university students are shown in Table 4. The results show that there is a significant relationship between the variables of age, time spent on the Internet and loneliness and Internet addiction scores of students ($R = .417$, $R^2 = .174$, $F = 30.584$, $p < .001$). Age, time spent on the Internet and loneliness together account for 17% of the total variance in Internet addiction.

The highest variable among the standardized regression coefficients β (beta) values is the most significant predictor (Büyüköztürk, 2011: 103). According to the standardized regression coefficient (β), the relative importance order of the independent variables on the Internet addiction is time spent on the Internet (β = - .30, $p < .001$) loneliness scores (β = -. 22, $p < .001$) and age (β = .13, $p < .01$). When the t-test results for the significance of the regression coefficients were examined, it was found that all three independent variables were significant predictors of Internet addiction (age: t = 2.943, $p < .01$; time spent on the Internet: t = -6.771, $p < .001$; UCLA_LS: t = -5.048, $p < .001$).

Table 2. The relationship between internet addiction and demographic variables

Demographic Variables	F	%	M	S	Statistical Analysis
Gender					t=1.509 df=438 p=.133
Female	287	65,2	131,9	20,2	
Male	153	34,8	128,7	23,5	
Grade					F=3.191 df=3-436 p=.024*
Freshmen	45	10,2	121,6	20,5	
Sophomore	158	35,9	131,3	19,3	Freshmen – Sophomore
Junior	103	23,4	132,0	22,3	Freshmen – Junior Freshmen – Senior
Senior	134	30,5	132,3	22,8	
Individuals Living With					F=0.006 df=3-436 p=.999
With their families	137	31,1	130,8	23,9	
With their friends	159	36,1	130,7	21,1	
Live alone	31	7,1	131,2	23,2	
Dormitory	113	25,7	130,8	18,1	
Students' Internet Usage Purposes					F=0.717 df=3-436 p=.542
To do research	40	9,1	133,2	25,4	
To read news	37	8,4	134,8	23,1	
To join social media	260	59,1	130,1	20,8	
To have fun	103	23,4	130,1	20,8	
Recreational Activity Level					F=0.994 df=4-435 p=.410
Very low	29	6,6	127,7	28,1	
Low	59	13,4	130,3	23,1	
Middle	204	46,4	129,4	20,5	
High	116	26,3	133,9	20,8	
Too high	32	7,3	132,0	18,9	

*P<0.05

Table 3. Pearson correlation

Variables	1	2	3	4
1. Age	1			
2. Time spent on the Internet	-,148**	1		
3. University of California Los Angeles Loneliness Scale (UCLA-LS)	,020	,068	1	
4. Turkish Internet Addiction Scale	,169**	-,333**	-,238**	1

**p<0.01

Table 4. Multiple regression analysis for internet addiction

Independent Variables	B	Beta	t	Sig.
(Constant)	128,508		9,352	,000
2. Age	1,93	,13	2,943	,003**
3. Time spent on the Internet	-,05	-,30	-6,771	,000***
4. University of California Los Angeles Loneliness Scale (UCLA-LS)	-,61	-,22	-5,048	,000***
R	.417			
R²	.174			
R² Adj.	.168			
F	30.584***			

**p<0.01; ***p<.001

DISCUSSION

Since 1990s Internet users rapidly increasing and it is become one of the most important topic for the research. On the one hand, the Internet has come to the fore as a source facilitating the access of individuals to information and perform research, therefore supporting the development of personal attributes such as problem solving, creativity and critical thinking (Berson and Berson, 2003); on the other hand causes an addiction in connection with excessive, uncontrolled and out of purpose use of Internet. According to the Turkish Statistical Institute (TSI) (2016) Household Use of Information Technologies Survey, the percentage of households with Internet access is 76.3% and the rate of Internet users (with an increase 6%) reached 61.2%. In the last three months of 2016, the ratio of regular Internet users is 94.9% (TSI, 2016). The group most affected by the adverse consequences of using the Internet is young people who easily adapt to innovations and developments to facilitate life (Selian, 2004). Undoubtedly, as in the rest of the world, young people in our country constitute a broad and diverse audience with values, habits, interests and behaviors on the use of Internet.

In the present study, the level of Internet addiction increases as the grade gets higher. On the other hand, there was no significant relationship between the gender of the students, the individuals they lived together with, the purpose of Internet use and recreational activity levels and Internet addiction. This may be due to the characteristics of the students included in the study or the structure of selected independent variables. On the other hand, it is possible to come across findings that are important determinants of Internet addiction regarding the demographics of students such as gender, age, frequency of Internet usage, etc. (Aksoy, 2015; Akdağ et al., 2014, Çakır, Ayas and Horzum, 2011; Üneri and Tanıdır, 2011).

In this study, we have found that loneliness is an important predictor of Internet addiction. The results display that there is a negative relationship between Internet addiction and loneliness. If the Internet addiction increases the loneliness decreases. This result can be explain by the fact that individuals who cannot develop sufficiently enough relationships with the people around them can develop Internet addiction to meet interpersonal needs and create alternative social channels (Papacharissi and Rubin, 2000). Individuals experiencing various obstacles in their social relations, and experience the anxiety of being obstructed, often resort to Internet to regenerate and maintain their personal relationships, and often substitute Internet with face-to-face communication (Inderbiten, Walters and Bukowski, 1997;

Kubey, Lavin and Barrows, 2001). This result shows that the internet is a tool for socializing and thus reducing loneliness among young people. It is possible to discover results both supporting and not supporting this result in the literature. For example, the study conducted by Hasmujaj (2016) have also found negative correlation between loneliness and Internet addiction, on the other hand students addicted to the Internet have significantly lower rates of loneliness. Hamburger and Ben-Artzi (2003) found that Internet addiction did not increase the level of loneliness and that Internet addiction emerged as a result of loneliness. Contrast to these results, there are many studies that the loneliness scores of individuals with pathological Internet use are significantly higher (Young, 1998; Moody, 2001; Bayraktar, 2001; Whang, Lee and Chang, 2003; Nalwa and Anand, 2003; Keser Özcan and Buzlu, 2007; Yellowlees and Marks 2007; Caplan 2007; Ceyhan and Ceyhan, 2008; Erdogan, 2008; Eijnden et al., 2008; Kelleci and İnal, 2010; Batıgün and Hasta, 2010; Gu, 2012). For example, Morahan-Martin and Schumacher (2000) surveyed 277 undergraduate Internet users and found that lonely participants use the Internet for emotional support and are more likely to describe disruption in their lives as consequences of Internet use. Lonely subjects tended to selfdisclose more, share more intimate details, and felt more accepted on the Internet when compared with non-lonely subjects (Morahan-Martin, 1999). Also, in Pawlaks' study (2002) it was stated that high school students who feel high level of loneliness can turn to the Internet to change these feelings, and in this context, the feeling of loneliness can make students become Internet addicts. Many studies which point to meaningful relationships between Internet addiction and the phenomenon of loneliness (Engelberg and Sjoberg, 2004; Kim et al., 2009; Ezoe and Toda, 2013; Ayas and Horzum, 2013; Demirer et al., 2013; Halley et al., 2014) have emphasized the strong influence that loneliness has over Internet addiction on the entire population, regardless of being a child, adolescent, or young adult. This difference between the study results may be aroused by the socio-economic and socio-cultural differences of the sample.

SOLUTIONS AND RECOMMENDATIONS

These findings should be able to shed light on families and experts who are interested in the cause, process, and treatment of Internet addiction. In the frame of these results, field experts and families can help keep children away from Internet addiction by increasing their social support and somehow eliminating youths' sense of loneliness. Also in the context of schools, students can be kept away from Internet addiction by strengthening their social aspects and by allowing them to establish bonds with each other that fulfill them in their social life.

LIMITATIONS

Some limitations of this paper are worth noting. First, given the cross-sectional research design of the study, no causal relationship among the variables can be inferred. Future studies should be designed on longitudinal to obtain further causality relationships among these variables. Second, the present study has some methodological limitations. The study sample included only students from the HU, which limits the generalizability of the results. Data from the different university should be included in future research.

CONCLUSION

In conclusion, this study shows that as individuals' sense of loneliness in everyday life increases, the sense of loneliness they feel in the virtual environment decreases. For those who are either unable to find or cannot develop self-satisfying relationships in social environments, to be able to rid themselves of this negative feeling, they are clearly seen to attempt socializing and sharing in virtual environments. Further, a sense of belonging that has not been met in social environments is provided in virtual environments.

REFERENCES

Akdağ, M., Şahan Yılmaz, B., Özhan, U., & San, I. (2014). Investigation of Internet dependences of university students in terms of variable variations (Inonu University Example). *Inonu University Journal of the Faculty of Education*, *15*(1), 73–96.

Aksoy, V. (2015). The degree of change of Internet addiction and social network use according to the demographic features of science high school students and its effect upon their academic success. *The Journal of Academic Social Science*, *3*(19), 365–383. doi:10.16992/ASOS.874

Ando, R., & Sakamoto, A. (2008). The effect of cyber-friends on loneliness and social anxiety: Differences between high and low self-evaluated physical attractiveness groups. *Computers in Human Behavior*, *24*(3), 993–1009. doi:10.1016/j.chb.2007.03.003

Aral, N., & Gürsoy, F. (2000). Levels of loneliness in young people. [in Turkish]. *Journal of Education and Science*, *25*(116), 8–12.

Ayas, T., & Horzum, M. B. (2013). Relation between depression, loneliness, self-esteem and Internet addiction. *Journal of Education*, *133*(3), 284–290.

Batıgün, A. D., & Hasta, D. (2010). Internet bağımlılığı: Yalnızlık ve kişilerarası ilişki tarzları açısından bir değerlendirme [Internet addiction: An evaluation in terms of loneliness and interpersonal relationship styles]. *Anatolian Journal of Psychiatry*, *11*(3), 213–219.

Bayraktar, F. (2001). *The role of Internet usage in the development of adolescents* (Unpublished master thesis). Ege University, Turkey.

Berson, I., & Berson, M. (2003). Digital literacy for effective citizenship. *Social Education*, *67*(3), 164–167.

Block, J. J. (2008). Issues for DSM-V: Internet addiction. *The American Journal of Psychiatry*, *165*(3), 306–307. doi:10.1176/appi.ajp.2007.07101556 PMID:18316427

Bricolo, F., Gentile, D. A., Smelser, R. L., & Serpelloni, G. (2007). Use of the computer and Internet among Italian families: First national study. *Cyberpsychology & Behavior*, *10*(6), 789–797. doi:10.1089/cpb.2007.9952 PMID:18085966

Büyüköztürk, Ş. (2007). *Sosyal Bilimler için Veri Analizi El Kitabı* [Data Analysis Handbook for Social Science] (7th ed.). Ankara, Turkey: Pegem A Yayıncılık. (in Turkish)

Çakır, O., Ayas, T., & Horum, M. B. (2011). An investigation of university students' Internet and game addiction with respect to several variables. *Ankara University Journal of Faculty of Educational Sciences, 44*(2), 95–117.

Caplan, S. E. (2007). Relations among loneliness, social anxiety, and problematic Internet use. *Cyberpsychology & Behavior, 10*(2), 234–242. doi:10.1089/cpb.2006.9963 PMID:17474841

Ceyhan, A. A. (2008). Predictors of problematic Internet use on Turkish university students. *Cyberpsychology & Behavior, 11*(3), 363–366. doi:10.1089/cpb.2007.0112 PMID:18537510

Ceyhan, A. A. (2011). University students' problematic Internet use and communication skills according to the Internet use purposes. *Educational Sciences: Theory and Practice, 11*(1), 59–77.

Ceyhan, A. A., & Ceyhan, E. (2008). Loneliness, depression and computer self-efficacy as predictors of problematic Internet use. *Cyberpsychology & Behavior, 11*(6), 699–701. doi:10.1089/cpb.2007.0255 PMID:19072150

Cıngı, H. (1994). *Ornekleme Kuramı* [Sampling Theory]. Ankara, Turkey: Hacettepe Üniversitesi Fen Fakültesi Basımevi. (in Turkish)

Cutrona, C. E. (1982). Transition to college: Loneliness and the process of social adjustment. In L. A. Peplau & D. Perlman (Eds.), *Loneliness: A sourcebook of current theory, research, and therapy* (pp. 291–309). New York: John Wiley & Sons.

Dağ, İ. (1991). The validity and reliability study of Rotter's Internal External Locus of Control for university students. [in Turkish]. *The Journal of Psychology, 7*(26), 10–16.

Davis, R. A. (2001). A cognitive-behavioral model of pathological Internet use. *Computers in Human Behavior, 17*(2), 187–195. doi:10.1016/S0747-5632(00)00041-8

Demir, A. (1989). Reliability and validity of the UCLA Loneliness Scale. *The Journal of Psychology, 7*(23), 14–18.

Demirer, V., Bozoglan, B., & Sahin, I. (2013). Pre-service teachers' Internet addiction in terms of gender, Internet access, loneliness, and life satisfaction. *International Journal of Education in Mathematics, Science and Technology, 1*(1), 56–63.

Duy, B. (2003). *The effect of cognitive-behavioral group counseling experience on loneliness and dysfunctional attitudes of university students* (Unpublished Doctoral dissertation). Ankara University, Turkey.

Eijnden, R. J. M., Meerkerk, G. J., Vermulst, A. A., Spijkerman, R., & Engels, C. M. E. (2008). Online communication, compulsive Internet use, and psychosocial well-being among adolescents: A longitudinal study. *Developmental Psychology, 44*(3), 655–665. doi:10.1037/0012-1649.44.3.655 PMID:18473634

Eker, D., & Arkar, H. (1995). Factorial structure, validity, and reliability of the Multidimensional Scale of Perceived Social Support. [in Turkish]. *Journal of Turkish Psychology, 101*(34), 45–55.

Eker, D., Arkar, H., & Yaldız, H. (2001). Factorial structure, validity, and reliability of revised form of the Multidimensional Scale of Perceived Social Support. [in Turkish]. *Journal of Turkish Psychiatry, 12*(1), 17–25.

Engelberg, E., & Sjoberg, L. (2004). Internet use, social skills, and adjustment. *Cyberpsychology & Behavior*, 7(1), 41–47. doi:10.1089/109493104322820101 PMID:15006168

Erdoğan, Y. (2008). Exploring the relationships among Internet usage, Internet attitudes and loneliness of Turkish adolescents. *Cyberpsychology (Brno)*, 2(2), 38–51.

Ezoe, S., & Toda, M. (2013). Relationships of loneliness and mobile phone dependence with Internet addiction in Japanese medical students. *Open Journal of Preventive Medicine*, 3(6), 407–412. doi:10.4236/ojpm.2013.36055

Ferraro, G., Caci, B., D'Amico, A., & Di Blasi, M. (2007). Internet addiction disorder: An Italian study. *Cyberpsychology & Behavior*, 10(2), 170–175. doi:10.1089/cpb.2006.9972 PMID:17474832

Geçtan, E. (1997). *İnsan olmak* [Being human] (18th ed.). İstanbul, Turkey: Remzi Kitabevi.

Gonzalez, N. A. (2002). *Internet addiction disorder and its relation to impulse control* (Unpublished master's thesis). Texas A&M University, Kingsville, TX.

Greenfield, D. N. (2000). Psychological characteristics of compulsive Internet use: A preliminary analysis. *Cyberpsychology & Behavior*, 5, 403–412. PMID:19178212

Griffiths, M. (2000). Does Internet and computer "Addiction" exist? Some case study evidence. *Cyberpsychology & Behavior*, 3(2), 217–218. doi:10.1089/109493100316067

Gu, M. (2012). *Study of adolescents' Internet use and Internet addiction in Shanghai, China: Implications for social work practice* (Unpublished Doctoral dissertation). The Chinese University of Hong Kong, Hong Kong.

Günüç, S. (2009). *Development of Internet Addiction Scale* (Unpublished master's thesis). Yüzüncü Yıl University, Van.

Hall, A. S., & Parsons, J. (2001). Internet addiction: College student case study using best practices in cognitive behavior therapy. *Journal of Mental Health Counseling*, 23(4), 312–327.

Halley, M. P., Mark, D. G., & Ivone, M. P. (2014). Internet addiction and loneliness among children and adolescents in the education setting: An empirical pilot study. *Aloma*, 32(1), 91–98.

Hamburger, A. Y., & Artzi, E. B. (2003). Loneliness and Internet use. *Computers in Human Behavior*, 9(1), 71–80. doi:10.1016/S0747-5632(02)00014-6

Hasmujaj, E. (2016). Internet addiction and loneliness among students of University of Shkodra. *European Scientific Journal*, 12(29), 1857–7881. doi:10.19044/esj.2016.v12n29p397

Hur, M. H. (2006). Demographic, habitual, and socioeconomic determinants of Internet addiction disorder: An empirical study of Korean teenagers. *Cyberpsychology & Behavior*, 9(5), 514–525. doi:10.1089/cpb.2006.9.514 PMID:17034317

Inderbiten, H. M., Walters, K. S., & Bukowski, A. L. (1997). The role of social anxiety in adolescent peer relations: Differences among sociometric status groups and rejected subgroups. *Journal of Clinical Child Psychology*, 26(4), 338–348. doi:10.1207/s15374424jccp2604_2 PMID:9418172

Jeon, J. H. (2005). *The effect of extent of Internet use and social supports for adolescent depression and self-esteem* (Unpublished master's thesis). Yonsei University, Seoul, South Korea.

Kaltiala-Heino, R., Lintonen, T., & Rimpela, A. (2004). Internet addiction: Potentially problematic use of the Internet in a population of 12–18 year-old adolescents. *Addiction Research and Theory, 12*(1), 89–96. doi:10.1080/1606635031000098796

Kandell, J. J. (1998). Internet addiction on campus: The vulnerability of college students. *Cyberpsychology & Behavior, 1*(1), 11–17. doi:10.1089/cpb.1998.1.11

Kelleci, M., Güler, N., Sezer, H., & Gölbaşı, Z. (2009). Lise öğrencilerinde internet kullanma süresinin cinsiyet ve psikiyatrik belirtiler ile ilişkisi [Relationships Gender and Psychiatric Symptoms with Duration of Internet Use among High School Students]. *Turk Silahli Kuvvetleri Koruyucu Hekimlik Bulteni, 8*(3), 223–230.

Kelleci, M., & İnal, S. (2010). Psychiatric symptoms in adolescents with and without Internet use. *Cyberpsychology, Behavior, and Social Networking, 13*(2), 191–194. doi:10.1089/cyber.2009.0026 PMID:20528277

Keser Özcan, N., & Buzlu, S. (2005). Problemli internet kullanımını belirlemede yardımcı bir araç: "İnternette Bilişsel Durum Ölçeği" nin üniversite öğrencilerinde geçerlik ve güvenirliği [An assistive tool in determining problematic Internet use: Validity and reliability of the "Online Cognition Scale" in a sample of university students]. *Bağimlik Dergisi, 6*, 19–26.

Keser Özcan, N., & Buzlu, S. (2007). Internet use and its relation with the psychosocial situation for a sample of university students. *Cyberpsychology & Behavior, 10*(6), 767–772. doi:10.1089/cpb.2007.9953 PMID:18085963

Kesici, Ş., & Şahin, İ. (2009). A comparative study of uses of the Internet among college students with and without Internet addiction. *Psychological Reports, 105*(3_suppl), 1103–1112. doi:10.2466/PR0.105.F.1103-1112 PMID:20229914

Kim, J., Larose, R., & Peng, W. (2009). Loneliness as the cause and the effect of problematic Internet use: The relationship between Internet use and psychological well-being. *Cyberpsychology, Behavior, and Social Networking, 12*(4), 451–455. doi:10.1089/cpb.2008.0327 PMID:19514821

King, S. A. (1996). *Is the Internet addictive or are addicts using the Internet?* Retrieved January 13, 2017, from http://giovanni-2000.tripod.com/mesh/selfaddict.html

Ko, C. H., Yen, J. Y., Chen, C. C., Chen, S. H., & Yen, C. F. (2005). Gender differences and related factors affecting online gaming addiction among Taiwanese adolescents. *The Journal of Nervous and Mental Disease, 193*(4), 273–277. doi:10.1097/01.nmd.0000158373.85150.57 PMID:15805824

Kraut, R., Patterson, M., Lundmark, V., Kiesler, S., Mukopadhyay, T., & Scherlis, W. (1998). Internet paradox: A social technology that reduces social involvement and psychological well-being? *The American Psychologist, 53*(9), 1017–1031. doi:10.1037/0003-066X.53.9.1017 PMID:9841579

Kubey, R. W., Lavin, M. J., & Barrows, J. R. (2001). Internet use and collegiate academic performance decrements: Early findings. *Journal of Communication, 51*(2), 366–382. doi:10.1111/j.1460-2466.2001.tb02885.x

Leung, L. (2004). Net-Generation attributes and seductive properties of the Internet as predictors of online activities and Internet addiction. *Cyberpsychology & Behavior, 7*(3), 333–347. doi:10.1089/1094931041291303 PMID:15257834

McWhirter, B. T. (1990). Loneliness: A review of current literature, with implications for counseling and research. *Journal of Counseling and Development, 68*(4), 417–422. doi:10.1002/j.1556-6676.1990.tb02521.x

Moody, E. J. (2001). Internet use and its relationship to loneliness. *Cyberpsychology & Behavior, 4*(3), 393–401. doi:10.1089/109493101300210303 PMID:11710265

Morahan-Martin, J. (1999). The relationship between loneliness and Internet use and abuse. *Cyberpsychology & Behavior, 2*(5), 431–440. doi:10.1089/cpb.1999.2.431 PMID:19178216

Morahan-Martin, J., & Schumacher, P. (2000). Incidence and correlates of pathological Internet use among college students. *Computers in Human Behavior, 16*(1), 13–29. doi:10.1016/S0747-5632(99)00049-7

Morahan-Martin, J., & Schumacher, P. (2003). Loneliness and social uses of the Internet. *Computers in Human Behavior, 19*(6), 659–671. doi:10.1016/S0747-5632(03)00040-2

Nalwa, K., & Anand, A. P. (2003). Internet addiction in students: A cause of concern. *Cyberpsychology & Behavior, 6*(6), 653–656. doi:10.1089/109493103322725441 PMID:14756932

Öz, F. (2010). *Sağlık alanında temel kavramlar* [Basic concept in healthcare field] (2nd ed.). Ankara, Turkey: Mattek Yayınları. (in Turkish)

Papacharissi, Z., & Rubin, A. M. (2000). Predictors of Internet use. *Journal of Broadcasting & Electronic Media, 44*(2), 175–196. doi:10.1207/s15506878jobem4402_2

Pawlak, C. (2002). Correlates of Internet use and addiction in adolescents. *Dissertation Abstracts International. A, The Humanities and Social Sciences, 63*(5-A), 1727.

Peplau, L. A., & Perlman, D. (1979). *Blueprint for a social psychological theory of loneliness. Love and Attraction.* Oxford, UK: Pergman.

Russell, D., Peplau, L. A., & Cutrona, C. E. (1980). The revised UCLA Loneliness Scale: Concurrent and discriminant validity evidence. *Journal of Personality and Social Psychology, 39*(3), 472–480. doi:10.1037/0022-3514.39.3.472 PMID:7431205

Selian, A. N. (2004). *Mobile phones and youth: A look at the US student market.* Retrieved January 13, 2017, from http://www.itu.int/osg/spu/ni/futuremobile/Youth.pdf

Shapira, N. A., Goldsmith, T. D., Keck, P. E. Jr, Khosla, U. M., & McElroy, S. L. (2000). Psychiatric features of individuals with problematic Internet use. *Journal of Affective Disorders, 57*(1-3), 267–272. doi:10.1016/S0165-0327(99)00107-X PMID:10708842

Shaver, P., Furman, W., & Buhrmester, D. (1985). Transition to college: Network changes, social skills, and loneliness. In S. Duck & D. Perlman (Eds.), *Understanding personal relationships: An interdisciplinary approach* (pp. 193–220). London: Sage Publications.

Sukunesan, S. (1999). *Internet addiction: An exploratory study amongst Malaysian Internet user* (Master's thesis). University Putra, Malaysia.

Sum, S., Mathews, R. M., Hughes, I., & Campbell, A. (2008). Internet use and loneliness in older adults. *Cyberpsychology & Behavior, 11*(2), 208–211. doi:10.1089/cpb.2007.0010 PMID:18422415

Turkish Statistical Institute (TSI). (2016). *Information and communication technology usage survey in households*. Retrieved January 13, 2017, from http://www.tuik.gov.tr

Üneri, O. S., & Tanıdır, C. (2011). Bir grup lise öğrencisinde internet bağımlılığı değerlendirmesi: Kesitsel bir çalışma [Evaluation of Internet addiction in a group of high school students: a cross-sectional study]. *Dusunen Adam The Journal of Psychiatry and Neurological Sciences, 24*(4), 265–272.

Wang, W. (2001). Internet dependency and psychosocial maturity among college students. *Human-Computer Studies, 55*(6), 919–938. doi:10.1006/ijhc.2001.0510

Weiss, R. S. (1973). *Loneliness: The experience of emotional and social isolation*. Cambridge, MA: MIT Press.

Whang, L. S. M., Lee, S., & Chang, G. (2003). Internet over-users' psychological profiles: A behavior sampling analysis on Internet addiction. *Cyberpsychology & Behavior, 6*(2), 143–150. doi:10.1089/109493103321640338 PMID:12804026

Yang, C. K., Choe, B. M., Baity, M., Lee, J.-H., & Cho, J.-S. (2005). SCL-90-R and 16PF profiles of senior high school students with excessive Internet use. *Canadian Journal of Psychiatry, 50*(7), 407–414. doi:10.1177/070674370505000704 PMID:16086538

Yang, S. C., & Tung, C. J. (2007). Comparison of Internet addicts and non-addicts in Taiwanese high school. *Computers in Human Behavior, 23*(1), 79–96. doi:10.1016/j.chb.2004.03.037

Yaparel, R. (1984). *The relationship between perceptions of success and failure in social relations and loneliness* (Unpublished master's thesis). Hacettepe University, Ankara, Turkey.

Yellowlees, P. M., & Marks, S. (2007). Problematic Internet use or Internet addiction? *Computers in Human Behavior, 23*(3), 1447–1453. doi:10.1016/j.chb.2005.05.004

You, H. S. (2007). *The effect of Internet addiction on elementary school student's self-esteem and depression* (Unpublished master's thesis). Kongju University, Chungnam.

Young, J. E. (1982). Loneliness, depression and cognitive therapy. In L. A. Peplau & D. Perlman (Eds.), *Loneliness: A sourcebook of current theory, research, and therapy* (pp. 379–406). New York: Wiley.

Young, K. S. (1998). *Caught in the net. How to recognize signs of Internet addiction and a winning strategy for recovery*. Wiley.

Young, K. S. (1999). *Internet addiction: Symptoms, evaluation and treatment*. Retrieved January 14, 2017, from http://netaddiction.com/articles/symptoms.pdf

Young, K. S. (2004). Internet addiction. *The American Behavioral Scientist, 48*(4), 402–441. doi:10.1177/0002764204270278

Young, K. S., & Case, C. J. (2004). Internet abuse in the workplace: New trends in risk management. *Cyberpsychology & Behavior, 7*(1), 105–111. doi:10.1089/109493104322820174 PMID:15006175

Young, K. S., & Rodgers, R. (1998). The relationship between depression and Internet addiction. *Cyberpsychology & Behavior, 1*(1), 25–28. doi:10.1089/cpb.1998.1.25

Young, K. S., & Rodgers, R. C. (1998, April). *Internet addiction: personality traits associated with its development.* Paper presented at the 69th annual meeting of the Eastern Psychological Association, Boston, MA.

KEY TERMS AND DEFINITIONS

Addiction: An irrepressible desire to an object, person, or an entity.

Excessive Internet Use: Loss of control of Internet usage, excessive usage.

Internet Addiction: Being unable to prevent the use of the Internet, making the Internet indispensable for life.

Internet: A constantly growing network.

Lone Individual: An individual who can not feel himself or herself belonging to a group, whose social relationships and perceived social support are low.

Loneliness: Inability to share, feel a sense of emptiness.

University Student: A person who is studying at a higher education institution.

Section 3
Social Aspects of Internet Addiction

This section covers social aspects of internet addiction.

Chapter 7
Socioeconomic Determinants of Internet Addiction in Adolescents:
A Scoping Review

Francisco Tsz Tsun Lai
The Chinese University of Hong Kong, China

Joyce Lok Yin Kwan
The Education University of Hong Kong, China

ABSTRACT

From a social epidemiological perspective, this chapter presents a new approach to conceptualizing the socioeconomic determinants of Internet Addiction (IA) in adolescents, followed by a rapid scoping review of the empirical research literature on the same topic which aims to provide an overview of the current body of knowledge. With a strict adherence to the established procedures, fifteen original research articles were retrieved for review and analysis. A wide range of socioeconomic risk factors was identified. The theoretical pathways of socioeconomic determinants suggested in the included studies were also tabulated and discussed. Finally, the chapter closes with several recommendations for future research on the potential socioeconomic determinants of IA based on the retrieved findings.

INTRODUCTION

Although researchers and psychiatrists are still in debates whether Internet Addiction (IA) should be treated as a psychiatric disorder (Pies, 2009), IA has been consistently found to be associated with numerous other mental conditions, such as anxiety disorder, alcohol dependence, and depression (Ko, Yen, Yen, Chen, & Chen, 2012). The conceptualization of IA incorporates a wide range of events associated with disturbances, or even harm, to normal life, for example, significant loss of productivity, mood modifications, and psychological conflicts (C. M. Lai et al., 2013). It is much less controversial, therefore, that IA is detrimental to adolescents' health and should thus be prevented. There also seems

DOI: 10.4018/978-1-5225-3477-8.ch007

to be little doubt that IA is mainly a problem of the youths judging from the clear majority of the current research that focuses on IA in children, adolescents, and young adults (Kuss & Lopez-Fernandez, 2016).

The identification of socioeconomic determinants of IA facilitates prevention in at least three ways. First, it extends our understanding of the shaping of IA towards one of the more upstream environmental antecedents of the causal path diagram of IA, i.e. socioeconomic background. Second, it connects socioeconomic status and intermediary determinants of IA to achieve a fuller explanation, such as peers relationships, self-esteem, and academic performance (F. T. T. Lai & Kwan, 2017b; Stavropoulos, Alexandraki, & Motti-Stefanidi, 2013; Yao, He, Ko, & Pang, 2013). Third, it helps better locate the adolescents who need additional assistance in managing their own Internet use in society. Nevertheless, unlike the various psychiatric disorders that IA is associated with (Green, Leyland, Sweeting, & Benzeval, 2016; Swartz, Hariri, & Williamson, 2017; Torikka, Kaltiala-Heino, Luukkaala, & Rimpelä, 2017), research on the socioeconomic determinants of IA in adolescents is relatively scarce despite the rapid growth of the size of the literature on IA (F. T. T. Lai & Kwan, 2017a). This scarcity possibly reflects the view that socioeconomic factors may not be of equal importance than other domains of determinants. One of the major reasons for such a view may be the fact that the prerequisite of IA is the adolescents' frequent access to the Internet through personal computers or other electronic devices, which may, to a certain extent, already suggests the absence of materialistic deprivation. This view is probably misguided. In many advanced societies in the world, the possession of devices with Internet access is not strongly associated with an upper socioeconomic position. For instance, income inequality in Hong Kong is one of the severest in the world, with the Gini coefficient estimated to be 0.540 in 2016 (Hong Kong Census and Statistics Department, 2017). However, the penetration rate of the Internet was estimated to be as high as 79.0% in the overall residential population, and 99.6% among citizens aged 10-24 years (Hong Kong Census and Statistics Department, 2016). This implies that regardless of socioeconomic status, most, especially young, citizens have access to the Internet in those societies. Moreover, even if the possession of devices with Internet access indicates the absence of deprivation, there may still be significant socioeconomic inequalities within those who possess those devices since socioeconomic status is essentially a relative concept (Kawachi, Subramanian, & Almeida-Filho, 2002). These inequalities may affect the vulnerability of adolescents to uncontrolled Internet use and IA through dictating the differing life exposures in similar ways they exert influence on other 'behavioral addictions' (Welte, Barnes, Tidwell, & Wieczorek, 2017).

This chapter aims to provide an overview of the current empirical research on the socioeconomic determinants of IA in adolescents through conducting a scoping review. It starts with a Background section which introduces the conceptualization of socioeconomic determinants of IA, discusses the previous efforts of synthesizing research findings on the topic, and accordingly derives the research questions to be addressed in the review. Subsequently, the methods of the literature search and screening are presented, followed by the description and interpretation of the retrieved findings. Based on these findings, the chapter closes with several recommendations on the relationship between socioeconomic status and IA in adolescents for future researchers. The overview of the literature generated from the scoping review presented in this chapter should hopefully facilitate further in-depth appraisal of the current research evidence and pave the way for more focused empirical research on the topic in the future.

BACKGROUND

Past and recent reviews of the literature on different topics regarding IA have consistently suggested the potential importance of the effects of socioeconomic factors. For instance, in a comprehensive systematic review of epidemiological research from 2001 to 2013 by Kuss, Griffiths, Karila, and Billieux (2013), a higher family income was identified as a likely risk factor of IA. More recently, Vondráčková and Gabrhelík (2016) conducted a systematic review of the scientific literature on IA prevention and classified socioeconomic factors such as family economic disadvantages as one of the six important domains of the biopsychosocial factors related to an elevated risk of IA. In another review article by Kayiş and colleagues (2016), the relationship between personality traits and IA was examined. Based on their findings, the authors recognized and recommended the potential moderating role of socioeconomic status as a future research direction. Although these research syntheses were not intended to directly answer research questions on the relationship between socioeconomic factors and IA, they all consistently reflect the possibly important role socioeconomic determinants may play in the shaping of IA as an upstream antecedent, or as a moderator between intermediary determinants and IA.

Conceptualizing Socioeconomic Determinants of IA

This chapter defines IA as *the psychological harm and disturbances to life caused by uncontrolled excessive access to the Internet* (F. T. T. Lai & Kwan, 2017a) and adheres to the American Psychological Association's definition of socioeconomic status: *the social standing or class of an individual or group which is often measured as a combination of education, income and occupation* (Destin, Rheinschmidt-Same, & Richeson, 2017). To understand why socioeconomic factors are important in determining IA, it is essential to discuss the possible paths through which socioeconomic factors may exert an effect. Social epidemiologists conceptualized a total of four pathways to explain the relationship between socioeconomic positions and health of individuals, namely Material, Psychosocial, Behavioral, and Biomedical Pathways (Skalická, van Lenthe, Bambra, Krokstad, & Mackenbach, 2009). Material Pathway focuses on the material conditions a higher socioeconomic status enables, such as a more comfortable living and working environment, access to goods and services that facilitate overall health condition, and less exposure to various risk factors that may cause diseases. Behavioral Pathway emphasizes the different health-related behaviors in different socioeconomic strata. While some unhealthy behaviors, such as smoking, are culturally acceptable among people with lower socioeconomic status, they are not accepted among those with higher socioeconomic status. Psychosocial Pathway represents the people's feelings under social inequality and how these feelings affect health. Specifically, a person with lower socioeconomic status may receive less social support, higher work demand, and a lower level of control. Biomedical Pathway is more downstream than the others and focuses on the unequal distribution of biological risk factors across socioeconomic strata because of behavioral and psychosocial differences. Figure 1 shows a graphical representation of this chapter's conceptualization of socioeconomic determinants of IA. Solid lines represent conventional social epidemiological theoretical pathways and dotted lines represent the hypothetical relationships between pathways as conceptualized in this chapter. While conventional social epidemiological theories described four different pathways as working in four different ways (solid lines), this chapter further conceptualized them as interconnected in the context of IA (dotted lines).

Figure 1. Conceptualization of socioeconomic determinants of internet addiction

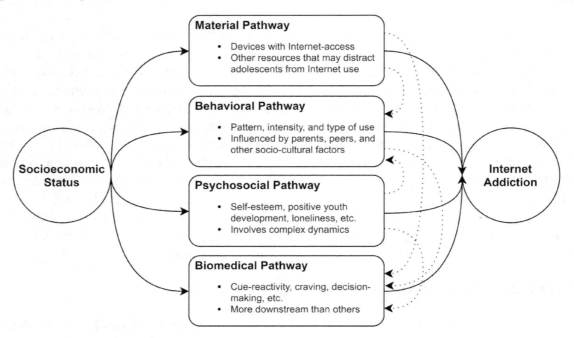

Material Pathway

In social epidemiological theory, material deprivation is generally associated with worse health outcomes. However, the effects of material deprivation on IA is slightly trickier. Is a positive association between material deprivation and IA really a plausible hypothesis? Should the absence of material deprivation not heighten the risk of IA because the person may have better access to the Internet and may have a better experience surfing the Internet because of better equipment and more advanced software? While there is indeed such a possibility, a better access to other goods and services such as better sports facilities and more convenient transportation for outdoor activities may also distract adolescents from excessive Internet use and hence reduce the psychological harm. It is, therefore, worth investigating in research studies whether material deprivation due to a lower socioeconomic status increases or decreases the risk of IA in adolescents. In addition to conventional measurements of socioeconomic status, data on the access to a variety of goods and services are required to answer this question.

Behavioral Pathway

The behavioral basis of IA is the excessive use of the Internet. Therefore, it is obvious that the amount, pattern, and manner of adolescents' Internet use represent the Behavioral Pathway between socioeconomic factors and IA. Like the Material Pathway, it is theoretically uncertain how a higher socioeconomic background may affect these behavioral dimensions of Internet use. On one hand, parents of higher socioeconomic status are probably better educated and may have a better control of their children's behaviors that could prevent overuse of the Internet. On the other hand, the better technological literacy of parents of higher socioeconomic status may be inherited by the adolescents and may be conducive to a better enjoyment of their use of the Internet, which may induce a significant increase in the amount of use and pave the way for IA. This behavioral basis of IA may also vary by different environmental factors that are related to socioeconomic factors, such as school environment, peer factors, and other socio-cultural contexts.

Psychosocial Pathway

The Psychosocial Pathway between socioeconomic status and IA is probably the most researched pathway among the four. Examples of previously examined factors include self-esteem (Bozoglan, Demirer, & Sahin, 2013), stress (Lam, Peng, Mai, & Jing, 2009), positive youth development (Shek & Yu, 2016), etc. As previous studies identified, these psychosocial variables are highly correlated with socioeconomic status (Kroenke, 2008; Twenge & Campbell, 2002). How these various psychosocial variables act as an intermediary determinant of IA that translate the influence of socioeconomic factors is a very complex question which incorporates numerous sub-questions. What psychosocial variables are relevant? How do they vary by socioeconomic status? How are they related to one another? How do they independently affect IA? How do they interact with one another in determining IA? While some of these questions have been addressed in existing research, there seems to be little attention on the role of these variables as mediators between socioeconomic background and IA.

Biomedical Pathway

Although IA is widely considered a mental condition, recent research has started to pay more attention to the biological/neurological aspects of IA. For example, in Brand, Young, and Laier's (2014) review, it was identified that findings from neuroimaging and other neuropsychological research illustrated that cue-reactivity, craving, and decision-making are important factors of Internet addiction. Nevertheless, there is extremely scarce evidence on the association between these neurological factors and socioeconomic background. It is also theoretically implausible that a different socioeconomic position can have a direct effect on these factors. Hence, as social epidemiologists conceptualize in their models of overall health status, the Biomedical Pathway may only represent the more downstream factors of IA: neurological factors may be affected by psychosocial or behavioral factors rather than directly by socioeconomic background.

Previous Research on Socioeconomic Determinants of IA

It is commonly recognized that the concept of IA was coined by Dr. Kimberly Young in the late 1990s (Young, 1998). Since then, research on IA has been rapidly expanding for almost 20 years. The field has now grown to be highly interdisciplinary, gathering researchers from psychiatry, psychology, epidemiology, communication, education, neurobiology, etc. In more recent years, numerous research syntheses have been conducted to evaluate the existing literature in various aspects, with part of those focusing on the risk factors of IA. In spite of the absence of a specialized review specifically conducted on socioeconomic determinants of IA, some of those reviews have already covered some of the socioeconomic factors that are potential determinants of IA.

For example, Kuss, Griffiths, Karila, and Billieux (2013) identified quite a number of factors in the literature of the past decade (2001-2013) as socioeconomic factors associated with IA. High family income, migrant status, and living in rural areas were among the socio-demographic factors of IA. However, since these factors were not identified in the same studies and multivariate adjustments may not have been properly made, these findings hardly send a clear message of whether a better socioeconomic background is associated with a higher /lower risk of IA. The authors of the review also noted that the included research did not account for the socio-cultural differences across populations and may thus be restricted in terms of generalizability. Lam's (2014) review had similar aims as Kuss et al.'s but was only focused on longitudinal studies. Among the risk factors identified by the eight retrieved studies, not living with one's mother, poor Internet-specific parenting practices, and parent conflicts were associated with IA. While these factors are not conventional socioeconomic factors, they have been consistently found associated with the socioeconomic background of the family (Conger, Conger, & Martin, 2010). In addition to these, Li, Garland, and Howard (2014) conducted a systematic review with a special focus on family factors of IA. Results on family socioeconomic status and IA were mixed. While some studies suggested a negative association, some reported none or even a positive association. Nevertheless, in general, a poorer family environment seems to be a risk factor of IA in children and adolescents.

Despite the insights generated from these studies, research on socioeconomic determinants of IA remains limited in several aspects. First, there is very little research specifically focused on socioeconomic determinants. In most cases, they were included only as a multivariate adjustment. Hence, potential confounders were not properly controlled, and interpretations were insufficiently discussed in the texts. Second, there is no guiding framework for the selection of variables and measurement. Without a hypothetical framework, it is difficult to organize a wide range of variables into statistical models. Also, a useful framework can effectively inform proper adjustment for confounders in the analyses. Third, there is little attention on the mediating role of intermediary variables between socioeconomic factors and IA. This is actually another consequence of the absence of a conceptual framework for the studies. Without a framework, it is hard to justify selecting variables arbitrarily for any mediation analyses. Fourth, the previous literature reviews did not apply specialized search strategies to exhaustively retrieve all relevant data for a good synthesis. There may be studies that consist of important information omitted during the search procedures only because the search strategy is not specialized for socioeconomic factors. All these inadequacies of the literature have restricted the understanding of the entirety of the mechanism by which IA is shaped, from upstream socioeconomic variables to mediators and to Internet use and IA.

Research Questions

The motivation of this scoping review of the literature on socioeconomic determinants of IA is to provide a clearer picture of the current knowledge on the topic for future researchers' reference. This review strives to correspond to the inadequacies of the literature as discussed above to better achieve this aim. Specifically, the research findings were evaluated based on the conceptualization of socioeconomic determinants as described earlier, and a specialized literature search strategy was adopted to retrieve all relevant data. The discussion of the findings will be more focused on the hypothesized pathways in accordance with the previously described conceptualization of the socioeconomic determinants of IA. Based on the findings, recommendations will also be made to facilitate future research. The following research questions can be answered in this review:

Question 1: What specific socioeconomic factors have been identified as associated with IA?
Question 2: How do these socioeconomic factors affect the risk of IA (though what pathways)?
Question 3: What are the research designs and methods of the studies on this topic?

METHOD

Literature Search and Screening

This chapter adheres to the framework of scoping reviews proposed by Arksey and O'Malley (2005). The study population of the review is young people aged 11-24 years. The inclusion criteria of the search and screening were i. quantitative study design, ii. measurement of IA with established tools, iii. including socioeconomic variables as exposure/independent variables, iv. including IA or degree of IA as the study outcome, v. having undergone the peer-review process. Socioeconomic variables were operationalized as any attributes one possessed that could directly indicate the social standing of that person. Non-English articles, non-empirical studies, qualitative studies, graduate dissertations, unpublished works, studies with a sample of patients with a particular disease, and studies on gaming addiction or problem gaming were excluded from this review. Publication date was limited within the range 2000-2017.

The search keywords adopted in this review are tabulated in Table 1. The same search strategy was applied to electronic databases PsycINFO, ERIC, Social Science Citation Index (SSCI), and MEDLINE to yield an exhaustive search result (Updated date of search: early August 2017). In addition, the gray literature was searched using web search engine Google. Finally, the bibliographies of the retrieved documents were also checked to identify any potentially relevant works.

All the documents retrieved from the described procedures were then screened by their title and abstract. After deleting irrelevant documents, the full texts were examined to make a judgement on the relevance of the remaining documents. Basic information and key findings of the eventually included studies were extracted and tabulated for a clearer presentation of data. Specifically, the identified socio-economic risk factors and suggested pathways of socioeconomic determinants were tabulated. No critical appraisal was conducted partly because of the heterogeneous methodologies adopted in the studies and partly because it goes beyond the aims of this review.

Table 1. Search keywords

Concept	Search Field	Keywords
Internet addiction	Title	'Internet addiction' OR 'problematic Internet use' OR 'pathological Internet use' OR 'addictive Internet use' OR 'excessive Internet use'
Socioeconomic background	Title/abstract	'Income' OR 'education level' OR 'educational attainment' OR 'socioeconomic' OR 'social status' OR 'deprivation' OR 'poverty' OR 'occupation'
Adolescents	Title/abstract	'adolescents' OR 'youth' OR 'young people' OR 'students' OR 'teenagers'

FINDINGS

Search Results

There were 154 initially yielded documents, of which 65 duplicates were removed. The screening by title and abstract eliminated 67 documents, and the full texts of the remaining 22 were examined with 15 of them finally included in the review. Most of the discarded studies during the screening process were removed due to the absence of a socioeconomic exposure variable. The gray literature search and bibliography check did not yield any relevant documents. Figure 2 shows the graphical illustration of the study selection procedures. The number of articles retrieved in the initial search, during the screening processes, and final results were reported in the corresponding boxes in the Figure connected with arrows indicating the sequence of the procedures. Reasons for discarding studies in the screening procedures were also clearly listed. For instance, during the full text screening, only one study was discarded because it did not use IA as the study outcome and six were removed because no socioeconomic exposure variables were included.

Figure 2. Literature search procedures

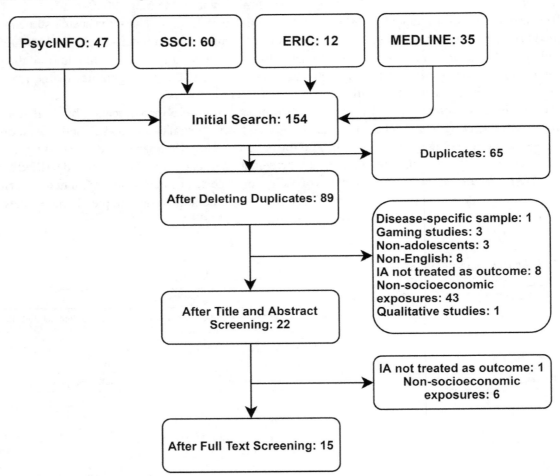

Study Characteristics

Table 2 shows the basic information of each of the 15 included studies. Sample size ranged from 375 to 73,238, implying reasonably strong statistical power. All these studies adopted a cross-sectional design whereby questionnaires were collected from school children and teenagers. Surprisingly, the 15 included studies were conducted in only six territories: four from China, three from Hong Kong, two from Korea, two from Turkey, two from Iran, and one from Jordan.

Study Findings

Table 3 shows the extracted key findings of the retrieved 15 studies. It is worth attention that the direction of the effect of socioeconomic status was not at all clear. In fact, while some studies suggested a higher socioeconomic status, indicated by some factors such as higher income, may be protective of IA, some other studies suggested otherwise. There are even contrasting results from the same studies, in which some indicators suggested a positive effect of socioeconomic status while some simultaneously suggested the opposite. The most commonly adopted socioeconomic indicators were income, parental education, and overall socioeconomic status scores. The Young's Internet Addiction Test (20 items) was found to be the most widely used questionnaire to measure IA. Regarding the mechanism by which socioeconomic status exerts influence on IA status, some of the retrieved studies have provided explanations that could actually be categorized under the conceptualization of socioeconomic determinants of IA as described earlier. The most commonly seen explanations could be classified as Material and Psychosocial Pathways, followed by Behavioral Pathway.

Table 2. Study characteristics

First Author (Year)	Sample	Study Design	Country
Ahmadi (2013)	4,342 high school or pre-college students (mean age=16.6)	Cross-sectional survey	Iran
Ahmadi (2014)	4,177 high school students aged 14-19	Cross-sectional survey	Iran
Ak (2013)	4,311 high school students (9th-12th grade)	Cross-sectional survey	Turkey
Demirer (2016)	375 high school students	Cross-sectional survey	Turkey
Heo (2014)	57,857 middle and high school students (13-18 years old)	Cross-sectional survey	Korea
Lai (2017a)	744 junior secondary school students (7th-10th grade)	Cross-sectional survey	Hong Kong
Lee (2015)	73,238 middle and high school students (mean age=15.10)	Web-based survey	Korea
Leung (2012)	718 children and adolescents aged 9-19	Cross-sectional survey	Hong Kong
Li (2013)	2,758 middle school adolescents (mean age=13.53)	Cross-sectional survey	China
Malak (2017)	716 school students (12-18 years old)	Cross-sectional survey	Jordan
Mei (2016)	1,552 adolescents with mean age=15.43	Cross-sectional survey	China
Seyrek (2017)	468 students aged 12-17	Cross-sectional survey	Turkey
Wu (2016)	2,021 secondary school students aged 12-18	Cross-sectional survey	Hong Kong
Xu (2014)	5,122 high school students (mean age=15.9)	Cross-sectional survey	China
Zhang (2015)	660 middle school students (7th-8th grade)	Cross-sectional survey	China

Table 3. Study findings

First Author (Year)	Socioeconomic Exposure	Confounder Control	Socioeconomic Risk Factors	IA Measurement	Suggested Pathways
Ahmadi (2013)	Parental education, family wealth	None	• Better educated parents • Smaller family wealth	Young's Internet Addiction Test (20 items)	None
Ahmadi (2014)	Financial status, mother's employment status	Family relationship, religious devotion	• Very good or very bad financial status • Mother with a job	Young's Internet Addiction Test (20 items)	Psychosocial and Behavioral
Ak (2013)	Family income, computer ownership, private room	Internet connection	• Higher income • Owning computer • Having private room	Young's Internet Addiction Test (20 items)	Material
Demirer (2016)	Family income	Purpose and intensity of Internet use, Grade Point Average	• Higher family income	Problematic Internet Use Scale	Material
Heo (2014)	Parental education	Substance abuse, exercise, school factors, psychiatric symptoms	• Poorer parental education level • Smaller family affluence	Korean Internet Addiction Self-Assessment Tool	Psychosocial and Behavioral
Lai (2017a)	Family income, parental education, housing type	School-related psychosocial variables, pattern of Internet use	• Higher family income • Better educated father • Less-educated mother	Young's Internet Addiction Test (20 items)	Material, Psychosocial, and Behavioral
Lee (2015)	Perceived socioeconomic status	Depression, suicidal ideation, academic performance, type of residence, school type, familial affluence score	• Lower socioeconomic status	Korean Internet Addiction Proneness Scale	None
Leung (2012)	Household income	Internet literacy, education, Internet use patterns	• Lower household income	Young's Internet Addiction Test (20 items)	None
Li (2013)	Family socioeconomic status	Deviant peer affiliation, school connectedness, parental attachment	None	Young's questionnaire (10 items)	None
Malak (2017)	Family income, parental education level	None	• Higher family income • Better educated father	Young's Internet Addiction Test (20 items)	Material
Mei (2016)	Parents' marital status, living expenses, family income	Personality traits, self-esteem, school level (grade)	• Single parent • Higher living expenses • Lower family income	Young's Diagnostic Questionnaire for IA	None
Seyrek (2017)	Family socioeconomic status	None	None	Young's questionnaire (10 items)	None
Wu (2016)	Parents' marital status, family income	Online friendship, relationship with parents, parenting style, family functioning	• Divorced parents • Lower family income	Young's Internet Addiction Test (20 items)	Material and Psychosocial
Xu (2014)	Family socioeconomic status, allowance, parents' marital status	Parents' attitude towards Internet use, family relationships	• Married but separated parents • Higher allowance	DRM-52 scale	Material and Psychosocial
Zhang (2015)	Family socioeconomic status	Parenting style, personality traits	• Higher family socioeconomic status	Young's questionnaire (10 items)	None

The comparison between these studies suggests that the conceptualized pathways of socioeconomic determinants of IA may be highly contextual. For instance, both Xu et al.(Xu et al., 2014) and Wu et al. (Wu et al., 2016) included a monetary indicator (income and expenses) and parental marital status as socioeconomic exposure variables with their explanations both categorized as Material and Psychosocial Pathways, but the specific interpretation were quite different. While Wu et al. (2016) explained the Material Pathway in the sense that lower-income families could afford fewer alternatives to Internet entertainments in Hong Kong, Xu et al. (2014) speculated that higher-income families in China could afford more advanced Internet-access devices and accessories such that Internet surfing was more fun and attractive so that the risk of IA increased. Hence, in different populations, different cultures, and even different time periods, the effects of socioeconomic determinants may vary.

DISCUSSION OF FINDINGS

The 15 retrieved studies represent the status quo of the current research on the potential socioeconomic determinants of IA. Although only a few of them made socioeconomic factors the primary exposure variables in the analyses (F. T. T. Lai & Kwan, 2017a; Lee & McKenzie, 2015), most of them provide a reasonable interpretation of the identified relationship between socioeconomic factors and IA. The examination and analysis of these studies answered the three research questions of this scoping review discussed earlier. First, as shown in the fourth column of Table 3, all identified socioeconomic risk factors were listed for and to prompt further research. Second, the Pathways of socioeconomic determ suggested in these studies were also tabulated in Table 3 (column six). ted a cross-sectional design. Nonetheless, the findings of this review ons of interest.

** ries Investigated**
** nts of IA?**

 of IA research in general has been slightly different than the more of a concentration of research in the Western populations, a huge from Asia (Kuss & Lopez-Fernandez, 2016). Therefore, it is no from Asian countries. However, the fact that there were only six s included both high-income and relatively low-income countries untries not conduct research on the socioeconomic determinants cioeconomic gradient in the six countries may be steeper than ention. For example, Hong Kong's Gini coefficient, an indicator , was ne of the highest in world. In China, the income inequality between al and rural populations has also been significant (Lui, 2016). This kind of social inequality can arouse the concern over the associated potential negative impacts on health status (Chung et al., 2015), including IA in adolescents. Although there is quite an abundance of research on IA from European populations (Durkee et al., 2012), it is possible that little research on socioeconomic determinants of IA was conducted because of a relatively more equal society given the better developed wealth redistribution policies, i.e. taxation and social welfare. Even high-income economies such as Korea and Hong Kong had much fewer similar policies to reduce the income gap. This may be the reason why there are no European studies, but 15 Asian studies, retrieved in this review.

Why Do the Retrieved Studies Point to Different Directions?

Table 3 clearly shows the identified socioeconomic risk factors of IA from the retrieved studies. However, the results seemed mixed regarding whether a higher socioeconomic status was associated with a lower risk of IA. Particularly, among the six studies which measured family income, three suggested higher income as a risk factor (Ak et al., 2013; Demirer & Bozoglan, 2016; F. T. T. Lai & Kwan, 2017a), while the other three suggested it as a protective factor (Leung & Lee, 2012; Mei et al., 2016; Wu et al., 2016). Among those measuring overall family socioeconomic status, Lee and McKenzie (2015) reported a negative association between socioeconomic status and the risk of IA, while D. Li et al. (2013) reported no significant association, and Zhang et al. (2015) reported a positive association. The only consistent result was that non-married status of the parents was identified as associated with the risk of IA (Mei et al., 2016; Wu et al., 2016; Xu et al., 2014). The inconsistency of socioeconomic influence across studies is not surprising because the socioeconomic factors are, causally speaking, more 'remote' antecedents that may only exert effects through intermediary factors. In fact, these mediations of socioeconomic effects are highly contextual and could be moderated by culture, environment, and behavioral factors, which could be very different across studies. The reason for the consistency of the results on non-married parents is, therefore, the more direct influence on psychosocial and behavioral variables, such as the reduced time spent monitoring the adolescents' behavior.

How Well Do the Interpretations in These Studies Fit With Our Conceptualization?

Although the conceptualization of socioeconomic determinants of IA is a newly introduced approach, it encompasses a wide range of mechanisms through which socioeconomic influence can be mediated. In fact, all explanations of the association between socioeconomic factors and IA identified in the 15 retrieved studies could be categorized under this conceptualization, i.e. one of the four pathways. For instance, Wu et al. (2016) explained the association between low family income and the risk of IA as due to the material deprivation and the lack of alternative entertainments for the adolescents. Thus, Internet use might become the only way to kill time and that increases the risk of IA. This could obviously be classified as one representation of the Material Pathway (see Figure 1). However, in the absence of an explicit adherence to the framework, the included studies did not compare possible pathways and derive the relative importance of each of them.

Why Did All the Included Studies Adopt a Cross-sectional Design?

The vast majority of IA research adopts a cross-sectional design. The same applies to the research on the socioeconomic determinants of IA as shown in the retrieved studies. Generally speaking, cross-sectional research design is probably the least costly and most convenient way of collecting information from adolescents. With the abundance of validated self-report measurement scales, it is in fact much less costly for researchers to ask preliminary research questions and conduct pilot studies. Nevertheless, there is one additional reason for research on socioeconomic determinants of IA to adopt a cross-sectional design. It is the fact that socioeconomic factors seldom change significantly within the same individual over time. Specifically, socioeconomic status probably precedes IA in terms of temporality. Hence, there is no need to recruit a cohort for longitudinal analysis to establish temporality between variables. There are actually also longitudinal studies discarded during the search and screening procedures. However, socioeconomic factors were not of the researchers' interest and were therefore not included (Lau, Gross, Wu, Cheng, & Lau, 2017; Yu & Shek, 2013).

Limitations of the Literature

Based on the review of the included studies, there seemed to be several limitations in the existing literature of the socioeconomic determinants of IA. First, as discussed earlier, the results of the socioeconomic influence on IA were mixed. Although it is expected since the socioeconomic factors might exert influence through a series of mediators which might be moderated by many factors, it is important that the mediators and moderators of the entire mechanism of the shaping of IA be captured in the statistical models in accordance to a comprehensive conceptual framework like the one discussed in this chapter. With these factors modelled in the analyses, results from different studies should show a higher level of consistency. For example, if researchers hypothesize that a higher socioeconomic status might elevate the risk of IA because of more advanced Internet-access devices and accessories, i.e. Material Pathway, the mediators, such as the possession of better devices, should also be measured and modelled in the analyses. Second, although cross-sectional design is well justified by the relatively low cost, administrative convenience, and the fact that socioeconomic factors precedes IA in terms of temporality, it is uncertain whether the mediators between socioeconomic factors and IA precede or follow IA in terms of temporal sequence. In more developed research designs, the temporal sequence between the exposure, the mediator, and the outcome must be well established to make sound inferences from the analyses. Therefore, a longitudinal research design with numerous follow-up surveys should probably be a more ideal design. Third, the diagnostic criteria are still not consistent across studies. This is because there is currently no official diagnosis of IA as a mental or psychiatric disorder. Without a common definition and operationalization, it is never certain whether different researchers are studying the same issue. In other words, the socioeconomic determinants might be associated with one conceptualization of IA but not with another.

Limitations of This Review

Although this review provides useful information on the current knowledge on the socioeconomic determinants of IA, there are several limitations to this review that should be taken into consideration when interpreting the results. First, the list of search keywords may not be sufficiently exhaustive to achieve an exhaustive search. There might be socioeconomic factors that are important in local contexts that were not included in the keywords for the literature search. Second, there is no objective operationalization of socioeconomic factors. There always is this question of what factors constitute a socioeconomic factor. The search and screening procedures were conducted based on the authors' subjective understanding of the concepts of socioeconomic status, which might be biased due to the authors' own cultures and education. Third, there was no critical appraisal of the include studies. Without a critical appraisal, it is impossible to tell good studies from bad ones. Nevertheless, the fact that all included studies were cross-sectional suggest that there might not be very good scientific evidence. An appraisal to distinguish between bad studies and very bad studies might not be meaningful.

Recommendations for Future Research

Adherence to a Comprehensive Conceptual Framework

The adherence to a well-established comprehensive framework of IA has several advantages. First, the selection of variables should be made much easier with a causal map which organizes a huge range of variables. Second, with similar selection of variables and theoretical construction of the mechanisms, studies could be much more comparable and results should be much more consistent. Third, the location of intervention entry points would also be easier because the mechanisms determining IA would be clearer.

Longitudinal Design

As mentioned earlier, although cross-sectional design may be justified by the motivations of relatively low cost, administrative convenience, and the fact that socioeconomic factors precedes IA in terms of temporality, it is unclear whether the intermediary determinants between socioeconomic status and IA precede or follow IA in terms of temporal sequence. An additional strength of longitudinal design is that the within-subject differences and between-subject differences could be well distinguished. In other words, within one person, there can be multiple measurements of IA and other variables for a more dynamic analysis.

Establishment of the Official Diagnostic Criteria of IA

Many of the limitations of the current literature on IA stemmed from the absence of an authoritative definition of IA. The most notable limitation is the inconsistency in the adoption of various instruments for the measurement of IA in research studies. Treatment for IA is also difficult to design because of the heterogeneous evidence which might be studying different outcomes, i.e. different measures of IA. Ultimately, clinicians would have to ask what exact condition they are treating. Hence, without a diagnosis, the prevention and treatment are extremely difficult to implement. Therefore, the top priority of the field should be the establishment of the official diagnostic criteria of IA.

CONCLUSION

This chapter presents a new approach to conceptualizing the socioeconomic determinants of IA from a social epidemiological perspective and described a rapid scoping review of the relevant literature. The findings presented in the review revealed the status quo of the existing literature. Studies were concentrated in Asia, did not agree on the direction of the effect of a higher socioeconomic position, and adopted cross-sectional designs. Limitations of the literature include mixed results on socioeconomic influence because of insufficient consideration of intermediary determinants, unclear temporality between variables, and the absence of an official diagnostic criteria of IA, and thus an absence of a commonly agreed definition for empirical research. Based on the findings, the authors recommended an adherence to a comprehensive theoretical framework of IA, longitudinal research design, and the establishment of a set of official diagnostic criteria for IA.

ACKNOWLEDGMENT

This research received no specific grant from any funding agency in the public, commercial, or not-for-profit sectors.

REFERENCES

Ahmadi, K. (2014). Internet addiction among Iranian adolescents: A nationwide study. *Acta Medica Iranica, 52*(6), 467–472. PMID:25130156

Ahmadi, K., & Saghafi, A. (2013). Psychosocial Profile of Iranian Adolescents' Internet Addiction. *Cyberpsychology, Behavior, and Social Networking, 16*(7), 543–548. doi:10.1089/cyber.2012.0237 PMID:23614793

Ak, Ş., Koruklu, N., & Yılmaz, Y. (2013). A study on Turkish adolescent's Internet use: Possible predictors of Internet addiction. *Cyberpsychology, Behavior, and Social Networking, 16*(3), 205–209. doi:10.1089/cyber.2012.0255 PMID:23253206

Arksey, H., & O'Malley, L. (2005). Scoping studies: Towards a methodological framework. *International Journal of Social Research Methodology, 8*(1), 19–32. doi:10.1080/1364557032000119616

Bozoglan, B., Demirer, V., & Sahin, I. (2013). Loneliness, self-esteem, and life satisfaction as predictors of Internet addiction: A cross-sectional study among Turkish university students. *Scandinavian Journal of Psychology, 54*(4), 313–319. doi:10.1111/sjop.12049 PMID:23577670

Brand, M., Young, K. S., & Laier, C. (2014). Prefrontal Control and Internet Addiction: A Theoretical Model and Review of Neuropsychological and Neuroimaging Findings. *Frontiers in Human Neuroscience, 8*, 375. doi:10.3389/fnhum.2014.00375 PMID:24904393

Chung, R. Y., Mercer, S., Lai, F. T. T., Yip, B. H. K., Wong, M. C. S., & Wong, S. Y. S. (2015). Socioeconomic Determinants of Multimorbidity: A Population-Based Household Survey of Hong Kong Chinese. *PLoS One, 10*(10), e0140040. doi:10.1371/journal.pone.0140040 PMID:26451589

Conger, R. D., Conger, K. J., & Martin, M. J. (2010). Socioeconomic Status, Family Processes, and Individual Development. *Journal of Marriage and the Family, 72*(3), 685–704. doi:10.1111/j.1741-3737.2010.00725.x PMID:20676350

Demirer, V., & Bozoglan, B. (2016). Purposes of Internet use and problematic Internet use among Turkish high school students. *Asia-Pacific Psychiatry, 8*(4), 269–277. doi:10.1111/appy.12219 PMID:26585686

Destin, M., Rheinschmidt-Same, M., & Richeson, J. A. (2017). Status-Based Identity. *Perspectives on Psychological Science, 12*(2), 270–289. doi:10.1177/1745691616664424 PMID:28346114

Durkee, T., Kaess, M., Carli, V., Parzer, P., Wasserman, C., Floderus, B., & Wasserman, D. et al. (2012). Prevalence of pathological internet use among adolescents in Europe: Demographic and social factors. *Addiction (Abingdon, England), 107*(12), 2210–2222. doi:10.1111/j.1360-0443.2012.03946.x PMID:22621402

Green, M. J., Leyland, A. H., Sweeting, H., & Benzeval, M. (2016). Socioeconomic position and early adolescent smoking development: evidence from the British Youth Panel Survey (1994–2008). *Tobacco Control, 25*(2), 203-210.

Heo, J., Oh, J., Subramanian, S. V., Kim, Y., & Kawachi, I. (2014). Addictive Internet Use among Korean Adolescents: A National Survey. *PLoS One, 9*(2), e87819. doi:10.1371/journal.pone.0087819 PMID:24505318

Hong Kong Census and Statistics Department. (2016). *Thematic Household Survey Report - Report No. 59.* Retrieved from http://www.statistics.gov.hk/pub/B11302592016XXXXB0100.pdf

Hong Kong Census and Statistics Department. (2017). *Hong Kong 2016 Population By-census – Thematic Report: Household Income Distribution in Hong Kong.* Retrieved from http://www.statistics.gov.hk/pub/B11200962016XXXXB0100.pdf

Kawachi, I., Subramanian, S. V, & Almeida-Filho, N. (2002). A glossary for health inequalities. *Journal of Epidemiology and Community Health, 56*(9), 647-652.

Kayiş, A. R., Satici, S. A., Yilmaz, M. F., Şimşek, D., Ceyhan, E., & Bakioğlu, F. (2016). Big five-personality trait and internet addiction: A meta-analytic review. *Computers in Human Behavior, 63*, 35–40. doi:10.1016/j.chb.2016.05.012

Ko, C. H., Yen, J. Y., Yen, C. F., Chen, C. S., & Chen, C. C. (2012). The association between Internet addiction and psychiatric disorder: A review of the literature. *European Psychiatry, 27*(1), 1–8. doi:10.1016/j.eurpsy.2010.04.011 PMID:22153731

Kroenke, C. (2008). Socioeconomic status and health: Youth development and neomaterialist and psychosocial mechanisms. *Social Science & Medicine, 66*(1), 31–42. doi:10.1016/j.socscimed.2007.07.018 PMID:17868964

Kuss, D. J., Griffiths, M. D., Karila, L., & Billieux, J. (2013). Internet Addiction: A Systematic Review of Epidemiological Research for the Last Decade. *Current Pharmaceutical Design, 1*(4), 397–413. PMID:24001297

Kuss, D. J., & Lopez-Fernandez, O. (2016). Internet addiction and problematic Internet use: A systematic review of clinical research. *World Journal of Psychiatry, 6*(1), 143–176. doi:10.5498/wjp.v6.i1.143 PMID:27014605

Lai, C. M., Mak, K.-K., Watanabe, H., Ang, R. P., Pang, J. S., & Ho, R. C. M. (2013). Psychometric Properties of the Internet Addiction Test in Chinese Adolescents. *Journal of Pediatric Psychology, 38*(7), 794–807. doi:10.1093/jpepsy/jst022 PMID:23671059

Lai, F. T. T., & Kwan, J. L. Y. (2017a). Socioeconomic influence on adolescent problematic Internet use through school-related psychosocial factors and pattern of Internet use. *Computers in Human Behavior, 68*, 121–136. doi:10.1016/j.chb.2016.11.021

Lai, F. T. T., & Kwan, J. L. Y. (2017b). The presence of heavy Internet using peers is protective of the risk of problematic Internet use (PIU) in adolescents when the amount of use increases. *Children and Youth Services Review, 73*, 74–78. doi:10.1016/j.childyouth.2016.12.004

Lam, L. T. (2014). Risk Factors of Internet Addiction and the Health Effect of Internet Addiction on Adolescents: A Systematic Review of Longitudinal and Prospective Studies. *Current Psychiatry Reports, 16*(11), 508. doi:10.1007/s11920-014-0508-2 PMID:25212714

Lam, L. T., Peng, Z., Mai, J., & Jing, J. (2009). Factors associated with Internet addiction among adolescents. *Cyberpsychology & Behavior, 12*(5), 551–555. doi:10.1089/cpb.2009.0036 PMID:19619039

Lau, J. T. F., Gross, D. L., Wu, A. M. S., Cheng, K., & Lau, M. M. C. (2017). Incidence and predictive factors of Internet addiction among Chinese secondary school students in Hong Kong: A longitudinal study. *Social Psychiatry and Psychiatric Epidemiology, 52*(6), 657–667. doi:10.1007/s00127-017-1356-2 PMID:28417158

Lee, C.-S., & McKenzie, K. (2015). Socioeconomic and Geographic Inequalities of Internet Addiction in Korean Adolescents. *Psychiatry Investigation, 12*(4), 559–562. doi:10.4306/pi.2015.12.4.559 PMID:26508969

Leung, L., & Lee, P. S. N. (2012). Impact of Internet Literacy, Internet Addiction Symptoms, and Internet Activities on Academic Performance. *Social Science Computer Review, 30*(4), 403–418. doi:10.1177/0894439311435217

Li, D., Li, X., Wang, Y., Zhao, L., Bao, Z., & Wen, F. (2013). School connectedness and problematic internet use in adolescents: A moderated mediation model of deviant peer affiliation and self-control. *Journal of Abnormal Child Psychology, 41*(8), 1231–1242. doi:10.1007/s10802-013-9761-9 PMID:23695186

Li, W., Garland, E. L., & Howard, M. O. (2014). Family factors in Internet addiction among Chinese youth: A review of English- and Chinese-language studies. *Computers in Human Behavior, 31*(1), 393–411. doi:10.1016/j.chb.2013.11.004

Lui, L. (2016). Gender, Rural-Urban Inequality, and Intermarriage in China. *Social Forces, 95*(2), 639–662. doi:10.1093/sf/sow076

Malak, M. Z., Khalifeh, A. H., & Shuhaiber, A. H. (2017). Prevalence of Internet Addiction and associated risk factors in Jordanian school students. *Computers in Human Behavior, 70*, 556–563. doi:10.1016/j.chb.2017.01.011

Mei, S., Yau, Y. H. C., Chai, J., Guo, J., & Potenza, M. N. (2016). Problematic Internet use, well-being, self-esteem and self-control: Data from a high-school survey in China. *Addictive Behaviors, 61*, 74–79. doi:10.1016/j.addbeh.2016.05.009 PMID:27249805

Pies, R. (2009). Should DSM-V Designate "Internet Addiction" a Mental Disorder? *Psychiatry (Edgmont)*, *6*(2), 31–37. PMID:19724746

Seyrek, S., Cop, E., Sinir, H., Ugurlu, M., & Şenel, S. (2017). Factors associated with Internet addiction: Cross-sectional study of Turkish adolescents. *Pediatrics International*, *59*(2), 218–222. doi:10.1111/ped.13117 PMID:27507735

Shek, D. T. L., & Yu, L. (2016). Adolescent Internet Addiction in Hong Kong: Prevalence, Change, and Correlates. *Journal of Pediatric and Adolescent Gynecology*, *29*(1), S22–S30. doi:10.1016/j.jpag.2015.10.005 PMID:26461526

Skalická, V., van Lenthe, F., Bambra, C., Krokstad, S., & Mackenbach, J. (2009). Material, psychosocial, behavioural and biomedical factors in the explanation of relative socio-economic inequalities in mortality: Evidence from the HUNT study. *International Journal of Epidemiology*, *38*(5), 1272–1284. doi:10.1093/ije/dyp262 PMID:19661280

Stavropoulos, V., Alexandraki, K., & Motti-Stefanidi, F. (2013). Recognizing internet addiction: Prevalence and relationship to academic achievement in adolescents enrolled in urban and rural Greek high schools. *Journal of Adolescence*, *36*(3), 565–576. doi:10.1016/j.adolescence.2013.03.008 PMID:23608781

Swartz, J. R., Hariri, A. R., & Williamson, D. E. (2017, February). An epigenetic mechanism links socioeconomic status to changes in depression-related brain function in high-risk adolescents. *Molecular Psychiatry*, *22*(2), 209–214. doi:10.1038/mp.2016.82 PMID:27217150

Torikka, A., Kaltiala-Heino, R., Luukkaala, T., & Rimpelä, A. (2017). Trends in Alcohol Use among Adolescents from 2000 to 2011: The Role of Socioeconomic Status and Depression. *Alcohol and Alcoholism (Oxford, Oxfordshire)*, *52*(1), 95–103. doi:10.1093/alcalc/agw048 PMID:27507821

Twenge, J. M., & Campbell, W. K. (2002). Self-esteem and socioeconomic status: A meta-analytic review. *Personality and Social Psychology Review*, *6*(1), 59–71. doi:10.1207/S15327957PSPR0601_3

Vondráčková, P., & Gabrhelík, R. (2016). Prevention of Internet addiction: A systematic review. *Journal of Behavioral Addictions*, *5*(4), 568–579. doi:10.1556/2006.5.2016.085 PMID:27998173

Welte, J. W., Barnes, G. M., Tidwell, M.-C. O., & Wieczorek, W. F. (2017). Predictors of Problem Gambling in the U.S. *Journal of Gambling Studies*, *33*(2), 327–342. doi:10.1007/s10899-016-9639-1 PMID:27557549

Wu, C. S. T., Wong, H. T., Yu, K. F., Fok, K. W., Yeung, S. M., Lam, C. H., & Liu, K. M. (2016). Parenting approaches, family functionality, and internet addiction among Hong Kong adolescents. *BMC Pediatrics*, *16*(1), 130. doi:10.1186/s12887-016-0666-y PMID:27538688

Xu, J., Shen, L.-X., Yan, C.-H., Hu, H., Yang, F., Wang, L., & Shen, X.-M. et al. (2014). Parent-adolescent interaction and risk of adolescent internet addiction: A population-based study in Shanghai. *BMC Psychiatry*, *14*(1), 112. doi:10.1186/1471-244X-14-112 PMID:24731648

Yao, M. Z., He, J., Ko, D. M., & Pang, K. (2013). The Influence of Personality, Parental Behaviors, and Self-Esteem on Internet Addiction: A Study of Chinese College Students. *Cyberpsychology, Behavior, and Social Networking*, *17*(2), 104–110. doi:10.1089/cyber.2012.0710 PMID:24003966

Young, K. S. (1998). Internet Addiction: The Emergence of a New Clinical Disorder. *Cyberpsychology & Behavior*, *1*(3), 237–244. doi:10.1089/cpb.1998.1.237

Yu, L., & Shek, D. T. L. (2013). Internet addiction in Hong Kong adolescents: A three-year longitudinal study. *Journal of Pediatric and Adolescent Gynecology*, *26*(3SUPPL), S10–S17. doi:10.1016/j.jpag.2013.03.010 PMID:23683821

Zhang, H., Li, D., & Li, X. (2015). Temperament and problematic Internet use in adolescents: A moderated mediation model of maladaptive cognition and parenting styles. *Journal of Child and Family Studies*, *24*(7), 1886–1897. doi:10.1007/s10826-014-9990-8

KEY TERMS AND DEFINITIONS

Behavioral Pathway: The theoretical pathway through which socioeconomic background exerts effects on a certain health condition through dictating the health behaviors of the individual.

Biomedical Pathway: The theoretical pathway through which socioeconomic background exerts effects on a certain health condition through biological factors.

Internet Addiction: The psychological harm and disturbances to life caused by uncontrolled excessive access to the Internet.

Material Pathway: The theoretical pathway through which socioeconomic background exerts effects on a certain health condition through materialistic factors such as access to resources, convenience, and better living environment.

Psychosocial Pathway: The theoretical pathway through which socioeconomic background exerts effects on a certain health condition through psychosocial variables, such as the feeling about social inequality and the associated stress.

Socioeconomic Determinant: A socioeconomic factor that is theorized as having a causal effect on a certain health condition.

Socioeconomic Status: The social standing or class of an individual or group which is often measured as a combination of education, income, and occupation.

Chapter 8

The Role of Family Factors in Internet Addiction Among Children and Adolescents:
An Overview

Bahadir Bozoglan
IF Weinheim Institute, Germany

ABSTRACT

As the Internet becomes increasingly integrated into everyday life, there is a growing concern on the antecedents that contribute to some of the adverse effects such as Internet addiction. Parents are important and influential agents, and their parenting practices may promote or prevent the development of Internet-related problems. This chapter provides a review of family factors surrounding child and adolescent Internet addiction such as parental monitoring and parental guidance, parental mediation, Internet parenting styles, parental norms and behaviors, parent and child characteristics, family functioning and parent marital conflict, quality of the parent-child and peer relationship and culture as highlighted in previous research. Common limitations on past research on family factors and child and adolescent Internet addiction are noted and future research directions are suggested. Finally, family-based solutions and recommendations to prevent children and adolescents from developing Internet addiction are provided in the light of previous findings.

INTRODUCTION

Today, Internet has become a widely used tool for network communication with a huge impact on daily life. Internet is considered to be one of the most popular leisure time activities for children and adolescents all over the world. However, along with the widespread use of Internet, there is also a growing concern on the antecedents that leads to adverse effects such as Internet addiction. Internet addiction prevalence rate in the United States and Europe has been reported as between 1.5% and 8.2% (Weinstein & Lejoyeux, 2010). In Asia, 10% of the adolescents in Park et al's (2008) study have been found to be

DOI: 10.4018/978-1-5225-3477-8.ch008

at high risk for Internet addiction. Internet addiction prevalence rates all around the world have called the researchers to better understand this new behavioral problem.

With an aim to shed light on Internet addiction, a plethora of studies have focused primarily on factors that may predispose individuals to Internet addiction. There is a consensus in literature that some personality traits such as social withdrawal, introversion, aggression, narcissism, shyness, low self-esteem and poor self-control are significant predictors of Internet addiction (Bozoglan, 2013; Griffth, 1995; Kim, 2008). Although the role of individual factors and personality in predicting Internet addiction have been widely investigated in literature, it is also important to look at the impact of environmental factors, such as family factors.

Elements of family life, such as parenting behaviors have a profound effect on the development of children and adolescents (Barker & Hunt, 2004). Family factors and parenting behaviors regarding child Internet use is necessary to consider when attempting to understand children with Internet addiction due to the central role of the family in the development of children and the important roles of family factors and parental attitudes and behaviors in child behavior (Van den Eijnden, Spijkerman, Vermulst, Van Rooij, & Engles, 2010; Yu, 2003). Studies conducted in developed countries reveal that Internet use is mainly home-based. While only 66% of children use Internet at school, 91.2% of primary school children surf on the Internet at home (Lee & Chae, 2007). The wide use of Internet at home also underlines the critical role of parents in providing a controlled and safe Internet use.

Despite the existence of empirical studies on Internet addiction, past research have shown that a complete understandings of how children and adolescents develop Internet addiction and effective prevention and intervention techniques are limited (Guan & Subrahmanyam, 2009; Willoughby, 2008). This chapter aims to provide an overview of the risk and protection factors for the occurrence of Internet addiction during childhood and adolescence in relation to family context and parenting behaviors. In this context, past research concerning the effect of family factors on Internet addiction among children and adolescents have been reviewed and frequently occurring points are explained.

BACKGROUND

Internet Addiction

Though an exact terminology to designate the pathological use of the Internet does not still exist, authors have used different terms to describe the harmful use of the Internet (Abreu, Karam, Góes & Spritzer, 2008) such as Internet addiction (Young, 1998), problematic Internet use (Shapira et al., 2003) or Internet use disorder (American Psychiatric Association [APA], 2013). Since this chapter approaches the pathological use of the Internet as a behavioral problem, the term "Internet addiction" has been chosen.

Within a medical framework, addiction is described as a psychological and physical dependency on a certain matter (Leung & Lee, 2012). However, no conclusive definition of Internet addiction has been adopted in literature yet. Young (2004) explains Internet addiction as compulsive behaviors associated with online activities that leads to sorrow and functional impairment (Young, 1999) and brings about stress on social relationships. Pathological Internet use is described as "a compulsive–impulsive spectrum disorder" that includes five main addiction types: information overload; computer addiction to programming or game playing; compulsions to online auctions; gambling or trading; and cyber-sexual relationship addictions (Young, 1998).

Internet addiction is associated with behaviors that negatively influence individual's social relations, health, mood, work, education, and occupation (Widyanto & Griffiths, 2009). According to Morahan-Martin and Schumacher (2000), Internet addicts are involved in online activities such as meeting new people, receiving emotional support, socializing, and playing online games more frequently than un-problematic users. Wallace (1999) has noted ecommunication as the primary factor related to Internet addiction. Young (1998) has concluded that problematic Internet users cannot easily limit their time online, and they spend quite a lot time sending or receiving e-mails or surfing the net. In parallel with the easy access to Internet, especially adolescents develop an "uncontrollable urge" to use it all day long. Today, Internet Addiction is widely assessed by a tool adopted from Diagnostic and Statistical Manual-IV (DSM-IV) criteria for pathological gambling by Young (1998).

Parenting and Parent Roles

The Psychodynamic Theory (Laslett, 1978) and the Social Learning Theory (Bandura, 1977) provide a theoretical framework for the relationship between Internet addiction and family factors. The Psychodynamic Theory and the Social Learning Theory look for the underlying reasons for problematic behaviors in children within the context of the relationships between the child and the parents. The Psychodynamic Theory suggests that inner conflicts and setbacks experienced in the immediate environment at early ages lead to problem behaviors in children. In a parallel vein, the Social Learning Theory relates problem behaviors to biological factors, family-related factors and school-related factors. In this context, parenting and parent roles are important in the psychosocial development and well-being of children and adolescents.

Parenting is described as "a complex activity that includes many specific behaviors that work individually and together to influence child outcomes" (Darling, 1999, p. 1). Parents are responsible for fostering the development of their children (Livingstone & Bober, 2004), and they take on several roles to achieve this goal. Parents are expected to take on a "material role", which includes providing the children with computer and Internet access at home, and a "symbolic role", which includes establishing rules about Internet use. However, ironically, percentage of the "digital natives" who feel confident about using the Internet is much higher compared to their parents (Livingstone, 2007). The "generational divide" in Internet usage (Mitchell, Finkelhor & Wolak, 2005) leads parents to see their children as a "home guru" in relation to Internet use and increases the side effects. Grossbart et al. (2002) suggest that this mediating role of children appears as a result of "reversed socialization". According to Grossbat et al. (2002) since children have better computer and Internet skills than their parents they are the most influential actors in installing hardware. In this regard, the symbolic role of parents includes ensuring that a filter software is used (Delver, 2003); monitoring the Internet use of children (Eastin et al., 2006); establishing the rules of Internet use (Barkin et al., 2006); talking about the Internet (Valkenburg, 2002); controlling Internet log files (Pardoen & Pijpers, 2006) and surfing with the children on the Internet (Eastin et al., 2006).

Especially for adolescents, parents play a protective role in keeping them away from problematic behavior (Miller & Plant, 2010). It has been reported that about 30% of parents are physically available when their children connect the Internet (Eastin et al., 2006). The rest mostly prefer to use filter-software, or check the Internet browser history (Beebe et al., 2004). Some parents check the Internet sites their children are surfing on the Internet (Valentine & Holloway, 2001). In case of any threat such as strangers trying to approach the kids, parents may stop Internet use (Walrave et al., 2008). Research reveals that parents prefer to control Internet use by limiting access time or establishing the hours to access the Internet (Wang et al., 2005). However, only a small number of parents state that they establish clear Internet usage rules at home (Duimel & de Haan, 2007). Thus, a majority of children can access the Internet freely and only 13.2% of parents provide guidance for their children in relation to Internet usage (Walrave et al., 2008).

Family plays a key role in the socialization of children. Parents are expected to provide their children with a respectful and communicative environment. Children should get the opportunity to talk about Internet with their parents (Fleming et al., 2006). Though research has shown that providing a respectful and open atmosphere to talk about the Internet (Young, 2008) and surfing together with children on the Internet diminishes the risks of Internet usage (Lee & Chae, 2007), less than 67% of parents talk with their children about the Internet (Duimel & de Haan, 2007) and only a small number of parents surf on the Internet with their children (Eurobarometer, 2008).

WHICH FAMILY FACTORS PROMOTE OR PREVENT THE DEVELOPMENT OF INTERNET ADDICTION AMONG CHILDREN AND ADOLESCENTS?

Internet addiction is mostly considered to be a behavioral problems syndrome like substance use (Yen et al, 2007). Some authors have addressed the impact of family factors on the development of problem behavior (e.g. Ahmadi & Saghafi, 2013; Lam, Peng, Mai & Jing, 2009; Van der Vorst et al., 2005) to indicate how parents can either prevent or promote or the development of Internet addiction among their children. Family variables such as broken family, family conflict, split homes, low family functionality and permissive or indulgent parenting styles have been highlighted by researchers as positive correlates of Internet addiction and other behavioral problems (Beal et al, 2001; Bogenschneider, 1998; Niaz et al, 2005). On the other hand, quality of the parent–child relationship has been noted as a negative correlate of Internet addiction among children (Liu & Kuo, 2007).

Family factors put forward in previous research on child Internet addiction can be listed as parental monitoring and parental guidance (Ko et al, 2015; Kwon, Chung, & Lee, 2011; Lin, Lin, & Wu, 2009; Park, Kim, & Cho, 2008; Van den Eijnden et al., 2010; Xu, Turel, & Yuan, 2012; Yang et al., 2013; Yen et al., 2007), parental mediation (Cho & Bae, 2010; Lee, 2012; Lee & Jeon, 2011; Tripp, 2011), Internet parenting styles (Huang et al., 2010; Kalaitzaki & Birtchnell, 2014; Liu et al., 2012; Xu et al., 2014; Valcke et al, 2010), parental norms and behaviors (Liu et al, 2012; Van den Eijnden et al., 2010; Yen et al, 2010), parent and child characteristics (Aunola et al., 2000; van Rooij & van den Eijden, 2007; Walrave et al., 2008; Wang et al., 2005), family functioning and parent marital conflict (Jang, & Ji, 2012; Lam et al., 2009; Tsitsika et al., 2011; Xu et al., 2014; Yen et al., 2007) and quality of the parent-child and peer relationship (Lam et al., 2009; Liu et al., 2012; Park, Kim, & Cho, 2008; Van den Eijnden et al., 2010; Yen et al., 2007).

Parental Monitoring and Parental Guidance

Parental monitoring refers to a set of parenting practices or behaviors through which parents learn about their children's whereabouts, peers, and activities (Borawski, Ievers-Landis, Lovegreen, & Trapl, 2003). Research has shown that the amount of parental monitoring perceived by children and adolescents can act as a shield against problematic behaviors such as alcohol and drug use (DiClemente et al., 2001).

Similarly, parental monitoring has been associated with lower rates of exposure to risky online content (Cho & Cheon, 2005) and Internet addiction among children and adolescents (Xu, Turel, & Yuan, 2012). Yen et al (2009) have found that low family monitoring predicted Internet addiction among adolescents. Previous studies have also indicated that Internet use that exceeds 20 h/day predicts the risk of Internet addiction (Ko et al., 2007; Ko et al., 2009). As also suggested by Ko et al. (2015) the no-limit use of the Internet is likely to increase the risk of Internet addiction later. Thus, it is important to monitor and regulate the Internet use of children and adolescents to prevent Internet addiction.

Parental guidance is described as establishing rules, giving advice, differentiating between the right and the wrong, providing direction, counseling and protection in daily life (Xiong, 2005). It includes all types of parental behaviors used to support the performance of children (Vandermaas, 2003). Bybee et al. (1982) have described three patterns of parental guidance for television viewing: restrictive, evaluative, and unfocused. Restrictive guidance is defined as putting limitations on the use of media such as limiting the amount of time spent watching tv. Evaluative parental guidance refers to talking about media with the children. For example, parents may sometimes comment on TV programs and explain their children why a specific tv program is beneficial or harmful. Unfocused parental guidance means accompanying the child while watching tv and encouraging proper behaviors.

Internet-specific parenting guidance has been differentiated from television guiding, though. Informative guidance is preferred instead of evaluative guidance. Additionally, since parents do not accompany children and adolescents surfing the Internet all the time, the term unfocused parental guidance is replaced with relational approaches. A relational approach promotes the use of the Internet by the parents and the children together to enhance a bidirectional interaction. Thus, use of the Internet supports parent-child relationship at the same time (Wu et al, 2016).

Parental Mediation

A discussion of parenting styles and behaviors in relation to addictive behaviors among children and adolescents has brought up the term, parental mediation. Previous research has revealed that parental mediation is also a crucial factor in preventing children and adolescents from negative effects of excessive Internet use. Parental mediation can be described as a set of strategies employed to mitigate children's excessive use of the media and its negative consequences (Clark, 2011). It includes three strategies: restrictive, active and co-use (Valkenburg et al., 1999). Restrictive mediation refers to establishing rules for media use such as time limit or content. Active mediation consists of instructive strategies which focus on explanations and discussions concerning the use of media. Co-use refers to sharing media time with children.

The framework of parental mediation has its roots in television research, but Internet mediation has also been included in this framework recently (Chang et al., 2015; Clark, 2009). Though parents are aware of the online opportunities and risks, parenting practices are mostly oriented toward restricting Internet use due to parental anxiety about online risks and related negative outcomes for their children (Cho & Bae, 2010; Lee, 2012; Lee & Jeon, 2011; Tripp, 2011). Livingstone and Helsper (2008) analysed data with 906 teens and their parents in the UK, and concluded that parental mediation techniques were not related to teens' online behavior, though restrictions on the use of social interactions such as chat or email decreased online risks. Sasson and Mesch (2014), on the other hand, found that social mediation such as checking emails resulted in increased online risks among Israeli youth. In this context, Kirwil (2009) studied Internet mediation practices in 18 European countries, and concluded that the relationship between parental mediation and risky online behaviors varied by country. However, in a majority of European countries social mediation strategies which include co-use and communication of rules between parents and the children were more effective than restrictive strategies.

Internet Parenting Styles

Parenting style can be a significant determiner of child and adolescent Internet behavior (Chou & Lee, 2007; Rosen, 2008). Especially parental control and parental warmth have been associated with effective parenting strategies concerning the use of Internet (Chou & Peng, 2007; Kerbs, 2005; Valcke et al., 2007). According to Baumrind (1991), "a parenting style is used to capture normal variations in parents' attempts to control and socialize their children" (p. 57). Eastin et al. (2006), on the other hand, highlight socialization involvement and control strictness and describe a parenting style as the "amount of involvement and strictness used by a parent to deal with their teen." (Eastin et al., 2006, p. 493). The early theory of Baumrind mainly stresses the role of parental control or demandingness, defined as "the extent to which parents desire children to become integrated into the family whole, by their maturity demands, supervision, disciplinary efforts and willingness to confront the child who disobeys" (Baumrind, 1991, p. 61). Following the further elaboration of the theory by Maccoby and Martin in 1983, Baumrind has added the concept of parental responsiveness or parental warmth which refers to "the extent to which parents intentionally foster individuality, self-regulation, and self-assertion by being attuned, supportive, and acquiescent to children's special needs and demands" (Baumrind, 1991, p. 62). Thus, while parental control is concerned with the level of guidance, parental warmth is mostly concerned with an investment in communication with the children and the level of support.

Parental control and socialization are considered to be at the center of parenting behaviors and styles (Baumrind, 1991; Eastin et al, 2006). However, there is no consensus among researchers on the relationship between parents' restrictive behavior and child and adolescent Internet use. On the one hand, some research findings indicate that parenting style has no effect on time online (Eastin et al., 2006) or actual Internet use (Lee & Chae 2007). On the other hand, some researchers (e.g. Lwin et al., 2008; Heim et al., 2007; Valcke et al., 2007) report that explicit parental control is associated with less Internet risk behavior. The role of parental warmth on Internet usage of children and adolescents seems to be clearer. Parental support and talking about the use of Internet have been related to a more positive and safer Internet usage (Fleming et al., 2006; Lee & Chae, 2007).

Valcke et al (2010) have put forward four Internet parenting styles based on Baumrind's (1991) taxonomy of parenting. The permissive parenting style includes the parents who do not establish explicit boundaries. Since they refrain from disputes with their children, they are willing to accept and fulfill any requests put forward by their children. They provide parental warmth, but hardly any guidance. The second type of Internet parenting style is laissez-faire, which reflects parents with limited control over and involvement. These parents neither support nor restrict Internet usage of their children. Parents with an authoritative parenting style, on the other hand, establish rules about the use of Internet clearly. Though they do not limit Internet use by the children explicitly, they expect children to take responsibility for their own actions and use the Internet in a self-regulated manner. Finally, authoritarian parents demand unconditional obedience. They prefer not to make explanations about the rules they put forward concerning the use of Internet. In their study, Valcke et al (2010) have investigated Internet parenting styles among parents of primary school children. They have concluded that the highest level of child Internet usage is observed among when parents adopt a permissive parenting style; whereas the lowest level of child

Internet usage is found when parents adopt an authoritarian Internet parenting style. However, they have also found that although parenting styles is related to the child Internet use, this relationship is mediated by parent educational background and parents' actual Internet usage. Thus, it seems that parenting style plays an important role in determining the level of Internet use by children and adolescents; but it is not the sole factor. Other factors will be discussed in the following parts of this chapter.

Parental Norms and Behaviors

Parental norms and behaviors have been proven to play a significant role on children's problem behaviors such as smoking (Tilson, Mcbride, Lipkus, & Catalano, 2004), drinking (Jones, Hussong, Manning, & Sterrett, 2008) and drug use (Yen et al., 2007). Since Internet addiction has been described as a behavioral problem, theories that explain other behavioral problems can be used to elucidate it (Shiin et al, 2011). In line with social learning theory, parents' behaviors model and shape future behaviors of their children. Children can observe and imitate not only positive but also negative behaviors of their parents such as smoking (Bandura, 1989). Similarly, recent research has indicated that parental Internet use can be a model for children and influence their use of Internet (Van den Eijnden et al., 2010). Though parents may use the Internet for different reasons such as for work, parents' Internet-specific norms can affect children's perceived parental attitude toward Internet use. Yen et al. (2007) have shown that adolescents' perceived positive parental attitudes toward substance use predicted both Internet overuse and substance abuse among adolescents in Taiwan. Van den Eijnden et al. (2010) have also indicated that parental rules about the use of the Internet can help to prevent Internet addiction among children. Liu et al. (2012) have also concluded that when parental norms comply with their Internet use behaviors, parental norms predict adolescent Internet addiction negatively; however, when parental norms do not comply with their Internet use behaviors, parental behaviors predict adolescent Internet addiction positively. Thus, parental norms and behaviors are significant factors in determining the level of Internet addiction among children and adolescents.

Parent and Child Characteristics

Past research has shown that some parent characteristics may also interact with the use of Internet and parenting styles. Parents' age can be a determining factor for Internet parenting styles. Wang et al. (2005) has found that elder parents are more likely to control more and guide less compared to younger parents. Similarly, Aunola et al. (2000) has reported that fathers use a more dominant authoritarian style, while mothers mostly prefer an authoritative style. Yao et al (2014) have also found that fathers' and mothers' behaviors influence children's online behaviors in different ways. The authors have concluded that fathers' rejection and overprotection, and mothers' rejection would increase the likelihood of Internet addiction. Biological parents are also more likely to control more than grandparents and other caretakers (van Rooij & van den Eijnden, 2007). Additionally, the education level of parents can also render their Internet parenting style. Pauwels et al. (2008) have found that parents with a higher education profile tend to employ parental control and warmth more. In a similar vein, parents who have a sound knowledge of Internet place more emphasis on the role of parental control and support for the Internet usage of children (Walrave et al., 2008). Finally, parental mental health can also be a predictor of Internet addiction among children and adolescents. Lam (2015) has noted a significant relationship between parental mental health, particularly depression, and the Internet addiction status of their children.

The characteristics of children can also interact with the use of Internet and parenting styles. The gender of the child is the first factor that could interact with the use of Internet and parenting styles. Parents prefer to employ an authoritative parenting style with girls, whereas a laissez-faire approach is taken towards boys (Aunola et al., 2000; van Rooij & van den Eijden, 2007). Thus, parents are more likely to define rules and talk about the Internet with their daughters rather than with their sons. Second, research has also shown that parental control is employed more on teenagers rather than on young children (Lwin et al., 2008; Wang et al., 2005).

Family Functioning and Parent Marital Conflict

Family functioning and parent marital conflict is another factor that can influence problematic Internet use among children. According to Bowen's (1966) family system theory, family is regarded as the primary emotional domain, and any kind of emotional conflict between the family members can affect the whole family triangulation. There is ample evidence showing that type and quality of family relations determines the quality and the level of Internet usage (De Leo & Wulfert, 2013; Li et al., 2014; Wu et al., 2016). Xu et al. (2014) have found a significant relationship between divorced parents, single parent household, and being the only child in the family and adolescent Internet addiction. Wu et al (2016) have examined the relationship between Internet addiction, parenting approaches and family functionality among Chinese adolescents in Hong Kong within a cross-sectional design study. The authors have concluded that adolescents from divorced families, low-income families, families in which family conflict exist, and severely dysfunctional families are more likely to develop Internet addiction.

Marital conflict, especially, may lead to problematic behaviors among children and adolescents (Stocker & Youngblade, 1999). When it comes to the Internet addiction, parent marital conflict again plays an important role (Zhang et al, 2017). Research has shown that perceived marital conflict among children is a significant predictor of children's addictive online behavior (De Leo & Wulfert, 2013; Wang et al., 2011; Yen et al., 2007). In this context, Li et al. (2014) have shown that conflictual family environments can trigger Internet addiction among adolescents and that adolescents with Internet addiction are more likely to come from families with dysfunctional family problems. Yang et al (2016) have also found that parent marital conflict is significantly related to college students' Internet addiction. The authors have also concluded that adolescents and college students grown in a more conflictual family environment are more likely to be at a higher risk for Internet addiction. They have also found that both mother-child and father-child attachment mediate the relationship between marital conflict and Internet addiction through peer attachment. Thus, it can be concluded that since parent marital conflict can contribute to problematic behavior among children and adolescents including Internet addiction, parents should avoid getting into conflicts in front of their children.

It is also important to note that there is a birectional relationship between family functioning and Internet addiction (Senormanci et al., 2014). Not only low family functioning renders individuals vulnerable to Internet addiction (Park et al, 2008; Yen et al, 2007), but also Internet addiction disrupts family functioning (Lin & Tsai, 2002; Young & Rogers, 1998). In this context, Ko et al. (2015) explored bidirectional associations between family factors and Internet addiction among adolescents in a prospective investigation. The results have revealed that inter-parental conflict and ineffective regulation of unessential Internet use predicted risk of Internet addiction, especially among adolescent girls. Thus, family intervention to prevent marital conflict and promote family function and Internet regulation is necessary to prevent Internet addiction.

Quality of the Parent-Child and Peer Relationship

Research has shown that there is a close relationship between problems in family communication and problematic behaviors among children such as alcohol use (Van der Vorst et al., 2005), and smoking (Harakeh et al., 2005). Similarly, studies point out a relationship between family communication and Internet addiction in children and adolescents (Gunuc & Dogan, 2013; Van den Eijnden et al., 2008; Xu et al, 2014). Displacement Theory has been used to explain the relationship between parent-child relationship and the Internet addiction in literature. The Displacement Theory suggests that the Internet has a negative effect on socialization and social relationships of the individuals (Valkenburg & Peter, 2011). Gunuc and Dogan (2013) have found that Turkish adolescents spending time with their mothers had a higher level of perceived social support and a lower level of Internet addiction. Furthermore, the authors have noted that though several activities including watching TV, eating, chatting, shopping and spending time outside the adolescents carried out with their mother have a positive effect on perceived social support, the level of Internet addiction does not change with respect to the types of activity. Interestingly, some authors have concluded that there is a positive relationship between parental communication and adolescents' problem behaviors (Van den Eijnden et al., 2008). Thus, they have concluded that frequent parental communication about problematic behaviors may increase adolescents' actual problematic behavior. As a response to this dilemma, recent studies have shown that quality of parental communication is more important in preventing adolescents' risk behaviors rather than frequency of communication (Harakeh et al. 2005; Van den Eijnden et al. 2010).

In a similar vein, Krout et al. (1998) have suggested that there is also a close relationship between problems in family communication and the Internet addiction among children. The relationship between the Internet addiction and quality of parent-child relationship can be explained on the basis of the need for social support. Children, and especially adolescents, need social support to sustain their social relationships and psychological well being and adapt to the society. Social support is described as fulfilling the basic needs such as love, appreciation and self realization and a feeling of belonging through interaction with others (Eker, Akar, & Yaldız, 2001;). Social support is a significant source of power for individuals. Through social support mechanisms, they overcome the problems in their life. Research has revealed that children and especially adolescents are involved into problem behaviors more when the level of perceived social support is low (Jessor et al., 2003). If the level of social support is not adequate, Internet can be used as a substitute for face to face communication (Papacharissi & Rubin, 2000). Andrade (2003) has shown that the Internet can provide emotional support and socialization for individuals. Additionally, it is possible to talk about a bidirectional relationship between parent-child relationship and Internet addiction. While poor parent-child relationship triggers addictive online behaviors among children, Internet addiction also seems to result in a poor parent-child relationship. Similarly, Park, Kim and Cho (2008) have found in their study that parent–child communications in Internet addict middle school students were significantly poorer than communications in non-Internet addict students in South Korea.

Parent-child attachment is another significant factor that contributes to children's addictive online behavior (Lei & Wu, 2007). Past research has shown that father-child and mother-child attachment may have different roles in children's addictive online behavior. Zhang et al (2011) have found that while father-child attachment can predict Internet addiction through loneliness both directly and indirectly, mother-child attachment can only predict Internet addiction through loneliness only indirectly. Apart from parent-child attachment, peer attachment can also have an effect on children's addictive online behavior. It has been well established in literature that the quality of peer attachment among adolescents contributes to Internet addiction (Li et al., 2014). Lei and Wu (2009) have also found that peer-attachment has a negative effect of Internet addiction among adolescents.

The protective role of effective parent-child communication against Internet addiction has been noted in different studies. A longitudinal study by Van den Eijnden et al. (2010) has indicated that qualitatively good communication about Internet use can help to protect teenagers against developing compulsive Internet use. Several studies have also found that parent–child communication can prevent adolescents from problematic Internet use (Kim & Kim, 2003; Nam, 2002).

Parenting, Internet Addiction and Culture

Culture is another crucial determiner of the relationship between family factors and children's Internet addiction. Research conducted mainly in Anglo-Saxon contexts generally identifies authoritative parenting as the optimal parenting style with optimum outcomes for children and adolescents (e.g. Lamborn et al., 1991; Steinberg et al., 1994). It has been found that children from authoritative families would have better developmental outcomes than children from neglectful families. As a combination of high levels of parental warmth (responsiveness) and strictness (demandingness) the authoritative style of parenting has been found to be the most preventive parenting style against several behavioral problems such as substance use or Internet addiction (Steinberg, 2001).

On the other hand, research on ethnic minority groups such as African Americans (Baumrind, 1972), Chinese Americans (Chao, 1994) and Hispanic Americans (Torres-Villa, 1995) have shown that the authoritative parenting style may not always be related with optimum adjustment outcomes among children and adolescents. Research conducted in Middle East and Asian societies has revealed that authoritarian parenting could also be an effective parenting style (e.g. Quoss & Zhao, 1995; Dwairy, Achoui, Abouserie & Farah, 2006). Additionally, research conducted in South European countries such as Spain (Martinez & Garcia, 2007) Turkey (Turkel & Tezer, 2008), and Italy (Marchetti, 1997) has indicated that permissive parenting can also lead to positive developmental outcomes for children. Thus, Calafat et al. (2011) have concluded that "the optimal parenting depends on the cultural backgrounds where parent-child relationships would generally develop" (p. 8).

SOLUTIONS AND RECOMMENDATIONS

Based on past research, it is possible to conclude that there is a close relationship between parenting behaviors and Internet usage of children and adolescents. Although it would be overoptimistic to expect parenting styles to counter all problematic online behaviors (Eastin et al., 2006), there is enough data to infer that parental control and parental warmth can help to develop an understanding of the risks of Internet (Chou & Peng, 2007; Kerbs, 2005; Valcke et al., 2007). Measures to regulate and control the Internet use of children and adolescents are essential to prevent Internet addiction. As also suggested by Ko et al. (2015), especially for non-essential Internet use, such as online gaming, a limit of no more than 2 h/day will be enough. Though research on restrictive parental behaviors and Internet usage of children seems to be inconclusive with conflicting findings (Lee & Chae, 2007; Valcke et al., 2007), research on parental warmth points to a clear relationship between parental support, talking about Internet and children's Internet usage (Fleming et al., 2006; Lee & Chae, 2007; Lwin et al., 2008). Parental mediation has also been noted as an effective strategy to deal with addictive online behaviors among children

(Livingstone & Helsper, 2008). Cultural orientations may create a difference, however, social mediation strategies that consist of co-use and communication of rules between parents and the children seem to be more protective against addictive online behaviors compared to restrictive strategies.

Research on problematic online behaviors of children also underlines the need for "net-education". Children and parents need to be informed about the risks of unsafe Internet usage such as of cyber-bullying (Chisholm, 2006; van Rooij & van den Eijden, 2007), exposure to pornography or violence, (Fleming, Greentree, Cocotti-Muller, Elias, & Morrison, 2006; Livingstone, 2003) and physical complaints (Vanlanduyt & De Cleyn, 2007; Wang et al., 2005). Media literacy education, which is provided at school, plays an important role in preventing the negative effects of Internet on children and adolescents. Additionally, awareness raising campaigns for parents could also offer more effective parenting approaches to Internet addiction.

Previous research findings on Internet addiction among children and adolescents sustain the importance of preventive action. However, a complete understanding of this new behavioral problem should involve the entire family. In this context, family-based prevention should consist of communication improvement techniques for parents, social skills development strategies for adolescents, counseling for family members to improve family functioning, fostering monitoring and discipline strategies for Internet addiction. Furthermore, managing leisure activities should also help avoid Internet addiction. Active participation in family and outdoor activities is likely to reduce the level of Internet addiction. Parents can enrich the contents of leisure activities and provide supportive control.

Family-based interventions can also help to reduce Internet addiction among children and adolescents. Family-based interventions are frequently employed for adolescent substance dependence and addiction, and there is amplitude of research to support its efficacy (e.g. Liddle, 2004). For instance, Liu et al.'s (2015) six-session multi-family group therapy has been found to be effective in reducing Internet addiction behaviors among adolescents. Thus, family-based interventions can help to foster positive parent–adolescent interaction. It is also necessary to examine parental mental health and, if necessary, provide treatment to parents. Family-based interventions such as multi-family group therapy can be included in preventive programs for Internet addiction in the future.

Past research has also shown that the promotion of family function is necessary among children and adolescents with Internet addiction. Family conflict, especially inter-parental conflict, is associated with increased risk of Internet addiction (e.g. Ko et al., 2015). In this regard, interventions to promote family functionality to educate family members in how to cope with family conflict are essential.

Finally, previous research implies that children's addiction to Internet should be approached in parallel with parents' own Internet addiction. If parents' own actions do not comply with their requests from children concerning the use of Internet, parental guidance is likely to be ineffective. As noted by Law et al. (2010, p.378), ''The most important monitoring and controlling that parents can do is to monitor their own behavior and control their own words and actions that discourage from being open and communicative''.

FUTURE RESEARCH DIRECTIONS

A glance at literature on Internet addiction reveals that there is a close relationship between parenting practices and Internet addiction of children and adolescents. Though Internet addiction research has come a long way in a short time, limitations are present. First, a majority of studies focusing on Internet addiction and parenting employ a cross-sectional design to examine the causality between the variables. Future studies can investigate the relationship between parenting and children's Internet addiction within longitudinal designs. Second, research on children's Internet addiction and parenting mostly collect data from only children. Future research can collect data from multiple sources including parents, other caretakers and peers. Third, a great deal of studies on Internet addiction use self-report questionnaires to gather data about characteristics of Internet addiction. Future studies can employ other data collection tools such as switching tasks to further investigate the psychological characteristics of children's Internet addiction. Additionally, though a plethora of research suggests that inappropriate parental rearing styles are closely related to children's Internet addiction, there are only a limited number of intervention studies. The role of Internet-specific parenting strategies in preventing Internet addiction among children and adolescents should be tested in intervention studies. These findings will help professionals in helping parents to attain more effective parenting styles. Additionally, future studies can investigate the feasibility of an integrated preventive intervention framework that includes school, community and family (Dodge & Godwin, 2013; Lovato et al., 2013). Finally, prospective research can investigate the effect of other mediating variables on children's Internet addiction such as socioeconomic status.

CONCLUSION

Internet plays a vital role in the lives of today's children, who are born into a cyber world. However, problematic Internet use or Internet addiction is often linked to several negative outcomes (Caplan & High, 2011; Ko et al., 2008; Yoo et al., 2004). Thus, an effort to reduce its prevalence and negative effects should start with an understanding of conditions that are associated with Internet addiction. Although parents have growing concerns about their children's excessive Internet use, little is known about the role parents can play to prevent their children from developing Internet addiction. A myriad of past research suggest that family factors are also important in understanding addictive online behaviors among children and that parents may both reduce as well as contribute to Internet addiction of their children. In this context, this chapter aimed to provide an overview of the risk and protection factors for the occurrence of Internet addiction during childhood and adolescence in relation to family context and parenting behaviors. The role of parental monitoring, parental guidance, Internet parenting styles, parental mediation, parental norms and behaviors, parent-and child characteristics, parent marital conflict, quality of the parent-child and peer relationship and culture have been explained as family factors in relation to children's Internet addiction. Several supportive and participative guidelines are provided for parents to help their children avoid Internet addiction in past studies such as maintaining open communication, being involved, finding other leisure time activities and encouraging outdoor activities, establishing clear limits and rules, monitoring computer use and being a good role model (Mindprison, 2007). Net-education and media-literacy education programs or campaigns designed for parents and children about the risks of excessive Internet use and effective parenting strategies also seem promising. In a nutshell: an effective and healthy use of Internet starts in the family and family should be in the core of any predictive, preventive or corrective acts about Internet addiction.

REFERENCES

Abreu, C. N. D., Karam, R. G., Góes, D. S., & Spritzer, D. T. (2008). Internet and videogame addiction: A review. *Revista Brasileira de Psiquiatria (Sao Paulo, Brazil), 30*(2), 156–167. doi:10.1590/S1516-44462008000200014 PMID:18592108

Ahmadi, K., & Saghafi, A. (2013). Psychosocial profile of Iranian adolescents' Internet addiction. *Cyberpsychology, Behavior, and Social Networking, 16*(7), 543–548. doi:10.1089/cyber.2012.0237 PMID:23614793

American Psychiatric Association. (2013). *Diagnostic and statistical manual of mental disorders (DSM-5®)*. American Psychiatric Pub.

Andrade, J. A. (2003). *The effect of Internet on children's perceived social support* (Unpublished doctorate dissertation). University of Hartford.

Aunola, K., Stattin, H., & Nurmi, J.-E. (2000). Parenting styles and adolescents' achievement strategies. *Journal of Adolescence, 23*(2), 205–222. doi:10.1006/jado.2000.0308 PMID:10831143

Bandura, A. (1977). Self-efficacy: Toward a unifying theory of behavioral change. *Psychological Review, 84*(2), 191–215. doi:10.1037/0033-295X.84.2.191 PMID:847061

Bandura, A. (1989). Human agency in social cognitive theory. *The American Psychologist, 44*(9), 1175–1184. doi:10.1037/0003-066X.44.9.1175 PMID:2782727

Barker, J. C., & Hunt, G. (2004). Representations of family: A review of the alcohol and drug literature. *The International Journal on Drug Policy, 15*(5), 347–356. doi:10.1016/j.drugpo.2004.07.002

Barkin, S., Ip, E., Richardson, I., Klinepeter, S., Finch, S., & Krcmar, M. (2006). Parental media mediation styles for children aged 2 to 11 years. *Archives of Pediatrics & Adolescent Medicine, 160*(4), 395–401. doi:10.1001/archpedi.160.4.395 PMID:16585485

Baumrind, D. (1972). An exploratory study of socialization effects on black children: Some black-white comparisons. *Child Development, 43*(1), 261–267. doi:10.2307/1127891 PMID:5027666

Baumrind, D. (1991). The influence of parenting style on adolescent competence and substance use. *The Journal of Early Adolescence, 11*(1), 56–95. doi:10.1177/0272431691111004

Beal, A. C., Ausiello, J., & Perrin, J. M. (2001). Social influences on health-risk behaviors among minority middle school students. *The Journal of Adolescent Health, 28*(6), 474–480. doi:10.1016/S1054-139X(01)00194-X PMID:11377991

Beebe, D. W., Ris, M. D., Brown, T. M., & Dietrich, K. N. (2004). Executive functioning and memory for the Rey-Osterreith complex figure task among community adolescents. *Applied Neuropsychology, 11*(2), 91–98. doi:10.1207/s15324826an1102_4 PMID:15477179

Bogenschneider, K., Wu, M. Y., Raffaelli, M., & Tsay, J. C. (1998). Parent influences on adolescent peer orientation and substance use: The interface of parenting practices and values. *Child Development, 69*(6), 1672–1688. doi:10.1111/j.1467-8624.1998.tb06184.x PMID:9914646

Borawski, E. A., Ievers-Landis, C. E., Lovegreen, L. D., & Trapl, E. S. (2003). Parental monitoring, negotiated unsupervised time, and parental trust: The role of perceived parenting practices in adolescent health risk behaviors. *The Journal of Adolescent Health, 33*(2), 60–70. doi:10.1016/S1054-139X(03)00100-9 PMID:12890596

Bowen, M. (1966). The use of family theory in clinical practice. *Comprehensive Psychiatry, 7*(5), 345–374. doi:10.1016/S0010-440X(66)80065-2 PMID:5922263

Bozoglan, B., Demirer, V., & Sahin, I. (2013). Loneliness, self-esteem, and life satisfaction as predictors of Internet addiction: A cross-sectional study among Turkish university students. *Scandinavian Journal of Psychology, 54*(4), 313–319. doi:10.1111/sjop.12049 PMID:23577670

Bybee, C. R., Robinson, D., & Turow, J. (1982). Determinants of parental guidance of children's television viewing for a special subgroup: Mass media scholars. *Journal of Broadcasting & Electronic Media, 26*(3), 697–710. doi:10.1080/08838158209364038

Calafat, A., García, F., Juan, M., Becoña, E., & Fernández-Hermida, J. R. (2014). Which parenting style is more protective against adolescent substance use? Evidence within the European context. *Drug and Alcohol Dependence, 138*, 185–192. doi:10.1016/j.drugalcdep.2014.02.705 PMID:24679841

Chang, F. C., Chiu, C. H., Miao, N. F., Chen, P. H., Lee, C. M., Chiang, J. T., & Pan, Y. C. (2015). The relationship between parental mediation and Internet addiction among adolescents, and the association with cyberbullying and depression. *Comprehensive Psychiatry, 57*, 21–28. doi:10.1016/j.comppsych.2014.11.013 PMID:25487108

Chao, J., & Nestler, E. J. (2004). Molecular neurobiology of drug addiction. *Annual Review of Medicine, 55*(1), 113–132. doi:10.1146/annurev.med.55.091902.103730 PMID:14746512

Chisholm, D., Chisholm, D., Doran, C., Chisholm, D., Doran, C., Shibuya, K., & Chisholm, D. et al. (2006). Comparative cost-effectiveness of policy instruments for reducing the global burden of alcohol, tobacco and illicit drug use. *Drug and Alcohol Review, 25*(6), 553–565. doi:10.1080/09595230600944487 PMID:17132573

Cho, C. H., & Cheon, H. J. (2005). Children's exposure to negative Internet content: Effects of family context. *Journal of Broadcasting & Electronic Media, 49*(4), 488–509. doi:10.1207/s15506878jobem4904_8

Cho, Y., & Bae, J. (2010). Study on parental mediation of children's digital media use within the home environment. *Media. Gender & Culture, 13*(13), 37–74.

Chou, C., & Lee, Y. H. (2017). The Moderating Effects of Internet Parenting Styles on the Relationship Between Internet Parenting Behavior, Internet Expectancy, and Internet Addiction Tendency. *The Asia-Pacific Education Researcher, 26*(3-4), 137–146. doi:10.1007/s40299-017-0334-5

Chou, C., & Peng, H. (2007). Net-friends: Adolescents' attitudes and experiences vs. teachers' concerns. *Computers in Human Behavior, 23*(5), 2394–2413. doi:10.1016/j.chb.2006.03.015

Clark, L. S. (2011). Parental mediation theory for the digital age. *Communication Theory*, *21*(4), 323–343. doi:10.1111/j.1468-2885.2011.01391.x

Clark, N., & Scott, P. S. (2009). *Game addiction: The experience and the effects*. McFarland.

Darling, N. (1999). *Parenting style and its correlates*. Retrieved on May 1, 2017 from. http://ceep.crc. uiuc.edu/eecearchive/digests/1999/darlin99.pdf

De Leo, J. A., & Wulfert, E. (2013). Problematic Internet use and other risky behaviors in college students: An application of problem-behavior theory. *Psychology of Addictive Behaviors*, *27*(1), 133–141. doi:10.1037/a0030823 PMID:23276311

Delver, B. (2003). *Pandora's mailbox*. Haarlem: E-com Publishing.

DiClemente, R. J., Wingood, G. M., Crosby, R., Sionean, C., Cobb, B. K., Harrington, K., & Oh, M. K. et al. (2001). Parental monitoring: Association with adolescents' risk behaviors. *Pediatrics*, *107*(6), 1363–1368. doi:10.1542/peds.107.6.1363 PMID:11389258

Dodge, K. A., & Godwin, J. (2013). The conduct problems prevention research group. Social-information-processing patterns mediate the impact of preventive intervention on adolescent antisocial behavior. *Psychological Science*, *24*(4), 456–465. doi:10.1177/0956797612457394 PMID:23406610

Dwairy, M., Achoui, M., Abouserie, R., Farah, A., Sakhleh, A. A., Fayad, M., & Khan, H. K. (2006). Parenting styles in Arab societies: A first cross-regional research study. *Journal of Cross-Cultural Psychology*, *37*(3), 230–247. doi:10.1177/0022022106286922

Eastin, M. S., Greenberg, B. S., & Hofschire, L. (2006). Parenting the Internet. *Journal of Communication*, *56*(3), 486–504. doi:10.1111/j.1460-2466.2006.00297.x

Eker, D., Arkar, H., & Yaldız, H. (2001). Factorial structure, validity, and reliability of revised form of the multidimensional scale of perceived social support. *Turkish Journal of Psychiatry*, *12*(1), 17–25.

Eurobarometer, F. (2008). *Towards a safer use of the Internet for children in the EU–a parents' perspective*. European Commission.

Fleming, M. J., Greentree, S., Cocotti-Muller, D., Elias, K. A., & Morrison, S. (2006). Safety in cyberspace: Adolescents' safety and exposure online. *Youth & Society*, *38*(2), 135–154. doi:10.1177/0044118X06287858

Griffiths, M. D., & Dancaster, I. (1995). The effect of type A personality on physiological arousal while playing computer games. *Addictive Behaviors*, *20*(4), 543–548. doi:10.1016/0306-4603(95)00001-S PMID:7484336

Grossbart, S., Hughes, S. M., Pryor, S., & Yost, A. (2002). *Socialization aspects of parents, children, and the Internet*. ACR North American Advances.

Guan, S. S. A., & Subrahmanyam, K. (2009). Youth Internet use: Risks and opportunities. *Current Opinion in Psychiatry*, *22*(4), 351–356. doi:10.1097/YCO.0b013e32832bd7e0 PMID:19387347

Gunuc, S., & Dogan, A. (2013). The relationships between Turkish adolescents' Internet addiction, their perceived social support and family activities. *Computers in Human Behavior*, *29*(6), 2197–2207. doi:10.1016/j.chb.2013.04.011

Harakeh, Z., Scholte, R. H., De Vries, H., & Engels, R. C. (2005). Parental rules and communication: Their association with adolescent smoking. *Addiction (Abingdon, England), 100*(6), 862–870. doi:10.1111/j.1360-0443.2005.01067.x PMID:15918816

Heim, J., Brandtzæg, P. B., Kaare, B. H., Endestad, T., & Torgersen, L. (2007). Children's usage of media technologies and psychosocial factors. *New Media & Society, 9*(3), 425–454. doi:10.1177/1461444807076971

Huang, X., Zhang, H., Li, M., Wang, J., Zhang, Y., & Tao, R. (2010). Mental health, personality, and parental rearing styles of adolescents with Internet addiction disorder. *Cyberpsychology, Behavior, and Social Networking, 13*(4), 401–406. doi:10.1089/cyber.2009.0222 PMID:20712498

Jang, M. H., & Ji, E. S. (2012). Gender differences in associations between parental problem drinking and early adolescents' Internet addiction. *Journal for Specialists in Pediatric Nursing, 17*(4), 288–300. doi:10.1111/j.1744-6155.2012.00344.x PMID:23009041

Jones, D. J., Hussong, A. M., Manning, J., & Sterrett, E. (2008). Adolescent alcohol use in context: The role of parents and peers among African American and European American youth. *Cultural Diversity & Ethnic Minority Psychology, 14*(3), 266–273. doi:10.1037/1099-9809.14.3.266 PMID:18624591

Kalaitzaki, A. E., & Birtchnell, J. (2014). The impact of early parenting bonding on young adults' Internet addiction, through the mediation effects of negative relating to others and sadness. *Addictive Behaviors, 39*(3), 733–736. doi:10.1016/j.addbeh.2013.12.002 PMID:24368006

Kerbs, R. W. (2005). Social and ethical considerations in virtual worlds. *The Electronic Library, 23*(5), 539–546. doi:10.1108/02640470510631254

Kim, E. J., Namkoong, K., Ku, T., & Kim, S. J. (2008). The relationship between online game addiction and aggression, self-control and narcissistic personality traits. *European Psychiatry, 23*(3), 212–218. doi:10.1016/j.eurpsy.2007.10.010 PMID:18166402

Kim, K. S., & Kim, J. H. (2003). A study on adolescent's level of Internet addiction by their perceived relationships with parents. *Korean J Hum Ecol, 6*(1), 15–25.

Kirwil, L. (2009). Parental mediation of children's Internet use in different European countries. *Journal of Children and Media, 3*(4), 394–409. doi:10.1080/17482790903233440

Ko, C. H., Wang, P. W., Liu, T. L., Yen, C. F., Chen, C. S., & Yen, J. Y. (2015). Bidirectional associations between family factors and Internet addiction among adolescents in a prospective investigation. *Psychiatry and Clinical Neurosciences, 69*(4), 192–200. doi:10.1111/pcn.12204 PMID:24836367

Ko, C. H., Yen, J. Y., Chen, C. S., Yeh, Y. C., & Yen, C. F. (2009). Predictive values of psychiatric symptoms for Internet addiction in adolescents: A 2-year prospective study. *Archives of Pediatrics & Adolescent Medicine, 163*(10), 937–943. doi:10.1001/archpediatrics.2009.159 PMID:19805713

Ko, C. H., Yen, J. Y., Yen, C. F., Lin, H. C., & Yang, M. J. (2007). Factors predictive for incidence and remission of Internet addiction in young adolescents: A prospective study. *Cyberpsychology & Behavior, 10*(4), 545–551. doi:10.1089/cpb.2007.9992 PMID:17711363

Kraut, R., Patterson, M., Lundmark, V., Kiesler, S., Mukophadhyay, T., & Scherlis, W. (1998). Internet paradox: A social technology that reduces social involvement and psychological well-being? *The American Psychologist*, *53*(9), 1017–1031. doi:10.1037/0003-066X.53.9.1017 PMID:9841579

Kwon, J. H., Chung, C. S., & Lee, J. (2011). The effects of escape from self and interpersonal relationship on the pathological use of Internet games. *Community Mental Health Journal*, *47*(1), 113–121. doi:10.1007/s10597-009-9236-1 PMID:19701792

Lam, L. T. (2015). Parental mental health and Internet Addiction in adolescents. *Addictive Behaviors*, *42*, 20–23. doi:10.1016/j.addbeh.2014.10.033 PMID:25462649

Lam, L. T., Peng, Z. W., Mai, J. C., & Jing, J. (2009). Factors associated with Internet addiction among adolescents. *Cyberpsychology & Behavior*, *12*(5), 551–555. doi:10.1089/cpb.2009.0036 PMID:19619039

Lamborn, S. D., Mounts, N. S., Steinberg, L., & Dornbusch, S. M. (1991). Patterns of competence and adjustment among adolescents from authoritative, authoritarian, indulgent, and neglectful families. *Child Development*, *62*(5), 1049–1065. doi:10.2307/1131151 PMID:1756655

Laslett, B. (1978). Family membership, past and present. *Social Problems*, *25*(5), 476–490. doi:10.2307/800097

Law, D. M., Shapka, J. D., & Olson, B. F. (2010). To control or not to control? Parenting behaviours and adolescent online aggression. *Computers in Human Behavior*, *26*(6), 1651–1656. doi:10.1016/j.chb.2010.06.013

Lee, S., & Jeon, S. (2011). Adolescent Internet use and parental mediation practice: Using parent-child interviews. *Media. Gender & Culture*, *17*, 5–42.

Lee, S. J. (2013). Parental restrictive mediation of children's Internet use: Effective for what and for whom? *New Media & Society*, *15*(4), 466–481. doi:10.1177/1461444812452412

Lee, S. J., & Chae, Y. G. (2007). Children's Internet use in a family context: Influence on family relationships and parental mediation. *Cyberpsychology & Behavior*, *10*(5), 640–644. doi:10.1089/cpb.2007.9975 PMID:17927531

Lei, L., & Wu, L. (2009). Adolescents peer attachment and their Internet use. *Studies of Psychology and Behavior*, *7*(2), 81–86.

Leung, L., & Lee, P. S. (2012). The influences of information literacy, Internet addiction and parenting styles on Internet risks. *New Media & Society*, *14*(1), 117–136. doi:10.1177/1461444811410406

Li, W., Garland, E. L., & Howard, M. O. (2014). Family factors in Internet addiction among Chinese youth: A review of English- and Chinese-language studies. *Computers in Human Behavior*, *31*, 393–411. doi:10.1016/j.chb.2013.11.004

Liddle, H. A. (2004). Family-based therapies for adolescent alcohol and drug use: Research contributions and future research needs. *Addiction (Abingdon, England)*, *99*(Suppl. 2), 76–92. doi:10.1111/j.1360-0443.2004.00856.x PMID:15488107

Lin, C. H., Lin, S. L., & Wu, C. P. (2009). The effects of parental monitoring and leisure boredom on adolescents' Internet addiction. *Adolescence, 44*, 993–1004. PMID:20432612

Lin, S. S., & Tsai, C. C. (2002). Sensation seeking and Internet dependence of Taiwanese high school adolescents. *Computers in Human Behavior, 18*(4), 411–426. doi:10.1016/S0747-5632(01)00056-5

Liu, C., Liao, M., & Smith, D. C. (2012). An empirical review of Internet addiction outcome studies in China. *Research on Social Work Practice, 22*(3), 282–292. doi:10.1177/1049731511430089

Liu, C. Y., & Kuo, F. Y. (2007). A study of Internet addiction through the lens of the interpersonal theory. *Cyberpsychology & Behavior, 10*(6), 799–804. doi:10.1089/cpb.2007.9951 PMID:18085967

Liu, Q. X., Fang, X. Y., Yan, N., Zhou, Z. K., Yuan, X. J., Lan, J., & Liu, C. Y. (2015). Multi-family group therapy for adolescent Internet addiction: Exploring the underlying mechanisms. *Addictive Behaviors, 42*, 1–8. doi:10.1016/j.addbeh.2014.10.021 PMID:25462646

Livingstone, S. (2003). Children's use of the Internet: Reflections on the emerging research agenda. *New Media & Society, 5*(2), 147–166. doi:10.1177/1461444803005002001

Livingstone, S. (2007). Strategies of parental regulation in the media-rich home. *Computers in Human Behavior, 23*(2), 920–941. doi:10.1016/j.chb.2005.08.002

Livingstone, S., & Bober, M. (2004). *UK Children Go Online: Surveying the experiences of young people and their parents.* Academic Press.

Livingstone, S., & Helsper, E. J. (2008). Parental mediation of children's Internet use. *Journal of Broadcasting & Electronic Media, 52*(4), 581–599. doi:10.1080/08838150802437396

Luque-Martínez, T., Alberto Castañeda-García, J., Frías-Jamilena, D. M., Muñoz-Leiva, F., & Rodríguez-Molina, M. A. (2007). Determinants of the use of the Internet as a tourist information source. *Service Industries Journal, 27*(7), 881–891. doi:10.1080/02642060701570586

Lwin, M. O., Stanaland, A. J., & Miyazaki, A. D. (2008). Protecting children's privacy online: How parental mediation strategies affect website safeguard effectiveness. *Journal of Retailing, 84*(2), 205–217. doi:10.1016/j.jretai.2008.04.004

Maccoby, E. E., & Martin, J. A. (1983). Socialization in the context of the family: Parent-child interaction. In Handbook of child psychology: formerly Carmichael's Manual of child psychology. Academic Press.

Marchetti, B. (1997). *Concetto di se' relazioni familiari e valori* (Unpublished master's thesis). Universita degli Studi di Bologna, Italy.

Miller, P., & Plant, M. (2010). Parental guidance about drinking: Relationship with teenage psychoactive substance use. *Journal of Adolescence, 33*(1), 55–68. doi:10.1016/j.adolescence.2009.05.011 PMID:19596424

Mitchell, K. J., Finkelhor, D., & Wolak, J. (2005). The Internet and family and acquaintance sexual abuse. *Child Maltreatment, 10*(1), 49–60. doi:10.1177/1077559504271917 PMID:15611326

Morahan-Martin, J., & Schumacher, P. (2000). Incidence and correlates of pathological Internet use among college students. *Computers in Human Behavior, 16*(1), 13–29. doi:10.1016/S0747-5632(99)00049-7

Nam, Y. O. (2002). A study on the psychosocial variables of the youth's addiction to Internet and cyber sex and their problematic behavior. *Korean Journal of Social Welfare, 50.*

Niaz, U., Siddiqui, S. S., Hassan, S., Husain, H., & Ahmed, S. (2005). A survey of psychosocial correlates of drug abuse in young adults aged 16-21 in Karachi: Identifying 'high risk'population to target intervention strategies. *Pakistan Journal of Medical Sciences, 21*(3), 271–277.

Papacharissi, Z., & Rubin, A. M. (2000). Predictors of Internet use. *Journal of Broadcasting & Electronic Media, 44*(2), 175–196. doi:10.1207/s15506878jobem4402_2

Pardoen, J. A., Pijpers, R., & Boeke, H. (2006). *Verliefd op Internet: over Internetgedrag van pubers.* SWP.

Park, S. K., Kim, J. Y., & Cho, C. B. (2008). Prevalence of Internet addiction and correlations with family factors among South Korean adolescents. *Adolescence, 43*(172), 895. PMID:19149152

Pauwels, C., Bauwens, J., & Vleugels, C. (2008). *Cyberteens: de betekenis van ICT in het dagelijkse leven van Belgische tieners* [Cyberteens: The relevance of ICT in daily life of Belgian teenagers]. Academic Press.

Quoss, B., & Zhao, W. (1995). Parenting styles and children's satisfaction with parenting in China and the United States. *Journal of Comparative Family Studies*, 265–280.

Rosen, L. D., Cheever, N. A., & Carrier, L. M. (2008). The association of parenting style and child age with parental limit setting and adolescent MySpace behavior. *Journal of Applied Developmental Psychology, 29*(6), 459–471. doi:10.1016/j.appdev.2008.07.005

Sasson, H., & Mesch, G. (2014). Parental mediation, peer norms and risky online behavior among adolescents. *Computers in Human Behavior, 33*, 32–38. doi:10.1016/j.chb.2013.12.025

Şenormancı, Ö., Şenormancı, G., Güçlü, O., & Konkan, R. (2014). Attachment and family functioning in patients with Internet addiction. *General Hospital Psychiatry, 36*(2), 203–207. doi:10.1016/j.genhospsych.2013.10.012 PMID:24262601

Shapira, N. A., Lessig, M. C., Goldsmith, T. D., Szabo, S. T., Lazoritz, M., Gold, M. S., & Stein, D. J. (2003). Problematic Internet use: Proposed classification and diagnostic criteria. *Depression and Anxiety, 17*(4), 207–216. doi:10.1002/da.10094 PMID:12820176

Shin, S. E., Kim, N. S., & Jang, E. Y. (2011). Comparison of problematic Internet and alcohol use and attachment styles among industrial workers in Korea. *Cyberpsychology, Behavior, and Social Networking, 14*(11), 665–672. doi:10.1089/cyber.2010.0470 PMID:21595524

Steinberg, L. (2001). We know some things: Parent–adolescent relationships in retrospect and prospect. *Journal of Research on Adolescence, 11*(1), 1–19. doi:10.1111/1532-7795.00001

Steinberg, L., Lamborn, S. D., Darling, N., Mounts, N. S., & Dornbusch, S. M. (1994). Over-time changes in adjustment and competence among adolescents from authoritative, authoritarian, indulgent, and neglectful families. *Child Development, 65*(3), 754–770. doi:10.2307/1131416 PMID:8045165

Stocker, C. M., & Youngblade, L. (1999). Marital conflict and parental hostility: Links with children's sibling and peer relationships. *Journal of Family Psychology, 13*(4), 598–609. doi:10.1037/0893-3200.13.4.598

Tilson, E. C., McBride, C. M., Lipkus, I. M., & Catalano, R. F. (2004). Testing the interaction between parent–child relationship factors and parent smoking to predict youth smoking. *The Journal of Adolescent Health, 35*(3), 182–189. doi:10.1016/S1054-139X(03)00532-9 PMID:15313499

Torres-Villa, M. S. (1995). *Parenting styles, language and parents1 education as predictors of school achievement for Hispanic students* (Unpublished doctoral dissertation). Georgia State University, Atlanta, GA.

Tripp, L. M. (2011). 'The computer is not for you to be looking around, it is for schoolwork': Challenges for digital inclusion as Latino immigrant families negotiate children's access to the Internet. *New Media & Society, 13*(4), 552–567. doi:10.1177/1461444810375293

Tsitsika, A., Critselis, E., Louizou, A., Janikian, M., Freskou, A., Marangou, E., & Kafetzis, D. A. et al. (2011). Determinants of Internet addiction among adolescents: A case-control study. *The Scientific World Journal, 11*, 866–874. doi:10.1100/tsw.2011.85 PMID:21516283

Türkel, Y. D., & Tezer, E. (2008). Parenting styles and learned resourcefulness of Turkish adolescents. *Adolescence, 43*(169), 143. PMID:18447086

Valcke, M., Bonte, S., De Wever, B., & Rots, I. (2010). Internet parenting styles and the impact on Internet use of primary school children. *Computers & Education, 55*(2), 454–464. doi:10.1016/j.compedu.2010.02.009

Valcke, M., Schellens, T., Van Keer, H., & Gerarts, M. (2007). Primary school children's safe and unsafe use of the Internet at home and at school: An exploratory study. *Computers in Human Behavior, 23*(6), 2838–2850. doi:10.1016/j.chb.2006.05.008

Valentine, G., & Holloway, S. (2001). On-line Dangers? Geographies of Parents' Fears for Children's Safety in Cyberspace. *The Professional Geographer, 53*(1), 71–83.

Valkenburg, P. (2002). *Beeldschermkinderen: Theorieën over kind en media* [Screen-kids: Theories 670 about children and media]. Amsterdam: Boom.

Valkenburg, P. M., Krcmar, M., Peeters, A. L., & Marseille, N. M. (1999). Developing a scale to assess three styles of television mediation: "Instructive mediation," "restrictive mediation," and "social coviewing". *Journal of Broadcasting & Electronic Media, 43*(1), 52–66. doi:10.1080/08838159909364474

Valkenburg, P. M., & Peter, J. (2011). Online communication among adolescents: An integrated model of its attraction, opportunities, and risks. *The Journal of Adolescent Health, 48*(2), 121–127. doi:10.1016/j.jadohealth.2010.08.020 PMID:21257109

Van den Eijnden, R. J., Meerkerk, G. J., Vermulst, A. A., Spijkerman, R., & Engels, R. C. (2008). Online communication, compulsive Internet use, and psychosocial well-being among adolescents: A longitudinal study. *Developmental Psychology, 44*(3), 655–665. doi:10.1037/0012-1649.44.3.655 PMID:18473634

Van Den Eijnden, R. J., Spijkerman, R., Vermulst, A. A., van Rooij, T. J., & Engels, R. C. (2010). Compulsive Internet use among adolescents: Bidirectional parent–child relationships. *Journal of Abnormal Child Psychology*, *38*(1), 77–89. doi:10.1007/s10802-009-9347-8 PMID:19728076

Van Der Vorst, H., Engels, R. C., Meeus, W., Deković, M., & Van Leeuwe, J. (2005). The role of alcohol-specific socialization in adolescents' drinking behaviour. *Addiction (Abingdon, England)*, *100*(10), 1464–1476. doi:10.1111/j.1360-0443.2005.01193.x PMID:16185208

Van Rooij, T., & Van den Eijnden, R. J. J. M. (2007). *Monitor Internet en Jongeren 2006 en 2007: Ontwikkelingen in Internetgebruik en de rol van opvoeding*. Rotterdam: IVO.

Vandermaas-Peeler, M., Way, E., & Umpleby, J. (2003). Parental guidance in a cooking activity with preschoolers. *Journal of Applied Developmental Psychology*, *24*(1), 75–89. doi:10.1016/S0193-3973(03)00025-X

Vanlanduyt, L., & De Cleyn, I. (2007). *Invloed van Internet bij jongeren: een uitdaging op school en thuis*. Academic Press.

Wallace, J. D. (1999). *Nameless in cyberspace: Anonymity on the Internet*. Cato Institute.

Walrave, M., Lenaerts, S., & De Moor, S. (2008). *Cyberteens@ risk? Tieners verknocht aan Internet, maar ook waakzaam voor risico's*. Academic Press.

Wang, H., Zhou, X., Lu, C., Wu, J., Deng, X., & Hong, L. (2011). Problematic Internet use in high school students in Guangdong Province, China. *PLoS One*, *6*(5), e19660. doi:10.1371/journal.pone.0019660 PMID:21573073

Wang, R., Bianchi, S. M., & Raley, S. B. (2005). Teenagers' Internet use and family rules: A research note. *Journal of Marriage and the Family*, *67*(5), 1249–1258. doi:10.1111/j.1741-3737.2005.00214.x

Weinstein, A., & Lejoyeux, M. (2010). Internet addiction or excessive Internet use. *The American Journal of Drug and Alcohol Abuse*, *36*(5), 277–283. doi:10.3109/00952990.2010.491880 PMID:20545603

Widyanto, L., & Griffiths, M. D. (2009). Unravelling the web: adolescents and Internet addiction. *Adolescent online social communication and behavior: Relationship formation on the Internet*, 29-49.

Willoughby, T. (2008). A short-term longitudinal study of Internet and computer game use by adolescent boys and girls: Prevalence, frequency of use, and psychosocial predictors. *Developmental Psychology*, *44*(1), 195–204. doi:10.1037/0012-1649.44.1.195 PMID:18194017

Wu, C. S. T., Wong, H. T., Yu, K. F., Fok, K. W., Yeung, S. M., Lam, C. H., & Liu, K. M. (2016). Parenting approaches, family functionality, and Internet addiction among Hong Kong adolescents. *BMC Pediatrics*, *16*(1), 130. doi:10.1186/s12887-016-0666-y PMID:27538688

Xiong, Z. B., Detzner, D. F., & Cleveland, M. J. (2005). Southeast Asian adolescents' perceptions of immigrant parenting practices. *Hmong Studies Journal, 5*, 1–20. Retrieved from http://hmongstudies.com/XiongDetznerClevelandHSJ5. pdf

Xu, J., Shen, L. X., Yan, C. H., Hu, H., Yang, F., Wang, L., & Zhang, J. et al. (2014). Parent-adolescent interaction and risk of adolescent Internet addiction: A population-based study in Shanghai. *BMC Psychiatry*, *14*(1), 112. doi:10.1186/1471-244X-14-112 PMID:24731648

Xu, Z., Turel, O., & Yuan, Y. (2012). Online game addiction among adolescents: Motivation and prevention factors. *European Journal of Information Systems*, *21*(3), 321–340. doi:10.1057/ejis.2011.56

Yang, C. Y., Sato, T., Yamawaki, N., & Miyata, M. (2013). Prevalence and risk factors of problematic Internet use: A cross-national comparison of Japanese and Chinese university students. *Transcultural Psychiatry*, *50*(2), 263–279. doi:10.1177/1363461513488876 PMID:23660582

Yang, X., Zhu, L., Chen, Q., Song, P., & Wang, Z. (2016). Parent marital conflict and Internet addiction among Chinese college students: The mediating role of father-child, mother-child, and peer attachment. *Computers in Human Behavior*, *59*, 221–229. doi:10.1016/j.chb.2016.01.041

Yao, M. Z., He, J., Ko, D. M., & Pang, K. (2014). The influence of personality, parental behaviors, and self-esteem on Internet addiction: A study of Chinese college students. *Cyberpsychology, Behavior, and Social Networking*, *17*(2), 104–110. doi:10.1089/cyber.2012.0710 PMID:24003966

Yen, J. Y., Yen, C. F., Chen, C. C., Chen, S. H., & Ko, C. H. (2007). Family factors of Internet addiction and substance use experience in Taiwanese adolescents. *Cyberpsychology & Behavior*, *10*(3), 323–329. doi:10.1089/cpb.2006.9948 PMID:17594255

Young, K. S. (1998). Internet addiction: The emergence of a new clinical disorder. *CyberPsycholgy & Behavior*, *1*(3), 237–244. doi:10.1089/cpb.1998.1.237

Young, K. S. (1999). Internet addiction: symptoms, evaluation and treatment. *Innovations in Clinical Practice: A Source Book, 17*, 19-31.

Young, K. S. (2004). Internet addiction: A new clinical phenomenon and its consequences. *The American Behavioral Scientist*, *48*(4), 402–415. doi:10.1177/0002764204270278

Young, K. S., & Rogers, R. C. (1998). The relationship between depression and Internet addiction. *Cyberpsychology & Behavior*, *1*(1), 25–28. doi:10.1089/cpb.1998.1.25

Yu, J. (2003). The association between parental alcohol-related behaviors and children's drinking. *Drug and Alcohol Dependence*, *69*(3), 253–262. doi:10.1016/S0376-8716(02)00324-1 PMID:12633911

Yu, L., & Shek, D. T. (2014). Family functioning, positive youth development, and Internet addiction in junior secondary school students: Structural equation modeling using AMOS. *International Journal on Disability and Human Development*, *13*(2), 227–238. doi:10.1515/ijdhd-2014-0308

Zhang, H., Spinrad, T. L., Eisenberg, N., Luo, Y., & Wang, Z. (2017). Young adults' Internet addiction: Prediction by the interaction of parental marital conflict and respiratory sinus arrhythmia. *International Journal of Psychophysiology*, *120*, 148–156. doi:10.1016/j.ijpsycho.2017.08.002 PMID:28800963

Zhang, Liu, Q. X., Deng, L. Y., Fang, X. Y., Liu, C. Y., & Lan, J. (2011). Parents-adolescents relations and adolescent's Internet addiction: the mediation effect of loneliness. *Psychological Development and Education, 6*, 641-64.

KEY TERMS AND DEFINITIONS

Family Functioning: The capacity of the family system to meet the needs of its members. Members in a functional family work together to improve relationships when they face challenges.

Marital Conflict: High levels of disagreement arising between the two parties in a marriage.

Parental Guidance: The attempts of parents to establish rules, give advice, offer direction, counseling and protection.

Parental Mediation: The attempts of parents to manage the relation between children and the media.

Parental Monitoring: The attempts of parents to supervise and understand the type of the activities their child is involved in. Parents can also monitor with who their children are communicating online.

Parental Norms: Informal guidelines that govern the behavior of parents.

Parenting Style: The strategies parents employ in rearing their child. While authoritative parents set rules and enforce boundaries based on open discussion and reasoning, authoritarian parents demand blind obedience. Permissive parents are reluctant to enforce rules and rarely set rules and boundaries. Parents with a laissez-faire parenting style, on the other hand, are indifferent to the needs of their child.

Chapter 9

Evaluating the Risk of Digital Addiction in Blended Learning Environments: Considering ICT Intensity, Learning Style, and Architecture

Jonathan Bishop
Crocels Community Media Group, UK

ABSTRACT

Digital addiction is a phenomenon where people who might take up addictive substances or other self-medicating activities do so instead with information and communications technology. The environment in which someone finds themselves is known to influence their behaviour. This might be as a result of the environment placing more demands on people with one cognitive set-up compared to those with a different one. One might not normally think of education environments as addictive, but the introduction of technology into them can affect different learners in different ways. Through computing a measure of brain activity called knol (k), this paper seeks to explore how learners with different learning styles react in environments that are differentiated according to the intensity of ICTs used and the physical architecture of the learning environment in which those ICTs are used.

INTRODUCTION

The concept of Internet addiction has been in existence for some time (Beard, 2005; Young, 1998a; Young, 1998b). However, the idea that people can be addicted to the Internet as a medium is less than satisfactory. This chapter looks at measuring 'digital addiction', which assumes not that digital technology is addictive, but that people with compulsive tendencies will use it as if it were. In other words, someone who has digital addiction is not addicted to technology, as they would engage in some other compulsion, such as smoking or drinking. Equally, it is unsatisfactory to use the term 'Internet gaming addiction'

DOI: 10.4018/978-1-5225-3477-8.ch009

because one would not say board gamers who play and drink at public houses have "pub addiction" as the public house is simply the venue for their compulsive game playing and drinking.

This chapter therefore seeks to assess the impact the environment in which a person is situated has on their propensity to be compulsive in their use of digital technologies. It is assumed throughout that addictive behaviours are caused as a result of disruption to the optimal regulation of a person's dopamine and serotonin levels, which creates a condition called serotonergic-dopaminergic asynchronicity, or 'SDA' (Bishop, 2011; Bishop, 2012).

BACKGROUND

This chapter looks at how digital addiction can manifest in educational environments through learners increasing the extent to which they are excited by or engaged with the environment in which they are located. To test this there are three variables that are controlled for. This includes the intensity of ICTs used in the environment, the learning style of the participant and the architecture of the environment in which the learning takes place.

ICT Intensity

The intensity of the use of information and communications technologies in a classroom can affect the extent to which learning outcomes are achieved and learners are able to feel a sense of community. Figure 1 sets out the blended learning continuum (Chew, Jones, & Turner, 2008), which is utilised in this chapter to design the learning environments in which the learners' level of engagement and propensity to experience digital addiction are measured.

Figure 1. The blended learning continuum

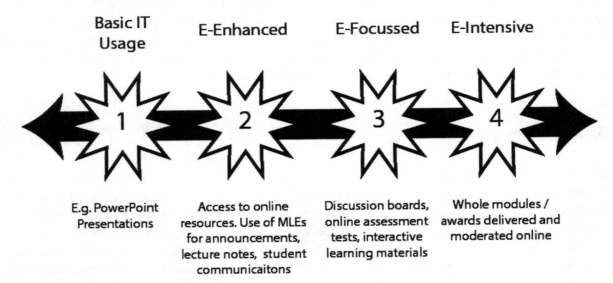

Learning Styles

Learning styles are a way of categorising the way learners learn so that it is possible for educators to change the way they teach to accommodate those learners' preferences (Shah & Gathoo, 2017). Learning styles have been seen as an effective means for educators to assess the individual development of learners (Rahman & Ahmar, 2017). However, learning styles have come under some criticism for encouraging a form of self-categorisation that is not based on actual learning preferences (Kirschner, 2017). Even so, in this chapter, learning styles are considered, but from a neurological stand point rather than the more socially constructed models that can be found elsewhere (Honey & Mumford, 1986; Kolb, 1984; Stubbs & Watkins, 1997).

Figure 2 sets out a neurological model of learning from which learning styles are extracted for this study. It is asserted that people whose SDA causes them to seek out learning environments where they work on their own have 'autistic' personality and those whose SDA makes them prefer learning in groups have an 'empathic' personality. Those whose SDA means they cannot tolerate things going against their own worldview are 'neurotic' and those who do not like being in environments where they do not know what is going on are 'psychotic' and those who like things kept simple are 'demotic' (Bishop, 2015b).

Whilst these labels in Figure 2 might not be ones that one might find in popular self-help books, at a clinical level they can be helpful in attributing neurological differences to learning preferences, in a way

Figure 2. A neurological model of learning

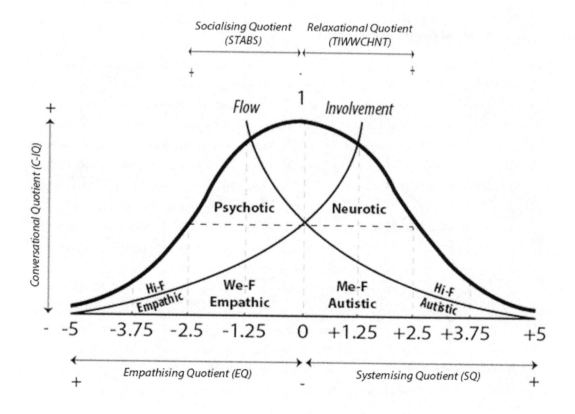

that traditional approaches to understanding learning styles fail to consider. For instance, someone who is an activist in one of the main learning style theories will behave differently depending on the manifestation of their SDA. A neurotic activist will want to campaign against those with a different version of the truth to them and argue their version of the truth is right. A psychotic activist will want to categorise people according to whether they agree with them or disagree with them and then support those who agree with them. An autistic activist will campaign strongly for those they support and against those they do not. An empathic activist will associate themselves with those who feel the same way about things as them, even if they do not achieve anything. And finally, a demotic activist will want to campaign on easy to understand and argue issues rather than support something that is multidimensional and complex.

Education Environment Architecture

The architectural design of classrooms has been important for public policy makers in order to ensure that learners can receive an education in the optimal context (Heschong, 1999). The use of energy efficiency policies are known to impact on the architectural design of school and the learning outcome of pupils (De Andrade, José Baltazar Salgueirinho Osório, Dutra, Schwinden, & de Andrade, 2015). The ability of some learners to feel included in an educational environment is in part influenced by the architecture of that environment (Rands, McDonald, & Clapp, 2013). Figure 3 shows the ecological cognition framework (Bishop, 2007a; Bishop, 2007b), which was used in this study in order to generate the variables used to conduct the 4-iteration study and can be seen as an effective model for understanding the environment in which learners are situated.

Figure 3. The ecological cognition framework

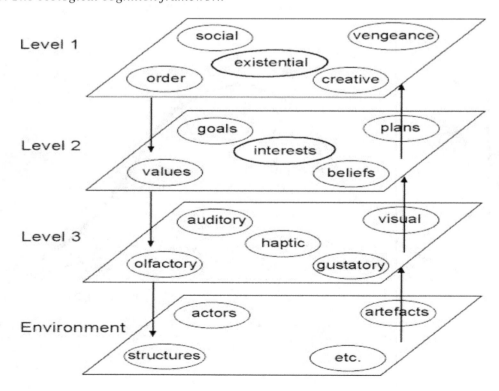

INVESTIGATION

This investigation comes in four iterations. The first is based on a field trip and workshop, more suited to empathics. The second is based on a cybercafé and workshop, more suited to autistics. The third is based on an ICT laboratory, more suited to people who are neither autistic nor empathic. The fourth, based on augmented learning, is normally accessible to both autistics and empathics, but does not especially benefit one or the other as much as the earlier approaches. Table 1 sets out how the dependent variables are organised across the four iterations. The independent variables consist of 27 questionnaire items relating to befriending, delurking and kudos (Bishop, 2016b).

Iteration 1: Field Trip and Church Hall

The first iteration of this study took the form of a field trip and workshop in a church hall in the village of Treforest in South Wales. Table 2 sets out the resources used in iteration one in terms of the ICT intensity.

Table 3 sets out the answers of learners to the questions in the category of "How much did you enjoy taking part in the workshop?" for sessions 1 and 2, which took place in the Taff Vale area of Taf Ely, specifically the village of Trefforest. The Mean refers to the average score out of 5 that a learner gave on their feedback form and the k refers to the "knol" (a measure of brain activity) for that activity for the autistic learner and the empathic learner. It shows that greatest satisfaction (M=5) was liking those who were in the class. Next was feeling they had access to the information they needed (M=4.58). Then it was feeling able to take part and to know and trust those in the group (M=4.44), followed by being able to trust their own abilities (M=4.31). The lowest was being able to help others who were stuck (M=2.78) and then being content with information provided, feeling helpful by participating and finding the equip-

Table 1. Dependent variables

#	Environment	ICT Intensity	Learning Styles
1	Field Trip and Church Hall	Mainly non-ICT	Empathic
2	Cybercafe	Mainly Basic ICT	Autistic
3	ICT Laboratory	Mainly E-enhanced	Demotic
4	Augmented Technology	Mainly E-intensive	Psychotic, neurotic

Table 2. Learning resources for iteration 1

Resource Type	Resources
Non-ICT	Flipchart paper, flipchart pens, flipchart easel, cellotape, scissors. Heritage artefacts., Consent form. Flipchart stand, flip chart paper, blutac, instant digital cameras Flipchart stand, flipchart paper, blutac miner's Davy Lamp, Pontypridd centenary coin, coins of Tony Blair and Winston Churchill, Several A2 card sorting grids, packs of perforated business cards, printer to print cards, Flipchart collages from earlier in the day, cards from earlier in the day, and encouraging the cards to be blutac-ed to the flipchart collages.
Basic ICT	Instant digital cameras, digital camera, printer.
E-enhanced	None.
E-focussed	None.
E-intensive	None.

Table 3 Learners' evaluations results for sessions 1 and 2 (How much did you enjoy taking part in the workshop?)

Q#	Question	Mean	Autistic k	Empathic k
1	I felt like I was always able to take part	4.44	0.814017	0.976705
2	I felt that the content of the information provided was relevant to me	3.89	0.817209	0.978409
3	I felt I was able to find out the others in the group and trust them	4.44	0.813218	0.980303
4	I felt I was being helpful each time I participated	3.89	0.813218	0.982197
5	I found the software and other equipment easy to use	3.89	0.829183	0.978409
6	I like the other members of the class and felt part of a community	5.00	0.813218	0.978409
7	I felt I was able to trust in my own abilities during the class	4.31	0.813218	0.980777
8	I felt I was able to help others who were stuck	2.78	0.841954	0.978409
9	I found I had access to all the information I needed	4.58	0.813218	0.979830

ment easy to use followed (M=3.89). The knol for the autistic learners were around 0.81, which is the optimal. For the empathic learner, the knol was between 0.97 and 0.98, suggesting the environment was most optimal for them, which is what was intended.

Table 4 sets out the answers of learners to the questions in the category of "How friendly was the workshop?" for sessions 1 and 2, which took place in the Taff Vale area of Taf Ely, specifically the village of Trefforest. The highest score (M=5) related to finding the activities to be meaningful and the lowest (M=3.47) related to feeling that everyone was kind and friendly and not feeling criticised. This was followed with feeling the class was welcoming, not hostile and tailored to the needs of the learner (M=3.89). Towards the higher end (M=4.44) was taking part in the class without feeling intimidated and taking part without feeling any tension. This was followed by feeling able to trust others in the class (M-4.61). In terms of the knol, the autistic participant was between 0.80 and 0.82 which is near the optimal of 0.81, whereas the empathic was between 0.97 and 1.0, which was to be expected because the session was designed for their learning style.

Table 5 sets out the answers of learners to the questions in the category of "Did you find it easy to make friends during the workshop?" for sessions 1 and 2. The lowest were feeling the class was interac-

Table 4. Learners' evaluations results for sessions 1 and 2 (How friendly was the workshop?)

Q#	Question	Mean	Autistic k	Empathic k
10	I felt that everyone was kind and friendly	3.47	0.808429	0.978598
11	I found the class was welcoming and not hostile or irrelevant	3.89	0.828118	1.000000
12	I felt I was able to trust others in the class to be friendly	4.61	0.813218	0.979646
13	I found the content of the course valuable and in tune with my beliefs	5.00	0.813218	0.978409
14	I found that the activities I was asked to do were meaningful	5.00	0.813218	0.978409
15	I found I was able to take part in activities without feeling criticised	3.47	0.828118	0.979735
16	I felt I was able to take part in the class without feeling intimidated	4.44	0.813218	0.980177
17	I felt the class was tailored to my needs and I was respected as me	3.89	0.828118	1.000000
18	I felt taking part in the class was easy without me feeling any tension	4.44	0.813218	0.980177

Table 5. Learners' evaluations results for sessions 1 and 2 (Did you find it easy to make friends during the workshop?)

Q#	Question	Mean	Autistic k	Empathic k
19	I felt I could be friends with everyone there	3.89	0.838761	0.994773
20	The class was relevant and unimportant things were avoided	4.44	0.836207	0.996288
21	I felt there was trust in the class and no inappropriate behaviours	1.67	0.838761	1.000833
22	Things in the class were fun and I agreed with what I was told	4.58	0.836207	0.833333
23	The technology was appropriate and considerate of my needs	4.58	0.836207	1.000000
24	The class was interactive without any behavioural issues from others	0.56	0.841315	1.000833
25	I felt safe in the class because everyone got on with each other	3.89	0.997803	0.997803
26	I felt changes were accommodated and my needs accounted for	3.47	0.838761	0.995909
27	I felt it was easy to take part in the class - it fitted around my life	5.00	0.836207	0.810556

tive without behavioural issues from others (M=0.57) and that there was trust in the class (M=1.67). The highest was that the class fitted around the learner's life (M=5.0). This was followed by feeling the class was fun and took account of the learner's needs (M=4.58) and then that it was relevant (M=4.44). Whether changes were accommodated was quite high (M=3.47), followed by being able to be friends with those present and feeling sage in the class (M=3.89).

Iteration 2: Cybercafé

Iteration 2 took part in a cybercafé environment in Tonyrefail in South Wales in which there was also a table present in addition to the computers. Table 6 sets out the resources used in terms of the ICT intensity.

Table 6 sets out the answers of learners to the questions in the category of "How much did you enjoy taking part in the workshop?" for sessions 3, 4 and 5. As can be seen, the lowest amount of satisfaction (M=1.11) is feeling able to help others who were stuck. The highest (M=4.44) related to feeling the information provided was relevant, trust in the group, finding the software easy to use and trust in own abilities. The next lowest (M=3.06) covered always being able to take part and being able to access all information needed. Second highest (M=3.33) included feeling that one was being helpful and feeling part of a community. In this context, the autistic participants went from a knol of 0.66 to 0.82, but on the whole, was much higher than in the group work setting. The empathic learners were between 0.79 and 0.80, which was much lower than with the group sessions. This is to be expected as there was a lot of individual learning in this iteration, which is more suited to autistic participants than empathic ones.

Table 8 sets out the answers of learners to the questions in the category of "How friendly was the workshop?" for sessions 3, 4, and 5. The lowest satisfaction (M=2.78) was for feeling everyone was kind and friendly and feeling the class was tailored to their needs, but this is still more than 50% satisfaction. The highest (M=5.0) was for being able to take part in the class without feeling intimidated and taking part without feeling any tension. The second highest (M=4.44) was for finding the class non-hostile and relevant, finding others in the class trustworthy and friendly, and finding the content of the course in tune with them believes. Finally, finding the activities meaningful seemed the mid-point (M=3.89). In

Table 6. ICT and other resources for iteration 2

Resource Type	Resources
Non-ICT	Real-world artefacts such as a copy of the Llantrisant Town Charter, coins on Magna Carta and Llantrisant.
Basic ICT	Digital camera and its contents. Microsoft Word
E-enhanced	Microsoft Word.
E-focussed	The manged learning environment and its contents.
E-intensive	N/A.

Table 7 Learners' evaluations results for sessions 3, 4 and 5 (How much did you enjoy taking part in the workshop?)

Q#	Question	Mean	Autistic k	Empathic k
1	I felt like I was always able to take part	3.06	0.820003	0.798534
2	I felt that the content of the information provided was relevant to me	4.44	0.817209	0.797994
3	I felt I was able to find out the others in the group and trust them	4.44	0.817209	0.797994
4	I felt I was being helpful each time I participated	3.33	0.825192	0.799537
5	I found the software and other equipment easy to use	4.44	0.817209	0.797994
6	I like the other members of the class and felt part of a community	3.33	0.666667	0.799537
7	I felt I was able to trust in my own abilities during the class	4.44	0.817209	0.797994
8	I felt I was able to help others who were stuck	1.11	0.797994	0.802623
9	I found I had access to all the information I needed	3.06	0.825192	0.800309

Table 8. Learners' evaluations results for sessions 3, 4 and 5 (How friendly was the workshop?)

Q#	Question	Mean	Autistic k	Empathic k
10	I felt that everyone was kind and friendly	2.78	0.823329	0.799177
11	I found the class was welcoming and not hostile or irrelevant	4.44	0.816943	0.797942
12	I felt I was able to trust others in the class to be friendly	4.44	0.816943	0.797942
13	I found the content of the course valuable and in tune with my beliefs	4.44	0.816943	0.797942
14	I found that the activities I was asked to do were meaningful	3.89	0.816943	0.799383
15	I found I was able to take part in activities without feeling criticised	4.44	0.816943	0.797942
16	I felt I was able to take part in the class without feeling intimidated	5.00	0.813218	0.797222
17	I felt the class was tailored to my needs and I was respected as me	2.78	0.828118	0.800103
18	I felt taking part in the class was easy without me feeling any tension	5.00	0.813218	0.797222

terms of the class, the empathics scored between 0.79 and 0.80 and the autistics between 0.81 and 0.82. This is to be expected as the class was more tailored to autistic people than empathics.

Table 9 sets out the answers of learners to the questions in the category of "Did you find it easy to make friends during the workshop?" for sessions 1 and 2. There were a lot of maximum scores in this category (M=5.0) including that things in the class were fund and agreeable, that the class was relevant

Table 9 Learners' evaluations results for session 1and 2 (Did you find it easy to make friends during the workshop?)

Q#	Question	Mean	Autistic k	Empathic k
19	I felt I could be friends with everyone there	2.78	0.838761	0.813025
20	The class was relevant and unimportant things were avoided	5.00	0.836207	0.810556
21	I felt there was trust in the class and no inappropriate behaviours	2.78	0.838761	0.813025
22	Things in the class were fun and I agreed with what I was told	5.00	0.836207	0.813025
23	The technology was appropriate and considerate of my needs	5.00	0.836207	0.810556
24	The class was interactive without any behavioural issues from others	0.56	0.841315	0.815494
25	I felt safe in the class because everyone got on with each other	5.00	0.836207	0.810556
26	I felt changes were accommodated and my needs accounted for	2.78	0.838761	0.813025
27	I felt it was easy to take part in the class - it fitted around my life	5.00	0.836207	0.810556

and unimportant things avoided, that the technology was appropriate and considerate of needs, that the class felt safe and that the class fitted around the learners' lives. The lowest score (M=0.56) was that the class was interactive without any behavioural issues. The mid-point scores (M=2.78) were for feeling they could be friends with those there, feeling there was trust in the class, and feeling changes accommodated needs. The autistic learners had a knol of between 0.83 and 0.84 and the empathic learners at the optimal of 0.81. This was to be expected as the class was designed more for autistic learners than empathic ones.

Iteration 3: ICT Laboratory

The third iteration, took place in an ICT laboratory with a virtual learning environment and is based on the concept of e-tivies (Salmon, 2003). Table 10 sets out the resources used in terms of the ICT intensity.

Table 11 sets out the answers of learners to the questions in the category of "How much did you enjoy taking part in the workshop?" for sessions 6, 7, 8. The interesting thing about this class was that the average scores were all in the above 50% satisfaction range. The lowest (M=2.67) was for having access to all the information and the next lowest (M=2.83) was for feeling able to help others who were stuck. The peak of 5.0 was not reached in this class. The highest (M=3.94) was for feeling always able to take part, then for finding the software easy to use (M=3.78), followed by feeling helpful each time

Table 10. ICT and other resources used in iteration 3

Resource Type	Resources
Non-ICT	Consent form, Flipchart stand, flip chart paper, blutac, miner's Davy Lamp, Pontypridd centenary coin, coins of Tony Blair and Winston Churchill. Photo paper to print collages.
Basic ICT	instant digital cameras. Video camera to record interviews with learners about their collages. Devices containing own images.
E-enhanced	Adobe Photoshop, images, text, comments and discussions created or referred to in VLE.
E-focussed	VLE containing pre-created and approved content relating to Heritage, Place, Community.
E-intensive	VLE containing comments section underneath each image or text based artefact

Table 11 Learners' evaluations results for sessions 6, 7 and 8 (How much did you enjoy taking part in the workshop?)

Q#	Question	Mean	Autistic k	Demotic k	Empathic k	Psychotic k
1	I felt like I was always able to take part	3.94	0.821999	0.954082	0.899524	0.963530
2	I felt that the content of the information provided was relevant to me	3.50	0.825192	0.972033	0.904550	0.972033
3	I felt I was able to find out the others in the group and trust them	3.11	0.829183	0.962585	0.904118	0.986206
4	I felt I was being helpful each time I participated	3.72	0.825192	0.962585	0.905753	0.983844
5	I found the software and other equipment easy to use	3.78	0.817209	0.962585	0.906139	0.962585
6	I like the other members of the class and felt part of a community	3.56	0.817209	0.962585	0.899737	0.983844
7	I felt I was able to trust in my own abilities during the class	3.11	0.825192	0.962585	0.906524	0.972033
8	I felt I was able to help others who were stuck	2.83	0.837165	0.962585	0.908839	0.983844
9	I found I had access to all the information I needed	2.67	0.829183	0.972033	0.905753	0.981481

they participated (M=3.72). The mid-points included feeling the content was relevant (M=3.50) and there was a community atmosphere (M=3.56). The next lower scores (M=3.11) included feeling able to find out and trust others in the ground and trusting their own abilities.

The class was intended to be mixed to cover all learning types, whether autistic, demotic, empathic or psychotic. The autistic learners ranged from the optimal of 0.81 to 0.82. The empathic ranged from 0.89 to 0.90. The demotic ranged from 0.95 to 0.97. The psychotic ranged from 0.96 to 0.98. There was no neurotic in the class. This shows that mixed environments are particularly suited to those type of learners that are neither autistic nor empathic, but that those who are autistic or empathic perform at an optimal level. As this class was intended to reflect a traditional school environment of mixed learning styles, it would strongly suggest that whilst mixed ability classes suit those who on the fringe of society, they do not help those who are in one of the two dominant groups, namely autistics and empathics, who best learn in environments suited to their specific way of learning, which is individually for autistics and in groups for empathics.

Table 12 Table 11 sets out the answers of learners to the questions in the category of "How friendly was the workshop?" for sessions 6, 7 and 8. In this part, the satisfaction was all above the 50 mark. The lowest score (M=3.28) was for finding the activities meaningful, the next lowest (M=3.39) for finding everyone to be kind and friendly. The highest was nowhere near 5.0 (M=3.61), being for finding the content of the course valuable and in keeping with beliefs as well as taking part without feeling any tension. This was followed (M=3.83) by finding the class welcoming and non-hostile and that it was possible to trust others to be friendly. The mid-points (M=3.44) were for feeling able to take part in activities without feeling criticised and being able to take part without feeling intimidated. And close to this was feeling the class was tailored to their needs (M=3.50).

In terms of knol, autistics scored between 0.81 and 0.83, empathics between 0.89 and 0.90, demotics between 0.95 and 0.96 and psychotics between 0.97 and 0.98. This shows once more that a class designed for mixed abilities is most suited to those who are not in one of the dominant groups of autistics and empathics. Whilst the empathics did better than the autistics, neither scored as high as the other two groups. The lessons were less structured, which might explain why autistics and empathics were not engaged with this class.

Table 12. Learners' evaluations results for sessions 6, 7 and 8 (How friendly was the workshop?)

Q#	Question	Mean	Autistic k	Demotic k	Empathic k	Psychotic k
10	I felt that everyone was kind and friendly	3.39	0.823329	0.956916	0.896385	0.974553
11	I found the class was welcoming and not hostile or irrelevant	3.83	0.816943	0.962585	0.899375	0.971403
12	I felt I was able to trust others in the class to be friendly	3.83	0.824393	0.962585	0.899375	0.971403
13	I found the content of the course valuable and in tune with my beliefs	3.61	0.816943	0.966994	0.901621	0.971403
14	I found that the activities I was asked to do were meaningful	3.28	0.820668	0.962585	0.899375	0.982426
15	I found I was able to take part in activities without feeling criticised	3.44	0.816943	0.962585	0.904990	0.975813
16	I felt I was able to take part in the class without feeling intimidated	3.44	0.824393	0.962585	0.903867	0.978017
17	I felt the class was tailored to my needs and I was respected as me	3.50	0.816943	0.962585	0.903867	0.975813
18	I felt taking part in the class was easy without me feeling any tension	3.61	0.824393	0.962585	0.906113	0.973608

Table 13 sets out the answers of learners to the questions in the category of "Did you find it easy to make friends during the workshop?" for sessions 6, 7 and 8. The lowest score (M=2.83) was for feeling they could be friends with everyone there. The next lowest (M=3.17) was for feeling the class was relevant, unimportant things were avoided, that the class was fun, agreeable and the technology use was appropriate and considerate of needs. The highest score was for believing the class was interactive without behavioural issues (M=4.67) followed by feeling there was trust and no inappropriate behaviours (M=4.39) and that they felt safe because everyone got on. The mid-points (M=3.67) were for feeling the changes were accommodated and the needs of the learners also, and that it was easy to take part because the class fitted around their lives.

As with the others, the autistics and empathics were lower than the others, but in this aspect – relating to finding easy to make friends, not as low. The autistic learner was between 0.83 and 0.84, which one might expect, and the empathic was around 0.91. The demotics learners were between 0.98 and 0.99 and the psychotic learners were at 0.99. Again, this shows that demotics and psychotics perform better in the less structured environments than autistics and empathics.

Table 13. Learners' evaluations results for session 6, 7 and 8 (Did you find it easy to make friends during the workshop?)

Q#	Question	Mean	Autistic k	Demotic k	Empathic k	Psychotic k
19	I felt I could be friends with everyone there	2.83	0.838761	0.989796	0.913174	0.993197
20	The class was relevant and unimportant things were avoided	3.17	0.836207	0.990552	0.912131	0.993197
21	I felt there was trust in the class and no inappropriate behaviours	4.39	0.836207	0.989796	0.911168	0.990552
22	Things in the class were fun and I agreed with what I was told	3.17	0.836845	0.990552	0.913828	0.993197
23	The technology was appropriate and considerate of my needs	3.17	0.836845	0.989796	0.912131	0.990552
24	The class was interactive without any behavioural issues from others	4.67	0.838123	0.989796	0.911055	0.991308
25	I felt safe in the class because everyone got on with each other	4.00	0.841315	0.989796	0.911981	0.992819
26	I felt changes were accommodated and my needs accounted for	3.67	0.836845	0.989796	0.912131	0.990552
27	I felt it was easy to take part in the class - it fitted around my life	3.67	0.838123	0.991308	0.912131	0.992063

Iteration 4: Augmented Technology

In this iteration, using the Wizard of Oz approach (Bishop, 2005), participants were shown videos of others participating in the project, on one occasions viewing on a laptop (session 9) as if by webcam (Reddy, 1997) and on the second occasion (session 10) using a VR headset as if using the AVEUGLE system (Bishop, 2015a; Bishop, 2016a). These resources are set out in Table 14.

Table 15 sets out the learner's evaluations for sessions 9 and 10 for the category, 'How much did you enjoy taking part in the workshop?' The lowest mean score was in terms of feeling able to take part (M=2.22). This is understandable, because watching others participating through VR technology or web cams is not expectantly engaging. As would be expected, the scores for the autistic participant (k=0.82) were above the optimal of 0.81 and the scores for the empathic participant (k=0.79) was below, as autistic people do not need to engage as much with others as empathics. Second lowest (M=2.50) was relating to not being able to help others when stuck, with the autistic being much higher (k=0.82) than the empathic (k=0.79). Taking part remotely makes engaging with others difficult, and it is to be expected this would be more problematic for empathics than autistics. The joint highest (M=4.44) related to feeling the information was relevant and the software and equipment was easy to use. In both cases the autistic score was above the optimal (k=0.82) and the empathic was below the optimal (k=0.79), suggesting autistic people prefer the remoteness of the ways of engaging in this iteration. Those that were the next highest (M=3.89) related to being able to find out information, feeling helpful participating and having

Table 14. ICT and other resources used in iteration 4

Resource Type	Resources
Non-ICT	None.
Basic ICT	Use of laptop for 'Webcam' session.
E-enhanced	None.
E-focussed	None.
E-intensive	VR Headset showing videos of earlier sessions in 'VR' session.

Table 15. Learners' evaluations results for sessions 9 and 10 (How much did you enjoy taking part in the workshop?)

Q#	Question	Mean	Autistic k	Empathic k
1	I felt like I was always able to take part	2.22	0.823994	0.796605
2	I felt that the content of the information provided was relevant to me	4.44	0.821201	0.797222
3	I felt I was able to find out the others in the group and trust them	3.89	0.829183	0.797222
4	I felt I was being helpful each time I participated	3.89	0.813218	0.800309
5	I found the software and other equipment easy to use	4.44	0.821201	0.797222
6	I like the other members of the class and felt part of a community	2.92	0.829183	0.799923
7	I felt I was able to trust in my own abilities during the class	3.61	0.829183	0.797994
8	I felt I was able to help others who were stuck	2.50	0.835568	0.799537
9	I found I had access to all the information I needed	3.89	0.829183	0.797222

access to information. The knol for the autistic participant ranged from 0.813218 to 0.829183 and for the empathic from 0.797222 to 0.800309. The autistic was thus above the optimal of 0.81 and the empathic below, which again is what one might expect in a mode of delivery that is remote. The remaining measure that was quite low (M=2.92) related to feeling part of the community with the autistic again being much higher (k=0.82) than the empathic (k=0.79), which is to be expected as it is often less easy to participate with others remotely.

Table 16 sets out the learner's evaluations for sessions 9 and 10 for the category, 'How friendly was the workshop?' The lowest scoring items (M=2.78) related to feeling everyone was kind and friendly, finding the class welcoming and being able to take part in the classes without feeling intimidated. This was to be expected, and with the autistic ranging from a knol of 0.81 to 0.82 and the empathic ranging from a knol of 0.79 to 0.81, it can be seen that it was not too different an experience. The highest scoring item, at the maximum of 5 was 'I felt taking part in the class was easy without me feeling any tension' with the autistic's knol being 0.81 and the empathic's being .

Table 17 sets out the learner's evaluations for sessions 9 and 10 for the category, 'Did you find it easy to make friends at the workshop?' The k-scores for the autistic participant were between 0.836

Table 16 Learners' evaluations results for sessions 9 and 10 (How friendly was the workshop?)

Q#	Question	Mean	Autistic k	Empathic k
10	I felt that everyone was kind and friendly	2.78	0.817742	0.817742
11	I found the class was welcoming and not hostile or irrelevant	2.78	0.828118	0.800103
12	I felt I was able to trust others in the class to be friendly	3.89	0.828118	0.797222
13	I found the content of the course valuable and in tune with my beliefs	4.44	0.828118	0.797222
14	I found that the activities I was asked to do were meaningful	4.17	0.828118	0.797942
15	I found I was able to take part in activities without feeling criticised	2.78	0.828118	0.798663
16	I felt I was able to take part in the class without feeling intimidated	3.19	0.828118	0.797582
17	I felt the class was tailored to my needs and I was respected as me	3.19	0.828118	0.797582
18	I felt taking part in the class was easy without me feeling any tension	5.00	0.813218	0.797222

Table 17. Learners' evaluations results for sessions 9 and 10 (Did you find it easy to make friends during the workshop?)

Q#	Question	Mean	Autistic k	Empathic k
19	I felt I could be friends with everyone there	3.89	0.838761	0.813796
20	The class was relevant and unimportant things were avoided	3.89	0.840038	0.812716
21	I felt there was trust in the class and no inappropriate behaviours	4.44	0.837484	0.813025
22	Things in the class were fun and I agreed with what I was told	3.89	0.840038	0.810864
23	The technology was appropriate and considerate of my needs	3.89	0.836207	0.810556
24	The class was interactive without any behavioural issues from others	4.44	0.837484	0.810556
25	I felt safe in the class because everyone got on with each other	2.92	0.838761	0.810864
26	I felt changes were accommodated and my needs accounted for	3.61	0.840038	0.810556
27	I felt it was easy to take part in the class - it fitted around my life	2.50	0.836207	0.810556

to 0.84 and the k-scores for the empathic were all in the 0.81 area. This is to be expected as autistic people are happier with mediated communication than in-person environments. The highest scoring answers (M=4.44) were feeling there was no inappropriate behaviour and that there was interaction without behavioural issues. This is of significant interest because it means both participants felt that this remote mode of learning meant that conflict was less likely to arise or be problematic. The lowest score related to the ease of taking part (M=2.5) and feeling safe because everyone got on (M=2.92), which is understandable because web cams and VR headsets do not yet offer the accessibility of being in person. The majority of the statements had a Mean of 3.89, covering feeling able to be friends with those there, feeling the class was relevant, that it was fun and agreeable and that the technology was appropriate, which is to be expected as the content was the same across the sessions. The third lowest answer (M=3.61) related to whether changes were accommodated, and with current VR and web cam technology this is not always easy to achieve.

IMPLICATIONS AND FUTURE RESEARCH DIRECTIONS

This chapter has looked heavily at questionnaire-derived data from a total of 10 teaching sessions that occurred over 4 iterations, looking at different intensities of ICT use in different types of educational building. The learning styles focussed on were autistic and empathic and showed that e-enhanced environments had a greater level of engagement and therefore higher chance of digital addiction than those environments that are either e-intensive or have no or basic use of ICTs. Those most useful conclusion from this finding is that the archetypal human-computer interaction approaches, using a PC, monitor and mouse have the greatest opportunities for digital addiction, and not the augmented technologies were either the participant interacts fully immersively, or otherwise remotely from the physical setting. Future research therefore needs to investigate whether this is a factor of the PC being the dominant interface for even the youngest of learners, or whether because it is multi-modal, namely it has a hand-driven pointing device, visual display of that movement, and entry through a fast keyboard, whether it is easier to engage with the system and that if augmented systems can be interacted with as much ease that they could become as digitally addictive.

CONCLUSION

This chapter has sought to investigate the interactions between ICT intensity, learning styles and education environment architecture. It was somewhat ethnographic in nature because it involved introducing learners into four different settings, namely a fieldtrip and church hall, a cybercafé, an ICT laboratory and augmented technology approach. The study found that there were key differences in what parts of these environments were most satisfactory to learners. In particular it found that learners felt more able to take part in the field-trip and workshop, they had better access to information in the cybercafé, the ICT laboratory was safer and more interactive, and the augmented technology was much better in terms of behavioural management. What was of most relevance was that the highest knols were found in the ICT laboratory across all learning styles. This might be because the PC has been the dominant means of human-computer interaction, even for the current generation, and that when other technologies, such as augmented and augmentive approaches become more accessible, then the k-scores for using these will increase also.

In terms of understanding digital addiction, the chapter has shown that the different environments offer different levels of engagement, which by using the measure of knol can assess the risk of each learning style compulsively using a particular intensity of ICT. As expected, autistic learners were more suited to environments that had a high level of ICT and that empathics were suited to environments that had a high level of in-person group work. Demotics were most suited to environments with the least amount of interaction required, psychotic those with the least dependence on social skills and neurotics those least dependent on technical skill.

REFERENCES

Beard, K. W. (2005). Internet addiction: A review of current assessment techniques and potential assessment questions. *Cyberpsychology & Behavior*, 8(1), 7–14. doi:10.1089/cpb.2005.8.7 PMID:15738688

Bishop, J. (2005). The role of mediating artifacts in the design of persuasive e-learning systems. *The 1st International Conference on Internet Technologies and Applications (ITA'05)*, 54-62.

Bishop, J. (2007a). Ecological cognition: A new dynamic for human-computer interaction. In B. Wallace, A. Ross, J. Davies & T. Anderson (Eds.), The mind, the body and the world: Psychology after cognitivism (pp. 327-345). Exeter, UK: Imprint Academic.

Bishop, J. (2007b). Increasing participation in online communities: A framework for human–computer interaction. *Computers in Human Behavior*, 23(4), 1881–1893. doi:10.1016/j.chb.2005.11.004

Bishop, J. (2011). *The role of the prefrontal cortex in social orientation construction: A pilot study.* Poster Presented to the BPS Welsh Conference on Wellbeing, Wrexham, UK.

Bishop, J. (2012). Taming the chatroom bob: The role of brain-computer interfaces that manipulate prefrontal cortex optimization for increasing participation of victims of traumatic sex and other abuse online. *Proceedings of the 13th International Conference on Bioinformatics and Computational Biology (BIOCOMP'12)*.

Bishop, J. (2015a). *An investigation into the extent and limitations of the GROW model for coaching and mentoring online: Towards 'prosthetic learning'.* The 14th International Conference on E-Learning, E-Business, Enterprise Information Systems, and E-Government (EEE'15), Las Vegas, NV.

Bishop, J. (2015b). Supporting communication between people with social orientation impairments using affective computing technologies: Rethinking the autism spectrum. In L. Bee Theng (Ed.), *Assistive technologies for physical and cognitive disabilities* (pp. 42–55). Hershey, PA: IGI Global. doi:10.4018/978-1-4666-7373-1.ch003

Bishop, J. (2016a). Enhancing the performance of human resources through E-mentoring: The role of an adaptive hypermedia system called "AVEUGLE". *International Management Review*, 12(1), 11–23.

Bishop, J. (2016b). *The impact of physical and virtual environments on human emotions: A pilot study in an adult and community education setting.* The 2016 International Conference on Computational Science and Computational Intelligence (CSCI'16), Las Vegas, NV.

Chew, E., Jones, N., & Turner, D. (2008). *Critical review of the blended learning models based on maslow's and vygotsky's educational theory.* Paper presented at the First International Conference on Hybrid Learning (ICHL 2008), Hong Kong. doi:10.1007/978-3-540-85170-7_4

De Andrade, J. B. S. O., Dutra, L., Schwinden, N. B. C., & de Andrade, S. F. (2015). Energy efficiency in the adoption of renewable energies in schools. In Implementing campus greening initiatives (pp. 183-201). Springer.

Heschong, L. (1999). *Daylighting in schools: An investigation into the relationship between daylighting and human performance.* Detailed Report.

Honey, P., & Mumford, A. (1986). *Manual of learning styles.* Maidenhead, UK: Peter Honey Publications.

Kirschner, P. A. (2017). Stop propagating the learning styles myth. *Computers & Education, 106,* 166–171. doi:10.1016/j.compedu.2016.12.006

Kolb, D. A. (1984). *Experiential learning: Experience as the source of learning and development.* London: Prentice Hall.

Rahman, A., & Ahmar, A. S. (2017). *Relationship between learning styles and learning achievement in mathematics based on genders.* Academic Press.

Rands, K., McDonald, J., & Clapp, L. (2013). *Landscaping classrooms toward queer utopias. In A critical inquiry into queer utopias* (pp. 149–172). Springer. doi:10.1057/9781137311979_7

Reddy, M. (1997). *Using the information superhighway to support the ACE initiative at level 12.* The 2nd BP International Conference on Students as Tutors and Mentors, London, UK.

Salmon, G. (2003). E-tivities: The key to active online learning. London: RoutledgeFalmer.

Shah, J., & Gathoo, V. (2017). *Learning styles and academic achievement of children with and without hearing impairment in primary inclusive classrooms in mumbai. Journal of Disability Management and Special Education, 1,* 1.

Stubbs, G., & Watkins, M. (1997). CBL: Assessing the student learning experience. *Proceedings of Frontiers in Education Conference, 1997. 27th Annual Conference. Teaching and Learning in an Era of Change, 2.*

Young, K. S. (1998a). *Caught in the net: How to recognize the signs of internet addiction--and a winning strategy for recovery.* Wiley.

Young, K. S. (1998b). Internet addiction: The emergence of a new clinical disorder. *Cyberpsychology & Behavior, 1*(3), 237–244. doi:10.1089/cpb.1998.1.237

KEY TERMS AND DEFINITIONS

Augmented Technology: Technology that changes what is visible to a person through their visual senses so that it is not what they would see unaided by the technology.

Augmentive Technology: Augmented technology where what is being augmented is complex information that would otherwise be inaccessible to the user.

Autism: A condition characteristic by a compulsion to take part in activities that are solitary and technical.

Blended Learning Continuum: A means of understanding ICT intensity in terms of how much technology is used to enhance a learning environment.

Demotism: A condition characterised by a compulsion to be in environments that are uncomplex and predictable.

Digital Addiction: The concept that it is not technology that is inherently addictive, but that those with compulsive tendencies turn to technology as an outlet that is an alternative to other habit-forming substances.

Empathism: A condition characterised by a compulsion to associate with people whose outlook on life is hyper-concordant with one's own.

Knol: A measure of the brain activity used to carry out a specific task or hold a particular worldview.

Neuroticism: A condition characterised by a compulsion to avoid situations that rely on technical abilities even though it is desirable to have these.

Psychoticism: A condition characterised by a compulsion to avoid social situations and those which rely on reading others intensions, even though this would be desirable.

Chapter 10
CyberPsycho Effect:
A Critical Study on the Impact of Internet Addiction

Manisha J. Nene
Defence Institute of Advanced Technology (DIAT), India

Prashant Gupta
Defence Institute of Advanced Technology (DIAT), India

ABSTRACT

The Internet has become a platform for different campaigns like political, social, cultural and marketing. Researchers are working on the effect of these services on human behavior and how the use of Internet and social network persuade the environment. This chapter focuses on the causes and effects of persuasive messages based on current trending news and events which can influence an individual's behavior. Cyberspace plus Psychological effect equals to CyberPsycho Effect leading to CyberPsycho attacks. In CyberPsycho attacks, an attacker uses cyberspace and social network to affect attitude or behavior of an individual or a targeted society, and achieve certain goals to attain political, religious, economical, and social gains. It motivates social media users towards a certain objective by spreading the persuasive messages in the form of texts, images or videos. The study is unique, valuable and compels the experts to understand the impact of Internet addiction.

INTRODUCTION

Present era is gradually becoming social media era. Human life is surrounded by machines and digital devices and gadgets. Inventions of low-cost digital devices like Internet of Things (IoTs) and robots make the digital world more useful and powerful; these are used in every field. People use them in every walk of life, scientists are working on to make these devices more intelligent and smart. With these devices, an individual can perform his work more effectively and efficiently and using the Internet one can share their work globally. The information shared over the Internet is useful and can be used by anyone from

DOI: 10.4018/978-1-5225-3477-8.ch010

any part of the world. But due to the rapid development of smart phones and Internet enabled devices, the Internet users are increasing exponentially and so are the different kinds of information shared by different kinds of persons. The information available is also used for different purposes, like betterment of the society or it may be used to harm someone or a targeted society. The social network sites play a key role in using the cyber world all the time, hence it can be said that everybody who is addicted to their smart devices is also addicted to the Internet to some extent.

Further, the extreme use of Internet also invites black hat adversaries, these adversaries may use information which is shared over the Internet and social network services for their benefit. Some of this activity falls under the category of cyber attacks which involves compromising the information. Cyber attack is defined as an attack initiated from a computer against a website, computer system or individual computer that compromises the confidentiality, integrity or availability of the computer system or information stored on it. Cyber attacks take many forms and are known as password trafficking, hacking, Internet fraud, SPAM, etc. Further, the Internet fraud using social engineering, exploitation malware, Internet harassment, extortion, bomb threats and blackmail impose varied challenges in the cyber world.

The study in this chapter analyzes the effects and their behavior leading to attacks which is completely different from previously defined cyber attacks. To date, most of the cyber attacks are either passive or active attacks whose objectives are to steal information or read information of users, these types of attacks do not attack onto the human mind or specifically attitude or behavior or perception or decision taking the ability of an individual in society. The study in this chapter discusses and categorizes cyber attacks where an attacker uses our cyber space and social network to affect our mental attitude or psychological behavior to achieve short-term or long-term goals. Further, the strategies in these attacks persuade an individual or society or community to attain certain objectives by spreading persuasive messages in the form of texts, images or videos to accomplish political, religious, socio-economic gains.

BACKGROUND

Recent advances in hardware and software technology are not only changing the dynamics of computing but, they are also changing the societal culture. In today's era computers are no longer used for storing, manipulating and retrieving information but, are used to influence our thoughts, relationships and decisions. The development in Smartphone and availability of the Internet in these devices plays a significant role in enlarging the impact of social network services in an individual's life and the society as a whole. It is a known fact that uses of social network, social media applications and websites are more used on the mobile platform as compared to the computer and laptop. Every individual who owns a Smartphone, approximately half of the total population in the world, are found to be actively involved on social networking sites. The social networking sites are known to affect users' behavior with themselves and others in the society on a daily basis, they are known to change an individual's or group's perspective of thinking and responsive nature.

The impact of this persuading magnitude of the social network in their daily lives is observed on volume of users. Many researchers and data analyst proposed many methods, architectures, approaches and techniques to observe this magnitude (Gupta et al. 2017; Mittal et al. 2013). Authors analysis the sentiments on social by tracing trending topics (Choi, 2014). Authors also examine the relationship of Social Networking Site (SNS) problematic usage with personality characteristics and depressive symptomatology (Giota et al. 2013). It is stated that social networking addict could be considered someone with a compulsion to use social media to excess by constantly checking and posting updates on social sites (Walker et al. 2017). People use and addicted to these social sites to fulfill their personal and professional needs which are categorized further in this chapter with respect to major domains of users involvement and interests.

As the social networking sites are dynamically growing, its presence and reachability is enveloping more number of users in its vicious cycle and grit grip, hence there is a requirement to give the necessary needed attention towards analyzing it. To analyze social media contents or social network, there should be many perspectives and dimensions. In these contexts, the author has analyzed social media contents with the perspective of effect in dimensions of cyber plus psychology plus social media which leads to attack.

CYBERPSYCHO EFFECT: A CRITICAL STUDY

Social Networking and Society

Growth in Internet usage and involvement of user's in the cyber world has increased multifold worldwide. The extensive reach of social media or social network has attracted entrepreneurs, politicians and other professionals to use this volume of the user base for their benefits. The cyber world provides many advantages and facilities to the users. These facilities range from online banking, reservation, shopping, trading, etc. With the advent of social networking services such as *Facebook, Twitter, YouTube* and *WhatsApp*, these services provide a platform to express stress, loneliness, happiness, depression, etc. The feelings expressed or shared by an individual on cyberspace are more compared to expressions shared with their real-world partners such as family and friends. The psychological compelling requirement for utilizing the smartphone, laptop or computer for connecting or sharing one's feelings with others in the cyber domain leads to the excessive use of social network services, such is the addiction. By spending more time, one may express more feelings, thoughts, views and activities over this virtual world than the real world. Since the feelings and expressions involved in this communication mode are persuading individual's decisions this brings in a methodology of manipulating those sentiments for other purposes also. The cyberspace and social network affects the psychological space of humans as it has features which present self, relationships and they also have features to explain experiences of human senses, reality or truth of life. These features have made the Internet and its services more interactive towards interpersonal interactions or human to computer interactions.

The social network provides an individual or a group a platform to present themselves in the cyber world. One can find their old school mate or classmates on Facebook or LinkedIn, or one can learn how things work by seeing videos in YouTube, or one can follow their role models on Twitter and many more aspects exist on the virtual web world. Social media services are used nowadays in both the social and professional lives of individual's. By far, using the social platforms to not only connect but also to communicate as part of their societal norms and professional requirements. By using social network individuals get a platform to support a cause or issue or else raise their voice against any matter which they deem as incorrect. They share what they know, what they get or how they feel about something or someone. They participate in events, discussions and debates based on what is happening in the world. It does not matter where the incident took place, it is always generally discussed in some other location, where the shards of the incident have never been realized. People share their views or opinions and react on issues based on their perception and dimension of understanding of the issue. It is embedded in every individual as part of his/ her human nature that everybody wants to share his or her thoughts, need to speak, wants that people should listen to them intently. In cyber space, social media platforms provide them the environment with the interactive platform to fulfill this extensive desire. On this social platform, one can share their views, express feelings, thoughts, qualities, facts in simple messages or articles, or can share in his or her voice, or share images or videos with the world.

The freedoms of expression in social network services are used to increase awareness about some societal issues such as women empowerment or environmental behaviors. These services are also used for uplifting the society by improving standards of living or by sharing health tips and are also used to increase knowledge, science and education in promoting ubiquitous learning. In today's world of hyper-connectivity these social media services are also used to identify victims, criminals, solve undisclosed crimes and in helping of people during crisis like floods, earthquakes, etc. Social networking sites such as *Facebook* include different features like banking, shopping, reviewing about places or services, helping users as well as government during social activities and finding hoaxes and spams. These all features, motivate more people to use them and become more active by spending more time on the virtual world connecting, communicating, contemplating and consuming every resource available.

People are keener to follow famous names in terms of either personalities or organizations. These famous personalities and organizations names are related to the political, business, entertainment, sports, religion and educational fields. People follow the works, views, news, and activities of these personalities' and also interested to know more about them. Profit or non-profit organizations engage their customers or users by keeping updated news, events and announcements about their products and services. There are different discussion forums based on categories like political, social, educational, technical, cultural etc. which are used by people according to their motives since it is (not) limited to the same intellect of people, but it restricts its user base. Through the interactive features of the social network, people use them as they deem it fit to use. These forums are used as a platform for exchange on topics like social gaming, marketing, job searching, event organizing, social gathering, social campaigns, social analysis etc. Overall, it becomes a community which connects more people together globally with local common interests. Social media may be used to get benefit from someone's knowledge, personality or social connection for the edification of one's knowledge and information. (Chiu et al. 2006) It may be used to exploit and manipulate sentiment of others to achieve his or her desired goals.

The insight of online social networking usage patterns, the motivation for excessive usage, the potential of addiction as a consequence of excessive use with what people are addicted to and what new features or tools measuring are done by Griffith et al (Griffith et al. 2011 & 2013). The authors also studied the impact of social networking sites on its users' privacy, security issues and their performances towards their work or academics. (Abdulahi et al. 2014)

In this literature, the new aspect of the Internet and social networking usage are highlighted that has made its users more addictive in terms of using it and attaching these aspects and dimensions of the virtual world with their personal, social or professional benefits which lead to affect psychological health of society that is termed as effect. Figure 1 describes the parameters of CyberPsycho effect. (Gupta et al. 2016)

Figure 1. CyberPsycho Effect

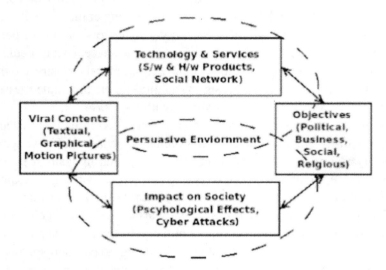

CyberPsycho Attacks

As smartphones and the Internet are already a requirement and needed in our social life, part of the society and people get all updates using their smartphones or connected devices. People get influenced by the contents shared or discussed over social media through the Internet. As news about surroundings are quickly updated and reachable to everyone on social media this feature of near instantaneous read consistency makes it addictive by causing a psychological dependency to check updates received periodically.

Keeping in mind the human nature, humans are more interested to know about what is happening around their environment and also make an endeavor to share his or her activities for appraisal and getting the feel good factor. This eagerness for social involvement and acknowledgment has been responsible for driving individuals towards the Internet and social network. The social network platform has also provided them a common ground to share his/her thoughts without any hesitation or fear of rejection or dejection. With these features of social media and Internet, this addiction has bloomed into an effect which is termed as CyberPsycho effect. In this effect, cyberspace or social media is used as a medium to influence others by persuading others thought process towards meeting certain objective or getting desired results. To attain some personal gains using this effect is termed as CyberPsycho attack.

In CyberPsycho attack, there are four phases (Gupta et al 2017) which are involved to enable it; media, medium, target and objective. Figure 2 describes the elements involved in CyberPsycho attack.

Media plays the most important role to enable this attack. The contents used to this effect are persuasive contents. These contents have sentiments and emotions and some have facts, incidents and content to trigger human sentiments. There are different mediums over the Internet to spread these contents like *Facebook, Twitter, WhatsApp, Instagram, Blogs* etc. Most of the mediums have cross-platform sharing features which make it easier to share contents to users of one platform to users of another platform. This makes it difficult for the publishers and the native users to verify the authenticity of the contents. The third element of this attack is "the target", in which attackers identify the target audience or user. It is similar to the marketing strategy where the target customer is identified and studied with respect to

Figure 2. Elements in CyberPsycho attack sources [Gupta et al. 2017]

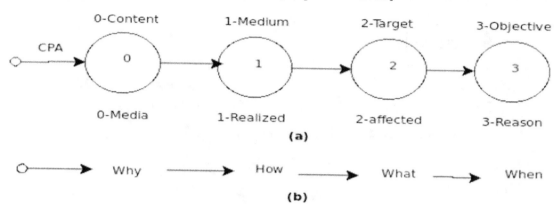

vulnerability analysis for the product so that the target's vulnerabilities are exploited effectively increasing profits or productivity. The fourth element of this attack is "objective" the purpose for which an attacker attacks his target to make personal gains after deploying this effect.

CyberPsycho Attack: Case Studies

There are many studies and researches that are being performed and are going on to identify the viral contents, spams/malicious URLs and malicious users for improving privacy and sense of security as well as identifying the sentiments within the messages, tweets, polls, review comments for identifying the users or customers views about the product, services or political leaders. Authors intend to motivate analysts, researchers, security agencies towards combining these two approaches to analyze social media or the Internet together to identify and counter the CyberPsycho attack (Gupta et al. 2016). Figure 3 describes the entities in action to realize CyberPsycho Attacks.

As a part of this book, this chapter introduces the term CyberPsycho attack and its effects with respect to different objectives which exploits the impacts of Internet addiction for business, politics, religion, etc. It involves identifying and exploiting the kinds of people and persuades their thoughts, decisions and behavior.

- **Business/ Economical Gains:** Nowadays, almost all business organization have made their presence felt on social platforms. They have been successful in increasing their online marketing budget as compared to the traditional marketing strategies. Many company campaigns on social network services use motivational or environmental messages as part of their marketing strategies to gain the attention of the masses, for example, safe driving, go green, save the girl child, patriotism, religion, sports or health matters. They carry out campaigns on social issues, trending news or on controversial topics which have no direct relation to their products or services offered by them, for example, a company which manufactures kids clothing and stationary running a campaign for safe driving or motivating people towards voting during political elections. These types of campaigns and social messages help the business organization to build up their brand value as well as engage more number of users. This increases their customer base as well as develops a perception in the customer or user's mind towards using their product or services which will increase their sales or productivity. The news

Figure 3. Entities in CyberPsycho attack

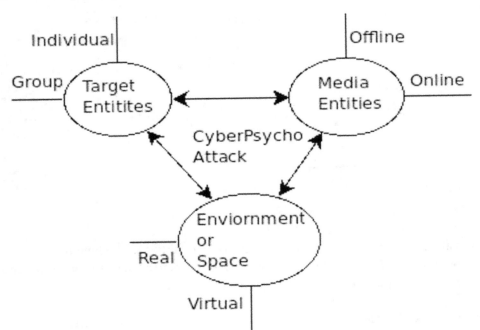

about the product, brand or services as well as the result of the campaign also affects its share value which will affect the company's overall market standing and also the shareholder's money. Social media and cyberspace may be used to affect that unsteady nature of business markets for gaining or dominating competitor's value by spreading the news on a global scale. Business organizations, as well as researchers, are continuously working out and finding new innovative ways to engage people and associate them more with their brand names and forge relationships with customers. There are many studies and strategies available on the Internet which not only help marketing experts or giant business organizations but also small enterprises to increase their business through social network services. (Cox et al. 2012; Rauch et al. 2001; Andzulis et al. 2012)

- **Political Gains:** Leaders from most of the countries, have been found to engage themselves on social networking sites so as to keep updates, give updates, pass their status, statements, news, events and most importantly connect with their followers in a manner desired by them, also formulate new strategies and campaigns to develop new fans and have a strong fan following. They have millions of followers which make them the most influencing nodes on the Internet. Social media has attracted politicians for election campaigns to influence their voters and develop renewed support among the masses. Most countries around the globe have witnessed the effect of social media and the Internet during the period of government elections. Political parties hire strategy makers, marketers for campaigning over social networks to manage perspective of the masses and improve their brand value to influence voters into voting for them. Traditional ways of political campaigns such as rallies, speeches etc., do not lose their resemblance with the impact of the digital medium or social media but both traditional and modern approaches are combined together for getting more involved with voters. In the present scenario, the availability of Internet and smartphones make the cyberspace domain media as important as print media. The contents which spread over social network sites are discussed offline same as the messages or speeches which are delivered offline and are spread over the Internet in the form of images, texts or videos. The contents which spread over the Internet domain sometimes have a direct objective that is to influence people to vote in favor of someone or else have indirect influence that may downgrade the image of rivals so that people have no choice but to vote against them. (Kaur et al. 2016; Biswas et al. 2014; Hampton et al. 2017; Narasimhamurthy et al. 2014; Shirky et al. 2011)

- **Religious Gains:** The followers of religion spread facts and figures about their religion and religious places to influence others to understand and follow their religion. Sometimes it is noticed that the messages or contents which hurt other religion followers are spread over cyberspace. The dissemination of these messages sometimes results in religious riots. The studies have shown that the perception and opinion of individuals about the religion are affected by media. Some of the contents shared over social media have religious sentiments, opinions and views which may influence people's opinion. It is also studied that social media effect religious and social values among it's users. (Emery et al. 2011; AI-Mosa et al. 2015; Lim et al. 2010; Everton et al. 2015)

- **Social Gains:** Everybody wants to be famous and want to be followed by the many followers or even want to showcase his or her talents. To become famous, individuals or groups even share their personal activities. This ambitious desire of individuals and groups of people is now fulfilled by the social networking sites. Users of these sites easily spread their views, thoughts, activities, skills without any extra expenditure to millions of viewers. (Sheedy et al. 2011)

- **International Gains:** Countries make strategies and policies for tourism, business and diplomacy. They also use the social media to spread contents about certain changes in policies or by spreading rumors about good or bad things about certain things about a country which may affect interpersonal relationships and communications between the people of countries and it will affect the overall growth of the country since it affects tourism and business as well. It is often noticed that whenever a government is changed the policies may be changed and it will affect the international democracy so at the time of this change one can spread certain things about the new rules or policies which will affect international societies, business or other countries as well as their people's work. It is observed that social media has powerful impact on international relations and foreign policies. Social media are effective to convey information to general public in any form either business, policies or it is also used to gain public support for a cause for example signing a petition against a country. It is also used to explain misconceptions about diplomacy or foreign policies. Social media also provide platform to the government to interact with citizens of other countries. (Harris et al. 2013; Martin et al. 2013; Funk et al. 2013; Zeitzoff et al. 2015).

- **Terrorism:** The terrorist groups also adopt this platform to influence people by motivating them to do something for their religion and people. As a result of this, many people join them or help them which increases terrorism. A study has shown that terrorist groups use social networking sites mostly to influence youngsters worldwide to persuade them to join their group and they use them for disseminating their propaganda. They make videos of their messages as well as their acts and spread it over the digital media. The video which shows their act of killing someone were even disseminated by many people who are not wanting to join them and who do not support their act, but they spread this with the intention of bringing social awareness and in a way help towards the objective of these groups which may make an impact on people's mind.(Liang, 2015)

Persuasive Technology

It is a field which is design to change attitude or perception or behavior of a person through social influence. It is widely used in different domains like marketing, health, training etc,. The importance of persuasion with technology is described as:

The world of persuasion has changed rapidly over the past 10 years. If you haven't noticed the shift, now is the time to recognize how technology opens doors across all sectors – to engage new customers, influence people's attitudes, and, most interesting of all, change their behaviors. Companies and individuals alike are writing software codes that render persuasive experiences, influencing what we think and do. Never before has the ability to automate persuasion been in the hands of so many. (Fogg, 2009)

People are surrounded by the products which have the ability to persuade them. Functionalities of these products or services are designed by using different factors like functionality, entertainment, ease of use, networking and persuasion. Internet and its services are creating persuading environment. If you are watching videos on YouTube then you may keep watching because of the links and suggestions are designed such a way same as with *Facebook*, it persuade its users to keep active by using its persuading features.

ARCHITECTURE AND TECHNIQUES TO QUANTIFY CYBERPSYCHO ATTACKS

The authors described an observation and approach to identify the CyberPsycho attacks in popular platforms like *Twitter, WhatsApp, Facebook* etc., (Gupta et al. 2017). It is observed and proposed that text analysis, data-log analysis, image content analysis, voice pattern analysis, video image analysis have to be performed using big data analysis techniques and framework to identify the nature of persuading contents as well as sentiments or emotions; where text-based content on trending topics, news and events with respect to different domains like business, politics, sports etc., are collected through social networks and processed to extract emotions and sentiments with user information. The information gained after the analysis has been used to predict the trend of the contents as well as predict the CyberPsycho attack.

FUTURE RESEARCH DIRECTIONS

The information which has been generated by the above process shows that contents mostly shared over the social network platforms contain a majority of positive words which can trigger humans' sentiments and make them act accordingly. Mostly contents shared in form of jokes or slogans fall under category of joy, and these are responsible for emotions that make individuals happy and trigger them to share this with others as this will not hurt anyone, but recursively it achieves its target by influencing many users and assist in making some kind of perceptions about the topic for which it is created. The features of this cyber world motivate cyber citizens to use it as they want to. There are need of more policies reviewer of these Internet services as well as the information shared using this services. The studies and researches have to move towards the different aspects of Internet usage and its effects. The technology and psychology used to persuade human towards awareness, productivity, learning need attention towards countering this persuasion. The categories described in this chapter in view of gains are studied by many researchers as single domain which could be cross linked.

CONCLUSION

Internet is addressed as Information Super Highway. It is a technology. It is used by millions of users from all around the world. The proliferation in the communication and software technology has provided convenient platforms addressed as 'Social Media' to an individual to express and exchange their feelings/ thoughts/ views/ perspectives. This medium has provided the range of platforms that assist an individual to search and seek opinions from the highly specialized/expert domains to the meaningless/casual/ carefree exchange of dialogues. As a result, these environments/media are the source of a voluminous information generation on Internet. It has the ability to enable efficient and effective communication between known and unknown entities/individual. It enables communications which is independent of caste/creed, religion, citizenship, gender, age group and profession, a few to mention.

The Internet and its services are used not only for the information exchange, but also has become an integral part of our daily travels, navigations, domestic/home control equipments, and commercial dealings. Apart from this, it has become a platform for different campaigns like political, social, cultural and marketing. Nowadays, government officials of most countries actively participate on Internet platforms like websites, social networks and blogs. Worldwide many researchers are working on analyzing the effect of these services on human behavior and how the use of Internet and social network persuade the environment. They also extract information from social network services to increase productivity, awareness and learning as well as finding malicious links, phishing mails, spams and trending viral contents.

The study in this chapter focuses on the causes and effects of persuasive messages based on current trending news and events which effectively can influence an individual's behavior. We name this effect as Cyberspace plus Psychological effect equals to CyberPsycho Effect leading to CyberPsycho attacks. In CyberPsycho attacks, an attacker uses cyberspace and social network to affect or change attitude or behavior of an individual or a targeted society, and achieve certain goals to attain political, religious, economical and social gains. It motivates social media users towards a certain objective by spreading the persuasive messages in the form of texts, images or videos. The study presented in this chapter is unique, valuable and compels the experts in academia, researchers, technologists and end-users to understand and acknowledge the serious impact of psychological, social and cultural aspects of Internet addiction.

The study states an observation that, many of its users who are actively involved in the exchange of thoughts via social media while expressing the views and dialogues are unaware of the direct/indirect consequences of their active participation. Even as the rules and policies for information exchange on Internet are getting matured, the unawareness for the need to know the media access rules, policies, security concerns, privacy aspects of information sharing are very inadequate. Further, illiteracy in its legal aspects, whether they are offending/defending certain entities in the society using such media are ignored. In some scenarios, these policies are not strictly followed and not verified because of the demographic issues and non uniformity of policy guidelines, globally.

The aspects enumerated in this chapter states the fact that since the cyberspace or virtual world unite the real world without any boundaries and limitations, there is a critical need of common laws and guidelines for all virtual world communities, globally.

REFERENCES

Abdulahi, A., Samadi, B., & Gharleghi, B. (2014). A study on the negative effects of social networking sites such as facebook among asia pacific university scholars in Malaysia. *International Journal of Business and Social Science*, *5*(10).

Al-Mosa, N. A. (2015). Role of Social Networks in Developing Religious and Social Values of the Students of the World Islamic Sciences & Education University. *International Education Studies*, *8*(9), 126. doi:10.5539/ies.v8n9p126

Andzulis, J. M., Panagopoulos, N. G., & Rapp, A. (2012). A review of social media and implications for the sales process. *Journal of Personal Selling & Sales Management*, *32*(3), 305–316. doi:10.2753/PSS0885-3134320302

Biswas, A., Ingle, N., & Roy, M. (2014). Influence of social media on voting behavior. *Journal of Power*, *2*(2), 127–155.

Chiu, C. M., Hsu, M. H., & Wang, E. T. (2006). Understanding knowledge sharing in virtual communities: An integration of social capital and social cognitive theories. *Decision Support Systems*, *42*(3), 1872–1888. doi:10.1016/j.dss.2006.04.001

Choi, D., Hwang, M., Kim, J., Ko, B., & Kim, P. (2014). Tracing trending topics by analyzing the sentiment status of tweets. *Computer Science and Information Systems*, *11*(1), 157–169. doi:10.2298/CSIS130205001C

Cox, S. L. (2012). *Social media marketing in a small business: A case study* (Doctoral dissertation). Purdue University.

Emery, M. D. (2011). A Case Study of Social and Media Influence on Religion. *Journal of International Students*, *1*(1), 18–24.

Everton, S. F. (2015). Networks and Religion: Ties that Bind, Loose, Build Up, and Tear Down. *Journal of Social Structure: JOSS*, *16*(10), 1–34.

Fogg, B. J. (2009). The new rules of persuasion. *RSA Journal*, *155*(5538), 24–29.

Funk, J. Q. (2013). The Power of 'Friending': How Social Media is. *juliannefunk.com* Retrieved from: http://www.juliannefunk.com/wp-content/uploads/2013/11/Julianne-Funk-Dissertation.pdf

Giota, K. G., & Kleftaras, G. (2013). The role of personality and depression in problematic use of social networking sites in Greece. *Cyberpsychology (Brno)*, *7*(3). doi:10.5817/CP2013-3-6

Griffiths, M. D. (2013). Social networking addiction: Emerging themes and issues. *Journal of Addiction Research & Therapy*, *4*(5). doi:10.4172/2155-6105.1000e118

Gupta, P., & Nene, M. J. (2017a) An Observation on Social Media Content to Analyze CyberPsycho Attack. *1st International Conference on Smart Computing & Informatics*. Springer.

Gupta, P., & Nene, M. J. (2017b) An Approach to Analyze CyberPsycho Attacks Enabled using Persuasive Messages. *1st International Conference on Smart Computing & Informatics*. Springer.

Gupta, P., & J, M. (2016). CyberPsycho Attacks: Techniques, Causes, Effects and Recommendations to End-Users. *International Journal of Computers and Applications, 156*(11), 11–16. doi:10.5120/ijca2016912556

Gupta, P., & Nene, M. J. (2017). Analysis of Text Messages in Social Media to Investigate CyberPsycho Attack. In *International Conference on Information and Communication Technology for Intelligent Systems* (pp. 581-587). Springer.

Hampton, K. N., Shin, I., & Lu, W. (2017). Social media and political discussion: When online presence silences offline conversation. *Information Communication and Society, 20*(7), 1090–1107. doi:10.1080/1369118X.2016.1218526

Harris, B. (2013). Diplomacy 2.0: The future of social media in nation branding. *Exchange: The Journal of Public Diplomacy, 4*(1), 3.

Kaur, M., & Verma, R. (2016). Social Media: An Emerging Tool for Political Participation. *International Journal of Social and Organizational Dynamics in IT, 5*(2), 31–38. doi:10.4018/IJSODIT.2016070103

Kuss, D. J., & Griffiths, M. D. (2011). Online social networking and addiction—a review of the psychological literature. *International Journal of Environmental Research and Public Health, 8*(9), 3528–3552. doi:10.3390/ijerph8093528 PMID:22016701

Liang, C. S. (2015). Cyber Jihad: Understanding and countering Islamic State propaganda. *GCSP Policy Papers*, (2), 2.

Lim, C., & Putnam, R. D. (2010). Religion, social networks, and life satisfaction. *American Sociological Review, 75*(6), 914–933. doi:10.1177/0003122410386686

Martin, C., Jagla, L., & Firestone, C. M. (2013). *Integrating Diplomacy and Social Media. A Report of the First Annual Aspen Institute Dialogue on Diplomacy and Technology*. Washington, DC: Aspen In-stitute.

Mittal, N., Agarwal, B., Agarwal, S., Agarwal, S., & Gupta, P. (2013). A hybrid approach for twitter sentiment analysis. *10th International Conference on Natural Language Processing (ICON-2013)*, 116-120.

Narasimhamurthy, N. (2014). *Use and Rise of Social media as Election Campaign medium in India*. Academic Press.

Rauch, J. E. (2001). Business and social networks in international trade. *Journal of Economic Literature, 39*(4), 1177–1203. doi:10.1257/jel.39.4.1177

Sheedy, C. S. (2011). Social media for social change: A case study of social media use in the 2011 Egyptian revolution. *Capstone Project, 28*(4), 1–58.

Shirky, C. (2011). The political power of social media: Technology, the public sphere, and political change. *Foreign Affairs*, 28–41.

Walker, L. (2017). What Is Social Networking Addiction? *About.com Guide*. Retrieved from: https://www.lifewire.com/what-is-social-networking-addiction-2655246

Zeitzoff, T., Kelly, J., & Lotan, G. (2015). Using social media to measure foreign policy dynamics: An empirical analysis of the Iranian–Israeli confrontation (2012–13). *Journal of Peace Research*, *52*(3), 368–383. doi:10.1177/0022343314558700

KEY TERMS AND DEFINITIONS

CyberPsycho Attack: In CyberPsycho attacks, an attacker uses cyberspace & social network to affect or change attitude or behavior of an individual or a targeted society, and achieve certain goals to attain political, religious, economical and social gains. That is, using Cyberspace + Psychological effect = *CyberPsycho Effect* may lead to 'CyberPsycho' attacks.

CyberPsycho Effect: The causes and effects of persuasive messages communicated using cyber-space or Internet based on current trending news and events which effectively can influence an individual's behavior. The authors of this chapter coin CyberPsycho effect as 'Cyberspace plus Psychological effect equals to CyberPsycho Effect', that is Cyberspace + Psychological effect = CyberPsycho Effect.

CyberPsychology: The study of behavior and mind of the cyber-citizens.

Internet Addiction: The psychological harm and disturbances to life caused by uncontrolled excessive access or use of the Internet.

Internet Services: Internet Services allows us to access huge amount of information such as text, graphics, sound and software over the internet.

Online Campaign: A series of activities performed over internet intended to achieve a goal, confined to a particular area, or involving a specified type of cause or purpose.

Persuasive Technology: The enabling technology used to persuade an individual.

Social Media: Social media are computer-mediated technologies that facilitate the creation and sharing of information, ideas, career interests and other forms of expression via virtual communities and *networks*.

Social Network Analysis: It is the process to analyze the relationships and flows between people, groups, organizations which are connected through computers and other information exchange devices and exchange information over the virtual communities such as Facebook, WhatsApp, Twitter, YouTube, etc.

Section 4
Cultural Aspects of Internet Addiction

This section covers cultural aspects of internet addiction.

Chapter 11
A Review of Internet Addiction on the Basis of Different Countries (2007–2017)

Ruya Samli
Istanbul University, Turkey

ABSTRACT

This chapter presents a review of Internet addiction on the basis of different countries between the years of 2007 and 2017. For this purpose, the term "addiction" is explained, some addiction types are examined, the differences between Internet addiction and the other ones are given and the Internet addiction status of different countries are presented. In today's world, Internet addiction is a privileged problem in almost all of the countries but especially a few countries have important number of studies about the subject. The most studies are completed in China, Turkey, Taiwan, Hong Kong and Korea. In this chapter, studies about these countries and some other ones are investigated. These studies show that the "Far East" is suffering from the problem a bit more than the others.

INTRODUCTION

The term "addiction" refers to a chronic and relapsing disease resulting from adaptive changes in brain structure and function (Al, 1997). People can be addicted to some materials such as cigarette, alcohol, drugs which have already addictivity property or some food such as chocolate, coffee or coke. These all stimulants have a common property and contain chemicals which makes dependency on brain. Based on the technological development in today's world, there is a new addiction without any chemicals defined for modern era: Internet addiction.

The term "Internet addiction" has been proposed as an explanation for uncontrollable and consequently damaging use of this technology (Beard and Wolf, 2001). Because it does not cause any physical symptom in a short time, it is very hard to determine whether a person is an Internet addict or not. For this reason, many researchers developed questionnaires that assessed Internet addiction. The most famous one of these questionnaires was developed in 1996 by a psychologist, Kimberly Young. In this Internet

DOI: 10.4018/978-1-5225-3477-8.ch011

Addiction Test, there are 20 questions based on the criteria used to diagnose compulsive gambling and alcoholism. The responders are expected to give a score between 0 – 5 to each question according to the frequency of the event in the question. The corresponding meanings of the scores are like this: 0 – does not reply, 1 – rarely, 2 – occasionally, 3 – frequently, 4 – often and 5 – always. After the response phase, the total of the scores is evaluated to determine the level of addiction. The questions are given below (Young, 2004):

- How often do you find that you stay online longer than you intended?
- How often do you neglect household chores to spend more time online?
- How often do you prefer the excitement of the Internet to intimacy with your partner?
- How often do you form new relationships with fellow online users?
- How often do others in your life complain to you about the amount of time you spend online?
- How often do your grades or school work suffer because of the amount of time you spend online?
- How often do you check your e-mail before something else that you need to do?
- How often does your job performance or productivity suffer because of the Internet?
- How often do you become defensive or secretive when anyone asks you what you do online?
- How often do you block out disturbing thoughts about your life with soothing thoughts of the Internet?
- How often do you find yourself anticipating when you will go online again?
- How often do you fear that life without the Internet would be boring, empty, and joyless?
- How often do you snap, yell, or act annoyed if someone bothers you while you are online?
- How often do you lose sleep due to late-night log-ins?
- How often do you feel preoccupied with the Internet when off-line, or fantasize about being online?
- How often do you find yourself saying "just a few more minutes" when online?
- How often do you try to cut down the amount of time you spend online and fail?
- How often do you try to hide how long you've been online?
- How often do you choose to spend more time online over going out with others?
- How often do you feel depressed, moody, or nervous when you are off-line, which goes away once you are back online?

The addiction level of a person is determined by the total points he/she gave to the question. After all the questions have been answered, the numbers for each response are added to eachother to obtain a final score. The higher the score, the greater the level of addiction. The severity impairment index is as follows:

- **NONE 0–30 Points:** If the person's questionnaire final score is between 0 and 30; it means that the person uses the Internet in normal levels, he/she doesn't have any addiction. But it must be known that, the Internet addiction and all of the addiction types are like spies and they can be shown up in a very short time period.
- **MILD 31–49 Points:** If the person's questionnaire final score is between 31 and 49; it means that the person is an average user. He/she may surf the Web a bit too long at times, but he/she has the control over his/her usage.
- **MODERATE 50–79 Points:** If the person's questionnaire final score is between 50 and 79; it means that the person is experiencing occasional or frequent problems because of the Internet. He/

she should consider the full impact of Internet on his/her life and this level can be thought as the beginning of the danger. In other words "Alarm bells start to ring ...".

- **SEVERE 80–100 Points:** If the person's questionnaire final score is between 80 and 100; the person's Internet usage is causing significant problems in the life. This type of people should evaluate the impact of the Internet on their life and determine the addiction problems directly caused by the Internet usage.

Internet addiction is not only an individual disease but also a reason of higher order diseases. These diseases can be grouped into two categories: physical and psychological (Table 1).

BACKGROUND

There are many studies in the literature that examine the relationship between diseases (especially the psychological ones) and Internet addiction. In 2000, Chou and Hsiao explores Internet addiction among some of the Taiwan's college students and found that addict group rated Internet impacts on their studies and daily life routines significantly more negatively than the non-addict group. Nalwa and Anand (2003) and Young (2004) suggested that Internet addicted stayed up late at night or even lost sleep for late – night logons. In 2004, Yoo et al. evaluated the relationship between Attention Deficit and Hyperactivity Disorder symptoms of 535 elemantary school students and Internet addiction and found that the presence of Attention Deficit and Hyperactivity Disorder symptoms may be one of the important risk factors for Internet addiction. Bernardi and Pallanti (2009) found that Internet addiction can cause different types of diseases such as borderline personality disorder, social anxiety disorder, dysthymia and obsessive compulsive personality disorder. Another study examined the Internet addiction – depression and Internet addiction – suicidal ideation relationships on 1573 Korean high – school students and showed that the levels of depression and suicide ideation were highest in the Internet – addicts group (Kim et al. 2006). In an interesting study which examines not only Internet addiction but also gaming addiction, ten patients who experienced epileptic seizures while games are investigated (Chuang, 2006). In 2007, Yen et al. examined the comorbid psychiatric symptoms of Internet addiction: Attention Deficit and Hyperactivity Disorder, depression, social phobia, and hostility by seperating the males and females as Internet addicted or not and found that higher Attention Deficit and Hyperactivity Disorder symptoms, depression, and hostility are associated with Internet addiction in male adolescents, and only higher Attention Deficit and Hyperactivity Disorder symptoms and depression are associated with Internet addiction in female students. In the same year, another study suggests that adolescents with Internet addiction

Table 1. Diseases caused by internet addiction

Physical	Psychological
* Neck pain	* Depression
* Lumbar pain	* Insomnia
* Eye burning	* Hyperactivity
* Hand numbness	* Social phobia
* Hernia	* Attention Deficit Andhyperactivity Disorder

exhibit more impulsivity than controls and have various comorbid psychiatric disorders, which could be associated with the psychopathology of Internet addiction (Cao et al. 2007). Cheung and Wong showed that Internet addicts had significantly longer sleep latency, lower habitual sleep efficiency, poorer sleep quality, more sleep disturbances, more daytime dysfunction and more frequent use of sleep mediaction than non–addicts (2011).

In this chapter, the literature studies are also classified according to the countries. There are more than 110 studies investigated for the countries, Australia, China, Germany, Greece, Hong Kong, India, Italy, Japan, Jordan, Korea, Norway, Poland, Portugal, Singapore, Taiwan, Turkey and Vietnam. Also, in some studies, comparisons between two or more countries were made. In these studies, there are novel, specific and local invetigations of the country (or countries) while there are also some reviews of previous studies. The author would like to point out that these are not all the studies in the literature. To search, find and investigate all studies is not possible so some samples of each group are handled.

China

China is the country in which most studies about Internet addiction were done. In these studies, the experimental people are generally college–university students, (Huang et al. 2007; Huang et al. 2009; Ni et al. 2009; Tsai et al. 2009; Su et al. 2011; Xu et al. 2012; Dong et al. 2013; Yao et al. 2013; Yao et al. 2014) and adolescents (Cao et al. 2007; Xu et al. 2012; Yang et al. 2014; Li et al. 2014; Wang et al. 2015). Also children (Guo et al. 2012), middle school students (Li et al. 2014) and samples of general population (Golub and Lingley, 2008; Szablewicz, 2010; Peng and Liu, 2010) were investigated. In these studies different numbers of people between the range of 524 and 24013 were examined and the relation between Internet addiction with mental health symptoms, psychological symptoms, adaptation problems, depression tendency, impulsivity, parental behaviour, self–control and self–esteem, nuroticism, psychoticism were analyzed.

In recent studies of China (2016 and the first half of 2017); attractive issues about Internet addiction hava been analyzed. For example, in a study by Yang et al. (2016), the effects of father-child and mother-child interactions on Internet addiction are emphasized and found that both father and mother are important people on the development of youth's peer attachment, which may in turn influence youth's Internet addiction. Liang et al. (2016) explored the role of gender in the association between Internet addiction and depression and as a result, they found that both males and females were prone to surfing the Internet alone, but males were more likely to go online with friends compared with females. In two different studies, the adolescents and vocational school students in only Anhui province are analyzed. In the first one, characteristics and prevalence of Internet addiction in adolescents so as to provide a scientific basis for the communities, schools, and families was to describe (Chen et al. 2016). There are some statistics obtained such as: the overall detection rate of Internet addicted in students was 8.7% (459/5249), the detection rate of Internet addicted people in males (12.3%) was higher than females (4.9%), the detection rate of Internet addicted students was statistically different between students from rural (8.2%) and urban (9.3%) areas, among students from different grades, between students from only-child families (9.5%) and non-only-child families (8.1%), and among students from different family types. In the second one, the hypothesis that "depression mediated the association between stressful life events and Internet addiction" was tested (Zhao et al. 2017) and the findings suggested that life events associated with Internet addiction both directly and indirectly, depression mediated the association between life events and Internet addiction. Wu et al. (2016) applied a questionnaire to a huge number of participants

(10158) which contains demographic characteristics, Internet use situation, Youth Internet Addiction Test, Youth Social Support Rating Scale (SSRS) and Zung Self-rating Depression Scale (SRDS). They concluded that, 10.40% of the adolescents surveyed exhibited Internet addiction among adolescents, social support had a significant negative predictive effect on Internet addiction and the mediating effect of depression between social support and Internet addiction was also significant. By using the same tests mentioned above (Internet Addiction Test, Zung's Self-Rating Anxiety Scale) and another one (Rosenberg Self-Esteem Scale–RSES) two different studies tried to determine two different parameter's effect on Internet addiction on Chinese college students: Tao et al. (2016) analyzed the relationship between binge eating and Internet addiction while Nie et al. (2017) explored depression, self-esteem and verbal fluency with different degrees of Internet addiction. Both of these studies unveiled that Internet addiction has relationships with some behaviour disorders.

Turkey

Turkey is another popular country of Internet addiction and there are high number of studies about this subject. Besides the general studies that examines Internet addiction (Tahiroglu et al. 2008; Aslanbay et al. 2009; Ak et al. 2013) there are also interesting ones that search the relationship between Internet addiction and different symptoms. One study investigates the health of the Internet addicted people in Turkey by using General Health Questionnaire (GHQ-28) (Koc and Gulyagci, 2013), while another similar one examines the correlation between Internet addiction and eating attitudes and body mass index (BMI) (Canan et al. 2014). Also, there are studies about

- Predictors of problematic Internet use (Ceyhan, 2008),
- Evaluation of psychometric properties (Canan et al. 2010),
- Social support and family activities (Gunuc and Dogan, 2013),
- Loneliness, self-esteem, and life satisfaction (Bozoglan et al. 2013),
- İmpulsivity and severity of psychopathology (Dalbudak et al. 2013),
- Relationship between Internet addiction and chronotype (Randler et al. 2013),
- Attention Deficit Hyperactivity Disorder symptoms (Dalbudak and Evren, 2014),
- Factors associated with Internet addiction (Seyrek et al. 2017),
- Relationship between Internet use and depression (Tekinarslan, 2017),
- Turkish version of the Internet Addiction Test (Boysan et al. 2017).

Taiwan

There are many studies investigating Internet addiction in Taiwan which is a precursor country of technology. These studies examine not only general Internet addiction but also online game addiction (Lee et al. 2015) and Internet cafe addiction (Wu and Cheng, 2007). The results of these studies can be summarized as follows:

- Students with personalities characterized by dependence, shyness, depression and low self-esteem had a high tendency to become addicted (Yang and Tung, 2007).
- Adolescent Internet addiction and substance use experience shared similar family factors (Yen et al. 2007).

- Both positive outcome expectancy and negative outcome expectancy were significantly and positively correlated with Internet addiction (Lin et al. 2008).
- Internet addiction effects differ from male adolescents to female adolescents (Yeh et al. 2008).
- More depressive symptoms, higher positive outcome expectancy of Internet use, higher Internet usage time (Lin et al. 2011).
- Online activities, depression, and substance use were important predictors of youth initiation and of the persistence of Internet addiction (Chang et al. 2014).

In a recent study of Taiwan, associations between child maltreatment, Post-Traumatic Stress Disorder (PTSD), and Internet addiction among the students has been examined (Hsieh et al. 2016) and demonstrated the effects of multiple types of maltreatment on the PTSD and Internet addiction of children and the importance of early prevention and intervention in addressing related public-health concerns.

Hong Kong

Although Hong Kong is inside China; because it is a self-reliant structure, there are studies which investigate only Hong Kong (not with China). Some of these studies can be given as follows in the chronologic order. In the study Shek et al. (2008) the psychometric properties of two developed measures of Internet addiction were examined through 6121 students. Leung (2008) tried to identify addiction symptoms that are uniquely associated with mobile phone use. Kim et al. (2010) examined the correlates of heavy Internet use and various health risk behaviors. Their results reveal that students with heavy Internet use were more likely to report poorer eating habits and sleeping behaviors. Cheung et al. (2011) investigates the effects of insomnia and Internet addiction on depression. Wang et al. (2016) applied health belief model and tried to find the relationship between model and Internet addiction. Ding et al. (2016) handled association between Internet addiction and highrisk sexual attitudes in Chinese university students from Hong Kong and Macau. Wu et al. (2016a) examined potential impact of Internet addiction and protective psychosocial factors onto depression among Hong Kong adolescents. Wu et al. (2016b) investigated the effects of parenting approaches and family functionality over Internet addiction.

Korea

The studies in Korea about Internet addiction have a wide range of subjects to examine. A study investigated the independent factors associated with Internet addiction in Korean adolescents and found that staff working in junior or senior high schools should pay closer attention to those students who have the risk factors for intermittent addiction and addiction to the Internet (Jang et al. 2008). Gyeong et al. (2012) analyzed the factors of the Young's Internet Addiction Test: in Korean college students.

In an adaptation study, Internet Addiction Test was translated into Korean language and the reliability and validity of this version was analyzed (Lee et al. 2013). In two different studies, cellular phone usage addiction (Ha et al. 2008) and online game addiction (Lee and Kim, 2014) of Korean adolescents were analyzed. The most interesting issue in the Korean studies generally is "the relationship between Internet addiction and physical properties of the addicted people". In the studies Kim et al. (2006), Lim et al. (2017) and Park and Lee (2017), the relationship between the obesity and Internet addiction in Korean adolescents was investigated and all of these studies mentioned that Internet addiction can cause nutrition disorders and obesity.

More Than 1 Country

In a few study in the literature, the Internet addiction issue was not investigated in one country; instead of this, some comparisons between two or more countries was made. Zhang et al. (2008) explored Internet addiction among university students in China and the United States to develop a better understanding of Internet addiction in a cross-national setting. In this study, 171 U.S. and 143 Chinese students were examined. The results indicate that Chinese students experience a higher rate of Internet addiction than their U.S. counterparts and Internet addiction may result as an artifact of the stage of Internet adoption within a society. Koski-Jannes and Simmat-Durand (2017) explored how treatment professionals' cultural and other background variables influence their beliefs about gambling and Internet addictions. Mailed surveys were conducted with addiction treatment professionals in Finland (520 participants) and France (472 participants). The results show that, Finnish professionals for the addiction potential of gambling and Internet use may make them less attentive to related disorders among their clients, on the other hand, the higher belief in untreated recovery from gambling by the French professionals together with their lack of trust in the efficacy of treatment for both of these behavioural addictions. Montag et al. (2015) investigated the relationship between generalized and specific Internet addiction in a cross-cultural study encompassing data from China, Taiwan, Sweden and Germany. There were totally 636 participants and addictive behaviour of online video gaming, online shopping, online social networks and online pornography were examined. The results show that online social network addiction correlates in large amounts with generalized Internet addiction. Mak et al. (2017) doesn't have a completely comparison but it applied a country's (Korea) scales for Internet addiction to another country's (Japan) high school students. In this study, Japanese versions for Korean Scale for Internet Addiction (K-Scale) and Smartphone Scale for Smartphone Addiction (S-Scale) were developed. After modification, K-Scale is a valid and reliable scale to be used in Japanese high school students for assessing addictive Internet behaviors. Błachnio et al. (2017) made an investigation about role of personality traits in Facebook and Internet addictions and it applied Bergen Facebook Addiction Scale, the Internet Addiction Test, and the Ten Item Personality Inventory to 1011 Facebook users from Poland, Turkey and Ukraine. The results presented that, personality plays an important role in determining Facebook use and certain activities on Facebook (Eftekhar et al. 2014) such as uploading photos, status updating, the number of friends displayed (Lee et al. 2014), photo-related activities, or the choice of profile pictures (Wu et al. 2015). They found that some different patterns were found in these countries and the highest level of Facebook addiction among Polish users as well as the highest number of hours spent online every day in the Ukrainian group.

Italy

Italy had a few studies about Internet addiction. In 2007, Ferraro et al. applied the Italian version of Internet Addiction Test to 236 Italian people. A more large scaled study applied this test to 2533 students (Poli and Agrimi, 2012). Scimeca et al. (2014) tried to determine the relationship between alexithymia, anxiety, depression and Internet addiction severity in a sample of Italian high school students. Servidio (2014) explored the effects of demographic factors, Internet usage and personality traits on Internet addiction in a sample of Italian university students. In the recent studies published in 2017, Servidio assesses the psychometric properties of the 20-item Internet Addiction Test among a sample of 659 Italian university students and Guglielmucci et al. investigate the relationship between specific personality profiles and Internet use in a sample of Italian adolescents.

Greece

In 2008, 2011, 2013 and 2017 there are some studies about Internet addiction of Greek people. Siomos et al. (2008) aimed to assess the prevalence of Internet addiction among Greek adolescent students, ages 12 to 18. The sample of 2200 students was recruited from 120 classes among 85 schools in Thessaly, Greece. Frangos et al. (2011) investigated the relationships between problematic Internet use among university students in Greece and factors such as gender, age, family condition, academic performance in the last semester of their studies, enrollment in unemployment programs, amount of Internet use per week (in general and per application), additional personal habits or dependencies (number of coffees, alcoholic drinks drunk per day, taking substances, cigarettes smoked per day), and negative psychological beliefs. Stavropoulos et al. (2013) estimated the prevalence of Internet addiction among adolescents of urban and rural areas in Greece, examined whether the Internet Addiction Test cut-off point is applicable to them and investigated the phenomenon's association with academic achievement. Stavropoulos et al. (2017) analyzed Internet addiction symptoms in adolescents were investigated longitudinally with specific focus on the individual's hostility, gaming use (of Massively Multiplayer Online Role Playing Games - MMORPGs) and gaming on the classroom level (calculated using the percentage of MMORPG players within classes).

India

India accounts for over 243 million Internet users and has the world's third largest population of Internet users after the United States and China (Dhir et al. 2015) but there are only a few studies about addiction. Yadav et al. (2013) and Sharma et al. (2016) investigated Internet addiction and its correlation with some parameters over Indian people of Ahmedabad and Mumbai respectively.

Germany

As similar to many languages, Internet addiction test has been translated to German (Barke et al. 2012). Apart from that, Müller et al. (2014) and Rehbein et al. (2015) examined Internet addiction in the general German population and Internet gaming addiction in German adolescents respectively.

Japan

There are two interesting studies in Japan about Internet addiction. In the first one, Ezoe and Toda (2013) investigated factors contributing to Internet addiction in 105 Japanese medical students. They handled relationships of loneliness and mobile phone dependence with Internet addiction in this group. Their findings suggest that university students with feelings of loneliness and mobile phone dependence are prone to have a higher level of Internet addiction. In the second one, Morioka et al. (2017) tried to find the association between alcohol use and problematic Internet use of adolescents in Japan.

Jordan

In a study about Jordan, 716 participants who are 12–18 years were selected randomly from ten public schools in Amman Governorate in Jordan. In order to determine the Internet addiction of this group, Socio-demographical data, patterns of Internet usage, the Internet Addiction Tool, the Symptom Checklist-Anxiety Scale and the Center for Epidemiological Studies Depression Scale for Children were used. The findings showed that the prevalence of severe Internet Addiction was 6.3% (Malak et al. 2017).

Singapore

The studies about Internet addiction of Singaporean people has been started recently. In this year, two different studies by Tang et al. (2017) and Lee et al. (2017) investigated especially online social network addiction. Tang et al. (2017) showed that social networking sites addiction has a high prevalence rate among college students in Singapore. Students with this addiction were vulnerable to experience other behavior addiction as well as affective disorder, especially among females. In the other study, findings suggest that it is important to account for both external and personal antecedent factors of social network site consumption.

Norway

In 2009, Bakken et al. investigated Internet addiction among Norwegian adults. 3399 people between 16 and 74 ages are handled according to their Internet usage. This population-based study showed that Internet addiction and at-risk Internet use is not confined to adolescents. Problematic Internet users spend large amounts of time on the Internet, especially for entertainment purposes, and more often report psychological impairments than non-problematic users.

Australia

In a study about Australia in 2010, video–arcade game, computer game and Internet activities of Australian students were investigated (Thomas & Martin, 2010).

Vietnam

In order to constitute this chapter, only one recent study of Internet addiction about Vietnam could be found. Tran et al. (2017) aimed to study the influence of Internet addiction and online activities on health-related quality of life (HRQOL) in young Vietnamese and this study also compared the frequencies of anxiety, depression and other addiction of young Vietnamese with and without Internet addiction. This study recruited 566 young Vietnamese (56.7% female, 43.3% male) ranging from 15 to 25 years of age. Regression analyses were used to examine the association between Internet usage characteristics and HRQOL. This study found that Internet addiction is a common problem in young Vietnamese and the prevalence of Internet addiction is among the highest as compared to other Asian countries.

Portugal

The only study about Internet addiction in Portugal reports an exploratory analysis of the relation between Internet addiction and patterns of use among 2617 Portuguese adolescents (Gamito et al. 2016).

Poland

There are not many studies about Internet addiction in Poland. In a recent study, Błachnio and Przepiorka (2016) tried to find an answer to the question of whether personality and positive orientation are linked to Internet and Facebook addiction. For this purpose, Bergen Facebook Addiction Scale, the Internet Addiction Test, the Short Personality Scale, and the Positive Orientation Scale were used over Poland participants and the results indicate that lower positive orientation, conscientiousness, emotional stability, and openness to experience are related to problematic use of both Internet and Facebook. Another study Błachnio et al. (2017) made an investigation about role of personality traits in Facebook and Internet addictions and it applied Bergen Facebook Addiction Scale, the Internet Addiction Test, and the Ten Item Personality Inventory to 1011 Facebook users from Poland, Turkey and Ukraine.

SOLUTIONS AND RECOMMENDATIONS

Prevention of Internet addiction is a troublesome and a long process. To prevent this effective addiction, early period preventive intervention programs are needed that consider the individual severity level of Internet addiction (Jang et al. 2008). Because an important percentage of Internet addicts are college students, there must be campus prevention programs focus on educating students about emotional regulation skills to decrease depressive symptoms (Lin et al. 2011) and also family-based preventive approach for Internet addiction should be implemented for students with negative family factors (Yen et al. 2007). This prevention should include skills training for parents to improve communication skills in helping adolescents to develop social skills, helping family members reduce maladaptive family function, fostering skills for healthy family interactions, and effective family monitoring and discipline focusing on Internet addiction (Lochman and Van den Steenhoven, 2006).

Internet addiction can cause nutrition disorders and obesity (Kim et al. 2010; Lim et al. 2017; Park and Lee, 2017). So, the Internet addicted people must be carefull about their food. Especially children should be educated as to what a balanced diet and optimum physical activity routine is to remain healthy and grow. Furthermore, the government should take an active role in designing and evaluating Internet addiction-related health intervention strategies (Kim et al. 2010). Also, special attention needs to be paid to the adolescents who deviate from normal body size and also have an inclination of heavy Internet use. Particularly, educational interventions for a healthy weight control behavior are highly recommended for those with inappropriate weight control behavior (Park and Lee, 2017).

If it is paid close attention, it can be easily seen that, nearly all of the studies about Internet addiction was about the psychology of the addicted people. The number, age, nation and other properties of participants are changed from one study to another; some studies handled 300 people while some other another one cares about 10000 people. These people can be children or adolescents; they can be Chinese, Japanese, Turkish, Polish, Ukranian, Taiwanese, Italian, German, French, Finn, Greek and so on. The parameter "that affected to Internet addiction" or "that is affected from Internet addiction" has a wide range too. It can be depression, anxiety, insomnia, obesity, sexuality, dysregulation of feelings and behaviors, emotional distress, health problems and so on. Of course these studies have a critical role to understand Internet addiction and prevent it. But, these studies are about the social type of the subject. There can be other types of studies which handle technical type of the addiction. For example, the computer program properties can be examined and there can be a decision about the programs whether it cause addiction or not. If the properties that cause addiction could be detected, the programmers can care about not to use this type of technical properties. Another example can be given about human – computer interaction and with this subject, the computer screen can be analyzed. Human eye is inclined to look some definite points on the screen and these points can be used to remove people from addiction. Finally, Internet addiction is an up and coming field to study not only for social investigators but also for technical investigators.

CONCLUSION

In this chapter, a review of Internet addiction on the basis of different countries between the years of 2007 and 2017 was presented. Over 110 papers in the literature were investigated in order to reveal the relationships between some parameters and Internet addiction. The results of these paper can be summarized as follows:

- Internet addiction is a problem which is getting more and more dangerous.
- There are sub-addictions such as online game addiction, online social network addiction, online shopping addiction, online pornography addiction, mobile telephone usage addiction and so on. The number of addiction types are increasing day by day.
- The "level of tendency" and the "level of effect" of a person for Internet addiction is depended to different criteria such as age and nationality.
- Internet addiction is followed by other diseases (physical and psychological). Some of these diseases are neck pain, depression, lumbar pain, insomnia, eye burning, hyperactivity, hand numbness, social phobia, hernia, Attention Deficit and Hyperactivity Disorder, depression and obesity.

If parents, governments, teachers could understand the level of danger and be careful , the Internet addiction could be reduced; otherwise, a problematical generation would meet us in the future.

REFERENCES

Ak, S., Koruklu, N., & Yilmaz, Y. (2013). A Study on Turkish Adolescent's Internet Use: Possible Predictors of Internet Addiction. *Cyberpsychology, Behavior, and Social Networking*, *16*(3), 205–209. doi:10.1089/cyber.2012.0255 PMID:23253206

American Psychiatric Association. (2013). *Diagnostic and Statistical Manual of Mental Disorders* (5th ed.). Arlington, VA: American Psychiatric Publishing.

Aslanbay, Y., Aslanbay, M., & Cobanoglu, E. (2009). Internet addiction among Turkish young consumers. *Young Consumers*, *10*(1), 60–70. doi:10.1108/17473610910940792

Frangos, C. C., Frangos, C. C., & Sotiropoulos, I. (2011). Problematic Internet Use Among Greek University Students: An Ordinal Logistic Regression with Risk Factors of Negative Psychological Beliefs, Pornographic Sites, and Online Games. *Cyberpsychology, Behavior, and Social Networking*, *14*(1-2), 51–58. doi:10.1089/cyber.2009.0306 PMID:21329443

Gamito, P. S., Morais, D. G., Oliveira, J. G. B., Rosa, R. P. J., & Matos, M. G. (2016). Frequency is not enough: Patterns of use associated with risk of Internet addiction in Portuguese adolescents. *Computers in Human Behavior*, *58*, 471–478. doi:10.1016/j.chb.2016.01.013

Golub, A., & Lingley, K. (2008). Internet Addiction, MMOGs, and Moral Crisis in Contemporary China. *Games and Culture*, *3*(1), 59–75. doi:10.1177/1555412007309526

Guglielmucci, F., Saroldi, M., Zullo, G., Munno, D., & Granieri, A. (2017). Personality Profiles and Problematic Internet Use in a Sample Of Italian Adolescents. *Clinical Neuropsychiatry*, *14*(1), 94–103.

Gunuc, S., & Dogan, A. (2013). The relationships between Turkish adolescents' Internet addiction, their perceived social support and family activities. *Computers in Human Behavior*, *29*(6), 2197–2207. doi:10.1016/j.chb.2013.04.011

Guo, J., Chen, L., Wang, X., Liu, Y., Chui, C. H. K., He, H., & Tian, D. et al. (2012). The Relationship Between Internet Addiction and Depression Among Migrant Children and Left-Behind Children in China. *Cyberpsychology, Behavior, and Social Networking*, *15*(11), 585–590. doi:10.1089/cyber.2012.0261 PMID:23002986

Gyeong, H., Lee, H. K., & Lee, K. (2012). Factor Analysis of the Young's Internet Addiction Test: In Korean College Students Group. *Journal of Korean Neuropsychiatric Association*, *51*(1), 45–51. doi:10.4306/jknpa.2012.51.1.45

Ha, J. H., Chin, B., Park, D. H., Ryu, S. H., & Yu, J. (2008). Characteristics of Excessive Cellular Phone Use in Korean Adolescents. *Cyberpsychology & Behavior*, *11*(6), 783–784. doi:10.1089/cpb.2008.0096 PMID:18991536

Hsieh, Y. P., Shen, A. C. T., Wei, H. S., Feng, J. Y., Huang, S. C. Y., & Hwa, H. L. (2016). Associations between child maltreatment, PTSD, and Internet addiction among Taiwanese students. *Computers in Human Behavior*, *56*, 209–214. doi:10.1016/j.chb.2015.11.048

Huang, R. L., Lu, Z., Liu, J. J., You, Y. M., Pan, Z. Q., Wei, Z., & Wang, Z. Z. et al. (2009). Features and predictors of problematic Internet use in Chinese college students. *Behaviour & Information Technology*, *28*(5), 485–490. doi:10.1080/01449290701485801

Huang, Z., Wang, M., Qian, M., Zhong, J., & Tao, R. (2007). Chinese Internet Addiction Inventory: Developing a Measure of Problematic Internet Use for Chinese College Students. *Cyberpsychology & Behavior*, *10*(6), 805–811. doi:10.1089/cpb.2007.9950 PMID:18085968

Jang, K. S., Hwang, S. Y., & Choi, J. Y. (2008). Internet Addiction and Psychiatric Symptoms Among Korean Adolescents. *The Journal of School Health*, *78*(3), 165–171. doi:10.1111/j.1746-1561.2007.00279.x PMID:18307612

Kim, J. H., Lau, C. H., Cheuk, K. K., Kan, P., Hui, H. L. C., & Griffiths, S. M. (2010). Brief report: Predictors of heavy Internet use and associations with health-promoting and health risk behaviors among Hong Kong university students. *Journal of Adolescence, 33*(1), 215–220. doi:10.1016/j.adolescence.2009.03.012 PMID:19427030

Kim, K., Ryu, E., Chon, M. Y., Yeun, E. J., Choi, S. Y., Seo, J. S., & Nam, B. W. (2006). Internet addiction in Korean adolescents and its relation to depression and suicidal ideation: A questionnaire survey. *International Journal of Nursing Studies, 43*(2), 185–192. doi:10.1016/j.ijnurstu.2005.02.005 PMID:16427966

Koc, M., & Gulyagci, S. (2013). Facebook Addiction Among Turkish College Students: The Role of Psychological Health, Demographic, and Usage Characteristics. *Cyberpsychology, Behavior, and Social Networking, 16*(4), 279–284. doi:10.1089/cyber.2012.0249 PMID:23286695

Koski-Ja¨nnes, A., & Simmat-Durand, L. (2017). Basic Beliefs About Behavioural Addictions Among Finnish and French Treatment Professionals. *Journal of Gambling Studies.* doi:10.1007/s10899-017-9672-8 PMID:28154957

Lee, E., Ahn, J., & Kim, Y. J. (2014). Personality traits and self-presentation at Facebook. *Personality and Individual Differences, 69*, 162–167. doi:10.1016/j.paid.2014.05.020

Lee, E. W. J., Ho, S. S., & Lwin, M. O. (2017). Extending the social cognitive model - Examining the external and personal antecedents of social network sites use among Singaporean adolescents. *Computers in Human Behavior, 67*, 240–251. doi:10.1016/j.chb.2016.10.030

Lee, K., Lee, H. K., Gyeong, H., Yu, B., Song, Y. M., & Kim, D. (2013). Reliability and Validity of the Korean Version of the Internet Addiction Test among College Students. *Journal of Korean Medical Science, 28*(5), 763–768. doi:10.3346/jkms.2013.28.5.763 PMID:23678270

Lee, Y. H., Ko, C. H., & Chou, C. (2015). Re-visiting Internet Addiction among Taiwanese Students: A Cross-Sectional Comparison of Students' Expectations, Online Gaming, and Online Social Interaction. *Journal of Abnormal Child Psychology, 43*(3), 589–599. doi:10.1007/s10802-014-9915-4 PMID:25079945

Leshner, A. I. (1997). Addiction is a brain disease, and it matters. *Science, 278*(5335), 45–47. doi:10.1126/science.278.5335.45 PMID:9311924

Leung, L. (2008). Linking psychological attributes to addiction and improper use of the mobile phone among adolescents in Hong Kong. *Journal of Children and Media, 2*(2), 93–113. doi:10.1080/17482790802078565

Li, C., Dang, J., Zhang, X., Zhang, Q., & Guo, J. (2014). Internet addiction among Chinese adolescents: The effect of parental behavior and self-control. *Computers in Human Behavior, 41*, 1–7. doi:10.1016/j.chb.2014.09.001

Liang, L., Zhou, D., Yuan, C., Shao, A., & Bian, Y. (2016). Gender differences in the relationship between Internet addiction and depression: A cross-lagged study in Chinese adolescents. *Computers in Human Behavior, 63*, 463–470. doi:10.1016/j.chb.2016.04.043

Lim, C. H., Kim, E. J., Kim, J. H., Lee, J. S., Lee, Y., & Park, S. H. (2017). The correlation of depression with Internet use and body image in Korean adolescents. *Korean Journal of Pediatrics*, *60*(1), 17–23. doi:10.3345/kjp.2017.60.1.17 PMID:28203256

Lin, M. P., Ko, H. C., & Wu, J. Y. W. (2008). The Role of Positive/Negative Outcome Expectancy and Refusal Self-Efficacy of Internet Use on Internet Addiction among College Students in Taiwan. *Cyberpsychology & Behavior*, *11*(4), 451–457. doi:10.1089/cpb.2007.0121 PMID:18721094

Lin, M. P., Ko, H. C., & Wu, J. Y. W. (2011). Prevalence and Psychosocial Risk Factors Associated with Internet Addiction in a Nationally Representative Sample of College Students in Taiwan. *Cyberpsychology, Behavior, and Social Networking*, *14*(12), 741–746. doi:10.1089/cyber.2010.0574 PMID:21651418

Lochman, J. E., & Van den Steenhoven, A. (2006). Family-based approaches to substance abuse prevention. *The Journal of Primary Prevention*, *23*(1), 49–114. doi:10.1023/A:1016591216363

Mak, K. K., Nam, J. K., Kim, D., Aum, N., Choi, J. S., Cheng, C., & Watanabe, H. et al. (2017). Cecilia Cheng, Huei-Chen Ko, Hiroko Watanabe, Cross-cultural adaptation and psychometric properties of the Korean Scale for Internet Addiction (K-Scale) in Japanese high school students. *Psychiatry Research*, *249*, 343–348. doi:10.1016/j.psychres.2017.01.044 PMID:28152469

Malak, M. Z., Khalifeh, A. H., & Shuhaiber, A. H. (2017). Prevalence of Internet Addiction and associated risk factors in Jordanian school students. *Computers in Human Behavior*, *70*, 556–563. doi:10.1016/j.chb.2017.01.011

Montag, C., Bey, K., Sha, P., Li, M., Chen, Y. F., Liu, W. Y., & Reuter, M. et al. (2015). Is it meaningful to distinguish between generalized and specific Internet addiction? Evidence from a cross - cultural study from Germany, Sweden, Taiwan and China. *Asia-Pacific Psychiatry*, *7*(1), 20–26. doi:10.1111/appy.12122 PMID:24616402

Morioka, H., Itani, O., Osaki, Y., Higuchi, S., Jike, M., Kaneita, Y., & Ohida, T. et al. (2017). The association between alcohol use and problematic Internet use: A large-scale nationwide cross-sectional study of adolescents in Japan. *Journal of Epidemiology*, *27*(3), 10–111. doi:10.1016/j.je.2016.10.004 PMID:28142042

Müller, K.W., Glaesmer, H., Brähler, E., Woelfling, K., & Beutel, M. E. (2014). *Prevalence of Internet addiction in the general population: Results from a German population-based survey*. Academic Press.

Nalwa, K., & Anand, A. P. (2003). Internet addiction in students: A cause of concern. *Cyberpsychology & Behavior*, *6*(6), 653–656. doi:10.1089/109493103322725441 PMID:14756932

Ni, X., Yan, H., Chen, S., & Liu, Z. (2009). Factors Influencing Internet Addiction in a Sample of Freshmen University Students in China. *Cyberpsychology, Behavior, and Social Networking*, *12*(3), 327–330. doi:10.1089/cpb.2008.0321 PMID:19445631

Nie, J., Zhang, W., & Liu, Y. (2017). Exploring depression, self-esteem and verbal fluency with different degrees of Internet addiction among Chinese college students. *Comprehensive Psychiatry*, *72*, 114–120. doi:10.1016/j.comppsych.2016.10.006 PMID:27810547

Park, S., & Lee, Y. (2017). Associations of body weight perception and weight control behaviors with problematic Internet use among Korean adolescents. *Psychiatry Research*, *251*, 275–280. doi:10.1016/j.psychres.2017.01.095 PMID:28222311

Peng, W., & Liu, M. (2010). Online Gaming Dependency: A Preliminary Study in China. *Cyberpsychology, Behavior, and Social Networking*, *13*(3), 329–333. doi:10.1089/cyber.2009.0082 PMID:20557254

Pierce, G. R., Lakey, B., & Sarason, I. G. (Eds.). (2013). *Sourcebook of Social Support and Personality*. Springer Science and Business Media Press.

Poli, R., & Agrimi, E. (2012). Internet addiction disorder: Prevalence in an Italian student population. *Nordic Journal of Psychiatry*, *66*(1), 55–59. doi:10.3109/08039488.2011.605169 PMID:21859396

Randler, C., Horzum, M. B., & Vollmer, C. (2013). Internet Addiction and Its Relationship to Chronotype and Personality in a Turkish University Student Sample. *Social Science Computer Review*, *32*(4), 1–12.

Rehbein, F., Kliem, S., Baier, D., Mößle, T., & Petry, N. M. (2015). Prevalence of Internet gaming disorder in German adolescents: Diagnostic contribution of the nine DSM-5 criteria in a state-wide representative sample. *Addiction (Abingdon, England)*, *110*(5), 842–851. doi:10.1111/add.12849 PMID:25598040

Rosenberg, M. (1965). *Society and the adolescent self-image*. Princeton, NJ: Princeton University Press. doi:10.1515/9781400876136

Scimeca, G., Bruno, A., Cava, L., Pandolfo, G., Muscatello, M. R. A., & Zoccali, R. (2014). The Relationship between Alexithymia, Anxiety, Depression, and Internet Addiction Severity in a Sample of Italian High School Students. *The Scientific World Journal*, *2014*, 1–8. doi:10.1155/2014/504376 PMID:25401143

Servidio, R. (2014). Exploring the effects of demographic factors, Internet usage and personality traits on Internet addiction in a sample of Italian university students. *Computers in Human Behavior*, *35*, 85–92. doi:10.1016/j.chb.2014.02.024

Servidio, R. (2017). Assessing the psychometric properties of the Internet Addiction Test: A study on a sample of Italian university students. *Computers in Human Behavior*, *68*, 17–29. doi:10.1016/j.chb.2016.11.019

Seyrek, S., Cop, E., Sinir, H., Ugurlu, M., & Senel, S. (2017). Factors associated with Internet addiction: Cross-sectional study of Turkish adolescents. *Pediatrics International*, *59*(2), 218–222. doi:10.1111/ped.13117 PMID:27507735

Sharma, P., Bharati, A., De Sousa, A., & Shah, N. (2016). Internet Addiction and Its Association With Psychopathology: A Study In School Children From Mumbai, India. *National Journal of Community Medicine*, *7*(1).

Shek, D. T. L., Tang, V. M. Y., & Lo, C. Y. (2008). Internet Addiction in Chinese Adolescents in Hong Kong: Assessment, Profiles, and Psychosocial Correlates. *The Scientific World Journal*, *8*, 776–787. doi:10.1100/tsw.2008.104 PMID:18690381

Siomos, K. E., Dafouli, E. D., Braimiotis, D. A., Mouzas, O. D., & Angelopoulos, N. V. (2008). Internet Addiction among Greek Adolescent Students. *Cyberpsychology & Behavior*, *11*(6), 653–657. doi:10.1089/cpb.2008.0088 PMID:18991535

Sroubek, A., Kelly, M., & Li, X. (2013). Inattentiveness in attention-deficit/hyperactivity disorder. *Neuroscience Bulletin*, *29*(1), 103–110. doi:10.1007/s12264-012-1295-6 PMID:23299717

Stavropoulos, V., Alexandraki, K., & Motti-Stefanidi, F. (2013). Recognizing Internet addiction: Prevalence and relationship to academic achievement in adolescents enrolled in urban and rural Greek high schools. *Journal of Adolescence*, *36*(3), 565–576. doi:10.1016/j.adolescence.2013.03.008 PMID:23608781

Stavropoulos, V., Kuss, D. J., Griffiths, M. D., Wilson, P., & Motti-Stefanidi, F. (2017). MMORPG gaming and hostility predict Internet Addiction symptoms in adolescents: An empirical multilevel longitudinal study. *Addictive Behaviors*, *64*, 294–300. doi:10.1016/j.addbeh.2015.09.001 PMID:26410795

Su, W., Fang, X., Miller, J. K., & Wang, Y. (2011). Internet-Based Intervention for the Treatment of Online Addiction for College Students in China: A Pilot Study of the Healthy Online Self-Helping Center. *Cyberpsychology, Behavior, and Social Networking*, *14*(9), 497–503. doi:10.1089/cyber.2010.0167 PMID:21294635

Szablewicz, M. (2010). The ill effects of "opium for the spirit": A critical cultural analysis of China's Internet addiction moral panic. *Chinese Journal of Communication*, *3*(4), 453–470. doi:10.1080/17544750.2010.516579

Tahiroglu, A. Y., Celik, G. G., Uzel, M., Ozcan, N., & Avci, A. (2008). Internet Use Among Turkish Adolescents. *Cyberpsychology & Behavior*, *11*(5), 537–543. doi:10.1089/cpb.2007.0165 PMID:18785800

Tang, C. S., & Koh, Y. Y. W. (2017). Online social networking addiction among college students in Singapore: Comorbidity with behavioral addiction and affective disorder. *Asian Journal of Psychiatry*, *25*, 175–178. doi:10.1016/j.ajp.2016.10.027 PMID:28262144

Tao, Z., Wu, G., & Wang, Z. (2016). The relationship between high residential density in student dormitories and anxiety, binge eating and Internet addiction: A study of Chinese college students. *SpringerPlus*, *5*(1), 1579–1587. doi:10.1186/s40064-016-3246-6 PMID:27652152

Tekinarslan, E. (2017). Relationship between Problematic Internet Use, Depression and Quality of Life Levels of Turkish University Students. *Journal of Education and Training Studies*, *5*(3), 167–175. doi:10.11114/jets.v5i3.2238

Thomas, N. J., & Martin, F. H. (2010). Video – arcade game, computer game and Internet activities of Australian students: Participation habits and prevalence of addiction. *Australian Journal of Psychology*, *62*(2), 59–66. doi:10.1080/00049530902748283

Tran, B. X., Huong, L. T., Hinh, N. D., Nguyen, L. H., Le, B. N., Nong, V. M., & Ho, R. C. M. et al. (2017). A study on the influence of Internet addiction and online interpersonal influences on health-related quality of life in young Vietnamese. *BMC Public Health*, *17*(1), 138. doi:10.1186/s12889-016-3983-z PMID:28143462

Tsai, H. F., Cheng, S. H., Yeh, T. L., Shih, C. C., Chen, K. C., Yang, Y. C., & Yang, Y. K. (2009). The risk factors of Internet addiction - A survey of university freshmen. *Psychiatry Research, 167*(3), 294–299. doi:10.1016/j.psychres.2008.01.015 PMID:19395052

Wang, C. W., Ho, R. T. H., Chan, C. L. W., & Tse, S. (2015). Exploring personality characteristics of Chinese adolescents with Internet-related addictive behaviors: Trait differences for gaming addiction and social networking addiction. *Addictive Behaviors, 42*, 32–35. doi:10.1016/j.addbeh.2014.10.039 PMID:25462651

Wang, Y., Wu, A. M. S., & Lau, J. T. F. (2016). The health belief model and number of peers with Internet addiction as interrelated factors of Internet addiction among secondary school students in Hong Kong. *BMC Public Health, 16*(1), 272–285. doi:10.1186/s12889-016-2947-7 PMID:26983882

Wu, C. H., & Cheng, F. F. (2007). Internet Café Addiction of Taiwanese Adolescents. *Cyberpsychology & Behavior, 10*(2), 220–225. doi:10.1089/cpb.2006.9965 PMID:17474839

Wu, C. S. T., Wong, H. T., Yu, K. F., Fok, K. W., Yeung, S. M., Lam, C. H., & Liu, K. M. (2016). Parenting approaches, family functionality, and Internet addiction among Hong Kong adolescents. *BMC Pediatrics, 16*(1), 130–140. doi:10.1186/s12887-016-0666-y PMID:27538688

Wu, X. S., Zhang, Z. H., Zhao, F., Wang, W. J., Li, Y. F., Bi, L., & Sun, Y. H. et al. (2016). Prevalence of Internet addiction and its association with social support and other related factors among adolescents in China. *Journal of Adolescence, 52*, 103–111. doi:10.1016/j.adolescence.2016.07.012 PMID:27544491

Wu, Y.C.J., Chang, W.H., & Yuan, C.H. (2015). Do facebook profile pictures reflect user's personality? *Computers in Human Behavior, 51*(Part B), 880–889.

Xu, J., Shen, L. X., Yan, C. H., Hu, H., Yang, F., Wang, L., & Shen, X. et al. (2012). Personal characteristics related to the risk of adolescent Internet addiction: A survey in Shanghai, China. *BMC Public Health, 12*(1), 3–10. doi:10.1186/1471-2458-12-1106 PMID:23259906

Yadav, P., Banwari, G., Parmar, C., & Maniar, R. (2013). Internet addiction and its correlates among high school students: A preliminary study from Ahmedabad, India. *Asian Journal of Psychiatry, 6*(6), 500–505. doi:10.1016/j.ajp.2013.06.004 PMID:24309861

Yang, L., Sun, L., Zhang, Z., Sun, Y., Wu, H., & Ye, D. (2014). Internet addiction, adolescent depression, and the mediating role of life events: Finding from a sample of Chinese adolescents. *International Journal of Psychology, 49*(5), 342–347. doi:10.1002/ijop.12063 PMID:25178955

Yang, S. C., & Tung, C. J. (2007). Comparison of Internet addicts and non-addicts in Taiwanese high school. *Computers in Human Behavior, 23*(1), 79–96. doi:10.1016/j.chb.2004.03.037

Yang, X., Zhu, L., Chen, Q., Song, P., & Wang, Z. (2016). Parent marital conflict and Internet addiction among Chinese college students: The mediating role of father-child, mother-child, and peer attachment. *Computers in Human Behavior, 59*, 221–229. doi:10.1016/j.chb.2016.01.041

Yao, B., Han, W., Zeng, L., & Guo, X. (2013). Freshman year mental health symptoms and level of adaptation as predictors of Internet addiction: A retrospective nested case-control study of male Chinese college students. *Psychiatry Research, 210*(2), 541–547. doi:10.1016/j.psychres.2013.07.023 PMID:23896352

Yao, M. Z., He, J., Ko, D. M., & Pang, K. (2014). The Influence of Personality, Parental Behaviors, and Self-Esteem on Internet Addiction: A Study of Chinese College Students. *Cyberpsychology, Behavior, and Social Networking, 17*(2), 104–110. doi:10.1089/cyber.2012.0710 PMID:24003966

Yeh, Y. C., Ko, H. C., Wu, J. Y. W., & Cheng, C. P. (2008). Gender Differences in Relationships of Actual and Virtual Social Support to Internet Addiction Mediated through Depressive Symptoms among College Students in Taiwan. *Cyberpsychology & Behavior, 11*(4), 485–487. doi:10.1089/cpb.2007.0134 PMID:18721099

Yen, J. Y., Yen, C. F., Chen, C. C., Chen, S. H., & Ko, C. H. (2007). Family Factors of Internet Addiction and Substance Use Experience in Taiwanese Adolescents. *Cyberpsychology & Behavior, 10*(3), 323–329. doi:10.1089/cpb.2006.9948 PMID:17594255

Yoo, H. J., Cho, S. C., Ha, J., Yune, S. K., Kim, S. J., Hwang, J., & Lyoo, I. K. et al. (2004). Attention deficit hyperactivity symptoms and Internet addiction. *Psychiatry and Clinical Neurosciences, 58*(5), 487–494. doi:10.1111/j.1440-1819.2004.01290.x PMID:15482579

Young, K. S. (2004). Internet addiction. A new clinical phenomenon and its consequences. *The American Behavioral Scientist, 48*(4), 402–415. doi:10.1177/0002764204270278

Zhang, L., Amos, C., & McDowell, W. C. (2008). A Comparative Study of Internet Addiction between the United States and China. *Cyberpsychology & Behavior, 11*(6), 727–729. doi:10.1089/cpb.2008.0026 PMID:18991530

Zhao, F., Zhang, Z. H., Bi, L., Wu, X. S., Wang, W. J., Li, Y. F., & Sun, Y. H. (2017). The association between life events and Internet addiction among Chinese vocational school students: The mediating role of depression. *Computers in Human Behavior, 70*, 30–38. doi:10.1016/j.chb.2016.12.057

KEY TERMS AND DEFINITIONS

Attention Deficit and Hyperactivity Disorder (ADHD): Attention Deficit and Hyperactivity Disorder is a mental disorder of the neurodevelopmental type. It is characterized by problems paying attention, excessive activity, or difficulty controlling behavior which is not appropriate for a person's age. These symptoms begin by age six to twelve, are present for more than six months, and cause problems in at least two settings (such as school, home, or recreational activities) (Sroubek et al. 2013).

General Health Questionnaire (GHQ): General Health Questionnaire is a screening device for identifying minor psychiatric disorders in the general population and within community or non-psychiatric clinical settings such as primary care or general medical out-patients. Suitable for all ages from adolescent upwards – not children, it assesses the respondent's current state and asks if that differs from his or her usual state. It is therefore sensitive to short-term psychiatric disorders but not to long-standing attributes of the respondent.

Internet Addiction Test (IAT): Internet Addiction Test (IAT) is a reliable and valid measure of addictive use of Internet, developed by Dr. Kimberly Young. It consists of 20 items that measures mild, moderate and severe level of Internet Addiction (Young, 2004).

Korean Scale for Internet Addiction (K-Scale): Korean Scale for Internet Addiction (K-Scale) was developed in Korea for assessing addictive Internet behaviors. It is a checklist for diagnosing and evaluating Internet addiction. Internet addiction has been recommended for inclusion in DSM-V (the American Psychiatric Association's Diagnostic and Statistical Manual of Mental Disorders, fifth revision) (Mak et al. 2017).

Post-Traumatic Stress Disorder (PTSD): Post-Traumatic Stress Disorder is a mental disorder that can develop after a person is exposed to a traumatic event, such as sexual assault, warfare, traffic collisions, or other threats on a person's life. Symptoms may include disturbing thoughts, feelings, or dreams related to the events, mental or physical distress to trauma-related cues, attempts to avoid trauma-related cues, alterations in how a person thinks and feels, and an increase in the fight-or-flight response (American Psychiatric Association, 2013).

Rosenberg Self-Esteem Scale (RSES): Rosenberg Self-Esteem Scale was designed Rosenberg M. To assess the self-esteem level. The scale is a ten item Likert scale with items answered on a four point scale - from strongly agree to strongly disagree. The original sample for which the scale was developed consisted of 5,024 high school juniors and seniors from 10 randomly selected schools in New York State (Rosenberg, 1965).

Smartphone Scale for Smartphone Addiction (S-Scale): Smartphone Scale for Smartphone Addiction is a scale used for assessing smartphone addiction levels of people.

Social Support Rating Scale (SSRS): Social Support Rating Scale (SSRS) is a measure of perveived social support. This measure has seperate subscales for the perceived helpfullness of peers, family and school personel (Pierce et al. 2013).

Chapter 12
Individual Differences and the Development of Internet Addiction:
A Nationally Representative Study

Mirna Macur
National Institute of Public Health, Slovenia

Halley M. Pontes
Nottingham Trent University, UK

ABSTRACT

Internet addiction (IA) has emerged as a universal issue, but its international estimates vary due to different screening instruments and different samples. The present study aims to estimate the risk of IA in a school-based nationally representative sample of Slovenian adolescents and ascertain the interplay between IA, sociodemographic factors, free-time activities, self-control, and perceived satisfaction with life. Overall, the present study found that adolescents at greater risk for developing IA tend to be more passive in their free time, since they watch TV and play video games more than their peers, as well as chat on social media. Adolescents presenting high risk of IA displayed poorer levels of self-control in most cases and reported to be generally less satisfied with their lives in comparison to adolescents presenting low risk of IA.

INTRODUCTION

Background

The Internet is an integral part of modern life that has brought about many advantages and benefits to its users. The Internet plays a key role as an essential tool for education, entertainment, communication, and information-sharing (Poli, 2017) with recent figures showing that the numbers of users are soaring to greater heights. Currently, around 40% of the world population has Internet access (Internet Live Stats

DOI: 10.4018/978-1-5225-3477-8.ch012

[ILS], 2017a), and from 1999 to 2013, the number of Internet users has increased tenfold during that period, with the first billion of users being reached in 2005 and the third billion in 2014 (ILS, 2017a). The use of the Internet varies across different world regions, with Asia (i.e., 48.4%), Americas (North and South) (i.e., 21.8%), and Europe (19%) presenting the largest number of users in the world. Given its ubiquity and wide applicability, alongside its evolving nature as a modern tool of society and issues surrounding its excessive and unhealthy use by a minority of individuals, Internet addiction (IA) has become an increasingly important topic for dedicated research agendas in the field of psychology, psychiatry, neuroscience, and communication studies (Pontes, Kuss, & Griffiths, 2015).

Although IA is currently not officially recognized as a *bona fide* addiction and terminological and conceptual conundrums still exist with regards to its legitimacy (Griffiths, Kuss, Billieux, & Pontes, 2015; Pies, 2009; Starcevic, 2010, 2013; Starcevic & Aboujaoude, 2016), a large body of research suggests that IA can lead to impaired psychosocial and physical health and detrimental interpersonal outcomes (M'hiri et al., 2015; Pontes, Kuss, et al., 2015). Notwithstanding the fact that conceptualization and definition of IA is not entirely consensual, several features have been suggested as being part of the experience related to IA. For instance, Starcevic (2010) suggested that IA is often described as "excessive or compulsive, along with preoccupation with and loss of control over the Internet use" (p. 92), with additional features including adverse consequences due to spending copious amount of time on the Internet, such as neglecting social activities, relationships, health and work or school-related duties, and altering sleep and eating habits in a detrimental way (Starcevic, 2010). Furtherly, Pontes and Kuss (in press) defined IA as "behavioral pattern of Internet use encompassing a dysfunctional craving for the use of the Internet for unregulated and excessive periods of time with accompanying significant psychosocial and functional impairments that are not accounted for by any other disorder." (p. 2).

The field of IA is rapidly evolving, and the latest developments in research helped shaping the conceptualization landscape of IA and new theoretical insights were provided by emerging empirical research. Accordingly, a recent study by Pontes and Griffiths (2017) on a large sample of Internet users found that the concept of IA could be adequately captured and operationalized using the diagnostic framework for Internet Gaming Disorder (IGD) that was developed by the American Psychiatric Association [APA] in the latest (fifth) edition of the *Diagnostic and Statistical Manual of Mental Disorders* (DSM-5) (APA, 2013). Based on this, the study by Pontes and Griffiths (2017) found that under these theoretical premises, the phenomenon of IA can be defined by four unique and distinct conceptual dimensions, with these being: (i) *escapism and dysfunctional emotional coping*, (ii) *withdrawal symptoms*, (iii) *impairments and dysfunctional self-regulation*, and (iv) *dysfunctional Internet-related self-control*. Additional empirical research by Pontes and Griffiths (2016) have further corroborated the validity and feasibility for conceptualizing and framing IA in light of the IGD diagnostic criteria, an approach that has been backed up by several scholars in the field (e.g., Rumpf et al., 2015).

Earlier views on the topic defined IA as an 'umbrella term' encompassing five specific sub-types of IA. These five sub-types of IA were described by (i) *'cybersexual addiction'* (i.e., compulsive use of adult contents for sexual purposes), (ii) *'cyber-relationship addiction'* (i.e., overinvolvement in online relationships), (iii) *'net compulsions'* (i.e., obsessive online gambling, shopping, or online trading), (iv) *'information overload'* (i.e., compulsive web surfing or database searches), and (v) *'computer addiction'* (i.e., obsessive computer game playing) (Young, Pistner, O'Mara, & Buchanan, 1999). According to recent empirical research (e.g., Griffiths & Szabo, 2014; Pontes, Szabo, & Griffiths, 2015), the concept of IA as an 'umbrella term' is problematic as it fails to take into account the focus of the object of addiction (e.g., gambling, videogaming, social networking, sex, work, shopping, etc.), further supporting early theoretical insights from the late 1990s suggesting that most Internet users spending excessive amounts of time on the Internet are not addicted to the medium itself, but use the Internet to fuel other specific addictions (i.e., most people have addictions *on* the Internet rather *to* it) (Griffiths, 1999, 2000).

Notwithstanding these inconsistencies and heterogeneity issues present in the conceptualization and assessment of IA, investigating the incidence and prevalence rates of IA in the general population is paramount to assessing the demand for consulting, treatments, and preventive measures as a consistent body of emerging research has shown that IA affects a small minority of Internet users (Griffiths, Pontes, & Kuss, 2016). Additionally, robust epidemiological studies on the prevalence rates of IA are still scarce and this type of research can facilitate further research and promote a better understanding of how IA may impact on societies. Pontes, Kuss, et al. (2015) recently reviewed the prevalence rates of IA across a number of nationwide representative studies and found that prevalence rates of IA can range from 1% to 18.7% according to the age of participants assessed, the cultural background in which studies are conducted, and also the type psychometric instrument and diagnostic approach utilized to assess IA.

Internet-Use and Related Behaviors in Slovenia

According to recent figures, Internet use in Slovenia is steadily increasing. The ILS (2017b) has reported that in 2016, 72% of the total population in Slovenia had Internet access. The Slovenian Statistical Office reported that 97% of individuals with ages between 16 to 24 years used the Internet in the last 12 months in 2016, this average is highly compared to the average in the European Union for this particular age group (Zupan, 2017).

Despite the growth of Internet use in Slovenia, little research on IA has been carried out in Slovenia. Jeriček (2001, 2002) conducted an early study on IA in a large sample (N = 1.194) of 3rd year high school adolescents in Ljubljana and found that around 3.7% of the sample exhibited high levels of IA symptoms. Jeriček (2001, 2002) investigated the differences amongst a high-severity IA group (i.e., total scores of 4 and 5, 10% of the total sample) and a low-severity IA group (i.e., total scores of 1 and 2, 10% of the total sample) and found that differences emerged with regards to these two types of users in terms of time spent on the Internet, place of Internet use, and school performance with gender and type of school being found to be key predictors of IA (Jeriček, 2001, 2002). Later in 2004, Šimek (2004) conducted a similar study on a smaller sample of adolescents from Maribor (N = 622) and found a prevalence rate of IA of 1.8% in the sample. Although these studies were important in promoting research on IA, the findings reported across these studies are not directly comparable as different approaches in the psychometric assessment (e.g., screening tools and cutoff points) of IA were employed.

Further research on IA was conducted by Primožič (2009) where the author examined the role of IA and emotional instability in a small sample of Internet users (N = 381). The findings of Primožič's (2009) study suggested that emotional instability was a risk factor predicting IA, and that individuals exhibiting greater preference for online social interactions were more prone to develop IA. More recently, two nationwide studies on IA in Slovenia were published, and prevalence rates of IA were found to be 3.1% in individuals with at least 18 years in one study (Macur, Király, Maraz, Nagygyörgy, & Demetrovics, 2016) and 3.8% in individuals with at least 15 years old another one (Macur, 2017). In Slovenia, Internet addicts tend to be male, not in a romantic relationship, and being highly educated (i.e., University degrees) and additional risk factors such as young age, unemployment status, and not being able to work due to health reasons have been identified as potential risk factor for IA in Slovenian samples (Macur et al., 2016).

Since research on IA is still on its infancy in Slovenia and that the field lacks robust findings from epidemiological studies carried out in nationally representative samples, the present study aims to: (i) estimate the risk of IA in a school-based nationally representative sample of Slovenian adolescents and (ii) ascertain the interplay between IA, sociodemographic factors, free-time activities, self-control, and perceived satisfaction with life.

METHOD

Sample and Procedures

This study was part of the project *"Healthy Lifestyle of Children and Youth Through the Empowerment of Youth Workers and the Establishment of Programs on a Local Level"* financed by Norway Grant and conducted by the National Institute of Public Health and NGO No Excuse. A total sample of 1.672 adolescents (Mean age = 18.2 years, SD = 1.3 years; 57% female) was randomly sampled from different schools and educational levels (see Table 1.) across the country representing the population of final year students in Slovenian high schools from various Nomenclature of Territorial Units for Statistics (NUTS3) regions. The sample reflected four high school programmes and 12 statistical regions in Slovenia. Schools were contacted and asked to participate in the study, and students were invited to fill out the study's questionnaire with the help of research assistants. Data were collected using the schools' computers (n = 1.130) in addition to paper-and-pencil data collection methods (n = 542). The data was cleaned and cases with severe missing values were excluded from the study, resulting in a total of 76 cases being removed. Weights were added in order to accurately represent the structure of the population (see Table 1.). In Slovenia, secondary schools fall into one of four different programmes: general education is acquired in gymnasium (i.e., four-year programme), technical education is acquired in four-year upper secondary technical education programmes; there is also a three-year vocational training (i.e. upper secondary vocational programme) that does not allow graduates to enter faculty programmes. If they students wish to continue studying at the faculty level, they need to finish a two-year short upper secondary vocational programme (fourth and fifth years of secondary school for them). The sample of the present study consisted of fourth year gymnasium students, fourth year technical education pro-

Table 1. The sample structure (N = 1.595)

	Eastern Slovenia		Western Slovenia		Samples
Educational Programme	n	%	n	%	N
Upper secondary vocational	163	58.0%	118	42.0%	281
Upper secondary technical education	311	55.5%	249	44.5%	560
General education - gimnazija	252	43.4%	329	56.6%	581
Short upper secondary vocational	95	54.9%	78	45.1%	173
Total	821	51.5%	774	48.5%	1595

grammes, third year upper secondary vocational programmes and fourth year short upper secondary vocational programmes.

In order to analyze the data collected, bivariate statistics with observable variables were used (e.g., chi-square tests and t-tests for independent samples) to investigate IA in the present sample.

Measures

Data on the sample's sociodemographic characteristics (i.e., age, gender, type of a school programme, location of the school) and free-time activities were collected. Participants were asked to specify using a 5-point Likert scale (1: '*Never*' to 5: '*Always*') how they usually spend their free time by choosing between a series of activities such as: spending time with friends, watching television, playing videogames, using online social networking sites, reading books, musical activities (e.g., choir), and doing sports.

Frequency of Internet use was measured by asking participants about their time spent on the Internet for leisure purposes in weekdays (Monday to Friday) and weekends (Saturdays and Sundays).

Problematic Internet use and risk of IA was measured with the Problematic Internet Use Questionnaire Short-Form (PIUQ-SF-6) (Demetrovics et al., 2016). The PIUQ-SF-6 (Demetrovics et al., 2016) is a shorter version of the Problematic Internet Use Questionnaire (PIUQ) (Demetrovics, Szeredi, & Rózsa, 2008), which is a psychometric tool that has been shown to possess adequate psychometric properties across different samples (Koronczai et al., 2011, Demetrovics et al., 2016). The PIUQ-SF-6 assesses three dimensions of problematic Internet use (i.e., obsession, neglect, and control disorder) and was developed by selecting two items from each of the three PIUQ factors. The six PIUQ-SF-6 items can be responded on a 5-point Likert scale (from '*never*' to '*always/almost always*') to estimate the severity of problematic Internet use. Scores obtained in this scale can range from 6 to 30, with higher scores indicating increased problematic use. For the present study, a Slovenian translation of the PIUQ-SF-6 was carried out and the scale presented with adequate internal consistency (Cronbach's α = .82).

Self-control was measured by seven items reflecting the tendency of low self-control. These items were based on previous studies (Cho, 2010; Rand, Stein, & Rand, 1998) and sample items include: "I wholeheartedly take part in exciting things even if I have to take an examination tomorrow", "I abandon a task once it becomes hard and laborious«, "I am apt to enjoy risky activities", "I enjoy teasing and harassing other people", "I feel like I am a ticking time bomb", "I lose my temper whenever I get angry" and "I habitually don't do my homework". Responses were measured on a Likert scale from 1 ('*Strongly agree*') to 5 ('*Strongly disagree*'). This scale has been shown to measure self-control in adolescents adequately in recent similar studies (i.e., Kim & Kim, 2015), and the Slovenian version of this measure used in the present study was found to possess adequate levels of internal consistency (Cronbach's α = .72).

Perceived life-satisfaction was measure by a single question asking participants to rate on a scale ranging from 1 ('*Completely dissatisfied*') to 10 ('*Totally satisfied*') how satisfied they were with their life. Greater scores were indicative of augmented levels of perceived life-satisfaction. This measure was employed in the present due to constraints related to time limits in the study.

RESULTS

Problematic Internet Use Scale in Adolescent Sample

After having cleaned the data, results from the descriptive statistics analysis revealed that average time spent on the Internet for leisure purposes in the sample during the weekdays was 3.43 hours (SD = 2.74) and 3.94 hours (SD = 2.97) during the weekend. The two most endorsed symptoms of IA as measured by the PIUQ-SF-6 were '*not being able to decrease the amount of time spent on the Internet*' (answers often & always/almost always combined 29.3%) and '*spending time online instead of sleeping*' (27% of answers often & always/almost always) (see Figure 1.). The least endorsed symptom of IA was measured by the following PIUQ-SF-6 item: "*How often does it happen to you that you feel depressed, moody, or nervous when you are not on the Internet and these feelings stop once you are back online?*" with 69.3% of the sample having responded to this item as "*never*" and 19% "*rarely*". In terms of the most endorsed PIUQ-SF-6 factor observed, "*obsession*" was the least pronounced factor in the sample while "control disorder" was the most salient factor.

Risk of IA and Descriptive Results

Overall, the results suggested that around 18.5% (95% CI:16.5%-20.5%; n = 260) of the sample presented with high risk for developing IA. Those individuals spent significantly more time on the Internet for leisure purposes on weekdays (Mean$_{IA}$ = 4.12, SD$_{IA}$ = 2.93) than non-problematic Internet users (Mean$_{non-ia}$ = 3.20, SD$_{non-ia}$ = 2.62; t[298.9] = -4.16, p < .001) and also on weekends (Mean$_{IA}$ = 4.83, SD$_{IA}$ = 3,00; Mean$_{non-ia}$ = 3.61, SD$_{non-ia}$ = 2.80; t[1116] = -5.76, p < .001). Furthermore, it was found

Figure 1. Distribution of answers in the scale assessing internet addiction

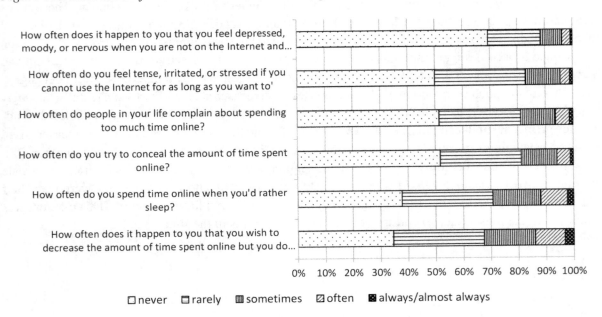

that risk of IA did not differ across male and females (χ^2 = .040; df=1; p = .84). The same result was found with regards to the different school programmes students were enrolled (χ^2 = 3.204; df=3; p =.36). Nevertheless, rates concerning risk of IA were found to be significantly higher among students enrolled in upper secondary vocational programmes (i.e., 20.7%, n = 50) in comparison to short upper secondary vocational programmes (13.6%, n = 20).

Risk of IA and Free-time Activities

In regards to how IA affects free-time activities, the analysis revealed that key differences between the high risk and low risk of IA groups emerged (see Figure 2.). More specifically, participants in the high risk group devoted significantly more time watching television (Mean$_{IA}$ = 2.95, SD$_{IA}$ = 1.01) than the low risk group (Mean$_{non-ia}$ = 2.71, SD$_{non-ia}$ = 0.97; t[1394] = -3.48, p = .001), playing videogames (Mean$_{IA}$ = 2.99, SD$_{IA}$ = 1.17; Mean$_{non-ia}$ = 2.58, SD$_{non-ia}$ = 1.13; t[1399] = -5.17, p < .001) and using online social networking sites (Mean$_{IA}$ = 3.87, SD$_{IA}$ = 0.96; Mean$_{non-ia}$ = 3.41, SD$_{non-ia}$ = 1.08; t[412.1] = -6.75, p < .001). Additionally, adolescents pertaining to the high risk group reported doing less sports (Mean$_{IA}$ = 3.05, SD$_{IA}$ = 1.13) than their low risk counterparts (Mean$_{non-ia}$ = 3.29, SD$_{non-ia}$ = 1.18; t[397.7] = 3.03, p = .003). Finally, both groups did not differ in terms of how they usually spend time with friends (Mean$_{IA}$ = 3.76, SD$_{IA}$ = 0.98; Mean$_{non-ia}$ = 3.86, SD$_{non-ia}$ = 0.86; t[353.8] = 1.43, p = .16), reading books (Mean$_{IA}$ = 2.15, SD$_{IA}$ = 1.01; Mean$_{non-ia}$ = 2.20, SD$_{non-ia}$ = 1.10; t[402.8] = 0.75, p = .45), and engaging in musical activities (Mean$_{IA}$ = 1.52, SD$_{IA}$ = 1.12; Mean$_{non-ia}$ = 1.49, SD$_{non-ia}$ = 1.11; t[1396] = -0.43, p = .67).

Figure 2. Risk of internet addiction and specific free time activities(from 1 "never" to 5 "almost always/ always")

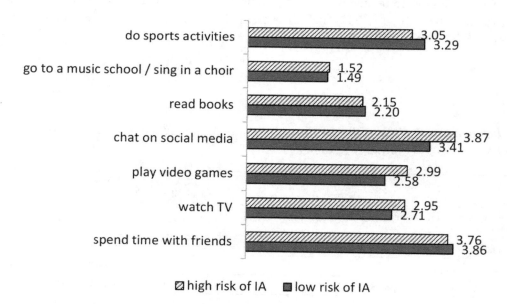

Risk of IA, Self-Control and Perceived Life-Satisfaction

The summary of the findings related to each aspect of self-control as measured by the seven items employed in this study is presented in Table 2. Overall, the most problematic aspect related to self-control in the sample was measured by the following items: "*I habitually don't do my homework*" (Mean = 2.66, SD = 1.34) and "*I wholeheartedly take part in exciting things even if I have to take an examination tomorrow*" (Mean = 2.75, SD = 1.14). Table 2 shows that the high risk group displayed overall poorer levels of self-control in comparison to the low risk group, with the exception of one domain of self-control (i.e., '*I am apt to enjoy risky activities*', $Mean_{IA}$ = 2.91, SD_{IA} = 1.14; $Mean_{non\text{-}ia}$ = 2.88, $SD_{non\text{-}ia}$ = 1.16 $t[1359]$ = -0.45, p = .65).

Finally, with regards to perceived general life satisfaction, participants belonging to high risk group ($Mean_{IA}$ = 6.70, SD_{IA} = 2.26) reported to be generally less satisfied with their lives in comparison to adolescents in the low risk group ($Mean_{non\text{-}ia}$ = 7.75, $SD_{non\text{-}ia}$ = 1.85 group, $t[328.9]$ = 6.85, p < .001).

Key Predictors of IA

A multiple linear regression analysis was carried in order to ascertain determine which variables mostly predicted risk of IA (measured by the total scores on the PIUQ-SF-6 score). Predictor variables were (i) watch TV during free-time, (ii) chat on social media during free time, (iii) '*to feel like a ticking time bomb*' (self-control-related variable), (iv) life satisfaction, and (v) time spent on the Internet for leisure purposes on weekends (see Table 3.). Taken together, these predictors explained 14.7% of the total variance in students' risk of IA (R^2 =.147; $F(2)$ = 37.52, p <.001). Further analysis of each predictor's contribution towards predicting risk of IA revealed that the strongest predictors (i.e., highest standardized beta coefficients) were related to high engagement in social media chats (ß = .17, p < .001), (ii) life dissatisfaction (ß = -.16, p < .001), and (iii) increased time spent on the Internet for leisure purposes on weekends (ß = .16, p < .001).

Table 2. Independent Samples T-Test regarding risk of IA and self-control scores (ranging from 1 = "Strongly Agree" to 5 = "Strongly Disagree")

	LRIA Mean (SD)	HRIA Mean (SD)	T-Test
I wholeheartedly take part in exciting things even if I have to take an examination tomorrow	2.78 (1.14)	2.63 (1.06)	$t[1370]$ = 1.98, p = .048
I abandon a task once it becomes hard and laborious	3.36 (1.08)	2.96 (0.93)	$t[431.1]$ = 6.07, p < .001
I am apt to enjoy risky activities	2.88 (1.16)	2.91 (1.14)	$t[1359]$ = -0.45, p = .654
I enjoy teasing and harassing other people	3.84 (1.24)	3.54 (1.24)	$t[1366]$ = 3.48, p = .001
I feel like I am a ticking time bomb	3.81 (1.23)	3.24 (1.13)	$t[401.8]$ = 7.18, p < .001
I lose my temper whenever I get angry	3.36 (1.28)	2.95 (1.14)	$t[417.6]$ = 5.03, p < .001
I habitually do not do my homework	2.69 (1.38)	2.47 (1.13)	$t[442.1]$ = 2.73, p = .007

Note: LRIA: Low risk of Internet addiction and **HRIA**: High risk of Internet addiction.

Table 3. Multiple regression analysis: Potential Internet addiction predictors = "Strongly Disagree")

Coefficients	Unstandardized Coefficients		Standardized Coefficients	t	p
	B	Std. Error	ß		
(Constant)	10.742	0.789		13.61	< .0001
Watch TV in free-time	0.403	0.123	0.094	3.27	.001
Chat on social media in free-time	0.657	0.119	0.166	5.533	< .0001
I feel like I am a ticking time bomb	-0.37	0.104	-0.107	-3.568	< .0001
Satisfaction with life in general	-0.358	0.065	-0.165	-5.489	< .0001
Number of hours on the Internet for leisure purposes on weekends	0.231	0.044	0.158	5.283	< .0001

Note: Dependent Variable: Risk of Internet addiction as a continuous variable.

CONCLUSION

The aim of the present study was to provide new findings regarding IA from a country in which relatively little is known about this phenomenon. More specifically, this study sought to (i) estimate risk of IA in a school-based nationally representative sample of Slovenian adolescents and (ii) ascertain the interplay between IA, sociodemographic factors, free-time activities, self-control, and perceived satisfaction with life.

In terms of risk of IA, it was found that almost one in five (i.e., 18.5%, n = 260) participants presented high risk of IA. Participants displaying high risk of IA spent significantly more time on the Internet for leisure purposes in comparison to students classed as low risk of IA, which is in line with previous studies. Demetrovics, Szeredi and Rosa (2008) increased time spent on the Internet related to non-work purposes is more related to IA. The present study has also shown that IA was not affected by gender differences and school programmes in contrast to previous studies in Slovenia (e.g., Jeriček, 2001,2002). Moreover, the present study investigated risk of IA and not IA per se, which might explain the differences observed in comparison to previous research in Slovenia that have investigated IA and its clinical significance (Demetrovics, Szeredi & Rozsa, 2008).

The present findings appear to be in line with previous similar studies. For instance, a study conducted by Evren, Dalbudak, Evren, and Demirci (2014) using a representative sample of 4.957 Turkish 10th graders found that around 16% of the total sample presented with high risk of IA, which is highly comparable to the proportion of high risk IA adolescents found in the present study (i.e., 18.5%). Additionally, in terms of geographical regions, studies from Asia reported rates of IA among adolescents and young people ranging from 2.4 to 37.9% as reported by a review study (Durkee et al., 2012). Previous research on IA in Europe reported prevalence rates of IA ranging from 3.1 to 18.3% (Durkee et al., 2012). As aforementioned, discrepancies in prevalence rates of IA might be the result of different research methodologies, cultural backgrounds, sampling techniques and/or assessment approach.

The findings presented concerning the interplay between IA, sociodemographic factors, free-time activities, self-control, and perceived life satisfaction also add to the broader discussion about the role of individual differences on the potential development of IA. These findings are important as they go beyond traditional personality traits that have been found to be implicated in IA. Recent research on personality characteristics found that neuroticism is positively related to IA while extraversion, agreeableness, conscientiousness, and openness to experience are negatively associated to IA (Kayiş et al., 2016).

Although other studies have reported different results on the role of personality traits in the development of IA (e.g., Aboujaoude, 2017; Zadra et al., 2016), these findings illustrate the intricacies between several personality traits and their contribution to explaining addictive Internet use.

Notwithstanding this, the results of the individual differences variables in the present study indicated that key differences emerged between the high risk and low risk of IA groups. More specifically, participants presenting high risk for developing IA spent significantly more time watching television, playing videogames, and using online social networking sites in comparison to participants presenting low risk for developing IA. Taken together, these findings could potentially illustrate common clinical course and shared etiology between different types of addictive behaviors. Furtherly, these results lend support to previous studies suggesting some underlying common risk factors between several technological addictions and related behaviors (Andreassen et al., 2016; Grant, Potenza, Weinstein, & Gorelick, 2010; Pontes, 2017; Robbins & Clark, 2015) and provide context to further understand why empirical studies often report positive associations between various addictive technological behaviors (Andreassen et al., 2016; Király et al., 2014; Pontes, 2017).

Another finding encountered in the present study related to the fact that participants in the high risk of IA engaged significantly less in sports in comparison to low risk participants and no significant differences emerged between the two groups in terms of how they usually spent time with their friends, read books, and participated in musical activities. A nationally representative study in Korea conducted by Heo, Oh, Subramanian, Kim, and Kawachi (2014) in a sample of 75.006 school-aged adolescents (13 to 18 years) revealed that IA was inversely associated to physical activity in the sample recruited while a more recent study conducted by Yayan, Arikan, Saban, and Özcan (2016) examining the relationship between IA and physical activities in a sample of 24.260 adolescents (11 to 15 years) found that adolescents engaging in exercise regularly exhibited lower levels of IA and social phobia. These results suggest that there is preliminary evidence indicating that IA can impair engagement in physical activities in adolescents, and that participation in exercise can also be used as a potential preventive strategy to curb levels of IA in the population.

The findings of the present study also suggest that IA may have differential effects across a wide range of social, leisure, and academic activities as no differences emerged between the high and low risk of IA groups in terms of spending time with friends, reading books, and engaging in musical activities. Future studies should investigate how IA may affect specific social, leisure, and academic activities as different effects were found in the present study. Although IA is generally associated with overall poor academic performance and achievement in adolescents (Dhir, Chen, & Nieminen, 2015; Jia, 2012; Kubey, Lavin, & Barrows, 2001; Stavropoulos, Alexandraki, & Motti-Stefanidi, 2013), the fact high risk of IA did not have a statistically significant effect on how often adolescents read books could be related to the fact that both groups of students dedicated significantly less time to read compared to other engagement in activities such as watching TV, playing videogames, chatting on social media, spending time with friends or engaging in sports activities.

Finally, with regards to self-control and overall life satisfaction, it was found that high risk of IA was associated to poor self-control and low levels of life satisfaction. In other words, adolescents exhibiting greater more symptoms of IA exhibited decreased levels of self-control and life satisfaction in comparison to adolescents presenting low risk of IA. These findings support previous small scale studies with non-probability samples that reported similar findings. Given the potential detrimental impact IA can have on adolescents, it is urgent to conduct further research to ascertain preventive factors that could boost adolescents' self-control and life satisfaction these factors may provide buffering effects against IA in adolescence.

Although the present study provided important insights on how IA may affect a wide range of experiences in school-aged adolescents, it is not without its limitations. First, the sample recruited had a very specific age range (from 14 to 25 years), thus it is unclear the findings encountered are generalizable to other age groups (e.g., children and elderly). Second, the use of self-report methodologies can be associated with several potential biases, such as social desirability and short-term recall biases which may have impacted on the results of the study. Despite these potential biases, the present study contributes to the ongoing discussion and field of IA by presenting timely and relevant data from a cultural background which relatively little is known, further allowing future studies to compare their findings with the ones reported in this study.

Taken as a whole, the findings of the present study draw attention to the problem of IA in adolescence and provides important insights into how IA may affect several aspects of life during this developmental stage. It is envisaged by the authors of this study that the findings reported will help progress the field towards a better understanding of IA as an emergent and less controversial clinical phenomenon.

ACKNOWLEDGMENT

Present work was funded by Norway Grant (Project nb: SI05-0007): http://eeagrants.org/project-portal/project/SI05-0007. The supporting agency had no role in the design and conduct of the study.

REFERENCES

Aboujaoude, E. (2017). The Internet's effect on personality traits: An important casualty of the "Internet addiction" paradigm. *Journal of Behavioral Addictions*, *6*(1), 1–4. doi:10.1556/2006.6.2017.009 PMID:28301969

American Psychiatric Association. (2013). *Diagnostic and Statistical Manual of Mental Disorders* (5th ed.). Arlington, VA: Author.

Andreassen, C. S., Billieux, J., Griffiths, M. D., Kuss, D. J., Demetrovics, Z., Mazzoni, E., & Ståle, P. (2016). The relationship between addictive use of social media and video games and symptoms of psychiatric disorders: A large-scale cross-sectional study. *Psychology of Addictive Behaviors*, *30*(2), 252–265. doi:10.1037/adb0000160 PMID:26999354

Cho, Y. J. (2010). A longitudinal study on the Internet delinquency in adolescents: The use of a latent growth model. *Korean Journal of Youth Studies*, *17*(6), 171–195.

Demetrovics, Z., Király, O., Koronczai, B., Griffiths, M. D., Nagygyörgy, K., Elekes, Z., & Urbán, R. et al. (2016). Psychometric properties of the Problematic Internet Use Questionnaire Short-Form (PIUQ-SF-6) in a nationally representative sample of adolescents. *PLoS One*, *11*(8), e0159409. doi:10.1371/journal.pone.0159409 PMID:27504915

Demetrovics, Z., Szeredi, B., & Rózsa, S. (2008). The three-factor model of Internet addiction: The development of the Problematic Internet Use Questionnaire. *Behavior Research Methods, 40*(2), 563–574. doi:10.3758/BRM.40.2.563 PMID:18522068

Dhir, A., Chen, S., & Nieminen, M. (2015). A repeat cross-sectional analysis of the psychometric properties of the Compulsive Internet Use Scale (CIUS) with adolescents from public and private schools. *Computers & Education, 86*, 172–181. doi:10.1016/j.compedu.2015.03.011

Durkee, T., Kaess, M., Carli, V., Parzer, P., Wasserman, C., Floderus, B., & Bobes, J. et al. (2012). Prevalence of pathological internet use among adolescents in Europe: Demographic and social factors. *Addiction (Abingdon, England), 107*(12), 2210–2222. doi:10.1111/j.1360-0443.2012.03946.x PMID:22621402

Evren, C., Dalbudak, E., Evren, B., & Demirci, A. C. (2014). High risk of Internet addiction and its relationship with lifetime substance use, psychological and behavioral problems among 10th grade adolescents. *Psychiatria Danubina, 26*(4), 330–339. PMID:25377367

Grant, J. E., Potenza, M. N., Weinstein, A., & Gorelick, D. A. (2010). Introduction to Behavioral Addictions. *The American Journal of Drug and Alcohol Abuse, 36*(5), 233–241. doi:10.3109/00952990.2010.491884 PMID:20560821

Griffiths, M. D. (1999). Internet addiction: Internet fuels other addictions. *Student BMJ, 7*, 428–429.

Griffiths, M. D. (2000). Internet addiction-time to be taken seriously? *Addiction Research, 8*(5), 413–418. doi:10.3109/16066350009005587

Griffiths, M. D., Kuss, D. J., Billieux, J., & Pontes, H. M. (2015). The evolution of Internet addiction: A global perspective. *Addictive Behaviors, 53*, 193–195. doi:10.1016/j.addbeh.2015.11.001 PMID:26562678

Griffiths, M. D., Pontes, H. M., & Kuss, D. J. (2016). Online addictions: Conceptualizations, debates, and controversies. *Addicta: The Turkish Journal on Addictions, 3*(2), 1–20. doi:10.15805/addicta.2016.3.0101

Griffiths, M. D., & Szabo, A. (2014). Is excessive online usage a function of medium or activity? An empirical pilot study. *Journal of Behavioral Addictions, 3*(1), 74–77. doi:10.1556/JBA.2.2013.016 PMID:25215216

Heo, J., Oh, J., Subramanian, S. V., Kim, Y., & Kawachi, I. (2014). Addictive Internet use among Korean adolescents: A national survey. *PLoS One, 9*(2), e87819. doi:10.1371/journal.pone.0087819 PMID:24505318

Internet Live Stats. (2017a). *Internet users*. Retrieved from: http://www.internetlivestats.com/internet-users/

Internet Live Stats. (2017b). *Slovenia Internet Users*. Retrieved from: http://www.internetlivestats.com/internet-users/slovenia/

Jeriček, H. (2001). Zasvojenost z internetom–sedanjost ali prihodnost. *Socialna Pedagogika, 5*(2), 141–168.

Jeriček, H. (2002). Internet i ovisnost o internetu u Sloveniji. *Medijska istraživanja, 8*(2), 85-101.

Jia, R. (2012). Computer playfulness, Internet dependency and their relationships with online activity types and student academic performance. *Journal of Behavioral Addictions, 1*(2), 74–77. doi:10.1556/JBA.1.2012.2.5 PMID:26165309

Kayiş, A. R., Satici, S. A., Yilmaz, M. F., Şimşek, D., Ceyhan, E., & Bakioğlu, F. (2016). Big five-personality trait and internet addiction: A meta-analytic review. *Computers in Human Behavior*, *63*, 35–40. doi:10.1016/j.chb.2016.05.012

Kim, J. E., & Kim, J. (2015). International note: Teen users' problematic online behavior: Using panel data from South Korea. *Journal of Adolescence*, *40*, 48–53. doi:10.1016/j.adolescence.2015.01.001 PMID:25621406

Király, O., Griffiths, M. D., Urbán, R., Farkas, J., Kökönyei, G., Elekes, Z., & Demetrovics, Z. et al. (2014). Problematic Internet use and problematic online gaming are not the same: Findings from a large nationally representative adolescent sample. *Cyberpsychology, Behavior, and Social Networking*, *17*(12), 749–754. doi:10.1089/cyber.2014.0475 PMID:25415659

Koronczai, B., Urban, R., Kökönyei, G., Paksi, B., Papp, K., Kun, B., & Demetrovics, Z. et al. (2011). Confirmation of the Three-Factor Model of Problematic Internet Use on Off-Line Adolescent and Adult Samples. *Cyberpsychology, Behavior, and Social Networking*, *14*(11), 657–664. doi:10.1089/cyber.2010.0345 PMID:21711129

Kubey, R. W., Lavin, M. J., & Barrows, J. R. (2001). Internet use and collegiate academic performance decrements: Early findings. *Journal of Communication*, *51*(2), 366–382. doi:10.1111/j.1460-2466.2001.tb02885.x

M'hiri, K., Constanza, A., Khazaal, Y., Khan, R., Zullino, D., & Achab, S. (2015). Problematic Internet use in older adults, a critical review of the literature. *Addiction Research and Theory*, *6*(4), 1000253. doi:10.4172/2155-6105.1000253

Macur, M. (2017). Can Internet use become problematic?: Presentation of Slovenian data. *International scientific conference Health Online - Book of papers with peer review and abstracts*. Retrieved from: http://www2.zf.uni-lj.si/images/stories/datoteke/Zalozba/Zdravje_na_spletu.pdf

Macur, M., Király, O., Maraz, A., Nagygyörgy, K., & Demetrovics, Z. (2016). Prevalence of problematic internet use in Slovenia. *Zdravstveno Varstvo*, *55*(3), 202–211. doi:10.1515/sjph-2016-0026 PMID:27703540

Pies, R. (2009). Should DSM-V designate "Internet addiction" a mental disorder? *Psychiatry (Edgmont)*, *6*(2), 31–37. PMID:19724746

Poli, R. (2017). Internet addiction update: Diagnostic criteria, assessment and prevalence. *Neuropsychiatry*, *7*(1), 4–8. doi:10.4172/Neuropsychiatry.1000171

Pontes, H. M. (2017). Investigating the differential effects of social networking site addiction and Internet Gaming Disorder on psychological health. *Cyberpsychology, Behavior, and Social Networking*. (under review)

Pontes, H. M., & Griffiths, M. D. (2016). The development and psychometric properties of the Internet Disorder Scale-Short Form (IDS9-SF). *Addicta: The Turkish Journal on Addictions*, *3*(2), 1–16. doi:10.15805/addicta.2016.3.0102

Pontes, H. M., & Griffiths, M. D. (2017). The development and psychometric evaluation of the Internet Disorder Scale (IDS-15). *Addictive Behaviors*, *64*, 261–268. doi:10.1016/j.addbeh.2015.09.003 PMID:26410796

Pontes, H. M., & Kuss, D. J. (in press). *Internet addiction*. Göttingen, Germany: Hogrefe Publishing.

Pontes, H. M., Kuss, D. J., & Griffiths, M. D. (2015). Clinical psychology of Internet addiction: A review of its conceptualization, prevalence, neuronal processes, and implications for treatment. *Neuroscience and Neuroeconomics*, *4*, 11–23. doi:10.2147/NAN.S60982

Pontes, H. M., Szabo, A., & Griffiths, M. D. (2015). The impact of Internet-based specific activities on the perceptions of Internet addiction, quality of life, and excessive usage: A cross-sectional study. *Addictive Behaviors Reports*, *1*, 19–25. doi:10.1016/j.abrep.2015.03.002

Primožič, A. (2009). *Zasvojenost z internetom (Bachelor thesis)*. University of Ljubljana. Retrieved from http://dk.fdv.uni-lj.si/diplomska/pdfs/primozic-anze.pdf

Rand, D. L., Stein, J. A., & Rand, S. T. (1998). Reliability and validity of a selfcontrol measure: Rejoinder. *Criminology*, *36*(1), 175–182. doi:10.1111/j.1745-9125.1998.tb01245.x

Robbins, T. W., & Clark, L. (2015). Behavioral addictions. *Current Opinion in Neurobiology*, *30*, 66–72. doi:10.1016/j.conb.2014.09.005 PMID:25262209

Rumpf, H.-J., Bischof, G., Bischof, A., Besser, B., Meyer, C., & John, U. (2015). *Applying DSM-5 criteria for Internet Gaming Disorder for the broader concept of Internet addiction*. Paper presented at the 2nd International Conference on Behavioral Addictions, Budapest, Hungary.

Šimek, D. (2004). Odvisnost od interneta. In *Vzgoja in izobraževanje v informacijski družbi: zbornik referatov* [Education in information society: conference proceedings]. Ljubljana: Ministrstvo za šolstvo, znanost in šport.

Starcevic, V. (2010). Problematic Internet use: A distinct disorder, a manifestation of an underlying psychopathology, or a troublesome behaviour? *World Psychiatry; Official Journal of the World Psychiatric Association (WPA)*, *9*(2), 92–93. doi:10.1002/j.2051-5545.2010.tb00280.x PMID:20671892

Starcevic, V. (2013). Is Internet addiction a useful concept? *The Australian and New Zealand Journal of Psychiatry*, *47*(1), 16–19. doi:10.1177/0004867412461693 PMID:23293309

Starcevic, V., & Aboujaoude, E. (2016). Internet addiction: Reappraisal of an increasingly inadequate concept. *CNS Spectrums*, 1–7. doi:10.1017/S1092852915000863 PMID:26831456

Stavropoulos, V., Alexandraki, K., & Motti-Stefanidi, F. (2013). Recognizing internet addiction: Prevalence and relationship to academic achievement in adolescents enrolled in urban and rural Greek high schools. *Journal of Adolescence*, *36*(3), 565–576. doi:10.1016/j.adolescence.2013.03.008 PMID:23608781

Yayan, E. H., Arikan, D., & Saban, F., N. G. B., & Özcan, Ö. (2016). Examination of the correlation between Internet addiction and social phobia in adolescents. *Western Journal of Nursing Research*, 1–15. doi:10.1177/0193945916665820 PMID:27561297

Young, K. S., Pistner, M., O'Mara, J., & Buchanan, J. (1999). Cyber disorders: The mental health concern for the new millennium. *Cyberpsychology & Behavior*, 2(5), 475–479. doi:10.1089/cpb.1999.2.475 PMID:19178220

Zadra, S., Bischof, G., Besser, B., Bischof, A., Meyer, C., John, U., & Rumpf, H.-J. (2016). The association between Internet addiction and personality disorders in a general population-based sample. *Journal of Behavioral Addictions*, 5(4), 691–699. doi:10.1556/2006.5.2016.086 PMID:28005417

Zupan, G. (2017). *16-24-year-olds and Safer Internet Day*. Statistical Office of the Republic of Slovenia. Retrieved from http://www.stat.si/StatWeb/en/News/Index/6478

KEY TERMS AND DEFINITIONS

Addiction: Addiction is a primary, chronic disease of brain reward, motivation, memory and related circuitry that leads to characteristic biological, psychological, social and spiritual manifestations. This is reflected in an individual pathologically pursuing reward and/or relief by substance use and other behaviors.

Behavioral Addictions: Any non-chemical behavior (e.g., gambling, work, sex, videogame playing, etc.) that contains all following six specific addictive features: salience, mood modification, tolerance, withdraw, conflict and relapse and causes several significant impairments in various domains of a person's life.

Internet Addiction: A behavioural addiction and umbrella term used to characterized generalized excessive or poorly controlled preoccupation, urges, and/or behaviors regarding Internet use that lead to significant psychosocial impariment or distress in several life domains.

Problematic Internet Use: A construct usually situated by cognitive-behavioral researchers in the middle range of the continuum of problem severity and emphasizes the mild, bnign nature of related negative outcomes (e.g., truancy, foregoing a social event). Problematic Internet Use comprises a distinct pattern of Internet-related cognitions and behaviors related to Internet use that are not linked to any specific content as individuals may develop problems due to the unique communicative context of the Internet.

Satisfaction With Life: refers to a cognitive judgment and a global assessment of a person's quality of life according to his/her chosen criteria. Judgements of satisfaction are usually dependent upon a comparison of one's circumstances with what is thought to be an appropriate standard.

Self-Control: A construct that reflects a person's ability to exert control over the self by the self. That is, self-control is said to occur when a erson attempts to change the way he or she would otherwise think, feel, or behave.

Chapter 13
Selfie–Objectification as a Facet of the Social Media Craze Among Youths in Nigeria:
A Socio–Cultural Discourse

Floribert Patrick Calvain Endong
University of Calabar, Nigeria

ABSTRACT

The advent of the social media in Nigeria has given rise to a plurality of information technology syndromes as well as multiple forms of social leprosies. One of these social leprosies has been selfie-objectification manifested by naked and highly sexualized selfies. As a form of social pathology, selfie-objectification has particularly engulfed the youths, corrupting the latter's innocence and affecting the positive relationship culture among them. Using observations and secondary sources, this chapter explores two opposing perspectives on selfie-objectification in Nigeria namely conservative and liberal. It criticizes the conservative reading of the self-objectification paradigm, arguing that any interpretation of selfie-objectification by Nigerian youths solely as a culturally insensitive act and a western cultural import is myopic and objectionable. The phenomenon should rather be read along the line of Nigerian youths' visible embrace of a liberal and postmodern philosophy of life.

INTRODUCTION

The advent of the social media in Nigeria has introduced a plurality of striking popular cultures thereby attracting the attention of critics from a variety of fields. Critics actually have various and sometimes concurrent appraisals or readings of the phenomenon. While some of them equate the ubiquity of the social media with a blessing, others describe it as a curse and a factor enabling a host of socio-cultural pathologies. Actors involved in the debate on the phenomenon are sometimes so dogmatic that it may seem futile to harmonize positions from both camps (Ajike & Nwakoby 2016; Ecomas & Ecomas 2015; Olawepo & Oyedepo, 2008; Uduma 2013). The positive appraisals mostly take into account the

DOI: 10.4018/978-1-5225-3477-8.ch013

fact that the social media have remarkably facilitated innovative forms of both inter personal and mass communication; they have equally been acting as an empowering tool for most segments of the Nigerian populace, particularly the youths. These digital media have for instance permitted young Nigerians with business acumen to initiate and maintain genuine online projects (for instance e-transactions, e-commerce and the like), which have been lucrative to them and have seriously empowered them to the bank. Furthermore, critics laud the social media on ground that, they have provided a forum for some unemployed Nigerians to be aware of international job opportunities and to even find permanent and well remunerated jobs abroad.

Other positive appraisals of the social networks are rooted in the fact that these media have the potential to facilitate digital (socio-political) activism and increase the populace's involvement in the governance of the country. Added to this is importance is the fact that they (the social media) may be very helpful instruments for research. In tandem with this, a number of recent studies have highlighted that the Nigerian youths increasingly resort to the social networking sites to gather data for educational or research assignments, as well as to blog, share, criticize and get engaged in various forms of political and social activism (Ajike & Nwakoby 2016; Edogor, Aladi & Idowu, 2015; Odu 2015). A case in point is the University of Lagos students' use of the social media in early 2016 to firmly resist the authority's intention to change the name of their school from University of Lagos to Mushu Abiola's University (Balarabe, 2015; Odu 2015). Another good example of social media driven activism is the one done by human rights advocates and (pro-)gay activists – such as Bisi Alimi, Olajide Marculay, Bisi Alimi and Yemisi among others through Facebook, Twitter, internet site, youtube and the like (Endong 2017; Endong & Vareba 2015). This digitally driven advocacy has been serious alternatives to street protests. It has even saved activists the danger of incurring the eventual brutality of government forces, for instance assaults by anti-protest police swards.

Despite the enormous positive dividends they have yielded in the Nigerian economy, the social media, have, according to skeptical observers, been representing an arsenal for the perpetration of multiple forms of economic frauds and socio-cultural abuses. Besides facilitating various typologies of cyber-criminality, these media are increasingly viewed by a considerable section of the Nigerian intelligentsia as some of the factors enabling what is often called "social media craze" among the Nigerian youths (Ajike & Nwakoby 2016; Edogor, Aladi & Idowu 2015). One of the manifestations of this "craze" has been the use of social networking sites by the youths, particularly the "wanna-be stars" and liberal/libertine Nigerian youths to share highly objectified or sexualized selfies. By definition, these types of selfies are unclad, offensive, sexually abusive or "pleasing" pictures. The tradition among youths of sharing unclad and controversial selfies has been labeled "selfie-objectification" by some psychologists, feminists and anthropologists (Gorman 2015; Kite & Kite 2014). Many conservative critics have "hastily" associated this phenomenon with westernization and have thus equated it to a bane of Nigerian cultural values. However, the dynamic and complex nature of the phenomenon calls for more nuanced observations and analyses.

Using critical observations and secondary sources, this chapter seeks to explore how selfie-objectification is a facet of the social-media craze in the Nigerian socio-cultural context. It begins with an exploration of the "social media craze" debate in Nigeria and proceeds by reviewing social interpretations of the selfie-objectification in Nigeria. It illustrates the fact that, in spite of its apparent incompatibility with the conservative and doctrinaire religious paradigms (which continues to govern the Nigerian society), the selfie-objectification is an index of the Nigerian youths' increasing fascination by foreign – mostly western – cultures and models of self-imaging. The book chapter is divided into four main sections.

The first section provides illuminations on some key conceptual and theoretical issues (namely self-objectification, social media craze, liberalism and African conservatism). The second part deals with showing how the selfie culture is progressively becoming a social "syndrome" in the Nigerian socio-cultural ecology. The third section provides a conservative perspective on self-objectification in Nigeria while the last section of the chapter critically discusses selfie-objectification as the manifestation of Nigerian youths' adherence to liberalism.

CONCEPTUAL AND THEORETICAL ISSUES

This section provides the conceptual and theoretical framework of this work. It is specifically devoted to the explanation of four key issues (theories and/or concepts) namely selfie-objectification, social media craze, liberalism and African Conservatism. Given the fact that most of these concepts are broad, the researcher will, in this section, endeavor to highlight the specific aspects or tenets of the terms that will be considered in this study.

Selfie-Objectification

This term is often used as a neologism or a kind of feminist-related theory. As a neologism, selfie-objectification is composed of the two terms "selfie" and "objectification". A selfie is a photograph one takes of him or herself with the use a smart phone, a camera or a selfie stick for posting on social networking sites notably Facebook, Instagram, and Twitter. Objectification on the other hand is the act of treating or seeing human beings as objects. Most often, objectification occurs in the sexual realm, hence the concept of sexual objectification. Varied typologies of objectification have been identified. Among these typologies/features, one notes *reduction to appearance* (which consists in treating a person primarily with respect to how he or she looks like or appears to the senses) and *reduction to the body* (which is the act of treating somebody as identified with his or her body or body parts. *Silencing* is also another important feature of objectification. It consists in treating a person as if he or she lacks the capabilities to speak. Nussbaum (1996) identified seven other features of objectification. These include:

- **Instrumentality:** The treatment of person as a tool existing for the purpose of the *objectifier*.
- **Ownership:** The treatment of somebody as if he or she is the propriety of the *objectifier*
- **Denial of Subjectivity:** Treating someone as if his or her feelings and experiences should not be taken into account.
- **Violability:** Treating someone as if he or she lacks integrity.
- **Denial of Autonomy:** Treating someone as if he or she lacks self-determination.
- **Inertness:** Treating someone as if he or she lack agency and activity
- **Fungibility:** Treating someone as if he/she is interchangeable with some objects.

Though most of the features outlined above point to the fact that objectification may be perpetrated on someone by an external human entity, it must be emphasized that objectification may also be done by the self; hence the concept of self-objectification. Self-objectification is therefore the act of presenting oneself as an object of sight or in some physical sense. It may involve viewing oneself from an outsider's perspective.

Selfie-objectification is generally considered as a (new) form of self-objectification which is manifested through – or is aided by – an objectionable use of selfies. According to Kite and Kite (2014), the process includes three stages namely: (i) capturing photos of oneself to admire and scrutinize, (ii) editing the captured photos to generate an acceptable final image and (iii) sharing these photos through social networking sites for peers to validate. An egregious illustration of selfie-objectification is the phenomenon of nude or *pornified* selfies. As Gorman (2015) explains, most youths (particularly the females) view themselves as brands. To them, the social media constitute a broadcasting tool with immense potential to create and advertise a personal brand. Their online avatar represents the image they want to sell to their peers. In tandem with this, looking hot and "fuckable" in a selfie is generally regarded as a big part of how desirable that brand is.

Social Media Craze

The term social media craze is mostly used in reference to (new) social media driven trends which society finds very popular and ephemeral. This is in tandem with the fact that the term craze is defined as a fashion which is taken up with great enthusiasm for a very short period of time (Mulhall 2016). At first sight, one may think that the term social media craze emanates from the idea that, specific social behaviors may be defined by analogy with forms of mental anomalies (craze). In Nigeria particularly, the term has often been construed by authors as any questionable use of the social media, particularly those uses which are clearly antithetical to African conservative principles (Ajike & Nwakoby 2016; Ecoma & Ecoma, 2015). Popular imaginations have thus tended to arguably associate the phenomenon with issues ranging from cyber crimes to selfie objectification and social media addictions (Adagbo, 2016; Ibidapo, 2014; Odu, 2015). It is however important to note here that social media craze is not inextricably related to internet addiction or social media addictions. In other words, the popular cultures often viewed (mostly by profanes) in the Nigeria socio-cultural context as social media craze are not in themselves recognized in psychology as social media addictions or technology related addictions. Popular imaginations in Nigeria for instance, associate the phenomenon of digitally driven scamming among young Nigerians with social media craze meanwhile, the culture is inherently not a social media or internet addiction. For a phenomenon to be considered internet or social media addiction, a number of symptoms must be observed. In the specific case of internet addiction, some of the symptoms include:

- Compulsive check by the addict of his or her text messages
- Frequent change of status on social networking sites
- Frequent uploading of selfies to social networking sites
- Social withdrawal
- A feeling of euphoria with the web
- Loss of interest in non-digitally driven activities
- A feeling of restlessness whenever he or she is disenabled to go online. (Cash, Rae, Steel & Wnkler, 2012; Shah 2015, Singh & Lippman 2017; Vats 2015).

As shown above, internet addiction is more complex than social media craze. The first is a recognized disorder (added in 2013 in the *Diagnostic and Statistical Manual of Mental Disorder* [DSMMD]); while the second is more of a social phenomenon (Singh & Lippman 2016). Being mindful of such a clear difference between the two terms, this paper merely adopts the definition of social media craze that places it among popular cultures which are being driven by the social media and which are mainly considered new, strange and to some extent culturally offensive by the conservative quarters of the Nigerian society. In other words, the chapter hinges on the conception of social media craze as any digitally driven cultures which, from a psychological point of view, should not be viewed inherently as disorders; but which are perceived by the conservative Nigerian society as constituting socio-cultural problems or pathologies.

African Conservatism

Otherwise called "conservativism", the concept of conservatism denotes a socio-political theory or philosophy which (i) celebrates traditions as a solution to external (aggressive) forces of change and (ii) is antithetical to the idea of radical social change. Agree (cited in Endong and Obongawan, 2015) associates conservatism with aristocracy. He notes that "the tactics of conservatism vary widely by place and time. But the most central feature of conservatism is deference: a psychologically internalized attitude on the part of the common people that the aristocracy are better people than they are". Proponents of the conservative theory advocate the preservation of the status quo, the progressive/slow reformation of the society or the return to old/traditional values. It is in line with this that some conservatives see enormous risks in attempts at changing society (the complex web of human interactions) overnight. They strongly advocate for an organic, rather than a revolutionary transformation of society. Revolutionary social transformations, they think, rather have the unwelcome potency to breed unintended consequences.

There exist various typologies of conservatism some of which include cultural, religious and social forms of conservatism. As its name indicates, cultural conservatism seeks to preserve the cultural heritage of a people or nation. Social conservatism seeks to preserve the social norms while religious conservatism preaches the preservation of religious ideologies either by advocating a return to traditional religious rituals or preserving certain beliefs in their original or pristine form (Mastin, 2008).

Conservatism therefore has geographical and cultural colorations, hence the concepts of African conservatism and Nigerian conservatives. Nigerian conservatives seek to preserve core African/Nigerian cultural values and traditions. Some of these core cultural values and traditions include communalism, respect for elders and authorities, modesfy, sense of proverbs and sense of sacredness of life. Proponents of this cultural current often preach Afro-centrism or African renaissance. They are usually staunchly opposed to the prevalence of Euro-centrism or westernization in African socio-cultural spheres (Akinpelu 1983). In tandem with their beliefs, they most often tend to see the ancestors and traditional African values as the answers to modern Africa's developmental equations. As Wambu (2009) puts it, in the face of any Euro-centrism, African conservative tend to romanticize African past. They also tend to default into the alternate Afro-centric space to valorize both traditional cultures and the institutions that protect/preserve them. African conservatives thus see African traditional values as an indispensable bridge to the past. From this premise, they posit that, core African values are not to be considered traditional and conservative (as the liberals may brand them), but rather progressive when contrasted with the imperialist-imposed present.

Though there exist many core traditional values which African conservatives seek to preserve, this essay will consider only aspects and tenets of African conservatism that border on physical appearance, gender relations and sexuality in the public space. This selective attention is justified by the fact that physical appearance, gender and sexuality are often emphasized in selfies. According to African conservatism, self-imaging and sexuality in public should be guided by the principle of modesty. In line with this, issues like pornography, mediated nudity, and mediated sex (notably naked and objectified selfies) are generally considered social leprosy and a bane to pure African/Nigerian traditional values. Many Nigerian conservatives arguably view these phenomena as cultural imports and pollution from the west (what is fondly termed westoxication – derived from a lexical fusion of "west" and "intoxication") (Endong 2016). And so, members of the society who embrace liberal views on sexuality and pornography are generally branded "social rebels" or simply viewed as social deviants.

Conservatives thus tend to perpetrate the shamming, ridicule, stigmatization and *ostracisation* of members of the society who "dare" to adopt liberal ideologies on sex and sexuality and self-imaging in public. For instance, women who openly speak about their sexuality or publicly expose their nudity are often branded by Nigerian conservatives as social deviants (Endong and Obongwan, 2015; Ojo 2005). Nigerian conservatism equates self-worth to being covered and so, any woman who dresses in a suggestive way is mostly viewed along various negative stereotypes. As Nigerian tabloid The *Capital* (2016) succinctly enthuses, Nigerian conservatives strongly believe that "a woman's femininity is best preserved and motherhood better ennobled if the contemporary woman could endeavor to keep her hidden graces covered and shielded from the glare of an increasingly nosy and narcissistic world" (para 3). It is based on the above mentioned index that some (radical feminist and modernist) scholars tend to regard Nigerian conservatism as a form of cultural fundamentalism which particularly bases women self-imaging in public on a set of patriarchal ideals rooted in doctrinaire religion and rigid traditionalism (Segoete, 2015).

Liberalism

Liberalism is most often defined as a political tradition. However, it may confusingly refer to a wide range of slightly different ideological positions. In effect, there exists a plurality of liberalisms and liberals some of which include social liberalism, neo-liberalism, libertarianism, objectivism, political liberalism, economic liberalism, anarcho-liberalism, classical liberalism and bleeding heart liberalism among others (Van de Haar, 2015). The existence of these varieties of liberals – and particularly the dichotomy between some of these typologies of liberalism – make the concept (of liberalism) to somehow be polysemic and slippery. As explained by Rooksby (2011), while a social liberal might advocate for generous welfare and redistribution of society's wealth, an "economic" or "classical" liberal will favor the adoption of *laisser faire* policies and minimal government intervention in an economy.

In spite of the small dichotomy that exists between some strands of liberalism, it remains clear that liberals share a number of core values, ideologies or ideals. On the basis of this premise, it can be enthused that liberalism has a number of essential proprieties. These include liberty, equal opportunities in life, tolerance, democracy, human rights and constitutionalism among others. Of all these core liberalist values, liberty and tolerance seem to be most cardinal. No doubt, the term "liberal" is classically employed to refer to a person who understands and respects other people's opinions and attitudes, even when they are different from his or her own.

Given the fact that liberalism is the dominant world view in the west, most Afro-centric observers tend to arguably regard liberal Africans (those who adopt liberal views on social and political issues) as products of western cultural imperialism or westernization (Student News Daily, 2010). In tandem with this, liberals in African societies (notably Nigeria) are most often contrasted with conservatives (Amadi 2005, Ojo 2005, Endong 2016, 2015). It is for instance popularly believed that only liberal Nigerians are liable to support issues like pornography, feminism, gender equality, children discretion/privacy, same-sex marriage and the LGBT (Lesbian, Gay, Bisexual and Transgender) right movement which arguably, are considered (by most Nigerian conservatives) as western imports and undisputable symbols of "westoxication" in Nigeria (Endong, 2016). Similarly, the apologists of such traditions as objectified selfies, nude selfies and other forms of sexualized self-imaging in public spaces are likely branded liberals and westernized members of the Nigerian society. This has been so, given the prevalence of the conservative current in the country.

A number of critics have argued that, with specific respect to sex or pornography, most Nigerians (young or not) tend to hypocritically claim to be conservative; meanwhile they have palpable liberalist inclination on such controversial issues. They actually often "pretend" to be conservative in public while sharing liberal views on pornography and mediated sex in secret circles (Endong and Vareba 2015; Ojo, 2005). They relish pornographic artifacts but will, in public spaces, profess to be anti-porn or too religious. It is based on such an observation that Nigerian porn star Judith Opara Mazagwu (alias Afrocandy) posits that though most Nigerians "pretend" to be too religious and conservative, they "pester" her for pornographic movies. In a humoristic tone, she states that, judging from the responses, requests and orders she has received so far, Nigerians are heavy consumers of porn though they will profess religious conservatism and Puritanism in public spaces. "You already know your people [Nigerians], they will criticise in public but go behind to buy it and hide in their bedrooms to watch it" (cited in *Osun Defender*, 2016). It could therefore be enthused that the growing magnitude at which Nigerian youths share nude selfies on social networking sites is a manifestation of the growing magnitude of liberal thinking among Nigerians in general and youths in particular. By such a liberal thinking, pornographic material (notably *pornified* selfie) is no longer sincerely frowned at.

SELFIE-OBJECTIFICATION AS A FACET OF THE SOCIAL MEDIA CRAZE IN NIGERIA

The advent of the social media in Nigeria has brought with it a plurality of both lauded and "problematic" /controversial cultures. One of these new and controversial cultures has been the selfie which, being variously embraced by the Nigerian youths, has led to some abysmal assessments of the social media by some conservative quarters. One easily observes that most negative reviews of the social impact of the new media in Nigeria hinge partially – and in some cases, dominantly – on the fact that the youths have mainly embraced questionable paradigms in their used of selfies. In tandem with this, the concept of selfie craze in the Nigerian context has most often conjured a pejorative idea. In the same logic, the term "social media craze" has, in the Nigerian context, been used to refer to the majority – nay totality – of new, "bizarre" and socially "inacceptable" or deviant traditions perpetrated by users on social networking sites and the internet (Chukwuka, 2016; Daily Post 2012; Dumo, 2016; Odu 2015; Onasanya, Olelekan, Ayelegba & Akingbemisilu, 2013).

One manifestation of social media craze has been the so called selfie craze seen in the tendency among many Nigerians to post or share sensational and controversial material on social networking sites. It has for instance been remarked that most Nigerians have preferred to exclusively and compulsively act as citizen journalists in the scenes of some accidents, rather than providing timely assistance to victims in distress. They have often preferred to shoot and capture the agonies and death of victims in such events as plane crashes, fatal motor accidents and other sad events just to have unique and sensational images to upload to social networking sites. Dumo (2016) underscores this somehow anti-social habit as he notes that unlike in the past where people rushed to scenes of accidents with the sole aim of helping the distressed victims, these days, capturing and filming their agonies on smartphones before uploading the photos to the Internet, appears to be not just in vogue but the norm. In most Nigerian metropolises, the selfie craze has progressively caused many individuals to act strangely and insensitively to the plight of others. "Many, in this bizarre habit, arrive at scenes of tragedies within minutes of their occurrences but do little or nothing to assist the dying victims". To further buttress his point, Dumo cites an informant who enthuses that smartphone craze (among other forms of social media craze) has subtly diluted – if not totally killed – humanity, modesty and other African values in many Nigerians. This informant anchors his position on some young Nigerians' display of insensitivity during a plane crash that occurred in 2012 in the country. He succinctly notes that:

Sadly, this new technology [the social media] has exposed a previously unnoticed aspect of the Nigerian society. There was a time when the concept of "dignity in death' was adhered to in Nigeria, but with technology, the dead are no longer given their respect. One of the most sickening displays of this insensitivity occurred in the aftermath of the June 2012 Dana Airline crash. Shortly after the plane crashed in Iju, (Lagos), thousands of people residing in the area rushed to the scene; however, instead of rescuing the people in the plane, people began using their phones to take images of the dying plane crash victims and recording the scenes. For me, it is a sad commentary of the harm this technology has and will continue to cause us except we put our humanity first. (p.35)

Another bizarre digitally driven trend has been the popular tradition among Nigerian youths to in share nude and objectified selfies on social networks. The female users seem arguably to be the principal actresses of this questionable tradition. In effect, like their western counterparts, many female Nigerian youths feel more and more pressured to appear "fuckable" (sexy) and promiscuous during their online interactions (Chukwuka, 2016; Dumo, 2016). Possessing such an appearance is believed by many of them to be a *sine qua non* condition to earn boys' attention and acceptance. Their self-representation and interactions on social networks are therefore, most often highly sexualized. The sharing of objectified selfies has, in this way, become a norm and an imperative for many young Nigerians. This is so as posting raunchy shots of boobs, curves, buttocks and complete nakedness is more and more viewed as a "must do" for many young girls who equate *pornified* self-imaging in public spaces with stardom. Twenty one-years-old Nigerian student Enitan Adeshola illustrates this youthful passion when she equates her nude selfies with creativity and evidences of her being talented. In effect, she posits that her sexually explicit selfies demonstrate that she possesses immense talent for theatrical performances and have what it takes in terms of boldness and physical attributes to be a good Nollywood actress. As she puts it,

I think there is something missing in the [Nollywood] industry and that's me. I seriously think so. I have got this talent and passion inside me that I want to show to everybody out there. I want the world to see what I have got inside me, the God-given talent inside me, and I know that the media are actually waiting for that young person that will come and blow everybody away. That's why I believe that they are looking for me. (Cited in Daily Post, 2012)

The phenomena of nude selfie and selfie-objectification are thus more accentuated among youths. Such youths view celebrities and Hollywood/Nollywood sexual personae – who have been notorious for nude selfies – as their role models. The likes of Kim Kardashian, Rihana, Meadee, Wizbiz, and Paris Hilton are models these young female Nigerians often attempt to emulate (Ecoma & Ecoma 2015; Mukhongo, 2014). The males are also not left out of this "latest craze in town" as many of them have progressively embraced the tradition of sharing what is popularly called "eggplant" selfies on social networks. This category of selfies includes shots of fully-erect or protruding penises. It goes without saying that such *pornified* shots are mainly aimed to tantalise viewers, particularly their female peers and remind the latter of the endowment hidden between the thighs of the selfie takers. Another popular typology of selfie-objectification among both young males and females in Nigeria has been the toilet selfie involving a youth appearing pants down and sitting on a toilet bowl and giving the impression to be answering a long or short nature's call.

The sharing of nude selfies by Nigerian youths arguably represents a visible index of the youthful desire/passion to cross borders, challenge established rules and be agents of socio-cultural avant-gardism or snobbism. It could therefore be enthused that there seems to be no significant difference between Nigerian youths and their western counterparts in terms of the use or sharing of these artefacts (nude selfies). As shall be argued in the subsequent sections of this discourse, Nigerian youths have mainly attempted to "flow with a global trend". This has implied that they struggle to be part of a "controversial" popular culture which prevails in almost all climes of the world. In other word, selfie-objectification among the youths is observable in the west the same as in Nigeria. It has over the years become the "universal language" of youths and celebrities. This imagination squares beautifully with Swiss artiste Moiré's contention which stipulates that:

I think naked selfies are a mix of narcissism, attention seeking and an emotional thrill. Porn pictures are nothing special anymore, however to show the own naked body is perceived as something forbidden. Social media platforms like Facebook document this view with censorships of nipples. Young people will always get the urge to cross borders; naked selfies is a quick, indirect way to explore. (cited in Patel, 2016, p.102)

Despite the prevalence of the conservative current in Nigeria, youths still feel the urge to deconstruct established societal norms, replicating the host of youthful cultures prevalent in foreign climes and enabling the globalisation of the selfie culture. This tends to rationalize the thesis that the selfie culture – be it selfie-objectification or not – more or less represents a universal phenomenon, particularly among the youths.

Objectified selfies have progressively become a symbol of "anticipated maturity" among many Nigerian teens. In line with this, the social media are considered to be "killing the child in children" in Nigeria. This coinage constantly used by some Nigerian observers vividly shows how these digital technologies push very young Nigerians to prematurely assume maturity. They actually assume adult roles, most often by imitation or by subtle instigation (Ajere & Oyinloye, 2011; Enukuomehim, 2011; Eze, 2001; Ihedoro, 2006; Onyeka, Sajoh & Balus, 2013). Corroborating this position, Chukwuka (2016) laments that the social media reduce all its users to a common denominator enabling a situation wherein, teens are made to take part in sexualized interactions with people (sex predators) who, most often, are old enough to be their parents. As he puts it, amoral men are shamefully using social media networks "to scout for young innocent girls, with promises as bait. Fraudsters lure children into despicable acts. Raw videos and images are easily transferred and children watch these items in their rooms and classrooms, unbeknownst to parents".

There has been a serious controversy over selfie-objectification – particularly sexting by youths – in almost all the societies of the world. Even in dominantly "liberal societies", such as the U.S., Britain, France, Germany, Switzerland and Australia among others, a host of schools of thought (mostly feminists, religious quarters and child/youth development experts) have censored these phenomena (Patel, 2016; Gorman, 2015; O'Brien & Torres, 2012; Sule, 2016). Nigeria has thus, not been exempted from this trend. In effect, selfie-objectification and sexting are subject to serious controversy. Though the country is dominantly conservative and religious in nature, a number of voices have expressed liberal views in favour of nude selfies sharing on social networking sites. The digitally driven tradition is progressively embraced by a good portion of the youth population as a symbol of modernity and universalism. There therefore exist two dominant schools of thought opposed on the issues of sexting and selfie-objectification: the conservative otherwise called traditionalist Nigerians (who are mostly composed of the older generations and the religious quarters) and those sharing liberal opinions (mostly composed of younger generations and acclaimed celebrities). This debate is explored in greater details in the subsequent portions of this essay.

CONSERVATIVE PERSPECTIVE ON SELFIE-OBJECTIFICATION BY NIGERIAN YOUTHS

African conservatism continues to be prevalent in Nigeria and so, selfie-objectification has mainly been viewed as a socio-cultural pathology in Nigerian societies (Ajike & Nwakoby 2016; Daily Post 2012; Ecoma & Ecoma 2015; The Capital 2016). To illustrate this fact, one just needs to consider the over growing number of gossip columns in newspapers or blogs which provide a forum for censuring the least incident of nude selfie perpetrated either by a Nigerian celebrity, a socialite or a "wanna-be star". Nigerian artistes and superstars such as Flavor, Wizbiz, Pretty Osaro, Afro Candy, Queeneth Hilbert, Tonto Dike, and Meadee among others, have tried the "daring" experiment of sharing their nude selfies on social media, only for them to receive torrential criticisms, abysmal profiling and labeling from religious and conservative quarters as well as from their fans (The Capital 2016; Udoma, 2013). Porn star Afro Candy is among the controversial superstars that have mostly been targeted by such conservatives and religious arbiters. Her personal Facebook pages, blogs and web sites have become veritable platforms for interminable quarrels between her critics/fans and her, over her nude selfies, explicit lifestyle and release of pornographic movies. Critics and fans' comments on these online platforms most often have conservative and religious undertone.

Another conservative criticism of selfie-objectification is offered by the Nigerian online magazine titled *The Capital* (2016). With great acerbity, this magazine censures the (new and) apparent compulsion among many Nigerian female artistes and Nollywood stars, of exposing their private parts at the least opportunity on social networking sites. The magazine thus laments that:

The rate at which local celebrities discard their clothing to reveal their bare skin covering their embryos would leave the conservative gasping for breath and clutching at norms with frenetic speed. The roll call of local female celebrities who are subscribing to this cultural import from Europe and America has become worrisome to folk who believe a woman's femininity is best preserved and motherhood better ennobled if the contemporary woman could endeavour to keep her hidden graces covered and shielded from the glare of an increasingly nosy and narcissistic world.

Just recently, Dior Chidera Adiele, shocked her fans and raised serious eyebrows by posing completely nude for a photo shoot celebrating her baby bump. [...] Probably lacking the courage and daring of

Adiele, Kaffy Ameh, otherwise known as Kaffy the Dance Queen, unclothed her belly to show off her baby bump to the world before she put to bed. And the roll keeps increasing to include more celebrities or wanna-be celebrities. (The Capital 2016, Para 3-6)

Nigerian conservatives and religious schools of thought view the phenomenon of selfie-objectification as an exocentric value (precisely a western cultural import) and a bane to "pure African" cultural values. As enthused by many Nigerian observers, nudity and lack of modesty in the public space are" un-African" or "un-Nigerian" (that is, they are antithetical to core Nigerian values). In effect, in no time are youths allowed to go nude in public spaces since such an act is liable to be interpreted as pornography or lack of modesty. Nigerian conservatives therefore tend to label adepts of nude selfies taking and sharing and tend to associate such "libertine" selfie users with westernized entities, and people who, knowingly or unknowingly, are off-rooted. In line with this, such adepts of sexting and *pornified* selfies are most often shamed, stigmatized and socially ostracized by their conservative counterparts (Ajere & Uyinloye, 2011; Endong & Vareba 2015; Segoete, 2015). As underscored by *The Capital* (mentioned above), the popular (conservative) imagination stipulates that adepts of selfie-objectification are blind imitators of the western lifestyle; and that, as blind imitators, they tend to jettison local cultural values in favor of exocentric cultural trends. Some conservative critics even think that this nude selfie culture is an inordinate, "exotic" and eccentric trend. A case in point is Ecoma and Ecoma (2015) who note that Nigerian youths' growing mania for selfie-objectification perfectly illustrates the latter's indiscriminate imitation of "models that look like extraterrestrial beings".

It must however be emphasized that the tendency of relegating any phenomenon related to pornography and overt nudity (notably selfie-objectification) to the western culture is somehow problematic and objectionable. One reality/fact which cultural and religious conservatives tend to ignore or overlook is the multidimensional influences of globalization and modernization on Nigerian communities. Some of these influences (notably *creolization* and *glocalization*) render more and more futile the definition of an essentialized youth identities. Inasmuch as some aspects of westernization (for instance the urge to copy western superstars, models and opinion leaders) may be viewed in the nude selfies of some Nigerian youths, it will be fairer to regard youths' mania for sexting and selfie-objectification – at least partially – as a consequence of globalization and the emergence and progressive proliferation of a global culture among youths. The selfie is becoming a universal paradigm and youths, irrespective of cultures, are tending to embrace it as a new language and contemporary lifestyle. As has been amply argued by some scholars, irrespective of cultures, youths are not unconscious of the possible adverse consequences of sexting and nude selfie sharing. They simply feel and react to the urge of flowing with the global trend (Daily Post 2012; The Capital 2016). As future media scholar Mark Brill puts it, smartphone addiction and selfie-objectification among youths in the world are driven by what he called "FOMO", the fear of missing out. As Brill further explains, "the thing about social media is that it creates a sense that you need to be involved with it and that if you're not, you're somehow missing out. So a lot of people do stuff on social media for the social recognition, the social value" (Cited in Patel 2016).

The tradition of sharing nude selfies may (arguably) have emanated from – or initially been prevalent in – the west; but that does not really make it an exclusively western cultural tradition – as the conservatives will want us believe. The conservative maxim stating that "porn is un-African" does not really hold waters as pornography sells in almost all cultures and is avidly consumed even in religious fundamentalist markets. An increasing portion of youths (even in conservative countries like Nigeria) have progressively resorted to objectified selfies as a way of challenging established norms and crossing borders. No doubt, West Africa NGO Network director, Tunji Lardner (cited in Ogbu, 2013) interprets selfie-objectification as another manifestation of the ongoing breakdown of Nigerian social order (the progressive triumph of liberal world views over conservative values). To him, Nigerian youths' engagement on social media platforms and the quality of their discourse are a direct reflection of prevailing norms within the [Nigerian] society. These prevailing norms have much to do with Nigerian citizens' progressive embrace of postmodern and liberal philosophies of life. This will be x-rayed in greater details in the subsequent part of this discourse.

SELFIE-OBJECTIFICATION AS A SIGN OF NIGERIAN YOUTHS' ADHERENCE TO LIBERALISM

It will be expedient from the outset to underline the fact that Nigerian youths tend to be more and more liberal on self-imaging in the public space as well as on sex related issues (notably on sexting and objectified selfie) (Endong & Vareba 2015). Compared to the older generations (which have mainly been conservatives), the youths have sometimes regarded nude selfie and other daring sex related traditions as forms of modern culture. Corroborating this position, Eze (2014) remarks that, Nigerian youths' growing exposure to sexual stimuli in the media of mass communication has pushed them to progressively embrace liberal and permissive attitudes towards sex. She further explains that, "the adolescents are exposed to sexual stimuli in magazines, television and the movies to a greater extent than before, thereby creating a general trend towards liberated attitudes and values that encourage open discussion on sexuality, once considered a taboo" (492).

Sex has long seized to be a taboo to most Nigerian youths and the social media are suitable platform to overtly talk, debate over or perform sexualized acts. The sharing of nude selfie (selfie-objectification) has thus become a suitable tool for such an exercise. In line with this, 22-years old Otoroh (an informant) notes that: "today, young Nigerian girls are no longer ashamed to fully embrace their bodies and their sexualities. The conservative norms which prevail in traditional Africa societies do not inform the ethical outlooks of many of them. This, to me, is good development [...] By the way, why should sex continue to be a taboo in the 21st century? Why should a young girl or woman be ashamed to exhibit her curves and graces in the name of religion or culture? It is absurd that religion and tradition subtly continue to render women sorts of prisoners"

Young Nigerians' involvement in selfie-objectification may therefore be viewed more as a generational trend than a cultural importation from the west. By such a generational trend, youths can be said to simply "act out their own age". As explained by Kwaghkondo (cited by Adagbo 2016), every generation tend to think their age is better than that of previous ones. Our forefathers thought their age was better, their children did not agree and our own children would not agree with us when we imply to them that our own time was better. Their own children will equally not agree with them. That is how it goes. Gorman (2013) shares corollaries as she notes that "selfies, sexting and twerking are all part of a teen continuum that has been outraging older generations". Following this logic, it may be enthused that selfie-objectification is just part of a contemporary youth culture or at best, a cultural revolution among the Nigerian youths.

It therefore goes without saying that, despite the prevalence of religious and cultural conservatism in the Nigerian society, youths appear more and more liberal in their ways of interacting on the social networks. This liberalism is very much facilitated by the nature of the social networks. Online settings (the social networks) are not only virtual in nature but loose as an environment. This nature of online settings subtly enables users to adopt varied identities and to enjoy the kind of freedom they may not experience in "off line settings" (the physical Nigerian society). One easily observes that on online settings, conditions are visibly conducive to libertarianism and postmodern thinking which, in turn, is propitious to liberal attitudes and even to libertinism. The virtual environment affords its users to have greater latitude to (re)construct their identities irrespective of the norms guiding interactions in the physical Nigerian space. These users can adopt attitudes which relatively conflict with their behaviors in offline cultural settings; but which clearly reveal their veritable attitude towards conservatism and liberal thinking. For instance, it has been demonstrated that, in offline settings, most young Nigerian women's construction of their image is more in conformity with patriarchal and conservative norms; meanwhile, in online or virtual settings, these women tend to circumstantially depart from conservative norms in favor of liberal ethical outlooks, hence the phenomenon of selfie objectification (Mukhongo, 2014). This is illustrated by 21-years-old Enitan who claims her motivation or "rationale" for taking and sharing nude selfies is to create controversy. She confides that: "I think because I am personally crazy. I love creativity. I love doing things that are so unusual. I don't want to be doing everyday things. When I take a picture and people keep wondering, who's that girl? I want to just create a controversy. That's why I love taking crazy pictures" (Cited in Daily Post, 2013).

The above mentioned line of reasoning squares with Sule's (2012) concept of Digital Technology Masturbation syndrome. According to this concept, the digital technology is used by some people (particularly the Nigerian youths) to stimulate the release of certain innermost desires, values and thoughts. Hinging on this thesis, it can be enthused that the absence of the postmodern channels to express "inordinate" and "deviationist" thoughts and desires, coupled with the prevalence of various conservative strictures in the Nigerian physical space, has pushed many youths to contain their innermost liberalist desire, thoughts and values. The advent and ubiquity of the social networks have permitted the liberal Nigerian internet users to have a channel through which they can manifest tendencies that are contrary to local societal norms. The social media have thus become suitable and viable tools for the youths – who technically may be viewed as "technology masturbators" – to release subconscious liberal thoughts, values and desires into their conscious world.

CONCLUSION

The advent of the social media in Nigeria has permitted the emergence of a plurality of information technology syndromes as well as various forms of social pathologies. One of these social pathologies has been the selfie-objectification indexed by factors such naked selfies. As a form of psycho-social pathology, selfie-objectification has particularly engulfed the youths, killing the child in the children, corrupting the latter's innocence and affecting the positive relationship culture among youths. This chapter has explored some of the manifestations of this psycho-social leprosy..

The chapter has equally explored two opposing perspectives on selfie-objectification in Nigeria namely conservative and liberal. It has observed that while Nigerians with liberal views tend to interpret selfie-objectification as a mode of expression and an index of the globalization or universality of the selfie phenomenon, the conservatives/traditionalists regard this type of objectification as yet another cultural import from the west and an agent of cultural malaise among the youths in Nigeria. However, interpreting selfie-objectification among the Nigerian youths solely as a cultural insensitive act and a western cultural import is visibly myopic and objectionable. The phenomenon should rather be read within a global perspective and along the line of Nigerian youths' visible embrace of liberal and post-modern philosophies of life.

REFERENCES

Adagbo, A. (2016, Oct.). Nollywood and Nigeria's challenge of reel geopolitics. *Intervention*, 11-21.

Ajere, O., & Oyinloye, O. A. (2011). Perspectives of youths on the interiorization of core-societal-values in the Nigerian society. *Akungba Journal of Research in Education*, *1*(1), 179–194.

Ajike, A. K., & Nwakoby, N. P. (2016). The impact of social networking sites on teenagers in Nigeria. *International Journal of Public Policy and Administration*, *11*(1), 35–64.

Akinpelu, J. A. (1983). Values in Nigerian society. In O. A. Nduka & E. O. Iheoma (Eds.), *New perspectives in moral education* (pp. 33–56). Ibadan: Evans Brothers Publishers Limited.

Amadi, E. (2005). *Ethics in Nigerian cultures*. Ibadan: Bookraft.

Balarabe, S. (2015). *Impact of social media on public discourse in Nigeria*. Paper presented at the International Conference on Communication, Media, Technology and Design, Dubai, UAE.

Cash, H., Rae, C., Steel, A. H., & Winkler, A. (2012). Internet addiction: A brief summary of research and practice. *Current Psychiatry Reviews*, *8*(4), 292–298. doi:10.2174/157340012803520513 PMID:23125561

Daily Post. (2012). NIJ student goes nude to break into Nollywood. *Daily Post*. Retrieved April 8, 2017, from http://www.nijstudent-goes-nude-to-break-into-nollywood-dailypost-htm

Ecoma, C. S., & Ecoma, B. C. (2015). Nigerian core values and social networking in contemporary times: A discourse. *The International Journal of Social Sciences and Humanities Inventions*, *2*(9), 1555–1565.

Edogor, I. O., Aladi, A. J., & Idowu, L. I. (2015). Influence of social media on youths' usage of traditional mass media in Nigeria. *New Media of Mass Communication*, *31*, 55–67.

Endong, F. P. (2017). Reconciling homosexuality and spirituality in Africa as a heresy and survival strategy: A study of House of Rainbow (LGBT Church) Nigeria. In P. Ana Maria (Ed.), *Multiculturalism and the Convergence of Faith and Practical Wisdom in Modern Society* (pp. 331–354). Hershey, PA: IGI Global. doi:10.4018/978-1-5225-1955-3.ch017

Endong, F. P. C. (2015). Framing the queers and the LGBT right movement in Africa: A study of Nigerian bloggers and web journalists. *Journal of Global Research in Education and Social Sciences*, *6*(4), 50–60.

Endong, F. P. C. (2016). The LGBT right movement in Africa and the myth of the Whiteman's superiority. *Journal of Globalization Studies*, *7*(1), 3–15.

Endong, F. P. C., & Obongawan, E. (2015). Sex in Christian movie: A study of Mel Gibson's *The Passion of the Christ* and Roger Young's *The Bible: Joseph*. *International Journal of Communication and Media Sciences*, *2*(2), 11–21.

Endong, F. P. C., & Vareba, A. L. (2015). Resisting anti-gay laws through media advocacy and online communities of meaning: A study of Nigerian homosexuals. *Journal for Studies in Management and Planning, 10*(2), 94–106.

Enukuomehin, O. A. (2011). ICT CGPA: Consequences of social networks in an internet driven learning society. *International Journal of Computer Trends and Technology, 2*(2), 101–124.

Eze, I. (2014). Adolescent attitude towards premarital sex. *Mediterranean Journal of Social Sciences, 5*(10), 491–496.

Eze, O. C. (2001). *Nigeria: Path to technological transformation*. Port Harcourt: Cass Publications.

Fallahi, V. (2011). Effect of ICT on the youth: A study about the relationship between internet usage and social isolation among Iranian Students. *Procedia: Social and Behavioral Sciences, 15*, 394–398. doi:10.1016/j.sbspro.2011.03.110

Gorman, V. (2015, March 31). Social media, sexualization and the selfie generation. The Drum. ABC News, 66-73.

Ibidapo, F. (2014, Oct. 6). Examining the impact of social media in Nigeria youth. *People Day*, 32-34.

Ihedoro, M. (2006). Value system, attitudes and knowledge of civic education as determinants of students performance in social studies (Unpublished M. Ed. Project). University of Ibadan.

Kite, L., & Kite, L. (2014). Selfies and self-objectification: Not-so-pretty picture. *Beauty Redefined*. Retrieved June 14, 2016 from http://www.beautyredefined.net/selfies-and-objectification/

Mastin, L. (2008). Conservatism. *The Basics of Philosophy*. Retrieved August 30, 2016, from http://www.philosophybasics.com/branch_conservatism.html

Mukhongo, L. L. (2014) Reconstructing gendered narratives online: Nudity for popularity on digital platforms. *Ada: A Journal of Gender, New Media, and Technology, 5*, 1-14.

Mulhall, J. P. (2016). *Social media: Fad, trend or much more*. New York: MIT Publishers.

Nussbaum, M. (1995). Objectification. *Philosophy & Public Affairs, 24*(4), 249–291. doi:10.1111/j.1088-4963.1995.tb00032.x

O'Brien, D., & Torres, A. M. (2012). Social networking and online privacy: Facebook users' perception. *Irish Journal of Management, 31*(2), 63–97.

Odu, O. (2016, June 18). Social media and the Nigerian youth. Nigerian Mirror, 21-23.

Ogbu, R. (2013). Trashy: More Nigerian girls pose nude to trend on twitter. *YNigeria*. Retrieved April 8, 2017, from http//:www.trashy.nigerian.girls.pose.nude.ynigeria.htm

Ojo, A. (2005). *Religion and Sexuality: Individuality, Choice and Sexual Rights in Nigerian Christianity*. Lagos: Africa Regional Sexuality Resource Center.

Olawepo, G. T., & Oyedepo, F. S. (2008). *Data communication and computer networks*. Adek Publisher.

Oluwatimilehin, M. (2016, August). The selfie syndrome danger. *Daily Times*, 16-19.

Onasanya, S. A., Olelekan, S.Y., Ayelegba, S.O., & Akingbemisilu, A.A. (2013). Online social network and academic achievement of university students – the experience of selected Nigerian Universities. *Information and Knowledge Management, 3*(5), 58-66.

Onyeka, N. C., Sajoh, D. I., & Bulus, L. D. (2013). The effect of social networking sites usage on the studies of Nigerian students. *International Journal of Engineering Science, 2*, 39–46.

Osun Defender. (2016, April 2). Nigerian pester me for sex movie. *Osun Defender*, 21-26.

Patel, R. (2016, March 23). Nude selfies: The latest trend sweeping the millennials. But there is a cost. *IBT: International Business Times*, 94-106.

Rooksby, E. (2011). What does it mean to be a liberal? *The Guardian*. Retrieved March 31, 2017 from https://www.theguardian.com/commentisfree/2011/aug/15/liberalism-political-economic-different-ideologies

Segoete, L. (2015). African female sexuality is past taboo. *This is Africa*. Retrieved June 10, 2017, from http://thisisafrica.me/sexuality-taboo/

Shah, P. B. (2015). Selfie – a new generation addiction disorder – literature review and updates. *International Journal of Emergency Mental Health and Human Resilience, 17*(3), 602. doi:10.4172/1522-4821.1000e227

Singh, D., & Lippman. (2017). Selfie addiction. *International Psychiatry: Bulletin of the Board of International Affairs of the Royal College of Psychiatrists, 4*(1), 11–27.

Student News Daily. (2010). Conservative Vs. liberal beliefs. *Student News Daily*. Retrieved March 31, 2017 from https://www.studentnewsdaily.com/conservative-vs-liberal-beliefs/

Sule, N. (2016). *The digital technology masturbation syndrome. A new craze in Nigeria.* Ibadan: Bookraft.

The Capital. (2016). Fad or faux pas? Nigerian celebrities strip nude to show baby bump. *The Capital*. Retrieved September 1, 2016 from http://www.thecapital.ng/?p=3184

Uduma, U. (2013). Youth and the internet: The dangers and the benefits. *Leadership Newspaper, 16*(June), 23–24.

Van de Haar, E. (2015). The meaning of "liberalism". *Liberaliam.org*. Retrieved March 31, 2017 from https://www.libertarianism.org/publications/essays/lets-clear-liberal-mess

Vats, M. (2015). Selfie syndrome: An infectious gift of IT to health care. *Journal of Lung. Pulmonary & Respiratory Rees, 2*(4), 48–49.

Wambu, O. (2015). Tradition versus modernity. *New African Magazine*. Retrieved August 30, 2016, from http://newafricanmagazine.com/tradition-versus-modernity/

KEY TERMS AND DEFINITIONS

African Conservatism: Term used in reference to a socio-cultural movement seeking to preserve core African cultural values and traditions. Some of these values include communalism, modesty, respect for elders and authorities, sense of proverbs and sense of sacredness of life among others. Proponents of this cultural current often preach Afro-centrism or African renaissance.

Liberalism: A socio-political doctrine which preaches values such as liberty, equal opportunity, tolerance, democracy, human rights and constitutionalism.

Objectification: The act of treating or viewing someone as an object. One typology of such tendency is sexual objectification which means treating someone as a sexual object.

Selfie: A type of self-portrait taken with a hand-held digital camera or a smartphone and uploaded to or social networking sites.

Sexting: This is a neologism which is derived from the fusion of the two words of "sex" and "texting". It is used to refer to the act of sending, receiving or forwarding sexually explicit images (photos) principally with the use of a telephone. It may however involve the use of computers.

Social Media Craze: Term used generally to mean social media driven cultures which are very popular. As used in the Nigerian context, the term is mostly derogatory and often refers to objectionable cultures aided by the social media.

Westernization: Social process whereby a given nation or society systematically comes under or adopts/absorbs western cultural values at multiple levels of its life.

Westoxication: A portmanteau composed of "west" and "intoxication". It is used by some Afro-centric scholars to refer to western cultural imperialism and the "adulteration" of local African cultures with typical western cultures.

Chapter 14
Problematic Linkages in Adolescents:
Italian Adaptation of a Measure for Internet-Related Problems

Valentina Boursier
University of Naples Federico II, Italy

Valentina Manna
Association for Social Promotion Roots in Action, Italy

ABSTRACT

Internet usage represents a risky opportunity for the youngest. Due to its social, communicative and emotional function in adolescents' lives, it may provide benefits and facilitations to their relationships. On the other hand, the excessive use of the Internet can harmfully affect their daily routines, with negative effects on their psychological state. Considering the widespread use of the Internet in everyday life during this developmental stage, the authors question the applicability of the concept of "addiction" and provide empirical data about the adaption of a useful instrument to measure problematic relationships with the Internet. The establishment of a cut-off procedure is proposed for screening purpose to identify at risk and problematic users. Moreover, differences by gender and age are explored and discussed. A comprehensive model of the Problematic Relationships with the Internet is presented and analyzed in comparison with the main perspectives and measures in literature.

INTRODUCTION

The Internet has become an essential part of our daily life. Compared to 2015, the number of *e-users* has increased by 10%, accounting more than 3 billion people in the world, around 39 million in Italy (We are social SRL, 2017). Particularly, the young users dominate the Internet usage: 95% of teenagers and 99% of young adults are web users (Online Safety Site, 2017; Pew Research Center, 2017). In Italy, more than 91% of people aged between 15 and 24 years are e-users (We Are Social SRL, 2017), and often they

DOI: 10.4018/978-1-5225-3477-8.ch014

are *always on*, or rather, connected all day long. Thus, the number of Internet young users is constantly increasing, providing them *risky opportunities* (Livingstone, 2008): on one hand, the web certainly may improve educational and social communication among adolescents, by enabling easier connections with friends, or by facilitating new relationships (Kraut et al., 2002; Van den Eijnden, Meerkerk, Vermulst, Spijkerman, & Engels, 2008). On the other hand, the excessive use of the Internet can negatively affect their daily routines, such as homework or revision, eating and family time, sporting activities, sleep patterns, and school attendance itself (Leung, 2006; Tam, 2016). Considering the widespread use of the Internet in everyday life and taking in account the specificity of the adolescence, as a stage of life during which the border between sanity and pathology is complex to define, the authors question the large applicability of the concept of "addiction" to the Internet misuse. In the authors' view, the problematic use needs a clearer definition, as it is not strictly related to a pathological behavior. Moreover, the need to distinguish a normal web usage from an addicted or problematic one lets the authors to provide empirical data about the adaption of a useful instrument to measure problematic relationships with the Internet especially among adolescents and preadolescents.

BACKGROUND

In the framework of psychopathology, several studies are concordant in identifying new forms of addictions, mostly behavioural (without substances). As noted by Bianchi & Phillips (2005), «the traditional concept of addiction was based on a medical model and referred to dependence associated with the ingestion of a substance, either drugs or alcohol. Lately, researchers have begun to question this medical model of addiction as the definitive model and have stated that the concept of addiction needs to cover a broader range of behaviors. Many researchers have thus argued for the validity of a behavioral addiction model» (p.40). Likely, among the non-chemical addictions (Marks, 1990), the Internet addiction is the most discussed.

According to Douglas and colleagues (2008), over the brief academic history on the Internet addiction, one of the most challenging tasks has been to get a unique definition of the concept. Researchers in the field have been unable to find a comprehensive term to describe the Internet overuse or abuse. Indeed, a standard and consensual definition of Internet addiction is still lacking (Laconi, Rodgers, & Chabrol, 2014; Spada, 2014) whilst various terms have been used to name the general "Problematic Internet Use" condition (Kuss, Griffiths, Karila, & Billieux, 2014; Tokunaga, & Rains, 2016). Among them, we can include: Internet Addiction Disorder (IAD) (Young, 1998b), Pathological Internet Use (Davis, 2001), Problematic Internet Use (Morahan-Martin, & Schumacher, 2000; Caplan, 2002), Excessive Internet Use (Widyanto, & Griffiths, 2006), and Compulsive Internet (or Computer) Use (Chou, & Hsiao, 2000; Johansson, & Götestam, 2004; Van den Eijnden, Meerkerk, Vermulst, Spijkerman, & Engels, 2008; Kuss, Griffiths, Karila, & Billieux, 2014).

The term "Internet Addiction" was provocatively proposed by Goldberg (1995) to describe an excessive and uncontrolled use of specific online applications (Müller et al., 2016), and gradually, attention has been increasingly focused on the potentially addictive features of the web.

Empirical evidence showed the web-related risks (Young, 1996; Brenner, 1997; Ferraro, Caci, D'amico, & Blasi, 2006; Byun et al., 2009; Kuss, Van Rooij, Shorter, Griffiths, & van de Mheen, 2013; Leung, 2014), until the American Psychological Association (APA), in 2013 included the Internet Gaming Disorder (IGD) in Section III (the research appendix) of the DSM-5. The inclusion of the IGD officialised the highly controversial topics of behavioural addictions and addictive potential of the Internet (Petry, & O'brien, 2013). This shows the need for making behavioral excesses more clinically identifiable, especially for the internet-related conditions, as stated by Griffiths (2005), because the addiction does not necessarily have to involve the abuse of a chemical intoxicant or substance (Griffiths, 1999; Young, 2004; Alavi et al., 2012). At the same time, strong empirical data are required to identify the defining features of the condition, obtaining cross-cultural data on reliability and validity of specific diagnostic criteria, determining rates of prevalence in representative epidemiological samples in different Countries, evaluating its natural history and examining its associated biological features.

The Internet Addiction, as well as other behavioral addictions (Holden, 2001), involves people in excessive activities, resulting in an uncontrollable desire and preoccupation with the Internet (King, Delfabbro, Griffiths, & Gradisar, 2011). Moreover, as for the substance-related addictions, several studies found that current Internet addiction consists of several common components or assessment tools, such as compulsive use, negative outcomes, salience, withdrawal symptoms, mood regulation, escapism and social comfort (Griffiths, 2005; Kuss, & Griffiths, 2011; Alavi et al., 2012; Lortie, & Guitton, 2013; Kuss et al., 2014; Tsitsika et al., 2014; Griffiths, Pontes, & Kuss, 2016).

Internet Mis-Use: An Addicted or Problematic Behavior?

Internet use is generally defined as "problematic" when an individual's psychological state (including both mental and emotional conditions, as well as scholastic, occupational and social interactions) is impaired by the overuse of the medium (Beard, 2005; Byun et al., 2009), in term of hours spent online and negative outcomes on the night and day activities (Tam, 2016). The problematic Internet use has been registered in any age, and social, educational or economic range (Beard, 2005), but adolescents and preadolescents have become a critical population to investigate. Indeed, some epidemiological studies showed that this period of life confers unique mental health risks, with special reference to the development of dependence-behaviors (Johnston, O'Malley, Bachman, & Schulenberg, 2005; Marcelli, & Bracconnier, 2006; Schepis, Adinoff, & Rao, 2008; Villella et al., 2011).

Despite impulsivity and non-control certainly have been central points in the addiction matter, the assessment of an Internet addicted behavior or misuse needs to refer to many other moods and related states of mind. This seems the reason why the addiction issue enacts several controversies among researchers. A first considerable debate is about whether the Internet is a medium to fuel other addictions (Griffiths, 2000; Griffiths, & Szabo, 2013; Pontes, Kuss, & Griffiths, 2015) or a causal factor of pathological conditions (Griffiths, 2000), such as depression (Kim et al., 2006; Ha et al., 2007), low self-esteem (Fioravanti, Dèttore, & Casale, 2012), high sensation-seeking (Armstrong, Phillips, & Saling, 2000), and loneliness and shyness (Caplan, 2002, 2003). Armstrong (2000), for example, noted that an addictive use of Internet appears to be more similar to impulse control disorders such as obsessive and compulsive, as it lacks chemical-based dependence. Studies have also explored the association with psychosocial well-being (Young, & De Abreu, 2010), and with various personality traits (Leung, 2006), as well as the Internet propensity to alleviate dysphoric moods and to allow coping with or compensate for real life problems (Young, 1998b). Many issues are still going to be discussed on this matter, such as if the Internet use can be considered as a compulsive (thus addicted) behaviour or a compensatory behaviour, i.e. the individual's reaction to his negative life situations, facilitated by the Internet application (Kardefelt-Winther, 2014). Nowadays, the scientific debate highlights the risk of overpathologyzing daily life (Billieux, Schimmenti, Khazaal, Maurage, & Heeren, 2015; De Timary, & Philippot, 2015; Griffiths, Pontes, & Kuss, 2016), through an addiction model; unlike chemical dependency and substance abuse, the Internet offers several psychological as well as functional benefits in modern lives. By comparison, alcohol or drugs are not an integral or necessary part of our personal and professional lives, nor do they offer any direct benefit. On the contrary, the Internet has so many practical uses that the signs of addiction can easily be masked or justified. It is a new tool used as an essential part of everyday life all over the world and its use increases especially among adolescents and youths (Maurya, & Singh, 2015). This is a matter of fact to be considered when analysing the Internet usage. Thus, the great availability and diffusion of the Internet, the unlimited and free Internet access for the adolescents, and the underestimate of negative features of the web could explain, on the one hand, the youth's risk for developing pathological Internet use, and, on the other hand, the need to distinguish a normal web usage from an addicted or problematic one.

MAIN FOCUS OF THE CHAPTER

Issues, Controversies, Problems

The large Internet addiction category easily gathers the "problematic" use of the Internet, often confusing each other (Beard, 2005; Laconi et al., 2014), and there is no standardized definition supported by all in the field (Anderson, Steen, & Stavropoulos, 2016). Actually, a problematic use is not strictly related to a pathological behavior. Obviously, the misuse and/or abuse of the Internet may lead to addictive behaviors; in this perspective, the construct of Internet addiction, which focuses on the behavioral repetitions, is useful to investigate the use/misuse of Internet. However, in accordance with Kardefelt-Winther (2014), this concept does not clarify the complexity of these phenomena, reducing them to a unique category. These issues lead to the question if we should research on problematic Internet use as just a maladaptive habit or a proper form of dependence, with special reference to adolescence, as a stage of life during which defining the border between sanity and pathology is complex. Moreover, specifically, age-related psychological factors can contribute to making a precise sense for Internet use (Kuss, Griffiths, & Binder, 2013). Thus, it is probably more useful to characterize individual differences that interact with environmental factors and lead to high Internet use, rather than diagnose Internet addiction (Van Rooij, & Prause, 2014).

Main Perspectives and Measures

The increasing research interest in the Internet abuse/misuse has led to the development of numerous scales to assess a probable disorder. Indeed, the self-report methodology is the most used in this framework because of its advantages over other methods: despite simple questions, lack of probing, limited control, and a relatively low response rate, the surveys decrease interview bias, are anonymous, allow for considered answers rather than immediate responses, and are accessible to wider samples (Kuss et al., 2014).

Tokunaga and Rains (2016) examined different traditions of problematic internet use (PIU) measures, which lead to conceptual and operational definitions of PIU. Through an articulate meta-analysis of scholar reports, the authors analyze the implications of different operational PIU definitions by also providing a useful classification of theoretical dimensions and related measures. Thus, they identify three different perspectives, considering PIU as: (a) a pathology related to substance dependence (Kandell, 1998), (b) an impulse control disorder similar to pathological gambling (Young, 1996, 1998b), and (c) a product of relational and relationship-building resource deficits (Davis, Flett, & Besser, 2002; Caplan, 2003).

According to Tokunaga and Rains' perspective (2016), three groups of measures can be consequently categorized: the *impulse control disorder group*, that operationally defines PIU by principally using the Internet Addiction Diagnostic Questionnaire (Young, 1996), the Internet Addiction Test (Young, 1998b), the Pathological Use Scale (Morahan-Martin, & Schumacher, 2000), and adaptations of the Diagnostic and Statistical Manual of Mental Disorders pathological gambling scale. To the second group, *substance dependence*, an operationalization of PIU principally using the Chen's Internet Addiction Scale (Chen, & Chou, 1999), the Internet-Related Addictive Behavior Inventory (Brenner, 1997), the Internet Addiction Scale (Nichols, & Nicki, 2004), and substantially adaptations of the DSM measures for substance dependence, has been attributed. Finally, the *relational resource deficits group* operationally defines PIU using above all the Generalized Problematic Internet Use Scale (GPIUS) (Caplan, 2002), Online Cognition Scale (OCS) (Davis et al., 2002), and Problematic Internet Usage Scale (Ceyhan, Ceyhan, & Gürcan, 2007).

Differences and similarities among these three main perspectives can be found.

Impulse Control Disorder Perspective

Referring to the first group/perspective, the *Internet Addiction Diagnostic Questionnaire* (IADQ) (Young, 1998b), was the first scale created for Internet addiction (Laconi et al., 2014). It is a 8-item self-report dichotomously measure based on the diagnostic symptoms of pathological gambling. The utilized criteria include preoccupation, tolerance, loss of control, withdrawal, denial, escapism, and negative consequences. In the last few years, this self-report measure was used by several studies to assess the adolescent Internet addiction (Durkee et al., 2012; Fisoun et al., 2012a; Fisoun, Floros, Siomos, Geroukalis, & Navridis, 2012b; Guo et al., 2012; Shek, & Yu, 2012; Siomos et al., 2012; Wang et al., 2013).

In the same perspective, the *Internet Addiction Test (IAT)* (Young, 1998a) emerged as the most evaluated and frequently used scale for Internet Addiction (Laconi et al., 2014). It is a 20-item self-report scale used for the Internet addiction assessment in adolescents and children aged 8 to 24 years. The pathological use of the web assessment, is based on criteria for substance dependence, including loss of control, neglecting everyday life, relationships and alternative recreation activities, behavioral and cognitive salience, negative consequences, escapism, and deception (Kuss et al., 2014). This measure is extremely widespread especially (not only) in Asian studies (Ha et al., 2006; Lam, Peng, Mai, & Jing, 2009; Cao, Sun, Wan, Hao, & Tao, 2011; Wang et al., 2011; Poli, & Agrimi, 2012; Ak, Koruklu, & Yılmaz, 2013; Lai et al., 2013; Watters, Keefer, Kloosterman, Summerfeldt, & Parker, 2013; Pontes, Patrao, & Griffiths, 2014; Lai et al., 2015). In Italy, Poli and Agrimi (2012) applied the IAT for their research aims, showing that only the 0,8% of the involved adolescents were considered to be seriously addicted, the lowest rate among those reported by other researches.

The *Pathological Internet Usage Scale (PIUS)* (Morahan-Martin, & Schumacher, 2000) is a 13-question scale developed to assess whether heavy Internet use negatively affects academic and other work, interpersonal relations, individual stress levels, social withdrawal, and mood alteration.

Substance Dependence Perspective

Within the second group/perspective, the *Chen's Internet Addiction Scale (CIAS)* (Chen, Weng, Su, Wu, & Yang, 2003) is a 26-item self-report instrument assessing the core Internet addiction symptoms, including: tolerance, compulsive use, withdrawal, and related problems in terms of negative impact on social activities, interpersonal relationships, physical condition, and time management (Kuss et al., 2014; Kuss, & Lopez-Fernandez, 2016). This instrument is extremely widespread in Asia and used in several, above all Chinese, studies including adolescent samples (Ko et al., 2006; Yen, Yen, Chen, Chen, & Ko, 2007; Ko, Yen, Yen, Chen, & Wang, 2008; Ko, Yen, Liu, Huang, & Yen, 2009; Yen, Ko, Yen, Chang, & Cheng, 2009; Ko et al., 2014; Mak et al., 2014; Yen, Chou, Liu, Yang, & Hu, 2014).

The *Internet-Related Addictive Behavior Inventory (IRABI)* (Brenner, 1997) has 32 true-false questions assessing users' Internet experiences. Further developments and refinements of this self-reported instrument for the identification of Internet addiction took place largely in Taiwan.

The *Internet Addiction Scale (IAS)* (Nichols, & Nicki, 2004), is a self-report 31-items instrument based on the 7 Diagnostic and Statistical Manual of Mental Disorders (4th ed.; American Psychiatric Association, 1994) substance dependence criteria and 2 additional criteria recommended by Griffiths (1998). The IAS has been tested on undergraduates, demonstrating that Family and Social Loneliness predicted IAS scores.

We could also include in this group the *Problematic Internet Use Questionnaire (PIUQ)* (Demetrovics, Szeredi, & Rózsa, 2008). The PIUQ was first published in 2006 and its psychometric properties were checked in a study by Kelley and Gruber (2010), confirming a three-factor model (obsession – neglect – control disorder). It's a 30-items scale based on the IAT and IAQ, used with adolescent, young adult and adult samples (Kelley, & Gruber, 2010; Koronczai et al., 2011). The age of participants in the original PIUQ study (Budapest, Hungary) ranged from 12 to 69. They were (approximately) for 50% students, and the mean age was 23 years, but it was a not gender-age-balanced sample. Moreover, discordant gender results are available: statistically significant sex differences were found in obsession and neglect by Demetrovics and colleagues (2008) but not by Kelly and Gruber (2010).

Several other self-report measures are widespread in academic literature.

In the middle of these two perspectives (*impulse control disorder and substance dependence*), the *Compulsive Internet Use Scale (CIUS)* (Meerkerk, Van Den Eijnden, Vermulst, & Garretsen, 2009) and the *Internet Related Problem Scale (IRPS)* (Armstrong et al., 2000) can be situated. The CIUS particularly and uniquely relates to the compulsive and impulsive element of the behavior. It is a 14-items self-report questionnaire based on the DSM-IV-TR diagnoses for substance dependence and pathological gambling. It has been utilized within adolescents in several European studies and to measure various types of internet addicted behaviors (Cartierre, Coulon, & Demerval, 2011; Khazaal et al., 2011; Sayed, Jannatifard, Eslami, & Rezapour, 2011; Guertler et al., 2013; Guertler et al., 2014; Wartberg, Petersen, Kammerl, Rosenkranz, & Thomasius, 2014; Dhir, Chen, & Nieminen, 2015). The IRPS (Armstrong et al., 2000) based on the Internet Related Addictive Behavior Inventory (IRABI) (Brenner, 1997), is an instrument to measure Internet-related problems, overcoming a strict definition of addiction. It is a 20-item scale assessing 8 factors: tolerance, escape from problems, loss of control, reduced activities, withdrawal, cravings, introversion, negative effects, that has been used with young adults (Boies, Cooper, & Osborne, 2004) and adults samples (Widyanto, Griffiths, Brunsden, & McMurran, 2008; Widyanto, Griffiths, & Brunsden, 2011).

The mentioned measures, belonging to these two perspective, are here expanded from the Tokunaga & Rains (2016) classification. As seen, these two groups use similar diagnostic criteria for the definition of PIU, sharing the inclusion of tolerance, withdrawal and negative outcomes dimensions. Differently, the third group/perspective (*relational resource deficits*) conceptualized PIU as a continuous variable, supporting the time spent online and the interpersonal efficacy online as core components of PIU (Tokunaga, & Rains, 2016):

Relational Resource Deficits Perspective

The *Online Cognition Scale* (*OCS*) (Davis et al., 2002) has been attributed to the this last group. The OCS scale reveals a four-dimensions model (diminished impulse control – loneliness/depression – comfort – distraction); it has been more used within college students and adult samples originally oriented to screen employers' cyberslacking (Ozcan, & Buzlu, 2005; Zec, 2005; Jun, 2007; Jia, & Jia, 2009).

The *Problematic Internet Usage Scale* (Ceyhan et al., 2007) is a 33-item "vertical scale" validate on University students. It shows a continuum from normal to pathologic Internet use, assuming the intensity of the Internet use as a central aspect. Thus, high scores from the scale indicate that individual's the Internet usage become unhealthy, it may affect their lives negatively and it may create tendency for the internet addiction. However, the scale must not be evaluated as a measure of problematic internet use to diagnose "the internet addiction" in individuals, and does not provide a specific cut-off.

Finally, basing on the cognitive-behavioral model (Davis, 2001; Caplan, 2010), proposed a new integrated model of Problematic Internet Use, that includes four core components: preference for online social interactions (POSI), mood regulation, deficient self-regulation, and negative outcomes. The first version of *Generalized Problematic Internet Use Scale* (*GPIUS*) (Caplan, 2002), a 29-item self-report questionnaire, was especially used in studies with young adults samples (Alavi, Jannatifard, Maracy, & Rezapour, 2009; Li, Wang, & Wang, 2009; Ang, Chong, Chye, & Huan, 2012).

The *Generalized Problematic Internet Use Scale 2* (*GPIUS2*) (Caplan, 2010) is a revised and updated version of the GPIUS, a 15-item self-report questionnaire largely used in studies including adolescents samples (Gámez-Guadix, Villa-George, & Calvete, 2012; Fioravanti, Primi, & Casale, 2013; Gámez-Guadix, Orue, & Calvete, 2013). As noted by Casale and colleagues (2016), this cognitive-behavioral model conceptualizes the Problematic Internet Use not as a behavioral addiction, but as a multidimensional syndrome consisting of cognitive, emotional, *and* behavioral symptoms that lead to difficulties in managing the offline life; moreover, it allows to account for what people are doing online. In comparison to the IAT (Young, 1998b), this instrument is specifically focused on problematic use that arises due to the unique communicative context of the internet (Casale et al., 2016). A recent Italian study proposed by Fioravanti and colleagues (2013) used this adaption of the GPIUS, involving a small and not gender-balanced sample, and including both adolescents and young adults, thus lacking a specific focus on preadolescents and adolescents. Moreover, it does not provide a specific cut-off.

Additionally, among these measures, the *Problematic Internet Use Scale for adolescents* (*PIUS-a*), (Rial Boubeta, Gomez Salgado, Isorna Folgar, Araujo Gallego, & Varela Mallou, 2015) and the *Cuestionario Experiencia Relation Internet* (*CERI*) (Beranuy, Oberst, Carbonell, & Chamarro, 2009) could be included. The PIUS-a is an 11-items scale specifically addressed to adolescents. It was developed on a sample of 1709 secondary-school students from Galicia (a region in northern Spain), aged 11 to 17.

The scale has satisfactory psychometric properties and, in the authors view, its use enables the gradation of adolescents on a risk or problematic Internet use continuum. However, they did not analyze data considering a balanced gender sample. The CERI is a 10-item questionnaire, assessing interpersonal and intrapersonal conflicts, which do not provide cut-off points.

Predictors of Problematic Internet Use: The Role of Gender and Age

For what concern gendered use and misuse of Internet, there are certainly differences in Web access and usage. Males use the Internet more for information searching and entertainment, whereas females use it more for communication purposes (Weiser, 2000; Jackson, Ervin, Gardner, & Schmitt, 2001). Female students tend to use the Internet primarily for interpersonal communication, while male students used the World Wide Web for entertainment and leisure activities (e.g., game websites, other specialist websites, and downloading material) (Joiner et al., 2005).

To provide a deeper comprehension of internet-related problems, the gender variable has been often analyzed, even though with controversial results.

Morahan-Martin and Schumacker (2000) reported that males were more likely than females to be pathological users (12% vs. 3%), whereas females were more likely than males to have no symptoms (28% vs. 26%) or have limited symptoms (69% vs. 61%) of behavioral pathology. Males are more likely to overindulge on the Internet than females (Ha, & Hwang, 2014)(Li et al., 2014), but the notion that males, or at least male college students, are more subject to Internet addiction shows different results. Some Asian studies reported that the negative effects of a problematic relationship with Internet are more severe in females than in males (Ko et al., 2014), e.g. attention deficit (Yen et al., 2009) or negative effects on depression (Liang et al., 2016). On the other hand, Ko, Yen, Chen, Chen, & Yen (2005) found that a problematic relationship with Internet was associated with lower self-esteem in males but not in females, and Li and collaborators (2010) reported that males scored lower in protective factors of problematic Internet use but higher in risk factors compared with females.

In a European cross-cultural study, Durkee (2012) provided evidence that girls with emotional difficulties had much higher risks of Internet addiction than did boys with similar problems. On the contrary, Kormas and colleagues (2011) on a sample of Greek adolescents (mean age: 14.7 years) provided evidence that males have more maladaptive (67.4%) or problematic internet use (84.6%) behaviors than females (maladaptive 32.6%; problematic 15.4%).

Thus, although different studies investigated the association between Internet problematic use and gender, their results are not conclusive and further studies appear necessary, especially in Italy where the gender variable was not deeply analyzed in samples of adolescents.

Furthermore, to the authors' knowledge, previous studies have lacked in examining potential differences in problematic Internet use depending on various moments of adolescence, in terms of clear differences between preadolescents, younger and older adolescents. Only Okwaraji and colleagues (2015) provided interesting suggestions in this direction by revealing that Nigerian older adolescents (16-19 years) appear more Internet-addicted than the younger (13-15 years).

SOLUTIONS AND RECOMMENDATIONS

Aims

Despite the clinical importance of evaluating risk during adolescence, knowledge about problematic relationships with the Internet among teens is not yet enough. Several instruments have been developed, even properly validated, but most refer to an addiction-model, based on a psychopathological perspective instead of a preventing approach related to the specificity of adolescence as a stage of life not likely to be categorized, during which, in the author's view, addiction is not something properly definable.

Moreover, there is little available information regarding validated measures of the construct of "problematic relationship with the Internet" in a sample of adolescents, especially in Italy, where adolescents' addiction has been barely explored and the lack of consensual definition led to inconsistencies in the assessment criteria. Particularly, little is known empirically about the validity of a possible clear cut-off threshold for problematic relationships with the Internet, while recently published studies provided interesting and yet conflicting results about the role of gender and age in the quality of the relationships teens have with this medium.

The focus in the current study is to validate a reliable instrument to identify maladaptive relationships with the Internet among preadolescents/adolescents, evaluating both behavioral and emotional conflicts.

The study aimed to:

- Evaluate the psychometric properties of a promising risk measure;
- Establish a cut-off threshold for defining "problematic" the relation teens have with the Internet;
- Estimate the prevalence of potential problematic users and define the profile of the typical problematic user;
- Verify the role of gender and age in influencing the quality of the relationship with Internet.

Participants

1220 participants aged 11-19 years (M = 14.14; SD = 2.519), were recruited in 12 secondary schools (I and II grade) from culturally different areas of Naples, equally distributed for gender (53.9% males and 46.1% females). All participants were Caucasian from Italian families. They all participated voluntary in the research and were informed about the confidentiality of the data and their anonymous treatment.

Measures

Data were collected via a self-report anonymous questionnaire administered to participants in groups during the school-time. It comprised four sections: (a) sociodemographics, (b) mobile phone/social networks/apps usage patterns, (c) the Cuestionario de Experiencias Relacionadas con el Móvil (CERM) (Beranuy et al., 2009) and (d) the Internet-Related Problems Scale (IRPS) (Armstrong et al., 2000; Boies et al., 2004) both adapted into Italian.

1. The recorded socio demographics were: gender; age (categorizing pupils into preadolescents 11–13 years: 47%, young adolescents 14-16 years: 24.3% and older adolescents 17–19 years: 28.7%); their school year and the school location (Town borough).

2. Under the section about mobile phone/social networks/apps usage patterns, participants were asked to indicate (1) if they have a smartphone; (2) why they use smartphones (to make phone calls, to message, to exchange photos/videos, to surf the Internet); (3) which social networks and apps they use to exchange messages and photos/videos.

3. CERM was developed to assess intra- and interpersonal conflicts related to the mobile use and to maladaptive emotional and communicational patterns, i.e. it refers both to behavioral and emotional aspects related to this phenomenon. Being consistent with a not-addiction perspective (Sánchez-Carbonell, Beranuy, Castellana, Chamarro y Oberst, 2008), here shared, it represents a useful tool to measure problematic relationships with the mobile. Here it has been used a 13–items revised version of this scale (Authors, in press), obtained by adding to the 10-items of the original version, 3 items directly linked to the trespassing of mobile use over other social activities, underestimated in the original version. All items were specifically referred to the use of smartphone (instead of generic mobile) and were scored on a 5-point Likert scale from 1 (never) to 5 (always), responding to the question "how often this happened to you?".

4. In IRPS, participants were asked to use a 5-point Likert scale to indicate "how much do you agree with the following statements about your relationship with Internet?"; statements refer to thoughts, feelings and experiences reflecting problematic emotional and behavioral aspects. To this study aims, the 11-items IRPS version, provided by Boies and colleagues (2004) in Canada, was here adopted. The scale, which showed a good internal consistency ($\alpha = .87$) was developed to overcome some shortcuts of Armstrong's original version and to reinforce a non-addiction perspective on this issue. Indeed, as Boies and colleagues (2004) noted, Armstrong and colleagues (2000), by correlating IRPS with the MMPI-2 Addiction Potential Scale, reintroduced the idea of dependency. This perspective risked to ignore the good properties of the Internet use for young adults, also evidenced by literature in terms of psychosocial well-being, such as: positive effects on depression, loneliness, social support and self-esteem (Shaw, & Gant, 2002). Thus, a variation of IRPS was introduced (Boies et al., 2004) and validated on 1100 young adults (older than 19 years). It assesses 7 of the original factors (tolerance, escape from problems, loss of control, reduced activities, withdrawal, cravings and negative effects), whilst excluding loss of control and introversion as components of the problematic use of the Internet. Even if the aim of discussing the dependance reintroduced by Armstrong was surely appreciable, neverthless no clear discussion and explanation of how this perspective can be applied to the measure is provided by the authors. For example, no cut off criteria has been established in relation to the scale, in order to use it for screening purpose about the problematicity with the Internet.

Analysis

First, the factorial properties and semantic structure of IRPS were explored by means of EFA in Mplus 6.11 (Muthén, & Muthén, 2010). Due to the non-normal distribution of the sample, we employed Robust Maximum Likehood with oblique Geomin rotation.

Factorial solutions were identified according to the criteria of minimal factorial saturation (at least 0.30), residuals analysis and avoiding high cross-loadings (Fabrigar, Wegener, MacCallum, & Strahan,

1999). The factorial solution is supported by scree-plot analysis, Bartlett's test of sphericity and KMO measure of sampling adequacy.

In order to verify the emerged structure solution and test dimensionality of our version of IRPS, a Confirmatory Factor Analysis (CFA) was used with Robust Maximum Likehood. The overall model fit was evaluated by CFI, RMSEA (90% CI), TLI and SRMR. To further verify the construct validity, we conducted a 2nd order CFA highlighting the existence of a single implicit psychological construct.

Internal reliability was calculated through Cronbach's α, item-total correlations and factor correlations also evaluating the internal coherence of each factor. Convergent validity was assessed by bivariate correlations between IRPS and CERM; it has been also applied a tentative statistical establishment of a cut-off score, by referring to the criteria used in the literature on problematic mobile phone use (Lopez-Fernandez, Honrubia-Serrano, Freixa-Blanxart, & Gibson, 2014): the 15th, 80th, and 90th percentiles are used to classify occasional, habitual, at risk, and problematic use respectively.

Then, an equivalent subsample of non-problematic users was randomly extracted to compare them with the group of problematic users and obtain the profile of a typical problematic user, by means of descriptive analysis and ANOVA; one-way ANOVAs (F; p < .001) were finally used to evaluate the role of gender and age.

Results

EFA yielded all factor loadings greater than 0.3, but one item, which was consequently eliminated. Based on theoretical considerations, a two-factor solution of the 10 remaining items was tested with CFA. The model provided a good fit to the data ($\chi2 = 884.448$ df = 45 p .0000; CFI = 0.970; TLI = 0.961; RMSEA = 0.035 [0.019–0.049]; Probability RMSEA <=.05: 0.957, SRMR=0.032).

Partially in line with literature (Caplan, 2010), the emerged structure (tab. 1) shows that the conflictual relation with the Internet is made up of behavior-related aspects and emotion-related ones:

- **Factor1 – Self and Mood Regulation:** emotional components of the problematic use of the Internet, used to regulate mood and moderate the exchange between the inner world and the outside one, also including difficulties in self-regulation with the device;
- **Factor2 – Negative Outcomes:** effects of Internet use on daily conducts (problematic aspects as resulting in behaviors), e.g. sleep, school performance, and friends/family perceptions of the ordinary use of Internet by the respondent.

Comparing these results to the previous version of the scale provided by Boies and colleagues, the second factor here obtained includes items originally referring to the use of Internet as a way to escape from problems, whilst the first factor gathers items related to the other dimensions identified by the authors. These results has been interpreted as follows: the first factor highlights a transversal component of the Internet usage that refers to an emotional interchange, whilst the second one is more specifically dealing with the negative consequences of this use. These different factorial structures are probably due to cultural differences between the Italian and Canadian culture, as well as to the age difference between this Italian sample and that one used by Boies and colleagues (2004). Indeed, here participants were younger and, then, probably more involved in preoccupation about the self and mood, where all the various other components converge. Self and mood appear to be the key preoccupations of this period of life.

Figure 1. Full model

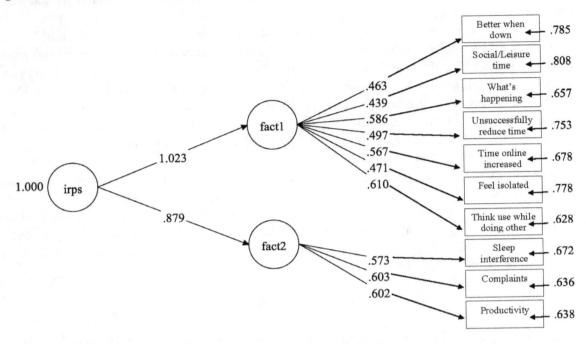

Cronbach's alphas indicated an excellent reliability of the scale (.809) and a good internal consistency for the subscales (F1: .753; F2: .646). The solution also showed high inter-item correlations (ranging from .205 to .427). Correlations between IRPS subscales were large (r =.601; .822; .949 p<.001). Moreover, bivariate correlations indicated that IRPS and CERM assess interrelated, yet distinct, constructs, confirming the convergent validity of the instrument (r =.740 p< .001). (tab. 2)

Our Italian sample showed a widespread use of the Internet: 97.8% participants have a smartphone, used to surf the Internet (87.2%), with special reference to Facebook for exchanging messages (68.6%) or photos (64.9%). A mean of 2.31 for IRPS scores was registered among participants (Mdn=2.20; SD=.777), with slightly higher scores on F1 than F2 (F1: M=2.33; SD=.790; F2: M= 2.24; SD=1.02). Participants mainly use Internet to:

- Talk to others when they feel isolated (M=2.85; SD=1.394)
- Make themselves feel better when they were down (M=2.64; SD=.288).

The time they spent on-line has increased during the last 12 months (M=2.71; SD=1.397) and they receive complaints about their use of Internet (M=2.33; SD=.790).

Following Lopez-Fernandez's (2014) procedure, the score of 34 was identified as a cut-off threshold for defining a problematic preadolescent/adolescent user. Particularly, the categories of occasional, habitual, at risk and problematic user correspond to scores of 0-15, 15-30, 30-34 and more than 34 respectively. The analysis revealed that 14.2% of participants were occasional users, 64.3% habitual users, 11.5% were at risk of problematic use and 10% problematic users. Findings are quite worrying if we sum at risk and problematic users, thus obtaining a 21.5% of participants showing potential excessive Internet use.

Then, an equivalent subsample of 122 non-problematic users was randomly extracted in order to compare them with problematic users. Considering the use of smartphones, apps and social networks, a clear profile of the Internet problematic user was not observed: problematic users do not differ in the *way* they use social media tools but in the *quality* of the relationship they establish with the Internet. The most problematic aspects of the relationship with Internet are the same in the two groups, but the problematic users show a specific tendency to think about going on-line while doing other things, also showing greater negative outcomes (F2), with average scores higher on all items. (tab. 3)

In order to define a potential profile of the typical problematic user, the collected socio-demographics were considered: problematic users are mostly preadolescents (50%) and female (59.8%), having a smartphone in almost all cases (97.5%). This indicate that the analysis of the relationship with the Internet in preadolescents/adolescents is strictly connected with their use of smartphone.

Our findings suggested a relevant role played by gender and age; thus, it was deeply analyzed it by ANOVAs. In this sample, the prevalence of problematic Internet use is 7.5% among boys, and 13% among girls. The mean IRPS score was 2.36 (SD=.805) for girls and 2.27 (SD=.751) for boys. Relevant gender differences were found on some items, revealing a major condition of risk among girls: they receive more complaints from others due to time spent online and they think at surfing the Internet more than boys do. A peculiar difference was also registered: girls use Internet to reinforce their offline-relationships whilst boys use Internet to substitute their relationships (tab. 4), while differences based on age, among the three groups (preadolescents, young adolescents and old adolescents) seem more relevant than those due to gender. Findings show that the younger is the participant, the more problematic is his/her relationship with Internet. Particularly, older adolescents have the lowest scores on all items; young adolescents reveal greater difficulties on behavioral aspects and their negative outcomes (F2) while preadolescents show specific difficulties on F1 (tab. 5). The latter result seems to confirm what above mentioned, i.e. the importance of regulating self and mood in the moment when the first psychic movements of adolescents occur, while, growing up, a more realistic attitude towards reality emerges, by showing greater preoccupations with the negative outcomes and greater difficulties on the relation with the outside.

FUTURE RESEARCH DIRECTIONS

This study has some limitations to be considered when interpreting the reported findings:

- Participants were recruited using a non-probability sampling technique, which potentially limits the external validity of the finding. However, to the best of the authors' knowledge, there are no data available on this issue in this context;
- Data were entirely collected using self-report questionnaires, which may producing potential biases (e.g., social desirability biases) but at the same time provide several advantages, such as: interpretability, richness of information, motivation to report and sheer practicality (Paulhus & Vazire, 2007);
- This is a situate study, i.e. locally based: in the future it would be interesting to compare different Italian regions to verify the existence of differences between North and South Italy, considering that Italy is a country with strong territorial differences. Cross-cultural research should also be conducted in the future.

Besides these potential limitations, the present study has some key strengths. It provides a short and psychometrically valid measure to assess the problematic relationship with internet, and given the strong psychometrics of the instrument, researchers are encouraged to consider using this tool to assess the quality of the relationship with the Internet within samples of preadolescents/adolescents. Thus, future research on this specific topic are suggested.

CONCLUSION

Focusing on the widespread Internet use and on the essential utility of the web nowadays, this study contributed to ongoing debate regards the usefulness of defining generally "addiction" the Internet misuse, especially among adolescents, who largely use technologies in a stage of life commonly predisposed to risks. Moreover, taking in account the need of clarifications of measures and related perspectives on the phenomenon, a contribution to this organization has been proposed and here expanded. Moving from this debate, this study presented the validation of a psychometric tool to assess problematic relationships with the Internet among Italian preadolescents/adolescents that overcomes the shortcomings of extant instruments. Considering that a clear profile of the "addicted" adolescent was not identified. To the best of the authors' knowledge, this is the first study to provide empirical information about the measurement of a cut-off threshold for preadolescents/adolescents.

The proposed two-factors model fitted the data adequately, highlighting self/mood regulation and negative outcomes as dimensions of *Internet Related Problems*. Thus these results, together with good sensitivity and reliability, could indicate the utility of the scale to measure whether a preadolescent/adolescent could develop a Problematic Relationship with Internet.

According to the prior classification of three perspectives/groups in the conceptualization and operationalization of PIU (Tokunaga, & Rains, 2016), this revised version of the IRPS seems to belong above all to the third one (*relational resource deficits*), even though considering central aspects of the first two groups. Indeed, this new model of Internet Related Problems proposes a more comprehensive framework, taking in account the importance of cognitive, emotional and behavioral symptoms, which converge into the ample dimensions of self and mood regulation or negative outcomes. What is here defined probably represent a more complete operationalization of the Internet misuse. In this perspective, the problematic relation with Internet defines a continuous (not dichotomous) measure which can identify lower, medium or higher level of risky net use.

The estimated prevalence of preadolescents/adolescents classified as problematic users, by using this criterion, was 10%, which is within the range of previous European studies.

Furthermore, this study indicated a greater risk of developing problematic relationships for the youngest and for girls, thus suggesting the need for early interventions differentiated by gender and age. Such differences seem to highlight a peculiarity of our context, being partially supported and partially contradicted by previous studies (Pezoa-Jares, Espinoza-Luna, & Vasquez-Medina, 2012; Laconi et al., 2014; Pontes et al., 2015).

REFERENCES

Ak, Ş., Koruklu, N., & Yılmaz, Y. (2013). A study on Turkish adolescent's Internet use: Possible predictors of Internet addiction. *Cyberpsychology, Behavior, and Social Networking*, *16*(3), 205–209. doi:10.1089/cyber.2012.0255 PMID:23253206

Alavi, S. S., Ferdosi, M., Jannatifard, F., Eslami, M., Alaghemandan, H., & Setare, M. (2012). Behavioral addiction versus substance addiction: Correspondence of psychiatric and psychological views. *International Journal of Preventive Medicine*, *3*(4), 290–294. PMID:22624087

Alavi, S. S., Jannatifard, F., Maracy, M., & Rezapour, H. (2009). The Psychometric properties Generalized pathological internet use Scale (GPIUS) in Internet users students of Isfahan Universities. *Journal of Knowledge & Research in Applied Psychology*, *0*(40), 38–51.

Anderson, E.L., Steen, E., & Stavropoulos, V. (2016). Internet use and Problematic Internet Use: a systematic review of longitudinal research trends in adolescence and emergent adulthood. *International Journal of Adolescence and Youth*, *3843*, 1-25.

Ang, R. P., Chong, W. H., Chye, S., & Huan, V. S. (2012). Loneliness and generalized problematic Internet use: Parents' perceived knowledge of adolescents' online activities as a moderator. *Computers in Human Behavior*, *28*(4), 1342–1347. doi:10.1016/j.chb.2012.02.019

Armstrong, L., Phillips, J. G., & Saling, L. L. (2000). Potential determinants of heavier Internet usage. *International Journal of Human-Computer Studies*, *53*(4), 537–550. doi:10.1006/ijhc.2000.0400

Beard, K. W. (2005). Internet addiction: A review of current assessment techniques and potential assessment questions. *Cyberpsychology & Behavior*, *8*(1), 7–14. doi:10.1089/cpb.2005.8.7 PMID:15738688

Beranuy, M., Oberst, U., Carbonell, X., & Chamarro, A. (2009). Problematic Internet and mobile phone use and clinical symptoms in college students: The role of emotional intelligence. *Computers in Human Behavior*, *25*(5), 1182–1187. doi:10.1016/j.chb.2009.03.001

Bianchi, A., & Phillips, J. G. (2005). Psychological predictors of problem mobile phone use. *Cyberpsychology & Behavior*, *8*(1), 39–51. doi:10.1089/cpb.2005.8.39 PMID:15738692

Billieux, J., Schimmenti, A., Khazaal, Y., Maurage, P., & Heeren, A. (2015). Are we overpathologizing everyday life? A tenable blueprint for behavioral addiction research. *Journal of Behavioral Addictions*, *4*(3), 119–123. doi:10.1556/2006.4.2015.009 PMID:26014667

Boies, S. C., Cooper, A., & Osborne, C. S. (2004). Variations in Internet-related problems and psychosocial functioning in online sexual activities: Implications for social and sexual development of young adults. *Cyberpsychology & Behavior*, *7*(2), 207–230. doi:10.1089/109493104323024474 PMID:15140364

Brenner, V. (1997). Psychology of computer use: XLVII. Parameters of Internet use, abuse and addiction: the first 90 days of the Internet Usage Survey. *Psychological Reports*, *80*(3), 879–882. doi:10.2466/pr0.1997.80.3.879 PMID:9198388

Byun, S., Ruffini, C., Mills, J. E., Douglas, A. C., Niang, M., Stepchenkova, S., & Blanton, M. et al. (2009). Internet addiction: Metasynthesis of 1996–2006 quantitative research. *Cyberpsychology & Behavior*, *12*(2), 203–207. doi:10.1089/cpb.2008.0102 PMID:19072075

Cao, H., Sun, Y., Wan, Y., Hao, J., & Tao, F. (2011). Problematic Internet use in Chinese adolescents and its relation to psychosomatic symptoms and life satisfaction. *BMC Public Health*, *11*(1), 802. doi:10.1186/1471-2458-11-802 PMID:21995654

Caplan, S. E. (2002). Problematic Internet use and psychosocial well-being: Development of a theory-based cognitive–behavioral measurement instrument. *Computers in Human Behavior*, *18*(5), 553–575. doi:10.1016/S0747-5632(02)00004-3

Caplan, S. E. (2003). Preference for online social interaction: A theory of problematic Internet use and psychosocial well-being. *Communication Research*, *30*(6), 625–648. doi:10.1177/0093650203257842

Caplan, S. E. (2010). Theory and measurement of generalized problematic Internet use: A two-step approach. *Computers in Human Behavior*, *26*(5), 1089–1097. doi:10.1016/j.chb.2010.03.012

Cartierre, N., Coulon, N., & Demerval, R. (2011). Validation d'une version courte en langue française pour adolescents de la Compulsive Internet Use Scale. *Neuropsychiatrie de l'Enfance et de l'Adolescence*, *59*(7), 415–419. doi:10.1016/j.neurenf.2011.06.003

Casale, S., Primi, C., & Fioravanti, G. (2016). Generalized Problematic Internet Use Scale 2: update on the psychometric properties among Italian young adults. In G. Riva, B. K. Wiederhold, & P. Cipresso (Eds.), *The Psychology of Social Networking: Identity and Relationships in Online Communities* (Vol. 2, pp. 202–2014). Berlin, Germany: De Gruyter.

Ceyhan, E., Ceyhan, A., & Gürcan, A. (2007). Problemli internet kullanımı ölçeği'nin geçerlik ve güvenirlik çalışmaları. *Kuram ve Uygulamada Eğitim Bilimleri Dergisi*, *7*(1), 387–416.

Chen, S., & Chou, C. (1999). *Development of Chinese Internet addiction scale in Taiwan*. Poster presented at the 107th american psychology annual convention, Boston, MA.

Chen, S., Weng, L., Su, Y., Wu, H., & Yang, P. (2003). Development of a Chinese Internet addiction scale and its psychometric study. *Chinese Journal of Psychology*, *45*(3), 279–294.

Chou, C., & Hsiao, M.-C. (2000). Internet addiction, usage, gratification, and pleasure experience: The Taiwan college students' case. *Computers & Education*, *35*(1), 65–80. doi:10.1016/S0360-1315(00)00019-1

Davis, R. A. (2001). A cognitive-behavioral model of pathological Internet use. *Computers in Human Behavior*, *17*(2), 187–195. doi:10.1016/S0747-5632(00)00041-8

Davis, R. A., Flett, G. L., & Besser, A. (2002). Validation of a new scale for measuring problematic Internet use: Implications for pre-employment screening. *Cyberpsychology & Behavior*, *5*(4), 331–345. doi:10.1089/109493102760275581 PMID:12216698

De Timary, P., & Philippot, P. (2015). Commentary on: Are we overpathologizing everyday life? A tenable blueprint for behavioral addiction research: Can the emerging domain of behavioral addictions bring a new reflection for the field of addictions, by stressing the issue of the context of addiction development? *Journal of Behavioral Addictions*, *4*(3), 148–150. doi:10.1556/2006.4.2015.024 PMID:26551903

Demetrovics, Z., Szeredi, B., & Rózsa, S. (2008). The three-factor model of Internet addiction: The development of the Problematic Internet Use Questionnaire. *Behavior Research Methods*, *40*(2), 563–574. doi:10.3758/BRM.40.2.563 PMID:18522068

Dhir, A., Chen, S., & Nieminen, M. (2015). A repeat cross-sectional analysis of the psychometric properties of the Compulsive Internet Use Scale (CIUS) with adolescents from public and private schools. *Computers & Education*, *86*(1), 172–181. doi:10.1016/j.compedu.2015.03.011

Douglas, A. C., Mills, J. E., Niang, M., Stepchenkova, S., Byun, S., Ruffini, C., & Atallah, M. et al. (2008). Internet addiction: Meta-synthesis of qualitative research for the decade 1996–2006. *Computers in Human Behavior*, *24*(6), 3027–3044. doi:10.1016/j.chb.2008.05.009

Durkee, T., Kaess, M., Carli, V., Parzer, P., Wasserman, C., Floderus, B., & Wasserman, D. et al. (2012). Prevalence of pathological internet use among adolescents in Europe: Demographic and social factors. *Addiction (Abingdon, England)*, *107*(12), 2210–2222. doi:10.1111/j.1360-0443.2012.03946.x PMID:22621402

Fabrigar, L. R., Wegener, D. T., MacCallum, R. C., & Strahan, E. J. (1999). Evaluating the use of exploratory factor analysis in psychological research. *Psychological Methods*, *4*(3), 272–299. doi:10.1037/1082-989X.4.3.272

Ferraro, G., Caci, B., D'amico, A., & Blasi, M. D. (2006). Internet addiction disorder: An Italian study. *Cyberpsychology & Behavior*, *10*(2), 170–175. doi:10.1089/cpb.2006.9972 PMID:17474832

Fioravanti, G., Dèttore, D., & Casale, S. (2012). Adolescent Internet addiction: Testing the association between self-esteem, the perception of Internet attributes, and preference for online social interactions. *Cyberpsychology, Behavior, and Social Networking*, *15*(6), 318–323. doi:10.1089/cyber.2011.0358 PMID:22703038

Fioravanti, G., Primi, C., & Casale, S. (2013). Psychometric evaluation of the generalized problematic internet use scale 2 in an Italian sample. *Cyberpsychology, Behavior, and Social Networking*, *16*(10), 761–766. doi:10.1089/cyber.2012.0429 PMID:23742149

Fisoun, V., Floros, G., Geroukalis, D., Ioannidi, N., Farkonas, N., Sergentani, E., & Siomos, K. et al. (2012a). Internet addiction in the island of Hippocrates: The associations between internet abuse and adolescent off-line behaviours. *Child and Adolescent Mental Health*, *17*(1), 37–44. doi:10.1111/j.1475-3588.2011.00605.x

Fisoun, V., Floros, G., Siomos, K., Geroukalis, D., & Navridis, K. (2012b). Internet addiction as an important predictor in early detection of adolescent drug use experience—implications for research and practice. *Journal of Addiction Medicine*, *6*(1), 77–84. doi:10.1097/ADM.0b013e318233d637 PMID:22227578

Gámez-Guadix, M., Orue, I., & Calvete, E. (2013). Evaluation of the cognitive-behavioral model of generalized and problematic Internet use in Spanish adolescents. *Psicothema*, *25*(3), 299–306. PMID:23910742

Gámez-Guadix, M., Villa-George, F. I., & Calvete, E. (2012). Measurement and analysis of the cognitive-behavioral model of generalized problematic Internet use among Mexican adolescents. *Journal of Adolescence*, *35*(6), 1581–1591. doi:10.1016/j.adolescence.2012.06.005 PMID:22789467

Goldberg, I. (1995). *Internet addiction disorder: Diagnostic criteria.* Retrieved March 17, 2017, from http:// http://users.rider.edu/~suler/psycyber/supportgp.html

Griffiths, M. (1998). Internet addiction: Does it really exist? In J. Gackenbach (Ed.), *Psychology and the Internet: Intrapersonal, interpersonal and transpersonal implications* (pp. 61–75). New York: Academic Press.

Griffiths, M. (1999). Internet addiction: Internet fuels other addictions. *Student BMJ, 7*(1), 428–429.

Griffiths, M. (2000). Internet addiction-time to be taken seriously? *Addiction Research, 8*(5), 413–418. doi:10.3109/16066350009005587

Griffiths, M. (2005). A 'components' model of addiction within a biopsychosocial framework. *Journal of Substance Use, 10*(4), 191–197. doi:10.1080/14659890500114359

Griffiths, M. D., Pontes, H. M., & Kuss, D. J. (2016). Online Addictions: Conceptualizations, Debates, and Controversies. *Addicta: the Turkish Journal on Addictions, 3*(2), 1–14.

Griffiths, M. D., & Szabo, A. (2013). Is excessive online usage a function of medium or activity? An empirical pilot study. *Journal of Behavioral Addictions, 3*(1), 74–77. doi:10.1556/JBA.2.2013.016 PMID:25215216

Guertler, D., Broda, A., Bischof, A., Kastirke, N., Meerkerk, G. J., John, U., & Rumpf, H. J. et al. (2014). Factor structure of the Compulsive Internet Use scale. *Cyberpsychology, Behavior, and Social Networking, 17*(1), 46–51. doi:10.1089/cyber.2013.0076 PMID:23962124

Guertler, D., Rumpf, H.-J., Bischof, A., Kastirke, N., Petersen, K. U., John, U., & Meyer, C. (2013). Assessment of problematic internet use by the compulsive internet use scale and the internet addiction test: A sample of problematic and pathological gamblers. *European Addiction Research, 20*(2), 75–81. doi:10.1159/000355076 PMID:24080838

Guo, J., Chen, L., Wang, X., Liu, Y., Chui, C. H. K., He, H., & Tian, D. et al. (2012). The relationship between Internet addiction and depression among migrant children and left-behind children in China. *Cyberpsychology, Behavior, and Social Networking, 15*(11), 585–590. doi:10.1089/cyber.2012.0261 PMID:23002986

Ha, J. H., Kim, S. Y., Bae, S. C., Bae, S., Kim, H., Sim, M., & Cho, S. C. et al. (2007). Depression and Internet addiction in adolescents. *Psychopathology, 40*(6), 424–430. doi:10.1159/000107426 PMID:17709972

Ha, J. H., Yoo, H. J., Cho, I. H., Chin, B., Shin, D., & Kim, J. H. (2006). Psychiatric comorbidity assessed in Korean children and adolescents who screen positive for Internet addiction. *The Journal of Clinical Psychiatry, 67*(5), 821–826. doi:10.4088/JCP.v67n0517 PMID:16841632

Ha, Y.-M., & Hwang, W. J. (2014). Gender differences in internet addiction associated with psychological health indicators among adolescents using a national web-based survey. *International Journal of Mental Health and Addiction, 12*(5), 660–669. doi:10.1007/s11469-014-9500-7

Holden, C. (2001). 'Behavioral'addictions: Do they exist? *Science, 294*(5544), 980–982. doi:10.1126/science.294.5544.980 PMID:11691967

Jackson, L. A., Ervin, K. S., Gardner, P. D., & Schmitt, N. (2001). Gender and the Internet: Women communicating and men searching. *Sex Roles, 44*(5-6), 363–379. doi:10.1023/A:1010937901821

Jia, R., & Jia, H. H. (2009). Factorial validity of problematic Internet use scales. *Computers in Human Behavior, 25*(6), 1335–1342. doi:10.1016/j.chb.2009.06.004

Johansson, A., & Götestam, K. G. (2004). Internet addiction: Characteristics of a questionnaire and prevalence in Norwegian youth (12–18 years). *Scandinavian Journal of Psychology, 45*(3), 223–229. doi:10.1111/j.1467-9450.2004.00398.x PMID:15182240

Johnston, L. D., O'Malley, P. M., Bachman, J. G., & Schulenberg, J. E. (2005). Monitoring the Future: National Survey Results on Drug Use, 1975-2004: Volume II. College Students & Adults Ages 19-45, 2004. Bethesda, MD: National Institutes of Health.

Joiner, R., Gavin, J., Duffield, J., Brosnan, M., Crook, C., Durndell, A., & Lovatt, P. et al. (2005). Gender, Internet identification, and Internet anxiety: Correlates of Internet use. *Cyberpsychology & Behavior, 8*(4), 371–378. doi:10.1089/cpb.2005.8.371 PMID:16092894

Jun, S., & Yang, F. (2007). The Usage of Online Cognitive Scale in 538 Medical Undergraduates. *Chinese Mental Health Journal, 8*, 526–528.

Kandell, J. J. (1998). Internet addiction on campus: The vulnerability of college students. *Cyberpsychology & Behavior, 1*(1), 11–17. doi:10.1089/cpb.1998.1.11

Kardefelt-Winther, D. (2014). A conceptual and methodological critique of internet addiction research: Towards a model of compensatory internet use. *Computers in Human Behavior, 31*, 351–354. doi:10.1016/j.chb.2013.10.059

Kelley, K. J., & Gruber, E. M. (2010). Psychometric properties of the problematic internet use questionnaire. *Computers in Human Behavior, 26*(6), 1838–1845. doi:10.1016/j.chb.2010.07.018

Khazaal, Y., Chatton, A., Atwi, K., Zullino, D., Khan, R., & Billieux, J. (2011). Arabic validation of the compulsive Internet use scale (CIUS). *Substance Abuse Treatment, Prevention, and Policy, 6*(1), 32. doi:10.1186/1747-597X-6-32 PMID:22126679

Kim, K., Ryu, E., Chon, M. Y., Yeun, E. J., Choi, S. Y., Seo, J. S., & Nam, B. W. (2006). Internet addiction in Korean adolescents and its relation to depression and suicidal ideation: A questionnaire survey. *International Journal of Nursing Studies, 43*(2), 185–192. doi:10.1016/j.ijnurstu.2005.02.005 PMID:16427966

King, D. L., Delfabbro, P. H., Griffiths, M. D., & Gradisar, M. (2011). Assessing clinical trials of Internet addiction treatment: A systematic review and CONSORT evaluation. *Clinical Psychology Review, 31*(7), 1110–1116. doi:10.1016/j.cpr.2011.06.009 PMID:21820990

Ko, C. H., Liu, T. L., Wang, P. W., Chen, C. S., Yen, C. F., & Yen, J. Y. (2014). The exacerbation of depression, hostility, and social anxiety in the course of Internet addiction among adolescents: A prospective study. *Comprehensive Psychiatry, 55*(6), 1377–1384. doi:10.1016/j.comppsych.2014.05.003 PMID:24939704

Ko, C. H., Yen, J. Y., Chen, C. C., Chen, S. H., Wu, K., & Yen, C. F. (2006). Tridimensional personality of adolescents with internet addiction and substance use experience. *Canadian Journal of Psychiatry, 51*(14), 887–894. doi:10.1177/070674370605101404 PMID:17249631

Ko, C. H., Yen, J. Y., Chen, C. C., Chen, S. H., & Yen, C. F. (2005). Gender differences and related factors affecting online gaming addiction among Taiwanese adolescents. *The Journal of Nervous and Mental Disease, 193*(4), 273–277. doi:10.1097/01.nmd.0000158373.85150.57 PMID:15805824

Ko, C. H., Yen, J. Y., Liu, S. C., Huang, C. F., & Yen, C. F. (2009). The associations between aggressive behaviors and Internet addiction and online activities in adolescents. *The Journal of Adolescent Health, 44*(6), 598–605. doi:10.1016/j.jadohealth.2008.11.011 PMID:19465325

Ko, C. H., Yen, J. Y., Yen, C. F., Chen, C. S., & Wang, S. Y. (2008). The association between Internet addiction and belief of frustration intolerance: The gender difference. *Cyberpsychology & Behavior, 11*(3), 273–278. doi:10.1089/cpb.2007.0095 PMID:18537496

Kormas, G., Critselis, E., Janikian, M., Kafetzis, D., & Tsitsika, A. (2011). Risk factors and psychosocial characteristics of potential problematic and problematic internet use among adolescents: A cross-sectional study. *BMC Public Health, 11*(1), 595. doi:10.1186/1471-2458-11-595 PMID:21794167

Koronczai, B., Urbán, R., Kökönyei, G., Paksi, B., Papp, K., Kun, B., & Demetrovics, Z. et al. (2011). Confirmation of the three-factor model of problematic internet use on off-line adolescent and adult samples. *Cyberpsychology, Behavior, and Social Networking, 14*(11), 657–664. doi:10.1089/cyber.2010.0345 PMID:21711129

Kraut, R., Kiesler, S., Boneva, B., Cummings, J., Helgeson, V., & Crawford, A. (2002). Internet paradox revisited. *The Journal of Social Issues, 58*(1), 49–74. doi:10.1111/1540-4560.00248

Kuss, D. J., & Griffiths, M. D. (2011). Online social networking and addiction—a review of the psychological literature. *International Journal of Environmental Research and Public Health, 8*(9), 3528–3552. doi:10.3390/ijerph8093528 PMID:22016701

Kuss, D. J., Griffiths, M. D., & Binder, J. F. (2013). Internet addiction in students: Prevalence and risk factors. *Computers in Human Behavior, 29*(3), 959–966. doi:10.1016/j.chb.2012.12.024

Kuss, D. J., Griffiths, M. D., Karila, L., & Billieux, J. (2014). Internet addiction: A systematic review of epidemiological research for the last decade. *Current Pharmaceutical Design, 20*(25), 4026–4052. doi:10.2174/13816128113199990617 PMID:24001297

Kuss, D. J., & Lopez-Fernandez, O. (2016). Internet addiction and problematic Internet use: A systematic review of clinical research. *World Journal of Psychiatry, 6*(1), 143–176. doi:10.5498/wjp.v6.i1.143 PMID:27014605

Kuss, D. J., Van Rooij, A. J., Shorter, G. W., Griffiths, M. D., & van de Mheen, D. (2013). Internet addiction in adolescents: Prevalence and risk factors. *Computers in Human Behavior, 29*(5), 1987–1996. doi:10.1016/j.chb.2013.04.002

Laconi, S., Rodgers, R. F., & Chabrol, H. (2014). The measurement of Internet addiction: A critical review of existing scales and their psychometric properties. *Computers in Human Behavior*, *41*, 190–202. doi:10.1016/j.chb.2014.09.026

Lai, C. M., Mak, K. K., Cheng, C., Watanabe, H., Nomachi, S., Bahar, N., & Griffiths, M. D. et al. (2015). Measurement Invariance of the Internet Addiction Test Among Hong Kong, Japanese, and Malaysian Adolescents. *Cyberpsychology, Behavior, and Social Networking*, *18*(10), 609–617. doi:10.1089/cyber.2015.0069 PMID:26468915

Lai, C.-M., Mak, K.-K., Watanabe, H., Ang, R. P., Pang, J. S., & Ho, R. C. (2013). Psychometric properties of the internet addiction test in Chinese adolescents. *Journal of Pediatric Psychology*, *38*(7), 794–807. doi:10.1093/jpepsy/jst022 PMID:23671059

Lam, L. T., Peng, Z., Mai, J., & Jing, J. (2009). Factors associated with Internet addiction among adolescents. *Cyberpsychology & Behavior*, *12*(5), 551–555. doi:10.1089/cpb.2009.0036 PMID:19619039

Leung, L. (2006). Stressful life events, motives for Internet use, and social support among digital kids. *Cyberpsychology & Behavior*, *10*(2), 204–214. doi:10.1089/cpb.2006.9967 PMID:17474837

Leung, L. (2014). Predicting Internet risks: A longitudinal panel study of gratifications-sought, Internet addiction symptoms, and social media use among children and adolescents. *Health Psychology and Behavioral Medicine*, *2*(1), 424–439. doi:10.1080/21642850.2014.902316 PMID:25750792

Li, D., Zhang, W., Li, X., Zhen, S., & Wang, Y. (2010). Stressful life events and problematic Internet use by adolescent females and males: A mediated moderation model. *Computers in Human Behavior*, *26*(5), 1199–1207. doi:10.1016/j.chb.2010.03.031

Li, H., Wang, J., & Wang, L. (2009). A survey on the generalized problematic Internet use in Chinese college students and its relations to stressful life events and coping style. *International Journal of Mental Health and Addiction*, *7*(2), 333–346. doi:10.1007/s11469-008-9162-4

Li, Y., Zhang, X., Lu, F., Zhang, Q., & Wang, Y. (2014). Internet addiction among elementary and middle school students in China: A nationally representative sample study. *Cyberpsychology, Behavior, and Social Networking*, *17*(2), 111–116. doi:10.1089/cyber.2012.0482 PMID:23971432

Liang, L., Zhou, D., Chunyong, Y., & Aihui, S. (2016). Gender differences in the relationship between internet addiction and depression: A cross-lagged study in Chinese adolescents. *Computers in Human Behavior*, *63*, 463–470. doi:10.1016/j.chb.2016.04.043

Livingstone, S. (2008). Taking risky opportunities in youthful content creation: Teenagers' use of social networking sites for intimacy, privacy and self-expression. *New Media & Society*, *10*(3), 393–411. doi:10.1177/1461444808089415

Lopez-Fernandez, O., Honrubia-Serrano, L., Freixa-Blanxart, M., & Gibson, W. (2014). Prevalence of problematic mobile phone use in British adolescents. *Cyberpsychology, Behavior, and Social Networking*, *17*(2), 91–98. doi:10.1089/cyber.2012.0260 PMID:23981147

Lortie, C. L., & Guitton, M. J. (2013). Internet addiction assessment tools: Dimensional structure and methodological status. *Addiction (Abingdon, England), 108*(7), 1207–1216. doi:10.1111/add.12202 PMID:23651255

Mak, K. K., Lai, C. M., Ko, C. H., Chou, C., Kim, D. I., Watanabe, H., & Ho, R. C. (2014). Psychometric properties of the revised chen internet addiction scale (CIAS-R) in Chinese adolescents. *Journal of Abnormal Child Psychology, 42*(7), 1237–1245. doi:10.1007/s10802-014-9851-3 PMID:24585392

Marcelli, D., & Bracconnier, A. (2006). *Adolescenza e psicopatologia*. Milano, Italy: Elsevier-Masson.

Marks, I. (1990). Behavioural (non-chemical) addictions. *British Journal of Addiction, 85*(11), 1389–1394. doi:10.1111/j.1360-0443.1990.tb01618.x PMID:2285832

Maurya, S., & Singh, K. (2015). Relationship between Psychological Aspects and Internet Addiction: A Review. *Journal of Advanced Research in Ayurveda, Yoga, & Homeopathy, 2*(1), 16–19.

Meerkerk, G.-J., Van Den Eijnden, R. J., Vermulst, A. A., & Garretsen, H. F. (2009). The compulsive internet use scale (CIUS): Some psychometric properties. *Cyberpsychology & Behavior, 12*(1), 1–6. doi:10.1089/cpb.2008.0181 PMID:19072079

Morahan-Martin, J., & Schumacher, P. (2000). Incidence and correlates of pathological Internet use among college students. *Computers in Human Behavior, 16*(1), 13–29. doi:10.1016/S0747-5632(99)00049-7

Müller, K. W., Dreier, M., Beutel, M. E., Duven, E., Giralt, S., & Wölfling, K. (2016). A hidden type of internet addiction? Intense and addictive use of social networking sites in adolescents. *Computers in Human Behavior, 55*, 172–177. doi:10.1016/j.chb.2015.09.007

Muthén, L. K., & Muthén, B. O. (2010). *Mplus User's Guide: Statistical Analysis with Latent Variables: User's Guide*. Los Angeles, CA: Muthén & Muthén.

Nichols, L. A., & Nicki, R. (2004). Development of a psychometrically sound internet addiction scale: A preliminary step. *Psychology of Addictive Behaviors, 18*(4), 381–384. doi:10.1037/0893-164X.18.4.381 PMID:15631611

Okwaraji, F. E., Aguwa, E. N., Onyebueke, G. C., & Shiweobi-Eze, C. (2015). Assessment of Internet Addiction and Depression in a Sample of Nigerian University Undergraduates. *International Neuropsychiatric Disease Journal, 4*(3), 114–122. doi:10.9734/INDJ/2015/19096

Online Safety Site. (2017). *Teen Internet Statistics*. Retrieved March 21, 2017, from http://www.online-safetysite.com/P1/Teenstats.htm

Ozcan, N. K., & Buzlu, S. (2005). An assistive tool in determining problematic internet use: Validity and reliability of the Online Cognition Scale in a sample of university students. *Journal of Dependence, 6*(1), 19–26.

Paulhus, D. L., & Vazire, S. (2007). The selfreport method. In R. W. Robins, R. C. Fraley, & R. F. Krueger (Eds.), *Handbook of research methods in personality psychology* (pp. 224–239). London: The Guilford Press.

Petry, N. M., & O'brien, C. P. (2013). Internet gaming disorder and the DSM-5. *Addiction (Abingdon, England), 108*(7), 1186–1187. doi:10.1111/add.12162 PMID:23668389

Pew Research Center. (2017). *Internet usage by age.* Retrieved March 21, 2017, from http://www.pewinternet.org/chart/internet-use-by-age/

Pezoa-Jares, R., Espinoza-Luna, I., & Vasquez-Medina, J. (2012). Internet addiction: A review. *Journal of Addiction Research & Therapy, S6*(004).

Poli, R., & Agrimi, E. (2012). Internet addiction disorder: Prevalence in an Italian student population. *Nordic Journal of Psychiatry, 66*(1), 55–59. doi:10.3109/08039488.2011.605169 PMID:21859396

Pontes, H. M., Kuss, D., & Griffiths, M. (2015). Clinical psychology of Internet addiction: A review of its conceptualization, prevalence, neuronal processes, and implications for treatment. *Neuroscience and Neuroeconomics, 4*, 11–23.

Pontes, H. M., Patrao, I. M., & Griffiths, M. D. (2014). Portuguese validation of the Internet Addiction Test: An empirical study. *Journal of Behavioral Addictions, 3*(2), 107–114. doi:10.1556/JBA.3.2014.2.4 PMID:25215221

Rial Boubeta, A., Gomez Salgado, P., Isorna Folgar, M., Araujo Gallego, M., & Varela Mallou, J. (2015). PIUS-a: Problematic Internet Use Scale in adolescents. Development and psychometric validation. *Adicciones, 27*(1), 47–63. doi:10.20882/adicciones.193 PMID:25879477

Sayed, S. A., Jannatifard, F., Eslami, M., & Rezapour, H. (2011). Validity, reliability and factor analysis of compulsive internet use scale in students of Isfahan's universities. *Health Information Management, 7*, 715–724.

Schepis, T. S., Adinoff, B., & Rao, U. (2008). Neurobiological processes in adolescent addictive disorders. *The American Journal on Addictions, 17*(1), 6–23. doi:10.1080/10550490701756146 PMID:18214718

Shaw, L. H., & Gant, L. M. (2002). In defense of the Internet: The relationship between Internet communication and depression, loneliness, self-esteem, and perceived social support. *Cyberpsychology & Behavior, 5*(2), 157–171. doi:10.1089/109493102753770552 PMID:12025883

Shek, D. T., & Yu, L. (2012). Internet addiction phenomenon in early adolescents in Hong Kong. *The Scientific World Journal, 2012*, 104304. doi:10.1100/2012/104304 PMID:22778694

Siomos, K., Floros, G., Fisoun, V., Evaggelia, D., Farkonas, N., Sergentani, E., & Geroukalis, D. et al. (2012). Evolution of Internet addiction in Greek adolescent students over a two-year period: The impact of parental bonding. *European Child & Adolescent Psychiatry, 21*(4), 211–219. doi:10.1007/s00787-012-0254-0 PMID:22311146

Spada, M. M. (2014). An overview of problematic Internet use. *Addictive Behaviors, 39*(1), 3–6. doi:10.1016/j.addbeh.2013.09.007 PMID:24126206

Tam, P. G. (2016). Problematic Internet Use in Youth: An Outline and Overview for Health Professionals. *Australian Clinical Psychologist, 2*(1), 20107.

Tokunaga, R. S., & Rains, S. A. (2016). A Review and Meta-Analysis Examining Conceptual and Operational Definitions of Problematic Internet Use. *Human Communication Research*, *42*(2), 165–169. doi:10.1111/hcre.12075

Tsitsika, A., Janikian, M., Schoenmakers, T. M., Tzavela, E. C., Olafsson, K., Wójcik, S., & Richardson, C. et al. (2014). Internet addictive behavior in adolescence: A cross-sectional study in seven European countries. *Cyberpsychology, Behavior, and Social Networking*, *17*(8), 528–535. doi:10.1089/cyber.2013.0382 PMID:24853789

Van den Eijnden, R. J., Meerkerk, G.-J., Vermulst, A. A., Spijkerman, R., & Engels, R. C. (2008). Online communication, compulsive Internet use, and psychosocial well-being among adolescents: A longitudinal study. *Developmental Psychology*, *44*(3), 655–665. doi:10.1037/0012-1649.44.3.655 PMID:18473634

Van Rooij, A., & Prause, N. (2014). A critical review of "Internet addiction" criteria with suggestions for the future. *Journal of Behavioral Addictions*, *3*(4), 203–213. doi:10.1556/JBA.3.2014.4.1 PMID:25592305

Villella, C., Martinotti, G., Di Nicola, M., Cassano, M., La Torre, G., Gliubizzi, M. D., & Conte, G. et al. (2011). Behavioural addictions in adolescents and young adults: Results from a prevalence study. *Journal of Gambling Studies*, *27*(2), 203–214. doi:10.1007/s10899-010-9206-0 PMID:20559694

Wang, H., Zhou, X., Lu, C., Wu, J., Deng, X., & Hong, L. (2011). Problematic Internet use in high school students in Guangdong Province, China. *PLoS One*, *6*(5), e19660. doi:10.1371/journal.pone.0019660 PMID:21573073

Wang, L., Luo, J., Bai, Y., Kong, J., Luo, J., Gao, W., & Sun, X. (2013). Internet addiction of adolescents in China: Prevalence, predictors, and association with well-being. *Addiction Research and Theory*, *21*(1), 62–69. doi:10.3109/16066359.2012.690053

Wartberg, L., Petersen, K.-U., Kammerl, R., Rosenkranz, M., & Thomasius, R. (2014). Psychometric validation of a German version of the compulsive Internet use scale. *Cyberpsychology, Behavior, and Social Networking*, *17*(2), 99–103. doi:10.1089/cyber.2012.0689 PMID:23988182

Watters, C. A., Keefer, K. V., Kloosterman, P. H., Summerfeldt, L. J., & Parker, J. D. (2013). Examining the structure of the Internet Addiction Test in adolescents: A bifactor approach. *Computers in Human Behavior*, *29*(6), 2294–2302. doi:10.1016/j.chb.2013.05.020

We Are Social, S. R. L. (2017). *Digital in 2017: In Italia e nel mondo*. Retrieved March 21, 2017, from http://wearesocial.com/it/blog/2017/01/digital-in-2017-in-italia-e-nel-mondo

Weiser, E. B. (2000). Gender differences in Internet use patterns and Internet application preferences: A two-sample comparison. *Cyberpsychology & Behavior*, *3*(2), 167–178. doi:10.1089/109493100316012

Widyanto, L., & Griffiths, M. (2006). 'Internet addiction': A critical review. *International Journal of Mental Health and Addiction*, *4*(1), 31–51. doi:10.1007/s11469-006-9009-9

Widyanto, L., Griffiths, M., Brunsden, V., & McMurran, M. (2008). The psychometric properties of the Internet related problem scale: A pilot study. *International Journal of Mental Health and Addiction*, *6*(2), 205–213. doi:10.1007/s11469-007-9120-6

Widyanto, L., Griffiths, M. D., & Brunsden, V. (2011). A psychometric comparison of the Internet Addiction Test, the Internet-Related Problem Scale, and self-diagnosis. *Cyberpsychology, Behavior, and Social Networking, 14*(3), 141–149. doi:10.1089/cyber.2010.0151 PMID:21067282

Yen, C.-F., Chou, W.-J., Liu, T.-L., Yang, P., & Hu, H.-F. (2014). The association of Internet addiction symptoms with anxiety, depression and self-esteem among adolescents with attention-deficit/hyperactivity disorder. *Comprehensive Psychiatry, 55*(7), 1601–1608. doi:10.1016/j.comppsych.2014.05.025 PMID:25015304

Yen, C. F., Ko, C. H., Yen, J. Y., Chang, Y. P., & Cheng, C. P. (2009). Multi-dimensional discriminative factors for Internet addiction among adolescents regarding gender and age. *Psychiatry and Clinical Neurosciences, 63*(3), 357–364. doi:10.1111/j.1440-1819.2009.01969.x PMID:19566768

Yen, J. Y., Ko, C. H., Yen, C. F., Wu, H. Y., & Yang, M. J. (2007b). The comorbid psychiatric symptoms of Internet addiction: Attention deficit and hyperactivity disorder (ADHD), depression, social phobia, and hostility. *The Journal of Adolescent Health, 41*(1), 93–98. doi:10.1016/j.jadohealth.2007.02.002 PMID:17577539

Yen, J. Y., Yen, C. F., Chen, C. C., Chen, S. H., & Ko, C. H. (2007a). Family factors of internet addiction and substance use experience in Taiwanese adolescents. *Cyberpsychology & Behavior, 10*(3), 323–329. doi:10.1089/cpb.2006.9948 PMID:17594255

Yen, J.Y., Yen, C.F., Cheng, C.P., Tang, Y.P., & Ko, C.H. (2009). The Association between Adult ADHD Symptoms and Internet Addiction among College Students: The Gender Difference. *Cyberpsychology & Behavior: The Impact of the Internet, Multimedia and Virtual Reality on Behavior and Society, 12*(2), 187-191.

Young, K. S. (1996). Psychology of computer use: XL. Addictive use of the Internet: a case that breaks the stereotype. *Psychological Reports, 79*(3), 899–902. doi:10.2466/pr0.1996.79.3.899 PMID:8969098

Young, K. S. (1998a). *Caught in the net: How to recognize the signs of internet addiction--and a winning strategy for recovery.* New York, NY: John Wiley & Sons.

Young, K. S. (1998b). Internet addiction: The emergence of a new clinical disorder. *Cyberpsychology & Behavior, 1*(3), 237–244. doi:10.1089/cpb.1998.1.237

Young, K. S. (2004). Internet addiction: A new clinical phenomenon and its consequences. *The American Behavioral Scientist, 48*(4), 402–415. doi:10.1177/0002764204270278

Young, K. S., & De Abreu, C. N. (2010). *Internet addiction: A handbook and guide to evaluation and treatment.* New York, NY: John Wiley & Sons.

Zec, G. (2005). *Faktorska struktura instrumenata Online Cognition Scale i predviđanje patološkog korištenja interneta* (Unpublished Diploma thesis). Filozofski fakultet u Zagrebu, Zagreb, Croatia.

KEY TERMS AND DEFINITIONS

Addiction: A strong and harmful need to regularly have something (such as a drug) or do something (such as gamble); it produces a brain or psychological disorder characterized by a persistent compulsive use.

Behavioral Addiction: A form of addiction that involves a compulsion to engage in a rewarding non-drug-related behavior, despite any negative consequences to the person's physical, mental, social or financial well-being.

Confirmatory Factor Analysis (CFA): A statistical method used to test whether measures of a construct are consistent with a researcher's understanding of the nature of that construct. The objective of confirmatory factor analysis is to test whether the data fit a hypothesized measurement model.

Exploratory Factor Analysis (EFA): A statistical method used to uncover the underlying structure of a relatively large set of variables. It is commonly used by researchers when developing a scale to identify a set of latent constructs underlying a battery of measured variables.

Problematic Internet Use: When an individual's psychological state (including both mental and emotional conditions, as well as scholastic, occupational and social interactions) is impaired by the overuse of the Internet, in terms of hours spent online and negative outcomes on the night and day activities.

Risk Measure: An instrument useful to statistically assess the probability of developing a problematic behavior. It allows the researcher to identify populations at risk and distinguish them from non-at-risk ones.

Scale: A collection of questions used to measure a particular research topic. The responses of a scale can be combined together into a single measure (a latent variable). The items of a scale can be dichotomous (e.g., yes/no, agree/disagree, correct/incorrect) or polytomous as in a Likert-scale (e.g., disagree strongly/disagree/neutral/agree/agree strongly).

APPENDIX

Table 1. Results from exploratory factor analysis

Items	F1	F2	Original Collocation	Item-tot Correlation	α if Item Removed
Factor 1: Self and Mood Regulation					
Per passare più tempo su Internet ho rinunciato a parte del mio tempo libero e del tempo che dedico alle relazioni sociali (offline) [I have given up some of my in-person social and leisure time so I can spend more time on the Internet]	.362	.177	Reduced activities	.418	.799
Quando non sono online mi ritrovo a domandarmi cosa sta accadendo in Internet [When I am not on-line, I find myself wondering what is happening on the Internet]	.788	-.192	Withdrawal	.508	.790
Ho provato senza successo a ridurre il mio uso di Internet [I have tried unsuccessfully to cut down my amount of Internet use]	.490	.089	Loss of control	.461	.795
Il tempo che spendo online è aumentato durante l'ultimo anno [The time I spend on-line has increased during the last 12 months]	.439	.237	Tolerance	.537	.786
Mi ritrovo a pensare che vorrei connettermi mentre sto facendo altre cose [I find myself thinking about going on-line when I am doing other things]	.477	.201	Craving	.550	.785
Ho usato Internet per sentirmi meglio quando ero giù di morale [I have used the Internet to make myself feel better when I was down]	.486	-.003	Escape from problems	.414	.800
Ho usato Internet per parlare con gli altri quando mi sentivo isolato/a [I have used the Internet to talk to others when I was feeling isolated]	.514	.017	Escape from problems	.441	.798
Factor 2: Negative Outcomes					
Il mio uso di Internet ha sostituito alcune delle mie abituali ore di sonno [My Internet use has replaced some of my usual sleeping hours]	.198	.468	Negative effects	.518	.788
I miei amici e la mia famiglia si lamentano dell'uso che faccio di Internet [My friends and family have complained about my use of the Internet]	.261	.407	Negative effects	.518	.788
La mia produttività al lavoro e a scuola è diminuita come risultato diretto del tempo che passo su Internet [My productivity at work or school has decreased as a direct result of the time I spend on the Internet]	-.001	.701	Reduced activities	.502	.790
Cronbach's α: .809	.743	.646			

Table 2. Correlations among scales and factors

	Correlations					
	CERM	**CERM-F1**	**CERM-F2**	**IRPS**	**IRPS-F1**	**IRPS-F2**
CERM	1					
CERM-F1 - *Behaviors*	.810**	1				
CERM-F2 - *Emotions*	.958**	.609**	1			
IRPS	.740**	.633**	.692**	1		
IRPS-F1 - *Self and mood regulation*	.733**	.651**	.674**	.949**	1	
IRPS-F2 – *Negative outcomes*	.476**	.339**	.479**	.822**	.601**	1
** The correlation is significant at level 0.01 (2-codes).						

Table 3. One-way ANOVAs: Problematic and Non-Problematic Users

		Mean	SD		Sum of Squares	Mean Square	F	Sig.
Better when down	Non problematic	2.50	1.24	Between groups	137.250	137.250	93.168	.000
	Problematic	4.00	1.18	Within groups	356.500	1.473		
Social/Leisure time	Non problematic	1.48	0.87	Between groups	129.852	129.852	99.739	.000
	Problematic	2.94	1.36	Within groups	315.066	1.302		
What's Happening	Non problematic	1.72	1.03	Between groups	180.500	180.500	134.389	.000
	Problematic	3.45	1.28	Within groups	322.347	1.343		
Unsuccessfully reduce time	Non problematic	1.88	1.12	Between groups	143.401	143,401	97.132	.000
	Problematic	3.42	1.31	Within groups	354.322	1,476		
Time online increased	Non problematic	2.56	1.47	Between groups	180.722	180.722	115.676	.000
	Problematic	4.30	1.00	Within groups	370.266	1.562		
Feel isolated	Non problematic	2.67	1.36	Between groups	137.250	137.250	94.287	.000
	Problematic	4.17	1.03	Within groups	352.270	1.456		
Sleep interference	Non problematic	1.82	1.13	Between groups	202.788	202.788	121.125	.000
	Problematic	3.65	1.44	Within groups	401.811	1.674		
Complaints	Non problematic	2.26	1.31	Between groups	256.148	256.148	179.274	.000
	Problematic	4.31	1.07	Within groups	345.770	1.429		
Productivity	Non problematic	1.78	1.05	Between groups	205.492	205.492	143.580	.000
	Problematic	3.62	1.32	Within groups	343.488	1.431		
Think use while doing other things	Non problematic	2.16	1.25	Between groups	197.470	197.470	135.649	.000
	Problematic	3.96	1.16	Within groups	350.834	1.456		
Factor 1: Self and mood regulation	Non problematic	2.14	0.74	Between groups	158.823	158.823	433.705	.000
	Problematic	3.75	0.43	Within groups	88.620	0.366		
Factor 2:Negative Outcomes	Non problematic	1.95	0.86	Between groups	222.814	222.814	316.156	.000
	Problematic	3.86	0.81	Within groups	170.552	0.705		
Internet Related Problems	Non problematic	2.08	0.66	Between groups	176.758	176.758	637.559	.000
	Problematic	3.78	0.34	Within groups	67.092	0.277		

Table 4. One-way ANOVAs by gender

		Mean	SD		Sum of Squares	Mean Square	F	Sig.
Better when down	Males	2.65	1.29	Between groups	0.161	0.161	0.097	.755
	Females	2.63	1.28	Within groups	2000.964	1.663		
Social/Leisure time	Males	2.64	1.28	Between groups	11.707	11.707	11.627	.001
	Females	1.76	1.05	Within groups	1215.273	1.007		
What's Happening	Males	1.56	0.95	Between groups	0.014	0.014	0.010	.919
	Females	1.94	1.16	Within groups	1669.471	1.391		
Unsuccessfully reduce time	Males	1.95	1.20	Between groups	7.716	7.716	5.180	.023
	Females	2.04	1.19	Within groups	1787.346	1.489		
Time online increased	Males	2.20	1.25	Between groups	12.018	12.018	6.175	.013
	Females	2.62	1.39	Within groups	2329.711	1.946		
Feel isolated	Males	2.82	1.41	Between groups	31.560	31.560	16.429	.000
	Females	2.70	1.36	Within groups	2303.354	1.921		
Sleep interference	Males	3.03	1.41	Between groups	0.030	0.030	0.017	.897
	Females	2.14	1.32	Within groups	2093.768	1.745		
Complaints	Males	2.13	1.33	Between groups	53.039	53.039	26.362	.000
	Females	2.40	1.35	Within groups	2422.427	2.012		
Productivity	Males	2.08	1.49	Between groups	6.525	6.525	4.217	.040
	Females	2.82	1.25	Within groups	1863.143	1.547		
Think use while doing other things	Males	1.94	1.23	Between groups	15.105	15.105	8.694	.003
	Females	2.32	1.31	Within groups	2095.266	1.737		
Factor 1: Self and mood regulation	Males	2.54	1.32	Between groups	2.889	2.889	4.627	.032
	Females	2.29	0.79	Within groups	754.285	0.624		
Factor 2: Negative Outcomes	Males	2.39	0.79	Between groups	2.430	2.430	2.337	.127
	Females	2.20	0.96	Within groups	1256.018	1.040		
Internet Related Problems	Males	2.27	1.09	Between groups	2.722	2.722	4.513	.034
	Females	2.36	0.75	Within groups	728.623	0.603		

Table 5. One-way ANOVAs by age

		Mean	SD		Sum of Squares	Mean Square	F	Sig.
Better when down	Young adolescents	2.68	1.33	Between groups	4.910	2.455	1.472	.230
	Old adolescents	2.54	1.22	Within groups	1993.588	1.668		
	Preadolescents	2.68	1.31					
Social/Leisure time	Young adolescents	1.65	0.97	Between groups	5.095	2.547	2.507	.082
	Old adolescents	1.58	0.96	Within groups	1218.443	1.016		
	Preadolescents	1.73	1.05					
What's Happening	Young adolescents	1.96	1.17	Between groups	23.861	11.931	8.735	.000
	Old adolescents	1.73	0.99	Within groups	1628.038	1.366		
	Preadolescents	2.06	1.26					
Unsuccessfully reduce time	Young adolescents	2.00	1.16	Between groups	36.734	18.367	12.526	.000
	Old adolescents	1.91	1.13	Within groups	1747.905	1.466		
	Preadolescents	2.29	1.28					
Time online increased	Young adolescents	2.75	1.39	Between groups	8.385	4.192	2.151	.117
	Old adolescents	2.58	1.39	Within groups	2318.846	1.949		
	Preadolescents	2.77	1.39					
Feel isolated	Young adolescents	2.87	1.40	Between groups	25.775	12.888	6.671	.001
	Old adolescents	2.63	1.29	Within groups	2300.986	1.932		
	Preadolescents	2.98	1.44					
Sleep interference	Young adolescents	2.26	1.32	Between groups	5.602	2.801	1.605	.201
	Old adolescents	2.09	1.29	Within groups	2080.214	1.745		
	Preadolescents	2.11	1.34					
Complaints	Young adolescents	2.78	1.44	Between groups	21.751	10.876	5.332	.005
	Old adolescents	2.41	1.39	Within groups	2439.443	2.040		
	Preadolescents	2.61	1.45					
Productivity	Young adolescents	2.36	1.33	Between groups	74.012	37.006	24.733	.000
	Old adolescents	2.14	1.25	Within groups	1789.507	1.496		
	Preadolescents	1.77	1.15					
Think use while doing other things	Young adolescents	2.52	1.31	Between groups	49.096	24.548	14.379	.000
	Old adolescents	2.10	1.22	Within groups	2045.239	1.707		
	Preadolescents	2.56	1.36					
Factor 1: Self and mood regulation	Young adolescents	2.35	0.81	Between groups	17.880	8.940	14.587	.000
	Old adolescents	2.15	0.74	Within groups	735.470	0.613		
	Preadolescents	2.44	079					
Factor 2: Negative Outcomes	Young adolescents	2.46	1.09	Between groups	18.061	9.030	8.768	.000
	Old adolescents	2.21	1.01	Within groups	1235.849	1.030		
	Preadolescents	2.16	0.97					
Internet Related Problems	Young adolescents	2.38	0.81	Between groups	9.634	4.817	8.031	.000
	Old adolescents	2.17	0.76	Within groups	719.768	0.600		
	Preadolescents	2.36	0.76					

Section 5
Putting It Together

This section provides a conclusion to internet addiction with treatment strategies and future research directions.

Chapter 15
Treatment of Internet Addiction

Libi Shen
University of Phoenix, USA

ABSTRACT

The birth of the Internet in 1969 has changed people's lives immensely in the past 48 years. Over the years, this invention has brought people connection, information, communication, business, entertainment, and so forth; however, researchers have found the impact of the Internet's byproduct, namely Internet addiction, in the past two decades as well. It was argued that Internet addiction might be detrimental to people's mental and physical health. The problem is that Internet addiction is not clearly defined, nor has it been included in Diagnostic and Statistical Manual for Mental Disorders (DSM-5) by American Psychiatric Association. If the definition is not clear and the symptoms are varied, the treatment for Internet addiction would become an issue. In this chapter, the researcher will focus on different approaches to the treatment of Internet addiction based on research after reviewing the definitions, theories, causes, consequences, and symptoms of Internet addiction.

INTRODUCTION

The Internet was born on October 29, 1969, when an UCLA team led by Dr. Leonard Kleinrock, a distinguished Computer Science professor, sent the first message over the ARPANET (the computer network) to Stanford Research Institute (Kromhout, 2009; Modesti, 2009). Over the years, the world has changed enormously due to the development of the Internet. This invention has brought convenience, communication, globalization, connection, online shopping, online banking, e-commerce, Information, entertainment, and so on to people's life all over the world. It has also precipitated cybercrimes, spam mails, phishing scams, data breaches, Trojan, virus, malware, hacking, and so forth to our world. The number of the Internet users has increased from 414,794,957 (6.8%) in 2000 to 3,424,971,237 (46.1%) in 2016 (Internet Live Stats, 2017). The top ten Internet users in the world are China, India, United States, Brazil, Japan, Russia, Nigeria, Germany, U.K., and Mexico in sequence (Internet Live Stats, 2017).

Since people's high-tech products (e.g., laptop computers, smartwatches, tablets), social networks (e.g., Facebook, LinkedIn, Twitter, Instagram, YouTube), communication apps (e.g., Skype, LINE, WeChat, WhatsApp, Snapchat), emails (e.g. Google, Yahoo) all rely on the Internet, many people are addicted

DOI: 10.4018/978-1-5225-3477-8.ch015

to the Internet without knowing it. Turkle (2012), a psychologist and an MIT professor, pointed out that we have sacrificed our conversation for mere connection with social media such as Facebook which has impoverished people's relationship and stripped out essential elements of human contact. The Internet brings us closer to people far from us, but also takes us away from the ones sitting next to us (Turkle, 2012). Gaille (2015) described that 27% of people used Facebook in the bathroom, 82% of people spent more time online than anticipated; 20% of people woke up at night to check their Facebook; and 20% surface area of brain shrinkage occurred for long-term Internet addiction.

Despite the critiques of Facebook as addictive, promoting narcissism, interfering with face-to-face contact between loved ones, Mark Zuckerberg insisted that "it's so clearly positive for people in terms of their ability to stay connected for folks…. Our mission is to connect every person in the world" (Grossman, 2014, p.40). On Facebook, Zuckerberg (2017) updated that approximately 1.9 billion people are in the online community now and 1.2 billion people are active using it every day, specifically more than 65 million small businesses use Facebook to connect with their customers nowadays. To build a global community online, Zuckerberg (2017) announced that 1.86 million people will be active on Facebook and 600 million on Instagram within three years; 1.2 billion people on WhatsApp and one billion on Messenger within 5 years; and more than 50 million people will be connected by internet.org within ten years.

In fact, the total number of social media users in the U.S. was 179.7 million in 2015 (Statista, 2016b). The total number of Facebook Users in 2016 by age groups was: 26.6 million for age 18-24, 33.2 million for age 25-34, 26.1 million for age 35-44, 23.2 million for age 45-54, 18.4 million for age 55-64, and 12.5 million for age 65 and over (Statista, 2016a). People between 25 and 34 years old are the top users. With this amount of Internet users, what should people do if they or their friends and family members are addicted to the Internet? The purpose of this chapter is to explore treatment for Internet addiction.

BACKGROUND

Internet addiction was defined as an impulse-control disorder that does not involve an intoxicant (Young, 1996). Beard and Wolf (2001) proposed that people who are preoccupied with the Internet, who are unable to control their use, and who are jeopardizing employment and relationships are Internet addicted. Based on Cheng and Li's (2014) meta-analysis of 80 reports (consisting of 89,281 participants from 31 countries across seven world regions), approximately 6% of the global population (i.e., 420 million people) was addicted to the Internet. Internet addiction has appeared in every age group, with 73% between age 13 to 17, 71% between age 18 to 24, 59% between age 25 to 34, 40% between age 45 to 54, 39% between age 55 to 64, and 44% above 65 years old (Addiction Facts, 2017). Approximately 64% females and 55% males were caught in the web (Addiction Facts, 2017).

In the past two decades, many researchers have found relationships between Internet addiction and risk factors, such as depression (Akin & Iskender, 2011; Şahin, 2014; Young & Rodgers, 1998), psychopathology (Koc, 2011), self-compassion (Iskender & Akin, 2011), shyness (Ayas, 2012; Doğan & Kaya, 2016), personality traits (Celik, Atak, & Basal, 2012), social networks (Cam & Isbulan, 2012; Simsek & Sali, 2014), psychological well-being (Cardak, 2013), loneliness (Demirer, Bozoglan, & Sahin, 2013; Pontes, Griffiths, & Patrao, 2014), social anxiety (Holm, 2013), drug use (Kurt, 2015), attitudes (Ilhan, Çelik, Gemcioğlu, & Çiftaslan, 2016), and social skills (Karimzadeh, 2015), etc. Others have explored the symptoms, evaluation, and treatment of Internet addiction (e.g., Beard, 2011; Caldwell &

Cunningham, 2010; Chrismore, Betzelberger, Bier, & Camacho, 2011; Conrad, 2016; Shaw & Black, 2008; Şenormanci, Konkan, & Sungur, 2012; Young, 1999; Young, 2011). Specifically, some researchers have found negative consequences of excessive Internet use (e.g., Akin & Iskender, 2011; Ben-Yehuda & Greenberg, & Weinstein, 2016; Griffiths, Kuss, & King, 2012; Ho, et al., 2014; Lam, 2016; Murali & George, 2007; Pontes, Griffiths, & Patrăo, 2014; Shaw & Black, 2008; Young, 1996; Uddin et al., 2016). The negative consequences of Internet addiction involve students' academic problems, relationship issues, financial problems, occupational problems, and physical problems.

Regardless of its benefits, the Internet is an abused medium for pornography, gambling, stock trading, shopping, auction, and cyber-sexual behaviors (Greenfield, 1999). Compulsive Internet use contributed to online progressive sexual behaviors, such as flirting, explicit sex talk, masturbation, online affair, phone contact, and real-time sex (Greenfield, 1999). Students failed academically due to long hours of surfing irrelevant websites, engaging in chat room gossip, and playing interactive games; people's marriages, dating relationships, parent-child relationships and friendships were disrupted due to excessive use of the Internet and misuse of time (Young, 1996). Young (2004) further indicated that online addiction is associated with online affairs, and the impact of online affairs included changing in sleep patterns, a demand for privacy, ignoring responsibilities, evidence of lying, personality change, loss of interest in sex, and declining investment in the relationship. Student's internet abuse was caused by free and unlimited Internet access, huge blocks of unstructured time, newly experienced freedom from parental control, no monitoring/censoring of what they say or do online, full encouragement from faculty and administrators, social intimidation and alienation, and a higher legal drinking age (Young, 2004). Employee Internet abuse consists of business epidemic, lost productivity, negative publicity, and legal liabilities (Young, 2004). In other words, the consequences of the Internet addiction are profound.

Although there were many research studies on Internet addiction, researchers have not defined the symptoms and the treatment systematically. How do people help Internet addicts if the definitions and symptoms are not clarified distinctly? In the following, the definitions, concepts, theories, causes, consequences, and symptoms of the Internet addiction over the past 20 years will be reviewed; issues and problems related to the Internet addiction will be examined; and solutions or approaches to treat Internet addicts will be sought as the main focus of the study.

LITERATURE REVIEW

Definitions of Internet Addiction

The concept of Internet addiction can be viewed through its definitions. Table 1 presented a list of definitions from year 1996 to 2016. The definition ranged from "an impulse-control disorder which does not involve any intoxicant" by Young (1996) to "a multi-faceted disorder" by Friebel & Kapoor (2016). Overall, the excessive use of the Internet, compulsive Internet use, problematic Internet use (PIU), and Internet Addiction Disorder (IAD) exemplify Internet addiction. Greenfield (2011) regarded the simple algorithm of addiction criteria as DIAR (desire to stop, inability to stop, attempts to stop, and relapse). "DIAR is a notable marker for Internet addiction, in addition to tolerance and withdrawal markers" (Greenfield, 2011). In Young's (2011) Clinical Assessment of Internet-Addicted Clients, there were three subtypes (i.e., excessive gaming, sexual preoccupations, and email/text messaging), four components

Table 1. Definitions of internet addiction

Source	Definition of Internet Addiction
Young (1996)	An impulse-control disorder which does not involve an intoxicant.
Griffiths (1998)	Excessive use of the Internet; a kind of technological addiction and a subset of behavioral addiction; technological addictions are nonchemical (behavioral) addictions that involve human-machine interaction.
Kandell (1998)	A psychological dependence on the Internet, regardless of the type of activity once logged on (p.12)
Greenfield (1999)	Compulsive Internet use, Internet abusers (e.g., electronic vagabonds; compulsive with chat rooms, personals, and emails; excessive stock trading, pornography, gambling, shopping, or auctioning)
Griffiths (2000)	Technological addictions, nonchemical (behavioral) addictions that involve human-machine interaction, are a subset of behavior addictions (i.e., salience, mood modification, tolerance, withdrawal, conflict and relapse).
Beard & Wolf (2001)	Problematic Internet users who use of the Internet excessively that creates psychological, social, school, and/or work difficulties in a person's life.
Nalwa & Anand (2003)	Psychological dependence on the Internet with the characteristics of an increasing investment of resources on Internet-related activities, unpleasant feelings when off-line, and denial of the problematic behaviors
Childnet International (2006)	People who spend excessive amounts of time online at the expense of and to the detriment of other aspects of their lives. The obsessive behavior takes the form of particular activities, and might include any or all of the followings: relationships, money, information searching, gaming, and sex.
Murali & George (2007)	Excessive maladaptive or problematic Internet use
Block (2008)	Compulsive-impulsive spectrum disorder that involves online and/or offline computer usage and consists of at least three subtypes: excessive gaming, sexual preoccupations, and email/text messaging. Four components: excessive use (i.e., loss of sentence of time, neglect of basic drives), withdrawal (i.e., feelings of anger, tension, and depression when the computer is inaccessible), tolerance (i.e., the need for better computer equipment, more software, or more hours of use), negative repercussions (i.e., arguments, lying, poor achievement, social isolation).
Shaw & Black (2008)	Excessive or poorly controlled preoccupations, urges or behaviors regarding computer use and internet access that lead to impairment or distress. (p.353)
Akin & Iskender (2011)	Internet addiction is typically characterized by psychomotor agitation, anxiety, craving (Ferraro, Caci, D'Amico et al., 2007), depression, hostility, substance experience (Ko, Yen, Chen et al., 2006; Yen, Ko, Yen et al., 2007), preoccupation, loss of control, withdrawal, impairment of function, reduced decision-making ability (Ko et al., 2005), and constant online surfing despite negative effects on social and psychological welfare (Shaw & Black, 2008; Tao et al., 2010).
Chrismore, Berger, Bier, & Camacho (2011)	Internet addiction, like chemical addiction, is a primary, progressive disease.
Çelik, Atak, & Başal (2012).	Internet dependency, pathological internet use, problematic internet use, extensive internet use, internet abuse, internet addiction disorder
Sahin (2014)	The excessive use of Internet in an uncontrolled way which causes various problems in individual, social and professional aspects.
Weinstein, Feder, Roseberg, & Dannon (2014)	Problematic Internet use (PIU), Internet Addiction Disorder (IAD), People who use the internet for extended periods, isolating themselves from other forms of social contact, and focus almost entirely on the Internet rather than broader life events.
Akar (2015)	Excessive Internet use
Griffiths (2015)	All addictions, irrespective of whether they are chemical or behavioral, comprise six components (salience, mood modification, tolerance, withdrawal, conflict, and relapse).
Breslau, Aharoni, Pedersen, & Miller (2015)	Problematic Internet use (PIU); compulsive use (i.e., staying online for long period of time and neglecting social responsibilities), tolerance (i.e., increasing intensity of engagement with online activities), withdrawal (i.e., distress or acute changes in functioning when s/he is unable to go online).
Conrad (2016)	If a person repeated goes online to avoid real world responsibilities or difficulties and this avoidance creates even more problems in their life, this may suggest the presence of an addiction to the Internet. Internet addiction can be psychological, physical, behavioral, and relational.
Gregory (2016)	Just because you use the Internet a lot (e.g., watch a lot of YouTube videos, shop online frequently, like to check social media) does not mean you suffer from Internet Addiction Disorder. The trouble comes when these activities start to interfere with your daily life. Most common categories of IAD include gaming, social networking, email, blogging, online shopping, and inappropriate Internet pornography use.
Teong & Ang (2016)	Longer Internet use and extreme engagement in interactive functions
Kuss & Lopez-Fernandez (2016)	Encompassing Internet-use related addictions and problematic Internet use, including Internet Gaming Disorder.
Ben-Yehuda, Greenberg, & Weinstein (2016)	The inability to control one's use of the Internet, a condition that causes severe impairment of various life functions
Friebel & Kapoor (2016)	A multi-faceted disorder

(i.e., excessive use, withdrawal, tolerance, negative repercussions), and eight criteria (i.e., preoccupied with the internet; increasing time on the Internet; unsuccessful control or stop the Internet use; feeling restless, moody, depressed, or irritable when cutting down the use; staying online longer than originally planned; jeopardizing relationship, job, or educational opportunity; lied to family members or therapists; escaping from problems) for conceptualizing the Internet addiction. Larose (2011) indicated that "to assess whether someone is in imminent danger of forming a problematic Internet habit, clinicians might explore whether the online behavior in question has become the primary means of relieving dysphoric moods and probe for signs of depression associated with mounting use" (p.66). If the individuals can maintain effective self-control when it is disrupted, it is not Internet addiction.

Theories and Models of Internet Addiction

The theories for Internet addiction have been interpreted in various ways. Over the years, there were a social psychological model, a cognitive-behavioral model, an interpersonal theory, a neuropsychological model, and a compensation theory, to name a few. The theories/models were illustrated as follows.

In 1999, Steven Stern assumed a social psychological model of the Internet addiction in which technology plays the role in the formation of maladaptive behaviors and psychopathologies. He compared two models of Internet addiction and concluded that technology increased our capacities and abilities, and enhance our ability to exhibit maladaptive behavior, fallibilities, and inabilities. He said, "The Internet, like other media technologies, has the effect of physically isolating people from one another. Another explanation of the Internet's capacity to promote compulsive behaviors could be rooted in the degree that it separates people from socially healthier contexts in which they could interact more appropriately" (Stern, 1999, p.423).

In Davis' (2001) cognitive-behavioral model, there were two types of pathological Internet use (PIU): the generalized and the specific. Generalized PIU consisted of a general, multidimensional overuse of the Internet, such as spending abnormal amounts of time on the Internet, wasting time online without clear objective, or spending lots of time in chat rooms (Davis, 2001). Generalized PIU was associated with the social aspect of the Internet, for instance, a lack of social support from family or friends and/or social isolation. This model suggested that psychopathology is a distal necessary cause of the symptoms of PIU (Davis, 2001). The specific PIU involved people who are dependent on a specific function of the Internet, including the overuse and abuse of specific Internet function, such as online auction services, online pornography, online stock trading, and online gambling (Davis, 2001). These dependencies are content-specific, and exist in the absence of the Internet (Davis, 2001). Specific PIU is assumed to be the result of pre-existing psychopathology that was associated with online activity (Davis, 2001). In the cognitive-behavioral theory, "if the cognitive symptoms of PIU are salient enough, they lead to behavioral symptoms that ultimately result in negative outcomes…. However, scholars have recognized that excessive use in and of itself is not necessarily problematic" (Caplan & High, 2011, p.47). Burnay, Billieux, Blairy, and Laroi (2015) believed that Internet addiction is a multidimensional phenomenon influenced by impulsivity and passion; age, urgency, lack of perseverance, obsessive passion, and depression were all predictors of Internet addiction. Psychological factors such as impulsivity and passion were found to be important to explain the Internet addiction (Burnay, et al., 2015).

The interpersonal theory was proposed by Sullivan in 1940 who suggested that people developed their personality within a social context in which the importance of different developmental stages in people's life (i.e., infancy, childhood, the juvenile era, preadolescence, early adolescence, late adolescence, and adulthood) was emphasized (Feist & Feist, 2005). In Sullivan's theory, needs and anxiety are two types of tensions. "Anxiety can interfere with satisfying interpersonal relations at any age" (Feist & Feist, 2005, p.213). "The transformation of potential energy into actual energy (behavior) for the purpose of satisfying needs or reducing anxiety was called energy transformations" (Feist & Feist, 2005, p.224). Energy transformations are tensions that transformed into actions and become typical behavior patterns (dynamisms), which are related to malevolence, intimacy, lust, and self-system (Feist & Feist, 2005). "People can never be isolated from the complex of interpersonal relations in which they live and have their own being"; additionally, "individual's level of anxiety is a direct product of the level of anxiety in that individual's early environment" (Liu & Kuo, 2007, p.800). In Sullivan's theory, the details of a patient's interpersonal interactions with others can provide insight into the causes and cures of mental disorder.

In neuropsychological model, there were one prerequisite and three conditions for Internet addiction. The prerequisite is that a person's Internet addiction must "severely jeopardize a young person's social functioning and interpersonal communication" (Young, Yue, & Ying, 2011, p.8). Three conditions to judge if a person is Internet addicted were: (a) "easier to achieve self-actualization online than in real life"; (b) "experience dysphoria or depression whenever access to the Internet is broken or cease to function"; and (c) "try to hide his or her true usage time from family members" (Young, Yue, & Ying, 2011, p.8). Thus, the major concept of the neuropsychological link of Internet addiction consists of primitive drive, euphoric experience, tolerance, abstinence reaction, passive cooping, and avalanche effect. Brand, Young, and Laier (2014) believed that the neuropsychological research findings showed that certain prefrontal functions, specifically the executive control functions are related to symptoms of the Internet addiction.

Compensation theory is proposed by the Institute of Psychology of the Chinese Academy of Sciences. Young people look for compensation for self-identity, self-esteem, and social networking by engaging in Internet activities (Tao's notes, as cited in Young, Yue, & Ying, 2011). In the past two decades, "Chinese young people have used poetry, the guitar, and sports to express their needs and feeling, whereas now they tend to use electronic games and other Web-based tools" (Young, Yue, & Ying, 2011, p.11). Internet addiction is associated with loneliness, social isolation, and depression. The use of the Internet can "overcome low self-esteem, social awkwardness, loneliness, and depression" as well as compensate the deficits of identity and relationships (Young, Yue, & Ying, 2011, p.12). "The theoretical argument is that by understanding how motivations mediate the relationship between psychosocial well-being and Internet addiction, we can draw conclusions about how online activities may compensate for psychosocial problems" (Kardefelt-Winther, 2014, p.351).

Causes of Internet Addiction

What are the major causes of Internet addiction? Researchers have discovered several reasons for Internet addiction. For example, some people increased their Internet use due to "low self-esteem, poor motivation, fear of rejection, and the need for approval associated with depressives" (Young & Rodgers, 1998, p.27). In Griffiths' (2000) case study of five participants, the motivation for excessive use of Internet included: "escapism into his own world where he can counteract his depression and forget about his social isolation and his medical condition (neurofibromatosis)" (p.213); "to socialize with other Internet users" (p.214); "for the fantasy role-playing games" (p.214); "no face-to-face communication takes place" (p.215); and "his desire to interact constantly with a new partner" (p.216).

"Many of the Internet users reported being depressed, lonely, having low self-esteem and anxiety" (Beard & Wolf, 2001, p.378). Young (2004) further specified that the major factors contributed to students' Internet abuse included free and unlimited Internet access; huge blocks of unstructured time in college; newly experienced freedom from parental control; no monitoring or censoring of what they say or do online; full encouragement from faculty and administrators to make full use of the Internet resources; social intimidation and alienation; and a higher legal drinking age. In Chou, Condron, and Belland's (2005) study, the nature of the Internet, Internet users themselves, and the interactions between users on the Internet make the Internet addictive.

Chait (2009) believed that some social causes (e.g., social connections, online relationship, and emotional attachments) and personality traits (e.g., the mix of an addictive personality, life stressors, and poor emotional health) contributed to the Internet addiction. Greenfield (2011) illustrated five main factors that lead to digital media attractiveness: content factors, process and access/availability factor, reinforcement/reward factors, social factors, and generation-digital factors. Griffiths (2011) examined different aspects of Internet gambling and illustrated the following factors that contributed to Internet gambling: accessibility, affordability, anonymity, convenience, escape, immersion and dissociation, disinhibition, event frequency, interactivity, simulation, and associability. "Excessive or problematic Internet use often stems from interpersonal difficulties such as introversion or social problems" (Ferris' notes, as cited in Young, 2011, p.29). She believed that some people might have limited social support systems in place, so they turn to virtual relationships as a substitute for the missing social connection in their lives (Young, 2011). In other words, real life relationships might be a cause for the Internet addiction.

In recent years, researchers have found more reasons for the Internet addiction. Pontes, Griffiths, and Patrao (2014) discovered that Internet addiction can be predicted because it is associated with weekly hours of Internet use, loneliness, social loneliness, ownership of a portable device with Internet access, increased subjective self-perceived victimization of bullying, cyberbullying, and disturbed classroom behavior. Internet addiction decreases psychological capital, but social media membership increases both university students' Internet addiction and psychological capital (Simsek & Sali, 2014). The causes of excessive Internet use are: learning and development needs, socialization needs, psychological reasons, and seeking entertainment (Akar, 2015). The factors associated with problematic Internet use were life stressors, comorbid mental health condition, low self-esteem, attention deficit hyperactivity disorder (ADHD), behavioral problems, loneliness, social anxiety, and social skills deficits (Breslau, Aharoni, Pedersen, & Miller, 2015).

Additionally, Ben-Yehuda, Greenberg, and Weinstein (2016) stated that the frequency of the Smartphone use may be associated with Internet addiction and is not influenced by any interest or involvement in daily activities. Further, there were effects of parental Internet use on adolescents Internet use (Dogan, Bozgeyikli, & Bozdas, 2015; Lam, 2016). In Kaya's (2016) study of 488 college students, shame predicts Internet addiction and social network usage; "Being shame may manifest itself in some behaviors such as avoidance of socialization and a preference to being alone" (p.1040). Internet addiction is associated with anxiety, depression, attention deficit hyperactivity disorder (ADHD), low self-esteem, and poor self-image (CRC health, 2016). In a systematic review of 46 studies, Kuss and Lopez-Fernandez (2016) summarized that the risk factors associated with Internet addiction were sociodemographic variables (e.g., gender, age, income), Internet use variables (i.e., time spent online, using social and gaming applications), psychosocial factors (e.g., impulsivity, neuroticism, loneliness), and comorbid symptoms (i.e., anxiety, depression, psychopathology in general). These factors all contribute to an increased Internet addiction.

Consequences of Internet Addiction

There are pros and cons for the Internet use. Alexander and Schweighofer (1988, p.154) believed that "addiction can be devastating, ultimately fatal condition, but it can also be harmless or even beneficial." The problems of excessive Internet use were classified into five categories: academic, relationship, financial, occupational, and physical (Young, 1996). Students had difficulty completing their assignments, studying for examinations, or getting enough sleep because they spent excessive hours surfing irrelevant web sites, engaging in chat room gossip, conversing with Internet pen-pals, and playing interactive games (Young, 1996). People's marriages, dating relationships, parent-child relationships, and close friendships were disrupted due to excessive use of the Internet (Young, 1996). Moreover, financial problems occurred due to paying for online service or buying more online games and game time; work-related problems happened because of employee's use of online access for personal use, and misuse of the time in work place; and excessive fatigue and sleep deprivation appeared due to excessive surfing online (Young, 1996). Earlier, Young (1999) has defined cyber-affair as a "romantic or sexual relationship that is initiated via online contact and maintained predominantly through electronic conversations that occur through email, chat rooms, or interactive games." Later, Young (2004) stated that "one of the most common consequences associated with online addiction is the problem of online affairs" (p.405); "online infidelity has accounted for a growing number of divorce cases" (p.406). These are all negative consequences of addictive use of the Internet.

In fact, "addictive use of the Internet directly leads to social isolation, increased depression, familial discord, divorce, academic failure, financial debt, and job loss (Nalwa & Anand, 2003). According to Childnet International (2006), the problems associated with Internet addiction included skipping meals, losing sleep, losing time for other things or responsibilities, rearranging daily routines and neglecting studies, influencing school performance, affecting relationships with friends and family, financial problems (e.g., paying for gambling and subscriptions), and physical problems (e.g., bad diet, lack of exercise, dry eyes, Carpal Tunnel Syndrome, and back ache). As Young (2007) described, clients lose significant real-life relationships with a spouse, a parent, or a close friend due to their Internet addiction. Murali and George (2007) summed up the negative consequences of Internet use as affecting people's life interpersonally, socially, occupationally, psychologically, and physically. Cyberwidow is a term for the neglected partners of Internet addicts (Murali & George, 2007). In addition, poor academic performance at schools, impaired functioning at work, loneliness, frustration, fatigue, sleep deprivation, backache, and carpal and radial tunnel syndromes are all related to Internet addiction (Murali & George 2007).

Chrismore, Betzelberger, Bier, and Camacho (2011) also pointed out that people who suffered from Internet addiction experience significant negative consequences in their lives, such as financial debt related to the cost of monthly video gaming services, missed work or school, suicidal ideations and attempts, lack of meaningful interpersonal relationships, social awkwardness, malnourishment, poor hygiene, family discord, lack of spirituality or emotional health, and failure to fulfill personal obligations/responsibilities. Sahin (2011) proved that "Internet addiction results in personal, family, academic, financial, and occupational problems" (p.65). Khazaal et al. (2012) summarized that Internet addiction is associated with anxiety, depression, loneliness, low self-esteem, depression, social phobia, hostility, lower frustration discomfort, substance use, harmful alcohol use, and higher impulsivity levels. The trouble of Internet addiction is also associated with negative consequences in a person's real life, such as academic activities, family, marriage, work, finance, time management, and sexual life (Khazaal et al., 2012).

Researchers in recent years have found similar problems raised by Young (1996). Adults who are using Internet excessively have interpersonal problem, behavioral problem, physical problem, psychological problem, and work problem (Alam et al., 2014). Ong and Tan (2014) reported the negative effects of Internet addiction as impaired psychological well-being, less peer and family interaction, poor academic performance, and impediment to achievement of psychosocial development tasks, obesity, aggression, back pain, eye strain, and carpal tunnel syndrome. Kurt (2015) manifested that college students' suicide risk is predicted by drug use and Internet addiction.

Excessive use of the Internet would cause negative effects on adolescents, such as social consequences, physical health problem, academic consequences, psychological problems, and mental problems (Akar, 2015). Breslau, Aharoni, Pedersen, and Miller (2015) indicated that the problematic Internet use (PIU) is associated with several risk factors, such as social withdrawal, victimization, emotional instability, anxiety, depression, aggression, substance abuse, and suicidal behavior. Additionally, the consequences of PIU can cause martial conflict, child neglect, financial difficulties, ruined college careers, unemployment, and physical illness due to insufficient sleep, eating, bathing, and exercise (Breslau, Aharoni, Pedersen, & Miller, 2015). In sum, Internet addiction seems to affect people extensively in academic, relational, financial, occupational, and physical ways.

Symptoms of the Internet Addiction

What symptoms exemplify the Internet addiction? Researchers and medical doctors perceived the symptoms of Internet addiction in diverse ways. The symptoms of online affair included change in sleep patterns, a demand for privacy, ignorance of other responsibilities, evidence of lying, personality changes, loss of interest in sex, and declining investment in the relationship (Young, 2004). The withdrawal symptoms by refraining from the Internet or gaming may include restlessness, irritability, lack of concentration, anger, aggression, and computer/internet/ technology seeking (ITAA, 2009). The "primary behavioral symptom of PIU is compulsive Internet use – an inability to control, or regulate, one's online behavior," so problematic Internet use is an impulse control disorder (Caplan & High, 2011, p.47).

Additionally, there's a significant relationship between daily Internet use and the degree of psychiatric symptoms, such as depression, obsessive compulsion, interpersonal sensitivity, anxiety, hostility phobic anxiety, paranoid ideation and psychoticism (Koc, 2011). Eidenbenz (2011) described the symptoms as decline in work or school performance, disinterest in social environment, decline in offline leisure interests, fatigue with chronic lack of sleep, and aggressiveness, nervousness if online usage is hindered. The symptoms of addiction to online role-playing games included salience, mood change, tolerance, withdrawal, conflict, and relapse and reinstatement (Belinka & Smahel, 2011). Salience can be cognitive (e.g., thinks about the activity in the game) and behavioral (e.g., ignore basic life routine such as food, sleep, or hygiene); tolerance happens when the player needs to play more and more; withdrawal is the negative feelings and sensations to terminate the activity; conflict could be interpersonal or intrapersonal caused by the carried-out activity; and relapse and reinstatement are to return to addictive behavior after periods of relative control (Belinka & Smahel, 2011).

Khazaal et al. (2012) described in further detail of the cognitive, behavioral, and emotional patterns in Internet addiction. The cognitive pattern covered time distortion, excessive worry, Internet-related ruminations, depression-related cognitions, denial, expectancies, self-efficacy, obsessive preoccupations, and rejection sensitivity in social situation (Khazaal et al., 2012). The behavioral patterns included escape, a deficit in natural behavior experiments, operant conditioning, pavlovian conditioning, impulsivity, and loneliness-related behaviors (Khazaal et al., 2012). The emotional pattern consisted of emotional relief, craving, withdrawal, feeling of guilt, and emotional disturbance related to specific psychopathology (Khazaal et al., 2012).

According to a survey of 1300 young adults by marketing agency Digital Clarity, 16% of the young adults between 18 to 25 years old had symptoms of Internet addiction (BBC News, 2014). This survey examined five signs of possible Internet addiction: spending hours online, becoming irritable when interrupted, feeling guilty about the time spent online, isolation from family and friends due to excessive online activity, and feeling euphoria online and panic offline (BBC News, 2014). The symptoms of PIU included preoccupation, regulation problems, functional impairment, social impairment, and experienced tolerance or withdrawal (Breslau, Aharoni, Pedersen, & Miller, 2015).

Gregory (2016) indicated that the emotional symptoms of Internet addiction disorder may include: depression, dishonesty, feeling of guilt, anxiety, feelings of euphoria when using the computer, inability to prioritize or keep schedules, isolation, no sense of time, defensiveness, avoidance of work, agitation, mood swings, fear, loneliness, boredom with routine tasks, and procrastination. The physical symptoms of Internet addiction disorder may include: backache, Carpal Tunnel Syndrome, headaches, insomnia, poor nutrition, poor personal hygiene, neck pain, vision problem, and weight gain or loss (Gregory, 2016). It is apparent that researchers have observed the major symptoms of Internet addiction which are significant and detrimental to people's health, mentally and physically. How do people help Internet addicts with different symptoms?

MAIN FOCUS OF THE CHAPTER

Issues, Controversies, Problems

Based on the aforementioned review, a few problems have surfaced for Internet addiction.

1. **Lack of Connection Between Internet Addicts and Sources of Treatment:** The definitions and symptoms are not categorized and leveled consistently. It appears that the definitions are varied and the symptoms exist emotionally, physically, and cognitively; however, there is no corresponding treatment for each symptom. Therapy and treatment would be needed due to those symptoms. If the symptoms persist or are ignored, it will become more chronic or systematical, and will naturally develop to a compulsive obsession. How should people help if their family or friends exhibit those symptoms? Where do the Internet addicts go for treatment? Do they go to the doctors, psychiatrists, teachers, and parents, or do they go online to search for help? There are numerous online sources to help treat Internet addicts, for example, goodtherapy.org, psychguides.com, techaddiction.ca, and so on. One of the retreat centers in the U.S. is ReStart (at http://www.netaddictionrecovery.com) for treating problematic Internet use, video game, and technology use; it is a 45-day residential care program and the clients have to go through 12-step meetings and spiritual recovery (e.g., individualized assessment, treatment of co-occurring mental health concerns, group counseling and

psychotherapy, life skills, mentoring and vocational coaching). However, do the Internet addicts know they are addicted? Will they use the online sources? Are they willing to accept any treatment? There's a need to build the connection or system between the clients and the sources of treatment.

2. **Lack of Help From the Society or the Community:** Lacking of help from the world around the Internet addicts makes the problem more complicated and serious. First, social media leaders do not have addiction preventive policies while promoting the use of social media through the Internet. It seems that their focus is on business and connection, so they don't care about young people's Internet addiction and how Internet addiction damages people's health. They promote connection all over the world through social media, but they do not care about the connection between family members at home. Second, the root of game addiction is the game itself. Who designed and developed the game? This involves moral and ethical issues. If the computer and internet game designers and manufacturers stop developing violent and sexy games for people to play, will there still be many Internet addicts? If they don't concern about the health and education of the youth, the society will be twisted and more people will become Internet addicted due to those unhealthy games. Third, parents spoil their children by buying all kinds of games for them or giving them money to buy whatever they like. They didn't screen what they bought or what their children played. Some parents do not have time for their children; others are addicted to the games too. Addiction cannot be avoided if parents don't care. Additionally, the consequence of Internet addiction not only influences personal life, but also the society. Violence occurs and the motives are embedded in the social media which affects million users' minds.

3. **Insufficient Information on Treatment for Different Internet Addicts:** Internet addiction is not recognized as a formal clinical disorder in all its forms in the fifth edition of the Diagnostic and Statistical Manual of Mental Disorders (DSM-5) (Trojak, Zullino, & Achab, 2015); however, Internet gaming disorder has been included in the appendix of DSM-5 (Kuss, 2016). There is lack of scientific knowledge concerning the effects of brain stimulation techniques on Internet addiction (Trojak, Zullino, & Achab, 2015). There is also insufficient information on how to treat different types of Internet addicts and what treatment works effectively for them. For example, how do people treat those Internet addicts with emotional symptoms, physical symptoms, or cognitive symptoms? Which treatment works better? Different treatment approaches should be implemented to cope with varied symptoms for the Internet addicts. The effectiveness of different types of treatment should be published for the public as well.

SOLUTIONS AND RECOMMENDATIONS

A Complete List of Symptoms and Treatment Is Needed

Since it is confusing what treatment for each can be used, a complete list of definitions, causes, consequences, symptoms, and treatment of Internet addiction need to be presented to the public. It is difficult to find solution or treatment for Internet addicts if the symptoms are obscure or varied. It is also difficult to help Internet addicts if the treatment for each symptom is not available. Therefore, the definitions and symptoms of Internet addiction should be established formally. A list of symptoms and treatments should be generated based on research.

Help From the Society and Community Is Crucial

Treating the Internet addicts is not the sole responsibility of medical doctors, researchers, and educators. Social media leaders, game designers, and parents should help too. If children are Internet addicted, parents have responsibility to help them. How social media leaders, game designers, and relevant policy makers help is crucial. Building connection between online sources and Internet addicts is essential as well. With software engineers', policy makers', and social media leaders' help, rules and appliances could be implemented to the website to avoid Internet addiction.

Treatment for the Internet Addicts

In the past two decades, many researchers have devoted efforts in exploring ways for treating the Internet addicts. Beard (2011, p.183) indicated that "the idea of just pulling the plug and going cold turkey for the Internet addict is not very realistic." The treatment focus should be on exploring ways to engage the Internet addict in controlled Internet use, especially by helping the adolescent define clear limits on his or her Internet use. In general, the approaches to Internet addiction treatment can be divided into psychological, physical, pharmaceutical, and combined therapies. It can also be categorized into pharmaceutical and non-pharmaceutical approaches. In the following, major researchers' approaches for Internet addiction treatment will be discussed.

Miller's (1983) Motivational Interviewing Approach

Motivational interviewing was developed by Miller (1983) and Miller and Rollnick (1991) in which "a goal-directed style of counseling for eliciting behavior change by helping clients to explore and resolve ambivalence" by "asking open-ended questions, giving affirmations, and reflective listening" (Young, 2015, p.11). "Motivational interviewing is an approach based upon principles of experimental social psychology, applying process such as attribution, cognitive dissonance, and self-efficacy" (Miller, 1983, p.147). This approach involves four principles (i.e., de-emphasis on labeling, individual responsibility, internal attribution of change, and cognitive dissonance) and four goals (i.e., increasing self-esteem, increasing self-efficacy, increasing dissonance, and direct dissonance reduction) toward behavior change in motivation (Miller, 1983). Miller (1983) stated that the strategies of motivational interviewing included affirmation (i.e., reflection as reinforcement and restructuring), awareness (i.e., eliciting self-motivational or positive motivational statements, integrating objective assessment, summarizing client's current situation), and alternatives (e.g., elicit awareness, ask the client what should be done, suggest additional interventions, self-directed change, discussion of treatment goal), so that the clients will move toward self-evaluation of the problem and motivation for implementation of change. The sequence to implement motivational interview consists of eliciting self-motivational statements, objective assessment, education, summary, transition, and negotiation of alternatives.

Although Miller (1983) raised motivational interviewing with problem drinkers, Griffiths, Kuss, and King (2012) believed that motivational interviewing can be used as part of a therapeutic intervention. It "borrows strategies from cognitive therapy, client-centered counseling, systems theory, and the social psychology of persuasion, and contains elements of both directive and non-directive therapeutic approaches" (Griffiths, Kuss, & King, 2012, p.311). Young (2011) proposed to use motivational interviewing to confront the client in a constructive manner to evoke change because it helps clients confront their ambivalence. The areas of clinical interview screening questions for the assessment of problematic video game use included presenting problem, biological areas, psychological areas, social areas, and relapse prevention areas (Beard, 2005; Griffiths, Kuss, & Pontes, 2016; King, Delfabbro, & Griffiths, 2012).

Young's (1999) Time Management and Family Therapy Approaches

Young (1999) believed that the traditional abstinence models with banned Internet use are not practical interventions, and the treatment should be focused on moderation and controlled use. She proposed the following strategies to treat Internet addiction: (1) practicing the opposite by reorganizing one's time for Internet use, (2) using external stoppers such as alarm clock or timer, (3) setting goals to trim the hours of Internet use, (4) restraining oneself from a particular application s/he is addicted, (5) using reminder cards to avoid problems and staying focused on their goals, (6) taking a personal inventory of what's being cut down or cut out and ranking the importance of those activities, (7) finding a real life social support group, and (8) using family therapy by intervention, education, and encouragement (Young, 1999). The first three are time management techniques; Time management techniques were used to help patients recognize, organize, and manage their time spent online as well as set rational goals of utilization and effective coping strategies (Young, 1999).

Rosenthal's (2008) Psychodynamic Psychotherapy

The psychodynamic model, psychoanalysis, and psychodynamic therapy came from Sigmund Freud (1856-1939) who asserted that our subconscious mind and innate impulses contributed to our abnormal behaviors and the mental issues we suffered. Freud believed that the human psyche consists of the id, ego, and superego that competed against one another for controlling over our behaviors (Waude, 2016). Psychodynamic psychotherapy (PDPT) consists of seven types of interventions or techniques: (a) a focus on affect and expression of the patient's emotions; (b) exploration of the patient's attempts to avoid topics or engage in activities that hinder the progress of therapy; (c) identification of patterns in the patient's actions, thoughts, feelings, experiences, and relationships; (d) an emphasis on past relationships; (e) a focus on interpersonal experiences; (f) an emphasis on the therapeutic relationship; and (g) an exploration of wishes, fantasies, and dreams (Rosenthal, 2008). In psychodynamic psychotherapy, it is assumed that

what people say and do has meaning, although it may be outside of conscious awareness; that there are patterns to one's behavior, and these repetitive patterns can be discerned from the individual's life narrative, and observed in the therapeutic relationship; and that although these behaviors become fixed, they can change with insight and understanding (Rosenthal, 2008, p.42).

Psychodynamic psychotherapy is effective for a variety of disorders; thus, it is sufficient to justify a clinical trial for pathological gambling (Rosenthal, 2008). However, it was argued that psychodynamic theory ignored our ability to use our own free will to control our behavior and ignored external factors (e.g., biological influences of genetics on our predisposition) to some mental problems (Waude, 2016).

Larose's (2011) UGs

In Young's (2011) *Internet Addiction: Handbook and Guide to Evaluation and Treatment*, LaRose (2011, p.69) suggested to use effective self-regulation to moderate the controlled online behavior; "restoring self-regulation to one form of media consumption (e.g., television) or even in completely different behavior domains (e.g., eating or exercise habits) might enhance the ability to regulate Internet behavior." LaRose (2011) also mentioned the uses and gratifications (UGs) paradigm. "Gratifications are assessed through responses to verbal statements about respondents' reasons for media consumption (e.g., enjoyment, social interaction), typically assessed on a multipoint rating scale" (LaRose, 2011, p.57). "The relationship of uses and gratifications (UGs) of Internet use to self-regulation of online behavior is thus crucial in the development of Internet habits that disrupt lives and also in the prevention of problematic forms of use" (LaRose, 2011, pp.69-70).

De Abreu and Goes' (2011) Structured Cognitive Psychotherapy Model - 18-Week Program

De Abreu and Goes (2011) developed a structured cognitive program for the therapy of Internet addicts. In their Structured Cognitive Psychotherapy Model for the treatment of Internet addiction, there were topics for an 18-week program: (1) application of inventories, (2) program presentation, (3) analysis of the Internet's positive aspects, (4-5) do I like to or need to navigate the Web? (6-7) what the experience of needing is like, (8) analysis of the most often visited web site and the subjective sensations experiences, (9) understanding the triggering mechanism, (10) life line technique, (11) deepening into deficient aspects, (12-14) working on emerging topics, (15-16) alternative actions coping process, (17) preparation for termination, and (18) termination and application of inventories (De Abreu & Goes, 2011, p.163).

Delmonico and Griffin's (2011) Three Approaches

Delmonico and Griffin (2011) proposed three approaches to manage problematic cybersex behavior: (a) computer and environment management, (b) electronic management, and (c) acceptable use policies. Strategies in computer and environmental management consisted of using the computer in high-traffic areas, limiting the days and times of use, avoid using computer alone at home, specifying where the Internet can or cannot be used, making sure the monitor is visible to others, and installing screen savers or backgrounds of family or partner (Delmonico & Griffin, 2011). Electronic management included filtering and blocking, and computer monitoring (Delmonico & Griffin, 2011). Acceptable use policies involved helping clients establish clear boundaries to use the Internet, such as setting the time of day, number of hours online, off-limit technologies, and use of filtering or monitoring software between the client and clinicians (Delmonico & Griffin, 2011).

Eidenbenz' (2011) Phase Model

Eidenbenz (2011) proposed a therapy process called Phase Model. In the Phase Model, there were start-up phase (one to three sessions), motivation phase (three to five sessions), exploratory phase (three to eight sessions), and stabilization and final phase (one to three sessions). The goal for the start-up phase was to "create a cooperative working relationship and to obtain information for conducting an individual and systemic analysis of the problem (diagnostics) and for forming hypothesis" (Eidenbenz, 2011, p.257). The purpose of the motivation phase was to understand the circumstances (e.g., lack of say, lack of respect, no sense of achievement) that cause and maintain addiction (Eidenbenz, 2011). The exploratory phase focused on promoting "an in-depth exploration of the causes of online addiction as well as active discussions and respect within the family and alliances at parental and sibling level" (Eidenbenz, 2011, p.259). Finally, the client will reach a level of satisfactory when he controls online times effectively, improves his academic performance, takes up other recreational activities, deals more constructively with conflicts, etc. (Eidenbenz, 2011).

Chrismore, Betzelberger, Bier, & Camacho's (2011) 12-Step Recovery in Inpatient Treatment

The first step in this treatment is to spend fathering information through psychological screenings, a biopsychosocial interview, medical history, and a concerned person questionnaire (CPQ). "Treating Internet and computer addiction is explained within the first day of treatment along with the 12-step concept and Third Tradition of Alcoholics Anonymous. All patients are expected to abstain from alcohol, drugs, and other addictive behaviors while in treatment. The client is given a copy of the Emotions Anonymous book, as well as copies of the Alcoholics Anonymous (AA) and Narcotics Anonymous (NA) texts to provide the origin and background of the 12-step philosophy" (Chrismore, Betzelberger, Bier, & Camacho, 2011, pp.214-215).

Young's (2007, 2011, 2015) Cognitive Behavior Therapy (CBT)

Cognitive-behavioral therapy was developed by Young (2007, 2011) which consisted of three approaches: behavioral modification to control Internet use; cognitive restricting to challenge and modify cognitive distortions; and harm reduction therapy to address co-morbid issues. Cognitive behavior therapy (CBT) was reinforced by other researchers. Khazaal et al. (2012) illustrated the major strategies for cognitive behavioral treatment, such as acknowledgement of the problem, auto observation, time management, development of off-line activities, relapse prevention, treatment setting and specifies, and effectiveness studies. Cognitive-behavior therapy for Internet addiction (CBT-IA) was a three-phase approach (initially involved behavior modification to control Internet use, cognitive restructuring to challenge and modify cognitive distortions, and harm reduction therapy to address co-morbid issues) (Young, 2015). The Re-Start program at www.netaddictionrecovery.com is one of the retreat centers that works with clients in a "45-day residential care program through individualized assessments, treatment of co-occurring mental health concerns, group counseling and psychotherapy, life skills, mentoring and vocational coaching, 12-step meetings and spiritual recovery (Young, 2015).

Griffiths' (2015) Combination Approaches

Griffiths (2015) pointed out that the treatment of behavioral addictions employed programs and approaches that were used in the treatment of chemical addictions, such as pharmacotherapy, cognitive-behavioral therapy, psychotherapy, and self-help therapy in the past decade. In Pharmacological intervention, the addicts were given a drug to help overcome their addiction, such as the use of opioid antagonists (Griffiths, 2015). In cognitive-behavioral therapy, rational emotional therapy, motivational interviewing, and relapse prevention were used (Griffiths, 2015). Psychotherapy included Freudian psychoanalysis, transactional analysis, drama therapy, family therapy, and minimalist intervention strategies (Griffiths, 2015). Self-help therapy involved the Minnesota Model 12-step program (Griffiths, 2015).

Research has proven the effectiveness of pharmacotherapy and psychotherapy. Shaw and Black (2008) reviewed some research studies (e.g., Hadley et al., 2006; Sattar & Ramaswamy, 2004, and Shapira et al., 2000) on the use of pharmacotherapy and found positive effects of using escitalopram and medication management. Winkler, Dörsing, Rief, Shen, and Glombiewski (2013) conducted a meta-analysis on 16 studies (including 17 treatments and 670 participants) between 2005 and 2010; they found that psychological and pharmacological interventions were highly effective for improving Internet addiction, anxiety, time spent online, and depression.

Breslau, Aharoni, Pedersen, and Miller's (2015) Combination Approaches

The treatment strategies mentioned by Breslau, Aharoni, Pedersen, and Miller (2015) included psychological interventions (e.g., cognitive-behavioral therapy), Pharmacological interventions, support groups, specialized outpatient and inpatient treatment centers, trainings and continuing education courses for providers in PIU treatment strategies, and applicability of Internet-based treatment approaches. Prevention is better than cure. Breslau et al. (2015) proposed the following prevention strategies for problematic Internet use: self-regulation (e.g., self-monitoring use, committing to self or others to limit use, rewarding oneself for meeting goals of limited use), workplace Internet policies (e.g., limit, block, or monitor employee Internet use), and cyber-wellness prevention programs (e.g., teach and train employees the safe and appropriate use of the Internet).

Cash, Rae, Steel, & Winkler's (2012) Multimodal Treatments

Cash, Rae, Steel, and Winkler (2012) divided the treatment of Internet addiction to non-psychological approaches, psychological approaches, multimodal treatments, and the restart program. In non-psychological approaches, pharmacological interventions for IAD have been used, such as serotonin-reuptake inhibitors for depression and anxiety, bupropion for decreasing the crave of Internet video game play, mood stabilizers for improving the symptoms, etc. (Cash, Rae, Steel, & Winkler, 2012). In Psychological approaches, motivational interviewing, community reinforcement and family training, reality therapy, acceptance and commitment therapy, and cognitive-behavioral approach were used (Cash et al., 2012). The multimodal treatment approach involves the uses of several treatments, such as pharmacology, psychotherapy, family counseling simultaneously or sequentially (Cash et al., 2012). The reSTART Program is an inpatient Internet addiction recovery program. Based on Cash et al. (2012), the reSTART Program integrates technology detoxification (no technology for 45 to 90 days), drug and alcohol treatment, 12-step work, cognitive behavioral therapy (CBT), experiential adventure based therapy, acceptance and commitment therapy (ACT), motivational interviewing (MI), mindfulness based relapse prevention (MBRP), mindfulness based stress reduction (MBSR), interpersonal group psychotherapy, individual psychotherapy, individualized treatments for co-occurring disorders, psycho-educational groups (life visioning, addiction education, communication and assertiveness training, social skills, life skills, Life balance plan), aftercare treatments (monitoring of technology use, ongoing psychotherapy and group work), and continuing care (outpatient treatment) in an individualized, holistic approach (p.295).

Kuss & Lopez-Fernandez' (2016) Psycho-Pharmacotherapy, Psychological Therapy, and Combined Treatment

Kuss and Lopez-Fernandez (2016) analyzed 46 studies on Internet addiction and classified them into four major categories: treatment seeker characteristics, psycho-pharmacotherapy, psychological therapy, and combined treatment. In psychopharmacotherapy, most researchers used antidepressant medication to treat the Internet addicts and received positive effects, for example, (1)Selective serotonin reuptake inhibitors (SSRI), antipsychotic medication; antidepressant citalopram; (2)Benzodiazepine clonazsparn; SSRI or tricyclic antidepressant clomipramine; fluroyamine, sertraline, fluoxetine clomipramine; fluvoxamine, fluoxetine, domipramine; (3) escitalopram; (4) Antidepressant bupropion (Atmaca, 2007; Bipeta et al., 2015; Dell'Ossp et al., 2008; Han et al., 2010). Kuss (2016) described the psychopharmacotherapy as a type of treatment including administering selective serotonin reuptake inhibitors (SSRIs) (e.g., OCD, stimulants for ADHD), and atypical antipsychotics for schizophrenia spectrum disorders. In psychological therapy, the Cognitive Behavioral Therapy (CBT) is the most common approach used for individual treatment; Multimodal School-based Group (MSBG), Multimodal School-Based Group (MSBG), Multi-family group therapy (MFGT), and a traditional family therapy are group approaches for Internet addiction treatment. Kuss and Lopez-Fernandez (2016) concluded that only two of four studies that adopted group approach showed significant effects of psychological therapy.

The combined therapy includes psychological treatment and one of the followings: pharmacotherapy, electro-acupuncture therapy in treatment. Griffiths, Kuss, and Pontes (2016, p.5) concluded that "therapy that combined different approaches was beneficial for all groups because Internet addiction symptomatology decreased at all measurement time points." As Griffiths et al. (2016, p.5) illustrated, "applying electroacupuncture in combination with a psychological treatment enhanced treatment outcomes for Internet addiction above CBT alone" which provided evidence for the effectiveness of the combined approaches. For the combined therapy, all of them were effective in treating Internet addicts; however, the benefits for comorbid psychopathology were limited (Kuss & Lopez-Fernandez, 2016).

FUTURE RESEARCH DIRECTIONS

Since more and more people are addicted to the Internet in problematic ways, research on the treatment of Internet addiction is always needed. The major direction is that researchers, clinical treatment doctors, and relevant individuals should work together to provide best possible care for the individuals who suffer from Internet addiction. There is a need to identify the definitions of Internet addiction, the symptoms and their treatment, the appropriate strategies or approaches to tackle with Internet addiction, and the right types of medicine for different types of Internet addiction. Therefore, a complete list of symptoms and treatment should be focused.

Additionally, research on the effectiveness of different treatment approaches to support varied types of Internet addicts is essential. Rowicka (2016) believed that the interventions of Internet addiction depend on therapeutic approaches, and the treatment can be divided into pharmacotherapy and psychotherapy. After reviewing several studies, Rowicka (2016) noted that "there has been no pharmacological agent identified to be effective in the treatment of primarily IAD symptoms, ... hence all the studies providing an indication for the application of pharmacotherapy in IAD treatment focus first on comorbid disorder" (p.57). "Even if CBT-IA is a comprehensive approach to IAD-related disorder treatment, there is not enough evidence-based data to support its effectiveness" (Rowicka, 2016, p.59). Rowicka (2016, p.62) proposed to address the following issues for further development of treatment: "(1) inhibition of the desire to engage excessively in Internet use; (2) improvement in cognitive capacities to inhibit participation in Internet use; and (3) overcoming maladaptive decision-making." These research directions might provide parents, Internet addicts, policy makers, educators, and healthcare providers some thoughts on the importance and effectiveness of the treatment for Internet addiction.

CONCLUSION

There are approximately 3,558,289,706 Internet users in the world today (Internet Live Stats, 2017). For many people, the Internet provides abundant information, quality of life, great opportunities for social connection, self-education, economic betterment, and freedom from shyness and loneliness. For others, it causes Internet addiction, which may jeopardize people's family relationship, academic performance, professional career, and personal health. In fact, many people are addicted to the Internet without knowing it. Treatment is needed to help gain control of the Internet use in beneficial way.

"Although there is no consensus regarding the clinical status of Internet Addiction Disorder (IAD), there is a growing demand for the development and examination of various treatment protocols for Internet-related addiction" (Rowicka, 2016, p.55). As Young (2015) summarized, the treatment approaches consisted of a variety of interventions and a mix of psychotherapy theories to treat the behaviors and psychological issues (e.g., social phobia, mood disorders, sleep disorders, marital dissatisfaction, or job burnout); the most commonly therapies included motivational interviewing, cognitive-behavioral therapy (CBT), and retreat or inpatient care. It is important to use the Internet with purpose in a reasonable amount of time and without behavioral or cognitive discomfort. As Davis (2001) indicated, "Healthy Internet users can separate Internet communication with real life communication. They employ the Internet as a helpful tool rather than a source of identity" (Davis, 2001, p.193).

In this chapter, definitions, theories, causes, consequences, and symptoms of Internet addiction were reviewed. Approaches for treating the Internet addicts were examined. More standard criteria for Internet addiction is needed; more approaches to tackle with each symptoms are welcome. Medical doctors' pharmacotherapy and psychiatrists' psychotherapy are all important. They can work together to advance the milestone of treatment for the Internet addiction, since no single treatment is best for all individuals. Family therapy, CBT, and psychoeducation are mainstream for the treatment of Internet addiction. Researchers, medical doctors, educators, parents, social media leaders, and policy makers should work together to create a healthy Internet community. Prevention is better than treatment/cure. Public awareness is essential. As Ong and Tan (2014, p.380) emphasized, "Public awareness of Internet addiction, parent education on Internet use and advocacy for proper parental supervision of Internet use and advocacy for proper parental supervision of Internet use are pertinent factors in prevention efforts." Only with people's conscious help from the society and the appropriate treatment implemented for the Internet addicts, Internet addiction will be reduced or diminished.

REFERENCES

Addiction Facts. (2017, March 24). *Internet addiction statistics*. Retrieved from http://www.aboutaddictionfacts.com/addiction-statistics/internet-addiction-statistics

Akar, F. (2015). Purposes, causes and consequences of excessive internet use among Turkish adolescents. *Eurasian Journal of Educational Research, 60*(60), 35–56. doi:10.14689/ejer.2015.60.3

Akin, A., & Iskender, M. (2011). Internet addiction and depression, anxiety and stress. *International Online Journal of Educational Sciences, 3*(1), 138–148.

Alam, S. S., Hashim, N. M. H. N., Ahmad, M., Wel, C. A. C., Nor, S. M., & Omar, N. A. (2014). Negative and positive impact of Internet addiction on young adults: Empirical study in Malaysia. *Intangible Capital, 10*(3), 619–638. doi:10.3926/ic.452

Alexander, B. K., & Schweighofer, A. R. F. (1988). Defining addiction. *Canadian Psychology, 29*(2), 151–162. doi:10.1037/h0084530

Atmaca, M. (2007). A case of problematic Internet use successfully treated with an SSRI-antipsychotic combination. *Progress in Neuro-Psychopharmacology & Biological Psychiatry, 31*(4), 961–962. doi:10.1016/j.pnpbp.2007.01.003 PMID:17321659

Ayas, T. (2012). The relationship between Internet and computer game addiction level and shyness among high school students. *Educational Sciences: Theory and Practice, 12*(2), 632–636.

BBC News. (2014). *Many young people addicted to net, survey suggests*. Retrieved from http://www.bbc.com/news/technology-29627896

Beard, K. W. (2011). Working with adolescents addicted to the Internet. In K. S. Young (Ed.), *Internet addiction: A handbook and guide to evaluation and treatment* (pp. 173–189). Hoboken, NJ: John Wiley & Sons, Inc.

Beard, K. W., & Wolf, E. M. (2001). Modification in the proposed diagnostic criteria for Internet addiction. *Cyberpsychology & Behavior, 4*(3), 377–383. doi:10.1089/109493101300210286 PMID:11710263

Ben-Yehuda, L., Greenberg, L., & Weinstein, A. (2016). Internet addiction by using the smartphone-Relationships between Internet addiction, frequency of smartphone use and the state of mind of male and female students. *Journal of Reward Deficiency Syndrome & Addiction Science, 2*(1), 22–27. doi:10.17756/jrdsas.2016-024

Bergmark, K. H., Stensson, E., & Bergmark, A. (2016). Internet addiction: The making of a new addiction. *Jacobs Journal of Addiction and Therapy, 3*(1), 1-10. Retrieved from https://su.diva-portal.org/smash/get/diva2:912153/FULLTEXT01.pdf

Block, J. J. (2008). Issues for DSM-V: Internet addiction. *The American Journal of Psychiatry, 165*(3), 306–308. doi:10.1176/appi.ajp.2007.07101556 PMID:18316427

Brand, M., Young, K. S., & Laier, C. (2014). Prefrontal control and Internet addiction: A theoretical model and review of neuropsychological and neuroimaging findings. *Frontiers in Human Neuroscience, 8*, 375–395. doi:10.3389/fnhum.2014.00375 PMID:24904393

Breslau, J., Aharoni, E., Pedersen, E. R., & Miller, L. L. (2015). *A review of research on problematic Internet use and well-being with recommendations for the U.S. Air Force.* Santa Monica, CA: RAND Corporation. Retrieved from http://www.rand.org/content/dam/rand/pubs/research_reports/RR800/RR849/RAND_RR849.pdf

Burnay, J., Billieux, J., Blairy, S., & Larøi, F. (2015). Which psychological factors influence Internet addiction? Evidence through an integrative model. *Computers in Human Behavior, 43*, 28–34. doi:10.1016/j.chb.2014.10.039

Caldwell, C. D., & Cunningham, T. J. (2010). *Internet addiction and students: Implications for school counselors.* American Counseling Association. Retrieved from http://www.counseling.org/resources/library/vistas/2010-v-online/Article_61.pdf

Caplan, S. E., & High, A. C. (2011). Online social interaction, psychosocial well-being, and problematic Internet use. In K. S. Young (Ed.), *Internet addiction: A handbook and guide to evaluation and treatment* (pp. 35–53). Hoboken, NJ: John Wiley & Sons, Inc.

Cash, H., Rae, C. D., Steel, A. H., & Winkler, A. (2012). Internet addiction: A brief summary of research and practice. *Current Psychiatry Reviews, 8*(4), 292–298. doi:10.2174/157340012803520513 PMID:23125561

Çelik, S., Atak, H., & Başal, A. (2012). Predictive role of personality traits on Internet addiction. *Turkish Online Journal of Distance Education, 13*(4), 10-24.

Chait, J. (2009). *Causes of Internet addiction.* Retrieved from http://addiction.lovetoknow.com/wiki/Causes_of_Internet_Addiction

Cheng, C., & Li, A. Y. (2014). Internet addiction prevalence and quality of real life: A meta-analysis of 31 nations across seven world regions. *Cyberpsychology, Behavior, and Social Networking, 17*(12), 755–760. doi:10.1089/cyber.2014.0317 PMID:25489876

Childnet International. (2006). *Internet addiction.* Retrieved from http://paneuyouth.eu/files/2013/07/factsheet_addiction.pdf

Chou, C., Condron, L., & Belland, J. C. (2005). A review of the research on Internet addiction. *Educational Psychology Review, 17*(4), 363–388. doi:10.1007/s10648-005-8138-1

Chrismore, S., Betzelberger, E., Bier, L., & Camacho, T. (2011). Twelve-step recovery in inpatient treatment for Internet addiction. In K. S. Young (Ed.), *Internet addiction: A handbook and guide to evaluation and treatment* (pp. 205–222). Hoboken, NJ: John Wiley & Sons, Inc.

Conrad, B. (2016a). Internet addiction –Symptoms, signs, treatment, and FAQs. *TECH Addiction.* Retrieved from http://www.techaddiction.ca/internet-addiction.html

Conrad, B. (2016b). *Internet addiction statistics – facts, figures, & numbers.* Retrieved from http://www. techaddiction.ca/internet_addiction_statistics.html

Davis, R. A. (2001). A cognitive-behavioral model of pathological Internet use. *Computers in Human Behavior, 17*(2), 187–195. doi:10.1016/S0747-5632(00)00041-8

De Abreu, C. N., & Goes, D. S. (2011). Psychotherapy for Internet addiction. In K. S. Young (Ed.), *Internet addiction: A handbook and guide to evaluation and treatment* (pp. 155–171). Hoboken, NJ: John Wiley & Sons, Inc.

Delmonico, D. L., & Griffin, E. J. (2011). Cybersex addiction and compulsivity. In K. S. Young (Ed.), *Internet addiction: A handbook and guide to evaluation and treatment* (pp. 113–131). Hoboken, NJ: John Wiley & Sons, Inc.

Demirer, V., Bozoglan, B., & Sahin, I. (2013). Preservice teachers' Internet addiction in terms of gender, Internet access, loneliness and life satisfaction. *International Journal of Education in Mathematics, Science and Technology, 1*(1), 56–63.

Dogan, H., Bozgeyikli, H., & Bozdas, C. (2015). Perceived parenting styles as predictor of Internet addiction in Adolescence. *International Journal of Research in Education and Science, 1*(2), 167–174. doi:10.21890/ijres.87952

Doğan, U., & Kaya, S. (2016). Mediation effects of Internet addiction on shame and social networking. *Universal Journal of Educational Research, 4*(5), 1037–1042. doi:10.13189/ujer.2016.040513

Eidenbenz, F. (2011). Systemic dynamics with adolescents addicted to the Internet. In K. S. Young (Ed.), *Internet addiction: A handbook and guide to evaluation and treatment* (pp. 245–266). Hoboken, NJ: John Wiley & Sons, Inc.

Feist, J., & Feist, G. J. (2005). *Theories of personality* (6th ed.). Columbus, OH: McGraw-Hill Higher Education.

Friebel, A. D., & Kapoor, H. (2016). Internet addiction: A multi-faceted disorder. *Journal of Addictive Behaviors, Therapy & Rehabilitation, 5*(1), 1–3. doi:10.4172/2324-9005.1000152

Gaille, B. (2015, Feb. 13). *32 interesting Internet addiction statistics.* Retrieved from http://brandongaille. com/32-interesting-internet-addiction-statistics/

Greenfield, D. (2011). The addictive properties of Internet usage. In K. S. Young (Ed.), *Internet addiction: A handbook and guide to evaluation and treatment* (pp. 135–153). Hoboken, NJ: John Wiley & Sons, Inc.

Greenfield, D. N. (1999). *Virtual addiction: Sometimes new technology can create new problems.* Retrieved from http://virtual-addiction.com/wp-content/pdf/nature_internet_addiction.pdf

Griffiths, M. (2011). Gambling addiction on the Internet. In K. S. Young (Ed.), *Internet addiction: A handbook and guide to evaluation and treatment* (pp. 91–111). Hoboken, NJ: John Wiley & Sons, Inc.

Griffiths, M. (2015). *Classification and treatment of behavioral addictions*. Retrieved from http://www.nursinginpractice.com/article/classification-and-treatment-behavioural-addictions

Griffiths, M. D. (1998). Internet addiction: Does it really exist? In J. Gackenbach (Ed.), *Psychology and the Internet: Intrapersonal, Interpersonal, and Transpersonal Applications* (pp. 61–75). New York, NY: Academic Press.

Griffiths, M. D. (2000). Does Internet and computer "addiction" exist? Some case study evidence. *Cyberpsychology & Behavior*, *3*(2), 211–218. doi:10.1089/109493100316067

Griffiths, M. D., Kuss, D. J., Billieux, J., & Pontes, H. M. (2016). The evolution of Internet addiction: A global perspective. *Addictive Behaviors*, *53*, 193–195. doi:10.1016/j.addbeh.2015.11.001 PMID:26562678

Griffiths, M. D., Kuss, D. J., & King, D. L. (2012). Video game addiction: Past, present and future. *Current Psychiatry Reviews*, *8*, 308–318. doi:10.2174/157340012803520414

Griffiths, M. D., Kuss, D. J., & Pontes, H. M. (2016). A brief overview of Internet gaming disorder and its treatment. *Australian Clinical Psychologist*, *2*(1), 20108.

Grossman, L. (2014, December 15). The man who wired the world; Mark Zuckerberg's crusade to put every single human being online. *Time Magazine*, 30-40.

Ho, R. C., Zhang, M. W., Tsang, T. Y., Toh, A. H., Pan, F., Lu, Y., . . . Holm, B. (2013, April 9). *Social anxiety and the Internet*. Retrieved from http://www.huffingtonpost.com/barbara-holm/social-anxiety-and-internet_b_2632610.html

Ilhan, A., Çelik, H. C., Gemcioğlu, M., & Çiftaslan, M. E. (2016). Examination of the relationship between Internet attitudes and Internet addictions of 13-18-year-old students: The case of Internet Live Stats. (2017, February). *Internet users by country (2016)*. Retrieved from http://www.internetlivestats.com/internet-users-by-country/

Iskender, M., & Akin, A. (2011). Self-compassion and Internet addiction. *TOJET: The Turkish Online Journal of Educational Technology*, *10*(3), 215–221.

ITAA. (2009, August 1). *Signs and symptoms of ITA*. Retrieved from http://www.netaddictionanon.org/category/about-itaa/

ITAA. (2016). *Internet and tech addiction anonymous. 12 steps and principles for Internet & technology addiction recovery*. Retrieved from http://www.netaddictionanon.org/about/itaa-12-steps/

Kandell, J. J. (1998). Internet addiction on campus: The vulnerability of college students. *Cyberpsychology & Behavior*, *3*(2), 211–218.

Kardefelt-Winther, D. (2014). A conceptual and methodological critique of internet addiction research: Towards a model of compensatory internet use. *Computers in Human Behavior*, *31*, 351–354. doi:10.1016/j.chb.2013.10.059

Karimzadeh, N. (2015). Investigating the relationship between Internet addiction and strengthening students' social skills. *Educational Research Review*, *10*(15), 2146–2152. doi:10.5897/ERR2015.2338

Khazaal, Y., Xirossavidou, C., Khan, R., Edel, Y., Zebouni, F., & Zullino, D. (2012). Cognitive-behavioral treatment for Internet addiction. *The Open Addiction Journal, 5*(1), 30–35. doi:10.2174/1874941001205010030

Koc, M. (2011). Internet addiction and psychopatology. *TOJET: The Turkish Online Journal of Educational Technology, 10*(1), 143–148.

Kromhout, W. W. (2009, Oct. 15). UCLA, birthplace of the Internet, celebrates 40th anniversary of network's creation. *UCLA Newsroom*. Retrieved from http://newsroom.ucla.edu/releases/birthplace-of-the-internet-celebrates-111333

Kurt, D. G. (2015). Suicide risk in college students: The effects of Internet addiction and drug use. *Educational Sciences: Theory and Practice, 15*(4), 841–848.

Kuss, D. J. (2016). Internet addiction: The problem and treatment. *Turkish Green Crescent Society, 3*(2), 185–192. doi:10.15805/addict.2016.3.0106

Kuss, D. J., & King, D. L. (2012). Video game addiction: Past, present and future. *Current Psychiatry Reviews, 8*(4), 308–318. doi:10.2174/157340012803520414

Kuss, D.J., & Lopez-Fernandez, O. (2016). Internet addiction and problematic Internet use: A systematic review of clinical research. *World Journal of Psychiatry, 6*(1), 143-176. doi: 105498/wjp.v6.i1.143

Lam, L. T. (2016). Parental Internet addictive behavior and Internet addiction in adolescents: A mediating model through parental mental health. *Austin Addiction Sciences, 1*(1), 1–5.

LaRose, R. (2011). Uses and gratifications of Internet addiction. In K. S. Young (Ed.), *Internet addiction: A handbook and guide to evaluation and treatment* (pp. 55–72). Hoboken, NJ: John Wiley & Sons, Inc.

Liu, C., & Kuo, F. (2007). A study of Internet addiction through the lens of the interpersonal theory. *Cyberpsychology & Behavior, 10*(6), 799–804. doi:10.1089/cpb.2007.9951 PMID:18085967

Miller, W. R. (1983). Motivational interviewing with problem drinkers. *Behavioural Psychotherapy, 11*(02), 147–172. doi:10.1017/S0141347300006583

Modesti, K. (2009, Oct. 29). How the Internet was born at UCLA. *Los Angeles Daily News*. Retrieved from http://www.dailynews.com/article/ZZ/20091029/NEWS/910299877

Murali, V., & George, S. (2007). Lost online: An overview of Internet addiction. *Advances in Psychiatric Treatment, 13*(1), 24–30. doi:10.1192/apt.bp.106.002907

Nalwa, K., & Anand, A. P. (2003). Internet addiction in students: A cause of concern. *Cyberpsychology & Behavior, 6*(6), 653–656. doi:10.1089/109493103322725441 PMID:14756932

Nykodym, N., Ariss, S., & Kurtz, K. (2008). Computer addiction and cybercrime. *Journal of Leadership, Accountability and Ethics, 35*, 55–59. Retrieved from http://na-businesspress.homestead.com/JLAE/nykodym.pdf

Ong, S. H., & Tan, Y. R. (2014). Internet addiction in young people. *Annals Academy of Medicine*, *43*(7), 378–382. PMID:25142474

Pontes, H. M., Griffiths, M. D., & Patrão, I. M. (2014). Internet addiction and loneliness among children and adolescents in the education setting: An empirical pilot study. *Aloma*, *32*(1), 91–98.

Rosenthal, R. J. (2008). Psychodynamic psychotherapy and the treatment of pathological gambling. *Revista Brasileira de Psiquiatria (Sao Paulo, Brazil)*, *30*(1), S41–S50. doi:10.1590/S1516-44462008005000004 PMID:17992358

Rowicka, M. (2016). Internet addiction treatment. In B. Lelonek-Kuleta & J. Chwaszcz (Eds.), *Gambling and Internet addictions – epidemiology and treatment* (pp. 55–64). Lublin, Poland: Natanaelum Association Institute for Psychopreventaion and Psychotherapy.

Şahin, C. (2014). An analysis of the relationship between Internet addiction and depression levels of high school students. *Participatory Educational Research*, *1*(2), 53–67. doi:10.17275/per.14.10.1.2

Şenormanci, Ö., Konkan, R., & Sungur, M. Z. (2012). Internet addiction and its cognitive behavior therapy. In I. R. De Oliveira (Ed.), *Standard and innovative strategies in cognitive behavior therapy*. Retrieved from http://www.intechopen.com/books/standard-and-innovative-strategies-in-cognitive-behavior-therapy/internet-addiction-and-its-cognitive-behavioral-therapy

Shaw, M., & Black, D. W. (2008). Internet addiction: Definition, assessment, epidemiology and clinical management. *CNS Drugs*, *22*(5), 353–365. doi:10.2165/00023210-200822050-00001 PMID:18399706

Simsek, E., & Sali, J. B. (2014). The role of Internet addiction and social media membership on university students' psychological capital. *Contemporary Educational Technology*, *5*(3), 239–256.

Statista. (2016a). *Number of Facebook users by age in the U.S. 2016*. Retrieved from https://www.statista.com/statistics/398136/us-facebook-user-age-groups/

Statista. (2016b). *Number social network users in the United States as of January 2015, by age (in millions)*. Retrieved from https://www.statista.com/statistics/243582/us-social-media-user-age-groups/

Teong, K. Y., & Ang, M. C. H. (2016). Internet use and addiction among students in Malaysian public universities in east Malaysia: Some empirical evidence. *Journal of Management Research*, *8*(2), 31–47. doi:10.5296/jmr.v8i2.9092

Trojak, B., Zullino, D., & Achab, S. (2015). Brain stimulation to treat Internet addiction: A commentary. *Addictive Behaviors*. doi:10.1016/j.addbeh.2015.11.006 PMID:26632195

Turkle, S. (2012). *Connected, but alone? TED ideas worth spreading*. Retrieved from https://www.ted.com/talks/sherry_turkle_alone_together/transcript?language=en

Uddin, M. S., Mamum, A. A., Iqbal, M. A., Nasrullah, M., Asaduzzaman, M., Sarwar, M. S., & Amran, M. S. (2016). Internet addiction disorder and its pathogenicity to psychological distress and depression among university students: A cross-sectional pilot study in Bangladesh. *Psychology (Irvine, Calif.)*, *7*(08), 1126–1137. doi:10.4236/psych.2016.78113

Waude, A. (2016). Psychodynamic approach. *Psychologist World*. Retrieved from https://www.psychologistworld.com/freud/psychodynamic-approach

Weinstein, A., Feder, L. C., Rosenberg, K. P., & Dannon, P. (2014). Internet addiction disorder: Overview and Controversies. In K. P. Rosenberg & L. C. Feder (Eds.), *Behavioral addictions criteria, evidence, and treatment* (pp. 99–117). Waltham, MA: Elserier, Inc. doi:10.1016/B978-0-12-407724-9.00005-7

Winkler, A., Dörsing, B., Rief, W., Shen, Y., & Glombiewski, J. A. (2013). Treatment of Internet addiction: A meta-analysis. *Clinical Psychology Review*, *33*(2), 317–329. doi:10.1016/j.cpr.2012.12.005 PMID:23354007

Young, K. (2015). The evolution of Internet addiction disorder. In C. Montag & M. Reuter (Eds.), *Internet addiction: Neuroscientific approaches and therapeutical interventions* (pp. 3–17). New York, NY: Springer International Publishing.

Young, K. S. (1996). Internet addiction: The emergence of a new clinical disorder. *Cyberpsychology & Behavior*, *1*(3), 237–244. doi:10.1089/cpb.1998.1.237

Young, K. S. (1998). *Caught in the Net*. New York, NY: John Wiley & Sons.

Young, K. S. (1999). Internet addiction: Symptoms, evaluation, and treatment. In L. VandeCreek & T. L. Jackson (Eds.), *Innovations in clinical practice* (Vol. 17). Sarasota, FL: Professional Resource Press. Retrieved from http://netaddiction.com/articles/symptoms.pdf

Young, K. S. (2004). Internet addiction: A new clinical phenomenon and its consequences. *The American Behavioral Scientist*, *48*(4), 402–415. doi:10.1177/0002764204270278

Young, K. S. (2007). Cognitive-behavioral therapy with Internet addicts: Treatment outcomes and implications. *Cyberpsychology & Behavior*, *10*(5), 671–679. doi:10.1089/cpb.2007.9971 PMID:17927535

Young, K. S. (2011). Clinical assessment of Internet-addicted clients. In K. S. Young (Ed.), *Internet addiction: A handbook and guide to evaluation and treatment* (pp. 19–34). Hoboken, NJ: John Wiley & Sons, Inc.

Young, K.S., & de Abreu. (2011). Closing thoughts and future implications. In K.S. Young (Ed.), *Internet addiction: A handbook and guide to evaluation and treatment* (pp. 267-273). Hoboken, NJ: John Wiley & Sons, Inc.

Young, K. S., & Rodgers, R. C. (1998). The relationship between depression and Internet addiction. *Cyberpsychology & Behavior*, *1*(1), 25–28. doi:10.1089/cpb.1998.1.25

Young, K. S., Yue, X. D., & Ying, L. (2011). Prevalence estimates and etiologic models of Internet addiction. In K. S. Young (Ed.), *Internet addiction: A handbook and guide to evaluation and treatment* (pp. 3–17). Hoboken, NJ: John Wiley & Sons, Inc.

Zuckerberg, M. (2017, February 1). *Facebook community update*. Retrieved from https://www.facebook.com/photo.php?fbid=10103472646530311&set=a.529237706231.2034669.4&type=3&theater

KEY TERMS AND DEFINITIONS

CBT: Cognitive-behavioral therapy; it consists of three approaches: behavioral modification to control Internet use; cognitive restricting to challenge and modify cognitive distortions; and harm reduction therapy to address co-morbid issues.

Combined Therapy: A psychological treatment with either pharmacotherapy or electro-acupuncture therapy in treatment.

DIAR: Raised by Greenfield (2011) to stand for desire to stop, inability to stop, attempt to stop, and relapse.

IAD: Internet Addiction Disorder; including addiction on gaming, social networking, email, blogging, online shopping, and inappropriate Internet pornography use.

Internet Addiction: The inability to control one's Internet use, which causes severe impairment of various life functions or disorder.

PDPT: Psychodynamic psychotherapy; a talking therapy that helps people identify past issues in subconscious mind and gain insights to resolve the unconscious conflicts.

PIU: Problematic Internet Use; use of the Internet excessively that creates psychological, social, school, and/or work difficulties in a person's life.

Psychopharmacotherapy: A therapy using antidepressant medication to treat the Internet addicts.

Conclusion

OVERVIEW

As research dwells deeper into Internet addiction, we are less likely to consider it a single phenomenon but rather an intersection of multiple psychological, social and cultural phenomena. This book has provided a synopsis of psychological, social and cultural aspects of Internet addiction. Here are the highlights of Internet addiction as noted by each chapter in this book:

INTERNET HAS BOTH A NEGATIVE AND A POSITIVE EFFECT ON THE TWENTY-FIRST CENTURY ADDICTIONS

In an era of digital technology, Internet makes individuals more vulnerable to different forms of chemical or behavioural addictions. Being involved in a virtual environment like the Internet for long hours works a catalyser for various behavioural addictions like online gaming, online gambling, compulsive shopping, and cyber sex etc. However Internet also provides a platform to manage addictions. Web based interventions can offer a cost effective and easily accessible platform for a vast number of individuals seeking help. Thus, as confirmed by Shilpa Suresh Bisen, in Chapter 1, the Internet has contributed both in a positive and negative way to addiction as a behavioural disorder.

INTERNET ADDICTION SHARES SEVERAL SYMPTOMS AND CONSEQUENCES WITH SUBSTANCE ADDICTIONS

The defining criteria which include salience, mood modification, tolerance, withdrawal symptoms, conflict, and relapse (Griffiths, 2005) is common to both Internet addiction and substance addiction.

THERE IS A GENERAL COMPLACENCY TOWARD THE USE OF INTERNET

Not only parents but also physicians do not seem to be aware of the potentials and risks of Internet. However, there is a potential to turn these risks into positive outcomes. The wide acceptance of the Internet can turn it into a powerful tool for identification of the at-risk individuals and for helping them with different treatment options.

THERE IS A NEED TO REACH CONSENSUS ON DEFINITION AND DIAGNOSTIC CRITERIA FOR INTERNET ADDICTION

As shown by Shaun Joseph Smyth, Kevin Curran and Nigel Mc Kelvey, in Chapter 2, agreement on diagnostic criteria for Internet addiction which will differentiate a pathological user from a normal user is important in terms of diagnosis and correct intervention to enable effective and efficient treatment approaches. However, there are still controversial academic and clinical opinions as to the concept and the definition of Internet addiction (Fu et al., 2010; Young, 2004; Young & Rodgers, 1998). The fact that Internet addiction does not appear independently but rather it is comorbid with other psychopathological conditions (Fu et al., 2010), further complicates the diagnosis of Internet addiction. Further research should be conducted to define Internet addiction and identify its diagnostic criteria.

THE ARGUMENT IS NO LONGER ABOUT THE EXISTENCE OF INTERNET ADDICTION BUT INSTEAD HOW PREVALENT IT IS

The rates of Internet addiction worldwide are usually high and sometimes alarming (Winkler & Dörsing, 2011). Since its outset in literature, various terms have been used to name the pathological use of Internet such as Internet dependency (te Wildt, 2011), compulsive computer use (Black, Belsare, & Schlosser, 1999), virtual addiction (Greenfield, 1999), problematic Internet use (Davis, Flett, & Besser, 2002), and Internet addiction disorder (Ko, Yen, Chen, Chen, & Yen, 2005). The inclusion of the term Internet addiction in the DSM-V as a psychiatric diagnosis suggests that there is more emphasis on Internet addiction as a serious behavioural condition (Fu et al., 2010).

MOST OF THE RESEARCH ON INTERNET ADDICTION IS BASED ON CROSS-SECTIONAL APPROACH

There is myriad cross-sectional research that focus on the association between Internet addiction and various psychological, social, and behavioural variables. There is need for further longitudinal studies to establish causal association between Internet addiction disorder and these variables.

UNDERSTANDING THE RISK AND PROTECTIVE FACTORS IN INTERNET ADDICTION IS NECESSARY TO PROMOTE INDIVIDUALS' POSITIVE DEVELOPMENT AND WELLBEING FROM CHILDHOOD TO ADULTHOOD

Internet addiction influences the positive development and wellbeing of the users. Individuals with Internet addiction experience several psychological (Arslan, 2017; Young, Yue, & Ying, 2011), social (Bozoglan, Demirer, & Sahin, 2014; Kamal & Mosallem, 2013; Lin et al., 2014; Milani, Osualdella, & Di Blasio, 2009; Müller et al., 2015; Odacı, 2013), academic or professional difficulties (Akhter, 2013; Eldeleklioğlu & Vural, 2013; Odacı, 2013). Understanding the risk and protective factors in Internet addiction will help to promote individuals' positive development and wellbeing from childhood to adulthood.

THERE IS A RELATIONSHIP BETWEEN INTERNET ADDICTION AND SPECIFIC PERSONALITY TRAITS, DISORDERS, AND CHARACTERISTICS

As noted by Zaheer Hussain and Halley M Pontes, in Chapter 3, distinct personality traits are associated with distinct online activities and individuals with specific personality features such as neuroticism, extraversion, and openness to experience, agreeableness, and conscientiousness may be particularly at risk for developing certain technological addictions such as Facebook addiction, videogame addiction, Internet addiction, and smartphone addiction (Andreassen et al., 2013). Moreover, the causal pathway between technological addictions and personality traits may be bi-directional. Thus, research on the identification and prevention of Internet addiction need to consider individual differences.

THERE IS A RELATIONSHIP BETWEEN INTERNET ADDICTION, TIME SPENT ONLINE, AND WELL-BEING

Higher time spent online is considered to be a fundamental indicator of Internet addiction (Chou, Condron, & Belland, 2005; Young, 1996). Time spent online can lead to differences in subjective well-being and sources of life satisfaction and dissatisfaction among Internet users (Kraut et al., 1998; Lenhart, 2015; Nie, Hillygus, and Erbring, 2002; Waldo, 2014). As noted by Tihana Brkljačić, Filip Majetić and Anja Wertag, in Chapter 4, heavy Internet users are likely to be less happy compared to light users, and they are more likely to find satisfaction in various entertainment activities, while light users tend to find satisfaction in love, life and family.

PSYCHOLOGICAL MALTREATMENT CAN BE A RISK FACTOR FOR INTERNET ADDICTION, AND IT MAY INCREASE VULNERABILITY TO INTERNET ADDICTION AND INTERNET-RELATED PROBLEMS

Research has shown that psychologically maltreated individuals are more inclined to develop addictive behaviours compared to non–maltreated ones (Arslan, 2016; Arslan, 2017; Elliott et al., 2014; Griffiths & Pontes, 2014). As suggested by Gökmen Arslan, in Chapter 5, psychologically maltreated individuals are also more inclined to develop Internet addiction. In line with General Theory of Addictions (Jacobs, 1986), negative life experiences during childhood such as maltreatment can act as risk factors in the development of Internet addiction and Internet–related problems (Felsher, Derevensky, & Gupta, 2010). However, there is still limited information on the relationship between psychological maltreatment and Internet addiction. There is need for further research to investigate short and long–term impacts of psychological maltreatment on Internet addiction.

LONELINESS IS AN IMPORTANT PREDICTOR OF INTERNET ADDICTION

Internet is a tool for socializing and thus reducing loneliness among young people. Individuals who fail to develop efficient relationships with the people around are more prone to develop Internet addiction to meet interpersonal needs and form alternative social channels (Papacharissi & Rubin, 2000). Thus,

Internet is used to substitute face-to-face communication (Kubey, Lavin & Barrows, 2001). As noted by Ayfer Aydiner Boylu and Gülay Günay, in Chapter 6, there seems to be a negative correlation between individuals' sense of loneliness in everyday life and the sense of loneliness they feel in the virtual environment. Those who cannot develop efficient relationships in social environments prefer to socialize in virtual environments, and experience a sense of belonging.

THE DIRECTION OF THE EFFECT OF SOCIOECONOMIC STATUS ON INTERNET ADDICTION IS NOT CLEAR

Socioeconomic determinants may affect Internet addiction in different ways in different populations, different cultures, and different time periods. Income, parental education and overall socioeconomic status scores are among the most commonly adopted socioeconomic indicators of Internet addiction. Additionally, not living with one's mother, poor Internet-specific parenting practices, and parent conflicts (Conger, Conger, & Martin, 2010), high family income, migrant status, and living in rural areas (Kuss, Griffiths, Karila, & Billieux, 2014) have been associated with Internet addiction. As noted by Francisco T.T. Lai and Joyce L.Y. Kwan, in Chapter 7, research on Internet addiction and socioeconomic factors does not clearly show whether a better socioeconomic background is associated with a higher or lower risk of Internet addiction.

THERE IS A CLOSE RELATIONSHIP BETWEEN FAMILY FACTORS AND INTERNET USAGE OF CHILDREN AND ADOLESCENTS

As highlighted, by me, in Chapter 8, family factors highlighted in previous research on child Internet addiction can be listed as parental monitoring and parental guidance, parental mediation, Internet parenting styles, parental norms and behaviours, parent and child characteristics, parent marital conflict, quality of the parent-child and peer relationship and culture. While family variables such as broken family, family conflict, split homes, low family functionality and permissive or indulgent parenting styles are positively correlated with Internet addiction (Beal et al, 2001; Bogenschneider, 1998), quality of the parent–child relationship is negatively correlated with Internet addiction among children and adolescents (Liu & Kuo, 2007).

AN EFFECTIVE AND HEALTHY USE OF INTERNET STARTS IN THE FAMILY AND FAMILY SHOULD BE IN THE CORE OF ANY PREDICTIVE, PREVENTIVE, OR CORRECTIVE ACTS ABOUT INTERNET ADDICTION

Some of the guidelines for parents to help their children avoid Internet addiction include employing parental control and parental warmth, maintaining open communication, being involved, finding other leisure time activities and encouraging outdoor activities, establishing clear limits and rules, monitoring computer use and being a good role model (Chou & Peng, 2007; Valcke et al., 2010). Net-education and media-literacy education programs or campaigns which aim at informing parents and children about the risks of excessive Internet use and effective parenting strategies can be promising, as well.

DIGITAL ADDICTION CAN MANIFEST ITSELF IN EDUCATIONAL ENVIRONMENTS IN DIFFERENT WAYS

As proposed by Jonathan Bishop, in Chapter 9, different environments offer different levels of engagement for individuals. With the introduction of technology, educational environments can be addictive for learners with different learning styles. Knol, a measure of brain activity, can be used to assess the risk of different learning styles using a particular intensity of ICT.

THE WIDESPREAD USE OF SOCIAL MEDIA AND INTERNET HAS BROUGHT UP THE TERMS *CYBERPSYCHO EFFECT* AND *CYBERPSYCHO ATTACK*

As described by Manisha Nene and Prashant Gupta, in Chapter 10, Cyberpsycho effect includes using the cyberspace or social media as a medium to influence others to meet certain objectives. *CyberPsycho attack* is described as the case when an attacker uses cyberspace and social network to manipulate the attitude or behaviour of an individual or a targeted society with an aim to achieve certain goals or to attain political, religious, economical, and social gains.

INTERNET ADDICTION HAS DISTINCT CULTURAL FEATURES AND IT CAN BE EXPERIENCED DIFFERENTLY ACROSS DIFFERENT CULTURES

As noted by Rüya Samlı, in Chapter 11, the "level of tendency" and the "level of effect" of a person for Internet addiction can change depending on the culture it is carried out. The discrepancies in prevalance rates of Internet addiction may result from different research methodologies, cultural backgrounds, sampling techniques and assessment approach (Pontes, Kuss, et al., 2015).

RESEARCH ON INTERNET ADDICTION HAS COMMONLY BEEN CONDUCTED IN ASIAN COUNTRIES AND "FAR EAST" COUNTRIES SEEM TO BE SUFFERING FROM INTERNET ADDICTION MORE THAN THE OTHERS

Internet addiction is a widespread problem researched all over the world. However, as shown by Rüya Samlı, in Chapter 11, Internet addiction research in some countries such as China, Turkey, Taiwan, Hong Kong and Korea have outnumbered the research conducted in the rest of the world. Internet addiction should be investigated in different countries or cultures with diverse samples.

THERE IS A RELATIONSHIP BETWEEN INTERNET ADDICTION AND THE PURPOSE OF INTERNET USE

The purpose of Internet use is an important factor to differentiate healthy and unhealthy users. (Ceyhan, 2008; Yang & Tung, 2007). While healthy users mostly use the Internet primarily for the purpose of obtaining information, problematic users are more likely to use the Internet more for entertainment and socialization. As confirmed, by Mirna Macur and Halley M. Pontes, in Chapter 12, college students with high risk of Internet addiction are more likely to spend time on the Internet for leisure purposes in comparison to students with low risk of Internet addiction. Additionally, Internet addiction may have different consequences on social, leisure, and academic activities. The purpose of Internet use is associated with the users' well-being, as well. While usage for communication purposes has been associated with beneficial effects, and usage for non-social purposes has been found to bring detrimental outcomes (e.g. Morgan & Cotten, 2003). It is also important to differentiate between the ones who are addicted to the Internet itself and those who use the Internet as a means of fuelling a different addiction (Griffiths, 1998).

THE ADVENT OF THE SOCIAL MEDIA HAS GIVEN RISE TO A PLURALITY OF INFORMATION TECHNOLOGY SYNDROMES AND MULTIPLE FORMS OF SOCIAL LEPROSIES SUCH AS SOCIAL MEDIA CRAZE AND SELFIE-OBJECTIFICATION

Though similar to social media addiction, social media craze is not completely associated with Internet addiction or social media addictions. Floribert Patrick Calvain Endong notes, in Chapter 13, that selfie-objectification is manifested by naked and highly sexualized selfies among Nigerians. It is considered to be a form of social pathology, observed particularly among the youths.

INTERNET USAGE SEEMS TO BE RISKY FOR THE YOUNGEST PARTICULARLY

Since Internet has social, communicative and emotional function in adolescents' lives, it contributes to their relationships. However, the excessive use of the Internet can have a negative effect on their daily routines and their psychological well-being, as well. As indicated by Valentina Boursier and Valentina Manna, in Chapter 14, there is a need to identify a clear profile of the "addicted" adolescent and develop psychometric tools to assess problematic relationships with the Internet for preadolescents/adolescents.

THERE IS A NEED TO IDENTIFY THE SYMPTOMS AND THEIR TREATMENT, THE APPROPRIATE STRATEGIES OR APPROACHES TO TACKLE WITH INTERNET ADDICTION, AND THE RIGHT TYPES OF MEDICINE FOR DIFFERENT TYPES OF INTERNET ADDICTION

As highlighted by Libi Shen, in Chapter 15, researchers and clinical doctors should work together to provide the best possible care for the individuals who suffer from Internet addiction. In addition to providing a complete list of symptoms and treatments for Internet addiction, research on the effectiveness of different treatment approaches for different types of Internet addiction is essential, as well. As underlined by Libi Shen, in Chapter 15, researchers, medical doctors, educators, parents, social media leaders, and policy makers should work in collaboration to form a healthy Internet community. Conscious help from the society and the appropriate treatment implemented for the Internet addicts seem to be the only solution to diminish Internet addiction.

NO SINGLE TREATMENT IS BEST FOR ALL INTERNET ADDICTS

Interventions of Internet addiction are mostly based on therapeutic approaches including pharmacotherapy and psychotherapy (Rowicka, 2016). Family therapy, Cognitive Behavioral Therapy, and psychoeducation are the mainstream treatments of Internet addiction. As indicated by Libi Shen, in Chapter 15, medical doctors' pharmacotherapy and psychiatrists' psychotherapy are all important to develop effective treatment strategies for Internet addiction.

Overall, as noted by Rudall (1996), the appearance of new behavioural situation should not surprise us at a time when technological advances are taking place so rapidly and revolutionarily. Internet has facilitated the modern life through several online activities, but it has also negative effects that may lead to problems for excessive users. As researchers, psychologists, sociologists or anthropologists, we should all face the fact that Internet is changing our lives but not always for better.

REFERENCES

Akhter, N. (2013). Relationship between Internet addiction and academic performance among university undergraduates. *Educational Research Review*, 8(19), 1793–1796.

Andreassen, C. S., Griffiths, M. D., Gjertsen, S. R., Krossbakken, E., Kvam, S., & Pallesen, S. (2013). The relationships between behavioral addictions and the five-factor model of personality. *Journal of Behavioral Addictions*, 2(2), 90–99. doi:10.1556/JBA.2.2013.003 PMID:26165928

Arslan, G. (2016). Psychological maltreatment, emotional and behavioral problems in adolescents: The mediating role of resilience and self-esteem. *Child Abuse & Neglect*, 52, 200–209. doi:10.1016/j.chiabu.2015.09.010 PMID:26518981

Arslan, G. (2017). Psychological maltreatment, forgiveness, mindfulness, and Internet addiction among young adults: A study of mediation effect. *Computers in Human Behavior*, 72, 57–66. doi:10.1016/j.chb.2017.02.037

Beal, A. C., Ausiello, J., & Perrin, J. M. (2001). Social influences on health-risk behaviors among minority middle school students. *The Journal of Adolescent Health*, 28(6), 474–480. doi:10.1016/S1054-139X(01)00194-X PMID:11377991

Black, D. W., Belsare, G., & Schlosser, S. (1999). Clinical features, psychiatric comorbidity, and health-related quality of life in persons reporting compulsive computer use behavior. *The Journal of Clinical Psychiatry*, 60(12), 839–844. doi:10.4088/JCP.v60n1206 PMID:10665630

Bogenschneider, K., Wu, M. Y., Raffaelli, M., & Tsay, J. C. (1998). Parent influences on adolescent peer orientation and substance use: The interface of parenting practices and values. *Child Development*, 69(6), 1672–1688. doi:10.1111/j.1467-8624.1998.tb06184.x PMID:9914646

Bozoglan, B., Demirer, V., & Sahin, I. (2013). Loneliness, self-esteem, and life satisfaction as predictors of Internet addiction: A cross-sectional study among Turkish university students. *Scandinavian Journal of Psychology*, 54(4), 313319. doi:10.1111/sjop.12049 PMID:23577670

Bozoglan, B., Demirer, V., & Sahin, I. (2014). Problematic Internet use: Functions of use, cognitive absorption, and depression. *Computers in Human Behavior*, *37*, 117–123. doi:10.1016/j.chb.2014.04.042

Ceyhan, A. A. (2008). Predictors of problematic Internet use on Turkish university students. *Cyberpsychology & Behavior*, *11*(3), 363–366. doi:10.1089/cpb.2007.0112 PMID:18537510

Chou, C., Condron, L., & Belland, J. C. (2005). A review of the research on Internet addiction. *Educational Psychology Review*, *17*(4), 363–388. doi:10.1007/s10648-005-8138-1

Chou, C., & Peng, H. (2007). Net-friends: Adolescents' attitudes and experiences vs. teachers' concerns. *Computers in Human Behavior*, *23*(5), 2394–2413. doi:10.1016/j.chb.2006.03.015

Conger, R. D., Conger, K. J., & Martin, M. J. (2010). Socioeconomic status, family processes, and individual development. *Journal of Marriage and the Family*, *72*(3), 685–704. doi:10.1111/j.1741-3737.2010.00725.x PMID:20676350

Davis, R. A., Flett, G. L., & Besser, A. (2002). Validation of a new scale for measuring problematic Internet use: Implications for pre-employment screening. *Cyberpsychology & Behavior*, *5*(4), 331–345. doi:10.1089/109493102760275581 PMID:12216698

Eldeleklioğlu, J., & Vural, M. (2013). Predictive effects of academic achievement, Internet use duration, loneliness and shyness on Internet addiction. *Hacettepe Üniversitesi Eğitim Fakültesi Dergisi*, *28*, 28–1.

Elliott, J. C., Stohl, M., Wall, M. M., Keyes, K. M., Goodwin, R. D., Skodol, A. E., & Hasin, D. S. et al. (2014). The risk for persistent adult alcohol and nicotine dependence: The role of childhood maltreatment. *Addiction (Abingdon, England)*, *109*(5), 842–850. doi:10.1111/add.12477 PMID:24401044

Felsher, J. R., Derevensky, J. L., & Gupta, R. (2010). Young adults with gambling problems: The impact of childhood maltreatment. *International Journal of Mental Health and Addiction*, *8*(4), 545–556. doi:10.1007/s11469-009-9230-4

Fu, K. W., Chan, W. S., Wong, P. W., & Yip, P. S. (2010). Internet addiction: Prevalence, discriminant validity and correlates among adolescents in Hong Kong. *The British Journal of Psychiatry*, *196*(6), 486–492. doi:10.1192/bjp.bp.109.075002 PMID:20513862

Greenfield, D. N. (1999). Psychological characteristics of compulsive Internet use: A preliminary analysis. *Cyberpsychology & Behavior*, *2*(5), 403–412. doi:10.1089/cpb.1999.2.403 PMID:19178212

Griffiths, M. (1998). Internet addiction: does it really exist? *Psychology and the Internet*, 61-75.

Griffiths, M. (2005). A 'components' model of addiction within a biopsychosocial framework. *Journal of Substance Use*, *10*(4), 191–197. doi:10.1080/14659890500114359

Griffiths, M. D., & Pontes, H. M. (2014). Internet addiction disorder and Internet gaming disorder are not the same. *Addiction Research & Therapy*, *5*(4), 1-3. DOI: 10.4172/2155-6105.1000e124

Kamal, N. N., & Mosallem, F. A. E. H. (2013). Determinants of problematic Internet use among el-minia high school students, Egypt. *International Journal of Preventive Medicine*, *4*(12), 1429–1437. PMID:24498499

Ko, C. H., Yen, J. Y., Chen, C. C., Chen, S. H., & Yen, C. F. (2005). Proposed diagnostic criteria of Internet addiction for adolescents. *The Journal of Nervous and Mental Disease, 193*(11), 728–733. doi:10.1097/01.nmd.0000185891.13719.54 PMID:16260926

Kraut, R., Patterson, M., Lundmark, V., Kiesler, S., Mukophadhyay, T., & Scherlis, W. (1998). Internet paradox: A social technology that reduces social involvement and psychological well-being? *The American Psychologist, 53*(9), 1017–1031. doi:10.1037/0003-066X.53.9.1017 PMID:9841579

Kubey, R. W., Lavin, M. J., & Barrows, J. R. (2001). Internet use and collegiate academic performance decrements: Early findings. *Journal of Communication, 51*(2), 366–382. doi:10.1111/j.1460-2466.2001.tb02885.x

Kuss, J., Griffiths, M., Karila, L., & Billieux, J. (2014). Internet addiction: A systematic review of epidemiological research for the last decade. *Current Pharmaceutical Design, 20*(25), 4026–4052. doi:10.2174/13816128113199990617 PMID:24001297

Lenhart, A. (2015). *Teens, Social Media & Technology: Overview 2015.* Retrieved March 17 2017 from http://www.pewInternet.org/2015/04/09/teens-social-media-technology-2015/

Lin, I. H., Ko, C. H., Chang, Y. P., Liu, T. L., Wang, P. W., Lin, H. C., & Yen, C. F. et al. (2014). The association between suicidality and Internet addiction and activities in Taiwanese adolescents. *Comprehensive Psychiatry, 55*(3), 504–510. doi:10.1016/j.comppsych.2013.11.012 PMID:24457034

Liu, C. Y., & Kuo, F. Y. (2007). A study of Internet addiction through the lens of the interpersonal theory. *Cyberpsychology & Behavior, 10*(6), 799–804. doi:10.1089/cpb.2007.9951 PMID:18085967

Milani, L., Osualdella, D., & Di Blasio, P. (2009). Quality of interpersonal relationships and problematic Internet use in adolescence. *Cyberpsychology & Behavior, 12*(6), 681–684. doi:10.1089/cpb.2009.0071 PMID:19788382

Morgan, C., & Cotten, S. R. (2003). The relationship between Internet activities and depressive symptoms in a sample of college freshmen. *Cyberpsychology & Behavior, 6*(2), 133–142. doi:10.1089/109493103321640329 PMID:12804025

Müller, K. W., Janikian, M., Dreier, M., Wölfling, K., Beutel, M. E., Tzavara, C., & Tsitsika, A. et al. (2015). Regular gaming behavior and Internet gaming disorder in European adolescents: Results from a cross-national representative survey of prevalence, predictors, and psychopathological correlates. *European Child & Adolescent Psychiatry, 24*(5), 565–574. doi:10.1007/s00787-014-0611-2 PMID:25189795

Nie, N., Hillygus, D. S., & Erbring, L. (2002). Internet use, interpersonal relations, and sociability: A time diary study. In B. Wellman & C. Haythornthwaite (Eds.), *The Internet in Everyday Life* (pp. 215–243). Oxford, UK: Blackwell. doi:10.1002/9780470774298.ch7

Odacı, H. (2013). Risktaking behavior and academic selfefficacy as variables accounting for problematic Internet use in adolescent university students. *Children and Youth Services Review, 35*(1), 183–187. doi:10.1016/j.childyouth.2012.09.011

Papacharissi, Z., & Rubin, A. M. (2000). Predictors of Internet use. *Journal of Broadcasting & Electronic Media, 44*(2), 175–196. doi:10.1207/s15506878jobem4402_2

Rowicka, M. (2016). Internet addiction treatment. In B. Lelonek-Kuleta & J. Chwaszcz (Eds.), *Gambling and Internet addictions – epidemiology and treatment* (pp. 55–64). Lublin, Poland: Natanaelum Association Institute for Psychopreventaion and Psychotherapy.

Rudall, B. H. (1996). Internet addiction syndrome. *Robotica, 14*, 510–511.

te Wildt, B. T., Putzig, I., Zedler, M., & Ohlmeier, M. D. (2007). Internet dependency as a symptom of depressive mood disorders. *Psychiatrische Praxis, 34*, S318–S322. doi:10.1055/s-2007-970973 PMID:17786892

Valcke, M., Bonte, S., De Wever, B., & Rots, I. (2010). Internet parenting styles and the impact on Internet use of primary school children. *Computers & Education, 55*(2), 454–464. doi:10.1016/j.compedu.2010.02.009

Waldo, A. (2014). Correlates of Internet addiction among adolescents. *Psychology (Irvine, Calif.), 5*(18), 1999–2008. doi:10.4236/psych.2014.518203

Winkler, A., & Dörsing, B. (2011). *Treatment of Internet addiction disorder: a first meta-analysis* (Diploma thesis). Marburg: University of Marburg.

Yang, S. C., & Tung, C. J. (2007). Comparison of Internet addicts and non-addicts in Taiwanese high school. *Computers in Human Behavior, 23*(1), 79–96. doi:10.1016/j.chb.2004.03.037

Young, K. S. (1996). Psychology of computer use: XL. Addictive use of the Internet: a case that breaks the stereotype. *Psychological Reports, 79*(3), 899–902. doi:10.2466/pr0.1996.79.3.899 PMID:8969098

Young, K. S., & Rodgers, R. C. (1998, April). Internet addiction: Personality traits associated with its development. *69th annual meeting of the Eastern Psychological Association*, 40-50.

Young, K. S. (2004). Internet addiction: A new clinical phenomenon and its consequences. *The American Behavioral Scientist, 48*(4), 402–415. doi:10.1177/0002764204270278

Young, K. S., Yue, X. D., & Ying, L. (2011). Prevalence estimates and etiologic models of Internet addiction. *Internet Addiction: A Handbook and Guide to Evaluation and Treatment*, 3-17.

Compilation of References

Abdulahi, A., Samadi, B., & Gharleghi, B. (2014). A study on the negative effects of social networking sites such as facebook among asia pacific university scholars in Malaysia. *International Journal of Business and Social Science*, *5*(10).

Aboujaoude, E. (2017). The Internet's effect on personality traits: An important casualty of the "Internet addiction" paradigm. *Journal of Behavioral Addictions*, *6*(1), 1–4. doi:10.1556/2006.6.2017.009 PMID:28301969

Abreu, C. N. D., Karam, R. G., Góes, D. S., & Spritzer, D. T. (2008). Internet and videogame addiction: A review. *Revista Brasileira de Psiquiatria (Sao Paulo, Brazil)*, *30*(2), 156–167. doi:10.1590/S1516-44462008000200014 PMID:18592108

Adagbo, A. (2016, Oct.). Nollywood and Nigeria's challenge of reel geopolitics. *Intervention*, 11-21.

Adalier, A. (2012). The relationship between Internet addiction and psychological symptoms. *International Journal of Global Education*, *1*, 42–49.

Addiction Facts. (2017, March 24). *Internet addiction statistics*. Retrieved from http://www.aboutaddictionfacts.com/addiction-statistics/internet-addiction-statistics

Ahmadi, J., Amiri, A., Ghanizadeh, A., Khademalhosseini, M., Khademalhosseini, Z., Gholami, Z., & Sharifian, M. (2014). Prevalence of addiction to the Internet, computer games, DVD, and video and its relationship to anxiety and depression in a sample of Iranian high school students. *Iranian Journal of Psychiatry and Behavioral Sciences*, *8*(2), 75. PMID:25053960

Ahmadi, K. (2014). Internet addiction among Iranian adolescents: A nationwide study. *Acta Medica Iranica*, *52*(6), 467–472. PMID:25130156

Ahmadi, K., & Saghafi, A. (2013). Psychosocial Profile of Iranian Adolescents' Internet Addiction. *Cyberpsychology, Behavior, and Social Networking*, *16*(7), 543–548. doi:10.1089/cyber.2012.0237 PMID:23614793

Ajere, O., & Oyinloye, O. A. (2011). Perspectives of youths on the interiorization of core-societal-values in the Nigerian society. *Akungba Journal of Research in Education*, *1*(1), 179–194.

Ajike, A. K., & Nwakoby, N. P. (2016). The impact of social networking sites on teenagers in Nigeria. *International Journal of Public Policy and Administration*, *11*(1), 35–64.

Akar, F. (2015). Purposes, causes and consequences of excessive internet use among Turkish adolescents. *Eurasian Journal of Educational Research*, *60*(60), 35–56. doi:10.14689/ejer.2015.60.3

Akdağ, M., Şahan Yılmaz, B., Özhan, U., & San, I. (2014). Investigation of Internet dependences of university students in terms of variable variations (Inonu University Example). *Inonu University Journal of the Faculty of Education*, *15*(1), 73–96.

Akhter, N. (2013). Relationship between internet addiction and academic performance among university undergraduates. *Educational Research Review, 8*(19), 1793–1796.

Akin, A., & Iskender, M. (2011). Internet addiction and depression, anxiety and stress. *International Online Journal of Educational Sciences, 3*(1), 138-148.

Akin, A., & Iskender, M. (2011). Internet addiction and depression, anxiety and stress. *International Online Journal of Educational Sciences, 3*(1), 138–148.

Akinpelu, J. A. (1983). Values in Nigerian society. In O. A. Nduka & E. O. Iheoma (Eds.), *New perspectives in moral education* (pp. 33–56). Ibadan: Evans Brothers Publishers Limited.

Ak, Ş., Koruklu, N., & Yılmaz, Y. (2013). A study on Turkish adolescent's Internet use: Possible predictors of Internet addiction. *Cyberpsychology, Behavior, and Social Networking, 16*(3), 205–209. doi:10.1089/cyber.2012.0255 PMID:23253206

Aksoy, V. (2015). The degree of change of Internet addiction and social network use according to the demographic features of science high school students and its effect upon their academic success. *The Journal of Academic Social Science, 3*(19), 365–383. doi:10.16992/ASOS.874

Alam, S. S., Hashim, N. M. H. N., Ahmad, M., Wel, C. A. C., Nor, S. M., & Omar, N. A. (2014). Negative and positive impact of Internet addiction on young adults: Empirical study in Malaysia. *Intangible Capital, 10*(3), 619–638. doi:10.3926/ic.452

Alavi, S. S., Ferdosi, M., Jannatifard, F., Eslami, M., Alaghemandan, H., & Setare, M. (2012). Behavioral addiction versus substance addiction: Correspondence of psychiatric and psychological views. *International Journal of Preventive Medicine, 3*(4), 290–294. PMID:22624087

Alavi, S. S., Jannatifard, F., Maracy, M., & Rezapour, H. (2009). The Psychometric properties Generalized pathological internet use Scale (GPIUS) in Internet users students of Isfahan Universities. *Journal of Knowledge & Research in Applied Psychology, 0*(40), 38–51.

Alexander, B. K., & Schweighofer, A. R. (1988). Defining addiction. *Canadian Psychology, 29*(2), 151–162. doi:10.1037/h0084530

Alf, E. F. Jr, & Abrahams, N. M. (1975). The use of extreme groups in assessing relationships. *Psychometrika, 40*(4), 563–572. doi:10.1007/BF02291557

Alminhana, L. O., & Farias, M. (2014). The missing link: What mediates the relationship between religiosity and alcohol use? *Revista Brasileira de Psiquiatria (Sao Paulo, Brazil), 36*(1), 3–3. doi:10.1590/1516-4446-2014-3602 PMID:24604457

Al-Mosa, N. A. (2015). Role of Social Networks in Developing Religious and Social Values of the Students of the World Islamic Sciences & Education University. *International Education Studies, 8*(9), 126. doi:10.5539/ies.v8n9p126

Alpaslan, A. H., Avci, K., Soylu, N., & Guzel, H. I. (2015). The association between problematic Internet use, suicide probability, alexithymia and loneliness among Turkish medical students. *Journal of Psychiatry, 18*(208).

Amadi, E. (2005). *Ethics in Nigerian cultures*. Ibadan: Bookraft.

American Psychiatric Association. (1994). *APA Diagnostic and Statistical Manual of Mental Disorders*. Author.

American Psychiatric Association. (1994). *Diagnostic and Statistical Manual for Mental Disorders* (4th ed.). Washington, DC: American Psychiatric Association.

American Psychiatric Association. (2013). *Diagnostic and Statistical Manual of Mental Disorders* (5th ed.). Arlington, VA: American Psychiatric Publishing.

Amichai-Hamburger, Y., & Vinitzky, G. (2010). Social network use and personality. *Computers in Human Behavior*, *26*(6), 1289–1295. doi:10.1016/j.chb.2010.03.018

Anderson, E.L., Steen, E., & Stavropoulos, V. (2016). Internet use and Problematic Internet Use: a systematic review of longitudinal research trends in adolescence and emergent adulthood. *International Journal of Adolescence and Youth*, *3843*, 1-25.

Andersson, E., Enander, J., Andrén, P., Hedman, E., Ljótsson, B., Hursti, T., & Rück, C. et al. (2012). Internet-based cognitive behavior therapy for obsessive–compulsive disorder: A randomized controlled trial. *Psychological Medicine*, *42*(10), 2193–2203. doi:10.1017/S0033291712000244 PMID:22348650

Ando, R., & Sakamoto, A. (2008). The effect of cyber-friends on loneliness and social anxiety: Differences between high and low self-evaluated physical attractiveness groups. *Computers in Human Behavior*, *24*(3), 993–1009. doi:10.1016/j.chb.2007.03.003

Andrade, J. A. (2003). *The effect of Internet on children's perceived social support* (Unpublished doctorate dissertation). University of Hartford.

Andreassen, C. S., Billieux, J., Griffiths, M. D., Kuss, D. J., Demetrovics, Z., Mazzoni, E., & Ståle, P. (2016). The relationship between addictive use of social media and video games and symptoms of psychiatric disorders: A large-scale cross-sectional study. *Psychology of Addictive Behaviors*, *30*(2), 252–265. doi:10.1037/adb0000160 PMID:26999354

Andreassen, C. S., Griffiths, M. D., Gjertsen, S. R., Krossbakken, E., Kvam, S., & Pallesen, S. (2013). The relationships between behavioral addictions and the five-factor model of personality. *Journal of Behavioral Addictions*, *2*(2), 90–99. doi:10.1556/JBA.2.2013.003 PMID:26165928

Andreassen, C. S., Pallesen, S., & Griffiths, M. D. (2017). The relationship between addictive use of social media, narcissism, and self-esteem: Findings from a large national survey. *Addictive Behaviors*, *64*, 287–293. doi:10.1016/j.addbeh.2016.03.006 PMID:27072491

Andzulis, J. M., Panagopoulos, N. G., & Rapp, A. (2012). A review of social media and implications for the sales process. *Journal of Personal Selling & Sales Management*, *32*(3), 305–316. doi:10.2753/PSS0885-3134320302

Ang, R. P., Chong, W. H., Chye, S., & Huan, V. S. (2012). Loneliness and generalized problematic Internet use: Parents' perceived knowledge of adolescents' online activities as a moderator. *Computers in Human Behavior*, *28*(4), 1342–1347. doi:10.1016/j.chb.2012.02.019

Antonius, J., Schoenmakers, T. M., & Regina, J. J. M. et al.. (2010). Compulsive Internet Use: The Role of Online Gaming and Other Internet Applications. *The Journal of Adolescent Health*, *47*(1), 51–57. doi:10.1016/j.jadohealth.2009.12.021 PMID:20547292

Aral, N., & Gürsoy, F. (2000). Levels of loneliness in young people. [in Turkish]. *Journal of Education and Science*, *25*(116), 8–12.

Argyle, M. (2001). *The Psychology of Happiness* (2nd ed.). London: Routledge.

Arksey, H., & O'Malley, L. (2005). Scoping studies: Towards a methodological framework. *International Journal of Social Research Methodology*, *8*(1), 19–32. doi:10.1080/1364557032000119616

Armstrong, L., Phillips, J. G., & Saling, L. L. (2000). Potential determinants of heavier Internet usage. *International Journal of Human-Computer Studies*, *53*(4), 537–550. doi:10.1006/ijhc.2000.0400

Arslan, G. (2016). Psychological maltreatment, emotional and behavioral problems in adolescents: The mediating role of resilience and self-esteem. *Child Abuse & Neglect*, *52*, 200–209. doi:10.1016/j.chiabu.2015.09.010 PMID:26518981

Arslan, G. (2017a). Psychological maltreatment, forgiveness, mindfulness, and internet addiction among young adults: A study of mediation effect. *Computers in Human Behavior*, *72*, 57–66. doi:10.1016/j.chb.2017.02.037

Arslan, G. (2017b). Psychological maltreatment, social acceptance, social connectedness, and subjective well-being in adolescents. *Journal of Happiness Studies*. doi:10.1007/s10902-017-9856-z

Arslan, G. (2017c). Psychological maltreatment, coping strategies, and mental health problems: A brief and effective measure of psychological maltreatment in adolescents. *Child Abuse & Neglect*, *68*, 96–106. doi:10.1016/j.chiabu.2017.03.023 PMID:28427000

Arslan, G., & Balkis, M. (2016). Ergenlerde Duygusal İstismar, Problem Davranışlar, Öz-Yeterlik ve Psikolojik Sağlamlık Arasındaki İlişki. *Sakarya University Journal of Education*, *6*(1), 8–22. doi:10.19126/suje.35977

Aslanbay, Y., Aslanbay, M., & Cobanoglu, E. (2009). Internet addiction among Turkish young consumers. *Young Consumers*, *10*(1), 60–70. doi:10.1108/17473610910940792

Assunção, R. S., & Matos, P. M. (2017). The Generalized Problematic Internet Use Scale 2: Validation and test of the model to Facebook use. *Journal of Adolescence*, *54*, 51–59. doi:10.1016/j.adolescence.2016.11.007 PMID:27871015

Atmaca, M. (2007). A case of problematic Internet use successfully treated with an SSRI-antipsychotic combination. *Progress in Neuro-Psychopharmacology & Biological Psychiatry*, *31*(4), 961–962. doi:10.1016/j.pnpbp.2007.01.003 PMID:17321659

Aunola, K., Stattin, H., & Nurmi, J.-E. (2000). Parenting styles and adolescents' achievement strategies. *Journal of Adolescence*, *23*(2), 205–222. doi:10.1006/jado.2000.0308 PMID:10831143

Ayas, T. (2012). The relationship between Internet and computer game addiction level and shyness among high school students. *Educational Sciences: Theory and Practice*, *12*(2), 632–636.

Ayas, T., & Horzum, M. B. (2013). Relation between depression, loneliness, self-esteem and Internet addiction. *Journal of Education*, *133*(3), 284–290.

Azher, M., Khan, R. B., Salim, M., Bilal, M., Hussain, A., & Haseeb, M. (2014). The relationship between internet addiction and anxiety among students of the University of Sargodha. *International Journal of Humanities and Social Science*, *4*(1), 288–293.

Aziz, S., & Tronzo, C. L. (2011). Exploring the relationship between workaholism facets and personality traits: A replication in American workers. *The Psychological Record*, *61*(2), 269–286. doi:10.1007/BF03395760

Bakken, I. J., Wenzel, H. G., Götestam, K. G., Johansson, A., & Øren, A. (2009). Internet addiction among Norwegian adults: A stratified probability sample study. *Scandinavian Journal of Psychology*, *50*(2), 121–127. doi:10.1111/j.1467-9450.2008.00685.x PMID:18826420

Balarabe, S. (2015). *Impact of social media on public discourse in Nigeria*. Paper presented at the International Conference on Communication, Media, Technology and Design, Dubai, UAE.

Balci, Ş., & Gülnar, B. (2009). Üniversite öğrencileri arasında internet bağımlılığı ve internet bağımlılarının profili. *Selçuk Üniversitesi İletişim Fakültesi Akademik Dergisi*, *6*(1), 5–22.

Bandura, A. (1977). Self-efficacy: Toward a unifying theory of behavioral change. *Psychological Review*, *84*(2), 191–215. doi:10.1037/0033-295X.84.2.191 PMID:847061

Bandura, A. (1989). Human agency in social cognitive theory. *The American Psychologist*, *44*(9), 1175–1184. doi:10.1037/0003-066X.44.9.1175 PMID:2782727

Bányai, F., Zsila, Á., Király, O., Maraz, A., Elekes, Z., Griffiths, M. D., & Demetrovics, Z. et al. (2017). Problematic social media use: Results from a large-scale nationally representative adolescent sample. *PLoS One, 12*(1), e0169839. doi:10.1371/journal.pone.0169839 PMID:28068404

Barber, A. (1997). Net's educational value questioned. *USA Today,* 4.

Barke, A., Nyenhuis, N., & Kroner-Herwig, B. (2012). The German Version of the Internet Addiction Test: A Validation Study. *Cyberpsychology, Behavior, and Social Networking, 15*(10), 534–542. doi:10.1089/cyber.2011.0616 PMID:23002984

Barker, J. C., & Hunt, G. (2004). Representations of family: A review of the alcohol and drug literature. *The International Journal on Drug Policy, 15*(5), 347–356. doi:10.1016/j.drugpo.2004.07.002

Barkin, S., Ip, E., Richardson, I., Klinepeter, S., Finch, S., & Krcmar, M. (2006). Parental media mediation styles for children aged 2 to 11 years. *Archives of Pediatrics & Adolescent Medicine, 160*(4), 395–401. doi:10.1001/archpedi.160.4.395 PMID:16585485

Bastani, S. (2008). Gender Division in Computer and Internet Application: Investigation of the Students of Tehran Universities. *Women's Studies, 5,* 45–64.

Batıgün, A. D., & Hasta, D. (2010). Internet bağımlılığı: Yalnızlık ve kişilerarası ilişki tarzları açısından bir değerlendirme [Internet addiction: An evaluation in terms of loneliness and interpersonal relationship styles]. *Anatolian Journal of Psychiatry, 11*(3), 213–219.

Baumrind, D. (1972). An exploratory study of socialization effects on black children: Some black-white comparisons. *Child Development, 43*(1), 261–267. doi:10.2307/1127891 PMID:5027666

Baumrind, D. (1991). The influence of parenting style on adolescent competence and substance use. *The Journal of Early Adolescence, 11*(1), 56–95. doi:10.1177/0272431691111004

Bayraktar, F. (2001). *The role of Internet usage in the development of adolescents* (Unpublished master thesis). Ege University, Turkey.

BBC News. (2014). *Many young people addicted to net, survey suggests.* Retrieved from http://www.bbc.com/news/technology-29627896

Beal, A. C., Ausiello, J., & Perrin, J. M. (2001). Social influences on health-risk behaviors among minority middle school students. *The Journal of Adolescent Health, 28*(6), 474–480. doi:10.1016/S1054-139X(01)00194-X PMID:11377991

Beard, K. W. (2005). Internet addiction: A review of current assessment techniques and potential assessment questions. *Cyberpsychology & Behavior, 8*(1), 7–14. doi:10.1089/cpb.2005.8.7 PMID:15738688

Beard, K. W. (2011). Working with adolescents addicted to the Internet. In K. S. Young (Ed.), *Internet addiction: A handbook and guide to evaluation and treatment* (pp. 173–189). Hoboken, NJ: John Wiley & Sons, Inc.

Beard, K. W., & Wolf, E. M. (2001). Modification in the proposed diagnostic criteria for Internet addiction. *Cyberpsychology & Behavior, 4*(3), 377–383. doi:10.1089/109493101300210286 PMID:11710263

Beebe, D. W., Ris, M. D., Brown, T. M., & Dietrich, K. N. (2004). Executive functioning and memory for the Rey-Osterreith complex figure task among community adolescents. *Applied Neuropsychology, 11*(2), 91–98. doi:10.1207/s15324826an1102_4 PMID:15477179

Bellis, M. A., Hughes, K., Jones, A., Perkins, C., & McHale, P. (2013). Childhood happiness and violence: A retrospective study of their impacts on adult well-being. *BMJ Open, 3*(9), 1–10. doi:10.1136/bmjopen-2013-003427 PMID:24056485

Ben-Yehuda, L., Greenberg, L., & Weinstein, A. (2016). Internet addiction by using the smartphone-Relationships between Internet addiction, frequency of smartphone use and the state of mind of male and female students. *Journal of Reward Deficiency Syndrome & Addiction Science*, 2(1), 22–27. doi:10.17756/jrdsas.2016-024

Beranuy, M., Oberst, U., Carbonell, X., & Chamarro, A. (2009). Problematic Internet and mobile phone use and clinical symptoms in college students: The role of emotional intelligence. *Computers in Human Behavior*, 25(5), 1182–1187. doi:10.1016/j.chb.2009.03.001

Bergevin, T., Gupta, R., Derevensky, J., & Kaufman, F. (2006). Adolescent gambling: Understanding the role of stress and coping. *Journal of Gambling Studies*, 22(2), 195–208. doi:10.1007/s10899-006-9010-z PMID:16838102

Bergmark, K. H., Stensson, E., & Bergmark, A. (2016). Internet addiction: The making of a new addiction. *Jacobs Journal of Addiction and Therapy*, 3(1), 1-10. Retrieved from https://su.diva-portal.org/smash/get/diva2:912153/FULLTEXT01.pdf

Bernardi, S., & Pallanti, S. (2009). Internet addiction: A descriptive clinical study focusing on comorbidities and dissociative symptoms. *Comprehensive Psychiatry*, 50(6), 510–516. doi:10.1016/j.comppsych.2008.11.011 PMID:19840588

Berson, I., & Berson, M. (2003). Digital literacy for effective citizenship. *Social Education*, 67(3), 164–167.

Bessière, K., Kiesler, S., Kraut, R., & Boneva, B. S. (2008). Effects of Internet use and social resources on changes in depression. *Information Communication and Society*, 11(1), 47–70. doi:10.1080/13691180701858851

Beutel, M. E., Brähler, E., Glaesmer, H., Kuss, D. J., Wölfling, K., & Müller, K. W. (2011). Regular and problematic leisure-time Internet use in the community: Results from a German population-based survey. *Cyberpsychology, Behavior, and Social Networking*, 14(5), 291–296. doi:10.1089/cyber.2010.0199 PMID:21067277

Beutel, M. E., Hoch, C., Woelfing, K., & Mueller, K. W. (2011). Clinical characteristics of computer game and Internet addiction in persons seeking treatment in an outpatient clinic for computer game addiction. *Psychosomatic Medecine & Psychotherapy*, 57, 77–90. PMID:21432840

Bianchi, A., & Phillips, J. G. (2005). Psychological predictors of problem mobile phone use. *Cyberpsychology & Behavior*, 8(1), 39–51. doi:10.1089/cpb.2005.8.39 PMID:15738692

Billieux, J., Schimmenti, A., Khazaal, Y., Maurage, P., & Heeren, A. (2015). Are we overpathologizing everyday life? A tenable blueprint for behavioral addiction research. *Journal of Behavioral Addictions*, 4(3), 119–123. doi:10.1556/2006.4.2015.009 PMID:26014667

Bishop, J. (2005). The role of mediating artifacts in the design of persuasive e-learning systems. *The 1st International Conference on Internet Technologies and Applications (ITA'05)*, 54-62.

Bishop, J. (2007a). Ecological cognition: A new dynamic for human-computer interaction. In B. Wallace, A. Ross, J. Davies & T. Anderson (Eds.), The mind, the body and the world: Psychology after cognitivism (pp. 327-345). Exeter, UK: Imprint Academic.

Bishop, J. (2011). *The role of the prefrontal cortex in social orientation construction: A pilot study.* Poster Presented to the BPS Welsh Conference on Wellbeing, Wrexham, UK.

Bishop, J. (2015a). *An investigation into the extent and limitations of the GROW model for coaching and mentoring online: Towards 'prosthetic learning'.* The 14th International Conference on E-Learning, E-Business, Enterprise Information Systems, and E-Government (EEE'15), Las Vegas, NV.

Bishop, J. (2016b). *The impact of physical and virtual environments on human emotions: A pilot study in an adult and community education setting.* The 2016 International Conference on Computational Science and Computational Intelligence (CSCI'16), Las Vegas, NV.

Bishop, J. (2007b). Increasing participation in online communities: A framework for human–computer interaction. *Computers in Human Behavior, 23*(4), 1881–1893. doi:10.1016/j.chb.2005.11.004

Bishop, J. (2012). Taming the chatroom bob: The role of brain-computer interfaces that manipulate prefrontal cortex optimization for increasing participation of victims of traumatic sex and other abuse online. *Proceedings of the 13th International Conference on Bioinformatics and Computational Biology (BIOCOMP'12)*.

Bishop, J. (2015b). Supporting communication between people with social orientation impairments using affective computing technologies: Rethinking the autism spectrum. In L. Bee Theng (Ed.), *Assistive technologies for physical and cognitive disabilities* (pp. 42–55). Hershey, PA: IGI Global. doi:10.4018/978-1-4666-7373-1.ch003

Bishop, J. (2016a). Enhancing the performance of human resources through E-mentoring: The role of an adaptive hypermedia system called "AVEUGLE". *International Management Review, 12*(1), 11–23.

Biswas, A., Ingle, N., & Roy, M. (2014). Influence of social media on voting behavior. *Journal of Power, 2*(2), 127–155.

Błachnio, A., & Przepiorka, A. (2016). Personality and positive orientation in Internet and Facebook addiction. An empirical report from Poland. *Computers in Human Behavior, 59*, 230–236. doi:10.1016/j.chb.2016.02.018

Blachnio, A., Przepiorka, A., Senol-Durak, E., Durak, M., & Sherstyuk, L. (2017). The role of personality traits in Facebook and Internet addictions: A study on Polish, Turkish, and Ukrainian samples. *Computers in Human Behavior, 68*, 269–275. doi:10.1016/j.chb.2016.11.037

Black, D. W., Belsare, G., & Schlosser, S. (1999). Clinical features, psychiatric comorbidity, and health-related quality of life in persons reporting compulsive computer use behavior. *The Journal of Clinical Psychiatry, 60*(12), 839–844. doi:10.4088/JCP.v60n1206 PMID:10665630

Blaszczynski, A., & Nower, L. (2002). A pathways model of problem and pathological gambling. *Addiction (Abingdon, England), 97*(5), 487–499. doi:10.1046/j.1360-0443.2002.00015.x PMID:12033650

Blinka, L., Škařupová, K., Ševčíková, A., Wölfling, K., Müller, K. W., & Dreier, M. (2015). Excessive Internet use in European adolescents: What determines differences in severity? *International Journal of Public Health, 60*(2), 249–256. doi:10.1007/s00038-014-0635-x PMID:25532555

Block, J. J. (2008). Issues for DSM-V: Internet addiction. *The American Journal of Psychiatry, 165*(3), 306–307. doi:10.1176/appi.ajp.2007.07101556 PMID:18316427

Boettcher, J., Åström, V., Påhlsson, D., Schenström, O., Andersson, G., & Carlbring, P. (2014). Internet-based mindfulness treatment for anxiety disorders: A randomized controlled trial. *Behavior Therapy, 45*(2), 241–253. doi:10.1016/j.beth.2013.11.003 PMID:24491199

Bogenschneider, K., Wu, M. Y., Raffaelli, M., & Tsay, J. C. (1998). Parent influences on adolescent peer orientation and substance use: The interface of parenting practices and values. *Child Development, 69*(6), 1672–1688. doi:10.1111/j.1467-8624.1998.tb06184.x PMID:9914646

Boies, S. C., Cooper, A., & Osborne, C. S. (2004). Variations in Internet-related problems and psychosocial functioning in online sexual activities: Implications for social and sexual development of young adults. *Cyberpsychology & Behavior, 7*(2), 207–230. doi:10.1089/109493104323024474 PMID:15140364

Borawski, E. A., Ievers-Landis, C. E., Lovegreen, L. D., & Trapl, E. S. (2003). Parental monitoring, negotiated unsupervised time, and parental trust: The role of perceived parenting practices in adolescent health risk behaviors. *The Journal of Adolescent Health, 33*(2), 60–70. doi:10.1016/S1054-139X(03)00100-9 PMID:12890596

Bourget, D., Ward, H., & Gagne, P. (2003). Characteristics of 75 gambling-related suicides in Quebec. *Canadian Psychiatric Association Bulletin*, *35*, 17–21.

Bowen, M. (1966). The use of family theory in clinical practice. *Comprehensive Psychiatry*, *7*(5), 345–374. doi:10.1016/S0010-440X(66)80065-2 PMID:5922263

Boyd, D. (2014). *It's complicated: The social lives of networked teens.* Yale University Press.

Boysan, M., Kuss, D. J., Barut, Y., Ayköse, N., Güleç, M., & Özdemir, O. (2017). Psychometric properties of the Turkish version of the Internet Addiction Test (IAT). *Addictive Behaviors*, *64*, 247–252. doi:10.1016/j.addbeh.2015.09.002 PMID:26421905

Bozoglan, B., & Demirer, V. (2015). The Association between internet addiction and psycho-social variables. In J. Bishop (Ed.), *Psychological and social issues surrounding internet and gaming addiction* (pp. 171–185). Hershey, PA: IGI Global. doi:10.4018/978-1-4666-8595-6.ch010

Bozoglan, B., Demirer, V., & Sahin, I. (2013). Loneliness, self-esteem, and life satisfaction as predictors of Internet addiction: A cross-sectional study among Turkish university students. *Scandinavian Journal of Psychology*, *54*(4), 313319. doi:10.1111/sjop.12049 PMID:23577670

Bozoglan, B., Demirer, V., & Sahin, I. (2014). Problematic Internet use: Functions of use, cognitive absorption, and depression. *Computers in Human Behavior*, *37*, 117–123. doi:10.1016/j.chb.2014.04.042

Brand, M., Laier, C., & Young, K. S. (2014). Internet addiction: Coping styles, expectancies, and treatment implications. *Frontiers in Psychology*, *5*, 1256. doi:10.3389/fpsyg.2014.01256 PMID:25426088

Brand, M., Young, K. S., & Laier, C. (2014). Prefrontal Control and Internet Addiction: A Theoretical Model and Review of Neuropsychological and Neuroimaging Findings. *Frontiers in Human Neuroscience*, *8*, 375. doi:10.3389/fnhum.2014.00375 PMID:24904393

Brand, M., Young, K. S., & Laier, C. (2014). Prefrontal control and Internet addiction: A theoretical model and review of neuropsychological and neuroimaging findings. *Frontiers in Human Neuroscience*, *8*. PMID:24904393

Brenner, V. (1997). Psychology of computer use: XLVII. Parameters of Internet use, abuse and addiction: the first 90 days of the Internet Usage Survey. *Psychological Reports*, *80*(3), 879–882. doi:10.2466/pr0.1997.80.3.879 PMID:9198388

Breslau, J., Aharoni, E., Pedersen, E. R., & Miller, L. L. (2015). *A review of research on problematic Internet use and well-being with recommendations for the U.S. Air Force.* Santa Monica, CA: RAND Corporation. Retrieved from http://www.rand.org/content/dam/rand/pubs/research_reports/RR800/RR849/RAND_RR849.pdf

Bricolo, F., Gentile, D. A., Smelser, R. L., & Serpelloni, G. (2007). Use of the computer and Internet among Italian families: First national study. *Cyberpsychology & Behavior*, *10*(6), 789–797. doi:10.1089/cpb.2007.9952 PMID:18085966

Brodski, S. K., & Hutz, C. S. (2012). The repercussions of emotional abuse and parenting styles on self-esteem, subjective well-being: A retrospective study with university students in Brazil. *Journal of Aggression, Maltreatment & Trauma*, *21*(3), 256–276. doi:10.1080/10926771.2012.666335

Bronfenbrenner, U., & Morris, P. A. (2006). The bioecological model of human development. In R. M. Lerner (Ed.), Handbook of child development: Vol. 1. Theoretical models of human development (6th ed.; pp. 793 – 828). Hoboken, NJ: Wiley.

Brooner, R. K., Schmidt, C. W., Jr., & Herbst, J. H. (1994). Personality trait characteristics of opioid abusers with and without comorbid personality disorders. In Personality disorders and the five-factor model of personality (pp. 131-148). Washington, DC: American Psychological Association. doi:10.1037/10140-025

Brown, R. I. F. (1993). Some contributions of the study of gambling to the study of other addictions. In W. R. Eadington & J. Cornelius (Eds.), *Gambling behavior and problem gambling*. Reno, NV: University of Nevada Press.

Brown, S., Fite, P. J., Stone, K., & Bortolato, M. (2016). Accounting for the associations between child maltreatment and internalizing problems: The role of alexithymia. *Child Abuse & Neglect*, *52*, 20–28. doi:10.1016/j.chiabu.2015.12.008 PMID:26774529

Bruno, A., Scimeca, G., Cava, L., Pandolfo, G., Zoccali, R. A., & Muscatello, M. R. (2014). Prevalence of internet addiction in a sample of southern Italian high school students. *International Journal of Mental Health and Addiction*, *12*(6), 708–715. doi:10.1007/s11469-014-9497-y

Bryant, J. A., Sanders-Jackson, A., & Smallwood, A. K. (2006). IMing, Text Messaging, and Adolescent Social Networks. *Journal of Computer-Mediated Communication*, *11*(2), 577–592. doi:10.1111/j.1083-6101.2006.00028.x

Buckner, J. E., Castille, C. M., & Sheets, T. L. (2012). The Five Factor Model of personality and employees' excessive use of technology. *Computers in Human Behavior*, *28*(5), 1947–1953. doi:10.1016/j.chb.2012.05.014

Buffardi, E. L., & Campbell, W. K. (2008). Narcissism and social networking web sites. *Perspectives in Social Psychology*, *34*, 1303–1314. PMID:18599659

Burnay, J., Billieux, J., Blairy, S., & Larøi, F. (2015). Which psychological factors influence Internet addiction? Evidence through an integrative model. *Computers in Human Behavior*, *43*, 28–34. doi:10.1016/j.chb.2014.10.039

Büyüköztürk, Ş. (2007). *Sosyal Bilimler için Veri Analizi El Kitabı* [Data Analysis Handbook for Social Science] (7th ed.). Ankara, Turkey: Pegem A Yayıncılık. (in Turkish)

Bybee, C. R., Robinson, D., & Turow, J. (1982). Determinants of parental guidance of children's television viewing for a special subgroup: Mass media scholars. *Journal of Broadcasting & Electronic Media*, *26*(3), 697–710. doi:10.1080/08838158209364038

Byun, S., Ruffini, C., Mills, J. E., Douglas, A. C., Niang, M., Stepchenkova, S., & Blanton, M. et al. (2009). Internet addiction: Metasynthesis of 1996–2006 quantitative research. *Cyberpsychology & Behavior*, *12*(2), 203–207. doi:10.1089/cpb.2008.0102 PMID:19072075

Cain, N. M., Pincus, A. L., & Ansell, E. B. (2008). Narcissism at the crossroads: Phenotypic description of pathological narcissism across clinical theory, social/personality psychology, and psychiatric diagnosis. *Clinical Psychology Review*, *28*(4), 638–656. doi:10.1016/j.cpr.2007.09.006 PMID:18029072

Çakır, O., Ayas, T., & Horum, M. B. (2011). An investigation of university students' Internet and game addiction with respect to several variables. *Ankara University Journal of Faculty of Educational Sciences*, *44*(2), 95–117.

Calafat, A., García, F., Juan, M., Becoña, E., & Fernández-Hermida, J. R. (2014). Which parenting style is more protective against adolescent substance use? Evidence within the European context. *Drug and Alcohol Dependence*, *138*, 185–192. doi:10.1016/j.drugalcdep.2014.02.705 PMID:24679841

Caldwell, C. D., & Cunningham, T. J. (2010). *Internet addiction and students: Implications for school counselors*. American Counseling Association. Retrieved from http://www.counseling.org/resources/library/vistas/2010-v-online/Article_61.pdf

Califano, J. A. Jr. (2008). *High society: How substance abuse ravages America and what to do about it*. Public Affairs.

Campbell, A. J., Cumming, S. R., & Hughes, I. (2006). Internet use of the socially fearful: Addiction or therapy? *Cyberpsychology & Behavior*, *9*(1), 69–81. doi:10.1089/cpb.2006.9.69 PMID:16497120

Campbell, W. K., Rudich, E. A., & Sedikides, C. (2002). Narcissism, self-esteem, and the positivity of self-views: Two portraits of self-love. *Personality and Social Psychology Bulletin, 28*(3), 358–368. doi:10.1177/0146167202286007

Canan, F., Ataoglu, A., Nichols, L. A., Yildirim, T., & Ozturk, O. (2010). Evaluation of Psychometric Properties of the Internet Addiction Scale in a Sample of Turkish High School Students. *Cyberpsychology, Behavior, and Social Networking, 13*(3), 317–320. doi:10.1089/cyber.2009.0160 PMID:20557252

Canan, F., Yildirim, O., Ustunel, T. Y., Sinani, G., Kaleli, A. H., Gunes, C., & Ataoglu, A. (2014). The Relationship Between Internet Addiction and Body Mass Index in Turkish Adolescents. *Cyberpsychology, Behavior, and Social Networking, 17*(1), 40–45. doi:10.1089/cyber.2012.0733 PMID:23952625

Cao, F. L., & Su, L. Y. (2007). Internet addiction among Chinese adolescents: Prevalence and psychological features. *Child: Care, Health and Development, 33*(3), 275–281. doi:10.1111/j.1365-2214.2006.00715.x PMID:17439441

Cao, F., Su, L., Liu, T. Q., & Gao, X. (2007). The relationship between impulsivity and Internet addiction in a sample of Chinese adolescents. *European Psychiatry, 22*(7), 466–471. doi:10.1016/j.eurpsy.2007.05.004 PMID:17765486

Cao, H., Sun, Y., Wan, Y., Hao, J., & Tao, F. (2011). Problematic Internet use in Chinese adolescents and its relation to psychosomatic symptoms and life satisfaction. *BMC Public Health, 11*(1), 2–8. doi:10.1186/1471-2458-11-802 PMID:21995654

Caplan, S. E. (2002). Problematic Internet use and psychosocial well-being: Development of a theory-based cognitive–behavioral measurement instrument. *Computers in Human Behavior, 18*(5), 553–575. doi:10.1016/S0747-5632(02)00004-3

Caplan, S. E. (2003). Preference for online social interaction A theory of problematic Internet use and psychosocial well-being. *Communication Research, 30*(6), 625–648. doi:10.1177/0093650203257842

Caplan, S. E. (2007). Relations among loneliness, social anxiety, and problematic Internet use. *Cyberpsychology & Behavior, 10*(2), 234–242. doi:10.1089/cpb.2006.9963 PMID:17474841

Caplan, S. E. (2010). Theory and measurement of generalized problematic Internet use: A two-step approach. *Computers in Human Behavior, 26*(5), 1089–1097. doi:10.1016/j.chb.2010.03.012

Caplan, S. E., & High, A. C. (2011). Online social interaction, psychosocial well-being, and problematic Internet use. In K. S. Young (Ed.), *Internet addiction: A handbook and guide to evaluation and treatment* (pp. 35–53). Hoboken, NJ: John Wiley & Sons, Inc.

Cardak, M. (2013). Psychological well-being and Internet addiction among university students. *TOJET: The Turkish Online Journal of Educational Technology, 12*(3), 134–141.

Carlbring, P., Westling, B.E., Ljungstrand, P., Ekselius, L., & Andersson, G. (2001) Treatment of panic disorder via the Internet: A randomized trial of a self-help program. *Behavior Therapy, 32*(4), 751-64.

Carlbring, P., & Andersson, G. (2006). The Internet and psychological treatment. How well can they be combined? *Computers in Human Behavior, 22*(3), 545–553. doi:10.1016/j.chb.2004.10.009

Cartierre, N., Coulon, N., & Demerval, R. (2011). Validation d'une version courte en langue française pour adolescents de la Compulsive Internet Use Scale. *Neuropsychiatrie de l'Enfance et de l'Adolescence, 59*(7), 415–419. doi:10.1016/j.neurenf.2011.06.003

Casale, S., Primi, C., & Fioravanti, G. (2016). Generalized Problematic Internet Use Scale 2: update on the psychometric properties among Italian young adults. In G. Riva, B. K. Wiederhold, & P. Cipresso (Eds.), *The Psychology of Social Networking: Identity and Relationships in Online Communities* (Vol. 2, pp. 202–2014). Berlin, Germany: De Gruyter.

Cash, H. D., Rae, C. H., Steel, A., & Winkler, A. (2012). Internet addiction: A brief summary of research and practice. *Current Psychiatry Reviews, 8*(4), 292–298. doi:10.2174/157340012803520513 PMID:23125561

Çelik, S., Atak, H., & Başal, A. (2012). Predictive role of personality traits on Internet addiction. *Turkish Online Journal of Distance Education, 13*(4), 10-24.

Çelik, Ç. B., & Odacı, H. (2013). The relationship between problematic internet use and interpersonal cognitive distortions and life satisfaction in university students. *Children and Youth Services Review, 35*(3), 505–508. doi:10.1016/j.childyouth.2013.01.001

Ceyhan, A. A. (2008). Predictors of problematic Internet use on Turkish university students. *Cyberpsychology & Behavior, 11*(3), 363–366. doi:10.1089/cpb.2007.0112 PMID:18537510

Ceyhan, A. A. (2011). University students' problematic Internet use and communication skills according to the Internet use purposes. *Educational Sciences: Theory and Practice, 11*(1), 59–77.

Ceyhan, A. A., & Ceyhan, E. (2008). Loneliness, depression and computer self-efficacy as predictors of problematic Internet use. *Cyberpsychology & Behavior, 11*(6), 699–701. doi:10.1089/cpb.2007.0255 PMID:19072150

Ceyhan, E. (2008). Ergen ruh sağlığı açısından bir risk faktörü: İnternet bağımlılığı. *Çocuk ve Gençlik Ruh Sağlığı Dergisi, 15*(2), 109–116.

Ceyhan, E., Ceyhan, A., & Gürcan, A. (2007). Problemli internet kullanımı ölçeği'nin geçerlik ve güvenirlik çalışmaları. *Kuram ve Uygulamada Eğitim Bilimleri Dergisi, 7*(1), 387–416.

Chait, J. (2009). *Causes of Internet addiction*. Retrieved from http://addiction.lovetoknow.com/wiki/Causes_of_Internet_Addiction

Chak, K., & Leung, L. (2004). Shyness and locus of control as predictors of internet addiction and internet use. *Cyberpsychology & Behavior, 7*(5), 559–570. doi:10.1089/cpb.2004.7.559 PMID:15667051

Chang, F. C., Chiu, C. H., Lee, C. M., Chen, P. H., & Miao, N. F. (2014). Predictors of the initiation and persistence of Internet addiction among adolescents in Taiwan. *Addictive Behaviors, 39*(10), 1434–1440. doi:10.1016/j.addbeh.2014.05.010 PMID:24930050

Chang, F. C., Chiu, C. H., Miao, N. F., Chen, P. H., Lee, C. M., Chiang, J. T., & Pan, Y. C. (2015). The relationship between parental mediation and Internet addiction among adolescents, and the association with cyberbullying and depression. *Comprehensive Psychiatry, 57*, 21–28. doi:10.1016/j.comppsych.2014.11.013 PMID:25487108

Chao, J., & Nestler, E. J. (2004). Molecular neurobiology of drug addiction. *Annual Review of Medicine, 55*(1), 113–132. doi:10.1146/annurev.med.55.091902.103730 PMID:14746512

Chappell, D., Eatough, V., Davies, M. N., & Griffiths, M. (2006). Everquest—It's just a computer game right? An interpretative phenomenological analysis of online gaming addiction. *International Journal of Mental Health and Addiction, 4*(3), 205–216. doi:10.1007/s11469-006-9028-6

Chebbi, P., Koong, K. S., Liu, L., & Rottman, R. (2001). Some observations on Internet addiction disorder research. *Journal of Information Systems Education, 1*(1), 3–4.

Chen, S., & Chou, C. (1999). *Development of Chinese Internet addiction scale in Taiwan*. Poster presented at the 107th american psychology annual convention, Boston, MA.

Cheng, C., & Li, A. Y. (2014). Internet addiction prevalence and quality of real life: A meta-analysis of 31 nations across seven world regions. *Cyberpsychology, Behavior, and Social Networking*, *17*(12), 755–760. doi:10.1089/cyber.2014.0317 PMID:25489876

Chen, S. Y., & Fu, Y. C. (2009). Internet use and academic achievement: Gender differences in early adolescence. *Adolescence*, *44*(176), 797–812. PMID:20432601

Chen, S., Weng, L., Su, Y., Wu, H., & Yang, P. (2003). Development of a Chinese Internet addiction scale and its psychometric study. *Chinese Journal of Psychology*, *45*(3), 279–294.

Chen, Y., Kang, Y., Gong, W., He, L., Jin, Y., Zhu, X., & Yao, Y. (2016). Investigation on Internet addiction disorder in adolescents in Anhui, People's Republic of China. *Neuropsychiatric Disease and Treatment*, *12*, 2233–2236. doi:10.2147/NDT.S110156 PMID:27621633

Cheung, L. M., & Wong, W. S. (2011). The effects of insomnia and Internet addiction on depression in Hong Kong Chinese adolescents: An exploratory cross-sectional analysis. *Journal of Sleep Research*, *20*(2), 311–317. doi:10.1111/j.1365-2869.2010.00883.x PMID:20819144

Chew, E., Jones, N., & Turner, D. (2008). *Critical review of the blended learning models based on maslow's and vygotsky's educational theory*. Paper presented at the First International Conference on Hybrid Learning (ICHL 2008), Hong Kong. doi:10.1007/978-3-540-85170-7_4

Chiao, C., Yi, C. C., & Ksobiech, K. (2014). Adolescent Internet use and its relationship to cigarette smoking and alcohol use: A prospective cohort study. *Addictive Behaviors*, *39*(1), 7–12. doi:10.1016/j.addbeh.2013.09.006 PMID:24140305

Childnet International. (2006). *Internet addiction*. Retrieved from http://paneuyouth.eu/files/2013/07/factsheet_addiction.pdf

Chisholm, D., Chisholm, D., Doran, C., Chisholm, D., Doran, C., Shibuya, K., & Chisholm, D. et al. (2006). Comparative cost-effectiveness of policy instruments for reducing the global burden of alcohol, tobacco and illicit drug use. *Drug and Alcohol Review*, *25*(6), 553–565. doi:10.1080/09595230600944487 PMID:17132573

Chiu, C. M., Hsu, M. H., & Wang, E. T. (2006). Understanding knowledge sharing in virtual communities: An integration of social capital and social cognitive theories. *Decision Support Systems*, *42*(3), 1872–1888. doi:10.1016/j.dss.2006.04.001

Cho, C. H., & Cheon, H. J. (2005). Children's exposure to negative Internet content: Effects of family context. *Journal of Broadcasting & Electronic Media*, *49*(4), 488–509. doi:10.1207/s15506878jobem4904_8

Choi, D., Hwang, M., Kim, J., Ko, B., & Kim, P. (2014). Tracing trending topics by analyzing the sentiment status of tweets. *Computer Science and Information Systems*, *11*(1), 157–169. doi:10.2298/CSIS130205001C

Choi, Y. H. (2007). Advancement of IT and seriousness of youth Internet addiction. In *2007 International Symposium on the Counseling and Treatment of Youth Internet Addiction* (Vol. 20, pp. 279-298). Seoul, South Korea: National Youth Commission .

Chou, C., Condron, L., & Belland, J. C. (2005). A Review of the Research on Internet Addiction. *Educational Psychology Review*, *17*(4), 363–388. doi:10.1007/s10648-005-8138-1

Chou, C., & Hsiao, M. C. (2000). Internet addiction, usage, gratification, and pleasure experience: The Taiwan college students' case. *Computers & Education*, *35*(1), 65–80. doi:10.1016/S0360-1315(00)00019-1

Chou, C., & Lee, Y. H. (2017). The Moderating Effects of Internet Parenting Styles on the Relationship Between Internet Parenting Behavior, Internet Expectancy, and Internet Addiction Tendency. *The Asia-Pacific Education Researcher*, *26*(3-4), 137–146. doi:10.1007/s40299-017-0334-5

Chou, C., & Peng, H. (2007). Net-friends: Adolescents' attitudes and experiences vs. teachers' concerns. *Computers in Human Behavior*, 23(5), 2394–2413. doi:10.1016/j.chb.2006.03.015

Cho, Y. J. (2010). A longitudinal study on the Internet delinquency in adolescents: The use of a latent growth model. *Korean Journal of Youth Studies*, 17(6), 171–195.

Cho, Y., & Bae, J. (2010). Study on parental mediation of children's digital media use within the home environment. *Media. Gender & Culture*, 13(13), 37–74.

Chrismore, S., Betzelberger, E., Bier, L., & Camacho, T. (2011). Twelve-step recovery in inpatient treatment for Internet addiction. In K. S. Young (Ed.), *Internet addiction: A handbook and guide to evaluation and treatment* (pp. 205–222). Hoboken, NJ: John Wiley & Sons, Inc.

Christakis, D. A., & Moreno, M. A. (2009). Trapped in the net: Will Internet addiction become a 21st-century epidemic? *Archives of Pediatrics & Adolescent Medicine*, 163(10), 959–960. doi:10.1001/archpediatrics.2009.162 PMID:19805719

Chuang, Y. C. (2006). Massively Multiplayer Online Role-Playing Game-Induced Seizures: A Neglected Health Problem in Internet Addiction. *Cyberpsychology & Behavior*, 9(4), 451–456. doi:10.1089/cpb.2006.9.451 PMID:16901249

Chung, R. Y., Mercer, S., Lai, F. T. T., Yip, B. H. K., Wong, M. C. S., & Wong, S. Y. S. (2015). Socioeconomic Determinants of Multimorbidity: A Population-Based Household Survey of Hong Kong Chinese. *PLoS One*, 10(10), e0140040. doi:10.1371/journal.pone.0140040 PMID:26451589

Cicchetti, D., & Lynch, M. (1993). Toward an ecological/transactional model of community violence and child maltreatment: Consequences for children's development. *Psychiatry*, 56(1), 96–118. doi:10.1080/00332747.1993.11024624 PMID:8488217

Cıngı, H. (1994). *Ornekleme Kuramı* [Sampling Theory]. Ankara, Turkey: Hacettepe Üniversitesi Fen Fakültesi Basımevi. (in Turkish)

Clark, L. S. (2011). Parental mediation theory for the digital age. *Communication Theory*, 21(4), 323–343. doi:10.1111/j.1468-2885.2011.01391.x

Clark, N., & Scott, P. S. (2009). *Game addiction: The experience and the effects*. McFarland.

Collins, E., Freeman, J., & Chamarro-Premuzic, T. (2012). Personality traits associated with problematic and non-problematic massively multiplayer online role playing game use. *Personality and Individual Differences*, 52(2), 133–138. doi:10.1016/j.paid.2011.09.015

Compas, B. E., Banez, G. A., Malcarne, V., & Worsham, N. (1991). Perceived control and coping with stress: A developmental perspective. *The Journal of Social Issues*, 47(4), 23–34. doi:10.1111/j.1540-4560.1991.tb01832.x

Conger, R. D., Conger, K. J., & Martin, M. J. (2010). Socioeconomic Status, Family Processes, and Individual Development. *Journal of Marriage and the Family*, 72(3), 685–704. doi:10.1111/j.1741-3737.2010.00725.x PMID:20676350

Conrad, B. (2016a). Internet addiction –Symptoms, signs, treatment, and FAQs. *TECH Addiction*. Retrieved from http://www.techaddiction.ca/internet-addiction.html

Conrad, B. (2016b). *Internet addiction statistics – facts, figures, & numbers*. Retrieved from http://www.techaddiction.ca/internet_addiction_statistics.html

Cooper, A. (1998). Sexuality and the Internet: Surfing into the new millennium. *Cyberpsychology & Behavior*, 1(2), 187–193. doi:10.1089/cpb.1998.1.187

Cooper, A. (Ed.). (2013). *Cybersex: The dark side of the force: A special issue of the Journal Sexual Addiction and Compulsion*. Routledge.

Cooper, A., Delmonico, D. L., & Griffin, S. E. (2004). Online sexual activity: An examination of potentially problematic behaviors. *Sexual Addiction & Compulsivity, 11*(3), 129–143. doi:10.1080/10720160490882642

Correa, T., Hinsley, A. W., & de Zuniga, H. G. (2010). Who interacts on the Web?: The intersection of users' personality and social media use. *Computers in Human Behavior, 26*(2), 247–253. doi:10.1016/j.chb.2009.09.003

Cox, S. L. (2012). *Social media marketing in a small business: A case study* (Doctoral dissertation). Purdue University.

Cummins, R. A., Walter, J., & Woerner, J. (2007). *Australian Unity Wellbeing Index: Report 16.1—The wellbeing of Australians—Groups with the highest and lowest wellbeing in Australia*. Melbourne: Australian Centre on Quality of Life, School of Psychology, Deakin University.

Cutrona, C. E. (1982). Transition to college: Loneliness and the process of social adjustment. In L. A. Peplau & D. Perlman (Eds.), *Loneliness: A sourcebook of current theory, research, and therapy* (pp. 291–309). New York: John Wiley & Sons.

Dağ, İ. (1991). The validity and reliability study of Rotter's Internal External Locus of Control for university students. [in Turkish]. *The Journal of Psychology, 7*(26), 10–16.

Daily Post. (2012). NIJ student goes nude to break into Nollywood. *Daily Post*. Retrieved April 8, 2017, from http://www.nijstudent-goes-nude-to-break-into-nollywood-dailypost-htm

Dalbudak, E., & Evren, C. (2014). The relationship of Internet addiction severity with Attention Deficit Hyperactivity Disorder symptoms in Turkish University students; impact of personality traits, depression and anxiety. *Comprehensive Psychiatry, 55*(3), 497–503. doi:10.1016/j.comppsych.2013.11.018 PMID:24374171

Dalbudak, E., Evren, C., Aldemir, S., Coskun, K. S., Ugurlu, H., & Yildirim, F. G. (2013). Relationship of Internet addiction severity with depression, anxiety, and alexithymia, temperament and character in university students. *Cyberpsychology, Behavior, and Social Networking, 16*(4), 272–278. doi:10.1089/cyber.2012.0390 PMID:23363230

Dalbudak, E., Evren, C., Topcu, M., Aldemir, S., Coskun, K. S., Bozkurt, M., & Canbal, M. et al. (2013). Relationship of Internet addiction with impulsivity and severity of psychopathology among Turkish university students. *Psychiatry Research, 210*(3), 1086–1091. doi:10.1016/j.psychres.2013.08.014 PMID:23998359

Darling, N. (1999). *Parenting style and its correlates*. Retrieved on May 1, 2017 from. http://ceep.crc.uiuc.edu/eecearchive/digests/1999/darlin99.pdf

Davis, R. A. (2001). A cognitive-behavioral model of pathological Internet use. *Computers in Human Behavior, 17*(2), 187–195. doi:10.1016/S0747-5632(00)00041-8

Davis, R. A., Flett, G. L., & Besser, A. (2002). Validation of a new scale for measuring problematic Internet use: Implications for pre-employment screening. *Cyberpsychology & Behavior, 5*(4), 331–345. doi:10.1089/109493102760275581 PMID:12216698

De Abreu, C. N., & Goes, D. S. (2011). Psychotherapy for Internet addiction. In K. S. Young (Ed.), *Internet addiction: A handbook and guide to evaluation and treatment* (pp. 155–171). Hoboken, NJ: John Wiley & Sons, Inc.

De Andrade, J. B. S. O., Dutra, L., Schwinden, N. B. C., & de Andrade, S. F. (2015). Energy efficiency in the adoption of renewable energies in schools. In Implementing campus greening initiatives (pp. 183-201). Springer.

De Leo, J. A., & Wulfert, E. (2013). Problematic Internet use and other risky behaviors in college students: An application of problem-behavior theory. *Psychology of Addictive Behaviors, 27*(1), 133–141. doi:10.1037/a0030823 PMID:23276311

De Timary, P., & Philippot, P. (2015). Commentary on: Are we overpathologizing everyday life? A tenable blueprint for behavioral addiction research: Can the emerging domain of behavioral addictions bring a new reflection for the field of addictions, by stressing the issue of the context of addiction development? *Journal of Behavioral Addictions*, *4*(3), 148–150. doi:10.1556/2006.4.2015.024 PMID:26551903

DeAngelis, T. (2000). Is Internet addiction real? Monitor on Psychology. *American Psychological Association Publication*, *31*, 4.

Delmonico, D. L., & Griffin, E. J. (2011). Cybersex addiction and compulsivity. In K. S. Young (Ed.), *Internet addiction: A handbook and guide to evaluation and treatment* (pp. 113–131). Hoboken, NJ: John Wiley & Sons, Inc.

Delver, B. (2003). *Pandora's mailbox*. Haarlem: E-com Publishing.

Demetrovics, Z., Király, O., Koronczai, B., Griffiths, M. D., Nagygyörgy, K., Elekes, Z., & Urbán, R. et al. (2016). Psychometric properties of the Problematic Internet Use Questionnaire Short-Form (PIUQ-SF-6) in a nationally representative sample of adolescents. *PLoS One*, *11*(8), e0159409. doi:10.1371/journal.pone.0159409 PMID:27504915

Demetrovics, Z., Szeredi, B., & Rózsa, S. (2008). The three-factor model of Internet addiction: The development of the Problematic Internet Use Questionnaire. *Behavior Research Methods*, *40*(2), 563–574. doi:10.3758/BRM.40.2.563 PMID:18522068

Demir, A. (1989). Reliability and validity of the UCLA Loneliness Scale. *The Journal of Psychology*, *7*(23), 14–18.

Demirer, V., & Bozoglan, B. (2016). Purposes of Internet use and problematic Internet use among Turkish high school students. *Asia-Pacific Psychiatry*, *8*(4), 269–277. doi:10.1111/appy.12219 PMID:26585686

Demirer, V., Bozoglan, B., & Sahin, I. (2013). Preservice teachers' Internet addiction in terms of gender, Internet access, loneliness and life satisfaction. *International Journal of Education in Mathematics, Science and Technology*, *1*(1), 56–63.

Derevensky, J., & Gupta, R. (1998). Child, and adolescent gambling problems: *A program of research. Canadian Journal of School Psychology*, *14*, 55–58. doi:10.1177/082957359801400106

Destin, M., Rheinschmidt-Same, M., & Richeson, J. A. (2017). Status-Based Identity. *Perspectives on Psychological Science*, *12*(2), 270–289. doi:10.1177/1745691616664424 PMID:28346114

Dhir, A., Chen, S., & Nieminen, M. (2015). A repeat cross-sectional analysis of the psychometric properties of the Compulsive Internet Use Scale (CIUS) with adolescents from public and private schools. *Computers & Education*, *86*, 172–181. doi:10.1016/j.compedu.2015.03.011

Dhir, A., Chen, S., & Nieminen, M. (2015). Psychometric Validation of Internet Addiction Test With Indian Adolescents. *Journal of Educational Computing Research*, *53*(1), 15–31. doi:10.1177/0735633115597491

Dickson, L., Derevensky, J., & Gupta, R. (2004). Harm reduction in the prevention of youth gambling problems: Lessons Learned from Adolescent High-Risk Behavior Prevention Programs. *Journal of Adolescent Research*, *19*(2), 233–263. doi:10.1177/0743558403258272

DiClemente, R. J., Wingood, G. M., Crosby, R., Sionean, C., Cobb, B. K., Harrington, K., & Oh, M. K. et al. (2001). Parental monitoring: Association with adolescents' risk behaviors. *Pediatrics*, *107*(6), 1363–1368. doi:10.1542/peds.107.6.1363 PMID:11389258

Diener, E., Emmons, R. A., Larsen, R. J., & Griffin, S. (1985). The satisfaction with life scale: A measure of life satisfaction. *Journal of Personality Assessment*, *49*(1), 71–75. doi:10.1207/s15327752jpa4901_13 PMID:16367493

Diener, E., Scollon, C. N., & Lucas, R. E. (2009). The evolving concept of subjective well-being: The multifaceted nature of happiness. In E. Diener (Ed.), *Assessing well-being* (pp. 67–100). Springer Netherlands; . doi:10.1007/978-90-481-2354-4_4

Diener, E., Suh, E. M., Lucas, R. E., & Lucas, H. E. (1999). Subjective well-being: Three decades of progress. *Psychological Bulletin, 125*(2), 276–302. doi:10.1037/0033-2909.125.2.276

Ding, Y. J., Lau, C. H., Sou, K. L., Abraham, A. A., Griffiths, S. M., & Kim, J. H. (2016). Association between Internet addiction and highrisk sexual attitudes in Chinese university students from Hong Kong and Macau. *Public Health, 132,* 60–63. doi:10.1016/j.puhe.2015.11.009 PMID:26743991

Dodge, K. A., & Godwin, J. (2013). The conduct problems prevention research group. Social-information-processing patterns mediate the impact of preventive intervention on adolescent antisocial behavior. *Psychological Science, 24*(4), 456–465. doi:10.1177/0956797612457394 PMID:23406610

Dogan, H., Bozgeyikli, H., & Bozdas, C. (2015). Perceived parenting styles as predictor of Internet addiction in Adolescence. *International Journal of Research in Education and Science, 1*(2), 167–174. doi:10.21890/ijres.87952

Doğan, U., & Kaya, S. (2016). Mediation effects of Internet addiction on shame and social networking. *Universal Journal of Educational Research, 4*(5), 1037–1042. doi:10.13189/ujer.2016.040513

Dong, G., Wang, J., Yang, X., & Zhou, H. (2013). Risk personality traits of Internet addiction: A longitudinal study of Internet-addicted Chinese university students. *Asia-Pacific Psychiatry, 5*(4), 316–321. doi:10.1111/j.1758-5872.2012.00185.x PMID:23857796

Donovan, N., Halpern, D., & Sargeant, R. (2002). *Life satisfaction: The state of knowledge and implications for government.* Cabinet Office, Strategy Unit.

Douglas, A. C., Mills, J. E., Niang, M., Stepchenkova, S., Byun, S., Ruffini, C., & Atallah, M. et al. (2008). Internet addiction: Meta-synthesis of qualitative research for the decade 1996–2006. *Computers in Human Behavior, 24*(6), 3027–3044. doi:10.1016/j.chb.2008.05.009

Dowling, N. A., Merkouris, S. S., Greenwood, C. J., Oldenhof, E., Toumbourou, J. W., & Youssef, G. J. (2017). Early risk and protective factors for problem gambling: A systematic review and meta-analysis of longitudinal studies. *Clinical Psychology Review, 51,* 109–124. doi:10.1016/j.cpr.2016.10.008 PMID:27855334

Durkee, T., Kaess, M., Carli, V., Parzer, P., Wasserman, C., Floderus, B., & Bobes, J. et al. (2012). Prevalence of pathological internet use among adolescents in Europe: Demographic and social factors. *Addiction (Abingdon, England), 107*(12), 2210–2222. doi:10.1111/j.1360-0443.2012.03946.x PMID:22621402

Duy, B. (2003). *The effect of cognitive-behavioral group counseling experience on loneliness and dysfunctional attitudes of university students* (Unpublished Doctoral dissertation). Ankara University, Turkey.

Dwairy, M., Achoui, M., Abouserie, R., Farah, A., Sakhleh, A. A., Fayad, M., & Khan, H. K. (2006). Parenting styles in Arab societies: A first cross-regional research study. *Journal of Cross-Cultural Psychology, 37*(3), 230–247. doi:10.1177/0022022106286922

Eastin, M. S., Greenberg, B. S., & Hofschire, L. (2006). Parenting the Internet. *Journal of Communication, 56*(3), 486–504. doi:10.1111/j.1460-2466.2006.00297.x

Eaton, L. G., & Funder, D. C. (2003). The creation and consequences of the social world: An interactional analysis of extraversion. *European Journal of Personality, 17*(5), 375–395. doi:10.1002/per.477

Ecoma, C. S., & Ecoma, B. C. (2015). Nigerian core values and social networking in contemporary times: A discourse. *The International Journal of Social Sciences and Humanities Inventions*, *2*(9), 1555–1565.

Edogor, I. O., Aladi, A. J., & Idowu, L. I. (2015). Influence of social media on youths' usage of traditional mass media in Nigeria. *New Media of Mass Communication*, *31*, 55–67.

Eftekhar, A., Fullwood, C., & Morris, N. (2014). Capturing personality from Facebook photos and photo-related activities: How much exposure do you need? *Computers in Human Behavior*, *37*, 162–170. doi:10.1016/j.chb.2014.04.048

Ehrenberg, A., Juckes, S., White, K. M., & Walsh, S. P. (2008). Personality and self-esteem as predictors of young people's technology use. *Cyberpsychology & Behavior*, *11*(6), 739–741. doi:10.1089/cpb.2008.0030 PMID:18991531

Eidenbenz, F. (2011). Systemic dynamics with adolescents addicted to the Internet. In K. S. Young (Ed.), *Internet addiction: A handbook and guide to evaluation and treatment* (pp. 245–266). Hoboken, NJ: John Wiley & Sons, Inc.

Eker, D., & Arkar, H. (1995). Factorial structure, validity, and reliability of the Multidimensional Scale of Perceived Social Support. [in Turkish]. *Journal of Turkish Psychology*, *101*(34), 45–55.

Eker, D., Arkar, H., & Yaldız, H. (2001). Factorial structure, validity, and reliability of revised form of the Multidimensional Scale of Perceived Social Support. [in Turkish]. *Journal of Turkish Psychiatry*, *12*(1), 17–25.

Eldeleklioğlu, J., & Vural, M. (2013). Predictive effects of academic achievement, internet use duration, loneliness and shyness on internet addiction. *Hacettepe Üniversitesi Eğitim Fakültesi Dergisi*, *28*(1), 141–152.

Elliott, J. C., Stohl, M., Wall, M. M., Keyes, K. M., Goodwin, R. D., Skodol, A. E., & Hasin, D. S. et al. (2014). The risk for persistent adult alcohol and nicotine dependence: The role of childhood maltreatment. *Addiction (Abingdon, England)*, *109*(5), 842–850. doi:10.1111/add.12477 PMID:24401044

Ellison, N. B. (2007). Social network sites: Definition, history, and scholarship. *Journal of Computer-Mediated Communication*, *13*(1), 210–230. doi:10.1111/j.1083-6101.2007.00393.x

Emery, M. D. (2011). A Case Study of Social and Media Influence on Religion. *Journal of International Students*, *1*(1), 18–24.

Endong, F. P. (2017). Reconciling homosexuality and spirituality in Africa as a heresy and survival strategy: A study of House of Rainbow (LGBT Church) Nigeria. In P. Ana Maria (Ed.), *Multiculturalism and the Convergence of Faith and Practical Wisdom in Modern Society* (pp. 331–354). Hershey, PA: IGI Global. doi:10.4018/978-1-5225-1955-3.ch017

Endong, F. P. C. (2015). Framing the queers and the LGBT right movement in Africa: A study of Nigerian bloggers and web journalists. *Journal of Global Research in Education and Social Sciences*, *6*(4), 50–60.

Endong, F. P. C. (2016). The LGBT right movement in Africa and the myth of the Whiteman's superiority. *Journal of Globalization Studies*, *7*(1), 3–15.

Endong, F. P. C., & Obongawan, E. (2015). Sex in Christian movie: A study of Mel Gibson's *The Passion of the Christ* and Roger Young's *The Bible: Joseph*. *International Journal of Communication and Media Sciences*, *2*(2), 11–21.

Endong, F. P. C., & Vareba, A. L. (2015). Resisting anti-gay laws through media advocacy and online communities of meaning: A study of Nigerian homosexuals. *Journal for Studies in Management and Planning*, *10*(2), 94–106.

Engelberg, E., & Sjoberg, L. (2004). Internet use, social skills, and adjustment. *Cyberpsychology & Behavior*, *7*(1), 41–47. doi:10.1089/109493104322820101 PMID:15006168

Enukuomehin, O. A. (2011). ICT CGPA: Consequences of social networks in an internet driven learning society. *International Journal of Computer Trends and Technology*, *2*(2), 101–124.

Erdoğan, Y. (2008). Exploring the relationships among Internet usage, Internet attitudes and loneliness of Turkish adolescents. *Cyberpsychology (Brno)*, *2*(2), 38–51.

Eşkisu, M., Hoşoğlu, R., & Rasmussen, K. (2017). An investigation of the relationship between Facebook usage, Big Five, self-esteem and narcissism. *Computers in Human Behavior*, *69*, 294–301. doi:10.1016/j.chb.2016.12.036

Eurobarometer, F. (2008). *Towards a safer use of the Internet for children in the EU–a parents' perspective*. European Commission.

Everton, S. F. (2015). Networks and Religion: Ties that Bind, Loose, Build Up, and Tear Down. *Journal of Social Structure: JOSS*, *16*(10), 1–34.

Evren, C., Dalbudak, E., Evren, B., & Demirci, A. C. (2014). High risk of Internet addiction and its relationship with lifetime substance use, psychological and behavioral problems among 10th grade adolescents. *Psychiatria Danubina*, *26*(4), 330–339. PMID:25377367

Eze, I. (2014). Adolescent attitude towards premarital sex. *Mediterranean Journal of Social Sciences*, *5*(10), 491–496.

Eze, O. C. (2001). *Nigeria: Path to technological transformation*. Port Harcourt: Cass Publications.

Ezoe, S., & Toda, M. (2013). Relationships of loneliness and mobile phone dependence with Internet addiction in Japanese medical students. *Open Journal of Preventive Medicine*, *3*(6), 407–412. doi:10.4236/ojpm.2013.36055

Fabrigar, L. R., Wegener, D. T., MacCallum, R. C., & Strahan, E. J. (1999). Evaluating the use of exploratory factor analysis in psychological research. *Psychological Methods*, *4*(3), 272–299. doi:10.1037/1082-989X.4.3.272

Fallahi, V. (2011). Effect of ICT on the youth: A study about the relationship between internet usage and social isolation among Iranian Students. *Procedia: Social and Behavioral Sciences*, *15*, 394–398. doi:10.1016/j.sbspro.2011.03.110

Farmer, A. D., Holt, C. B., Cook, M. J., & Hearing, S. D. (2009). Social networking sites: A novel portal for communication. *Postgraduate Medical Journal*, *85*(1007), 455–459. doi:10.1136/pgmj.2008.074674 PMID:19734511

Feist, J., & Feist, G. J. (2005). *Theories of personality* (6th ed.). Columbus, OH: McGraw-Hill Higher Education.

Felsher, J. R., Derevensky, J. L., & Gupta, R. (2010). Young adults with gambling problems: The impact of childhood maltreatment. *International Journal of Mental Health and Addiction*, *8*(4), 545–556. doi:10.1007/s11469-009-9230-4

Ferraro, G., Caci, B., D'Amico, A., & Di Blasi, M. (2007). Internet addiction disorder: An Italian study. *Cyberpsychology & Behavior*, *10*(2), 170–175. doi:10.1089/cpb.2006.9972 PMID:17474832

Fioravanti, G., Dèttore, D., & Casale, S. (2012). Adolescent Internet addiction: Testing the association between self-esteem, the perception of Internet attributes, and preference for online social interactions. *Cyberpsychology, Behavior, and Social Networking*, *15*(6), 318–323. doi:10.1089/cyber.2011.0358 PMID:22703038

Fioravanti, G., Primi, C., & Casale, S. (2013). Psychometric evaluation of the generalized problematic internet use scale 2 in an Italian sample. *Cyberpsychology, Behavior, and Social Networking*, *16*(10), 761–766. doi:10.1089/cyber.2012.0429 PMID:23742149

Fisher, D. R., & Boekkooi, M. (2010). Mobilizing Friends and Strangers: Understanding the role of the Internet in the Step It Up day of action. *Information Communication and Society*, *13*(2), 193–208. doi:10.1080/13691180902878385

Fisher, L. A., Elias, J. W., & Ritz, K. (1998). Predicting relapse to substance abuse as a function of personality dimensions. *Alcoholism, Clinical and Experimental Research*, *22*(5), 1041–1047. doi:10.1111/j.1530-0277.1998.tb03696.x PMID:9726270

Fisoun, V., Floros, G., Geroukalis, D., Ioannidi, N., Farkonas, N., Sergentani, E., & Siomos, K. et al. (2012a). Internet addiction in the island of Hippocrates: The associations between internet abuse and adolescent off-line behaviours. *Child and Adolescent Mental Health*, *17*(1), 37–44. doi:10.1111/j.1475-3588.2011.00605.x

Fisoun, V., Floros, G., Siomos, K., Geroukalis, D., & Navridis, K. (2012). Internet addiction as an important predictor in early detection of adolescent drug use experience—implications for research and practice. *Journal of Addiction Medicine*, *6*(1), 77–84. doi:10.1097/ADM.0b013e318233d637 PMID:22227578

Fleming, M. J., Greentree, S., Cocotti-Muller, D., Elias, K. A., & Morrison, S. (2006). Safety in cyberspace: Adolescents' safety and exposure online. *Youth & Society*, *38*(2), 135–154. doi:10.1177/0044118X06287858

Floros, G., & Siomos, K. (2014). Excessive Internet use and personality traits. *Current Behavioral Neuroscience Reports*, *1*(1), 19–26. doi:10.1007/s40473-014-0006-1

Floros, G., Siomos, K., Stogiannidou, A., Giouzepas, I., & Garyfallos, G. (2014). The relationship between personality, defense styles, internet addiction disorder, and psychopathology in college students. *Cyberpsychology, Behavior, and Social Networking*, *17*(10), 672–676. doi:10.1089/cyber.2014.0182 PMID:25225916

Fogg, B. J. (2009). The new rules of persuasion. *RSA Journal*, *155*(5538), 24–29.

Fordyce, M. W. (1988). A review of research on the happiness measures: A sixty second index of happiness and mental health. *Social Indicators Research*, *20*(4), 355–381. doi:10.1007/BF00302333

Forman, R. F., Marlowe, D. B., & McLellan, A. T. (2006). The Internet as a source of drugs of abuse. *Current Psychiatry Reports*, *8*(5), 377–382. doi:10.1007/s11920-006-0039-6 PMID:16968618

Frangos, C. C., Frangos, C. C., & Sotiropoulos, I. (2011). Problematic Internet use among Greek university students: An ordinal logistic regression with risk factors of negative psychological beliefs, pornographic sites, and online games. *Cyberpsychology, Behavior, and Social Networking*, *14*(1-2), 51–58. doi:10.1089/cyber.2009.0306 PMID:21329443

Fredricks, J. A., & Eccles, J. S. (2006). Is extracurricular participation associated with beneficial outcomes? Concurrent and longitudinal relationships. *Developmental Psychology*, *42*(4), 698–713. doi:10.1037/0012-1649.42.4.698 PMID:16802902

Friebel, A. D., & Kapoor, H. (2016). Internet addiction: A multi-faceted disorder. *Journal of Addictive Behaviors, Therapy & Rehabilitation*, *5*(1), 1–3. doi:10.4172/2324-9005.1000152

Fu, K. W., Chan, W. S., Wong, P. W., & Yip, P. S. (2010). Internet addiction: Prevalence, discriminant validity and correlates among adolescents in Hong Kong. *The British Journal of Psychiatry*, *196*(6), 486–492. doi:10.1192/bjp.bp.109.075002 PMID:20513862

Funk, J. Q. (2013). The Power of 'Friending': How Social Media is. *juliannefunk.com* Retrieved from: http://www.juliannefunk.com/wp-content/uploads/2013/11/Julianne-Funk-Dissertation.pdf

Gaille, B. (2015, Feb. 13). *32 interesting Internet addiction statistics*. Retrieved from http://brandongaille.com/32-interesting-internet-addiction-statistics/

Gámez-Guadix, M., Calvete, E., Orue, I., & Las Hayas, C. (2015). Problematic Internet use and problematic alcohol use from the cognitive–behavioral model: A longitudinal study among adolescents. *Addictive Behaviors*, *40*, 109–114. doi:10.1016/j.addbeh.2014.09.009 PMID:25244690

Gámez-Guadix, M., Orue, I., & Calvete, E. (2013). Evaluation of the cognitive-behavioral model of generalized and problematic Internet use in Spanish adolescents. *Psicothema*, *25*(3), 299–306. PMID:23910742

Gámez-Guadix, M., Villa-George, F. I., & Calvete, E. (2012). Measurement and analysis of the cognitive-behavioral model of generalized problematic Internet use among Mexican adolescents. *Journal of Adolescence*, *35*(6), 1581–1591. doi:10.1016/j.adolescence.2012.06.005 PMID:22789467

Gamito, P. S., Morais, D. G., Oliveira, J. G. B., Rosa, R. P. J., & Matos, M. G. (2016). Frequency is not enough: Patterns of use associated with risk of Internet addiction in Portuguese adolescents. *Computers in Human Behavior*, *58*, 471–478. doi:10.1016/j.chb.2016.01.013

Geçtan, E. (1997). *İnsan olmak* [Being human] (18th ed.). İstanbul, Turkey: Remzi Kitabevi.

Gervasi, A. M., La Marca, L., Lombardo, E., Mannino, G., Iacolino, C., & Schimmenti, A. (2017). Maladaptive Personality Traits and Internet Addiction Symptoms among Young Adults: A Study based on the alternative DSM-5 Model for Personality Disorders. *Clinical Neuropsychiatry*, *14*(1), 20–28.

Gibbons, R. D., Brown, C. H., Hur, K., Davis, J. M., & Mann, J. J. (2012). Suicidal thoughts and behavior with antidepressant treatment: Reanalysis of the randomized placebo-controlled studies of fluoxetine and venlafaxine. *Archives of General Psychiatry*, *69*(6), 580–587. doi:10.1001/archgenpsychiatry.2011.2048 PMID:22309973

Giota, K. G., & Kleftaras, G. (2013). The role of personality and depression in problematic use of social networking sites in Greece. *Cyberpsychology (Brno)*, *7*(3). doi:10.5817/CP2013-3-6

Glaser, D. (2002). Emotional abuse and neglect (psychological maltreatment): A conceptual framework. *Child Abuse & Neglect*, *26*(6), 697–714. doi:10.1016/S0145-2134(02)00342-3 PMID:12201163

Goldberg, I. (1995). *Internet addiction disorder: Diagnostic criteria*. Retrieved March 17, 2017, from http:// http://users.rider.edu/~suler/psycyber/supportgp.html

Goldberg, I. (1996). *Internet addictive disorder (IAD) diagnostic criteria*. Retrieved March 17, 2017 from http://www.webcitation.org/query?url=http%3A%2F%2Fwww.psycom.net%2Fiadcriteria.html&date=2013-02-06

Golub, A., & Lingley, K. (2008). Internet Addiction, MMOGs, and Moral Crisis in Contemporary China. *Games and Culture*, *3*(1), 59–75. doi:10.1177/1555412007309526

Gong, J., Chen, X., Zeng, J., Li, F., Zhou, D., & Wang, Z. (2009). Adolescent addictive Internet use and drug abuse in Wuhan, China. *Addiction Research and Theory*, *17*(3), 291–305. doi:10.1080/16066350802435152

Gonzalez, N. A. (2002). *Internet addiction disorder and its relation to impulse control* (Unpublished master's thesis). Texas A&M University, Kingsville, TX.

Gorman, V. (2015, March 31). Social media, sexualization and the selfie generation. The Drum. ABC News, 66-73.

Graham, A. L., Cobb, N. K., Raymond, L., Sill, S., & Young, J. (2007). The effectiveness of an Internet-based worksite smoking cessation intervention at 12 months. *Journal of Occupational and Environmental Medicine*, *49*(8), 821–828. doi:10.1097/JOM.0b013e3180d09e6f PMID:17693778

Grant, J. E., Potenza, M. N., Weinstein, A., & Gorelick, D. A. (2010). Introduction to behavioral addictions. *The American Journal of Drug and Alcohol Abuse*, *36*(5), 233–241. doi:10.3109/00952990.2010.491884 PMID:20560821

Green, M. J., Leyland, A. H., Sweeting, H., & Benzeval, M. (2016). Socioeconomic position and early adolescent smoking development: evidence from the British Youth Panel Survey (1994–2008). *Tobacco Control, 25*(2), 203-210.

Greenfield, D. N. (1999). *Virtual addiction: Sometimes new technology can create new problems*. Academic Press.

Greenfield, D. N. (1999). *Virtual addiction: Sometimes new technology can create new problems*. Retrieved from http://virtual-addiction.com/wp-content/pdf/nature_internet_addiction.pdf

Greenfield, D. (2011). The addictive properties of Internet usage. In K. S. Young (Ed.), *Internet addiction: A handbook and guide to evaluation and treatment* (pp. 135–153). Hoboken, NJ: John Wiley & Sons, Inc.

Greenfield, D. N. (1999). Psychological characteristics of compulsive Internet use: A preliminary analysis. *Cyberpsychology & Behavior*, *2*(5), 403–412. doi:10.1089/cpb.1999.2.403 PMID:19178212

Griffiths, M. (1995) Technological addictions. *Clinical Psychology Forum, 76,* 14-19.

Griffiths, M. (1998). Internet addiction: does it really exist? *Psychology and the Internet*, 61-75.

Griffiths, M. (2015). *Classification and treatment of behavioral addictions*. Retrieved from http://www.nursinginpractice.com/article/classification-and-treatment-behavioural-addictions

Griffiths, M. D. (1996). Internet addiction: An issue for clinical psychology? *Clinical Psychology Forum, 97,* 32-6.

Griffiths, M. D., & Pontes, H. M. (2014). Internet addiction disorder and internet gaming disorder are not the same. *Addiction Research & Therapy, 5*(4), 1-3. DOI: 10.4172/2155-6105.1000e124

Griffiths, M. (1997). Psychology of computer use: XLIII. Some comments on 'addictive use of the Internet' by Young. *Psychological Reports*, *80*(1), 81–82. doi:10.2466/pr0.1997.80.1.81 PMID:9122355

Griffiths, M. (1998). Internet addiction: Does it really exist? In J. Gackenbach (Ed.), *Psychology and the Internet: Intrapersonal, interpersonal and transpersonal implications* (pp. 61–75). New York: Academic Press.

Griffiths, M. (2000). Does Internet and computer" addiction" exist? Some case study evidence. *Cyberpsychology & Behavior*, *3*(2), 211–218. doi:10.1089/109493100316067

Griffiths, M. (2000). Internet addiction-time to be taken seriously? *Addiction Research*, *8*(5), 413–418. doi:10.3109/16066350009005587

Griffiths, M. (2003). Internet gambling: Issues, concerns, and recommendations. *Cyberpsychology & Behavior*, *6*(6), 557–568. doi:10.1089/109493103322725333 PMID:14756922

Griffiths, M. (2011). Gambling addiction on the Internet. In K. S. Young (Ed.), *Internet addiction: A handbook and guide to evaluation and treatment* (pp. 91–111). Hoboken, NJ: John Wiley & Sons, Inc.

Griffiths, M. D. (1998). Internet addiction: Does it really exist? In J. Gackenbach (Ed.), *Psychology and the Internet: Intrapersonal, Interpersonal, and Transpersonal Applications* (pp. 61–75). New York, NY: Academic Press.

Griffiths, M. D. (1999). Internet addiction: Internet fuels other addictions. *Student BMJ, 7,* 428–429.

Griffiths, M. D. (2005). A components model of addiction within a biopsychosocial framework. *Journal of Substance Use*, *10*(4), 191–197. doi:10.1080/14659890500114359

Griffiths, M. D. (2013). Social networking addiction: Emerging themes and issues. *Journal of Addiction Research & Therapy*, *4*(5). doi:10.4172/2155-6105.1000e118

Griffiths, M. D., & Dancaster, I. (1995). The effect of type A personality on physiological arousal while playing computer games. *Addictive Behaviors*, *20*(4), 543–548. doi:10.1016/0306-4603(95)00001-S PMID:7484336

Griffiths, M. D., Kuss, D. J., Billieux, J., & Pontes, H. M. (2015). The evolution of Internet addiction: A global perspective. *Addictive Behaviors*, *53*, 193–195. doi:10.1016/j.addbeh.2015.11.001 PMID:26562678

Griffiths, M. D., Kuss, D. J., & King, D. L. (2012). Video game addiction: Past, present and future. *Current Psychiatry Reviews, 8*, 308–318. doi:10.2174/157340012803520414

Griffiths, M. D., Kuss, D. J., & Pontes, H. M. (2016). A brief overview of Internet gaming disorder and its treatment. *Australian Clinical Psychologist, 2*(1), 20108.

Griffiths, M. D., & Larkin, M. (2004). Conceptualizing addiction: The case for a 'complex systems' account. *Addiction Research and Theory, 12*(2), 99–102. doi:10.1080/16066350420000193211

Griffiths, M. D., Pontes, H. M., & Kuss, D. J. (2016). Online Addictions: Conceptualizations, Debates, and Controversies. *Addicta: the Turkish Journal on Addictions, 3*(2), 1–14.

Griffiths, M. D., Pontes, H. M., & Kuss, D. J. (2016). Online addictions: Conceptualizations, debates, and controversies. *Addicta: The Turkish Journal on Addictions, 3*(2), 1–20. doi:10.15805/addicta.2016.3.0101

Griffiths, M. D., & Szabo, A. (2014). Is excessive online usage a function of medium or activity? An empirical pilot study. *Journal of Behavioral Addictions, 3*(1), 74–77. doi:10.1556/JBA.2.2013.016 PMID:25215216

Gross, A. B., & Keller, H. R. (1992). Long-term consequences of childhood physical and psychological maltreatment. *Aggressive Behavior, 18*(3), 171–185. doi:10.1002/1098-2337(1992)18:3<171::AID-AB2480180302>3.0.CO;2-I

Grossbart, S., Hughes, S. M., Pryor, S., & Yost, A. (2002). *Socialization aspects of parents, children, and the Internet.* ACR North American Advances.

Gross, E. F. (2004). Adolescent Internet use: What we expect, what teens report. *Journal of Applied Developmental Psychology, 25*(6), 633–649. doi:10.1016/j.appdev.2004.09.005

Gross, E. F., Juvonen, J., & Gable, S. L. (2002). Internet use and well-being in adolescence. *The Journal of Social Issues, 58*(1), 75–90. doi:10.1111/1540-4560.00249

Grossman, L. (2014, December 15). The man who wired the world; Mark Zuckerberg's crusade to put every single human being online. *Time Magazine*, 30-40.

Gu, M. (2012). *Study of adolescents' Internet use and Internet addiction in Shanghai, China: Implications for social work practice* (Unpublished Doctoral dissertation). The Chinese University of Hong Kong, Hong Kong.

Guan, S. S. A., & Subrahmanyam, K. (2009). Youth Internet use: Risks and opportunities. *Current Opinion in Psychiatry, 22*(4), 351–356. doi:10.1097/YCO.0b013e32832bd7e0 PMID:19387347

Guertler, D., Broda, A., Bischof, A., Kastirke, N., Meerkerk, G. J., John, U., & Rumpf, H. J. et al. (2014). Factor structure of the Compulsive Internet Use scale. *Cyberpsychology, Behavior, and Social Networking, 17*(1), 46–51. doi:10.1089/cyber.2013.0076 PMID:23962124

Guertler, D., Rumpf, H.-J., Bischof, A., Kastirke, N., Petersen, K. U., John, U., & Meyer, C. (2013). Assessment of problematic internet use by the compulsive internet use scale and the internet addiction test: A sample of problematic and pathological gamblers. *European Addiction Research, 20*(2), 75–81. doi:10.1159/000355076 PMID:24080838

Guglielmucci, F., Saroldi, M., Zullo, G., Munno, D., & Granieri, A. (2017). Personality Profiles and Problematic Internet Use in a Sample Of Italian Adolescents. *Clinical Neuropsychiatry, 14*(1), 94–103.

Günüç, S. (2009). *Development of Internet Addiction Scale* (Unpublished master's thesis). Yüzüncü Yıl University, Van.

Gunuc, S., & Dogan, A. (2013). The relationships between Turkish adolescents' Internet addiction, their perceived social support and family activities. *Computers in Human Behavior, 29*(6), 2197–2207. doi:10.1016/j.chb.2013.04.011

Guo, J., Chen, L., Wang, X., Liu, Y., Chui, C. H. K., He, H., & Tian, D. et al. (2012). The Relationship Between Internet Addiction and Depression Among Migrant Children and Left-Behind Children in China. *Cyberpsychology, Behavior, and Social Networking*, *15*(11), 585–590. doi:10.1089/cyber.2012.0261 PMID:23002986

Gupta, P., & Nene, M. J. (2017a) An Observation on Social Media Content to Analyze CyberPsycho Attack. *1st International Conference on Smart Computing & Informatics*. Springer.

Gupta, P., & Nene, M. J. (2017b) An Approach to Analyze CyberPsycho Attacks Enabled using Persuasive Messages. *1st International Conference on Smart Computing & Informatics*. Springer.

Gupta, P., & J, M. (2016). CyberPsycho Attacks: Techniques, Causes, Effects and Recommendations to End-Users. *International Journal of Computers and Applications*, *156*(11), 11–16. doi:10.5120/ijca2016912556

Gupta, P., & Nene, M. J. (2017). Analysis of Text Messages in Social Media to Investigate CyberPsycho Attack. In *International Conference on Information and Communication Technology for Intelligent Systems* (pp. 581-587). Springer.

Gyeong, H., Lee, H. K., & Lee, K. (2012). Factor Analysis of the Young's Internet Addiction Test: In Korean College Students Group. *Journal of Korean Neuropsychiatric Association*, *51*(1), 45–51. doi:10.4306/jknpa.2012.51.1.45

Haagsma, M. C., Caplan, S. E., Peters, O., & Pieterse, M. E. (2013). A cognitive-behavioral model of problematic online gaming in adolescents aged 12–22 years. *Computers in Human Behavior*, *29*(1), 202–209. doi:10.1016/j.chb.2012.08.006

Hahn, E., Reuter, M., Spinath, F. M., & Montag, C. (2017). Internet addiction and its facets: The role of genetics and the relation to self-directedness. *Addictive Behaviors*, *65*, 137–146. doi:10.1016/j.addbeh.2016.10.018 PMID:27816039

Hahn, E., & Spinath, F. M. (2017). Quantitative behavior genetics of Internet addiction. In C. Montag & M. Reuter (Eds.), *Internet addiction: Neuroscientific approaches and therapeutical implications including smartphone addiction* (2nd ed.; pp. 125–140). Cham, Switzerland: Springer International Publishing. doi:10.1007/978-3-319-46276-9_8

Ha, J. H., Chin, B., Park, D. H., Ryu, S. H., & Yu, J. (2008). Characteristics of Excessive Cellular Phone Use in Korean Adolescents. *Cyberpsychology & Behavior*, *11*(6), 783–784. doi:10.1089/cpb.2008.0096 PMID:18991536

Ha, J. H., Kim, S. Y., Bae, S. C., Bae, S., Kim, H., Sim, M., & Cho, S. C. et al. (2007). Depression and Internet addiction in adolescents. *Psychopathology*, *40*(6), 424–430. doi:10.1159/000107426 PMID:17709972

Ha, J. H., Yoo, H. J., Cho, I. H., Chin, B., Shin, D., & Kim, J. H. (2006). Psychiatry comorbidity assessed in Korean children and adolescents who screen positive for Internet addiction. *The Journal of Clinical Psychiatry*, *67*(05), 821–826. doi:10.4088/JCP.v67n0517 PMID:16841632

Hall, A. S., & Parsons, J. (2001). Internet addiction: College student case study using best practices in cognitive behavior therapy. *Journal of Mental Health Counseling*, *23*(4), 312–327.

Halley, M. P., Mark, D. G., & Ivone, M. P. (2014). Internet addiction and loneliness among children and adolescents in the education setting: An empirical pilot study. *Aloma*, *32*(1), 91–98.

Hamburger, A. Y., & Artzi, E. B. (2003). Loneliness and Internet use. *Computers in Human Behavior*, *9*(1), 71–80. doi:10.1016/S0747-5632(02)00014-6

Hampton, K. N., Shin, I., & Lu, W. (2017). Social media and political discussion: When online presence silences offline conversation. *Information Communication and Society*, *20*(7), 1090–1107. doi:10.1080/1369118X.2016.1218526

Harakeh, Z., Scholte, R. H., De Vries, H., & Engels, R. C. (2005). Parental rules and communication: Their association with adolescent smoking. *Addiction (Abingdon, England)*, *100*(6), 862–870. doi:10.1111/j.1360-0443.2005.01067.x PMID:15918816

Hardie, E., & Tee, M. Y. (2007). Excessive Internet use: The role of personality, loneliness and social support networks in Internet Addiction. *Australian Journal of Emerging Technologies and Society*, 5(1).

Harris, B. (2013). Diplomacy 2.0: The future of social media in nation branding. *Exchange: The Journal of Public Diplomacy*, 4(1), 3.

Hart, S. N., Binggeli, N. J., & Brassard, M. R. (1998). Evidence for the effects of psychological maltreatment. *Journal of Emotional Abuse*, 1(1), 27–58. doi:10.1300/J135v01n01_03

Hasmujaj, E. (2016). Internet addiction and loneliness among students of University of Shkodra. *European Scientific Journal*, 12(29), 1857–7881. doi:10.19044/esj.2016.v12n29p397

Ha, Y.-M., & Hwang, W. J. (2014). Gender differences in internet addiction associated with psychological health indicators among adolescents using a national web-based survey. *International Journal of Mental Health and Addiction*, 12(5), 660–669. doi:10.1007/s11469-014-9500-7

Hayes, S. C., Luoma, J. B., Bond, F. W., Masuda, A., & Lillis, J. (2006). Acceptance and commitment therapy: Model, processes, and outcomes. *Behaviour Research and Therapy*, 44(1), 1–25. doi:10.1016/j.brat.2005.06.006 PMID:16300724

Hedman, E., Ljótsson, B., & Lindefors, N. (2012). Cognitive behavior therapy via the Internet: A systematic review of applications, clinical efficacy, and cost–effectiveness. *Expert Review of Pharmacoeconomics & Outcomes Research*, 12(6), 745–764. doi:10.1586/erp.12.67 PMID:23252357

Heim, J., Brandtzæg, P. B., Kaare, B. H., Endestad, T., & Torgersen, L. (2007). Children's usage of media technologies and psychosocial factors. *New Media & Society*, 9(3), 425–454. doi:10.1177/1461444807076971

Heo, J., Chun, S., Lee, S., Lee, K. H., & Kim, J. (2015). Internet use and well-being in older adults. *Cyberpsychology, Behavior, and Social Networking*, 18(5), 268–272. doi:10.1089/cyber.2014.0549 PMID:25919967

Heo, J., Oh, J., Subramanian, S. V., Kim, Y., & Kawachi, I. (2014). Addictive Internet Use among Korean Adolescents: A National Survey. *PLoS One*, 9(2), e87819. doi:10.1371/journal.pone.0087819 PMID:24505318

Hersh, W. (1999). A world of knowledge at your fingertips": The promise, reality, and future directions of on-line information retrieval. *Academic Medicine*, 74(3), 240–243. doi:10.1097/00001888-199903000-00012 PMID:10099643

Heschong, L. (1999). *Daylighting in schools: An investigation into the relationship between daylighting and human performance*. Detailed Report.

Ho, R. C., Zhang, M. W., Tsang, T. Y., Toh, A. H., Pan, F., Lu, Y., . . . Holm, B. (2013, April 9). *Social anxiety and the Internet*. Retrieved from http://www.huffingtonpost.com/barbara-holm/social-anxiety-and-internet_b_2632610.html

Hodgins, D. C., Schopflocher, D. P., el-Guebaly, N., Casey, D. M., Smith, G. J., Williams, R. J., & Wood, R. T. (2010). The association between childhood maltreatment and gambling problems in a community sample of adult men and women. *Psychology of Addictive Behaviors*, 24(3), 548–554. doi:10.1037/a0019946 PMID:20853942

Holden, C. (2001). 'Behavioral' addictions: Do they exist? *Science*, 294(5544), 980–982. doi:10.1126/science.294.5544.980 PMID:11691967

Holdoš, J. (2016). Type D personality in the prediction of Internet addiction in the young adult population of Slovak Internet users. *Current Psychology (New Brunswick, N.J.)*, 1–8.

Honey, P., & Mumford, A. (1986). *Manual of learning styles*. Maidenhead, UK: Peter Honey Publications.

Hong Kong Census and Statistics Department. (2016). *Thematic Household Survey Report - Report No. 59*. Retrieved from http://www.statistics.gov.hk/pub/B11302592016XXXXB0100.pdf

Hong Kong Census and Statistics Department. (2017). *Hong Kong 2016 Population By-census – Thematic Report: Household Income Distribution in Hong Kong*. Retrieved from http://www.statistics.gov.hk/pub/B11200962016XXXXB0100.pdf

Howard, C. J., Wilding, R., & Guest, D. (2016). Light video game play is associated with enhanced visual processing of rapid serial visual presentation targets. *Perception, 46,* 2. PMID:27697909

Hsiao, K. L., Lee, C. H., Chiang, H. S., & Wang, J. Y. (2016). Exploring the Antecedents of Technostress and Compulsive Mobile Application Usage: Personality Perspectives. In *International Conference on Human Aspects of IT for the Aged Population* (pp. 320-328). Springer International Publishing. doi:10.1007/978-3-319-39943-0_31

Hsieh, Y. P., Shen, A. C. T., Wei, H. S., Feng, J. Y., Huang, S. C. Y., & Hwa, H. L. (2016). Associations between child maltreatment, PTSD, and internet addiction among Taiwanese students. *Computers in Human Behavior, 56,* 209–214. doi:10.1016/j.chb.2015.11.048

Huang, R. L., Lu, Z., Liu, J. J., You, Y. M., Pan, Z. Q., Wei, Z., & Wang, Z. Z. et al. (2009). Features and predictors of problematic Internet use in Chinese college students. *Behaviour & Information Technology, 28*(5), 485–490. doi:10.1080/01449290701485801

Huang, Z., Wang, M., Qian, M., Zhong, J., & Tao, R. (2007). Chinese Internet Addiction Inventory: Developing a Measure of Problematic Internet Use for Chinese College Students. *Cyberpsychology & Behavior, 10*(6), 805–811. doi:10.1089/cpb.2007.9950 PMID:18085968

Huan, V. S., Ang, R. P., & Chye, S. (2014). Loneliness and shyness in adolescent problematic internet users: The role of social anxiety. *Child and Youth Care Forum, 43*(5), 539–551. doi:10.1007/s10566-014-9252-3

Humphreys, K., & Tucker, J. A. (2002). Toward a more responsive and effective intervention systems for alcohol-related problems. *Addiction (Abingdon, England), 97*(2), 126–132. doi:10.1046/j.1360-0443.2002.00004.x PMID:11860378

Hur, M. H. (2006). Demographic, habitual, and socioeconomic determinants of Internet addiction disorder: An empirical study of Korean teenagers. *Cyberpsychology & Behavior, 9*(5), 514–525. doi:10.1089/cpb.2006.9.514 PMID:17034317

Hwang, Y. (2014). Personal Characters and Addictive Use of Facebook. *Journal of the Korea Society of IT Services, 13*(4), 45-63.

Hwang, J. Y., Shin, Y. C., Lim, S. W., Park, H. Y., Shin, N. Y., Jang, J. H., & Kwon, J. S. et al. (2012). Multidimensional comparison of personality characteristics of the Big Five Model, impulsiveness, and affect in pathological gambling and obsessive–compulsive disorder. *Journal of Gambling Studies, 28*(3), 351–362. doi:10.1007/s10899-011-9269-6 PMID:21938524

Hyman, S. M., Garcia, M., & Sinha, R. (2006). Gender specific associations between types of childhood maltreatment and the onset, escalation and severity of substance use in cocaine dependent adults. *The American Journal of Drug and Alcohol Abuse, 32*(4), 655–664. doi:10.1080/10623320600919193 PMID:17127554

Ibidapo, F. (2014, Oct. 6). Examining the impact of social media in Nigeria youth. *People Day,* 32-34.

Ihedoro, M. (2006). Value system, attitudes and knowledge of civic education as determinants of students performance in social studies (Unpublished M. Ed. Project). University of Ibadan.

Ilhan, A., Çelik, H. C., Gemcioğlu, M., & Çiftaslan, M. E. (2016). Examination of the relationship between Internet attitudes and Internet addictions of 13-18-year-old students: The case of Internet Live Stats. (2017, February). *Internet users by country (2016)*. Retrieved from http://www.internetlivestats.com/internet-users-by-country/

Inderbiten, H. M., Walters, K. S., & Bukowski, A. L. (1997). The role of social anxiety in adolescent peer relations: Differences among sociometric status groups and rejected subgroups. *Journal of Clinical Child Psychology, 26*(4), 338–348. doi:10.1207/s15374424jccp2604_2 PMID:9418172

Infurna, M. R., Reichl, C., Parzer, P., Schimmenti, A., Bifulco, A., & Kaess, M. (2016). Associations between depression and specific childhood experiences of abuse and neglect: A meta-analysis. *Journal of Affective Disorders, 190*, 47–55. doi:10.1016/j.jad.2015.09.006 PMID:26480211

International Telecommunication Union. (2012). *Internet users.* International Telecommunication Union. Retrieved 14 December 2016 from http://www.itu.int/ITU-D/ict/statistics/index.html

Internet Live Stats. (2017a). *Internet users.* Retrieved from: http://www.internetlivestats.com/internet-users/

Internet Live Stats. (2017b). *Slovenia Internet Users.* Retrieved from: http://www.internetlivestats.com/internet-users/slovenia/

Iskender, M., & Akin, A. (2011). Self-compassion and Internet addiction. *TOJET: The Turkish Online Journal of Educational Technology, 10*(3), 215–221.

ITAA. (2009, August 1). *Signs and symptoms of ITA.* Retrieved from http://www.netaddictionanon.org/category/about-itaa/

ITAA. (2016). *Internet and tech addiction anonymous. 12 steps and principles for Internet & technology addiction recovery.* Retrieved from http://www.netaddictionanon.org/about/itaa-12-steps/

Iwaniec, D. (2006). *The emotionally abused and neglected child: Identification, assessment and intervention: A practice handbook.* Chichester, UK: John Wiley & Son,Ltd.

Iwaniec, D., Larkin, E., & Higgins, S. (2006). Research review: Risk and resilience in cases of emotional abuse. *Child & Family Social Work, 11*(1), 73–82. doi:10.1111/j.1365-2206.2006.00398.x

Jackson, L. A., Ervin, K. S., Gardner, P. D., & Schmitt, N. (2001). Gender and the Internet: Women communicating and men searching. *Sex Roles, 44*(5-6), 363–379. doi:10.1023/A:1010937901821

Jacobs, D. F. (1986). A general theory of addictions: A new theoretical model. *Journal of Gambling Behavior, 2*(1), 15-31.

Jafarkarimi, H., Sim, A. T. H., Saadatdoost, R., & Hee, J. M. (2016). Facebook addiction among Malaysian students. *International Journal of Information and Education Technology (IJIET), 6*(6), 465–469. doi:10.7763/IJIET.2016.V6.733

Jang, K. S., Hwang, S. Y., & Choi, J. Y. (2008). Internet Addiction and Psychiatric Symptoms Among Korean Adolescents. *The Journal of School Health, 78*(3), 165–171. doi:10.1111/j.1746-1561.2007.00279.x PMID:18307612

Jang, M. H., & Ji, E. S. (2012). Gender differences in associations between parental problem drinking and early adolescents' Internet addiction. *Journal for Specialists in Pediatric Nursing, 17*(4), 288–300. doi:10.1111/j.1744-6155.2012.00344.x PMID:23009041

Jansz, J., & Tanis, M. (2007). Appeal of playing online first person shooter games. *Cyberpsychology & Behavior, 10*(1), 133–136. doi:10.1089/cpb.2006.9981 PMID:17305460

Jena, A. B., & Goldman, D. P. (2011). Growing Internet use may help explain the rise in prescription drug abuse in the United States. *Health Affairs*, 10–1377. PMID:21565838

Jeon, J. H. (2005). *The effect of extent of Internet use and social supports for adolescent depression and self-esteem* (Unpublished master's thesis). Yonsei University, Seoul, South Korea.

Jeriček, H. (2002). Internet i ovisnost o internetu u Sloveniji. *Medijska istraživanja, 8*(2), 85-101.

Jeriček, H. (2001). Zasvojenost z internetom–sedanjost ali prihodnost. *Socialna Pedagogika, 5*(2), 141–168.

Jeske, D., Briggs, P., & Coventry, L. (2016). Exploring the relationship between impulsivity and decision-making on mobile devices. *Personal and Ubiquitous Computing, 20*(4), 545–557. doi:10.1007/s00779-016-0938-4

Jia, R. (2012). Computer playfulness, Internet dependency and their relationships with online activity types and student academic performance. *Journal of Behavioral Addictions, 1*(2), 74–77. doi:10.1556/JBA.1.2012.2.5 PMID:26165309

Jia, R., & Jia, H. H. (2009). Factorial validity of problematic Internet use scales. *Computers in Human Behavior, 25*(6), 1335–1342. doi:10.1016/j.chb.2009.06.004

Johansson, A., & Götestam, K. G. (2004). Internet addiction: Characteristics of a questionnaire and prevalence in Norwegian youth (12–18 years). *Scandinavian Journal of Psychology, 45*(3), 223–229. doi:10.1111/j.1467-9450.2004.00398.x PMID:15182240

Johnston, L. D., O'Malley, P. M., Bachman, J. G., & Schulenberg, J. E. (2005). Monitoring the Future: National Survey Results on Drug Use, 1975-2004: Volume II. College Students & Adults Ages 19-45, 2004. Bethesda, MD: National Institutes of Health.

Joiner, R., Gavin, J., Duffield, J., Brosnan, M., Crook, C., Durndell, A., & Lovatt, P. et al. (2005). Gender, Internet identification, and Internet anxiety: Correlates of Internet use. *Cyberpsychology & Behavior, 8*(4), 371–378. doi:10.1089/cpb.2005.8.371 PMID:16092894

Jones, D. J., Hussong, A. M., Manning, J., & Sterrett, E. (2008). Adolescent alcohol use in context: The role of parents and peers among African American and European American youth. *Cultural Diversity & Ethnic Minority Psychology, 14*(3), 266–273. doi:10.1037/1099-9809.14.3.266 PMID:18624591

Jung, C. G. (1964). *Man and his symbols*. New York: Dell.

Jun, S., & Choi, E. (2015). Academic stress and Internet addiction from general strain theory framework. *Computers in Human Behavior, 49*, 282–287. doi:10.1016/j.chb.2015.03.001

Jun, S., & Yang, F. (2007). The Usage of Online Cognitive Scale in 538 Medical Undergraduates. *Chinese Mental Health Journal, 8*, 526–528.

Kaare, P. R., Mõttus, R., & Konstabel, K. (2009). Pathological gambling in Estonia: Relationships with personality, self-esteem, emotional states and cognitive ability. *Journal of Gambling Studies, 25*(3), 377–390. doi:10.1007/s10899-009-9119-y PMID:19234772

Kabasakal, Z. (2015). Life satisfaction and family functions as-predictors of problematic Internet use in university students. *Computers in Human Behavior, 53*, 294–304. doi:10.1016/j.chb.2015.07.019

Kabasakal, Z., & Erdem, Ş. (2015). Üniversite öğrencilerinde çocukluk dönemi istismar yaşantilari ve psikolojik iyi olma. *Eğitim ve Öğretim Araştırmaları Dergisi, 4*(1), 14–23.

Kairys, S. W., & Johnson, C. F. (2002). The psychological maltreatment of children—Technical report. *Pediatrics, 109*(4), 1–3. doi:10.1542/peds.109.4.e68 PMID:11927741

Kalaitzaki, A. E., & Birtchnell, J. (2014). The impact of early parenting bonding on young adults' Internet addiction, through the mediation effects of negative relating to others and sadness. *Addictive Behaviors, 39*(3), 733–736. doi:10.1016/j.addbeh.2013.12.002 PMID:24368006

Kaltiala-Heino, R., Lintonen, T., & Rimpela, A. (2004). Internet addiction: Potentially problematic use of the Internet in a population of 12–18 year-old adolescents. *Addiction Research and Theory, 12*(1), 89–96. doi:10.1080/16066350310000987796

Kamal, N. N., & Mosallem, F. A. E. H. (2013). Determinants of problematic internet use among el-minia high school students, Egypt. *International Journal of Preventive Medicine, 4*(12), 1429–1437. PMID:24498499

Kamal, N. N., & Mosallem, F. A. E. H. (2013). Determinants of problematic Internet use among el-minia high school students, Egypt. *International Journal of Preventive Medicine, 4*(12), 1429–1437. PMID:24498499

Kandell, J. J. (1998). Internet addiction on campus: The vulnerability of college students. *Cyberpsychology & Behavior, 1*(1), 11–17. doi:10.1089/cpb.1998.1.11

Kardefelt-Winther, D. (2014). A conceptual and methodological critique of Internet addiction research: Towards a model of compensatory Internet use. *Computers in Human Behavior, 31*, 351–354. doi:10.1016/j.chb.2013.10.059

Karimzadeh, N. (2015). Investigating the relationship between Internet addiction and strengthening students' social skills. *Educational Research Review, 10*(15), 2146–2152. doi:10.5897/ERR2015.2338

Kaur, M., & Verma, R. (2016). Social Media: An Emerging Tool for Political Participation. *International Journal of Social and Organizational Dynamics in IT, 5*(2), 31–38. doi:10.4018/IJSODIT.2016070103

Kawachi, I., Subramanian, S. V, & Almeida-Filho, N. (2002). A glossary for health inequalities. *Journal of Epidemiology and Community Health, 56*(9), 647-652.

Kawa, M. H., & Shafi, H. (2015). Evaluation of Internet addiction and psychological distress among university students. *International Journal of Modern Social Sciences, 4*(1), 29–41.

Kayiş, A. R., Satici, S. A., Yilmaz, M. F., Şimşek, D., Ceyhan, E., & Bakioğlu, F. (2016). Big five-personality trait and internet addiction: A meta-analytic review. *Computers in Human Behavior, 63*, 35–40. doi:10.1016/j.chb.2016.05.012

Kelleci, M., Güler, N., Sezer, H., & Gölbaşı, Z. (2009). Lise öğrencilerinde internet kullanma süresinin cinsiyet ve psikiyatrik belirtiler ile ilişkisi [Relationships Gender and Psychiatric Symptoms with Duration of Internet Use among High School Students]. *Turk Silahli Kuvvetleri Koruyucu Hekimlik Bulteni, 8*(3), 223–230.

Kelleci, M., & İnal, S. (2010). Psychiatric symptoms in adolescents with and without Internet use. *Cyberpsychology, Behavior, and Social Networking, 13*(2), 191–194. doi:10.1089/cyber.2009.0026 PMID:20528277

Kelley, K. J., & Gruber, E. M. (2010). Psychometric properties of the problematic internet use questionnaire. *Computers in Human Behavior, 26*(6), 1838–1845. doi:10.1016/j.chb.2010.07.018

Kerbs, R. W. (2005). Social and ethical considerations in virtual worlds. *The Electronic Library, 23*(5), 539–546. doi:10.1108/02640470510631254

Keser Özcan, N., & Buzlu, S. (2005). Problemli internet kullanımını belirlemede yardımcı bir araç: "İnternette Bilişsel Durum Ölçeği" nin üniversite öğrencilerinde geçerlik ve güvenirliği [An assistive tool in determining problematic Internet use: Validity and reliability of the "Online Cognition Scale" in a sample of university students]. *Bağimlik Dergisi, 6*, 19–26.

Keser Özcan, N., & Buzlu, S. (2007). Internet use and its relation with the psychosocial situation for a sample of university students. *Cyberpsychology & Behavior, 10*(6), 767–772. doi:10.1089/cpb.2007.9953 PMID:18085963

Kesici, Ş., & Şahin, İ. (2009). A comparative study of uses of the Internet among college students with and without Internet addiction. *Psychological Reports, 105*(3_suppl), 1103–1112. doi:10.2466/PR0.105.F.1103-1112 PMID:20229914

Khazaal, Y., Chatton, A., Atwi, K., Zullino, D., Khan, R., & Billieux, J. (2011). Arabic validation of the compulsive Internet use scale (CIUS). *Substance Abuse Treatment, Prevention, and Policy, 6*(1), 32. doi:10.1186/1747-597X-6-32 PMID:22126679

Khazaal, Y., Xirossavidou, C., Khan, R., Edel, Y., Zebouni, F., & Zullino, D. (2012). Cognitive-behavioral treatment for Internet addiction. *The Open Addiction Journal*, *5*(1), 30–35. doi:10.2174/1874941001205010030

Kim, E. J., Namkoong, K., Ku, T., & Kim, S. J. (2008). The relationship between online game addiction and aggression, self-control and narcissistic personality traits. *European Psychiatry*, *23*(3), 212–218. doi:10.1016/j.eurpsy.2007.10.010 PMID:18166402

Kim, H., & Chung, Y. W. (2014). The use of social networking services and their relationship with the Big Five personality model and job satisfaction in Korea. *Cyberpsychology, Behavior, and Social Networking*, *17*(10), 658–663. doi:10.1089/cyber.2014.0109 PMID:25127246

Kim, J. E., & Kim, J. (2015). International note: Teen users' problematic online behavior: Using panel data from South Korea. *Journal of Adolescence*, *40*, 48–53. doi:10.1016/j.adolescence.2015.01.001 PMID:25621406

Kim, J. H. (2017). Smartphone-mediated communication vs. face-to-face interaction: Two routes to social support and problematic use of smartphone. *Computers in Human Behavior*, *67*, 282–291. doi:10.1016/j.chb.2016.11.004

Kim, J. H., Lau, C. H., Cheuk, K. K., Kan, P., Hui, H. L. C., & Griffiths, S. M. (2010). Brief report: Predictors of heavy Internet use and associations with health-promoting and health risk behaviors among Hong Kong university students. *Journal of Adolescence*, *33*(1), 215–220. doi:10.1016/j.adolescence.2009.03.012 PMID:19427030

Kim, J., & Cicchetti, D. (2004). A longitudinal study of child maltreatment, mother–child relationship quality and maladjustment: The role of self-esteem and social competence. *Journal of Abnormal Child Psychology*, *32*(4), 341–354. doi:10.1023/B:JACP.0000030289.17006.5a PMID:15305541

Kim, J., Larose, R., & Peng, W. (2009). Loneliness as the cause and the effect of problematic Internet use: The relationship between Internet use and psychological well-being. *Cyberpsychology, Behavior, and Social Networking*, *12*(4), 451–455. doi:10.1089/cpb.2008.0327 PMID:19514821

Kim, K. S., & Kim, J. H. (2003). A study on adolescent's level of Internet addiction by their perceived relationships with parents. *Korean J Hum Ecol*, *6*(1), 15–25.

Kim, K., Ryu, E., Chon, M. Y., Yeun, E. J., Choi, S. Y., Seo, J. S., & Nam, B. W. (2006). Internet addiction in Korean adolescents and its relation to depression and suicidal ideation: A questionnaire survey. *International Journal of Nursing Studies*, *43*(2), 185–192. doi:10.1016/j.ijnurstu.2005.02.005 PMID:16427966

King, S. A. (1996). *Is the Internet addictive or are addicts using the Internet?* Retrieved January 13, 2017, from http://giovanni-2000.tripod.com/mesh/selfaddict.html

King, D. L., Delfabbro, P. H., Griffiths, M. D., & Gradisar, M. (2011). Assessing clinical trials of Internet addiction treatment: A systematic review and CONSORT evaluation. *Clinical Psychology Review*, *31*(7), 1110–1116. doi:10.1016/j.cpr.2011.06.009 PMID:21820990

Király, O., Griffiths, M. D., Urbán, R., Farkas, J., Kökönyei, G., Elekes, Z., & Demetrovics, Z. et al. (2014). Problematic Internet use and problematic online gaming are not the same: Findings from a large nationally representative adolescent sample. *Cyberpsychology, Behavior, and Social Networking*, *17*(12), 749–754. doi:10.1089/cyber.2014.0475 PMID:25415659

Kirschner, P. A. (2017). Stop propagating the learning styles myth. *Computers & Education*, *106*, 166–171. doi:10.1016/j.compedu.2016.12.006

Kirschner, P. A., & Karpinski, A. C. (2010). Facebook and academic performance. *Computers in Human Behavior*, *26*(6), 1237–1245. doi:10.1016/j.chb.2010.03.024

Kirwil, L. (2009). Parental mediation of children's Internet use in different European countries. *Journal of Children and Media*, *3*(4), 394–409. doi:10.1080/17482790903233440

Kite, L., & Kite, L. (2014). Selfies and self-objectification: Not-so-pretty picture. *Beauty Redefined*. Retrieved June 14, 2016 from http://www.beautyredefined.net/selfies-and-objectification/

Klimmt, C., & Hartmann, T. (2006). Effectance, self-efficacy, and the motivation to play video games. *Playing Video Games: Motives, Responses, and Consequences*, 133-145.

Ko, C. H., Hsiao, S., Liu, G. C., Yen, J. Y., Yang, M. J., & Yen, C. F. (2010). The characteristics of decision making, potential to take risks, and personality of college students with Internet addiction. *Psychiatry Research*, *175*(1), 121–125. doi:10.1016/j.psychres.2008.10.004 PMID:19962767

Ko, C. H., Liu, T. L., Wang, P. W., Chen, C. S., Yen, C. F., & Yen, J. Y. (2014). The exacerbation of depression, hostility, and social anxiety in the course of Internet addiction among adolescents: A prospective study. *Comprehensive Psychiatry*, *55*(6), 1377–1384. doi:10.1016/j.comppsych.2014.05.003 PMID:24939704

Ko, C. H., Wang, P. W., Liu, T. L., Yen, C. F., Chen, C. S., & Yen, J. Y. (2015). Bidirectional associations between family factors and Internet addiction among adolescents in a prospective investigation. *Psychiatry and Clinical Neurosciences*, *69*(4), 192–200. doi:10.1111/pcn.12204 PMID:24836367

Ko, C. H., Yen, J. Y., Chen, C. C., Chen, S. H., Wu, K., & Yen, C. F. (2006). Tridimensional personality of adolescents with Internet addiction and substance use experience. *Canadian Journal of Psychiatry*, *51*(14), 887–894. doi:10.1177/070674370605101404 PMID:17249631

Ko, C. H., Yen, J. Y., Chen, C. C., Chen, S. H., & Yen, C. F. (2005). Gender differences and related factors affecting online gaming addiction among Taiwanese adolescents. *The Journal of Nervous and Mental Disease*, *193*(4), 273–277. doi:10.1097/01.nmd.0000158373.85150.57 PMID:15805824

Ko, C. H., Yen, J. Y., Chen, C. C., Chen, S. H., & Yen, C. F. (2005). Proposed diagnostic criteria for Internet addiction for adolescents. *The Journal of Nervous and Mental Disease*, *193*(11), 728–733. doi:10.1097/01.nmd.0000185891.13719.54 PMID:16260926

Ko, C. H., Yen, J. Y., Chen, C. S., Yeh, Y. C., & Yen, C. F. (2009). Predictive values of psychiatric symptoms for Internet addiction in adolescents: A 2-year prospective study. *Archives of Pediatrics & Adolescent Medicine*, *163*(10), 937–943. doi:10.1001/archpediatrics.2009.159 PMID:19805713

Ko, C. H., Yen, J. Y., Liu, S. C., Huang, C. F., & Yen, C. F. (2009). The associations between aggressive behaviors and Internet addiction and online activities in adolescents. *The Journal of Adolescent Health*, *44*(6), 598–605. doi:10.1016/j.jadohealth.2008.11.011 PMID:19465325

Ko, C. H., Yen, J. Y., Yen, C. F., Chen, C. S., & Chen, C. C. (2012). The association between Internet addiction and psychiatric disorder: A review of the literature. *European Psychiatry*, *27*(1), 1–8. doi:10.1016/j.eurpsy.2010.04.011 PMID:22153731

Ko, C. H., Yen, J. Y., Yen, C. F., Chen, C. S., & Wang, S. Y. (2008). The association between Internet addiction and belief of frustration intolerance: The gender difference. *Cyberpsychology & Behavior*, *11*(3), 273–278. doi:10.1089/cpb.2007.0095 PMID:18537496

Ko, C. H., Yen, J. Y., Yen, C. F., Chen, C. S., Weng, C. C., & Chen, C. C. (2008). The association between Internet addiction and problematic alcohol use in adolescents: The problem behavior model. *Cyberpsychology & Behavior*, *11*(5), 571–576. doi:10.1089/cpb.2007.0199 PMID:18785835

Ko, C. H., Yen, J. Y., Yen, C. F., Lin, H. C., & Yang, M. J. (2007). Factors predictive for incidence and remission of Internet addiction in young adolescents: A prospective study. *Cyberpsychology & Behavior*, *10*(4), 545–551. doi:10.1089/cpb.2007.9992 PMID:17711363

Koc, M. (2011). Internet addiction and psychopatology. *TOJET: The Turkish Online Journal of Educational Technology*, *10*(1), 143–148.

Koc, M., & Gulyagci, S. (2013). Facebook Addiction Among Turkish College Students: The Role of Psychological Health, Demographic, and Usage Characteristics. *Cyberpsychology, Behavior, and Social Networking*, *16*(4), 279–284. doi:10.1089/cyber.2012.0249 PMID:23286695

Kolb, D. A. (1984). *Experiential learning: Experience as the source of learning and development*. London: Prentice Hall.

Kormas, G., Critselis, E., Janikian, M., Kafetzis, D., & Tsitsika, A. (2011). Risk factors and psychosocial characteristics of potential problematic and problematic internet use among adolescents: A cross-sectional study. *BMC Public Health*, *11*(1), 595. doi:10.1186/1471-2458-11-595 PMID:21794167

Kornør, H., & Nordvik, H. (2007). Five-factor model personality traits in opioid dependence. *BMC Psychiatry*, *7*(1), 37. doi:10.1186/1471-244X-7-37 PMID:17683593

Koronczai, B., Urban, R., Kökönyei, G., Paksi, B., Papp, K., Kun, B., & Demetrovics, Z. et al. (2011). Confirmation of the Three-Factor Model of Problematic Internet Use on Off-Line Adolescent and Adult Samples. *Cyberpsychology, Behavior, and Social Networking*, *14*(11), 657–664. doi:10.1089/cyber.2010.0345 PMID:21711129

Koski-Ja¨nnes, A., & Simmat-Durand, L. (2017). Basic Beliefs About Behavioural Addictions Among Finnish and French Treatment Professionals. *Journal of Gambling Studies*. doi:10.1007/s10899-017-9672-8 PMID:28154957

Kotov, R., Gamez, W., Schmidt, F., & Watson, D. (2010). Linking "big" personality traits to anxiety, depressive, and substance use disorders: A meta-analysis. *Psychological Bulletin*, *136*(5), 768–821. doi:10.1037/a0020327 PMID:20804236

Kraut, R., Kiesler, S., Boneva, B., Cummings, J., Helgeson, V., & Crawford, A. (2002). Internet paradox revisited. *The Journal of Social Issues*, *58*(1), 49–74. doi:10.1111/1540-4560.00248

Kraut, R., Patterson, M., Lundmark, V., Kiesler, S., Mukophadhyay, T., & Scherlis, W. (1998). Internet paradox: A social technology that reduces social involvement and psychological well-being? *The American Psychologist*, *53*(9), 1017–1031. doi:10.1037/0003-066X.53.9.1017 PMID:9841579

Krishnamurthy, S., & Chetlapalli, S. K. (2015). Internet addiction: Prevalence and risk factors: A cross-sectional study among college students in Bengaluru, the Silicon Valley of India. *Indian Journal of Public Health*, *59*(2), 115–121. doi:10.4103/0019-557X.157531 PMID:26021648

Kroenke, C. (2008). Socioeconomic status and health: Youth development and neomaterialist and psychosocial mechanisms. *Social Science & Medicine*, *66*(1), 31–42. doi:10.1016/j.socscimed.2007.07.018 PMID:17868964

Kromhout, W. W. (2009, Oct. 15). UCLA, birthplace of the Internet, celebrates 40th anniversary of network's creation. *UCLA Newsroom*. Retrieved from http://newsroom.ucla.edu/releases/birthplace-of-the-internet-celebrates-111333

Krusche, A., Cyhlarova, E., & Williams, J. M. G. (2013). Mindfulness online: An evaluation of the feasibility of a web-based mindfulness course for stress, anxiety, and depression. *BMJ Open*, *3*(11), e003498. doi:10.1136/bmjopen-2013-003498 PMID:24293203

Kubey, R. W., Lavin, M. J., & Barrows, J. R. (2001). Internet use and collegiate academic performance decrements: Early findings. *Journal of Communication*, *51*(2), 366–382. doi:10.1111/j.1460-2466.2001.tb02885.x

Kuntsche, E., von Fischer, M., & Gmel, G. (2008). Personality factors and alcohol use: A mediator analysis of drinking motives. *Personality and Individual Differences*, *45*(8), 796–800. doi:10.1016/j.paid.2008.08.009

Kurt, D. G. (2015). Suicide risk in college students: The effects of Internet addiction and drug use. *Educational Sciences: Theory and Practice*, *15*(4), 841–848.

Kuss, D.J., & Lopez-Fernandez, O. (2016). Internet addiction and problematic Internet use: A systematic review of clinical research. *World Journal of Psychiatry*, *6*(1), 143-176. doi: 105498/wjp.v6.i1.143

Kuss, D. J. (2013). Internet gaming addiction: Current perspectives. *Psychology Research and Behavior Management*, *6*, 125. doi:10.2147/PRBM.S39476 PMID:24255603

Kuss, D. J. (2016). Internet Addiction: The Problem and Treatment. *Addicta-The Turkish Journal on Addictions*, *3*(2), 185–192. doi:10.15805/addicta.2016.3.0106

Kuss, D. J. (2016). Internet addiction: The problem and treatment. *Turkish Green Crescent Society*, *3*(2), 185–192. doi:10.15805/addict.2016.3.0106

Kuss, D. J., & Billieux, J. (2016). Technological addictions: Conceptualisation, measurement, etiology and treatment. *Addictive Behaviors*, *30*(16), 147–152. PMID:27136694

Kuss, D. J., & Griffiths, M. D. (2011). Online social networking and addiction—a review of the psychological literature. *International Journal of Environmental Research and Public Health*, *8*(9), 3528–3552. doi:10.3390/ijerph8093528 PMID:22016701

Kuss, D. J., & Griffiths, M. D. (2012). Internet gaming addiction: A systematic review of empirical research. *International Journal of Mental Health and Addiction*, *10*(2), 278–296. doi:10.1007/s11469-011-9318-5

Kuss, D. J., Griffiths, M. D., & Binder, J. F. (2013). Internet addiction in students: Prevalence and risk factors. *Computers in Human Behavior*, *29*(3), 959–966. doi:10.1016/j.chb.2012.12.024

Kuss, D. J., Griffiths, M. D., Karila, L., & Billieux, J. (2013). Internet Addiction: A Systematic Review of Epidemiological Research for the Last Decade. *Current Pharmaceutical Design*, *1*(4), 397–413. PMID:24001297

Kuss, D. J., Griffiths, M. D., Karila, L., & Billieux, J. (2014). Internet addiction: A systematic review of epidemiological research for the last decade. *Current Pharmaceutical Design*, *20*(25), 4026–4052. doi:10.2174/13816128113199990617 PMID:24001297

Kuss, D. J., & Lopez-Fernandez, O. (2016). Internet addiction and problematic Internet use: A systematic review of clinical research. *World Journal of Psychiatry*, *6*(1), 143. doi:10.5498/wjp.v6.i1.143 PMID:27014605

Kuss, D. J., Van Rooij, A. J., Shorter, G. W., Griffiths, M. D., & van de Mheen, D. (2013). Internet addiction in adolescents: Prevalence and risk factors. *Computers in Human Behavior*, *29*(5), 1987–1996. doi:10.1016/j.chb.2013.04.002

Kwee, A. W., Komoru-Venovic, E., & Kwee, J. L. (2010). Treatment Implications from Etiological and Diagnostic Considerations of Internet Addiction: Cautions with the Boot Camp Approach. *Proceedings of the International Conference of e-CASE*.

Kwon, J. H., Chung, C. S., & Lee, J. (2011). The effects of escape from self and interpersonal relationship on the pathological use of Internet games. *Community Mental Health Journal*, *47*(1), 113–121. doi:10.1007/s10597-009-9236-1 PMID:19701792

La Barbera, D., La Paglia, F., & Valsavoia, R. (2009). Social network and addiction. *Cyberpsychology & Behavior*, *12*, 628–629. PMID:19592725

Laconi, S., Andréoletti, A., Chauchard, E., Rodgers, R. F., & Chabrol, H. (2016). Problematic Internet use, time spent online and personality traits. *L'Encéphale*, *42*(3), 214–218. doi:10.1016/j.encep.2015.12.017 PMID:26827120

Laconi, S., Rodgers, R. F., & Chabrol, H. (2014). The measurement of Internet addiction: A critical review of existing scales and their psychometric properties. *Computers in Human Behavior*, *41*, 190–202. doi:10.1016/j.chb.2014.09.026

Ladd, G. T., & Petry, N. M. (2002). Disordered gambling among university-based medical and dental patients: A focus on Internet gambling. *Psychology of Addictive Behaviors*, *16*(1), 76–79. doi:10.1037/0893-164X.16.1.76 PMID:11934091

Lai, C. M., Mak, K. K., Cheng, C., Watanabe, H., Nomachi, S., Bahar, N., & Griffiths, M. D. et al. (2015). Measurement Invariance of the Internet Addiction Test Among Hong Kong, Japanese, and Malaysian Adolescents. *Cyberpsychology, Behavior, and Social Networking*, *18*(10), 609–617. doi:10.1089/cyber.2015.0069 PMID:26468915

Lai, C. M., Mak, K. K., Watanabe, H., Ang, R. P., Pang, J. S., & Ho, R. C. (2013). Psychometric properties of the Internet addiction test in Chinese adolescents. *Journal of Pediatric Psychology*, *38*(7), 794–807. doi:10.1093/jpepsy/jst022 PMID:23671059

Lai, F. T. T., & Kwan, J. L. Y. (2017). Socioeconomic influence on adolescent problematic Internet use through school-related psychosocial factors and pattern of Internet use. *Computers in Human Behavior*, *68*, 121–136. doi:10.1016/j.chb.2016.11.021

Lai, F. T. T., & Kwan, J. L. Y. (2017b). The presence of heavy Internet using peers is protective of the risk of problematic Internet use (PIU) in adolescents when the amount of use increases. *Children and Youth Services Review*, *73*, 74–78. doi:10.1016/j.childyouth.2016.12.004

Lamborn, S. D., Mounts, N. S., Steinberg, L., & Dornbusch, S. M. (1991). Patterns of competence and adjustment among adolescents from authoritative, authoritarian, indulgent, and neglectful families. *Child Development*, *62*(5), 1049–1065. doi:10.2307/1131151 PMID:1756655

Lam, L. T. (2014). Risk factors of Internet addiction and the health effect of Internet addiction on adolescents: A systematic review of longitudinal and prospective studies. *Current Psychiatry Reports*, *16*(11), 1–9. doi:10.1007/s11920-014-0508-2 PMID:25212714

Lam, L. T. (2015). Parental mental health and Internet Addiction in adolescents. *Addictive Behaviors*, *42*, 20–23. doi:10.1016/j.addbeh.2014.10.033 PMID:25462649

Lam, L. T. (2016). Parental Internet addictive behavior and Internet addiction in adolescents: A mediating model through parental mental health. *Austin Addiction Sciences*, *1*(1), 1–5.

Lam, L. T., Peng, Z. W., Mai, J. C., & Jing, J. (2009). Factors associated with Internet addiction among adolescents. *Cyberpsychology & Behavior*, *12*(5), 551–555. doi:10.1089/cpb.2009.0036 PMID:19619039

Lane, W., Sacco, P., Downton, K., Ludeman, E., Levy, L., & Tracy, J. K. (2016). Child maltreatment and problem gambling: A systematic review. *Child Abuse & Neglect*, *58*, 24–38. doi:10.1016/j.chiabu.2016.06.003 PMID:27337693

Lange, A., Rietdijk, D., Hudcovicova, M., Van De Ven, J. P., Schrieken, B., & Emmelkamp, P. M. (2003). Interapy: A controlled randomized trial of the standardized treatment of posttraumatic stress through the internet. *Journal of Consulting and Clinical Psychology*, *71*(5), 901–909. doi:10.1037/0022-006X.71.5.901 PMID:14516238

LaRose, R. (2011). Uses and gratifications of Internet addiction. In K. S. Young (Ed.), *Internet addiction: A handbook and guide to evaluation and treatment* (pp. 55–72). Hoboken, NJ: John Wiley & Sons, Inc.

Laslett, B. (1978). Family membership, past and present. *Social Problems*, *25*(5), 476–490. doi:10.2307/800097

Lau, J. T. F., Gross, D. L., Wu, A. M. S., Cheng, K., & Lau, M. M. C. (2017). Incidence and predictive factors of Internet addiction among Chinese secondary school students in Hong Kong: A longitudinal study. *Social Psychiatry and Psychiatric Epidemiology*, *52*(6), 657–667. doi:10.1007/s00127-017-1356-2 PMID:28417158

Lavin, M., Marvin, K., McLarney, A., Nola, V., & Scott, L. (1999). Sensation seeking and collegiate vulnerability to Internet dependence. *Cyberpsychology & Behavior*, *2*(5), 425–430. doi:10.1089/cpb.1999.2.425 PMID:19178215

Law, D. M., Shapka, J. D., & Olson, B. F. (2010). To control or not to control? Parenting behaviours and adolescent online aggression. *Computers in Human Behavior*, *26*(6), 1651–1656. doi:10.1016/j.chb.2010.06.013

Layard, R. (2011). *Happiness: Lessons from a new science*. Penguin UK.

Lee, C.-S., & McKenzie, K. (2015). Socioeconomic and Geographic Inequalities of Internet Addiction in Korean Adolescents. *Psychiatry Investigation*, *12*(4), 559–562. doi:10.4306/pi.2015.12.4.559 PMID:26508969

Lee, E. W. J., Ho, S. S., & Lwin, M. O. (2017). Extending the social cognitive model - Examining the external and personal antecedents of social network sites use among Singaporean adolescents. *Computers in Human Behavior*, *67*, 240–251. doi:10.1016/j.chb.2016.10.030

Lee, E., Ahn, J., & Kim, Y. J. (2014). Personality traits and self-presentation at Facebook. *Personality and Individual Differences*, *69*, 162–167. doi:10.1016/j.paid.2014.05.020

Lee, K., Lee, H. K., Gyeong, H., Yu, B., Song, Y. M., & Kim, D. (2013). Reliability and Validity of the Korean Version of the Internet Addiction Test among College Students. *Journal of Korean Medical Science*, *28*(5), 763–768. doi:10.3346/jkms.2013.28.5.763 PMID:23678270

Lee, S. J. (2013). Parental restrictive mediation of children's Internet use: Effective for what and for whom? *New Media & Society*, *15*(4), 466–481. doi:10.1177/1461444812452412

Lee, S. J., & Chae, Y. G. (2007). Children's Internet use in a family context: Influence on family relationships and parental mediation. *Cyberpsychology & Behavior*, *10*(5), 640–644. doi:10.1089/cpb.2007.9975 PMID:17927531

Lee, S., & Jeon, S. (2011). Adolescent Internet use and parental mediation practice: Using parent-child interviews. *Media. Gender & Culture*, *17*, 5–42.

Lee, Y. H., Ko, C. H., & Chou, C. (2015). Re-visiting Internet Addiction among Taiwanese Students: A Cross-Sectional Comparison of Students' Expectations, Online Gaming, and Online Social Interaction. *Journal of Abnormal Child Psychology*, *43*(3), 589–599. doi:10.1007/s10802-014-9915-4 PMID:25079945

Lee, Y. S., Han, D. H., Kim, S. M., & Renshaw, P. F. (2013). Substance abuse precedes internet addiction. *Addictive Behaviors*, *38*(4), 2022–2025. doi:10.1016/j.addbeh.2012.12.024 PMID:23384457

Lei, L., & Wu, L. (2009). Adolescents peer attachment and their Internet use. *Studies of Psychology and Behavior*, *7*(2), 81–86.

Leiner, B. M., Cerf, V. G., Clark, D. D., Kahn, R. E., Kleinrock, L., Lynch, D. C., & Wolff, S. S. (1997). The past and future history of the Internet. *Communications of the ACM, 40*(2), 102–108. doi:10.1145/253671.253741

Lenhart, A. (2015). *Teens, Social Media & Technology: Overview 2015.* Retrieved March 17 2017 from http://www.pewInternet.org/2015/04/09/teens-social-media-technology-2015/

Lenhart, A., Purcell, K., Smith, A., & Zickuhr, K. (2010). *Social Media and Young Adults.* Retrieved 14 November 2016 from http://www.pewinternet.org/2010/02/03/social-media-and-young-adults/

Lenhart, A., Duggan, M., Perrin, A., Stepler, R., Rainie, H., & Parker, K. (2015). *Teens, social media and technology overview 2015. Smartphones facilitate shifts in communication landscape for teens.* Washington, DC: Pew Internet & American Life Project.

Lerner, R. M., Rothbaum, F., Boulos, S., & Castellino, D. R. (2002). Developmental systems perspective on parenting. In M. H. Bornstein (Ed.), Handbook of parenting (2nd ed.; pp. 315–344). Mahwah, NJ: Erlbaum.

Leshner, A. I. (1997). Addiction is a brain disease, and it matters. *Science, 278*(5335), 45–47. doi:10.1126/science.278.5335.45 PMID:9311924

Leung, L. (2004). Net-generation attributes and seductive properties of the Internet as predictors of online activities and Internet addiction. *Cyberpsychology & Behavior, 7*(3), 333–348. doi:10.1089/1094931041291303 PMID:15257834

Leung, L. (2006). Stressful life events, motives for Internet use, and social support among digital kids. *Cyberpsychology & Behavior, 10*(2), 204–214. doi:10.1089/cpb.2006.9967 PMID:17474837

Leung, L. (2008). Linking psychological attributes to addiction and improper use of the mobile phone among adolescents in Hong Kong. *Journal of Children and Media, 2*(2), 93–113. doi:10.1080/17482790802078565

Leung, L. (2014). Predicting Internet risks: A longitudinal panel study of gratifications-sought, Internet addiction symptoms, and social media use among children and adolescents. *Health Psychology and Behavioral Medicine, 2*(1), 424–439. doi:10.1080/21642850.2014.902316 PMID:25750792

Leung, L., & Lee, P. S. (2012). The influences of information literacy, Internet addiction and parenting styles on Internet risks. *New Media & Society, 14*(1), 117–136. doi:10.1177/1461444811410406

Leung, L., & Lee, P. S. N. (2012). Impact of Internet Literacy, Internet Addiction Symptoms, and Internet Activities on Academic Performance. *Social Science Computer Review, 30*(4), 403–418. doi:10.1177/0894439311435217

Liang, C. S. (2015). Cyber Jihad: Understanding and countering Islamic State propaganda. *GCSP Policy Papers*, (2), 2.

Liang, L., Zhou, D., Yuan, C., Shao, A., & Bian, Y. (2016). Gender differences in the relationship between Internet addiction and depression: A cross-lagged study in Chinese adolescents. *Computers in Human Behavior, 63*, 463–470. doi:10.1016/j.chb.2016.04.043

Li, B., Friston, K. J., Liu, J., Liu, Y., Zhang, G., Cao, F., & Hu, D. et al. (2014). Impaired frontal-basal ganglia connectivity in adolescents with Internet addiction. *Scientific Reports, 4*. PMID:24848380

Li, C., Dang, J., Zhang, X., Zhang, Q., & Guo, J. (2014). Internet addiction among Chinese adolescents: The effect of parental behavior and self-control. *Computers in Human Behavior, 41*, 1–7. doi:10.1016/j.chb.2014.09.001

Li, D., Li, X., Wang, Y., Zhao, L., Bao, Z., & Wen, F. (2013). School connectedness and problematic internet use in adolescents: A moderated mediation model of deviant peer affiliation and self-control. *Journal of Abnormal Child Psychology, 41*(8), 1231–1242. doi:10.1007/s10802-013-9761-9 PMID:23695186

Li, D., Zhang, W., Li, X., Zhen, S., & Wang, Y. (2010). Stressful life events and problematic Internet use by adolescent females and males: A mediated moderation model. *Computers in Human Behavior*, 26(5), 1199–1207. doi:10.1016/j.chb.2010.03.031

Liddle, H. A. (2004). Family-based therapies for adolescent alcohol and drug use: Research contributions and future research needs. *Addiction (Abingdon, England)*, 99(Suppl. 2), 76–92. doi:10.1111/j.1360-0443.2004.00856.x PMID:15488107

Li, H., Wang, J., & Wang, L. (2009). A survey on the generalized problematic Internet use in Chinese college students and its relations to stressful life events and coping style. *International Journal of Mental Health and Addiction*, 7(2), 333–346. doi:10.1007/s11469-008-9162-4

Li, H., Zou, Y., Wang, J., & Yang, X. (2016). Role of Stressful Life Events, Avoidant Coping Styles, and Neuroticism in Online Game Addiction among College Students: A Moderated Mediation Model. *Frontiers in Psychology*, 7. PMID:27920734

Lim, C. H., Kim, E. J., Kim, J. H., Lee, J. S., Lee, Y., & Park, S. H. (2017). The correlation of depression with Internet use and body image in Korean adolescents. *Korean Journal of Pediatrics*, 60(1), 17–23. doi:10.3345/kjp.2017.60.1.17 PMID:28203256

Lim, C., & Putnam, R. D. (2010). Religion, social networks, and life satisfaction. *American Sociological Review*, 75(6), 914–933. doi:10.1177/0003122410386686

Lin, C. H., Lin, S. L., & Wu, C. P. (2009). The effects of parental monitoring and leisure boredom on adolescents' Internet addiction. *Adolescence*, 44, 993–1004. PMID:20432612

Lin, I. H., Ko, C. H., Chang, Y. P., Liu, T. L., Wang, P. W., Lin, H. C., & Yen, C. F. et al. (2014). The association between suicidality and internet addiction and activities in Taiwanese adolescents. *Comprehensive Psychiatry*, 55(3), 504–510. doi:10.1016/j.comppsych.2013.11.012 PMID:24457034

Lin, M. P., Ko, H. C., & Wu, J. Y. W. (2008). The Role of Positive/Negative Outcome Expectancy and Refusal Self-Efficacy of Internet Use on Internet Addiction among College Students in Taiwan. *Cyberpsychology & Behavior*, 11(4), 451–457. doi:10.1089/cpb.2007.0121 PMID:18721094

Lin, M. P., Ko, H. C., & Wu, J. Y. W. (2011). Prevalence and Psychosocial Risk Factors Associated with Internet Addiction in a Nationally Representative Sample of College Students in Taiwan. *Cyberpsychology, Behavior, and Social Networking*, 14(12), 741–746. doi:10.1089/cyber.2010.0574 PMID:21651418

Lin, S. S., & Tsai, C. C. (2002). Sensation seeking and Internet dependence of Taiwanese high school adolescents. *Computers in Human Behavior*, 18(4), 411–426. doi:10.1016/S0747-5632(01)00056-5

Liu, C. Y., & Kuo, F. Y. (2007). A study of Internet addiction through the lens of the interpersonal theory. *Cyberpsychology & Behavior*, 10(6), 799–804. doi:10.1089/cpb.2007.9951 PMID:18085967

Liu, C., Liao, M., & Smith, D. C. (2012). An empirical review of Internet addiction outcome studies in China. *Research on Social Work Practice*, 22(3), 282–292. doi:10.1177/1049731511430089

Liu, M., & Luo, J. (2015). Relationship between peripheral blood dopamine level and Internet addiction disorder in adolescents: A pilot study. *International Journal of Clinical and Experimental Medicine*, 8(6), 9943. PMID:26309680

Liu, Q. X., Fang, X. Y., Yan, N., Zhou, Z. K., Yuan, X. J., Lan, J., & Liu, C. Y. (2015). Multi-family group therapy for adolescent Internet addiction: Exploring the underlying mechanisms. *Addictive Behaviors*, 42, 1–8. doi:10.1016/j.addbeh.2014.10.021 PMID:25462646

Liu, T., & Potenza, M. N. (2007). Problematic Internet use: Clinical implications. *CNS Spectrums*, *12*(6), 453–466. doi:10.1017/S1092852900015339 PMID:17545956

Livingstone, S., & Bober, M. (2004). *UK Children Go Online: Surveying the experiences of young people and their parents*. Academic Press.

Livingstone, S. (2003). Children's use of the Internet: Reflections on the emerging research agenda. *New Media & Society*, *5*(2), 147–166. doi:10.1177/1461444803005002001

Livingstone, S. (2007). Strategies of parental regulation in the media-rich home. *Computers in Human Behavior*, *23*(2), 920–941. doi:10.1016/j.chb.2005.08.002

Livingstone, S. (2008). Taking risky opportunities in youthful content creation: Teenagers' use of social networking sites for intimacy, privacy and self-expression. *New Media & Society*, *10*(3), 393–411. doi:10.1177/1461444808089415

Livingstone, S., & Helsper, E. J. (2008). Parental mediation of children's Internet use. *Journal of Broadcasting & Electronic Media*, *52*(4), 581–599. doi:10.1080/08838150802437396

Li, W., Garland, E. L., & Howard, M. O. (2014). Family factors in Internet addiction among Chinese youth: A review of English- and Chinese-language studies. *Computers in Human Behavior*, *31*(1), 393–411. doi:10.1016/j.chb.2013.11.004

Li, Y., Zhang, X., Lu, F., Zhang, Q., & Wang, Y. (2014). Internet addiction among elementary and middle school students in China: A nationally representative sample study. *Cyberpsychology, Behavior, and Social Networking*, *17*(2), 111–116. doi:10.1089/cyber.2012.0482 PMID:23971432

Lochman, J. E., & Van den Steenhoven, A. (2006). Family-based approaches to substance abuse prevention. *The Journal of Primary Prevention*, *23*(1), 49–114. doi:10.1023/A:1016591216363

Lopez-Fernandez, O., Honrubia-Serrano, L., Freixa-Blanxart, M., & Gibson, W. (2014). Prevalence of problematic mobile phone use in British adolescents. *Cyberpsychology, Behavior, and Social Networking*, *17*(2), 91–98. doi:10.1089/cyber.2012.0260 PMID:23981147

Lortie, C. L., & Guitton, M. J. (2013). Internet addiction assessment tools: Dimensional structure and methodological status. *Addiction (Abingdon, England)*, *108*(7), 1207–1216. doi:10.1111/add.12202 PMID:23651255

Lui, L. (2016). Gender, Rural-Urban Inequality, and Intermarriage in China. *Social Forces*, *95*(2), 639–662. doi:10.1093/sf/sow076

Luque-Martínez, T., Alberto Castañeda-García, J., Frías-Jamilena, D. M., Muñoz-Leiva, F., & Rodríguez-Molina, M. A. (2007). Determinants of the use of the Internet as a tourist information source. *Service Industries Journal*, *27*(7), 881–891. doi:10.1080/02642060701570586

Lwin, M. O., Stanaland, A. J., & Miyazaki, A. D. (2008). Protecting children's privacy online: How parental mediation strategies affect website safeguard effectiveness. *Journal of Retailing*, *84*(2), 205–217. doi:10.1016/j.jretai.2008.04.004

Lyubomirsky, S., & Lepper, H. S. (1999). A measure of subjective happiness: Preliminary reliability and construct validation. *Social Indicators Research*, *46*(2), 137–155. doi:10.1023/A:1006824100041

M'hiri, K., Constanza, A., Khazaal, Y., Khan, R., Zullino, D., & Achab, S. (2015). Problematic Internet use in older adults, a critical review of the literature. *Addiction Research and Theory*, *6*(4), 1000253. doi:10.4172/2155-6105.1000253

Maccoby, E. E., & Martin, J. A. (1983). Socialization in the context of the family: Parent-child interaction. In Handbook of child psychology: formerly Carmichael's Manual of child psychology. Academic Press.

Macur, M. (2017). Can Internet use become problematic?: Presentation of Slovenian data. *International scientific conference Health Online - Book of papers with peer review and abstracts*. Retrieved from: http://www2.zf.uni-lj.si/images/stories/datoteke/Zalozba/Zdravje_na_spletu.pdf

Macur, M., Király, O., Maraz, A., Nagygyörgy, K., & Demetrovics, Z. (2016). Prevalence of problematic internet use in Slovenia. *Zdravstveno Varstvo*, *55*(3), 202–211. doi:10.1515/sjph-2016-0026 PMID:27703540

Mak, K. K., Lai, C. M., Ko, C. H., Chou, C., Kim, D. I., Watanabe, H., & Ho, R. C. (2014). Psychometric properties of the revised chen internet addiction scale (CIAS-R) in Chinese adolescents. *Journal of Abnormal Child Psychology*, *42*(7), 1237–1245. doi:10.1007/s10802-014-9851-3 PMID:24585392

Mak, K. K., Nam, J. K., Kim, D., Aum, N., Choi, J. S., Cheng, C., & Watanabe, H. et al. (2017). Cecilia Cheng, Huei-Chen Ko, Hiroko Watanabe, Cross-cultural adaptation and psychometric properties of the Korean Scale for Internet Addiction (K-Scale) in Japanese high school students. *Psychiatry Research*, *249*, 343–348. doi:10.1016/j.psychres.2017.01.044 PMID:28152469

Malak, M. Z., Khalifeh, A. H., & Shuhaiber, A. H. (2017). Prevalence of Internet Addiction and associated risk factors in Jordanian school students. *Computers in Human Behavior*, *70*, 556–563. doi:10.1016/j.chb.2017.01.011

Maltby, J., Day, L., & Macaskill, A. (2010). *Personality, individual differences and intelligence* (2nd ed.). Essex, UK: Pearson Education Limited.

Marcelli, D., & Bracconnier, A. (2006). *Adolescenza e psicopatologia*. Milano, Italy: Elsevier-Masson.

Marchetti, B. (1997). *Concetto di se'relazioni familiari e valori* (Unpublished master's thesis). Universita degli Studi di Bologna, Italy.

Marks, I. (1990). Behavioural (non-chemical) addictions. *British Journal of Addiction*, *85*(11), 1389–1394. doi:10.1111/j.1360-0443.1990.tb01618.x PMID:2285832

Martin, C., Jagla, L., & Firestone, C. M. (2013). *Integrating Diplomacy and Social Media. A Report of the First Annual Aspen Institute Dialogue on Diplomacy and Technology*. Washington, DC: Aspen In-stitute.

Mastin, L. (2008). Conservatism. *The Basics of Philosophy*. Retrieved August 30, 2016, from http://www.philosophy-basics.com/branch_conservatism.html

Maurya, S., & Singh, K. (2015). Relationship between Psychological Aspects and Internet Addiction: A Review. *Journal of Advanced Research in Ayurveda, Yoga, & Homeopathy*, *2*(1), 16–19.

Mazhari, S. (2012). The prevalence of problematic internet use and the related factors in medical students, Kerman, Iran. *Addiction & Health*, *4*(3-4), 87. PMID:24494141

McIntyre, E., Wiener, K. K. K., & Saliba, A. J. (2015). Compulsive Internet use and relations between social connectedness, and introversion. *Computers in Human Behavior*, *48*, 569–574. doi:10.1016/j.chb.2015.02.021

McWhirter, B. T. (1990). Loneliness: A review of current literature, with implications for counseling and research. *Journal of Counseling and Development*, *68*(4), 417–422. doi:10.1002/j.1556-6676.1990.tb02521.x

Meerkerk, G. J., Van den Eijnden, R. J. J. M., Franken, I. H. A., & Garretsen, H. F. L. (2010). Is compulsive Internet use related to sensitivity to reward and punishment, and impulsivity? *Computers in Human Behavior*, *26*(4), 729–735. doi:10.1016/j.chb.2010.01.009

Meerkerk, G.-J., Van Den Eijnden, R. J., Vermulst, A. A., & Garretsen, H. F. (2009). The compulsive internet use scale (CIUS): Some psychometric properties. *Cyberpsychology & Behavior*, *12*(1), 1–6. doi:10.1089/cpb.2008.0181 PMID:19072079

Mehdizadeh, S. (2010). Self-presentation 2.0: Narcissism and self-esteem on Facebook. *Cyberpsychology, Behavior, and Social Networking*, *13*(4), 357–364. doi:10.1089/cyber.2009.0257 PMID:20712493

Mehroof, M., & Griffiths, M. D. (2010). Online gaming addiction: The role of sensation seeking, self-control, neuroticism, aggression, state anxiety, and trait anxiety. *Cyberpsychology, Behavior, and Social Networking*, *13*(3), 313–316. doi:10.1089/cyber.2009.0229 PMID:20557251

Mei, S., Yau, Y. H. C., Chai, J., Guo, J., & Potenza, M. N. (2016). Problematic Internet use, well-being, self-esteem and self-control: Data from a high-school survey in China. *Addictive Behaviors*, *61*, 74–79. doi:10.1016/j.addbeh.2016.05.009 PMID:27249805

Milani, L., Osualdella, D., & Di Blasio, P. (2009). Quality of interpersonal relationships and problematic Internet use in adolescence. *Cyberpsychology & Behavior*, *12*(6), 681–684. doi:10.1089/cpb.2009.0071 PMID:19788382

Miller, K. J., & Mesagno, C. (2014). Personality traits and exercise dependence: Exploring the role of narcissism and perfectionism. *International Journal of Sport and Exercise Psychology*, *12*(4), 368–381. doi:10.1080/1612197X.2014.932821

Miller, P., & Plant, M. (2010). Parental guidance about drinking: Relationship with teenage psychoactive substance use. *Journal of Adolescence*, *33*(1), 55–68. doi:10.1016/j.adolescence.2009.05.011 PMID:19596424

Miller-Perrin, C. L., & Perrin, R. D. (2007). *Child maltreatment: An introduction*. London: Sage Publications.

Miller, W. R. (1983). Motivational interviewing with problem drinkers. *Behavioural Psychotherapy*, *11*(02), 147–172. doi:10.1017/S0141347300006583

Mitchell, K. J., Finkelhor, D., & Wolak, J. (2005). The Internet and family and acquaintance sexual abuse. *Child Maltreatment*, *10*(1), 49–60. doi:10.1177/1077559504271917 PMID:15611326

Mitchell, P. (2000). Internet addiction: Genuine diagnosis or not? *Lancet*, *355*(9204), 632. doi:10.1016/S0140-6736(05)72500-9 PMID:10696991

Mittal, N., Agarwal, B., Agarwal, S., Agarwal, S., & Gupta, P. (2013). A hybrid approach for twitter sentiment analysis. *10th International Conference on Natural Language Processing (ICON-2013)*, 116-120.

Modesti, K. (2009, Oct. 29). How the Internet was born at UCLA. *Los Angeles Daily News*. Retrieved from http://www.dailynews.com/article/ZZ/20091029/NEWS/910299877

Montag, C., & Reuter, M. (2015). Molecular Genetics, Personality and Internet Addiction. In C. Montag & M. Reuter (Ed.), Internet Addiction (pp. 93–109). Springer International Publishing.

Montag, C., Bey, K., Sha, P., Li, M., Chen, Y. F., Liu, W. Y., & Reuter, M. et al. (2015). Is it meaningful to distinguish between generalized and specific Internet addiction? Evidence from a cross - cultural study from Germany, Sweden, Taiwan and China. *Asia-Pacific Psychiatry*, *7*(1), 20–26. doi:10.1111/appy.12122 PMID:24616402

Moody, E. J. (2001). Internet use and its relationship to loneliness. *Cyberpsychology & Behavior*, *4*(3), 393–401. doi:10.1089/109493101300210303 PMID:11710265

Morahan, M. J., & Schumacher, P. (2000). Incidence and correlates of pathological Internet use among college students. *Computers in Human Behavior*, *16*(1), 13–29. doi:10.1016/S0747-5632(99)00049-7

Morahan-Martin, J. (1999). The relationship between loneliness and Internet use and abuse. *Cyberpsychology & Behavior*, *2*(5), 431–440. doi:10.1089/cpb.1999.2.431 PMID:19178216

Morahan-Martin, J. (2007). Internet use and abuse and psychological problems. In J. Joinson, K. McKenna, T. Postmes, & U. Reips (Eds.), *Oxford Handbook of Internet Psychology* (pp. 331–345). Oxford, UK: Oxford University Press.

Morahan-Martin, J., & Schumacher, P. (2003). Loneliness and social uses of the Internet. *Computers in Human Behavior*, *19*(6), 659–671. doi:10.1016/S0747-5632(03)00040-2

Morgan, C., & Cotten, S. R. (2003). The relationship between Internet activities and depressive symptoms in a sample of college freshmen. *Cyberpsychology & Behavior*, *6*(2), 133–142. doi:10.1089/109493103321640329 PMID:12804025

Morioka, H., Itani, O., Osaki, Y., Higuchi, S., Jike, M., Kaneita, Y., & Ohida, T. et al. (2017). The association between alcohol use and problematic Internet use: A large-scale nationwide cross-sectional study of adolescents in Japan. *Journal of Epidemiology*, *27*(3), 10–111. doi:10.1016/j.je.2016.10.004 PMID:28142042

Morsünbül, Ü. (2014). The association of internet addiction with attachment styles, personality traits, loneliness and life satisfaction. *Journal of Human Sciences*, *11*(1), 357–372.

Mottram, A. J., & Fleming, M. J. (2009). Extraversion, impulsivity, and online group membership as predictors of problematic Internet use. *Cyberpsychology & Behavior*, *12*(3), 319–321. doi:10.1089/cpb.2007.0170 PMID:19445635

Mueller, A., Mitchell, J. E., Peterson, L. A., Faber, R. J., Steffen, K. J., Crosby, R. D., & Claes, L. (2011). Depression, materialism, and excessive Internet use in relation to compulsive buying. *Comprehensive Psychiatry*, *52*(4), 420–424. doi:10.1016/j.comppsych.2010.09.001 PMID:21683178

Mukhongo, L. L. (2014) Reconstructing gendered narratives online: Nudity for popularity on digital platforms. *Ada: A Journal of Gender, New Media, and Technology, 5*, 1-14.

Mulhall, J. P. (2016). *Social media: Fad, trend or much more*. New York: MIT Publishers.

Mullen, P. E., Martin, J. L., Anderson, J. C., Romans, S. E., & Herbison, G. P. (1996). The long-term impact of the physical, emotional, and sexual abuse of children: A community study. *Child Abuse & Neglect*, *20*(1), 7–21. doi:10.1016/0145-2134(95)00112-3 PMID:8640429

Müller, K.W., Glaesmer, H., Brähler, E., Woelfling, K., & Beutel, M. E. (2014). *Prevalence of Internet addiction in the general population: Results from a German population-based survey*. Academic Press.

Müller, K. W., Dreier, M., Beutel, M. E., Duven, E., Giralt, S., & Wölfling, K. (2016). A hidden type of Internet addiction? Intense and addictive use of social networking sites in adolescents. *Computers in Human Behavior*, *55*, 172–177. doi:10.1016/j.chb.2015.09.007

Müller, K. W., Janikian, M., Dreier, M., Wölfling, K., Beutel, M. E., Tzavara, C., & Tsitsika, A. et al. (2015). Regular gaming behavior and internet gaming disorder in European adolescents: Results from a cross-national representative survey of prevalence, predictors, and psychopathological correlates. *European Child & Adolescent Psychiatry*, *24*(5), 565–574. doi:10.1007/s00787-014-0611-2 PMID:25189795

Müller, K. W., Koch, A., Dickenhorst, U., Beutel, M. E., Duven, E., & Wölfling, K. (2013). Addressing the question of disorder-specific risk factors of internet addiction: A comparison of personality traits in patients with addictive behaviors and comorbid internet addiction. *BioMed Research International*, *2013*, 1–7. doi:10.1155/2013/546342 PMID:23865056

Murali, V., & George, S. (2007). Lost online: An overview of Internet addiction. *Advances in Psychiatric Treatment*, *13*(1), 24–30. doi:10.1192/apt.bp.106.002907

Muthén, L. K., & Muthén, B. O. (2010). *Mplus User's Guide: Statistical Analysis with Latent Variables: User's Guide.* Los Angeles, CA: Muthén & Muthén.

Myers, D. G., & Diener, E. (1996). The pursuit of happiness. *Scientific American, 274*(5), 70–72. doi:10.1038/scientificamerican0596-70 PMID:8934647

Nalwa, K., & Anand, A. P. (2003). Internet addiction in students: A cause of concern. *Cyberpsychology & Behavior, 6*(6), 653–656. doi:10.1089/109493103322725441 PMID:14756932

Nam, Y. O. (2002). A study on the psychosocial variables of the youth's addiction to Internet and cyber sex and their problematic behavior. *Korean Journal of Social Welfare, 50.*

Narasimhamurthy, N. (2014). *Use and Rise of Social media as Election Campaign medium in India.* Academic Press.

Niaz, U., Siddiqui, S. S., Hassan, S., Husain, H., & Ahmed, S. (2005). A survey of psychosocial correlates of drug abuse in young adults aged 16-21 in Karachi: Identifying 'high risk' population to target intervention strategies. *Pakistan Journal of Medical Sciences, 21*(3), 271–277.

Nichols, L. A., & Nicki, R. (2004). Development of a psychometrically sound internet addiction scale: A preliminary step. *Psychology of Addictive Behaviors, 18*(4), 381–384. doi:10.1037/0893-164X.18.4.381 PMID:15631611

Nie, J., Zhang, W., & Liu, Y. (2017). Exploring depression, self-esteem and verbal fluency with different degrees of Internet addiction among Chinese college students. *Comprehensive Psychiatry, 72*, 114–120. doi:10.1016/j.comppsych.2016.10.006 PMID:27810547

Nie, N., Hillygus, D. S., & Erbring, L. (2002). Internet use, interpersonal relations, and sociability: A time diary study. In B. Wellman & C. Haythornthwaite (Eds.), *The Internet in Everyday Life* (pp. 215–243). Oxford, UK: Blackwell. doi:10.1002/9780470774298.ch7

Ni, X., Yan, H., Chen, S., & Liu, Z. (2009). Factors Influencing Internet Addiction in a Sample of Freshmen University Students in China. *Cyberpsychology, Behavior, and Social Networking, 12*(3), 327–330. doi:10.1089/cpb.2008.0321 PMID:19445631

Noh, D., & Kim, S. (2016). Dysfunctional attitude mediates the relationship between psychopathology and Internet addiction among Korean college students: A cross-sectional observational study. *International Journal of Mental Health Nursing, 25*(6), 588–597. doi:10.1111/inm.12220

Norman, R. E., Byambaa, M., De, R., Butchart, A., Scott, J., & Vos, T. (2012). The long-term health consequences of child physical abuse, emotional abuse, and neglect: A systematic review and meta-analysis. *PLoS Medicine, 9*(11), e1001349. doi:10.1371/journal.pmed.1001349 PMID:23209385

Nussbaum, M. (1995). Objectification. *Philosophy & Public Affairs, 24*(4), 249–291. doi:10.1111/j.1088-4963.1995.tb00032.x

Nykodym, N., Ariss, S., & Kurtz, K. (2008). Computer addiction and cybercrime. *Journal of Leadership, Accountability and Ethics, 35*, 55–59. Retrieved from http://na-businesspress.homestead.com/JLAE/nykodym.pdf

O'Brien, D., & Torres, A. M. (2012). Social networking and online privacy: Facebook users' perception. *Irish Journal of Management, 31*(2), 63–97.

Oberst, U., Wegmann, E., Stodt, B., Brand, M., & Chamarro, A. (2017). Negative consequences from heavy social networking in adolescents: The mediating role of fear of missing out. *Journal of Adolescence, 55*, 51–60. doi:10.1016/j.adolescence.2016.12.008 PMID:28033503

Odacı, H. (2013). Risktaking behavior and academic selfefficacy as variables accounting for problematic internet use in adolescent university students. *Children and Youth Services Review, 35*(1), 183–187. doi:10.1016/j.childyouth.2012.09.011

Odacı, H., & Çelik, Ç. B. (2013). Who are problematic internet users? An investigation of the correlations between problematic internet use and shyness, loneliness, narcissism, aggression and self-perception. *Computers in Human Behavior, 29*(6), 2382–2387. doi:10.1016/j.chb.2013.05.026

Odacı, H., & Çıkrıkçı, Ö. (2014). Problematic internet use in terms of gender, attachment styles and subjective well-being in university students. *Computers in Human Behavior, 32*, 61–66. doi:10.1016/j.chb.2013.11.019

Odu, O. (2016, June 18). Social media and the Nigerian youth. Nigerian Mirror, 21-23.

Ogbu, R. (2013). Trashy: More Nigerian girls pose nude to trend on twitter. *YNigeria*. Retrieved April 8, 2017, from http//:www.trashy.nigerian.girls.pose.nude.ynigeria.htm

Ojo, A. (2005). *Religion and Sexuality: Individuality, Choice and Sexual Rights in Nigerian Christianity*. Lagos: Africa Regional Sexuality Resource Center.

Okwaraji, F. E., Aguwa, E. N., Onyebueke, G. C., & Shiweobi-Eze, C. (2015). Assessment of Internet Addiction and Depression in a Sample of Nigerian University Undergraduates. *International Neuropsychiatric Disease Journal, 4*(3), 114–122. doi:10.9734/INDJ/2015/19096

Olawepo, G. T., & Oyedepo, F. S. (2008). *Data communication and computer networks*. Adek Publisher.

Oluwatimilehin, M. (2016, August). The selfie syndrome danger. *Daily Times*, 16-19.

Onasanya, S. A., Olelekan, S.Y., Ayelegba, S.O., & Akingbemisilu, A.A. (2013). Online social network and academic achievement of university students – the experience of selected Nigerian Universities. *Information and Knowledge Management, 3*(5), 58-66.

Ong, S. H., & Tan, Y. R. (2014). Internet addiction in young people. *Annals Academy of Medicine, 43*(7), 378–382. PMID:25142474

Online Safety Site. (2017). *Teen Internet Statistics*. Retrieved March 21, 2017, from http://www.onlinesafetysite.com/P1/Teenstats.htm

Onyeka, N. C., Sajoh, D. I., & Bulus, L. D. (2013). The effect of social networking sites usage on the studies of Nigerian students. *International Journal of Engineering Science, 2*, 39–46.

Orr, E. S., Ross, C., Simmering, M. G., Arsenault, J. M., & Orr, R. R. (2009). The influence of shyness on the use of Facebook in an undergraduate sample. *Cyberpsychology & Behavior, 12*(3), 337–340. doi:10.1089/cpb.2008.0214 PMID:19250019

Oshio, T., Umeda, M., & Kawakami, N. (2011). *Childhood adversity and adulthood happiness: Evidence from Japan (No. 529)*. Center for Intergenerational Studies, Institute of Economic Research, Hitotsubashi University.

Osun Defender. (2016, April 2). Nigerian pester me for sex movie. *Osun Defender*, 21-26.

Ozcan, N. K., & Buzlu, S. (2005). An assistive tool in determining problematic internet use: Validity and reliability of the Online Cognition Scale in a sample of university students. *Journal of Dependence, 6*(1), 19–26.

Özdemir, Y., Kuzucu, Y., & Ak, Ş. (2014). Depression, loneliness and Internet addiction: How important is low self-control? *Computers in Human Behavior, 34*, 284–290. doi:10.1016/j.chb.2014.02.009

Öz, F. (2010). *Sağlık alanında temel kavramlar* [Basic concept in healthcare field] (2nd ed.). Ankara, Turkey: Mattek Yayınları. (in Turkish)

Özge, E., & Gölge, Z. B. (2015). Üniversite öğrencilerinde riskli davranışlar ile çocukluk çağı istismar, dürtüsellik ve riskli davranışlar arasındaki ilişki. *Journal of Psychiatry, 16*(3), 189–197.

Öztürk, E., & Özmen, S. K. (2016). The relationship of self-perception, personality and high school type with the level of problematic internet use in adolescents. *Computers in Human Behavior, 65*, 501–507. doi:10.1016/j.chb.2016.09.016

Palen, L. A., & Coatsworth, J. D. (2007). Activity-based identity experiences and their relations to problem behaviour and psychological well-being in adolescence. *Journal of Adolescence, 30*(5), 721–737. doi:10.1016/j.adolescence.2006.11.003 PMID:17222899

Papacharissi, Z., & Rubin, A. M. (2000). Predictors of Internet use. *Journal of Broadcasting & Electronic Media, 44*(2), 175–196. doi:10.1207/s15506878jobem4402_2

Pardoen, J. A., Pijpers, R., & Boeke, H. (2006). *Verliefd op Internet: over Internetgedrag van pubers*. SWP.

Park, S. K., Kim, J. Y., & Cho, C. B. (2008). Prevalence of Internet addiction and correlations with family factors among South Korean adolescents. *Adolescence, 43*(172), 895–909. PMID:19149152

Park, S., & Lee, Y. (2017). Associations of body weight perception and weight control behaviors with problematic Internet use among Korean adolescents. *Psychiatry Research, 251*, 275–280. doi:10.1016/j.psychres.2017.01.095 PMID:28222311

Patel, R. (2016, March 23). Nude selfies: The latest trend sweeping the millennials. But there is a cost. *IBT: International Business Times*, 94-106.

Paulhus, D. L., & Vazire, S. (2007). The selfreport method. In R. W. Robins, R. C. Fraley, & R. F. Krueger (Eds.), *Handbook of research methods in personality psychology* (pp. 224–239). London: The Guilford Press.

Pauwels, C., Bauwens, J., & Vleugels, C. (2008). *Cyberteens: de betekenis van ICT in het dagelijkse leven van Belgische tieners* [Cyberteens: The relevance of ICT in daily life of Belgian teenagers]. Academic Press.

Pawlak, C. (2002). Correlates of Internet use and addiction in adolescents. *Dissertation Abstracts International. A, The Humanities and Social Sciences, 63*(5-A), 1727.

Peng, W., & Liu, M. (2010). Online Gaming Dependency: A Preliminary Study in China. *Cyberpsychology, Behavior, and Social Networking, 13*(3), 329–333. doi:10.1089/cyber.2009.0082 PMID:20557254

Peplau, L. A., & Perlman, D. (1979). *Blueprint for a social psychological theory of loneliness. Love and Attraction*. Oxford, UK: Pergman.

Peters, C. S., & Malesky, L. A. Jr. (2008). Problematic usage among highly-engaged players of massively multiplayer online role playing games. *Cyberpsychology & Behavior, 11*(4), 481–484. doi:10.1089/cpb.2007.0140 PMID:18721098

Petry, N. M. (2005). *Pathological Gambling: Etiology, Comorbidity, and Treatments*. Washington, DC: American Psychological Association Press. doi:10.1037/10894-000

Petry, N. M. (2006). Internet gambling: An emerging concern in family practice medicine? *Family Practice, 23*(4), 421–426. doi:10.1093/fampra/cml005 PMID:16621919

Petry, N. M., & O'brien, C. P. (2013). Internet gaming disorder and the DSM-5. *Addiction (Abingdon, England), 108*(7), 1186–1187. doi:10.1111/add.12162 PMID:23668389

Petry, N. M., & Steinberg, K. L. (2005). Childhood maltreatment in male and female treatment-seeking pathological gamblers. *Psychology of Addictive Behaviors, 19*(2), 226–229. doi:10.1037/0893-164X.19.2.226 PMID:16011396

Pew Research Center. (2017). *Internet usage by age*. Retrieved March 21, 2017, from http://www.pewinternet.org/chart/internet-use-by-age/

Pezoa-Jares, R., Espinoza-Luna, I., & Vasquez-Medina, J. (2012). Internet addiction: A review. *Journal of Addiction Research & Therapy, S6*(004).

Pierce, G. R., Lakey, B., & Sarason, I. G. (Eds.). (2013). *Sourcebook of Social Support and Personality*. Springer Science and Business Media Press.

Pies, R. (2009). Should DSM-V designate "Internet addiction" a mental disorder? *Psychiatry (Edgmont), 6*(2), 31–37. PMID:19724746

Pies, R. (2009). Should DSM-V Designate "Internet Addiction" a Mental Disorder? *Psychiatry (Edgmont), 6*(2), 31–37. PMID:19724746

Poli, R. (2017). Internet addiction update: Diagnostic criteria, assessment and prevalence. *Neuropsychiatry, 7*(1), 4–8. doi:10.4172/Neuropsychiatry.1000171

Poli, R., & Agrimi, E. (2012). Internet addiction disorder: Prevalence in an Italian student population. *Nordic Journal of Psychiatry, 66*(1), 55–59. doi:10.3109/08039488.2011.605169 PMID:21859396

Pontes, H. M., & Kuss, D. J. (in press). *Internet addiction*. Göttingen, Germany: Hogrefe Publishing.

Pontes, H. M., Griffiths, M. D., & Patrão, I. M. (2014). Internet addiction and loneliness among children and adolescents in the education setting: An empirical pilot study. *Aloma: Revista de Psicologia, Ciències de l'Educació I de l'Esport, 32*(1), 91-98.

Pontes, H. M., Griffiths, M. D., & Patrão, I. M. (2014). Internet addiction and loneliness among children and adolescents in the education setting: an empirical pilot study. *Aloma: Revista de Psicologia, Ciències de l'Educació i de l'Esport, 32*(1).

Pontes, H. M. (2016). Current practices in the clinical and psychometric assessment of internet gaming disorder in the era of the DSM-5: A mini review of existing assessment tools. *Mental Health and Addiction Research, 1*(1), 18–19. doi:10.15761/MHAR.1000105

Pontes, H. M. (2017). Investigating the differential effects of social networking site addiction and Internet Gaming Disorder on psychological health. *Cyberpsychology, Behavior, and Social Networking*. (under review)

Pontes, H. M., Caplan, S. E., & Griffiths, M. D. (2016). Psychometric validation of the Generalized Problematic Internet Use Scale 2 in a Portuguese sample. *Computers in Human Behavior, 63*, 823–833. doi:10.1016/j.chb.2016.06.015

Pontes, H. M., & Griffiths, M. D. (2014). Internet addiction disorder and Internet gaming disorder are not the same. *Journal of Addiction Research & Therapy, 5*(4).

Pontes, H. M., & Griffiths, M. D. (2015). Measuring DSM-5 Internet Gaming Disorder: Development and validation of a short psychometric scale. *Computers in Human Behavior, 45*, 137–143. doi:10.1016/j.chb.2014.12.006

Pontes, H. M., & Griffiths, M. D. (2016a). The development and psychometric properties of the Internet Disorder Scale-Short Form (IDS9-SF). *Addicta: The Turkish Journal on Addictions, 3*(2), 1–16.

Pontes, H. M., & Griffiths, M. D. (2016b). Portuguese validation of the Internet Gaming Disorder Scale–Short-Form. *Cyberpsychology, Behavior, and Social Networking, 19*(4), 288–293. doi:10.1089/cyber.2015.0605 PMID:26974853

Pontes, H. M., & Griffiths, M. D. (2017). The development and psychometric evaluation of the Internet Disorder Scale (IDS-15). *Addictive Behaviors, 64*, 261–268. doi:10.1016/j.addbeh.2015.09.003 PMID:26410796

Pontes, H. M., Király, O., Demetrovics, Z., & Griffiths, M. D. (2014). The conceptualisation and measurement of DSM-5 Internet Gaming Disorder: The development of the IGD-20 Test. *PLoS One, 9*(10), e110137. doi:10.1371/journal.pone.0110137 PMID:25313515

Pontes, H. M., Kuss, D. J., & Griffiths, M. D. (2015). Clinical psychology of Internet addiction: A review of its conceptualization, prevalence, neuronal processes, and implications for treatment. *Neuroscience and Neuroeconomics, 4*, 11–23.

Pontes, H. M., Patrão, I. M., & Griffiths, M. D. (2014). Portuguese validation of the Internet Addiction Test: An empirical study. *Journal of Behavioral Addictions, 3*(2), 107–114. doi:10.1556/JBA.3.2014.2.4 PMID:25215221

Pontes, H. M., Szabo, A., & Griffiths, M. D. (2015). The impact of Internet-based specific activities on the perceptions of Internet addiction, quality of life, and excessive usage: A cross-sectional study. *Addictive Behaviors Reports, 1*, 19–25. doi:10.1016/j.abrep.2015.03.002

Poon, S. (2000). Business environment and Internet commerce benefit—a small business perspective. *European Journal of Information Systems, 9*(2), 72–81. doi:10.1057/palgrave.ejis.3000361

Primack, B. A., Swanier, B., Georgiopoulos, A. M., Land, S. R., & Fine, M. J. (2009). Association between media use in adolescence and depression in young adulthood: A longitudinal study. *Archives of General Psychiatry, 66*(2), 181–188. doi:10.1001/archgenpsychiatry.2008.532 PMID:19188540

Primožič, A. (2009). *Zasvojenost z internetom (Bachelor thesis)*. University of Ljubljana. Retrieved from http://dk.fdv.uni-lj.si/diplomska/pdfs/primozic-anze.pdf

Quoss, B., & Zhao, W. (1995). Parenting styles and children's satisfaction with parenting in China and the United States. *Journal of Comparative Family Studies*, 265–280.

Rahman, A., & Ahmar, A. S. (2017). *Relationship between learning styles and learning achievement in mathematics based on genders*. Academic Press.

Rand, D. L., Stein, J. A., & Rand, S. T. (1998). Reliability and validity of a selfcontrol measure: Rejoinder. *Criminology, 36*(1), 175–182. doi:10.1111/j.1745-9125.1998.tb01245.x

Randler, C., Horzum, M. B., & Vollmer, C. (2013). Internet Addiction and Its Relationship to Chronotype and Personality in a Turkish University Student Sample. *Social Science Computer Review, 32*(4), 1–12.

Rands, K., McDonald, J., & Clapp, L. (2013). *Landscaping classrooms toward queer utopias. In A critical inquiry into queer utopias* (pp. 149–172). Springer. doi:10.1057/9781137311979_7

Rauch, J. E. (2001). Business and social networks in international trade. *Journal of Economic Literature, 39*(4), 1177–1203. doi:10.1257/jel.39.4.1177

Reddy, M. (1997). *Using the information superhighway to support the ACE initiative at level 12*. The 2nd BP International Conference on Students as Tutors and Mentors, London, UK.

Reed, P., Osborne, L. A., Romano, M., & Truzoli, R. (2015). Higher impulsivity after exposure to the Internet for individuals with high but not low levels of self-reported problematic Internet behaviours. *Computers in Human Behavior, 49*, 512–516. doi:10.1016/j.chb.2015.03.064

Reer, F., & Krämer, N. C. (2017). The connection between introversion/extraversion and social capital outcomes of playing World of Warcraft. *Cyberpsychology, Behavior, and Social Networking, 20*(2), 97–103. doi:10.1089/cyber.2016.0439 PMID:28170308

Rehbein, F., Kliem, S., Baier, D., Mößle, T., & Petry, N. M. (2015). Prevalence of Internet gaming disorder in German adolescents: Diagnostic contribution of the nine DSM-5 criteria in a state-wide representative sample. *Addiction (Abingdon, England), 110*(5), 842–851. doi:10.1111/add.12849 PMID:25598040

Rehman, A., Shafi, H., & Rizvi, T. (2016). Internet Addiction and Psychological Well-being among Youth of Kashmir. *The International Journal of Indian Psychology, 3*(3), 6–11.

Rial Boubeta, A., Gomez Salgado, P., Isorna Folgar, M., Araujo Gallego, M., & Varela Mallou, J. (2015). PIUS-a: Problematic Internet Use Scale in adolescents. Development and psychometric validation. *Adicciones, 27*(1), 47–63. doi:10.20882/adicciones.193 PMID:25879477

Robbins, T. W., & Clark, L. (2015). Behavioral addictions. *Current Opinion in Neurobiology, 30*, 66–72. doi:10.1016/j.conb.2014.09.005 PMID:25262209

Romano, M., Osborne, L. A., Truzoli, R., & Reed, P. (2013). Differential psychological impact of Internet exposure on Internet addicts. *PLoS One, 8*(2), e55162. doi:10.1371/journal.pone.0055162 PMID:23408958

Rooksby, E. (2011). What does it mean to be a liberal? *The Guardian.* Retrieved March 31, 2017 from https://www.theguardian.com/commentisfree/2011/aug/15/liberalism-political-economic-different-ideologies

Rosenberg, M. (1965). *Society and the adolescent self-image.* Princeton, NJ: Princeton University Press. doi:10.1515/9781400876136

Rosenkranz, S. E., Muller, R. T., & Henderson, J. L. (2012). Psychological maltreatment in relation to substance use problem severity among youth. *Child Abuse & Neglect, 36*(5), 438–448. doi:10.1016/j.chiabu.2012.01.005 PMID:22622223

Rosen, L. D., Cheever, N. A., & Carrier, L. M. (2008). The association of parenting style and child age with parental limit setting and adolescent MySpace behavior. *Journal of Applied Developmental Psychology, 29*(6), 459–471. doi:10.1016/j.appdev.2008.07.005

Rosen, L. D., Whaling, K., Rab, S., Carrier, L. M., & Cheever, N. A. (2013). Is Facebook creating "iDisorders"? The link between clinical symptoms of psychiatric disorders and technology use, attitudes, and anxiety. *Computers in Human Behavior, 29*(3), 1243–1254. doi:10.1016/j.chb.2012.11.012

Rosenthal, R. J. (2008). Psychodynamic psychotherapy and the treatment of pathological gambling. *Revista Brasileira de Psiquiatria (Sao Paulo, Brazil), 30*(1), S41–S50. doi:10.1590/S1516-44462008005000004 PMID:17992358

Ross, C., Orr, E. S., Sisic, M., Arseneault, J. M., Simmering, M. G., & Orr, R. R. (2009). Personality and Motivations associated with Facebook Use. *Computers in Human Behavior, 25*(2), 578–586. doi:10.1016/j.chb.2008.12.024

Rowicka, M. (2016). Internet addiction treatment. In B. Lelonek-Kuleta & J. Chwaszcz (Eds.), *Gambling and Internet addictions – epidemiology and treatment* (pp. 55–64). Lublin, Poland: Natanaelum Association Institute for Psychoprevenaion and Psychotherapy.

Roy, A., & Ferguson, C. J. (2016). Competitively versus cooperatively? An analysis of the effect of game play on levels of stress. *Computers in Human Behavior, 56*, 14–20. doi:10.1016/j.chb.2015.11.020

Rücker, J., Akre, C., Berchtold, A., & Suris, J. C. (2015). Problematic Internet use is Associated with substance use in young adolescents. *Acta Paediatrica (Oslo, Norway), 104*(5), 504–507. doi:10.1111/apa.12971 PMID:25662370

Rudall, B. H. (1996). Internet addiction syndrome. *Robotica, 14,* 510–511.

Ruggiero, T. E. (2000). Uses and gratifications theory in the 21st century. *Mass Communication & Society, 3*(1), 3–37. doi:10.1207/S15327825MCS0301_02

Rumpf, H.-J., Bischof, G., Bischof, A., Besser, B., Meyer, C., & John, U. (2015). *Applying DSM-5 criteria for Internet Gaming Disorder for the broader concept of Internet addiction.* Paper presented at the 2nd International Conference on Behavioral Addictions, Budapest, Hungary.

Rumpf, H. J., Vermulst, A. A., Bischof, A., Kastirke, N., Gürtler, D., Bischof, G., & Meyer, C. et al. (2014). Occurence of Internet addiction in a general population sample: A latent class analysis. *European Addiction Research, 20*(4), 159–166. doi:10.1159/000354321 PMID:24401314

Russell, D., Peplau, L. A., & Cutrona, C. E. (1980). The revised UCLA Loneliness Scale: Concurrent and discriminant validity evidence. *Journal of Personality and Social Psychology, 39*(3), 472–480. doi:10.1037/0022-3514.39.3.472 PMID:7431205

Ryan, R. M., & Deci, E. L. (2001). On happiness and human potentials: A review of research on hedonic and eudaimonic well-being. *Annual Review of Psychology, 52*(1), 141–166. doi:10.1146/annurev.psych.52.1.141 PMID:11148302

Ryan, T., & Xenos, S. (2011). Who uses Facebook? An investigation into the relationship between the Big Five, shyness, narcissism, loneliness, and Facebook usage. *Computers in Human Behavior, 27*(5), 1658–1664. doi:10.1016/j.chb.2011.02.004

Şahin, C. (2014). An analysis of the relationship between Internet addiction and depression levels of high school students. *Participatory Educational Research, 1*(2), 53–67. doi:10.17275/per.14.10.1.2

Salmon, G. (2003). E-tivities: The key to active online learning. London: RoutledgeFalmer.

Sariyska, R., Reuter, M., Bey, K., Sha, P., Li, M., Chen, Y. F., & Feldmann, M. et al. (2014). Self-esteem, personality and Internet addiction: A cross-cultural comparison study. *Personality and Individual Differences, 61,* 28–33. doi:10.1016/j.paid.2014.01.001

Sariyska, R., Reuter, M., Lachmann, B., & Montag, C. (2015). Attention deficit/hyperactivity disorder is a better predictor for problematic Internet use than depression: Evidence from Germany. *Journal of Addiction Research & Therapy, 6*(209), 1–6. PMID:26925299

Şaşmaz, T., Öner, S., Kurt, A. Ö., Yapıcı, G., Buğdaycı, R., & Şiş, M. (2013). Prevalence and risk factors of Internet addiction in high school students. *European Journal of Public Health, 24*(1), 15–20. doi:10.1093/eurpub/ckt051 PMID:23722862

Sasson, H., & Mesch, G. (2014). Parental mediation, peer norms and risky online behavior among adolescents. *Computers in Human Behavior, 33,* 32–38. doi:10.1016/j.chb.2013.12.025

Sato, T. (2009). *Internet Addiction among Students: Prevalence and Psychological Problems in Japan.* Retrieved March 17, 2017 from www.med.or.jp/english/pdf/2006_07+/279_283.pdf

Saulsman, L. M., & Page, A. C. (2004). The five-factor model and personality disorder empirical literature: A meta-analytic review. *Clinical Psychology Review, 23*(8), 1055–1085. doi:10.1016/j.cpr.2002.09.001 PMID:14729423

Sayed, S. A., Jannatifard, F., Eslami, M., & Rezapour, H. (2011). Validity, reliability and factor analysis of compulsive internet use scale in students of Isfahan's universities. *Health Information Management, 7,* 715–724.

Scannapieco, M., & Connell-Carrick, K. (2005). *Understanding child maltreatment: An ecological and developmental perspective.* New York, NY: Oxford University Press. doi:10.1093/acprof:oso/9780195156782.001.0001

Schepis, T. S., Adinoff, B., & Rao, U. (2008). Neurobiological processes in adolescent addictive disorders. *The American Journal on Addictions, 17*(1), 6–23. doi:10.1080/10550490701756146 PMID:18214718

Schmidt, M. M., Sharma, A., Schifano, F., & Feinmann, C. (2011). "Legal highs" on the net—Evaluation of UK-based Web sites, products, and product information. *Forensic Science International, 206*(1), 92–97. doi:10.1016/j.forsciint.2010.06.030 PMID:20650576

Schou Andreassen, C., & Pallesen, S. (2014). Social network site addiction-an overview. *Current Pharmaceutical Design, 20*(25), 4053–4061. doi:10.2174/13816128113199990616 PMID:24001298

Scimeca, G., Bruno, A., Cava, L., Pandolfo, G., Muscatello, M. R. A., & Zoccali, R. (2014). The Relationship between Alexithymia, Anxiety, Depression, and Internet Addiction Severity in a Sample of Italian High School Students. *The Scientific World Journal, 2014*, 1–8. doi:10.1155/2014/504376 PMID:25401143

Scimeca, G., Bruno, A., Cava, L., Pandolfo, G., Muscatello, M. R. A., & Zoccali, R. (2014). The relationship between alexithymia, anxiety, depression, and Internet addiction severity in a sample of Italian high school students. *The Scientific World Journal*. PMID:25401143

Scimeca, G., Bruno, A., Cava, L., Pandolfo, G., Muscatello, M. R. A., & Zoccali, R. (2014). The Relationship between Alexithymia, Anxiety, Depression, and Internet Addiction Severity in a Sample of Italian High School Students. *The Scientific World Journal*. PMID:25401143

Segal, Z. V., Teasdale, J. D., & Williams, J. M. G. (2004). Mindfulness-based cognitive therapy: Theoretical rationale and empirical status. In S. Hayes, V. Follette, & M. Linehan (Eds.), *Mindfulness and acceptance: Expanding the cognitivebehavioral tradition*. New York: Guilford Press.

Segal, Z. V., Teasdale, J. D., Williams, J. M., & Gemar, M. C. (2002). The mindfulness-based cognitive therapy adherence scale: Inter-rater reliability, adherence to protocol and treatment distinctiveness. *Clinical Psychology & Psychotherapy, 9*(2), 131–138. doi:10.1002/cpp.320

Segoete, L. (2015). African female sexuality is past taboo. *This is Africa*. Retrieved June 10, 2017, from http://thisisafrica.me/sexuality-taboo/

Selian, A. N. (2004). *Mobile phones and youth: A look at the US student market*. Retrieved January 13, 2017, from http://www.itu.int/osg/spu/ni/futuremobile/Youth.pdf

Şenormancı, Ö., Konkan, R., & Sungur, M. Z. (2012) Internet addiction and its cognitive behavioral therapy. In Standard and Innovative Strategies in Cognitive Behavior Therapy. Intech.

Şenormanci, Ö., Konkan, R., & Sungur, M. Z. (2012). Internet addiction and its cognitive behavior therapy. In I. R. De Oliveira (Ed.), *Standard and innovative strategies in cognitive behavior therapy*. Retrieved from http://www.intechopen.com/books/standard-and-innovative-strategies-in-cognitive-behavior-therapy/internet-addiction-and-its-cognitive-behavioral-therapy

Şenormancı, Ö., Şenormancı, G., Güçlü, O., & Konkan, R. (2014). Attachment and family functioning in patients with internet addiction. *General Hospital Psychiatry, 36*(2), 203–207. doi:10.1016/j.genhosppsych.2013.10.012 PMID:24262601

Servidio, R. (2014). Exploring the effects of demographic factors, Internet usage and personality traits on Internet addiction in a sample of Italian university students. *Computers in Human Behavior, 35*, 85–92. doi:10.1016/j.chb.2014.02.024

Servidio, R. (2017). Assessing the psychometric properties of the Internet Addiction Test: A study on a sample of Italian university students. *Computers in Human Behavior, 68*, 17–29. doi:10.1016/j.chb.2016.11.019

Seyrek, S., Cop, E., Sinir, H., Ugurlu, M., & Şenel, S. (2017). Factors associated with Internet addiction: Cross-sectional study of Turkish adolescents. *Pediatrics International*, *59*(2), 218–222. doi:10.1111/ped.13117 PMID:27507735

Shaffer, D. R., & Kipp, K. (2013). *Developmental psychology: Childhood and adolescence*. Wadsworth, Cengage Learning.

Shah, J., & Gathoo, V. (2017). *Learning styles and academic achievement of children with and without hearing impairment in primary inclusive classrooms in mumbai. Journal of Disability Management and Special Education*, 1, 1.

Shah, P. B. (2015). Selfie – a new generation addiction disorder – literature review and updates. *International Journal of Emergency Mental Health and Human Resilience*, *17*(3), 602. doi:10.4172/1522-4821.1000e227

Shapira, N. A., Goldsmith, T. D., Keck, P. E. Jr, Khosla, U. M., & McElroy, S. L. (2000). Psychiatric features of individuals with problematic internet use. *Journal of Affective Disorders*, *57*(1-3), 267–272. doi:10.1016/S0165-0327(99)00107-X PMID:10708842

Shapira, N. A., Lessig, M. C., Goldsmith, T. D., Szabo, S. T., Lazoritz, M., Gold, M. S., & Stein, D. J. (2003). Problematic Internet use: Proposed classification and diagnostic criteria. *Depression and Anxiety*, *17*(4), 207–216. doi:10.1002/da.10094 PMID:12820176

Sharma, G. (2014). Effect of demographic variables on psychological well-being and quality of life. *International Journal of Social Science and Humanities Research*, *2*(3), 290–298.

Sharma, P., Bharati, A., De Sousa, A., & Shah, N. (2016). Internet Addiction and Its Association With Psychopathology: A Study In School Children From Mumbai, India. *National Journal of Community Medicine*, *7*(1).

Shaver, P., Furman, W., & Buhrmester, D. (1985). Transition to college: Network changes, social skills, and loneliness. In S. Duck & D. Perlman (Eds.), *Understanding personal relationships: An interdisciplinary approach* (pp. 193–220). London: Sage Publications.

Shaw, L. H., & Gant, L. M. (2002). In defense of the Internet: The relationship between Internet communication and depression, loneliness, self-esteem, and perceived social support. *Cyberpsychology & Behavior*, *5*(2), 157–171. doi:10.1089/109493102753770552 PMID:12025883

Shaw, W., & Black, D. W. (2008). Internet addiction: Definition, assessment, epidemiology and clinical management. *CNS Drugs*, *22*(5), 353–365. doi:10.2165/00023210-200822050-00001 PMID:18399706

Sheedy, C. S. (2011). Social media for social change: A case study of social media use in the 2011 Egyptian revolution. *Capstone Project*, *28*(4), 1–58.

Shek, D. T. L., Tang, V. M. Y., & Lo, C. Y. (2008). Internet Addiction in Chinese Adolescents in Hong Kong: Assessment, Profiles, and Psychosocial Correlates. *The Scientific World Journal*, *8*, 776–787. doi:10.1100/tsw.2008.104 PMID:18690381

Shek, D. T. L., & Yu, L. (2016). Adolescent Internet Addiction in Hong Kong: Prevalence, Change, and Correlates. *Journal of Pediatric and Adolescent Gynecology*, *29*(1), S22–S30. doi:10.1016/j.jpag.2015.10.005 PMID:26461526

Shek, D. T., & Yu, L. (2012). Internet addiction phenomenon in early adolescents in Hong Kong. *The Scientific World Journal*, *2012*, 104304. doi:10.1100/2012/104304 PMID:22778694

Shin, S. E., Kim, N. S., & Jang, E. Y. (2011). Comparison of problematic Internet and alcohol use and attachment styles among industrial workers in Korea. *Cyberpsychology, Behavior, and Social Networking*, *14*(11), 665–672. doi:10.1089/cyber.2010.0470 PMID:21595524

Shirky, C. (2011). The political power of social media: Technology, the public sphere, and political change. *Foreign Affairs*, 28–41.

Shotton, M. A. (1991). The costs and benefits of "computer addiction". *Behaviour & Information Technology*, *10*(3), 219–230. doi:10.1080/01449299108924284

Šimek, D. (2004). Odvisnost od interneta. In *Vzgoja in izobraževanje v informacijski družbi: zbornik referatov* [Education in information society: conference proceedings]. Ljubljana: Ministrstvo za šolstvo, znanost in šport.

Simsek, E., & Sali, J. B. (2014). The role of Internet addiction and social media membership on university students' psychological capital. *Contemporary Educational Technology*, *5*(3), 239–256.

Singh, D., & Lippman. (2017). Selfie addiction. *International Psychiatry: Bulletin of the Board of International Affairs of the Royal College of Psychiatrists*, *4*(1), 11–27.

Siomos, K. E., Dafouli, E. D., Braimiotis, D. A., Mouzas, O. D., & Angelopoulos, N. V. (2008). Internet addiction among Greek adolescent students. *Cyberpsychology & Behavior*, *11*(6), 653–657. doi:10.1089/cpb.2008.0088 PMID:18991535

Siomos, K., Floros, G., Fisoun, V., Evaggelia, D., Farkonas, N., Sergentani, E., & Geroukalis, D. et al. (2012). Evolution of Internet addiction in Greek adolescent students over a two-year period: The impact of parental bonding. *European Child & Adolescent Psychiatry*, *21*(4), 211–219. doi:10.1007/s00787-012-0254-0 PMID:22311146

Skalická, V., van Lenthe, F., Bambra, C., Krokstad, S., & Mackenbach, J. (2009). Material, psychosocial, behavioural and biomedical factors in the explanation of relative socio-economic inequalities in mortality: Evidence from the HUNT study. *International Journal of Epidemiology*, *38*(5), 1272–1284. doi:10.1093/ije/dyp262 PMID:19661280

Skues, J. L., Williams, B., & Wise, L. (2012). The effects of personality traits, self-esteem, loneliness, and narcissism on Facebook use among university students. *Computers in Human Behavior*, *28*(6), 2414–2419. doi:10.1016/j.chb.2012.07.012

Soule, L. C., Shell, L. W., & Kleen, B. A. (2003). Exploring Internet addiction: Demographic characteristics and stereotypes of heavy Internet users. *Journal of Computer Information Systems*, *44*(1), 64–73.

Southern, S. (2008). Treatment of compulsive cybersex behavior. *The Psychiatric Clinics of North America*, *31*(4), 697–712. doi:10.1016/j.psc.2008.06.003 PMID:18996308

Spada, M. M. (2014). An overview of problematic Internet use. *Addictive Behaviors*, *39*(1), 3–6. doi:10.1016/j.addbeh.2013.09.007 PMID:24126206

Sroubek, A., Kelly, M., & Li, X. (2013). Inattentiveness in attention-deficit/hyperactivity disorder. *Neuroscience Bulletin*, *29*(1), 103–110. doi:10.1007/s12264-012-1295-6 PMID:23299717

Starcevic, V. (2016). *Internet addiction: Rarely an addiction and not the Internet that one is addicted to.* Paper presented at the 3rd International Conference on Behavioral Addictions, Geneva, Switzerland.

Starcevic, V. (2010). Problematic Internet use: A distinct disorder, a manifestation of an underlying psychopathology, or a troublesome behaviour? *World Psychiatry; Official Journal of the World Psychiatric Association (WPA)*, *9*(2), 92–93. doi:10.1002/j.2051-5545.2010.tb00280.x PMID:20671892

Starcevic, V. (2013). Is Internet addiction a useful concept? *The Australian and New Zealand Journal of Psychiatry*, *47*(1), 16–19. doi:10.1177/0004867412461693 PMID:23293309

Starcevic, V., & Aboujaoude, E. (2016). Internet addiction: Reappraisal of an increasingly inadequate concept. *CNS Spectrums*, 1–7. PMID:26831456

Statista. (2016a). *Number of Facebook users by age in the U.S. 2016*. Retrieved from https://www.statista.com/statistics/398136/us-facebook-user-age-groups/

Statista. (2016b). *Number social network users in the United States as of January 2015, by age (in millions)*. Retrieved from https://www.statista.com/statistics/243582/us-social-media-user-age-groups/

Stavropoulos, V., Alexandraki, K., & Motti-Stefanidi, F. (2013). Recognizing internet addiction: Prevalence and relationship to academic achievement in adolescents enrolled in urban and rural Greek high schools. *Journal of Adolescence*, *36*(3), 565–576. doi:10.1016/j.adolescence.2013.03.008 PMID:23608781

Stavropoulos, V., Kuss, D. J., Griffiths, M. D., & Motti-Stefanidi, F. (2016). A longitudinal study of adolescent Internet addiction: The role of conscientiousness and classroom hostility. *Journal of Adolescent Research*, *31*(4), 442–473. doi:10.1177/0743558415580163

Stavropoulos, V., Kuss, D. J., Griffiths, M. D., Wilson, P., & Motti-Stefanidi, F. (2017). MMORPG gaming and hostility predict Internet Addiction symptoms in adolescents: An empirical multilevel longitudinal study. *Addictive Behaviors*, *64*, 294–300. doi:10.1016/j.addbeh.2015.09.001 PMID:26410795

Steinberg, L. (2001). We know some things: Parent–adolescent relationships in retrospect and prospect. *Journal of Research on Adolescence*, *11*(1), 1–19. doi:10.1111/1532-7795.00001

Steinberg, L., Lamborn, S. D., Darling, N., Mounts, N. S., & Dornbusch, S. M. (1994). Over-time changes in adjustment and competence among adolescents from authoritative, authoritarian, indulgent, and neglectful families. *Child Development*, *65*(3), 754–770. doi:10.2307/1131416 PMID:8045165

Stepanikova, I., Nie, N. H., & He, X. (2010). Time on the Internet at home, loneliness, and life satisfaction: Evidence from panel time-diary data. *Computers in Human Behavior*, *26*(3), 329–338. doi:10.1016/j.chb.2009.11.002

Stocker, C. M., & Youngblade, L. (1999). Marital conflict and parental hostility: Links with children's sibling and peer relationships. *Journal of Family Psychology*, *13*(4), 598–609. doi:10.1037/0893-3200.13.4.598

Stubbs, G., & Watkins, M. (1997). CBL: Assessing the student learning experience. *Proceedings of Frontiers in Education Conference, 1997. 27th Annual Conference. Teaching and Learning in an Era of Change, 2*.

Student News Daily. (2010). Conservative Vs. liberal beliefs. *Student News Daily*. Retrieved March 31, 2017 from https://www.studentnewsdaily.com/conservative-vs-liberal-beliefs/

Sukunesan, S. (1999). *Internet addiction: An exploratory study amongst Malaysian Internet user* (Master's thesis). University Putra, Malaysia.

Sule, N. (2016). *The digital technology masturbation syndrome. A new craze in Nigeria*. Ibadan: Bookraft.

Sum, S., Mathews, R. M., Hughes, I., & Campbell, A. (2008). Internet use and loneliness in older adults. *Cyberpsychology & Behavior*, *11*(2), 208–211. doi:10.1089/cpb.2007.0010 PMID:18422415

Su, W., Fang, X., Miller, J. K., & Wang, Y. (2011). Internet-Based Intervention for the Treatment of Online Addiction for College Students in China: A Pilot Study of the Healthy Online Self-Helping Center. *Cyberpsychology, Behavior, and Social Networking*, *14*(9), 497–503. doi:10.1089/cyber.2010.0167 PMID:21294635

Swartz, J. R., Hariri, A. R., & Williamson, D. E. (2017, February). An epigenetic mechanism links socioeconomic status to changes in depression-related brain function in high-risk adolescents. *Molecular Psychiatry*, *22*(2), 209–214. doi:10.1038/mp.2016.82 PMID:27217150

Swickert, R. J., Rosentreter, C. J., Hittner, J. B., & Mushrush, J. E. (2002). Extraversion, social support processes, and stress. *Personality and Individual Differences*, *32*(5), 877–891. doi:10.1016/S0191-8869(01)00093-9

Szablewicz, M. (2010). The ill effects of "opium for the spirit": A critical cultural analysis of China's Internet addiction moral panic. *Chinese Journal of Communication*, *3*(4), 453–470. doi:10.1080/17544750.2010.516579

Tahiroğlu, A. Y., Çelik, G. G., Fettahoğlu, Ç., Yildirim, V., Toros, F., Avci, A., ... Uzel, M. (2010). Psikiyatrik Bozukluğu Olan ve Olmayan Ergenlerde Problemli İnternet Kullanımı. *Archives of Neuropsychiatry/Noropsikiatri Arsivi, 47*(3), 241-246.

Tahiroglu, A. Y., Celik, G. G., Uzel, M., Ozcan, N., & Avci, A. (2008). Internet Use Among Turkish Adolescents. *Cyberpsychology & Behavior*, *11*(5), 537–543. doi:10.1089/cpb.2007.0165 PMID:18785800

Tait, R. J., Spijkerman, R., & Riper, H. (2013). Internet and computer based interventions for cannabis use: A meta-analysis. *Drug and Alcohol Dependence*, *133*(2), 295–304. doi:10.1016/j.drugalcdep.2013.05.012 PMID:23747236

Tam, P. G. (2016). Problematic Internet Use in Youth: An Outline and Overview for Health Professionals. *Australian Clinical Psychologist*, *2*(1), 20107.

Tang, C. S., & Koh, Y. Y. W. (2017). Online social networking addiction among college students in Singapore: Co-morbidity with behavioral addiction and affective disorder. *Asian Journal of Psychiatry*, *25*, 175–178. doi:10.1016/j.ajp.2016.10.027 PMID:28262144

Tang, J. H., Chen, M. C., Yang, C. Y., Chung, T. Y., & Lee, Y. A. (2016). Personality traits, interpersonal relationships, online social support, and Facebook addiction. *Telematics and Informatics*, *33*(1), 102–108. doi:10.1016/j.tele.2015.06.003

Tao, R., Huang, X., Wang, J., Zhang, H., Zhang, Y., & Li, M. (2010). Proposed diagnostic criteria for internet addiction. *Addiction (Abingdon, England)*, *105*(3), 556–564. doi:10.1111/j.1360-0443.2009.02828.x PMID:20403001

Tao, Z., Wu, G., & Wang, Z. (2016). The relationship between high residential density in student dormitories and anxiety, binge eating and Internet addiction: A study of Chinese college students. *SpringerPlus*, *5*(1), 1579–1587. doi:10.1186/s40064-016-3246-6 PMID:27652152

te Wildt, B. T., Putzig, I., Zedler, M., & Ohlmeier, M. D. (2007). Internet dependency as a symptom of depressive mood disorders. *Psychiatrische Praxis*, *34*, S318–S322. doi:10.1055/s-2007-970973 PMID:17786892

Teague, E., Simoncic, K., & Vargas, J. (2014). On the internet no one knows I am Introvert".Extraversion, Neuroticism and Internet Interaction. *Cyberpsychology & Behavior*, *5*(2), 125–128.

Tekinarslan, E. (2017). Relationship between Problematic Internet Use, Depression and Quality of Life Levels of Turkish University Students. *Journal of Education and Training Studies*, *5*(3), 167–175. doi:10.11114/jets.v5i3.2238

Telef, B. B. (2016). Investigating the relationship among internet addiction, positive and negative effects, and life satisfaction in Turkish adolescents. *International Journal of Progressive Education*, *12*(1), 128–135.

Teng, C. I. (2008). Personality Differences between Online Game Players and Nonplayers in a Student Sample. *Cyberpsychology & Behavior*, *11*(2), 232–234. doi:10.1089/cpb.2007.0064 PMID:18422420

Teong, K. Y., & Ang, M. C. H. (2016). Internet use and addiction among students in Malaysian public universities in east Malaysia: Some empirical evidence. *Journal of Management Research*, *8*(2), 31–47. doi:10.5296/jmr.v8i2.9092

Terracciano, A., & Costa, P. T. Jr. (2004). Smoking and the Five-Factor Model of personality. *Addiction (Abingdon, England)*, *99*(4), 472–481. doi:10.1111/j.1360-0443.2004.00687.x PMID:15049747

The Capital. (2016). Fad or faux pas? Nigerian celebrities strip nude to show baby bump. *The Capital*. Retrieved September 1, 2016 from http://www.thecapital.ng/?p=3184

Thomas, J. C. (2016). A humanistic approach to problematic online sexual behavior. *Journal of Humanistic Psychology*, *56*(1), 3–33. doi:10.1177/0022167814542286

Thomas, N. J., & Martin, F. H. (2010). Video – arcade game, computer game and Internet activities of Australian students: Participation habits and prevalence of addiction. *Australian Journal of Psychology*, *62*(2), 59–66. doi:10.1080/00049530902748283

Thompson, R. A. (2008). Early attachment and later development. In J. Cassidy & P. R. Shaver (Eds.), *Handbook of attachment: Theory, research, and clinical applications* (pp. 265–286). New York: Guilford.

Thorens, G., Achab, S., Billieux, J., Khazaal, Y., Khan, R., Pivin, E., & Zullino, D. et al. (2014). Characteristics and treatment response of self-identified problematic Internet users in a behavioral addiction outpatient clinic. *Journal of Behavioral Addictions*, *3*(1), 78–81. doi:10.1556/JBA.3.2014.008 PMID:25215217

Tilson, E. C., McBride, C. M., Lipkus, I. M., & Catalano, R. F. (2004). Testing the interaction between parent–child relationship factors and parent smoking to predict youth smoking. *The Journal of Adolescent Health*, *35*(3), 182–189. doi:10.1016/S1054-139X(03)00532-9 PMID:15313499

Titov, N., Andrews, G., Davies, M., McIntyre, K., Robinson, E., & Solley, K. (2010). Internet treatment for depression: A randomized controlled trial comparing clinician vs. technician assistance. *PLoS One*, *5*(6), e10939. doi:10.1371/journal.pone.0010939 PMID:20544030

Toda, M., Monden, K., Kubo, K., & Morimoto, K. (2006). Mobile phone dependence and health-related lifestyle of university students. *Social Behavior and Personality*, *34*(10), 1277–1284. doi:10.2224/sbp.2006.34.10.1277

Tokunaga, R. S. (2015). Perspectives on Internet addiction, problematic Internet use, and deficient self-regulation: Contributions of communication research. In E. L. Cohen (Ed.), *Communication Yearbook 30* (pp. 131–161). New York, NY: Routledge. doi:10.1080/23808985.2015.11679174

Tokunaga, R. S., & Rains, S. A. (2016). A Review and Meta-Analysis Examining Conceptual and Operational Definitions of Problematic Internet Use. *Human Communication Research*, *42*(2), 165–169. doi:10.1111/hcre.12075

Torikka, A., Kaltiala-Heino, R., Luukkaala, T., & Rimpelä, A. (2017). Trends in Alcohol Use among Adolescents from 2000 to 2011: The Role of Socioeconomic Status and Depression. *Alcohol and Alcoholism (Oxford, Oxfordshire)*, *52*(1), 95–103. doi:10.1093/alcalc/agw048 PMID:27507821

Torres-Villa, M. S. (1995). *Parenting styles, language and parents1 education as predictors of school achievement for Hispanic students* (Unpublished doctoral dissertation). Georgia State University, Atlanta, GA.

Tran, B. X., Huong, L. T., Hinh, N. D., Nguyen, L. H., Le, B. N., Nong, V. M., & Ho, R. C. M. et al. (2017). A study on the influence of Internet addiction and online interpersonal influences on health-related quality of life in young Vietnamese. *BMC Public Health*, *17*(1), 138. doi:10.1186/s12889-016-3983-z PMID:28143462

Tripp, L. M. (2011). 'The computer is not for you to be looking around, it is for schoolwork': Challenges for digital inclusion as Latino immigrant families negotiate children's access to the Internet. *New Media & Society*, *13*(4), 552–567. doi:10.1177/1461444810375293

Trojak, B., Zullino, D., & Achab, S. (2015). Brain stimulation to treat Internet addiction: A commentary. *Addictive Behaviors*. doi:10.1016/j.addbeh.2015.11.006 PMID:26632195

Tsai, C. C., & Lin, S. S. (2001). Analysis of attitudes toward computer networks and Internet addiction of Taiwanese adolescents. *Cyberpsychology & Behavior, 4*(3), 373–376. doi:10.1089/109493101300210277 PMID:11710262

Tsai, C. C., & Lin, S. S. (2003). Internet addiction of adolescents in Taiwan: An interview study. *Cyberpsychology & Behavior, 6*(6), 649–652. doi:10.1089/109493103322725432 PMID:14756931

Tsai, H. F., Cheng, S. H., Yeh, T. L., Shih, C. C., Chen, K. C., Yang, Y. C., & Yang, Y. K. (2009). The risk factors of Internet addiction—a survey of university freshmen. *Psychiatry Research, 167*(3), 294–299. doi:10.1016/j.psychres.2008.01.015 PMID:19395052

Tsitsika, A., Critselis, E., Louizou, A., Janikian, M., Freskou, A., Marangou, E., & Kafetzis, D. A. et al. (2011). Determinants of Internet addiction among adolescents: A case-control study. *The Scientific World Journal, 11*, 866–874. doi:10.1100/tsw.2011.85 PMID:21516283

Tsitsika, A., Janikian, M., Schoenmakers, T. M., Tzavela, E. C., Olafsson, K., Wójcik, S., & Richardson, C. et al. (2014). Internet addictive behavior in adolescence: A cross-sectional study in seven European countries. *Cyberpsychology, Behavior, and Social Networking, 17*(8), 528–535. doi:10.1089/cyber.2013.0382 PMID:24853789

Türkel, Y. D., & Tezer, E. (2008). Parenting styles and learned resourcefulness of Turkish adolescents. *Adolescence, 43*(169), 143. PMID:18447086

Turkish Statistical Institute (TSI). (2016). *Information and communication technology usage survey in households.* Retrieved January 13, 2017, from http://www.tuik.gov.tr

Turkle, S. (2012). *Connected, but alone? TED ideas worth spreading.* Retrieved from https://www.ted.com/talks/sherry_turkle_alone_together/transcript?language=en

Turner, N. E., Jain, U., Spence, W., & Zangeneh, M. (2008). Pathways to pathological gambling: Component analysis of variables related to pathological gambling. *International Gambling Studies, 8*(3), 281–298. doi:10.1080/14459790802405905

Twenge, J. M., & Campbell, W. K. (2002). Self-esteem and socioeconomic status: A meta-analytic review. *Personality and Social Psychology Review, 6*(1), 59–71. doi:10.1207/S15327957PSPR0601_3

Uddin, M. S., Mamum, A. A., Iqbal, M. A., Nasrullah, M., Asaduzzaman, M., Sarwar, M. S., & Amran, M. S. (2016). Internet addiction disorder and its pathogenicity to psychological distress and depression among university students: A cross-sectional pilot study in Bangladesh. *Psychology (Irvine, Calif.), 7*(08), 1126–1137. doi:10.4236/psych.2016.78113

Uduma, U. (2013). Youth and the internet: The dangers and the benefits. *Leadership Newspaper, 16*(June), 23–24.

Üneri, O. S., & Tanıdır, C. (2011). Bir grup lise öğrencisinde internet bağımlılığı değerlendirmesi: Kesitsel bir çalışma [Evaluation of Internet addiction in a group of high school students: a cross-sectional study]. *Dusunen Adam The Journal of Psychiatry and Neurological Sciences, 24*(4), 265–272.

Vaknin, S. (2003). *Malignant self-love: Narcissism revisited.* Prague: Narcissus Publications.

Valcke, M., Bonte, S., De Wever, B., & Rots, I. (2010). Internet parenting styles and the impact on Internet use of primary school children. *Computers & Education, 55*(2), 454–464. doi:10.1016/j.compedu.2010.02.009

Valcke, M., Schellens, T., Van Keer, H., & Gerarts, M. (2007). Primary school children's safe and unsafe use of the Internet at home and at school: An exploratory study. *Computers in Human Behavior, 23*(6), 2838–2850. doi:10.1016/j.chb.2006.05.008

Valentine, G., & Holloway, S. (2001). On-line Dangers? Geographies of Parents' Fears for Children's Safety in Cyberspace. *The Professional Geographer, 53*(1), 71–83.

Valkenburg, P. (2002). *Beeldschermkinderen: Theorieën over kind en media* [Screen-kids: Theories 670 about children and media]. Amsterdam: Boom.

Valkenburg, P. M., Krcmar, M., Peeters, A. L., & Marseille, N. M. (1999). Developing a scale to assess three styles of television mediation: "Instructive mediation," "restrictive mediation," and "social coviewing". *Journal of Broadcasting & Electronic Media*, *43*(1), 52–66. doi:10.1080/08838159909364474

Valkenburg, P. M., & Peter, J. (2007). Online communication and adolescent well-being: Testing the stimulation versus the displacement hypothesis. *Journal of Computer-Mediated Communication*, *12*(4), 1169–1182. doi:10.1111/j.1083-6101.2007.00368.x

Valkenburg, P. M., & Peter, J. (2011). Online communication among adolescents: An integrated model of its attraction, opportunities, and risks. *The Journal of Adolescent Health*, *48*(2), 121–127. doi:10.1016/j.jadohealth.2010.08.020 PMID:21257109

Van de Haar, E. (2015). The meaning of "liberalism". *Liberaliam.org*. Retrieved March 31, 2017 from https://www.libertarianism.org/publications/essays/lets-clear-liberal-mess

van den Eijnden, R. J., Meerkerk, G. J., Vermulst, A. A., Spijkerman, R., & Engels, R. C. (2008). Online communication, compulsive Internet use, and psychosocial well-being among adolescents: A longitudinal study. *Developmental Psychology*, *44*(3), 655–665. doi:10.1037/0012-1649.44.3.655 PMID:18473634

Van Den Eijnden, R. J., Spijkerman, R., Vermulst, A. A., van Rooij, T. J., & Engels, R. C. (2010). Compulsive Internet use among adolescents: Bidirectional parent–child relationships. *Journal of Abnormal Child Psychology*, *38*(1), 77–89. doi:10.1007/s10802-009-9347-8 PMID:19728076

Van der Aa, N., Overbeek, G., Engels, R. C., Scholte, R. H., Meerkerk, G. J., & Van den Eijnden, R. J. (2009). Daily and compulsive internet use and well-being in adolescence: A diathesis-stress model based on big five personality traits. *Journal of Youth and Adolescence*, *38*(6), 765–776. doi:10.1007/s10964-008-9298-3 PMID:19636779

Van Der Vorst, H., Engels, R. C., Meeus, W., Deković, M., & Van Leeuwe, J. (2005). The role of alcohol-specific socialization in adolescents' drinking behaviour. *Addiction (Abingdon, England)*, *100*(10), 1464–1476. doi:10.1111/j.1360-0443.2005.01193.x PMID:16185208

Van Rooij, A., & Prause, N. (2014). A critical review of "Internet addiction" criteria with suggestions for the future. *Journal of Behavioral Addictions*, *3*(4), 203–213. doi:10.1556/JBA.3.2014.4.1 PMID:25592305

Van Rooij, T., & Van den Eijnden, R. J. J. M. (2007). *Monitor Internet en Jongeren 2006 en 2007: Ontwikkelingen in Internetgebruik en de rol van opvoeding*. Rotterdam: IVO.

Vandermaas-Peeler, M., Way, E., & Umpleby, J. (2003). Parental guidance in a cooking activity with preschoolers. *Journal of Applied Developmental Psychology*, *24*(1), 75–89. doi:10.1016/S0193-3973(03)00025-X

Vanlanduyt, L., & De Cleyn, I. (2007). *Invloed van Internet bij jongeren: een uitdaging op school en thuis*. Academic Press.

Vats, M. (2015). Selfie syndrome: An infectious gift of IT to health care. *Journal of Lung. Pulmonary & Respiratory Rees*, *2*(4), 48–49.

Villella, C., Martinotti, G., Di Nicola, M., Cassano, M., La Torre, G., Gliubizzi, M. D., & Conte, G. et al. (2011). Behavioural addictions in adolescents and young adults: Results from a prevalence study. *Journal of Gambling Studies*, *27*(2), 203–214. doi:10.1007/s10899-010-9206-0 PMID:20559694

Vondráčková, P., & Gabrhelík, R. (2016). Prevention of Internet addiction: A systematic review. *Journal of Behavioral Addictions*, *5*(4), 568–579. doi:10.1556/2006.5.2016.085 PMID:27998173

Waldo, A. (2014). Correlates of Internet addiction among adolescents. *Psychology (Irvine, Calif.)*, *5*(18), 1999–2008. doi:10.4236/psych.2014.518203

Walker, L. (2017). What Is Social Networking Addiction? *About.com Guide*. Retrieved from: https://www.lifewire.com/what-is-social-networking-addiction-2655246

Wallace, J. D. (1999). *Nameless in cyberspace: Anonymity on the Internet*. Cato Institute.

Walrave, M., Lenaerts, S., & De Moor, S. (2008). *Cyberteens@ risk? Tieners verknocht aan Internet, maar ook waakzaam voor risico's*. Academic Press.

Wambu, O. (2015). Tradition versus modernity. *New African Magazine*. Retrieved August 30, 2016, from http://newafricanmagazine.com/tradition-versus-modernity/

Wang, C. W., Ho, R. T., Chan, C. L., & Tse, S. (2015). Exploring personality characteristics of Chinese adolescents with internet-related addictive behaviors: Trait differences for gaming addiction and social networking addiction. *Addictive Behaviors*, *42*, 32–35. doi:10.1016/j.addbeh.2014.10.039 PMID:25462651

Wang, H., Zhou, X., Lu, C., Wu, J., Deng, X., & Hong, L. (2011). Problematic Internet use in high school students in Guangdong Province, China. *PLoS One*, *6*(5), e19660. doi:10.1371/journal.pone.0019660 PMID:21573073

Wang, L., Luo, J., Bai, Y., Kong, J., Luo, J., Gao, W., & Sun, X. (2013). Internet addiction of adolescents in China: Prevalence, predictors, and association with well-being. *Addiction Research and Theory*, *21*(1), 62–69. doi:10.3109/16066359.2012.690053

Wang, R., Bianchi, S. M., & Raley, S. B. (2005). Teenagers' Internet use and family rules: A research note. *Journal of Marriage and the Family*, *67*(5), 1249–1258. doi:10.1111/j.1741-3737.2005.00214.x

Wang, W. (2001). Internet dependency and psychosocial maturity among college students. *Human-Computer Studies*, *55*(6), 919–938. doi:10.1006/ijhc.2001.0510

Wang, Y., Wu, A. M. S., & Lau, J. T. F. (2016). The health belief model and number of peers with Internet addiction as interrelated factors of Internet addiction among secondary school students in Hong Kong. *BMC Public Health*, *16*(1), 272–285. doi:10.1186/s12889-016-2947-7 PMID:26983882

Warmerdam, L., Riper, H., Klein, M. C., van de Ven, P., Rocha, A., Henriques, M. R., & Cuijpers, P. et al. (2012). Innovative ICT solutions to improve treatment outcomes for depression: The ICT4Depression project. *Annual Review of Cybertherapy and Telemedicine*, *181*(1), 339–343. PMID:22954884

Wartberg, L., Kammerl, R., Bröning, S., Hauenschild, M., Petersen, K. U., & Thomasius, R. (2015). Gender-related consequences of Internet use perceived by parents in a representative quota sample of adolescents. *Behaviour & Information Technology*, *34*(4), 341–348. doi:10.1080/0144929X.2014.928746

Wartberg, L., Kriston, L., Kammerl, R., Petersen, K. U., & Thomasius, R. (2015). Prevalence of pathological Internet use in a representative German sample of adolescents: Results of a latent profile analysis. *Psychopathology*, *48*(1), 25–30. doi:10.1159/000365095 PMID:25342152

Wartberg, L., Petersen, K.-U., Kammerl, R., Rosenkranz, M., & Thomasius, R. (2014). Psychometric validation of a German version of the compulsive Internet use scale. *Cyberpsychology, Behavior, and Social Networking*, *17*(2), 99–103. doi:10.1089/cyber.2012.0689 PMID:23988182

Wästlund, E., Norlander, T., & Archer, T. (2001). Internet blues revisited: Replication and extension of an Internet paradox study. *Cyberpsychology & Behavior*, *4*(3), 385–391. doi:10.1089/109493101300210295 PMID:11710264

Watson, J. C. (2015). Internet addiction. *Treatment Strategies for Substance Abuse and Process Addictions*, 293.

Watters, C. A., Keefer, K. V., Kloosterman, P. H., Summerfeldt, L. J., & Parker, J. D. (2013). Examining the structure of the Internet Addiction Test in adolescents: A bifactor approach. *Computers in Human Behavior*, *29*(6), 2294–2302. doi:10.1016/j.chb.2013.05.020

Waude, A. (2016). Psychodynamic approach. *Psychologist World*. Retrieved from https://www.psychologistworld.com/freud/psychodynamic-approach

We Are Social, S. R. L. (2017). *Digital in 2017: In Italia e nel mondo*. Retrieved March 21, 2017, from http://wearesocial.com/it/blog/2017/01/digital-in-2017-in-italia-e-nel-mondo

Weinstein, A., Dorani, D., Elhadif, R., Bukovza, Y., & Yarmulnik, A. (2015). Internet addiction is associated with social anxiety in young adults. *Annals of Clinical Psychiatry*, *27*(1), 4–9. PMID:25696775

Weinstein, A., Feder, L. C., Rosenberg, K. P., & Dannon, P. (2014). Internet addiction disorder: Overview and Controversies. In K. P. Rosenberg & L. C. Feder (Eds.), *Behavioral addictions criteria, evidence, and treatment* (pp. 99–117). Waltham, MA: Elserier, Inc. doi:10.1016/B978-0-12-407724-9.00005-7

Weinstein, A., & Lejoyeux, M. (2010). Internet addiction or excessive Internet use. *The American Journal of Drug and Alcohol Abuse*, *36*(5), 277–283. doi:10.3109/00952990.2010.491880 PMID:20545603

Weiser, E. B. (2000). Gender differences in Internet use patterns and Internet application preferences: A two-sample comparison. *Cyberpsychology & Behavior*, *3*(2), 167–178. doi:10.1089/109493100316012

Weiss, R. S. (1973). *Loneliness: The experience of emotional and social isolation*. Cambridge, MA: MIT Press.

Welte, J. W., Barnes, G. M., Tidwell, M.-C. O., & Wieczorek, W. F. (2017). Predictors of Problem Gambling in the U.S. *Journal of Gambling Studies*, *33*(2), 327–342. doi:10.1007/s10899-016-9639-1 PMID:27557549

Whang, L. S. M., Lee, S., & Chang, G. (2003). Internet over-users' psychological profiles: A behavior sampling analysis on Internet addiction. *Cyberpsychology & Behavior*, *6*(2), 143–150. doi:10.1089/109493103321640338 PMID:12804026

Widyanto, L., & Griffiths, M. D. (2009). Unravelling the web: adolescents and Internet addiction. *Adolescent online social communication and behavior: Relationship formation on the Internet*, 29-49.

Widyanto, L., & Griffiths, M. (2006). 'Internet addiction': A critical review. *International Journal of Mental Health and Addiction*, *4*(1), 31–51. doi:10.1007/s11469-006-9009-9

Widyanto, L., & Griffiths, M. (2007). Internet addiction: Does it really exist? (revisited). In J. Gackenbach (Ed.), *Psychology and the Internet: Intrapersonal, interpersonal, and transpersonal implications* (2nd ed.; pp. 141–163). San Diego, CA: Academic Press. doi:10.1016/B978-012369425-6/50025-4

Widyanto, L., Griffiths, M. D., & Brunsden, V. (2011). A psychometric comparison of the Internet Addiction Test, the Internet-Related Problem Scale, and self-diagnosis. *Cyberpsychology, Behavior, and Social Networking*, *14*(3), 141–149. doi:10.1089/cyber.2010.0151 PMID:21067282

Widyanto, L., Griffiths, M., Brunsden, V., & McMurran, M. (2008). The psychometric properties of the Internet related problem scale: A pilot study. *International Journal of Mental Health and Addiction*, *6*(2), 205–213. doi:10.1007/s11469-007-9120-6

Wiederhold, B. K. (2017). Beyond direct benefits: Indirect health benefits of social media use. *Cyberpsychology, Behavior, and Social Networking, 20*(1), 1–2. doi:10.1089/cyber.2016.29059.bkw PMID:28080148

Williams, J. M., Teasdale, J. D., Segal, Z. V., & Soulsby, J. (2000). Mindfulness-based cognitive therapy reduces over general autobiographical memory in formerly depressed patients. *Journal of Abnormal Psychology, 109*(1), 150–155. doi:10.1037/0021-843X.109.1.150 PMID:10740947

Willoughby, T. (2008). A short-term longitudinal study of Internet and computer game use by adolescent boys and girls: Prevalence, frequency of use, and psychosocial predictors. *Developmental Psychology, 44*(1), 195–204. doi:10.1037/0012-1649.44.1.195 PMID:18194017

Wingo, A. P., Wrenn, G., Pelletier, T., Gutman, A. R., Bradley, B., & Ressler, K. J. (2010). Moderating effects of resilience on depression in individuals with a history of childhood abuse or trauma exposure. *Journal of Affective Disorders, 126*(3), 411–414. doi:10.1016/j.jad.2010.04.009 PMID:20488545

Winkler, A., & Dörsing, B. (2011). *Treatment of Internet addiction disorder: a first meta-analysis* (Diploma thesis). Marburg: University of Marburg.

Winkler, A., Dörsing, B., Rief, W., Shen, Y., & Glombiewski, J. A. (2013). Treatment of Internet addiction: A meta-analysis. *Clinical Psychology Review, 33*(2), 317–329. doi:10.1016/j.cpr.2012.12.005 PMID:23354007

Wu, Y.C.J., Chang, W.H., & Yuan, C.H. (2015). Do facebook profile pictures reflect user's personality? *Computers in Human Behavior, 51*(Part B), 880–889.

Wu, C. H., & Cheng, F. F. (2007). Internet Café Addiction of Taiwanese Adolescents. *Cyberpsychology & Behavior, 10*(2), 220–225. doi:10.1089/cpb.2006.9965 PMID:17474839

Wu, C. S. T., Wong, H. T., Yu, K. F., Fok, K. W., Yeung, S. M., Lam, C. H., & Liu, K. M. (2016). Parenting approaches, family functionality, and internet addiction among Hong Kong adolescents. *BMC Pediatrics, 16*(1), 130. doi:10.1186/s12887-016-0666-y PMID:27538688

Wu, C. Y., Lee, M. B., Liao, S. C., & Chang, L. R. (2015). Risk factors of Internet addiction among Internet users: An online questionnaire survey. *PLoS One, 10*(10), e0137506. doi:10.1371/journal.pone.0137506 PMID:26462196

Wu, J. Y. W., Ko, H. C., & Lane, H. Y. (2016). Personality disorders in female and male college students with internet addiction. *The Journal of Nervous and Mental Disease, 204*(3), 221–225. doi:10.1097/NMD.0000000000000452 PMID:26731123

Wu, J. Y. W., Ko, H. C., Tung, Y. Y., & Li, C. C. (2016). Internet use expectancy for tension reduction and disinhibition mediates the relationship between borderline personality disorder features and Internet addiction among college students–One-year follow-up. *Computers in Human Behavior, 55*, 851–855. doi:10.1016/j.chb.2015.09.047

Wu, X. S., Zhang, Z. H., Zhao, F., Wang, W. J., Li, Y. F., Bi, L., & Sun, Y. H. et al. (2016). Prevalence of Internet addiction and its association with social support and other related factors among adolescents in China. *Journal of Adolescence, 52*, 103–111. doi:10.1016/j.adolescence.2016.07.012 PMID:27544491

Xiong, Z. B., Detzner, D. F., & Cleveland, M. J. (2005). Southeast Asian adolescents' perceptions of immigrant parenting practices. *Hmong Studies Journal, 5*, 1–20. Retrieved from http://hmongstudies. com/XiongDetznerClevelandHSJ5. pdf

Xiuqin, H., Huimin, Z., Mengchen, L., Jinan, W., Ying, Z., & Ran, T. (2010). Mental health, personality, and parental rearing styles of adolescents with Internet addiction disorder. *Cyberpsychology, Behavior, and Social Networking, 13*(4), 401–406. doi:10.1089/cyber.2009.0222 PMID:20712498

Xu, J., Shen, L. X., Yan, C. H., Hu, H., Yang, F., Wang, L., & Ouyang, F. X. et al. (2012). Personal characteristics related to the risk of adolescent Internet addiction: A survey in Shanghai, China. *BMC Public Health*, *12*(1), 1106–1116. doi:10.1186/1471-2458-12-1106 PMID:23259906

Xu, J., Shen, L.-X., Yan, C.-H., Hu, H., Yang, F., Wang, L., & Shen, X.-M. et al. (2014). Parent-adolescent interaction and risk of adolescent internet addiction: A population-based study in Shanghai. *BMC Psychiatry*, *14*(1), 112. doi:10.1186/1471-244X-14-112 PMID:24731648

Xu, Z., Turel, O., & Yuan, Y. (2012). Online game addiction among adolescents: Motivation and prevention factors. *European Journal of Information Systems*, *21*(3), 321–340. doi:10.1057/ejis.2011.56

Yadav, P., Banwari, G., Parmar, C., & Maniar, R. (2013). Internet addiction and its correlates among high school students: A preliminary study from Ahmedabad, India. *Asian Journal of Psychiatry*, *6*(6), 500–505. doi:10.1016/j.ajp.2013.06.004 PMID:24309861

Yang, C. K. (2001). Sociopsychiatric characteristics of adolescents who use computers to excess. *Acta Psychiatrica Scandinavica*, *104*(3), 217–222. doi:10.1034/j.1600-0447.2001.00197.x PMID:11531659

Yang, C. K., Choe, B. M., Baity, M., Lee, J.-H., & Cho, J.-S. (2005). SCL-90-R and 16PF profiles of senior high school students with excessive internet use. *Canadian Journal of Psychiatry*, *50*(7), 407–414. doi:10.1177/070674370505000704 PMID:16086538

Yang, C. Y., Sato, T., Yamawaki, N., & Miyata, M. (2013). Prevalence and risk factors of problematic Internet use: A cross-national comparison of Japanese and Chinese university students. *Transcultural Psychiatry*, *50*(2), 263–279. doi:10.1177/1363461513488876 PMID:23660582

Yang, L., Sun, L., Zhang, Z., Sun, Y., Wu, H., & Ye, D. (2014). Internet addiction, adolescent depression, and the mediating role of life events: Finding from a sample of Chinese adolescents. *International Journal of Psychology*, *49*(5), 342–347. doi:10.1002/ijop.12063 PMID:25178955

Yang, S. C., & Tung, C. J. (2007). Comparison of Internet addicts and non-addicts in Taiwanese high school. *Computers in Human Behavior*, *23*(1), 79–96. doi:10.1016/j.chb.2004.03.037

Yang, X., Zhu, L., Chen, Q., Song, P., & Wang, Z. (2016). Parent marital conflict and Internet addiction among Chinese college students: The mediating role of father-child, mother-child, and peer attachment. *Computers in Human Behavior*, *59*, 221–229. doi:10.1016/j.chb.2016.01.041

Yan, W., Li, Y., & Sui, N. (2014). The relationship between recent stressful life events, personality traits, perceived family functioning and Internet addiction among college students. *Stress and Health*, *30*(1), 3–11. doi:10.1002/smi.2490 PMID:23616371

Yao, B., Han, W., Zeng, L., & Guo, X. (2013). Freshman year mental health symptoms and level of adaptation as predictors of Internet addiction: A retrospective nested case-control study of male Chinese college students. *Psychiatry Research*, *210*(2), 541–547. doi:10.1016/j.psychres.2013.07.023 PMID:23896352

Yao, M. Z., He, J., Ko, D. M., & Pang, K. (2014). The influence of personality, parental behaviors, and self-esteem on Internet addiction: A study of Chinese college students. *Cyberpsychology, Behavior, and Social Networking*, *17*(2), 104–110. doi:10.1089/cyber.2012.0710 PMID:24003966

Yao, M. Z., & Zhong, Z.-J. (2014). Loneliness, social contacts and Internet addiction: A cross-lagged panel study. *Computers in Human Behavior*, *30*, 164–170. doi:10.1016/j.chb.2013.08.007

Yaparel, R. (1984). *The relationship between perceptions of success and failure in social relations and loneliness* (Unpublished master's thesis). Hacettepe University, Ankara, Turkey.

Yates, T. M., Gregor, M. A., & Haviland, M. G. (2012). Child maltreatment, alexithymia, and problematic internet use in young adulthood. *Cyberpsychology, Behavior, and Social Networking*, *15*(4), 219–225. doi:10.1089/cyber.2011.0427 PMID:22313343

Yayan, E. H., Arikan, D., & Saban, F., N. G. B., & Özcan, Ö. (2016). Examination of the correlation between Internet addiction and social phobia in adolescents. *Western Journal of Nursing Research*, 1–15. doi:10.1177/0193945916665820 PMID:27561297

Yee, N. (2006). Motivations for play in online games. *Cyberpsychology & Behavior*, *9*(6), 772–775. doi:10.1089/cpb.2006.9.772 PMID:17201605

Yeh, Y. C., Ko, H. C., Wu, J. Y. W., & Cheng, C. P. (2008). Gender Differences in Relationships of Actual and Virtual Social Support to Internet Addiction Mediated through Depressive Symptoms among College Students in Taiwan. *Cyberpsychology & Behavior*, *11*(4), 485–487. doi:10.1089/cpb.2007.0134 PMID:18721099

Yellowlees, P. M., & Marks, S. (2007). Problematic Internet use or Internet addiction? *Computers in Human Behavior*, *23*(3), 1447–1453. doi:10.1016/j.chb.2005.05.004

Yen, J.Y., Yen, C.F., Cheng, C.P., Tang, Y.P., & Ko, C.H. (2009). The Association between Adult ADHD Symptoms and Internet Addiction among College Students: The Gender Difference. *Cyberpsychology & Behavior: The Impact of the Internet, Multimedia and Virtual Reality on Behavior and Society, 12*(2), 187-191.

Yen, C. F., Ko, C. H., Yen, J. Y., Chang, Y. P., & Cheng, C. P. (2009). Multi-dimensional discriminative factors for Internet addiction among adolescents regarding gender and age. *Psychiatry and Clinical Neurosciences*, *63*(3), 357–364. doi:10.1111/j.1440-1819.2009.01969.x PMID:19566768

Yen, C.-F., Chou, W.-J., Liu, T.-L., Yang, P., & Hu, H.-F. (2014). The association of Internet addiction symptoms with anxiety, depression and self-esteem among adolescents with attention-deficit/hyperactivity disorder. *Comprehensive Psychiatry*, *55*(7), 1601–1608. doi:10.1016/j.comppsych.2014.05.025 PMID:25015304

Yen, J. Y., Ko, C. H., Yen, C. F., Wu, H. Y., & Yang, M. J. (2007). The comorbid psychiatric symptoms of Internet addiction: Attention deficit and hyperactivity disorder (ADHD), depression, social phobia, and hostility. *The Journal of Adolescent Health*, *41*(1), 93–98. doi:10.1016/j.jadohealth.2007.02.002 PMID:17577539

Yen, J. Y., Yen, C. F., Chen, C. C., Chen, S. H., & Ko, C. H. (2007). Family factors of internet addiction and substance use experience in Taiwanese adolescents. *Cyberpsychology & Behavior*, *10*(3), 323–329. doi:10.1089/cpb.2006.9948 PMID:17594255

Yen, J. Y., Yen, C. F., Chen, C. S., Tang, T. C., & Ko, C. H. (2009). The association between adult ADHD symptoms and internet addiction among college students: The gender difference. *Cyberpsychology & Behavior*, *12*(2), 187–191. doi:10.1089/cpb.2008.0113 PMID:19072077

Yoo, H. J., Cho, S. C., Ha, J., Yune, S. K., Kim, S. J., Hwang, J., & Lyoo, I. K. et al. (2004). Attention deficit hyperactivity symptoms and internet addiction. *Psychiatry and Clinical Neurosciences*, *58*(5), 487–494. doi:10.1111/j.1440-1819.2004.01290.x PMID:15482579

You, H. S. (2007). *The effect of Internet addiction on elementary school student's self-esteem and depression* (Unpublished master's thesis). Kongju University, Chungnam.

Young, K. S. (1996). *Internet addiction: The emergence of a new clinical disorder.* Poster presented at the 104th American Psychological Association Annual Convention, Toronto, Canada.

Young, K. S. (1999). Internet addiction: symptoms, evaluation and treatment. *Innovations in Clinical Practice: A Source Book, 17,* 19-31.

Young, K. S. (1999). *Internet addiction: Symptoms, evaluation and treatment.* Retrieved January 14, 2017, from http://netaddiction.com/articles/symptoms.pdf

Young, K. S. (1999). Internet addiction: Symptoms, evaluation, and treatment. *Innovations in Clinical Practice: A Source Book, 17,* 19-31.

Young, K. S., & Rodgers, R. C. (1998, April). Internet addiction: Personality traits associated with its development. *69th annual meeting of the Eastern Psychological Association*, 40-50.

Young, K. S., & Rodgers, R. C. (1998, April). *Internet addiction: personality traits associated with its development.* Paper presented at the 69th annual meeting of the Eastern Psychological Association, Boston, MA.

Young, K. S., Yue, X. D., & Ying, L. (2011). Prevalence estimates and etiologic models of Internet addiction. *Internet Addiction: A Handbook and Guide to Evaluation and Treatment*, 3-17.

Young, K.S., & de Abreu. (2011). Closing thoughts and future implications. In K.S. Young (Ed.), *Internet addiction: A handbook and guide to evaluation and treatment* (pp. 267-273). Hoboken, NJ: John Wiley & Sons, Inc.

Young, J. E. (1982). Loneliness, depression and cognitive therapy. In L. A. Peplau & D. Perlman (Eds.), *Loneliness: A sourcebook of current theory, research, and therapy* (pp. 379–406). New York: Wiley.

Young, K. (1996). Psychology of computer use. Addictive use of the Internet: A case that breaks the stereotype. *Psychological Reports*, *79*(3), 899–902. doi:10.2466/pr0.1996.79.3.899 PMID:8969098

Young, K. (2010). Internet addiction over the decade: A personal look back. *World Psychiatry; Official Journal of the World Psychiatric Association (WPA)*, *9*(2), 91–91. doi:10.1002/j.2051-5545.2010.tb00279.x PMID:20671891

Young, K. (2015). The evolution of Internet addiction disorder. In C. Montag & M. Reuter (Eds.), *Internet addiction: Neuroscientific approaches and therapeutical interventions* (pp. 3–17). New York, NY: Springer International Publishing.

Young, K. S. (1998). *Caught in the net. How to recognize signs of Internet addiction and a winning strategy for recovery.* Wiley.

Young, K. S. (1998). *Caught in the Net.* New York, NY: John Wiley & Sons.

Young, K. S. (1998). Internet addiction: The emergence of a new clinical disorder. *Cyberpsychology & Behavior*, *1*(3), 237–244. doi:10.1089/cpb.1998.1.237

Young, K. S. (1998a). *Caught in the net: How to recognize the signs of internet addiction--and a winning strategy for recovery.* Wiley.

Young, K. S. (1999). Internet addiction: Symptoms, evaluation, and treatment. In L. VandeCreek & T. L. Jackson (Eds.), *Innovations in clinical practice* (Vol. 17). Sarasota, FL: Professional Resource Press. Retrieved from http://netaddiction.com/articles/symptoms.pdf

Young, K. S. (1999). The research and controversy surrounding Internet addiction. *Cyberpsychology & Behavior*, *2*(5), 381–383. doi:10.1089/cpb.1999.2.381 PMID:19178209

Young, K. S. (2004). Internet addiction: A new clinical phenomenon and its consequences. *The American Behavioral Scientist, 48*(4), 402–415. doi:10.1177/0002764204270278

Young, K. S. (2007). Cognitive behavior therapy with Internet addicts: Treatment outcomes and implications. *Cyberpsychology & Behavior, 10*(5), 671–679. doi:10.1089/cpb.2007.9971 PMID:17927535

Young, K. S. (2008). Internet Sex Addiction: Risk Factors, Stages of Development, and treatment. *The American Behavioral Scientist, 52*(1), 21–37. doi:10.1177/0002764208321339

Young, K. S. (2011). Clinical assessment of Internet-addicted clients. In K. S. Young (Ed.), *Internet addiction: A handbook and guide to evaluation and treatment* (pp. 19–34). Hoboken, NJ: John Wiley & Sons, Inc.

Young, K. S., & Case, C. J. (2004). Internet abuse in the workplace: New trends in risk management. *Cyberpsychology & Behavior, 7*(1), 105–111. doi:10.1089/109493104322820174 PMID:15006175

Young, K. S., & De Abreu, C. N. (2010). *Internet addiction: A handbook and guide to evaluation and treatment*. New York, NY: John Wiley & Sons.

Young, K. S., Pistner, M., O'Mara, J., & Buchanan, J. (1999). Cyber disorders: The mental health concern for the new millennium. *Cyberpsychology & Behavior, 2*(5), 475–479. doi:10.1089/cpb.1999.2.475 PMID:19178220

Young, K. S., & Rogers, R. C. (1998). The relationship between depression and Internet addiction. *Cyberpsychology & Behavior, 1*(1), 25–28. doi:10.1089/cpb.1998.1.25

Young, K. S., Yue, X. D., & Ying, L. (2011). Prevalence estimates and etiologic models of Internet addiction. In K. S. Young & C. N. de Abreu (Eds.), *Internet addiction: A handbook and guide to evaluation and treatment* (pp. 3–18). Hoboken, NJ: John Wiley & Sons.

Yu, J. (2003). The association between parental alcohol-related behaviors and children's drinking. *Drug and Alcohol Dependence, 69*(3), 253–262. doi:10.1016/S0376-8716(02)00324-1 PMID:12633911

Yu, L., & Shek, D. T. (2014). Family functioning, positive youth development, and Internet addiction in junior secondary school students: Structural equation modeling using AMOS. *International Journal on Disability and Human Development, 13*(2), 227–238. doi:10.1515/ijdhd-2014-0308

Yu, L., & Shek, D. T. L. (2013). Internet addiction in Hong Kong adolescents: A three-year longitudinal study. *Journal of Pediatric and Adolescent Gynecology, 26*(3SUPPL), S10–S17. doi:10.1016/j.jpag.2013.03.010 PMID:23683821

Yu, Q., Zhang, L., Wu, S., Guo, Y., Jin, S., & Sun, Y. (2017). The influence of juvenile preference for online social interaction on problematic Internet use: The moderating effect of sibling condition and the moderated moderating effect of age cohort. *Computers in Human Behavior, 68*, 345–351. doi:10.1016/j.chb.2016.11.026

Yu, T. K., & Chao, C. M. (2016). Internet misconduct impact adolescent mental health in Taiwan: The moderating roles of Internet addiction. *International Journal of Mental Health and Addiction, 14*(6), 921–936. doi:10.1007/s11469-016-9641-y

Zadra, S., Bischof, G., Besser, B., Bischof, A., Meyer, C., John, U., & Rumpf, H.-J. (2016). The association between Internet addiction and personality disorders in a general population-based sample. *Journal of Behavioral Addictions, 5*(4), 691–699. doi:10.1556/2006.5.2016.086 PMID:28005417

Zafar, S. N. (2016). Internet Addiction or Problematic Internet Use: Current Issues and Challenges in Conceptualization, Measurement and Treatment. *Journal of Islamic International Medical College, 11*(2), 46–47.

Zec, G. (2005). *Faktorska struktura instrumenata Online Cognition Scale i predviđanje patološkog korištenja interneta* (Unpublished Diploma thesis). Filozofski fakultet u Zagrebu, Zagreb, Croatia.

Zeitzoff, T., Kelly, J., & Lotan, G. (2015). Using social media to measure foreign policy dynamics: An empirical analysis of the Iranian–Israeli confrontation (2012–13). *Journal of Peace Research, 52*(3), 368–383. doi:10.1177/0022343314558700

Zhang, Liu, Q. X., Deng, L. Y., Fang, X. Y., Liu, C. Y., & Lan, J. (2011). Parents-adolescents relations and adolescent's Internet addiction: the mediation effect of loneliness. *Psychological Development and Education, 6,* 641-64.

Zhang, Z. H., Yang, L. S., Hao, J. H., Huang, F., Zhang, X. J., & Sun, Y. H. (2012). Relationship of childhood physical abuse and Internet addiction disorder in adolescence: The mediating role of self-esteem. *Zhonghua liu xing bing xue za zhi= Zhonghua liuxingbingxue zazhi, 33*(1), 50-53.

Zhang, H., Li, D., & Li, X. (2015). Temperament and problematic Internet use in adolescents: A moderated mediation model of maladaptive cognition and parenting styles. *Journal of Child and Family Studies, 24*(7), 1886–1897. doi:10.1007/s10826-014-9990-8

Zhang, H., Spinrad, T. L., Eisenberg, N., Luo, Y., & Wang, Z. (2017). Young adults' Internet addiction: Prediction by the interaction of parental marital conflict and respiratory sinus arrhythmia. *International Journal of Psychophysiology, 120*, 148–156. doi:10.1016/j.ijpsycho.2017.08.002 PMID:28800963

Zhang, L., Amos, C., & McDowell, W. C. (2008). A Comparative Study of Internet Addiction between the United States and China. *Cyberpsychology & Behavior, 11*(6), 727–729. doi:10.1089/cpb.2008.0026 PMID:18991530

Zhao, F., Zhang, Z. H., Bi, L., Wu, X. S., Wang, W. J., Li, Y. F., & Sun, Y. H. (2017). The association between life events and Internet addiction among Chinese vocational school students: The mediating role of depression. *Computers in Human Behavior, 70*, 30–38. doi:10.1016/j.chb.2016.12.057

Zhu, Y., Zhang, H., & Tian, M. (2015). Molecular and functional imaging of Internet addiction. *BioMed Research International*. PMID:25879023

Zilman, D. (2000). Influence of unrestrained access to erotica on adolescents' and young adults' dispositions toward sexuality. *The Journal of Adolescent Health, 27*(2), 41–44. doi:10.1016/S1054-139X(00)00137-3 PMID:10904205

Zimmer-Gembeck, M. J., & Locke, E. M. (2007). The socialization of adolescent coping behaviours: Relationships with families and teachers. *Journal of Adolescence, 30*(1), 1–16. doi:10.1016/j.adolescence.2005.03.001 PMID:16837040

Zuckerberg, M. (2017, February 1). *Facebook community update*. Retrieved from https://www.facebook.com/photo.php?fbid=10103472646530311&set=a.529237706231.2034669.4&type=3&theater

Zupan, G. (2017). *16-24-year-olds and Safer Internet Day*. Statistical Office of the Republic of Slovenia. Retrieved from http://www.stat.si/StatWeb/en/News/Index/6478

Zywica, J., & Danowski, J. (2008). The faces of Facebookers: Investigating social enhancement and social compensation hypotheses: Predicting Facebook and offline popularity from sociability and self-esteem, and mapping the meanings of popularity with semantic networks. *Journal of Computer-Mediated Communication, 14*(1), 1–34. doi:10.1111/j.1083-6101.2008.01429.x

About the Contributors

Bahadır Bozoglan is a licensed psychotherapist of Weinheim Systemic Therapy Institute. He received his Ph.D. in Psychological Counseling and Guidance. He has taught graduate and undergraduate courses as an Assistant Professor at different universities in Turkey. His major research interests include Internet Addiction, Psychological Variables, Systemic Therapy, Family Issues, Retirement and Measurement. His research works have been published in high-impact journals, including Scandinavian Journal of Psychology, Computers in Human Behavior, Psychological Reports, European Journal of Psychological Assessment, Asia Pacific Psychiatry and Turkish Journal of Geriatrics. He is a contributing author for the IGI book, "Psychological and Social Implications Surrounding Internet and Gaming Addiction". He has also reviewed tens of articles for distinguished journals such as Journal of Personality and Individual Differences and Journal of Clinical Psychology. He is a member of EFTA (European Family Therapy Association), Weinheim Family Therapy Institute, Germany and Turkish Psychological Counseling and Guidance Association.

* * *

Gökmen Arslan has a PhD degree in Psychological Counseling and Guidance and is an independent scholar in Turkey. Dr. Arslan's research areas are broadly in the areas of parenting and the prevention of child maltreatment. Dr. Arslan's research focuses on psychological maltreatment, particularly adolescents and its short and long-term outcomes across physical and mental health domains and wellbeing. He is invested in supporting health and resilience within psychologically maltreated populations, and disseminates actively to policy and practice. Her research interests, presented at international conferences and publications, include the effects of psychological maltreatment on mental health and wellbeing, resilience, wellbeing at school, identity processes, and internet–related problems in adolescents. His recent research seeks to understand the role of psychological maltreatment, as a risk factor, in the development of the internet addiction and internet–related problems. He is the editor-in-chief of Journal of Positive Psychology & Welbeing and also an active member of the Turkish Psychological Counseling Association.

Shilpa Bisen, Ph.D., has been working as a Research Scholar since 2013. She did a Masters in clinical psychology from the University of Pune (India) and is pursuing a Doctorate from National Institute of Technology Nagpur (India). She is a University Grant Commission Junior Research fellowship Holder In clinical psychology. Her research interest is in the area of Information Technology Addiction, schizophrenia, Depression and personality disorders. She is recipient of International scientist award in Applied Psychology. She worked as a consultant clinical psychologist, teacher of forensic psychology and mentor to undergraduate Psychology students.

Jonathan Bishop is an information technology executive, researcher and writer. He founded the Centre for Research into Online Communities and E-Learning Systems in 2005, now part of the Crocels Community Media Group. Jonathan's research and development work generally falls within human-computer interaction. He has over 75 publications in this area, including on Internet trolling, cyber-stalking, gamification, cyberlaw, multimedia forensics, Classroom 2.0 and Digital Teens. In addition to his BSc(Hons) in Multimedia Studies and various postgraduate degrees, including in law, economics and computing, Jonathan serves in local government as a councillor, and has been a school governor and contested numerous elections, including to the UK Parliament and Welsh Assembly. He is a fellow of BCS, CILIP, the InstAM, the RAI, the RSS and the RSA, senior member of IEEE and a member of the IMarEST with MarTech. Jonathan has won prizes for his literary skills and been a finalist in national and local competitions for his environmental, community and equality work, which often form part of action research studies. In his spare time Jonathan enjoys listening to music, swimming and chess.

Valentina Boursier, Clinical Psychologist, PhD, Researcher at University of Naples "Federico II" (Italy), Psychotherapist for Children and Adolescents, Member of the Winnicott's Institute (iW) and of the Italian Psychoanalytical Psychotherapy Society for Children and Adolescents (SIPsIA). Her occupational fields and research areas include Clinical Psychology and Development Psychoanalysis, Gender Studies, Feminine Identity, Mother-Infant interactions, Children's psychopathology prevention, Direct observation for training, intervention and clinical research tools. One specific study direction focuses on the web use and misuse among parents as e-health users and adolescents, underlying related risks and opportunities. Many of these studies have been presented at international conferences and publications.

Ayfer Aydıner Boylu is an Associate Professor at Hacettepe University, Faculty of Economics and Administrative Sciences, Department of Family and Consumer Sciences. Dr. Aydıner Boylus' research interests include, quality of life, family quality of life, family crisis, and crisis intervention.

Tihana Brkljačić received PhD at the Department of Psychology, Faculty of Philosophy, University of Zagreb in 2003. She currently works as senior research associate at Institute of Social Sciences Ivo Pilar (from 1998) and at Croatian Catholic University (from 2013). Apart from scientific work at Institute, from 1999, she is continuously teaching at Croatian studies, Faculty of electrical engineering and computing and from 2013 at Croatian Catholic University. Tihana Brkljačić primarily scientific interests are in the area of positive psychology, specifically, human well-being and specific indicators of quality of life among specific and challenged groups; and psychology of communication with emphasis on interaction of online communication and well-being. Tihana Brkljačić participated at numerous national and international scientific projects, published over 20 scientific articles, and attended over 20 scientific congresses and meetings.

Kevin Curran is a Professor of Cyber Security and group leader for the Ambient Intelligence & Virtual Worlds Research Group at Ulster University. He is also a senior member of the IEEE. Prof Curran is perhaps most well-known for his work on location positioning within indoor environments and Internet security. His expertise has been acknowledged by invitations to present his work at international conferences, overseas universities and research laboratories. He is a regular contributor on TV & radio and in trade and consumer IT magazines.

Yogesh Deshpande is an Associate professor of Psychology in Visvesvaraya national Institute of Technology, Nagpur (India). His Area of interest is positive psychology, Human values in Higher Education, Indology & Hypermedia culture. Currently he is Associate Dean of public relations at Visvesvaraya National Institute of Technology, Nagpur (India).

Floribert Patrick C. Endong (PhD) is a research consultant in the humanities and social sciences. He is a reviewer and editor with many scientific journals in the social sciences. His current research interest focuses on international communication, gender studies, digital media, media laws, international relations, culture and religious communication He is author of numerous peer-reviewed articles and book chapters in the above-mentioned areas of interest.

Gülay Günay is an Associate Professor at Karabük University, Faculty of Economics and Administrative Sciences, Department of Social Work. Dr. Gülay Günay was burn in Germany at 1975. Dr. Günay received her MS in Family and Consumers Sciences from the Hacettepe University in 1996. She was a Research Assistant of Family and Consumer Sciences at Hacettepe University Faculty of Economics and Administrative Sciences (1996 – 2006). She writes and presents widely on issues of preretirement planning, post retirement life, ageing, family life. she has published in a variety of social science journals.

Prashant Gupta completed Master of Technology in Cyber Security from Defence Institute of Advanced Technology(DIAT), India and Master of Science in Information Technology from Mahatma Gandhi University(MGU), Meghalaya, India. He is currenty working for the Defence Institute of Psychological Research(DIPR), Delhi, India. His research area includes analysis of cyberpsycho attacks and cyberpsycho effect including sentiment analysis, social media analysis and persuasive technology.

Zaheer Hussain is a Psychologist, Researcher, and Senior Lecturer in Psychology at the University of Derby, UK. He is internationally known for his work in the area of behavioural addictions, social media, and technology use. He is regarded as a technology and addiction specialist. He has published many research papers and presented at well-known conferences. Dr Zaheer Hussain regularly contributes to leading journals in his field as Associate Editor and Reviewer. He has also appeared on radio programmes and engages in consultancy work for government and non-government organisations.

Joyce Lok Yin Kwan obtained her PhD in Psychology from the Chinese University of Hong Kong. She is an assistant professor in the Department of Psychology and is the associate director of the Assessment Research Center at the Education University of Hong Kong. Her research centers on quantitative research methodology and her main areas of research interest include structural equation modeling, moderation and mediation analysis, and latent growth curve analysis. She recently also dedicated her research to problematic Internet use. She is the co-developer of VS (Variable System), a computer software program for the analysis of conditional path models.

Francisco Tsz Tsun Lai is a PhD student at The Jockey Club School of Public Health and Primary Care, The Chinese University of Hong Kong. His research centers on the mechanisms through which adolescent Internet addiction is shaped by various social determinants. His previous works have been published in international scholarly journals such as Teaching and Teacher Education, Computers in Human Behavior, and Children and Youth Services Review.

Mirna Macur is a researcher at National Institute of Public Health, Slovenia and Associate Professor at School of Advanced Social Studies, where she teaches social science research methodology and evaluation methods. She is a sociologist, working as a methodologist on various projects in a Health Data Centre of the institute. Her research interests in last years encompass various behavioural addictions and she presented her work in several international and national conferences. In 2015, she conducted a big school based study on various types of behavioural addictions. She is presenting the results on problematic internet use in one of the samples in the chapter of this book.

Filip Majetić holds an MA and PhD in Sociology from the University of Zagreb and an MSc in Entrepreneurship from Uppsala University. Currently he is a Research Associate at the Institute of Social Sciences Ivo Pilar in Zagreb. He did short-term research stays at the University of Ljubljana (2012) and at the University of Stockholm (2017). His main field of research interest is social entrepreneurship.

Valentina Manna, PhD, post-doctoral fellow at Naples University, is clinical psychologist and post-graduate student in Psychoanalyitic Psychotherapy of the child, adolescent and parents (Winnicott Institute, ASNE-SIPsIA). She mostly works with schoolers and preschoolers, also being engaged as educator at a nursery school. She was project manager in several national/international projects about prevention of risk in childhood and adolescence, equal opportunities and gender issues. She was awarded (2015) by the Italian Order of Psychologists for the project Dear Sibling, addressed to young siblings of children with Down Syndrome. She has been enrolled in home visiting programs for at-risk-children, and currently runs help-desks for parents. She is vicepresident of Roots in Action Association, active in the field of psychosocial interventions for children with disabilities and developmental disorders. Her research interests, presented at international conferences and publications, include sibling relationships in disabilities, psychodynamic observation, videobservation/videofeedback, identity processes and technologies in adolescence, and infant psychoanalysis.

Nigel McKelvey (Ed.D., MSc., BSc., PGCE, MICS) is a lecturer in Computing at the Letterkenny Institute of Technology and specialises in teaching secure programming techniques at both undergraduate and postgraduate level. Other areas of interest include ethical gaming, performance based programming and digital forensics. Nigel is an advocate of CoderDojos and encourages community programming initiatives.

Manisha J. Nene received the Ph.D. degree in Computer Science and Engineering from the Defence Institute of Advanced Technology(DIAT), a Defence Research and Development Organization (DRDO) establishment under the Ministry of Defence, India. With eighteen plus years of experience in academia and research; currently, she is a faculty in the Department of Computer Science and Engineering, DIAT. Her areas of interest are cyber physical systems, sensor networks, cognitive radio, analysis of algorithms, data analytics, high performance computing, social network analysis, and modeling and simulation. She is recipient of national awards for her contribution on research and ICT contributions to the society.

Halley Pontes (PhD, CPsychol) is a chartered psychologist and a lecturer at Nottingham Trent University. His main research interest relates to the use psychometrics and advanced statistical modelling to assess and further understand the diagnostic criteria of behavioural addictions such as Internet addiction and Internet Gaming Disorder. Dr. Pontes has worked as a clinical psychologist in Portugal where he treated patients with Internet Gaming Disorder. Dr. Pontes is an experienced social scientist with over 60 refereed studies across a wide range of high impact refereed international journals specialized in addictive behaviours and cyberpsychology. Dr. Pontes has extensively disseminated his work at several international congresses and conferences related to his area of research and has also published in other closely related areas such as: sex addiction, work addiction, and game transfer phenomena.

Ruya Samli was born in 1983, in Turkey. She received her MSc and PhD degrees in Istanbul University Computer Engineering department in 2006 and 2011 respectively. She is working in the Engineering Faculty of Istanbul University. She has many Sci/Sci-expanded papers, journals in conference proceedings and projects etc. She is interested in many different subjects of computer engineering such as artificial intelligence, neural networks, stability, optimization, modelling and software engineering. She is also interested in social subjects such as information technology law, cybercrimes, and internet addiction.

Libi Shen has a Ph.D. in Instruction and Learning from University of Pittsburgh, PA. She started her college teaching career in 1989. She has been an online faculty for University of Phoenix since 2010. Libi is a contributing author for the following IGI Global books: (1) Educational, Behavioral, Psychological Considerations in Niche Online Communities; (2) Cases on Critical and Qualitative Perspectives in Online Higher Education; (3) Online Tutor 2.0: Methodologies and Case Studies for Successful Learning; (4) Emerging Priorities and Trends in Distance Education: Communication, Pedagogy, and Technology; (5) Identification, Evaluation, and Perceptions of Distance Education Experts; (6) Cybersecurity Breaches and Issues Surrounding Online Threat Protection; and (7) Handbook of Research on Human Factors in Contemporary Workforce Development. She is also an author for Technology in the Classroom for Now and the Future. Her research interests include reading skills, curriculum design, distance education, online learning, communication, and instructional technology.

Shaun Smyth (BSc, MSc) has an educational background from Ulster University whose achievements include both a BSc in Computer Science and an MSc in Computational Intelligence. Shaun is currently involved in the research and writing of several papers and the collaboration with other lecturers and colleagues from the computing faculty on several papers on a range of different subjects with a view to future publication.

Anja Wertag received PhD at Department of Psychology, Faculty of Philosophy, University of Zagreb in 2015. She currently works as a research assistant at Institute of Social Sciences Ivo Pilar in Zagreb, and was an assistant on courses Introduction to Psychology, and The basis of social behavior at Department of Psychology, Centre for Croatian Studies, University of Zagreb. Her major area of research is personality and individual differences. She has participated in several national and international scientific projects such as The determinants of risk and deviant behaviour in a national and global context and International Father Acceptance - Rejection Project (IFARP), and published 5 scientific papers.

Index

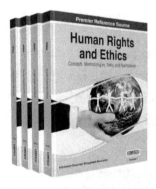
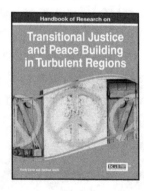
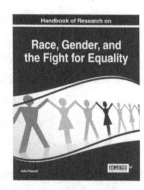 

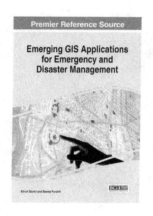
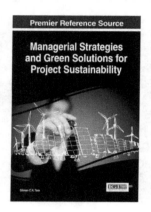

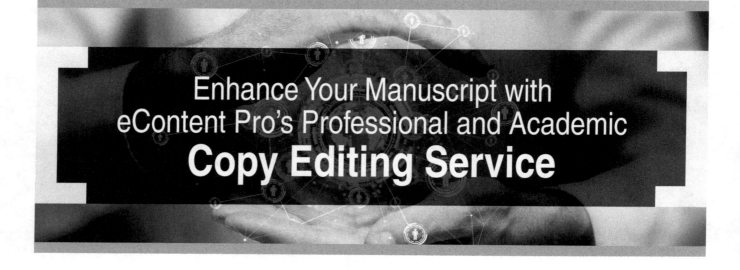

Information Resources Management Association

Advancing the Concepts & Practices of Information Resources Management in Modern Organizations

Become an IRMA Member

Members of the **Information Resources Management Association (IRMA)** understand the importance of community within their field of study. The Information Resources Management Association is an ideal venue through which professionals, students, and academicians can convene and share the latest industry innovations and scholarly research that is changing the field of information science and technology. Become a member today and enjoy the benefits of membership as well as the opportunity to collaborate and network with fellow experts in the field.

IRMA Membership Benefits:

- **One FREE Journal Subscription**

- **30% Off Additional Journal Subscriptions**

- **20% Off Book Purchases**

- Updates on the latest events and research on Information Resources Management through the IRMA-L listserv.

- Updates on new open access and downloadable content added to Research IRM.

- A copy of the Information Technology Management Newsletter twice a year.

- A certificate of membership.

IRMA Membership $195

Scan code or visit **irma-international.org** and begin by selecting your free journal subscription.

Membership is good for one full year.

CPSIA information can be obtained
at www.ICGtesting.com
Printed in the USA
LVHW101501050519
616707LV00016B/264/P

DATE DUE

			PRINTED IN U.S.A.